LONDON

EMILY BARBER

SOMERSET · LONDON

Eighteenth edition

Published by Blue Guides Limited, a Somerset Books Company
Winchester House, Deane Gate Avenue, Taunton, Somerset TA1 2UH
www.blueguides.com. 'Blue Guide' is a registered trademark.

ISBN 978-1-905131-63-1

A CIP catalogue record of this book is available from the British Library.

Distributed in the United States of America by
W.W. Norton & Company, Inc.
500 Fifth Avenue, New York, NY 10110.

The author and the publishers have made reasonable efforts to ensure the accuracy of all the
information in *Blue Guide London*; however, they can accept no responsibility for any loss,
injury or inconvenience sustained by any traveller as a result of information or advice
contained in the guide.

Blue Guides, their authors and editors, are prohibited from accepting any payment from any
restaurant, hotel, gallery or other establishment for its inclusion in this guide, or for a more
favourable mention than would otherwise have been made.

Every effort has been made to contact the copyright owners of material reproduced in this
guide. We would be pleased to hear from any copyright owners we have been unable to reach.

Design by Stephen Reid and Blue Guides. Image research by Hadley Kincade.
Maps by Dimap Bt. © Crown copyright 2014 Ordnance Survey 100043799.
Architectural line drawings: Michael Mansell RIBA & Gabriella Juhász © Blue Guides.
Floor plans: Imre Bába © Blue Guides.
All material prepared for press by Anikó Kuzmich.

Printed in Hungary by Dürer Nyomda Kft., Gyula.

Your views on this book would be much appreciated. We welcome not only specific
comments, suggestions or corrections, but any more general views you may have: how
this book enhanced your visit, how it could have been more helpful. Blue Guides authors
and editorial and production team work hard to bring you what we hope are the best-
researched and best-presented cultural guide books in the English language. Please
write to us by email (*editorial@blueguides.com*), via the comments page on our website
(*www.blueguides.com*) or at the address given above. We will be happy to acknowledge
useful contributions in the next edition, and to offer a free copy of one of our titles.

This is the 18th edition of *Blue Guide London*, a work which has almost a century of history, written, edited and compiled under the care of many hands. The first edition was published in 1918, edited by Findlay Muirhead. Since then it has gone through numerous re-editions, successively updated by L. Russell Muirhead, Stuart Rossiter, Ylva French (12th–16th eds) and Roger Woodley (17th ed.). The text of this edition has been compiled, updated and rewritten by Emily Barber, with contributions and assistance from Annabel Howells, Michael Partington and Charles Freeman.

   Emily Barber studied History of Art at UCL and is a Fellow of the Gemmological Association of Great Britain and independent jewellery valuer for the Treasure Valuation Committee of Great Britain. She is currently Department Director of the London Jewellery Department at Bonhams Auctioneers. She has been involved with the research and sale of many valuable and historic jewellery collections and has taught and lectured at leading institutions, including the V&A in London. **Annabel Howells** is Editorial Director of the Blue Guides. **Michael Partington** is a historian and art historian with a special interest in the early Stuarts and the Italian Renaissance. He has worked for the University of Ferrara and Hertford College, Oxford and is a volunteer coin handler at the Ashmolean Museum. He is the author of the *Oxford Dictionary of National Biography* entry on the travel writer Edward Hutton. **Charles Freeman** is a freelance academic historian. His *Egypt, Greece and Rome, Civilizations of the Ancient Mediterranean* (Oxford University Press, 3rd ed. 2014) is widely used as an introductory textbook to the ancient world and is supported by his *Sites of Antiquity: 50 Sites that Explain the Classical World* (Blue Guides, 2009). He is a Fellow of the Royal Society of Arts.

   Some of the entries on museums have been revised, adapted and updated from *Blue Guide Museums and Galleries of London* (4th ed.) by Tabitha Barber and Charles Godfrey-Faussett. **Tabitha Barber** is Curator of British Art 1550–1750 at Tate Britain. **Charles Godfrey-Faussett** is a previous Deputy Editor of the Blue Guides, a former theatre reviewer, and author of books on England and London.

With grateful thanks to Bill Forse, Timothy Duke, Chester Herald and Sue Allison, Matthew Blythe, Andrew Culverwell, Kate Edwards, Peter Fiennes, Jean Ghika, Phil Manning (St Olave's, Hart St), Guy Savill, Patrick Short, Stephen Startup, Mark Tilley, Amy Vosburgh-Savill.

Cover: St Paul's Cathedral, Michael Mansell RIBA & Gabriella Juhász © Blue Guides; Frontispiece: Mosaic detail of the Royal Albert Hall. Photo: A. Howells © Blue Guides. Interior photos: Emily Barber pp. 50, 185, 431; Hadley Kincade pp. 125, 278; © Mike Kemp/ In Pictures/Corbis/Profimedia p. 19; ©Jonathan Blair/Corbis/Profimedia p. 90; ©Steve Vidler/Superstock/Corbis/Profimedia p. 102; ©Jeremy Lightfoot/Robert Harding World Imagery/Corbis/Profimedia p. 128; ©Rudy Sulgan/Corbis/Profimedia p. 140; ©Purcell-Holmes/Robert Harding World Imagery/Corbis/Profimedia p. 164; ©istockphoto.com/ compassandcamera p. 192; ©istockphoto.com/decisiveimages p. 206; ©Mark Sykes/JAI/ Corbis/Profimedia p. 250; ©istockphoto.com/Amanda Lewis p. 257; ©istockphoto.com/ double_p p. 273; ©istockphoto.com/fazon1 p. 286; Wikicommons pp. 346, 523; eustonarch. org p. 363; ©Ethel Davies/Robert Harding World Imagery/Corbis/Profimedia p. 371; ©istockphoto.com/cristapper p. 408; ©David Noton Photography/Alamy/Profimedia p. 436; ©Neil Emmerson/Robert Harding World Imagery/Corbis/Profimedia p. 467; ©Marcus Peel/VIEW/Corbis/Profimedia p. 480; ©Angelo Hornak/Corbis/Profimedia p. 485; ©Paul Hackett/In Pictures/Corbis/Profimedia p. 500; ©Sandro Vannini/Corbis/Profimedia p. 512; ©Steve Vidler/Alamy/Profimedia p. 524. All other photographs by A. Howells ©Blue Guides.

CONTENTS

PRACTICAL INFORMATION

MAPS & PLANS

Introduction to London

London's history spans two millennia. Ever since the Romans set up camp on the banks of the Thames in AD 43 this great city has sprawled along the river in both directions, up and down residual Roman roads and over the intervening fields and countryside, swallowing up disparate villages whole. This is London's essence: its complex, complicated, convoluted spread.

London is the seat of the British government as well as the British monarchy and as a consequence is rich in tradition, pomp and ceremony. By 1800 London was the largest and most important city in the world; throughout the 19th century the Victorians built on these advantages and London became the nucleus of the vast British Empire.

London is a global financial centre as well as a cultural capital. In London you will find four World Heritage sites, internationally famous attractions and some of the best art, theatre, music, entertainment and shopping in the world. London has hosted the Olympic Games three times in its history and is still riding high from the successes of 2012. London is also a food-lovers paradise and has over 60 Michelin-starred restaurants. It has numerous parks and green spaces and its river and waterways are open for boating, walking and cycling. It has one of the most extensive public transport systems of any modern metropolis as well as the world's busiest international airport. Here too you will find the finest taxi drivers, who have passed the rigorous and celebrated 'Knowledge' exam, which demands an intimate acquaintance with London's complicated street layout. London cabbies pride themselves on being able to pick you up and take you anywhere you want via the best route.

London has formulated and distilled many great inventions: penicillin, fire insurance, the daily newspaper, canned food, traffic lights, the electrical generator, the first television, the Internet—the list is impressive. London is so proud of its luminaries that buildings are riddled with plaques proclaiming the great and the good who have once lived in them.

Today, London is truly a stimulating, cosmopolitan and thoroughly modern metropolis. Over eight million people live here. Thousands of daily commuters work here. Foreign visitors arrive here as both tourists and expatriates. London is always busy, always crowded, always buzzing. Londoners seldom conform to stereotype: they rarely form an orderly queue for the bus, never wear bowler hats and generally prefer coffee to tea; but what they excel at is adapting to change. As the modern city strives to accommodate its burgeoning population and update its infrastructure, London is constantly evolving and transforming itself. Geographically, London may not be in the centre of Europe, but in terms of diversity, it is at the centre of the world.

London Chronology

55–54 BC Julius Caesar's invasions of
Britain

AD 43 The Romans invade Britain again.
They find the Thames to be ford-
able, near the present site of London
Bridge.

AD c. 50 The Romans found Londinium,
on the site of the City of London

AD 61 Roman London is burnt by
Boudica

410 Rome is sacked by the Goths. The
Romans begin their withdrawal from
Britain, leaving the people to organ-
ise their own defence. Decline of
Londinium begins

597 St Augustine lands in Kent on
a mission to convert the people to
Christianity

604 Augustine appoints Mellitus Bishop
of London

619 Mellitus becomes Archbishop of
Canterbury. As soon as he leaves
London, the people resume their
pagan ways

731 Bede describes Ludenwic, on the
site of today's Covent Garden, as 'a
trading centre for many nations'

872 The Danes occupy London

886 Alfred the Great takes London and
recognises Danish control of eastern
England. Watling Street is the frontier

c. 960 Founding of the Benedictine
Abbey of Westminster

1014 Battle of London Bridge. King Olaf
II of Norway joins forces with the

Saxon Ethelred against the Danes

1066 Death of Edward the Confessor.
Harold fails to retain the crown, and
William the Conqueror is crowned in
Westminster Abbey

1106 Building of Southwark Cathedral
begins

1123 Foundation of St Bartholomew's
Hospital and priory

1161 Henry II orders the building of a
new shrine to Edward the Confessor

1176 Old London Bridge is begun, on the
site of an ancient crossing

c. 1078 William begins the White Tower

1215 King John signs the Magna Carta

1225 Franciscans arrive in London,
establishing themselves at Greyfriars

1269 Consecration of Henry III's splendid new Westminster Abbey

1274 Edward I makes a grant of land to
the Dominicans, who build a friary in
the area now known as Blackfriars

1290 Edward I begins his attempts to
conquer Scotland. He turns to Italian
money-lenders for funding and expels
the Jews from London

1296 Edward I removes the Stone of
Destiny from Scone and brings it to
London

1305 William Wallace is executed at
Smithfield. The following year Robert
the Bruce becomes King of Scotland
and open revolt begins against King
Edward I

1348 The first outbreak of plague,

known as the Black Death

1362 English replaces French as the official language of Parliament

1381 The Peasants' Revolt enters London, demanding an end to serfdom. Richard II negotiates with them and their leader, Wat Tyler, is killed

1397 Richard Whittington becomes Mayor of London for the first time

1411 Building of the London Guildhall begins

1414 Lollards seize London and attempt to capture Henry V

1440 Foundation of Eton College

1450 Jack Cade's rebellion against Henry VI. Fierce fighting in London

1460 The Duke of York arrives in London announcing a claim to the throne. Beginning of the Wars of the Roses

1471 Lancastrian defeat at the Battle of Barnet secures the throne for Edward IV

1476 William Caxton sets up his printing press at Westminster

1483 Mysterious death of the Princes in the Tower

1496 Henry VII empowers John Cabot to set up trading links with those countries he discovers on his voyages of exploration

1500 Wynkyn de Worde sets up a printing press in Fleet Street

1509 Henry VII's death at Richmond is met with public rejoicing. The canny king, who had done so much to set England on her mercantile career, is succeeded by Henry VIII. Little do the people know what is in store

1510 Founding of St Paul's School

1512 After a fire at Westminster, Henry VIII moves his court to Whitehall

1513 Henry VIII establishes the Royal Naval Docks at Deptford

1521 Lutheran books are burned in London and Henry VIII receives the title 'Defender of the Faith' from Pope Leo X

1527 Copies of Tyndale's Bible are burned in St Paul's

1529 Wolsey fails to obtain a divorce for Henry VIII. Thomas More becomes Chancellor

1534 Act of Supremacy: Henry VIII is supreme head of the Church of England

1536 The Dissolution of the Monasteries begins, with the crown seizing Church land and property. Many areas of London that are public parks today are appropriated by Henry VIII as hunting grounds

1547 The House of Commons makes the Palace of Westminster its meeting place instead of the Chapter House of Westminster Abbey

1552 Edward VI founds St Thomas's Hospital

1553 Mary I becomes Queen and sets about restoring the old religion

1558 Elizabeth I succeeds to the throne and re-suppresses the religious houses re-opened by Mary

1565 Thomas Gresham founds the Royal Exchange

1576 The Theatre playhouse opens in Shoreditch

1577 An institute for the teaching of science is established by the will of Sir Thomas Gresham

1581 Francis Drake is knighted at Deptford. He returned from his circumnavigation the previous year

1582 The first houses in London to receive pumped water

1585 Shakespeare arrives in London

1587 Mary, Queen of Scots is executed, having been implicated in a plot to kill

Elizabeth I, the culmination of many decades of intriguing, with alliances signed and broken, between England, Scotland and France

1588 Defeat of the Spanish Armada. English dominance of the seas is assured

1595 Hungry Londoners riot

1598 John Stow publishes his *Survey of London*

1599 The Globe Theatre opens in Southwark

1600 Founding of the East India Company on Leadenhall Street

1603 James VI of Scotland becomes James I of England, thus uniting the two kingdoms; Sir Walter Raleigh founds the Mermaid Tavern club

1604 The Treaty of London brings peace with Spain and a trade agreement with France

1605 The Gunpowder Plot, a Catholic conspiracy to blow up Parliament

1608 Foundation of the Royal Blackheath Golf Club

1613 The New River is constructed, to bring drinking water from Stoke Newington

1615 Tobacco vending machines are introduced in taverns; James I issues a proclamation to the effect that London is to be transformed into a 'truly magnificent city comparable to the Rome of the Emperor Augustus'

1617 The first attempt is made to create one-way streets in London

1619 Inigo Jones begins the Banqueting House

1620 The *Mayflower* sets sail for Plymouth from Rotherhithe

1621 John Donne is appointed Dean of St Paul's

1632 Van Dyck becomes court painter to Charles I

1633 Bananas are first displayed in a London shop window by the herbalist Thomas Johnson

1634 Opening of Covent Garden Market

1642 Parliament takes control of the army; Charles I leaves London; beginning of the Civil War

1645 The group of scientists who are later to become the Royal Society begin to meet informally in London and Oxford

1649 Charles I is beheaded at Whitehall. The loyal Scots promptly declare Charles II king

1654 Treaty of Westminster ends the first Anglo-Dutch war over trade routes

1657 Velho Sephardic cemetery opened on Mile End Road

1658 Oliver Cromwell dies at Whitehall. He is buried in Westminster Abbey. The effigy in his funeral procession is dressed in full royal regalia. He is succeeded by his son

1660 Pepys writes the first entries in his diary; Charles II enters London and the monarchy is restored

1661 The first postmarks in the world are struck in London

1662 Queen Catherine of Braganza introduced tea-drinking to the London court

1665 The Great Plague

1666 The Great Fire

1676 The 'Little Fire of London' devastates Southwark

1671 Captain Blood attempts to steal the Crown Jewels from the Tower

1673 The Test Act: Catholics and nonconformists may not hold public office

1674 Treaty of Westminster brings peace with the Dutch. New Amsterdam becomes New York

1675 The Royal Observatory is founded

at Greenwich

1677 The Monument, the tallest free-standing column in the world, is inaugurated as a memorial to the Great Fire

1680 Henry Purcell becomes organist at Westminster Abbey

1681 Charles II offers sanctuary to the Huguenots, French Protestants facing persecution at home

1682 Spitalfields Market is established

1685 The Duke of Monmouth's rebellion against James II is crushed. Judge Jeffreys presides over the Bloody Assizes, condemning his supporters to death. Monmouth himself is beheaded

1688 James II attempts to force Church leaders to support his Liberty of Conscience declaration; William of Orange is invited to take over the throne; James leaves for the Continent: the 'Glorious Revolution' is over

1693 William III borrows £1 million, with interest, to fund the war with France: this signals the beginning of the National Debt, which Disraeli in his novels will excoriate as the 'Dutch system'

1694 The Bank of England is founded, to obtain interest on government money

1696 Great Howland Dock is built, the largest commercial dock in the world

1698 Opening of White's, London's oldest gentlemen's club

1699 Free fish market established at Billingsgate

1702 Britain's first daily newspaper, the *Daily Courant*, is founded in Fleet Street

1704 Britain is victorious over France at Blenheim

1706 Thomas Twining starts his tea importing business

1707 Union of the English and Scottish parliaments

1711 The new St Paul's Cathedral is formally declared complete; the New Churches Act is passed, more churches are to be built to serve the rapidly growing city: they become known as 'Queen Anne churches'

1720 The South Sea Bubble hoax ruins many London investors

1721 Robert Walpole becomes the first British Prime Minister

1723 Handel is appointed composer to the Chapel Royal

1731 Downing Street becomes the official residence of the Prime Minister

1734 A group of Grand Tourists found the Dilettanti Society, aimed at promoting a taste for Classical antiquities

1739 Establishment of the Foundling Hospital, the first secular institution of its kind

1750 The first umbrella is sported in London by Jonas Hanway. He is roundly ridiculed

1751 Robert Clive establishes control of southern India

1753 Founding of the British Museum

1754 Outbreak of the Seven Years' War, a tussle between the Great Powers over colonisation and the division of territory

1755 Samuel Johnson publishes his Dictionary

1761 Ashkenazi burial ground opens on Brady Street

1764 London introduces a system of house numbering

1768 Founding of the Royal Academy

1770 Construction of London's first canal, the Limehouse Cut; Captain Cook lands at Botany Bay and claims it for Britain

1776 American Declaration of

Independence

1780 Outbreak of anti-Catholic protests, known as the Gordon Riots

1783 The last execution at Tyburn

1787 Founding of the Association for the Abolition of the Slave Trade

1788 The first shipment of convicts from Millbank arrives in Australia

1799 Death of Tipu Sultan; the British consolidate their position in south India

1801 Birth of the United Kingdom with the union of Britain and Ireland; Pitt wants to make provisions for Catholics but George III refuses

1802 Madame Tussaud arrives in London; West India Dock is built: it will quickly be followed by a succession of others; following the Treaty of Alexandria signed with France the previous year, treasures including the Rosetta Stone arrive at the British Museum

1805 Battle of Trafalgar: victory over Napoleon; Nelson is killed

1807 Pall Mall is the first London street to be lit by gas

1813 Bryan Donkin sets up the fist meat cannery in Bermondsey; Spencer Perceval, the only British Prime Minister to be assassinated, is shot

1815 Battle of Waterloo ends the Napoleonic Wars

1816 The British Museum purchases the Parthenon Marbles from Lord Elgin; economic depression following the Napoleonic Wars leads to poverty and rioting, which is met by increasingly repressive government measures

1817 Dulwich Picture Gallery opens, the first public art gallery in Britain

1820 The Cato Street conspiracy, a plot to assassinate the entire Cabinet, is foiled; the cause of reform is retarded by fears of public radicalism

1824 Founding of the National Gallery

1829 Catholic Emancipation Act: the first Catholic MP takes his seat in Parliament; London begins its first scheduled omnibus services

1832 The Reform Bill is passed, greatly augmenting the electorate

1833 Abolition of the Slave Trade

1836 The first London railway is built between Deptford and Bermondsey (London Bridge)

1837 Queen Victoria makes Buckingham Palace her London residence

1840 The last ever Bartholomew Fair is held at Smithfield

1841 Fenchurch Street Station is the first to be built in the City

1843 Opening of the Thames Tunnel between Rotherhithe and Wapping

1846 Famine strikes Ireland; the first operation under ether to be performed in Europe is carried out at University College Hospital

1847 The British Museum opens

1848 Founding of the Pre-Raphaelite Brotherhood; Chartist meeting on Kennington Common, a prelude to delivering to Parliament a petition demanding better rights and enfranchisement for the working man

1849 Charles Henry Harrod sets up his famous store in Knightsbridge

1851 The Great Exhibition is held in Hyde Park

1853 Beginning of the Crimean War

1857 The Indian Mutiny (Uprising)

1858 Queen Victoria is proclaimed sovereign of India; the *Great Eastern* is launched

1860 Henry Poole invents the dinner jacket (renamed the 'tuxedo' in New York) in Savile Row

1861 Lagos in Nigeria is proclaimed a crown colony

1863 The churchyard of St Botolph-without-Bishopsgate is the first to open as a public garden; the first Tube line, the Metropolitan, runs from Paddington to Farringdon

1864 The first Christmas Day swim in the Serpentine takes place

1865 The Salvation Army is founded in Whitechapel

1868 Britain's last public execution takes place outside Newgate; its first traffic roundabout comes into operation at Parliament Square

1875 London's first commemorative plaque is set up (in Leicester Square, to Sir Joshua Reynolds)

1876 Alexander Graham Bell makes the first UK demonstration of his telephone from Brown's Hotel

1877 Queen Victoria is declared Empress of India; Dr Barnardo opens his 'Ragged School' in the East End

1880 All clocks in the country are set to Greenwich Mean Time

1895 Oscar Wilde is sentenced to Pentonville Prison

1897 Queen Victoria celebrates her Diamond Jubilee

1901 Death of Queen Victoria

1904 'Entente Cordiale' between France and Britain, aimed at solving colonial disputes in Africa

1907 The 5th Russian Labour Party congress is held in Whitechapel

1909 Selfridges opens on Oxford Street

1912 Suffragettes invade the House of Commons

1913 A suffragette plot to bomb St Paul's is foiled

1914 A suffragette slashes the *Rokeby Venus* with a meat cleaver; Britain declares war on Germany following the German invasion of Belgium

1916 The Easter Rising in Ireland; Daylight Saving is introduced; Battle of the Somme; Mark Gertler paints his *Merry-go-Round*

1917 The Royal Family abandon their German title, becoming the House of Windsor; the Balfour Declaration supports the founding of a Jewish homeland in Palestine

1918 Women over 30 are enfranchised; the German army surrenders on 11th Nov: the date is still commemorated every year as Remembrance Day

1919 The Irish Republican Army (IRA) is founded and begins a campaign of political murders and aggression against British targets; the Cenotaph is unveiled on Whitehall; Nancy Astor becomes the first female MP

1920 The Unknown Soldier is buried in Westminster Abbey

1921 The province of Northern Ireland is formed; Gandhi stages a mass repudiation of the Prince of Wales in Calcutta

1922 Founding of the BBC and of the Irish Free State

1924 Britain elects its first ever Labour government: one of its first acts is to recognise Bolshevik Russia, which Lloyd George had previously refused to do

1925 British Summer Time is instituted on a permanent basis; J.L. Baird gives the first public demonstration of his new television, at Selfridges

1926 The British Commonwealth recognises a number of dominions as being exempt from British legislative control

1928 The Thames floods, drowning four people in London. Many artworks are damaged at Tate Britain

1929 The Dorothy Warren Gallery in Mayfair is raided by police: it is exhibiting erotic art by D.H. Lawrence which is deemed obscene

1932 Oswald Mosley founds the British Union of Fascists; Sir Thomas Beecham founds the London Philharmonic Orchestra

1934 The Bauhaus architect Walter Gropius comes to London, fleeing Nazi persecution. He stays in the capital for three years

1936 The first high-definition TV broadcasts are made from Alexandra Palace; Battle of Cable Street in the East End between police and opponents of the Fascists; Edward VIII abdicates

1938 Sigmund Freud comes to London, fleeing persecution in his native Vienna

1939 IRA bombs are detonated at Tottenham Court Road and Leicester Square Underground stations; Britain declares war on Germany following the latter's invasion of Poland

1940–1 London is badly damaged in the Blitz

1943 The *Scharnhorst* is sunk by British ships, among them HMS *Belfast*

1945 The end of the Second World War

1946 The newly-elected Labour government begins a programme of sweeping nationalisation

1947 George VI renounces the title Emperor of India; India gains independence

1948 The *Empire Windrush* brings 500 Jamaican immigrants to London; London hosts the Olympic Games; end of the British mandate in Palestine: the state of Israel is declared; the National Health Service is set up

1949 Strike by London dockworkers

1950 Britain sends troops to Korea; Scottish nationalists steal the Stone of Destiny from Westminster Abbey (it is recovered soon after)

1951 The Festival of Britain opens

1952 Accession of Queen Elizabeth II; Agatha Christie's *The Mousetrap* begins its theatre run

1954 Roman temple of Mithras discovered in the City

1956 The Clean Air Act is passed in an attempt to deal with London's notorious 'pea-souper' smogs; the Suez Crisis results in the Prime Minister's resignation

1957 Ghana and Malaya achieve independence

1958 Race riots in Notting Hill

1961 Closure of the Victualling Yard at Deptford

1963 Kenya achieves independence

1964 Martin Luther King preaches at St Paul's Cathedral

1965 Winston Churchill is accorded a state funeral

1967 London Bridge is sold to an oil magnate in Arizona

1968 Closure of St Katharine Docks

1969 The Aviva Tower becomes the first building to be taller than St Paul's; abolition of the death penalty for murder

1971 Decimal currency is introduced in Britain and Ireland

1972 Ugandan Asians arrive in Britain, expelled from their country by President Amin

1973 Britain joins the EEC, the forerunner of the EU; IRA bombs are discovered at Baker Street and Sloane Square Tube; the government promises to tax the rich 'until the pips squeak'; the three-day week comes into force

1974 Covent Garden Market moves to Nine Elms, Battersea

1976 More IRA bomb attacks on the London Tube; the Brick Lane synagogue becomes a mosque; the National Theatre is opened

1977 The Queen celebrates her Silver Jubilee

1978 'Winter of Discontent': freezing temperatures and repeated strikes and Trades Union disputes

1979 Margaret Thatcher becomes Britain's first female Prime Minister

1981 A development corporation is set up to repurpose the London docks; Tower 42 becomes the tallest office block in Europe; race riots in Brixton

1982 Billingsgate fish market moves to West India Dock; opening of the Barbican Centre; beginning of the Falklands War; opening of the Thames Barrier; an intruder is found in the Queen's bedroom in Buckingham Palace

1983 IRA bombs explode on Oxford Street and outside Harrods

1985 The East London Mosque opens on Whitechapel Road; further riots in Brixton

1986 The 'Big Bang' deregulation of the London Stock Market: the resulting boom leads to many companies moving from the cramped City to former dockyard premises; Richard Rogers's Lloyd's Building is opened; the first newspaper companies move from Fleet Street to Wapping

1987 Smoking is banned on the Underground following a fire at King's Cross

1989 The Truman Brewery on Brick Lane ceases production

1990 Crowds take to the streets to demonstrate against the government's Community Charge or 'poll tax'

1991 More IRA bomb attacks on the London Tube; One Canada Square becomes the tallest building in Europe; beginning of the Gulf War

1992–3 Irish terrorist bombs explode in the City causing fatalities and damage to historic buildings; fruit and vegetables cease to be traded at Spitalfields Market; fire at Windsor Castle; Buckingham Palace is opened to visitors

1996 The Stone of Destiny is officially moved from London to Edinburgh

1997 The Prime Minster, Tony Blair, throws a 'Cool Britannia' party in Downing Street, to which rock stars, fashion designers and left-leaning literary luminaries are invited; Diana, Princess of Wales dies in a car crash in Paris

2000 London celebrates the Millennium

2003 Britain supports the US invasion of Iraq

2004 Norman Foster's 'Gherkin' opens

2005 Islamic terrorists detonate bombs on the London Underground: over 50 people are killed and many more injured; Reuters moves out of Fleet Street, the last remaining newspaper business to do so

2011 Heron Tower becomes the tallest building in the City

2012 Renzo Piano's Shard is the tallest building in the European Union; London hosts the Olympic Games; HM The Queen celebrates her Diamond Jubilee

2013 The 'Pompeii of the North' is discovered under Walbrook Square; former Prime Minister Margaret Thatcher is granted a ceremonial funeral

2014 London's first 'kinetic façade' comes to Debenhams on Oxford Street

THE GUIDE

The City of London

The City is London's most ancient quarter and a global financial centre, closely connected with international trade and commerce for over two millennia. The tightly built 'Square Mile' of small streets, crooked alleys, squares, courts, churches, civic buildings, offices and high-rises stretches from the Royal Courts of Justice in the Strand (Temple Bar) to Aldgate in the east and from the Thames in the south to City Road in the north.

London first became a port of wealth and prominence under Roman occupation (AD 43–410). In the 2nd century, the Romans built a towering defence wall around the City, 20ft high and 8ft wide, as impressive as Hadrian's Wall in the North. It formed the foundations for the medieval city wall that was restored by King Alfred in the 9th century and remained standing until the 18th and 19th centuries. The legacy of this defensive circuit is that

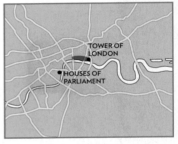

it loosely defines the perimeters of the City to this day and significant remains may still be seen at Tower Hill, the Barbican and on the modern road called London Wall.

After the Norman Conquest of 1066, William the Conqueror built three mighty fortresses in the City to subdue its citizens (the Tower, officially outside the City's limits, is the only one that remains). However, William also recognised the City's value to the wealth of the country and approved a London charter which upheld previous Saxon rights and privileges. In the 12th century, the City was granted the autonomy of self government, a privilege that continues today. Many of the City's grand livery companies (*see overleaf*) were founded in the 12th–13th centuries. By the 15th century the City was home to flourishing trading firms and in 1600 the great East India Company was established. In 1565, Sir Thomas Gresham founded the Royal Exchange, opened by Elizabeth I. The Plague of 1665 reduced the population by one fifth and then in 1666 the Great Fire reduced five-sixths of the medieval city to ashes, destroying 86 out of 107 parish churches and the halls of 44 livery companies. Although the chief architect, Christopher Wren, wished to restructure along more planned, Enlightenment lines, the urgent need to rebuild meant that the City was re-erected over its medieval footprint, within the outline of the old Roman walls.

After the Fire many wealthy inhabitants moved west, but the City remained a great commercial centre. The Bank of England was founded in 1694 and this and other

major civic buildings such as the Mansion House, the official residence of the Lord Mayor, were constructed. By the 19th century, the Port of London was the largest in the world and the pivot of the British Empire. The expansion of the Victorian era saw the demolition of residential areas, including many historic buildings, to make way for commercial premises and the railway. Fenchurch Street, Cannon Street, Blackfriars and Liverpool Street stations were constructed and with them came new, wider streets such as Queen Victoria Street, lined with banks and warehouses.

In the Second World War, the City was subjected to terrific assault during the Blitz. German aircraft used the Thames to navigate their way to London and whole areas were laid waste by incendiary bombs. After the War the City was painstakingly rebuilt and since the 1980s, high-rise buildings have changed the landscape once more.

Today the City is one of the most important financial centres in the world, with over 300,000 financial-sector workers making the Monday–Friday commute from outside its boundaries. In comparison, few people actually live here; the City only has about 7,000 residents. The City of London Corporation is keen to attract visitors and investment is being made in hotels and shopping complexes in order to swell the population. Weekends offer quiet, empty streets—and though most tourist attractions are open, many bars, restaurants and shops are closed. Weekdays are the best time to visit the City's churches and during this time the streets and alleyways hum with business—a contrast to the quiet, leafy courtyards and gardens, small oases where office and construction workers take a break or smoke a quick cigarette. It is a concentrated area in constant flux, where ancient jostles with modern, and with much to explore.

THE CITY OF LONDON CORPORATION AND LORD MAYOR

In the 12th century, in recognition of its importance as a trading centre, the City of London was granted the right to run its own affairs by the Crown. Today it is still a city in its own right and a ceremonial county, with its own local government and police force. The City's boundaries are delineated by plaques bearing its coat of arms: the shield of St George borne by dragons. The City motto, *Domine dirige nos* (Lord, direct us), is to be seen inscribed upon many buildings and monuments. The City is divided into 25 districts, known as Wards, each of which is represented by elected councillors and an Alderman.

The City of London Corporation is headed by the Lord Mayor (a role distinct from the Mayor of London), who is elected annually and whose role is unsalaried and non-party political. Only the Sovereign takes precedence over the Lord Mayor in the City. The Lord Mayor's role is essentially that of an ambassador, promoting the City's interests both abroad and at home, and he (or she) presides over of the Court of Aldermen and the Court of Common Council (the Ward representatives), who meet in the Guildhall. The City Corporation is proud to be the oldest continuously elected governing body in the world.

The Lord Mayor's Show, held annually in November since 1215, is the official procession from the City to the Royal Courts of Justice in Westminster, where the Lord Mayor takes the oath of office and swears allegiance to the Crown. The procession is over three miles long and the Lord Mayor rides in a historic gilded state coach, accompanied by sheriffs, aldermen, the Sword Bearer and the Common Cryer. The City's livery companies and regiments also participate. On the way, the procession stops at St Paul's Cathedral, where the Lord Mayor is blessed by the Dean.

The livery companies

The City currently has 108 livery companies, all of which are linked to its medieval trading past when guilds were set up as fraternities for its tradesmen. The guilds maintained professional standards, regulated crafts and provided support, education and places of worship for their members. They were also fiercely protectionist, limiting all activity in each sphere to guild members. In the 21st century they no longer hold a monopoly over trade but are committed to upholding excellence and funding educational and charitable projects. The Worshipful Company of Goldsmiths is still responsible for regulating the gold standard and its Hall is home to the London Assay Office. Some livery companies, such as Maltmen, Bonnet Makers, Pinmakers, Soapmakers, Hatband Makers and Galochemakers, have ceased to exist.

The order of precedence, originally based on financial and political influence, is now based on the antiquity of the company. The Great Twelve are as follows:

1. **Mercers**. Hall on Ironmonger Lane (*map p. 607, D3*)
2. **Grocers**. Hall on Princes Street (*map p. 607, D3*)
3. **Drapers**. Hall on Throgmorton Avenue (*map p. 607, E2*)
4. **Fishmongers**. Hall at London Bridge (*map p. 607, D4–E4*)
5. **Goldsmiths**. Hall on Foster Lane (*map p. 606, C2*)
6. **Skinners**. Hall on Dowgate Hill (*map p. 607, D3*)
7. **Merchant Taylors**. Hall on Threadneedle Street (*map p. 607, E3*)
8. **Haberdashers**. Hall on West Smithfield (*map p. 606, B2*)
9. **Salters**. Hall on Fore Street (*map p. 607, D2*)
10. **Ironmongers**. Hall in Shaftesbury Place (*map p. 606, C2*)
11. **Vintners**. Hall on Upper Thames Street (*map p. 607, D3*)
12. **Clothworkers**. Hall in Dunster Court (*map p. 607, E3*).

Freedom of the City gave a member of a guild or livery company the right to carry out their trade within the Square Mile, the right to vote, immunity from conscription into the armed forces and the right to marry in St Paul's Cathedral. Freedom is still granted and ancient surviving privileges still permit a freeman (or woman) of the City to herd a flock of sheep over London Bridge and a flock of geese down Cheapside. Entry to the livery companies' premises is not open to the public; to visit their halls one must apply in person directly. See the website for further details (*www. cityoflondon.gov.uk*) or ask at the City Information Centre.

City Information Centre

St Paul's Churcyhard. Map p. 606, C3. Open Mon–Fri 9.30–5.30, Sun 10–4. It supplies information on all aspects of the City, including open days of livery halls, City churches, City walks. It also sells travel cards and tickets to the major attractions. For details, see www.cityoflondon.gov.uk.

FLEET STREET & WHITEFRIARS

Map p. 606, A3–B3. Underground: Temple, Blackfriars.

Fleet Street, from Temple Bar to Ludgate Circus, is the ancient road that linked Westminster with the City of London. It derives its name from the River Fleet or Holbourne, a large underground river (parts of which are now a sewer) which rises at Hampstead and Highgate Ponds, flows down the Holborn Valley and joins the Thames near Blackfriars Bridge.

Fleet Street has long been associated with both the legal profession and the printing trade, hence its names the 'Street of Shame' and the 'Street of Ink'. Legal London continues to survive, thrive and expand here and until the late 1980s, Fleet Street was the centre of Britain's newspaper industry (the first newspaper, *The Daily Courant*, was set up in 1702). At one time nearly all national newspapers and international journals were printed in the area. In its 20th-century editorial heyday, when hard-bitten, hard-drinking journalists delivered copy either longhand or banged it out on old-fashioned typewriters, the line between workplace and watering hole was remarkably blurred. Each newspaper had a pub regarded by its staff as its own and many had a nickname. For example, the *Mirror*'s hacks could be found in the 'Stab in the Back' (the White Hart, off Fetter Lane; now demolished). The neighbourhood was especially frenzied late at night, when the dailies went to press with their first editions and the great presses rumbled in the basements. Today, all newspapers have moved their printing plants and editorial offices to Docklands, Wapping and elsewhere. Reuters, the last to remain, left in 2005. Fleet Street is now an ordinary Monday-to-Friday working area of London with some interesting sights and a few historic pubs on the way to St Paul's Cathedral.

FROM TEMPLE BAR TO YE OLD CHESHIRE CHEESE

The Strand ends and Fleet Street begins at the Royal Courts of Justice (*see p. 193*). Here, the **Temple Bar Monument**, the tall column in the middle of the road surmounted by a spiny dragon rampant, marks the boundary between the City of London and the City of Westminster. It was designed by Sir Horace Jones and erected in 1880. The statues of Queen Victoria and Edward VII (as Prince of Wales) are by Sir Joseph Boehm. The bronze dragon, proffering the arms of the City, is by Charles Birch. The two bronze reliefs depicting Queen Victoria visiting the City are by Charles H. Mabey and Charles Kelsey and refer to the ancient custom of the Lord Mayor granting the sovereign permission to visit the City and 'pass Temple Bar'. The custom is still observed on state occasions, when the Lord Mayor presents the sovereign with the Pearl Sword. The frontal relief, depicting Time and Fortune drawing a curtain over old Temple Bar, is also by Mabey. Old Temple Bar was a stone gateway erected on this site after the Great Fire and popularly believed to have been by Wren. By the 1870s it had become a traffic obstacle and was carefully taken down stone by stone. It was later re-erected at Theobalds Park in Hertfordshire, the country estate of Sir Henry Bruce Meux, where it mouldered for over a century. Since its rescue and restoration, it has been re-sited at the entrance to Paternoster Square, north of St Paul's Cathedral (*see p. 40*).

At no. 1 Fleet St (on the south side) is **Child's Bank**. Child & Co. was founded in the 17th century and was one of the UK's oldest private banks. It is now amalgamated with the Royal Bank of Scotland and the current building dates from 1878–80. (The Child family home at Osterley, with interiors by Adam, can be visited; *see p. 487*.) The blue plaque on the wall confirms that this was also the site of the Devil Tavern, demolished in 1787, a literary haunt where Ben Jonson reigned supreme in the 'Apollo Club'. A mock ode under a bust of the god apostrophised wine as 'the true Phoebeian liquor: cheers the brains, makes wit the quicker.' Luminaries of the succeeding generation who drank here included John Aubrey and John Evelyn.

At **no. 17 Fleet St**, the half-timbered house of 1610, with a projecting upper storey and pairs of oriel windows, is one of the few to have escaped the Great Fire. Its lower floor is built of stone and is the entrance to the Inner Temple (*see p. 202*). Built as the Prince Henry pub (presumably named after the elder son of James I), the first floor, known as Prince Henry's Room, has a Jacobean plaster ceiling with the Prince of Wales's feathers and the initials PH. In the 17th century, the pub was known as the Fountain Inn and was visited by Samuel Pepys in 1661, who 'stayed till 12 at night drinking and singing'. The building was closed to the public at the time of writing.

The **Cock Tavern**, a short way on at no. 22, preserves some 17th-century interior fittings from the original inn that stood on the other side of the road. In the 1880s it was rebuilt on the current site. Also on the south side is **Hoare's Bank** (no. 37), founded in 1672 by Richard Hoare, a goldsmith and dealer in precious gems, who moved to Fleet Street in 1690. It is the only remaining private bank in the UK, still run by the Hoare family. The Neoclassical building of Bath stone was designed by Charles Parker in 1829–30 to incorporate an office, strongroom and living space. Famous customers have included Catherine of Braganza, Sir Godfrey Kneller, Samuel Pepys, Lord Byron and Jane Austen. The marvellously old-fashioned banking hall exudes an air of quiet gentility and old-world Englishness. Further along on the same side, **El Vino's wine bar**, founded in 1879 and a Fleet Street institution, served generations of newspapermen, who thronged the bar each evening, mingling with barristers and lawyers, picking up useful gossip. Until 1982, women were not allowed to stand and drink with male colleagues and would only be served at tables in the back room. Still highly regarded as a throwback to bygone days, it has an extensive wine list and serves uncomplicated fare, including breakfast.

Opposite Hoare's Bank is the neo-Gothic church of **St Dunstan-in-the-West**, which has a fine openwork lantern tower and centralised octagonal interior lit by windows high up in the walls. The medieval church, founded c. 1170, was rebuilt by John Shaw in 1830–3 and completed by his son. John Donne was vicar here in 1624–31. The tower was restored in 1950 after bomb damage during World War Two. The famous clock to the right of the tower is by Thomas Harris. Dating from 1671, it was the first clock in London to have a minute hand. It is also the oldest performing clock in London: the hours and quarters are struck by two club-wielding giants (thought to represent Gog and Magog) who turn their heads. The church is also famed for its exterior statue of Elizabeth I (1586), the only one known to have been carved during her reign and which previously stood on top of the Ludgate (an entrance to the City demolished in 1760). Inside, the carved wooden high altar and reredos date from the 17th century and many of the monuments are from the original church. St Dunstan's is home to the Romanian Orthodox Church in London and the limewood painted iconostasis (c. 1860) was brought from Antim Monastery near Bucharest in 1966.

CITY CHURCHES

In 1665, at the time of the outbreak of the Great Fire, there were 107 churches in the City of London. 86 were destroyed and only 51 rebuilt, many of them by Sir Christopher Wren, his pupil Nicholas Hawksmoor, and his assistant, the exceptionally gifted Robert Hooke. Of the resultant new total of 72 churches, 25 were demolished during the rapid development and expansion of London in the later 19th century, reducing the number of churches to 47. Luftwaffe bombs wreaked havoc during the Second World War. Eighteen churches were utterly destroyed, and of those, eight were never rebuilt: at certain points in the City, isolated towers still stand, forlorn reminders of a former church. Today there are 39 churches in the City. The most complete surviving examples by Wren are St Martin-within-Ludgate and St Margaret Lothbury. St Mary Woolnoth is the only City church entirely by Hawksmoor (though altered) and the only one to have escaped the Blitz unscathed. Generally the City churches are open on weekdays (there is typically a half-hour Communion service at lunchtime). Not all are used for regular Anglican worship: some have become study centres or spiritual retreats; others offer a home to other congregations (Romanian Orthodox at St Dunstan-in-the-West, for example). For information about services, worship and events, see *london-city-churches.org.uk*.

Sweeney Todd, the Demon Barber of Fleet Street, is reputed to have had his shop near St Dunstan's, where he murdered his clients and made them into pies. Fetter Lane, leading north (left) to Holborn, beyond St Dunstan's, derives its name either from the *'faitours'* (beggars) with which it used to swarm, or from a colony of *'feutriers'* (felt-makers). Keep on this side of the road as you round the bend in Fleet Street, to appreciate the celebrated view of St Paul's Cathedral rising over the Fleet valley, accompanied now by the Gherkin (*see p. 71*) and the Cheesegrater (*see p. 70*). The small courts and alleys on this side of the road, between Fetter Lane and Shoe Lane, date from the late 17th century and probably originated as gardens. They are full of literary and historical associations and make interesting diversions from Fleet Street.

Ye Old Cheshire Cheese (*145 Fleet St; entrance on Wine Office Court*) is an atmospheric 17th-century pub with 18th-century additions and lashings of modern sawdust on the floor. Although evidence is slim, it is believed that one of its famous patrons was Samuel Johnson, who lived in Gough Square just beyond it (*see below*). Other luminaries who certainly drank here include Dickens, Tennyson, Thackeray, Mark Twain, Conan Doyle and W.B. Yeats. Inside, the fittings are mainly 19th-century and the myriad small rooms are hung with mementoes. The parrot, Polly (d. 1926, now stuffed), was notoriously foul-mouthed and enjoyed imitating customers. On Armistice Night,

1918, she apparently mimicked the sound of popping champagne corks as bottles were opened to celebrate the end of the First World War.

DR JOHNSON'S HOUSE

Map p. 606, A2–A3. Open May–Sept Mon–Sat 11–5.30; Oct–April Mon–Sat 11–5. Closed bank holidays. Admission charge. Shop. T: 020 7353 3745, drjohnsonshouse.org.

Tucked behind Fleet Street in Gough Square, approached via a number of passages—Hind Court, St Dunstan's Court, Wine Office Court or Johnson's Court—which are part of London's pre-Great Fire street pattern, is the handsome red-brick house (c. 1700) where the great lexicographer Dr Samuel Johnson lived from 1748–59. Visiting the house is a pleasure: no compulsory guided tours, no staff in period costume, and plenty of places to sit and read the excellent handbills that are placed in every room.

Originally from Lichfield in Staffordshire, Johnson moved to London with his friend, the actor David Garrick. A struggling journalist when he first occupied the house, he produced *The Rambler* here and wrote *The Vanity of Human Wishes*. It was also while living here that he was commissioned to compile the celebrated Dictionary. Published in two volumes in 1755, it went through four editions in Johnson's lifetime and instantly became the standard authority. A congenial man with a wide circle of friends, Johnson nevertheless did not enjoy great wealth. He lived simply at Gough Square with his wife, Elizabeth Porter, 20 years his senior, until her death in 1752, and later his Jamaican servant, Francis Barber, joined him.

The house is unostentatious and pleasing. On the ground floor is the **Parlour**, with a portrait of Francis Barber. The stairs lead to a landing with hinged partitions, allowing the staircase to be blocked off and one large room created from the **Withdrawing Room** and **Miss Williams's Room**. The authoress Anna Williams was a friend of Mrs Johnson and companion to Dr Johnson after his wife's death. The portrait of her was painted by Sir Joshua Reynolds' sister Frances. By all accounts Miss Williams became foul tempered in later life, perhaps owing to a failed cataract operation which left her blind. Francis Barber fled the household twice because of her; but the breach was healed and 'Frank' was the main beneficiary of Johnson's will.

At the top of the house is the **Garret**, where the Dictionary was written and where, at long tables, six clerks took down Johnson's succinct and often witty definitions. A facsimile copy is available for browsing. Throughout the rooms are period furnishings and objects, several of them personal to Johnson or to his close friends. Johnson's own walking stick is on show, as is his piece of 'healing gold', a medal he received when as a young child he was touched for the King's Evil by Queen Anne.

Facing the house, at the east end of Gough Square, is a modern **sculpture of Dr Johnson's cat**, Hodge, sitting with oyster shells by his side. Johnson regularly bought oysters for him; in those days they were cheap, not the luxury they have become.

SOME SPLENDID FORMER PRESS PALACES

The **former Daily Telegraph building** (135–141 Fleet St), now the London headquarters of Goldman Sachs, was completed in 1931 by Elcock & Sutcliffe with Thomas

FLEET STREET
Mercury figures fly from the British Isles, spreading news
around the globe. Detail of the façade of the former
Daily Telegraph building (1931).

Tait and is a fusion of monumental classical motifs (twin Mercurys scurrying East and West, with a map of Britain and Ireland behind them) and giant Egyptian-style columns. The huge clock is by the Birmingham Guild of Handicraft.

Further down, at 120–129, across Shoe Lane, are the **former offices of _The Daily Express_**, a sleek and sensational Art Deco building with bands of clear glass and black Vitrolite (opaque tinted glass made by Pilkington) set in chromium strips. Designed by Sir Owen Williams in 1930–3, it is London's earliest curtain-walled building and has a particularly sumptuous Art Deco entrance hall by Robert Atkinson. Although closed to the public, it is usually open as part of London Open House Weekend (_for dates, see londonopenhouse.org_). It was built when the _Daily Express_, owned by the press baron Lord Beaverbrook, was Britain's most popular paper. Evelyn Waugh briefly worked here in 1938 and went on to lampoon the experience in his novel _Scoop_.

Directly opposite the _Daily Express_ building, on the north side, the huge stone edifice with an oculus above the doorway occupied by a bugle-blowing herald angel is the **former headquarters of Reuters**, designed by Sir Edwin Lutyens in 1935. Reuters left in 2005 and the building is now legal and financial offices with a ground-floor restaurant called Lutyens.

ST BRIDE'S

Directly behind the Reuters building is Wren's church of St Bride (_map p. 606, B3; usually open daily except Sat_), the 'spiritual home of the media' since Wynkyn de Worde, the first printer to set up in Fleet Street in 1500, was buried in the churchyard. Samuel Pepys was baptised here. The church was rebuilt after the Great Fire, in 1671–8, and the soaring, telescopic steeple was added 1701–3. It is the tallest of all Wren's spires

(226ft) and has launched a thousand similes, the most famous of which likens it to a tiered wedding cake. The church was gutted by bombs in 1940 but the steeple remained standing despite a raging fire which caused its bells to melt and fall. The church was rebuilt from 1954 by Godfrey Allen, an authority on Wren. The *trompe l'oeil* behind the altar, giving the impression of an apse, is by Glyn Jones. Prior to reconstruction, the site was excavated by F.W. Grimes and Roman remains were discovered, along with the foundations of six previous churches on the site as well as thousands of human skeletons, many believed to have been victims of the Great Plague. An exhibition in the **crypt** displays the finds. In the northeast chapel is the **Journalists' Altar**, commemorating those in the news industry who have died, been kidnapped or are missing in the field.

Behind the church, in St Bride's Passage, is the red-brick **St Bride Foundation**, founded in 1891 as a social, cultural and recreational centre for locals and for those in the printing trade. On the upper level is the St Bride Library, with important collections relating to printing, publishing, typography and the graphic arts.

FROM FLEET STREET TO THE RIVER

The area south of Fleet Street, between Bouverie Street and Whitefriars Street (*map p. 606. B3*), was once the **site of the medieval monastery of Whitefriars**, so-called because the Carmelite monks wore white. Remains of the crypt may be seen behind a glass wall in a sunken courtyard off Magpie Alley (from Bouverie St) or Ashentree Court (from Whitefriars St).

New Bridge Street leads south to the Thames and Blackfriars station and bridge. The building at no. 14 is on the **site of Bridewell Palace**, possibly founded in Norman times but renovated by Henry VIII for official use during the early years of his reign. Holbein's *The Ambassadors*, which hangs in the National Gallery, was painted in Bridewell Palace. Edward VI granted the palace to the City of London and it became a house of correction for wayward women and afterwards the notorious Bridewell Prison. It was pulled down in the 19th century.

Further down on the same side, curving round the corner of New Bridge Street and Victoria Embankment, is **Unilever House** (1932), with its long Ionic loggia, commissioned by the Lancashire soap manufacturers Lever Brothers after their merger with the Dutch margarine company Margarine Unie. Next door (beyond the curve), the neo-Renaissance building is the former City of London School for Boys (Davis & Emmanuel, 1882). Further on, overlooking the Embankment, is the neo-Gothic **Sion College** (Sir Arthur Blomfield, 1887), founded c. 1630 for the benefit of the Anglican clergy. Its chief glory was its library of 300,000 volumes, which possessed many rarities but suffered considerable war damage. The building was sold in 1996 and the books and manuscripts were split between Lambeth Palace and King's College Library.

On the river here is moored the HMS *President* (1918), a Royal Navy battleship which served during the First World War (and one of only three such to survive). The view across the water takes in the London Eye and Oxo Tower and, in the other direction, Tate Modern and the Shard.

BLACKFRIARS & LUDGATE HILL

Map p. 606, B3. Underground: Blackfriars.

Blackfriars, the southwest corner of the City, occupies the area around Blackfriars Station, a major terminus with entrances on both the north and sound sides of Blackfriars Bridge. Blackfriars Millennium Pier is a stop for river bus services. Blackfriars takes its name from the Dominicans, who wore black habits and who established extensive monastic buildings between the Thames and Ludgate Hill. Edward I granted them the land in 1274 and allowed them to rebuild the City Wall around this area. It was customary in medieval cities for the two mendicant orders to set up houses close to the city walls. Thus the Dominicans were at Blackfriars, near Ludgate and the mouth of the Fleet river, while the Franciscans (Greyfriars) occupied the areas around Newgate and Aldgate. The Blackfriars buildings were used for state occasions and meetings of the Privy Council. A synod here in 1382 condemned Wycliffe's teaching as heretical. It was also here that a decree of divorce was heard between Henry VIII and Queen Katherine of Aragon. The friary was closed in 1538, during the Dissolution of the Monasteries.

BLACKFRIARS LANE AND CARTER LANE

When the wide thoroughfare of Queen Victoria Street was created in 1867–71, it sliced through many ancient streets and alleys and as a result created wedge-shaped sites on which triangular buildings were built. One of the last remaining is the **Black Friar pub**, opposite the station on the corner of New Bridge Street. The sculpture over the main door is of a rotund, black-robed friar smiling beatifically down on passing traffic. Built in the 1870s, the pub has a unique Arts and Crafts interior dating from 1905 (restored 1983) of polychrome marble slabs and beaten bronze bas-reliefs of jolly friars at work. In the restaurant, there are red marble columns, an arched mosaic ceiling and further decorative figures.

From the pub, cross under the railway bridge and immediately on the left is Blackfriars Lane, leading into Playhouse Yard (*map p. 606, B3*), where Richard Burbage's theatre once stood. Further up Blackfriars Lane on the right is the **Apothecaries' Hall**, dating partly from the 1660s, partly from the 1780s. It is built on the site of the friary guest house.

Carter Lane, off Blackfriars Lane to the right, is an atmospheric street of mainly pre-20th-century buildings with narrow alleys leading off it. It has so far managed to escape development and is favoured by TV crews when a location redolent of yesteryear is required. The **former St Paul's Choir School** (F.C. Penrose, 1874–5) at the end of the street on the left (corner of Dean's Court; *map p. 606, C3*) has been a youth hostel since 1975. The neo-Renaissance building is reminiscent of an Italian *palazzo* and would not look out of place amongst the buildings commissioned by Prince Albert in South Kensington. The sgraffito Latin frieze running along the first storey is from St Paul's letter to the Galatians, 6:14: 'MIHI AUTEM ABSIT GLORIARI NISI IN CRUCE

QUEEN VICTORIA STREET
Detail of the decoration of the Black Friar pub.

DOMINI NOSTRI JESU CHRISTI / PER QUEM MIHI MUNDUS CRUCIFIXUS EST ET EGO MUNDO' (But God forbid that I should glory, save in the cross of our Lord Jesus Christ, by whom the world is crucified unto me, and I unto the world).

In Dean's Court itself, the **former St Paul's Deanery** (1672) was designed by Wren. The two-tone red-brick façade, with sash and dormer windows, is a vision of restrained elegance. John Donne, when Dean, lived in the earlier house on the site. Since 1996, it has been the official residence of the Bishop of London. From here you can either continue up Dean's Court to St Paul's (*see p. 33*) or, from Carter Lane, go down Addle Hill and then Wardrobe Terrace to reach the church of **St Andrew-by-the-Wardrobe**

NEW BRIDGE STREET
Detail of Unilever House (1932).

(*standrewbythewardrobe.net; map p. 606, B3–C3*) perched above Queen Victoria Street. It was rebuilt by Wren in 1685–94 and is one of his plainer churches (restored in 1961 after war damage). It took its name from the proximity of the King's Great Wardrobe, the Crown's store of arms and clothing that used to be in the area until 1666, when it was destroyed by the Great Fire. The only part of the Royal Household to remain in the City is the College of Arms (*see below*). On Sunday mornings, St Andrew's is used by the St Gregorios Indian Orthodox Church (also known as the Malankara Church), an ancient congregation founded by St Thomas the Apostle in AD 52.

QUEEN VICTORIA STREET

The **College of Arms** (*map p. 606, C3*), occupying a handsome building on Queen Victoria Street with the dome of St Paul's rising immediately behind it, is the official heraldic authority for the UK and much of the Commonwealth (*open Mon–Fri 10–4; the Officer in Waiting is available to deal with enquiries; souvenirs and heraldic books may be purchased from reception*). The College was first incorporated by Richard III in 1484 and its heralds received a new charter from Queen Mary I (and a building on the present site) in 1555. This was destroyed in the Great Fire and the present building (1671–88) was designed by Francis Sandford, Rouge Dragon Pursuivant, and Morris Emmett, the King's bricklayer. Splendid 19th-century wrought-iron gates, formerly at Goodrich Court, Herefordshire (demolished), were given to the College in 1956.

The Officers of Arms are appointed by the Crown on the advice of the Duke of Norfolk as hereditary Earl Marshal, whom they assist in planning and participating in ancient and splendid ceremonies including the State Opening of Parliament, state funerals and the monarch's coronation. They consist of three Kings of Arms (Garter, Clarenceux and Norroy & Ulster), six Heralds (Windsor, Somerset, Richmond, York, Chester and Lancaster) and four Pursuivants (Bluemantle, Portcullis, Rouge Croix and Rouge Dragon). Since the 15th century at least, the Kings of Arms have been responsible for granting coats of arms on behalf of the Crown to eminent persons and organisations. A right to arms by inheritance is established by proving and recording at the College a descent from someone already on record as being entitled to bear arms. Suitably qualified American citizens who can prove descent from someone once a subject of the Crown may be granted honorary arms. Visitors can see the Earl Marshal's Court with its throne (Court of Chivalry). The heraldic and genealogical records and collections compiled over the course of more than five centuries are unique (*not available to the public except for groups by prior arrangement*). The officers will make searches and undertake genealogical enquiries.

The church of **St Benet Paul's Wharf** stands marooned in traffic between Queen Victoria Street and Upper Thames Street, a roaring modern thoroughfare not particularly pleasant for the pedestrian. The original 12th-century church was destroyed in the Great Fire and its successor was built by Wren's associate Robert Hooke in 1678–84. It is now used by Welsh Anglicans and services are in Welsh. Henry Fielding was married here in 1748 and Inigo Jones (d. 1652) was buried in the earlier church (monument destroyed in the Fire). The 17th-century Restoration interior is notable because it escaped both Victorian improvements and Luftwaffe bombing.

At no. 101 Queen Victoria Street is the **international headquarters of the Salvation Army**, a quasi-military Christian movement founded in 1865 by the Methodists William and Catherine Booth, to help those in need. The current building, the third on the site (Sheppard Robson, 2004), fulfils the brief 'modern in design, frugal in operation, evangelical in purpose'. Footfall has increased since the opening of the Millennium Bridge (*see p. 421*) and each year millions pass by the fritted glass premises with Gospel texts on its windows.

Beyond, on the other side of the road, is the church of **St Nicholas Cole Abbey**, an elegant balustraded box with elaborately pedimented arched windows, built by Wren in 1672–8 on the site of its pre-Fire predecessor. The church had been closed for many years but is recently reopened after a full renovation it is now a centre for religious education and hosts the 'St Nick's Talks', lunchtime Bible discussions aimed at City workers. Coffee is served in The Wren café. Note the richly-coloured glass of the east windows, by Keith New (1962), who also contributed to the new Coventry Cathedral.

South down Lambert Hill is the surviving tower of **St Mary Somerset**, in a small garden on Upper Thames Street. The rest of the church, built by Wren in 1695, was taken down c. 1870. The eight Baroque pinnacles are noteworthy.

LUDGATE HILL AND THE APPROACH TO ST PAUL'S

Ludgate Circus (*map p. 606, B3*) is no more than a busy traffic junction of Farringdon Street, Ludgate Hill and Fleet Street. Fleet Place on Limeburner Lane commemorates the site of the **Fleet Prison**, which stood on the east side of the Fleet river and was used for those committed by the Star Chamber and for debtors. The prison was twice rebuilt, after destruction in the Great Fire (1666) and again in the Gordon Riots (1780); it was finally pulled down in 1844–6.

Ludgate Hill to the east rises towards St Paul's Cathedral. Some way up on the left, next to Ye Olde London pub, is the church of **St Martin-within-Ludgate** (*open weekdays 11–3, services on Thur*), with a slender lead spire. The church was rebuilt by Wren, probably with Robert Hooke, in 1677–86 and has fine woodwork with an original reredos and pulpit. A Chinese Christian congregation gathers here every Sunday. Although the roof was damaged during the Blitz, the church was the least damaged of Wren's City's churches during World War Two. The 17th-century breadshelves, originally from St Mary Magdalen, Fish Street, display fake bread for effect. Wealthy parishioners would leave food for poorer members of the parish on these shelves. Captain (later Admiral Sir) William Penn, father of the founder of Pennsylvania, was married in the former church in 1643. The old church stood just within the Roman wall close to Lud Gate, the first curfew gate in London to be closed at night. Statues from the gate, notably that of Elizabeth I, may be seen at St Dunstan-in-the-West on Fleet Street (*see p. 23*). The gate is popularly believed to be named after King Lud, mythical founder of London, but the name is more likely to derive from the Old English *hlid*, a gap or opening, or *hlið*, a slope or hillside.

Further up again, in Ave Maria Lane, is **Stationers' Hall**, the guildhall of the Stationers' Company. The fine Neoclassical stone-faced east front, facing the outer courtyard, is by Robert Mylne (1800). The Stationers' Company, founded c. 1402, was incorporated by royal charter in 1557 and for a time it preserved the sole right of printing in England (apart from the presses at Oxford and Cambridge), while it had a monopoly of the publishing of almanacs until 1771. Until the passing of the Copyright Act of 1911, every work published in Great Britain had to be registered for copyright at Stationers' Hall. In 1933 the company was amalgamated with that of the Newspaper Makers. A plane tree in the court behind the Hall marks the spot where seditious books used to be burnt.

Behind Stationers' Hall is **Amen Court**, a quiet little nook that escaped World War Two bombing, with private entrances on Ave Maria Lane and Warwick Lane. Nos 1–3 were built in 1671–3 as dwellings for the Canons Residentiary of St Paul's. The Black Dog of Newgate, a fearsome ghostly hound, is reputed to haunt the high wall that backs onto the site of Newgate Prison.

At the top of Ludgate Hill is the entrance to St Paul's Cathedral.

ST PAUL'S CATHEDRAL

Map p. 606, C3. Underground: St Paul's. Open Mon–Sat 8.30–4.30, last tickets at 4pm. No visitors on Sun. T: 020 7246 8357, stpauls.co.uk. This is a very popular destination; it is worth booking online to avoid the queue. Ticket prices are hefty. Leave plenty of time for your visit: visitors are ejected promptly at 4.30 and even before that, vergers begin roping off sections of the building. Photography is not allowed, and silence is supposed to be observed in the Whispering Gallery. These rules are sometimes noisily enforced by cathedral staff. Guided tours of the cathedral and crypt can be taken for no extra charge (ask at the guiding desk; no advance bookings). The Triforium Tour (fee payable) includes the Trophy Room with Wren's Great Model (to book, see phone number above).

St Paul's Cathedral stands on the top of Ludgate Hill, which at 58ft above sea level shares with the summit of Cornhill the accolade of being the highest point in the City. St Paul's is the largest and most famous of all the City's many churches, the cathedral of the Bishop of London and the English Baroque masterpiece of Sir Christopher Wren, built between 1675 and 1711. Wren deliberately designed it to dominate the City landscape and until the construction of the Aviva Tower in 1969, it was the tallest building in the City, complemented by the myriad spires of surrounding churches, designed by Wren and others. Today, despite the St Paul's Cathedral Preservation Act of 1935, its impact is drastically lessened by recent high-rise eruptions. Nevertheless, St Paul's is a true icon of London and fulfils Wren's belief that architecture, especially public architecture, has the power not only to establish a nation but also to induce its people to love their country. The surrounding area was devastated during the Blitz but St Paul's survived thanks to the St Paul's Watch, a group of volunteers who defended it during incendiary bombing raids. The cathedral has recently undergone a £40 million programme of repair and conservation: the Portland stone of which it is built gleams once more and cleaning has revealed the fine workmanship of the 17th-century carving. It is worth spending several hours in this magnificent place—but be prepared for large crowds at all times of year and queues to climb the dome.

There is no evidence to support the theory that a Roman temple stood on the commanding site now occupied by St Paul's, although Roman artefacts have been found in the area and Londinium's western hilltop would have been a logical site for a capitolium. What is certain is that a Christian church was founded here in AD 604 by Mellitus, a missionary companion of St Augustine who later became Archbishop of Canterbury. The earliest buildings were frequently destroyed by fire and Viking attacks. In 1087 Bishop Maurice, chaplain to William the Conqueror, founded the church which went on to become, after much rebuilding, the splendid medieval cathedral of Old St Paul's. It was the longest cathedral in England (600ft) and the central tower was surmounted by a steeple which at the lowest estimate was 460ft high—but destroyed by lightning in 1561 and never re-erected. Today St Paul's is one of the great churches of the Protestant world, but it is worth remembering that until the reign of Henry VIII it was a Catholic cathedral where Mass was celebrated and where saints were venerated. In Old St Paul's John Wycliffe was tried for heresy in 1377 and Tyndale's New Testament was publicly burned here in 1527. By the 17th century it had become sadly neglected and restorations were begun under Charles I. Inigo Jones added a classical portico to the west front, one of his objects being to banish from the church the 'secular rabble' that for over a century had used the nave (Paul's Walk) as a place of business (and frequently intrigue). Jones's restorations were halted by the outbreak of Civil War in 1642. Parliamentarians seized control of the cathedral and it was used as a barracks for 800 horses. After the Restoration in 1660, plans to restore and repair the cathedral were once again considered until the cathedral practically burned down in the Great Fire of 1666. Wren conceived several designs for a new building, including the so-called Great Model, (housed in the Trophy Room), which, like Michelangelo's design for St Peter's, was in the form of a Greek Cross. As had happened with St Peter's likewise, the design was modified to a Latin Cross and finally, nine years after the Fire, work commenced on Sir Christopher Wren's new St Paul's; the first cathedral to be built in England since the Reformation. Building costs were largely met by a tax on sea-borne coal entering London. The cathedral was declared complete in 1711.

EXTERIOR OF ST PAUL'S

The exterior of St Paul's consists throughout of two orders, the lower Corinthian, the upper Composite. On the north and south sides the upper order is merely a curtain wall, not corresponding with the height of the aisles and concealing the flying buttresses that support the clerestory of the nave. The balustrade along the top was added against the wishes of Wren, who cynically remarked that 'ladies think nothing well without an edging'. The west front, approached by a broad flight of steps and flanked by two towers, has a lower colonnade of twelve columns and an upper one of eight. In the pediment, sculpture by Francis Bird (1706) depicts the Conversion of St Paul. Above the pediment stands the figure of St Paul, flanked by other apostles and the four Evangelists, also by Bird. Bird also carved the statue of Queen Anne that stood by the west front (the current statue is a copy). Anne was the reigning monarch at the time of the cathedral's completion. In the northeast tower is a peal of bells and in the south-west tower are Great Paul (a bell weighing nearly 17 tons, the largest bell in the UK) and Great Tom, a bell tolled on the death of senior members of the Royal Family, the Archbishop of Canterbury, the Bishop of London, the Dean of St Paul's or the Lord Mayor of London.

The famous **dome**, built to rival that of St Peter's in Rome and one of the largest cathedral domes in the world, lifts its cross 365ft above the City. The outer dome is of wood covered with lead. Between it and the painted inner dome is a cone of brick which rises between them and bears the weight of the elegant lantern on the top.

ST PAUL'S CATHEDRAL: WEST FAÇADE

INTERIOR OF ST PAUL'S

The interior, though 'classical' in detail, still retains the general ground plan of a Gothic church—nave and aisles with triforium and clerestory, transepts and a deep choir—with, however, the great dome-space at the crossing. Against the massive piers rise Corinthian pilasters and stone enrichments relieve the wall-spaces.

On entering St Paul's, the visitor should first walk up the centre of the nave to the great space beneath the dome, where the huge proportions of the church are especially impressive.

The dome (A): The inner cupola of the dome soars 218ft above you, resting upon massive supports, of which the four chief ones, at the angles, afford room in their interiors for the vestries and the library staircase. Nineteenth-century mosaics executed by Salviati of Venice fill the spandrels, traditionally seen as linking spaces between the heavenly realm above and the earthly realm below and thus decorated with images of those who transmitted God's message to mankind: here on the west we see Old Testament prophets (from south to north, Isaiah, Jeremiah, Ezekiel and Daniel, designed by Alfred Stevens and partly executed by W.E.F. Britten). The other spandrels show the Evangelists: SS Matthew and John (by G.F. Watts) and SS Mark and Luke (by Britten). In the quarter-domes, at a lower level, are more recent mosaics by Sir W.B. Richmond (d. 1921).

Above the arches is the Whispering Gallery (*see p. 40*), above which again are recesses with 19th-century marble statues of the Fathers of the Church. The cupola, above, was decorated by Sir James Thornhill with eight scenes in monochrome from the life of St Paul. Monochrome was used deliberately in a carefully planned scheme for the decoration of the new church, which was to be Anglican in spirit: dignified, dedicated to the glory of God, neither Roman Catholic (too gaudy) nor Puritan (too plain). Later decorations have eclipsed the original intent to a great degree. The spandrel mosaics are a marked example.

Quire (B): Although a Luftwaffe bomb struck the east end of the quire, bringing down tons of masonry onto the sanctuary, the priceless carvings escaped almost undamaged. Above the high altar is a carved and gilded baldachin of marble and oak, by Godfrey Allen and S.E. Dykes Bower, replacing the reredos damaged in 1941 and serving as a memorial to Commonwealth citizens of all creeds and races who lost their lives in the two World Wars. The tall bronze candlesticks in front are copied from four now in St-Bavon in Ghent, which were made by Benedetto da Rovezzano for the tomb of Henry VIII at Windsor but were sold under the Commonwealth.

The beautiful carved choir stalls and organ case are by Grinling Gibbons. The organ was originally built in 1695 by Father Smith (*see p. 204*) to John Blow's direction, and was played by Jeremiah Clarke at its inauguration.

The mosaics which decorate the vaulting of the quire were designed by Sir W.B. Richmond and were executed in 1891–1912. The central panel of the great apse shows *Christ in Majesty*, seated upon the rainbow: 'Behold, a throne was set in heaven, and one sat on the throne. And he that sat was to look upon like a jasper and a sardine stone: and there was a rainbow round about the throne, in sight like unto an emerald.' (Revelation 4:2–3) In the shallow cupolas above the choir proper are (from west to east) the *Creation of the Beasts*, *Creation of the Birds* and *Creation of the Fishes*.

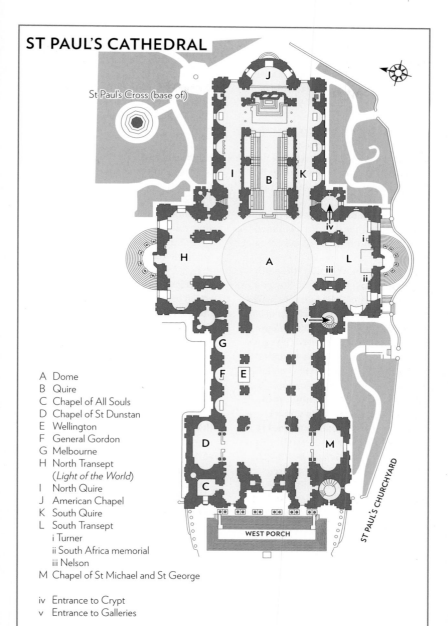

ST PAUL'S CATHEDRAL

St Paul's Cross (base of)

WEST PORCH

ST PAUL'S CHURCHYARD

A Dome
B Quire
C Chapel of All Souls
D Chapel of St Dunstan
E Wellington
F General Gordon
G Melbourne
H North Transept
   (*Light of the World*)
I North Quire
J American Chapel
K South Quire
L South Transept
   i Turner
   ii South Africa memorial
   iii Nelson
M Chapel of St Michael and St George

iv Entrance to Crypt
v Entrance to Galleries

Monuments on the north side: The monuments in the cathedral are eloquent of the nation's history, commemorating men of art and invention as well as victors in war. The most important are as follows:

The **Chapel of All Souls (C)** was dedicated in 1925 to the memory of Field Marshal Earl Kitchener of Khartoum (d. 1916), with a recumbent figure by Reid Dick and a roll of honour of the Royal Engineers.

The **Chapel of St Dunstan (D)** has a memorial (under the first window) to Lord Leighton (d. 1896), painter and sculptor.

The **Monument to the Duke of Wellington (E)** is by Alfred Stevens. Above the pediments at either end are allegorical groups: *Truth Plucking out the Tongue of Falsehood* and *Valour Thrusting down Cowardice*. The equestrian statue on the top was executed by Tweed in 1912 from a sketch-model by Stevens.

Opposite it is the **Monument to General Gordon (F)** and further down on the left is the **Memorial to Lord Melbourne** (d. 1848) **(G)**, with *Two Angels at the Gate of Death* by Marochetti.

North transept (H): This part of the church was severely damaged by a bomb in April 1941, when the transept dome and the whole of the north porch, with the famous inscription from Wren's tomb: '*Si monumentum requiris, circumspice*' ('If you would see his monument, look around you'), fell into the crypt below. Here is William Holman Hunt's third version of his painting **The Light of the World** (1900). Commemorated here are the composer Sir Arthur Sullivan, of the Gilbert and Sullivan light operas; and Sir Joshua Reynolds, with a monument by Flaxman. The statue of Turner by Patrick McDowell (1862) had its palette and brushes restored in 1992 after they had been missing for over 100 years.

North quire (I): At the entrance to the north quire aisle are gates by Jean Tijou (c. 1712) and a statue of Samuel Johnson in a Roman toga, by Bacon. The choir screen, formed of the original altar rails, is also by Tijou. The Chapel of the Modern Martyrs commemorates Anglican martyrs since 1850.

American Chapel (J): The chapel which occupies the cathedral apse is the memorial to America's fallen in the Second World War, with a roll of honour containing 28,000 names of those who fell in operations based on Britain.

South quire (K): In the aisle is the figure (clad in a shroud) of John Donne (1573–1631), poet and Dean of St Paul's, the only comparatively uninjured monument (by Nicholas Stone) to have survived the destruction of Old St Paul's. It still shows traces of fire.

South transept (L): Here is the entrance to the crypt (*see below*), beyond which, at the angle of the dome-space, is a statue of the prison reformer John Howard (1726–90), the first monument admitted into the new St Paul's.

On the south wall of the transept is a memorial to J.M.W. Turner **(i)**. On the other side of the door is a bronze memorial **(ii)** by Princess Louise, the sculptor daughter of Queen Victoria, to the

Colonial Troops who fell in the second South African War. On the west wall of the transept is a monument to Lord Nelson, shown leaning on an anchor, by John Flaxman **(iii)**; the reliefs on the pedestal represent the Arctic Ocean, the North Sea, the Nile and the Mediterranean.

Chapel of St Michael and St George (M): This chapel has since 1906 been occupied by the Most Distinguished Order of St Michael and St George, with the banners of the Knights Grand Cross (GCMG). The order (instituted in 1818) is conferred for distinguished services in colonial or foreign affairs. The prelate's throne is a memorial to Lord Forrest (d. 1918) of Bunbury, Western Australia, the first Australian peer. On the left is the door to the Geometrical Staircase—a spiral of 92 stone steps and an iron balustrade by Tijou (*accessible only on a guided tour*).

St Paul's Crypt and former Treasury

The crypt (*entrance in the south transept*) corresponds in size with the upper church. Here are the graves of many of those whose monuments are above, as well as many additional monuments and graves to those who made outstanding contributions to the nation. Below the south choir aisle, at the foot of the staircase, is a bust of Sir John Macdonald (1815–91), first Prime Minister of Canada. In the second bay are monuments to the painter Sir Edwin Landseer and the hymn-writer and Bishop of Calcutta Reginald Heber (d. 1826), by Chantrey. In the pavement is the tomb of Sir Lawrence Alma-Tadema. In the next bay is the tombstone of Sir Christopher Wren, above which is the original tablet with its famous epitaph (*see North Transept, above*).

This bay and the one to the north are known as 'Painters' Corner', for here rest Lord Leighton, Benjamin West, Sir Thomas Lawrence, Landseer, Millais, Turner, Reynolds and Holman Hunt. On the walls are memorials to William Blake, Van Dyck, Constable and Lutyens. John Singer Sargent is commemorated by a relief group of the *Redemption*, which he designed.

The chapel at the east end of the crypt, formerly called St Faith's, was dedicated in 1960 as the Chapel of the Order of the British Empire. Further west a wall tablet marks the grave of Sir Alexander Fleming (d. 1955), discoverer of penicillin.

In the west portion of the crypt is Wellington's colossal porphyry sarcophagus and further on a memorial to Florence Nightingale (1820–1910). Below the centre of the dome, Lord Nelson rests in a coffin made from the mainmast of the French ship *L'Orient*, enclosed in a sarcophagus of black and white marble originally designed for Cardinal Wolsey. In recesses to the south and north are other military heroes and a bust of Lawrence of Arabia (d. 1935).

A plaque commemorates 5,746 men of the garrison of Kut (Iraq) who died in 1916. In the adjoining recess is a memorial to the Labour politician Sir Stafford Cripps (d. 1952), with a fine bust by Epstein. Opposite is a bust of George Washington near a tablet to William Fiske, Olympic bobsleigh medallist and the first US citizen to join the RAF. He lost his life in the Battle of Britain, 'an American citizen who died that England might live'. The memorial to the poet and critic W.E. Henley (d. 1903) has a bust by Rodin.

The **former Treasury** is home to 'Oculus: an eye into St Paul's', a 270° film covering the history of the cathedral from its earliest foundation and offering virtual tours of the dome and galleries as well as of Wren's Great Model, the vast maquette of the projected cathedral that was produced for King Charles II.

The galleries

The upper parts of the cathedral are reached by a staircase from the south aisle (*marked on the plan on p. 37*). Be warned: once committed to the ascent, it is not possible to turn back. First (easy to climb to) is the **Whispering Gallery**, 112ft in diameter, which runs within the lower dome. It takes its name from the fact that words whispered near the wall on one side can be distinctly heard at the other side: but the pressure of crowds often makes it difficult to test this. However, this is the best point from which to admire Thornhill's monochrome paintings in the dome.

Further up is the **Stone Gallery**, the exterior gallery around the base of the dome, which commands a fine view of London. Finally, up 528 steps from ground level (not recommended to anyone who suffers from claustrophobia or vertigo), is the **Golden Gallery**, a narrow ledge running around the base of the lantern. From here one is rewarded by panoramic views.

PATERNOSTER SQUARE & ST PAUL'S CHURCHYARD

North of the cathedral is **Paternoster Square** (*map p. 606, C3*), where printing and publishing warehouses were based until their annihilation during the Blitz. Post-war rebuilding was contentious and generally disliked, until redevelopment by Sir William Whitfield in 2000 finally created a worthy setting for Wren's great masterpiece. At the entrance to the square is **Old Temple Bar**, the stone gateway originally erected in Fleet Street after the Great Fire (*see p. 23*). In the pedestrian-only piazza, modern buildings fan out from a central column topped by a flaming gilded urn. *Paternoster*, the bronze sculpture of Christ and his sheep, is by Elizabeth Frink (1975). The London Stock Exchange relocated to Paternoster Square in 2004.

In the northeast churchyard stood **St Paul's Cross** (a column topped by a gilded statue of St Paul). In the 16th century it functioned as an open-air rallying point where members of the public could come to hear the Word.

East of the cathedral is New Change, where St Paul's Cathedral School (founded 1123; current buildings 1960s, incorporating the surviving tower of St Augustine, Watling Street) is based. Over the road squats the bulky new shopping complex One New Change, nicknamed the 'Stealth Bomber'. The public roof terrace affords good views of the cathedral façade.

The street on the north and south sides of St Paul's is known as **St Paul's Churchyard**. Across the south section on the right, the distinctive tent-like structure is the **City of London Information Centre**, with useful visitor information on all things City-related (*see p. 21*). In front of the cathedral are attractively planted public gardens with fountains and sculpture. Standing with your back to the south porch and looking straight ahead along the stepped St Peter's Hill (at the top of which is a monument to City firefighters of World War Two), you can see down to the Millennium Bridge (*described on p. 421*), built to connect St Paul's with Tate Modern and the South Bank. From here, it is an easy stroll to see the Old Deanery in Dean's Court and the old Choir School in Carter Lane (*described on pp. 28–9*).

NORTH OF ST PAUL'S: KING EDWARD STREET

On the junction of Newgate and King Edward streets stands the shell of **Christ Church Newgate Street** (*map p. 606, C2*), on the site of Greyfriars church, a Franciscan foundation of 1225 and the largest church in London after St Paul's Cathedral until its destruction in the Fire. Wren and Hooke re-built the church in 1667–87 on a reduced footprint over the old choir, and the tall trees in the churchyard to the west mark where the former 300ft medieval nave was. The church was badly bombed in World War Two, but the tower was restored in 1960 and is now a private house. The ruined nave is now Christchurch Greyfriars Garden and the pergolas with their tumbling wisteria and roses mark where the nave piers once stood. The remains of the east wall were lost during road-widening in the 1970s but a low wall, erected in 2001 by Merill Lynch, marks the line.

THE OLD POSTAL BUILDINGS AND POSTMAN'S PARK

North up King Edward Street (with St Paul's behind you; *map p. 606, C2*), the former General Post Office building, the **King Edward Building** (1911), is by Sir Henry Tanner and the foundation stone was laid by King Edward VII. The statue in front is of Sir Rowland Hill, whose postal reforms led to the introduction of the first postage stamp, the Penny Black. The King Edward Building stands on the site of Christ's Hospital, the famous 'Blue Coat School', founded by Edward VI in 1552 to educate City orphans. The foundation included St Thomas's Hospital for the sick and Bridewell Hospital for idle vagabonds. The school moved to Horsham in West Sussex in 1902. The bust of a famous former pupil, the essayist Charles Lamb, was moved to the Watch House, Giltspur Street, in 1962 (*see p. 44*). Opposite is another former post office building, originally known as **GPO North** (Sir Henry Tanner, c. 1895), with a façade extending onto St Martin's le-Grand.

Next door, **Postman's Park** occupies the area between King Edward Street and St Martin's le-Grand. It was laid out in the 1880s in the churchyard of St Botolph-without-Aldersgate (*see below*) and the former burial grounds of Christ Church Newgate Street and St Leonard Foster (a church not rebuilt after the Fire). It is higher than street level because, due to overcrowding, bodies were laid flat and covered with earth rather than buried. On the north side (left as you enter from King Edward Street) is the Watts Memorial, a lean-to with a wall covered in Arts and Crafts ceramic tiles made by Royal Doulton. Each tile commemorates 'those who have heroically lost their lives trying to save another'. The idea was suggested by the painter G.F. Watts, who believed 'everyday heroes provide models of exemplary behaviour and character', and unveiled in 1900. The tributes are charming: we read, for example, of a 19-year-old railway clerk who drowned while 'trying to save a lad from a dangerous entanglement of weed'.

St Botolph-without-Aldersgate escaped the Great Fire but was entirely rebuilt in 1788–91. It is noted for its 18th-century interior (*open every Tues at 1pm for a talk with buffet afterwards*). The Aldersgate of the name refers to the old north City gate (pulled down in 1761).

THE OLD BAILEY & NEWGATE

Map p. 606, B2. Underground: Chancery Lane, St Paul's.

The crimson and gold cast-iron **Holborn Viaduct**, a road bridge 1400ft long and 80ft wide, was constructed at the cost of over 4,000 dwellings and over £2 million in 1863–9. It was designed by William Haywood to carry the thoroughfare over the depression of the Holbourne stream. The two bronze figures at each end are *Agriculture* and *Commerce* by H. Bursill and *Science* and *Fine Arts* by Farmer and Brindley (1868). The bridge makes a good starting point for exploring historic but disparate parts of the City. To the south, just beyond Holborn Circus, is the **church of St Andrew** (*open Mon–Fri 9–5*) re-built by Wren in 1684–7, the largest of his City churches, with a lovely light interior. It was ruined in the Second World War and largely rebuilt, though the interior of the medieval tower, dating from 1446 and unaltered by Wren, survives. Immediately inside to the left is the tomb of Captain Thomas Coram, erected when his remains were brought here from the Foundling Hospital (*see p. 351*). In this church William Hazlitt was married in 1808 (Mary Lamb was bridesmaid and Charles Lamb the best man). In 1817 Benjamin Disraeli (at the age of 12) was received into the Christian Church here. Next door to St Andrew's is the **City Temple** (Congregational), opened in 1874 under Dr Joseph Parker, for a congregation founded in 1640. Burnt out in 1941, it was rebuilt (apart from the façade) by Seely & Paget in 1956–8.

THE OLD BAILEY
Map p. 606, B2. Open Mon–Fri 10–1 & 2–5, closed bank holidays and the day immediately after, reduced court sitting in Aug. Public galleries open for viewing of trials in session; no reserved seating. No children under 14, no electronic devices, bags, food or drink. No public access to the precincts of the Central Criminal Court.

The neo-English Baroque Central Criminal Court, its façade inscribed with the motto 'Defend the Children of the Poor and Punish the Wrongdoer', is known as The Old Bailey. It is built on the site of the former Newgate Prison, which in turn stood on the site of New Gate, one of the gates in the Roman city wall. Newgate was an infamous and 'dreadful place of incarceration' from the 12th century until its closure in the early 20th century. A reconstruction of a Newgate cell with original iron doors may be seen at the Museum of London (*see p. 55*). Typhus, or 'gaol fever', was rife due to squalid conditions and overcrowding and in 1750 several judges, members of the jury and even the Lord Mayor died of it. Thereafter, strong-smelling herbs were spread around the court and judges carried posies. In 1768–75, new buildings by George

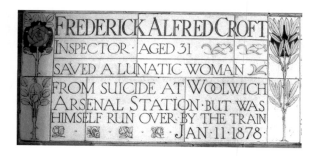

POSTMAN'S PARK
One of the commemorations of 'everyday heroes' on the Watts Memorial.

Dance the Younger were erected in forbidding *Architecture terrible* style, designed to intimidate prisoners and deter would-be felons. Public executions, previously carried out at Tyburn (Marble Arch), took place in front of Newgate from 1783–1868 and then within the prison until 1901. Elizabeth Fry, prison reformer, Quaker and helper of the homeless, helped found the Association for the Reformation of the Female Prisoners in Newgate in 1817.

Dance's buildings were demolished and replaced by the new Old Bailey (the current building) by Edward Mountford in 1900–7. The figure of *Justice* by F.W. Pomeroy (1907), cast in bronze and covered with gold leaf, stands on top of the dome. She wears a five-pointed star on her head and holds the Sword of Retribution in one hand and the Scales of Justice in the other. Pomeroy also sculpted the figures over the main entrance; the Recording Angels with *Fortitude* and *Truth* on either side. The main entrance is only used when the Lord Mayor visits in state as Chief Justice of the City. The Edwardian splendour of the Grand Hall is rarely open to the public. The extension on the south side of the Old Bailey is by McMorran and Whitby, completed in 1972.

ST SEPULCHRE-WITHOUT-NEWGATE

Map p. 606, B2. Open Mon–Fri 11–3, closed weekends.
On the corner of Newgate and Giltspur streets is the church of St Sepulchre-without-Newgate, the largest of the City's parish churches and once closely associated with Newgate Prison. Until 1890 the bells of St Sepulchre (the 'Bells of Old Bailey' in the nursery rhyme 'Oranges and Lemons') were tolled when a prisoner was executed. Today it has happier connections and is the National Musicians' Church.

The church, dating back to the 12th century and named after the Holy Sepulchre in Jerusalem, was rebuilt in the 15th century and again after the Fire in neo-Gothic manner. In the Musicians' Chapel in the north aisle, a bust commemorates Sir Henry Wood (d. 1943), first conductor of the Proms (*see p. 553*), who at the age of twelve deputised for the organist. His ashes are buried here. A 1960s' stained-glass window commemorates the singer Dame Nellie Melba and the dessert named after her. In the same chapel, the remains of an Easter sepulchre are thought to mark the tomb of Roger Ascham (1515–68), tutor to Queen Elizabeth I. Captain John Smith, first governor of the state of Virginia, who sailed to America in 1607, is buried in the south aisle. A stained-glass window recalls how Princess Pocahontas freed him after his capture by Native Americans. Nearby, in a glass case, is displayed the Execution Bell. The bellman of St Sepulchre's would pass along an underground passage to Newgate Prison and ring it at midnight outside the condemned prisoner's cell, at the same time reciting a rhyme, the transcript of which is exhibited with it. The south aisle and chapel and the garden serve as a memorial to the Royal Fusiliers.

GILTSPUR STREET

Giltspur Street (*map p. 606, B2*) leads north to West Smithfield and St Bartholomew's Hospital. In 1381 King Richard II met the leaders of the Peasants' Revolt in Giltspur Street. On the corner, at 126 Newgate St, is the **Viaduct Tavern** (*closed weekends*), opened in 1869, the same year as the Holborn Viaduct, and well worth a pit stop. It occupies the site of the Giltspur Street Compter, a debtor's prison (there are still some cells in the basement), and was once a Victorian gin palace. Its ornate interior includes three gilded and painted panels of graceful, pre-Raphaelitesque maidens.

A short way up Giltspur Street, attached to the church of St Sepulchre, is the **Watch House** (1791, destroyed in the Blitz, rebuilt 1962), erected to deter the body snatchers who stole corpses from Newgate in order to sell them for dissection to St Bartholomew's Hospital opposite. The bust of English essayist Charles Lamb bears the inscription, 'Perhaps the most loved name in English literature who was a bluecoat boy here for 7 years. B·1775, D·1834.' It was moved here in 1962 from near the site of Christ's Hospital School (*see p. 41*), where Lamb was educated.

The junction of Giltspur Street with Cock Lane is known as **Pye Corner**. Mounted on the wall is a 17th-century gilded chubby cherub, known as the Golden Boy of Pye Corner, marking the spot where the Great Fire of 1666 supposedly stopped. The inscription beneath the monument reads, 'This Boy is in Memmory Put up for the late FIRE of LONDON Occasion'd by the Sin of Gluttony 1666' (a reference to the fire starting in Pudding Lane). In medieval times, prostitution was legal in Cock—Cokkes—Lane. John Bunyan, writer of *The Pilgrim's Progress*, died here in 1688.

SMITHFIELD & ST BARTHOLOMEW'S

Map p. 606, B2–C2. Underground: St Paul's, Barbican.

At the top of Giltspur Street is Smithfield, properly West Smithfield, an area that escaped both the Great Fire and the Blitz. Originally a spacious 'smoothfield' just outside the Roman city walls, it was used for events and tournaments. From 1133 until 1840 Smithfield was the scene of the annual Bartholomew Fair, horse and cloth fairs combined with several days of revelry, held around the feast of St Bartholomew (24th Aug), and until 1855 it was the chief live cattle market of London. It was also a place of execution. A memorial on the exterior wall of St Bartholomew's Hospital commemorates the Scottish patriot William Wallace, 'hanged, drawn and quartered' here in 1305. In 1381 the rebel Wat Tyler, leader of the Peasants' Revolt, was slain here by Sir William Walworth, the Mayor, in the presence of Richard II. Protestant martyrs were burnt at the stake here in the reign of Mary I.

Today the wide, circular space is surrounded by eateries and cafés. On the west side is the **Haberdashers' Hall** (2002) by the Hopkins partnership. In the centre are the Smithfield Rotunda Gardens, with a fountain and a figure of *Peace* by J.B. Philip (1873). The north side is filled with the elaborate building of the **Central Meat Market** (Sir Horace Jones, 1867). A meat market has existed here for a thousand years and it is the only surviving wholesale meat market in Central London. It is also the largest in the country and one of the largest in Europe. Refrigerated lorries unload their carcasses, which are then prepared by 'cutters' ready for selling from the very early morning. The market is open Mon–Fri and remains lively until midday, although most of the action is from 3am–9am. The hall has been beautifully restored by the City of London. In Charterhouse Street, skirting the north side of the market, is the **Fox and Anchor**, one of the many pubs with early opening hours. It has an Art Nouveau façade and serves a full breakfast from 7am. Many of the old warehouses that line the streets in this area have façades adorned with reliefs of livestock: bulls, sheep and cows.

ST BARTHOLOMEW'S HOSPITAL

St Bartholomew's Hospital (St Bart's; *map p. 606, C2*), a premier teaching and specialised treatment hospital, occupies the southeast side of Smithfield. It was founded, together with a priory for Augustinian canons, in 1123 by Rahere, a favourite courtier of Henry I, in fulfilment of a vow made by him when on pilgrimage in Rome. Having fallen ill, Rahere had a vision of St Bartholomew and vowed to found a hospital for the poor on his return. It is the oldest charitable institution in London still extant on its original site. Dick Whittington, the famous mayor, bequeathed money for its repair in 1423. At the Dissolution, the priory was closed but the hospital was spared by Henry VIII, who granted it to the City and in 1547 endowed it with properties and income. Dr Roderigo Lopez became the hospital's first regular physician in 1567, later succeeded by Peter Turner (*see p. 86*). Lopez, a Portuguese Jew, was afterwards implicated in a plot against Elizabeth I and executed. It has been suggested that he was the inspiration for Shakespeare's Shylock. William Harvey, who discovered the circulation of the blood, was chief physician in 1609–43. In the 18th century a medical school was founded here and in 1877 a school of nursing. St Bart's was threatened with closure in the 1990s but was saved and now specialises in cancer and cardiac care.

The hospital buildings

The fine **Henry VIII Gate**, with a statue of Henry in a niche, is by Edward Strong the Younger (1702) and is the oldest surviving part of the hospital. It was restored by Philip Hardwick in the 1830s. Just inside the gate (hard left) is the small octagonal church of

St Bartholomew the Less, rebuilt (except for the striking 15th-century tower) in the 1790s by George Dance the Younger and restored in the 19th century by Thomas and Philip Hardwick. Inigo Jones was baptised here in 1573.

Continue through the gatehouse to see the hospital itself. Although it escaped the Great Fire, the medieval buildings were demolished and the hospital rebuilt, in the name of medical modernity, as a quadrangle by James Gibbs, architect of St Martin-in-the-Fields, in 1730–69. Three out of Gibbs's four buildings survive. As you come through the gatehouse, straight ahead is his historic **North Wing** (1732). Pause in the archway and straight ahead again, the area with the fountain playing at the centre is what remains of the quadrangle; the two hospital wings left and right (east and west) were designed to house the hospital wards.

The museum and Hogarth paintings

The hospital has a small museum which is entered via the left-hand door under the North Wing archway (*open Tues–Fri 10–4, closed over Christmas and New Year, Easter and public holidays; entry free but donations welcome; it is staffed by volunteers and opening hours may be subject to change; to check, T: 020 3465 5798/6798*). Walk through the museum to a cordoned-off section, from where you can view the grand staircase, hung with two vast paintings by William Hogarth, who was born nearby in Bartholomew Close and who donated them to the hospital. Both were painted in 1735–7. *The Pool of Bethesda* apparently features patients from the wards suffering from different sicknesses; the other painting depicts *The Good Samaritan*. (*To view the paintings in greater detail and to see more of this historic part of the hospital, ask at the museum reception for details of guided tours.*)

ST BARTHOLOMEW THE GREAT

Map p. 606, C2. Open Mon–Fri 8.30–5 (4 in winter), Sat 10.30–4, Sun 8.30–8; admission charge; nominal extra charge for photography; no visitors or tours during services, for times, see greatstbarts.com.

The priory church of St Bartholomew the Great is the most important surviving 12th-century monument in London and is noted for its music. The church lies tucked away behind a small stone gateway with a half-timbered Tudor gatehouse above, adorned with a statue of St Bartholomew and his flaying knife. This takes you into the churchyard. On Good Friday, in accordance with a Victorian custom, 21 poor widows each received an old sixpence, which was laid on a flat tombstone here. The ceremony is now symbolic and the sixpences have been substituted by baskets of buttered hot cross buns, which are shared with the crowd who come to watch. The church is entered beneath a brick tower built in 1628 to take the place of the tower over the crossing. The five pre-Reformation bells date from 1510.

History of St Bartholomew's

The church was part of a priory founded in 1123 by Rahere, a canon of St Paul's, and

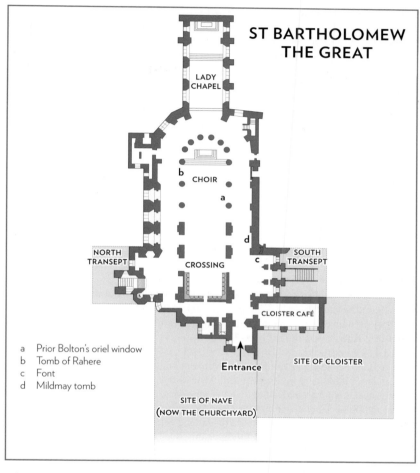

ST BARTHOLOMEW THE GREAT

LADY CHAPEL

b CHOIR

a

d

NORTH TRANSEPT

CROSSING

c SOUTH TRANSEPT

CLOISTER CAFÉ

a Prior Bolton's oriel window
b Tomb of Rahere
c Font
d Mildmay tomb

Entrance

SITE OF CLOISTER

SITE OF NAVE
(NOW THE CHURCHYARD)

exists in fragment form. After the priory was dissolved in 1539, the Augustinian buildings and much of the church were pulled down or alienated, and of the original priory church only the choir, the crossing, one bay of the nave and the Lady Chapel remain. The stone gateway at the entrance to the churchyard was once the west door; another survival. The churchyard itself occupies the site of the nave (*see plan*). Restoration in the second half of the 19th century was mainly carried out by Sir Aston Webb, architect of the Victoria & Albert Museum.

Interior of St Bartholomew's

The shadowy, majestic choir of Rahere's priory church, with massive columns, piers and round arches, is in pure Norman style. The triforium is interrupted on the south side by **Prior Bolton's oriel window (a)**, added c. 1517 to communicate as a sort of oratory with the prior's adjoining house. It bears Prior Bolton's rebus, a bolt and a tun (barrel). On the north side of the sanctuary is the early 15th-century **tomb of Rahere** (d. 1143) **(b)**, with a coloured effigy beneath a rich canopy. Little is known of the facts of Rahere's life, though there are many legends about him and he appears as the king's jester in Rudyard Kipling's short story *The Tree of Justice*. In the south transept stands the **font** (c. 1405) **(c)**, one of only two pre-Reformation fonts in London, at which Hogarth (born nearby) was baptised in 1697. In the south aisle is the alabaster **tomb of Sir Walter Mildmay** (d. 1589) **(d)**, founder of Emmanuel College, Cambridge, and his wife, Lady Mary Mildmay.

The **Lady Chapel**, the third on the site, was rebuilt in the 1890s. From 1539 it served variously as a private house, a printing press (where Benjamin Franklin worked in 1724) and as premises for lace and fringe makers until the property was bought back in 1885 and restored. The **north transept** was a blacksmith's forge, where the clanging of hammer on anvil could be heard until 1884.

What survives of the **cloister** (12th century, rebuilt c. 1405 and reconstructed in 1905–28), entered from the southwest porch entrance, is now the Cloister Café. The arches in the wall mark the entrance to the former chapter house.

LITTLE BRITAIN AND CLOTH FAIR

To the south of St Bartholomew's is the street called **Little Britain** (*map p. 606, C2*), where the poet John Milton lived in hiding after the Restoration in 1660. Off it is Bartholomew Close, where William Hogarth was born in 1697. At nos 87–88 is **Butchers' Hall** (1960), the livery hall of the Butchers' company.

Cloth Fair, a tiny street skirting the north side of St Bartholomew's church, marks the site once occupied by the booths of drapers and clothiers at Bartholomew Fair. You can enter it either from West Smithfield or via a small gate from St Bartholomew's churchyard. At nos 41 and 42 are fine examples of early 17th-century merchant's houses which have been well preserved and restored. The poet John Betjeman lived in Cloth Court (no. 43; blue plaque). At the far end of Cloth Fair, at no. 3 Cloth St, is the **livery hall of the Farmers and Fletchers** (Michael Twigg Brown, 1987).

CHEAPSIDE, POULTRY & OLD JEWRY

Map pp. 606, C3–607, D3. Underground: Mansion House.

Cheapside was a busy market from Saxon times (*chepe* in Old English means market) and a higgledy-piggledy medieval street of retailers that was laid waste by the Great Fire. The names of the cross-streets indicate the position of the different traders: bakers in Bread Street, ironmongers in Ironmonger Lane, fishmongers in Friday Street, dairymen in Milk Street, etc. The 'prentices of Chepe,' Chaucer tells us, 'were long notorious for their turbulence'. Today, retailing is coming home to Cheapside: One

New Change, Jean Nouvel's mall complex (2010) with shops, restaurants, bars, offices and a public roof gallery, is open seven days a week from early until late. The glass panels are designed to reflect the sky and a cut in the building frames a view of St Paul's Cathedral (the roof gallery offers a fine prospect of St Paul's dome).

Cheapside also runs through the heart of Roman London. A public bath of c. AD 100 was found just off Cheapside, and to the south the main Roman road through the City was discovered during excavations. Watling Street was a major thoroughfare, leading from Londinium to Dubris, the port of Dover. In 1912, a priceless cache of 16th- and 17th-century jewels and gems was discovered hidden in a Cheapside basement. The collection is part of a major display at the Museum of London (*see p. 55*).

Two of London's famous Elizabethan taverns, The Mitre and the Bull Head, were located here. In Bread Street, to the south, stood a third, the Mermaid Tavern, famous for the club founded in 1603 by Sir Walter Raleigh, whose members included Ben Jonson, Donne and Shakespeare. All three taverns were destroyed in the Great Fire.

John Milton was born in Bread Street in 1608 and Sir Thomas More in Milk Street, nearly opposite, in 1478. In Bread Street stood Wren's St Mildred's church, where Shelley and Mary Godwin were married in 1816. It was destroyed in World War Two.

ST VEDAST ALIAS FOSTER

In Foster Lane, the first turning off Cheapside to the north, opposite One New Change, stands the boxy church of St Vedast alias Foster (*map p. 606, C2*), noted for its Baroque steeple with obelisk spire that has been attributed to Wren's pupil, Hawksmoor. The unusual dedication to a 6th-century Frankish bishop from Arras, northern Gaul, points to a post-Conquest founding. St Vedast was venerated in England from the 12th century where he was known as St Foster. The church was rebuilt after the Fire by Wren's office in 1695–1701 (steeple 1709–12) and it was restored after the Blitz in 1953–63 under the direction of its rector, Canon Mortlock, and architect Stephen Dykes Bower. The pews face the nave, collegiate style. Cleaning in 1992–3 revealed the medieval fabric of the walls. On the list of vicars in the entrance, note Foulke Bellers (1643–61), presented as a 'Commonwealth Intruder'. The *Journal of the House of Commons* for August 1643 notes that, 'an Order for sequestring the Rectory of the Parish Church of St Vedast, alias Fosters, London, whereof James Batty is Rector, to the Use and Benefit of Foulke Bellers, Master of Arts, a godly and orthodox Divine; who is thereby authorized and required to officiate the said Cure, as Rector; and to preach diligently there; was this Day read; and, by Vote upon the Question, assented unto.' The ousted Batty had been a staunch Royalist.

The quiet courtyard, Fountain Court, with entrances from the church and the street, displays a section of Roman mosaic pavement, a profile in carved stone of Canon Mortlock by Jacob Epstein and an ancient Syrian brick presented to Canon Mortlock and found during Sir Max Mallowan's (Agatha Christie's husband's) dig at Nimrud in the 1950s/60s. The cuneiform inscription translates: 'Shalmaneser Mighty King, King of the World, King of Assyria, Son of Ashurnasirpal, Mighty King, King of the World, King of Assyria, son of Tukulti-Ninurta who was also King of the World, The facing of the Ziggurat of the City of Kalhu.'

On the corner of Cheapside and Wood Street are three small shops, all re-fronted, though what lies behind the frontages are rare 17th-century survivors of post-Fire rebuilding. Behind them, an immense plane tree grows on the **site of the church of St Peter Cheap**, destroyed in the Fire and not rebuilt. The tree is believed to have inspired Wordsworth's 'The Reverie of Poor Susan' (1797), a poem about a country girl working in London in whom visions of remembered bucolic sweetness are awakened by the dawn trilling of a thrush from a tree at the corner of Wood Street.

ST MARY-LE-BOW

According to tradition, 'Cockneys' are born within the sound of Bow Bells, the bells of St Mary-le-Bow (*map p. 607, D3*). At one time they could be heard in Hackney Marshes but today, surrounded as the church is by tall buildings, not many Londoners get an opportunity to be born real Cockneys. The famous bells also called back Dick Whittington to be four times Mayor of London. They were destroyed in the Great Fire and their successors suffered in the Blitz, but new ones have been recast from those salvaged. The Pearly Costermongers' Harvest Festival, held at the church on the last Sun in Sept, affords an opportunity to hear the bells ring out: and ring out they do, gloriously, for several hours. Pearly kings and queens from various London boroughs, along with donkeys and dogs pulling carts of autumnal produce, gather at Guildhall before processing with City dignitaries behind a marching band along Cheapside to the church.

PEARLY KINGS AND QUEENS

Pearly Kings and Pearly Queens have their origins in London's costermongers, the itinerant traders, barrow boys and vendors whose famous cries of 'Come and buy!', 'Cherry ripe!' once filled the City streets—and on market days in some areas, still do. In the 19th century the costermongers of each borough began to elect a 'king' to represent them to the authorities and to defend their patches against other traders. They began to distinguish their dress by stitching rows of mother-of-pearl buttons along the seams of their trousers. The full Pearly costumes that are seen today evolved after the 1880s, when a rat-catcher named Henry Croft covered an entire suit with pearl buttons arranged to form patterns and the slogan 'All For Charity'. Soon all the 'Pearlys' were at it, constructing ever more elaborate attire for themselves to be worn in their pageants and processions. Today there are several Pearly groups, all of which devote their efforts to raising money for the city.

St Mary-le-Bow was one of the first churches to be rebuilt after the Fire, by Wren, in 1670–80. It succeeds the older medieval church of Sancta Maria de Arcubus, 'of the arches'. The name derives from the Deanery of the Arches, a group of thirteen parish churches under the jurisdiction of the Archbishop of Canterbury, not the Bishop of London. Their council, the Court of Arches, traditionally met here.

ST MARY-LE-BOW
Post-war photograph showing the church (on the left) as a
bombed-out shell.

The fine Neoclassical **steeple**, erected in 1678–80, is 224ft high, second in height of the London steeples after St Bride's. Inside the tower entrance, a haunting photograph taken after the Blitz shows the area's devastation. The church was gutted in 1941 and the interior restoration, completed in 1964 by Laurence King, is to Wren's design, though the furnishings are in a very different style. The decorative, brightly-coloured **east windows** are the work of John Hayward (1964). The northeast window represents the bombed City churches grouped around the Virgin, who holds the church of St Mary-le-Bow in her arms. Note the bosses on the keystones of the arches, carved with the portraits of past rectors. At the west end is the **memorial bust of Admiral Arthur Phillip** (1738–1814), founder and governor of the first colony of British settlers in Australia (1788), who was born in Bread Street. The bust was salvaged from St Mildred's church.

Below the church, the Norman **crypt** (c. 1077–87, incorporating Roman bricks) is one of the oldest and most important ecclesiastical structures in the City (now also home to the church's restaurant, Café Below). The Chapel of the Holy Spirit occupies the part formerly used as a burying place and as the meeting place of the ecclesiastical Court of Arches (*see above*). In 1914 an ancient stone from the crypt of Bow Church was placed in Trinity Church, New York, in reference to the fact that William III granted to the vestry of that church the same privileges as those of St Mary-le-Bow.

John Milton is commemorated by a tablet on the church's exterior west wall. In the **churchyard** is a statue of Captain John Smith, founder of the Colony of Virginia, erected in 1960. It is a copy of the statue in Jamestown by William Couper. Smith is buried in St Sepulchre-without-Newgate (*see p. 43*).

OLD JEWRY

Beyond Bow Church, King Street leads left to the Guildhall. A plaque on the corner of Ironmonger Lane, just beyond King Street, states that St Thomas à Becket was born in a house near this spot. Also on Ironmonger Lane stands **Mercers' Hall**, the livery hall of the Mercers, one of the richest of the City livery companies and the first in order of civic precedence, still committed to education and charitable works. The **tower of St Olave's** just beyond is a relic of a Wren church demolished in 1887 and since 1986 restored as offices. A Roman pavement and vessels were discovered beneath it.

St Olave's Court leads between Ironmonger Lane and **Old Jewry** (*map p. 607, D3*), the area set aside for Jews since William the Conqueror encouraged them to settle in England soon after 1066. In 1290, after two centuries of intermittent support punctuated by outbreaks of persecution, they were expelled by King Edward I, an edict that remained in place until Oliver Cromwell formally invited Jews back to England from 1655, in the hope that they would reinvigorate the country's finances. A blue plaque on the wall opposite the entrance to St Olave's Court commemorates the site of the Great Synagogue that stood here until 1272. In Frederick's Place, a small Georgian cul-de-sac, Disraeli worked at no. 6 from 1821–4.

POULTRY

The short continuation of Cheapside eastwards towards Bank is known as Poultry (*map p. 607, D3*), from its early occupation by the shops of poulterers, who drove their flocks from Essex with special cloth coverings over their webbed feet. Directly opposite is **No. 1 Poultry**, a pink Post-modern office building by James Stirling (which Prince Charles once deprecated as looking like a radio). The Coq d'Argent restaurant is at the top, with a roof terrace and garden. At 27–35 Poultry and 5 Prince's St is the **former Midland Bank headquarters** by Lutyens. Elizabeth Fry, the women's prison reformer, lived on this site in 1800–9. The church of St Mildred, Poultry was also here (it was pulled down in 1872). Grocer's Hall Court, off Poultry, leads to the **hall of the Worshipful Company of Grocers**, second in order of precedence and one of the original twelve (*see p. 21*). Its main entrance is on Princes Street. At no. 1 Princes St, on the corner plot wedged against Lutyens' former Midland Bank, is Sir Edwin Cooper's **National Westminster Bank** (1929–32), overlooking the Bank of England, Royal Exchange and Mansion House, with the Gherkin, Cheesegrater and Walkie-Talkie skyscrapers looming behind. On this site the world's first postmarks were struck in 1661 (plaque on the Princes Street side of building).

GRESHAM STREET AND THE APPROACH TO LONDON WALL

Gresham Street (*map p. 606, C2*) takes its name from the old Gresham College (now based at Barnard's Inn; *see p. 201*). On the corner of Foster Lane stands the neo-Renaissance **Goldsmiths' Hall**, by Philip Hardwick (1835). The Worshipful Company of Goldsmiths was founded in 1327 and is one of the original twelve great livery companies (*see p. 21*). It is also one of the richest and its hall has a fitting gilded interior and an opulent collection of plate, which is brought up from the vaults for sumptuous livery dinners. The Goldsmiths' Company is responsible for maintaining standards in gold, silver, platinum and palladium and its headquarters are home to the London Assay Office. Although it is not open to the public, it holds bi-annual exhibitions and entry to these is usually free (*see www.thegoldsmiths.co.uk*).

Opposite the livery hall is a small public garden on the **site of St John Zachary**, a church destroyed by the Fire and not rebuilt. Left of the garden, on the corner of Gresham and Noble streets, is the small red-brick **church of St Anne and St Agnes**, designed on a Greek cross plan by Wren's office (1680) and restored in 1963–8. Noble Street itself boasts a large exposed section of the **old City wall** (*see p. 57*). Opposite it, Oat Lane takes you past the **Pewterers' Hall** (1961), next to which a small garden in the midst of a modern office block commemorates the **site of St Mary Staining**, a church destroyed in the Fire and not rebuilt. A passage (St Alban's Court) leads through the office block to Wood Street. Here, directly opposite, is the **tower of St Alban**, the only remaining part of Wren's neo-Gothic church rebuilt after the Fire in 1685. It is now a private house and notoriously difficult to let, marooned as it is on a traffic island. Look left: at **no. 88 Wood Street** stands an 18-storey office block with floor-to-ceiling glass walls in a cascading design, by Richard Rogers, completed in 2001. The huge blue and red funnels at ground level that look like comedy periscopes are for ventilation.

Wood Street leads onto **London Wall** and the Museum of London (*see overleaf*). Nearby, substantial sections of the **old City wall** may be seen (*see p. 57*).

THE BARBICAN

Map p. 607, D1–D2. Underground: Barbican. The Barbican Centre can be approached via the walkway system from Wood Street (follow the signs and yellow lines in the floor), or direct from the main entrance in Silk Street. The Centre is open Mon–Sat 9am–11pm, Sun and Bank Holidays noon–11pm. T: 020 7638 8891, barbican.org.uk.

John Betjeman has a famous mock-heroic image of a commuter slogging out his days in the City and dreaming as he does so of his cosy suburban home: 'And all that day in murky London Wall, the thought of Ruislip kept him warm inside...' London Wall *is* very murky indeed. The realigned modern road running between Aldersgate, Moorgate and Bishopsgate was constructed in 1957–76 after extensive damage during World War Two. It very loosely follows the boundary of the old Roman wall. The post-war plan for redevelopment of the area, inspired by the ideas of Le Corbusier, had aimed at segregating pedestrians and traffic. An integrated series of identical high-rise blocks lined London Wall. Parking was underground and pedestrian access was at first-floor level via staircases, high walkways and bridges over the road. The result was to allow traffic free rein along London Wall, turning it into a pounding, dual-carriage highway. The 1960s' raised 'pedways', with decks for shops, gave the historic buildings and gardens remaining at ground level an abandoned, sunken appearance (*see church of St Alphage below*). By the 1980s, the taste for Modernism had soured and many walkways have since been abandoned and demolished, although the network around the Barbican Centre still remains. Much of the original 1960s' architecture is being, or has been, replaced, such as at **Alban Gate** (125 London Wall), where a great behemoth by Terry Farrell (1992) now spans the road where it crosses Wood Street in the form of two huge Post-modern blocks set at 90 degrees to each other. Inside, walkways lead to the Museum of London and to the Barbican. Among the shops and restaurants is a two-floor Pizza Express which stays open at weekends. Foster & Partners designed **One London Wall** (corner of Aldersgate Street; completed 2004), which incorporates **Plaisterers' Hall** (1972). The **Ironmongers' Hall**, a neo-Tudor edifice of 1925, is in Shaftesbury Place (east off Aldersgate Street between the Museum of London and Barbican Tube).

On Fore Street, which leads off Wood Street north of London Wall, is **Salters' Hall** (1976; based on designs by Sir Basil Spence). Behind it, the atmospheric 1960s' St Alphage Highwalk had become an atmospheric ghost town of overgrown grasses in raised beds and empty buildings including shops, offices and a NatWest bank. At the time of writing the entire complex was roped off and scheduled for demolition. Within the concrete embrace are the sunken ruins of the **church of St Alphage**, with a collapsing 14th-century tower. Over all the devastation, Michael Ayrton's bronze sculpture *Minotaur* keeps forbidding watch. The subject of the statue may be more appropriate than was intended: the Barbican highwalk is notoriously labyrinthine and finding one's way around it is difficult: painted lines on the floor help show you where to go, standing in for Theseus' unravelling ball of string.

HISTORY AND DEVELOPMENT OF THE BARBICAN CENTRE

In 1940 this whole area, the parish of Cripplegate, was razed to the ground by Luftwaffe bombs and only the church of St Giles-without-Cripplegate was left standing. During the 1950s, designs were proposed to redevelop the 60-acre site as a centre for the arts and entertainment and also as living and recreation space for several thousand residents and City workers. Building of the controversial complex, in concrete Brutalist style, by Chamberlin, Powell and Bon, went ahead in 1971–81. The complicated structure on eight levels, three of which are underground, was opened by HM The Queen in March 1982: she dubbed it 'one of the modern wonders of the world'.

Today the Barbican is proudly Europe's largest multi-arts and conference venue, with theatres that can be adapted for opera and dance, a concert hall that seats 2,000, cinemas, a library, exhibition halls and bars and restaurants. It is home to the London Symphony Orchestra and the Guildhall School of Speech and Drama. It is also home to over 4,000 residents, who live in the three towers and in 21 residential blocks. The Conservatory (*open most Sundays; see barbican.org.uk*) is the second largest in London and houses 2,000 species of tropical plant along with finches, quail and fish. The rather beautiful L-shaped artificial lake, with fountains, gardens and lakeside seating, alleviates the concrete harshness. Prominent remains of a Roman/medieval bastion (the 'barbican' of the name) lie to the south across the lake extension. (*See barbican.org.uk to download a free walking tour and for information on guided architecture tours which last approx. 90mins; fee payable.*)

ST GILES TERRACE

Lying at the heart of the Barbican complex, on the south side of the lake terrace, this paved piazza is the site of the restored church of **St Giles-without-Cripplegate** (*map p. 607, D2; open Mon–Fri 11–4, stgilesnewsite.co.uk*), opposite the City of London School for Girls. St Giles is the Barbican's parish church and one of the few remaining medieval churches in the City. When built, it originally stood outside the City's walls, near the Cripplegate (the name probably deriving from the Old English *crepel*, a burrow or low opening). The piazza has been formed from its churchyard and weathered tombstones have been set into raised rectangular sections.

The stone tower and the nave belong to the church of 1390 (the brick top storey of the tower was added in 1682–4 by John Bridges). After a fire in 1545 and alterations in the 17th–18th centuries, the church was badly damaged by bombs in 1940 but amazingly remained standing when everything else within a half-mile radius was destroyed. In the 1960s it was restored; the east and west windows were renewed and the organ (incorporating an 18th-century case) was installed.

Few monuments survive and most are in fragment form. A plaque beside the north (entrance) door recalls 'Men of Mark' connected with the parish, who include Sir Martin Frobisher, seaman and explorer (d. 1594); John Foxe, martyrologist (d. 1587); John Bunyan (d. 1688) and Daniel Defoe (d. 1731; the parish register records his burial in Bunhill Fields). In the south aisle another plaque records the burial of John Milton, whose *Paradise Lost* was printed by an Aldersgate printer. He died in Bunhill Row in 1674 but lived in several houses in the area and was buried in the same grave as his father. One night in 1790, a group of scamps, growing warm with beer at the home of the church overseer in nearby Beech Street, hatched a plot to disinter the poet's remains. According to Philip Neve in his *A Narrative of the Disinterment of Milton's Coffin*, the unearthed sarcophagus was concealed under a pew and Mrs Grant the gravedigger charged visitors tuppence to view the body. The bust of Milton that now surmounts the plaque was made by John Bacon, three years after this ignominious event.

In this church, Shakespeare attended the baptism of his nephew in 1604, while lodging in Silver Street (now subsumed by the Barbican) with Christopher Montjoy, a Huguenot and 'tire maker' whom he had known 'for the space of tenne yeres or thereaboutes'. Oliver Cromwell was married here in 1620. The Great Plague was at its worst in the parish of St Giles, and plague burials fill nearly a folio volume of the parish register for 1665. The documents are now in the Guildhall Library.

THE MUSEUM OF LONDON

Map p. 606, C2. Open daily 10–6. Free. T: 020 7001 9844, museumoflondon.org.uk.

The museum, housed in a building which in its day was a vision incarnate of Modernism (Powell & Moya 1968–76), white-tiled above and of black bricks below, possesses over 1.1 million objects pertaining to the physical and social history of London, from its origins in prehistory to the present day. The early displays are chronological and excellently captioned. Later displays are themed. Selected highlights are given below.

Chronological displays

The **Prehistory section** displays tools and ritual objects, some of them of exquisite craftsmanship, including flint hand axes and Mesolithic picks of a type known as the 'Thames pick' from the sheer numbers of them dredged from London's river. The **Roman section** explores Londinium, at one time the largest city in Roman Britain. Artefacts include items of jewellery, sections of mosaic floor, three curses scratched on lead found in the drains of the Roman amphitheatre, and a famous pair of girl's leather underpants found at the bottom of an old well in Queen Street. The marble sculptures from the Temple of Mithras were discovered under Queen Victoria Street in 1954. The bust of Mithras himself dates to AD 180–220. Among the **Saxon artefacts** is a King Alfred the Great silver penny of c. 886. An 11th-century grave slab, beautifully carved with a lion and serpent in battle and with a Norse runic inscription, was possibly part of the tomb of an individual connected to the court of King Canute.

Items from **medieval London** demonstrate the cultural flowering of the capital and its extensive overseas mercantile links. Pilgrim badges are on show, mementoes brought back from holy shrines, the most popular being that of St Thomas à Becket at Canterbury. A tangle of window leading from the vandalised stained glass of Merton Priory is a potent relic of the Reformation. The unquestionable highlight of the **Tudor display**, however, are the items from the astonishing Cheapside Hoard, a collection of over 230 pieces of jewellery recovered in 1912 from the site of Wakefield House, probably part of a goldsmith's trade stock.

Themed displays

Early Stuart and Reformation London comes under the heading of '**War, Plague and Fire**'. Mortality bills from the time of the 1665 Great Plague can be seen. Oliver Cromwell's death mask is one of the highlights. '**Expanding City**' (1666–1850s) begins by showing how a modern metropolis rose from the ashes of the Great Fire. London became home to wealthy merchants and financiers, made rich through the great trading companies and the emerging financial market. The city developed into a centre for luxury trades, such as silk-weaving centred on Spitalfields. Inevitably the wealth and taste of the few is contrasted with the penury of the many, and there is plenty of material on poverty and exploitation. A Newgate Prison cell has been recreated, using a genuine door recovered from that notorious place of incarceration. Slavery is explored. The theme is continued in '**People's City**' (1850s–1940s), where the extremes of wealth and indigence are contrasted: the Selfridge's department store lift symbolises the pampered lives of the well-to-do; poverty maps remind us that much of the East End was covered in slum tenements. '**World City**' (1950s–today) celebrates London, to quote the museum's own words, as a 'vibrant modern city for the masses'.

THE ALDERSGATE FLAME

Directly outside the main entrance to the Museum of London stands the **Aldersgate Flame**, a bronze sculpture erected in 1981 on the approximate site of the house where Wesley felt himself converted to faith in Christ on 24th May 1730. In Wesley's own words: 'In the evening I went very unwillingly to a Society in Aldersgate Street, where one was reading Luther's Preface to the Epistle to the Romans. About a quarter before nine, while he was describing the Change which God works in the heart thro' Faith in Christ, I felt my heart strangely warm'd. I felt I *did* trust in Christ, Christ alone for Salvation: and an Assurance was given me, that He had taken away my sins, even mine, and saved me from the Law of Sin and Death.'

THE OLD CITY WALL

London was first encircled by walls by the Romans c. AD 200. These defences, pierced by numerous gates and posterns, were maintained throughout the Middle Ages. Only in the 18th century did they begin to be dismantled, as the capital expanded and its walls and gates became obstacles to traffic. Sizeable sections of wall can still be seen and the London Wall Walk may be downloaded from the Museum of London's website (*www.museumoflondon.org.uk*). It follows the line of the wall from the Tower of London to the Museum of London and is about two miles long with a series of panels pointing out sites of interest along the way. The main gates were as follows (clockwise from the west): Newgate, Aldersgate, Cripplegate, Bishopsgate, Aldgate and Ludgate. Moorgate was added in medieval times. There were also water-gates on the Thames, such as Billingsgate, Queenhithe, Dowgate and Bridegate.

GUILDHALL

Map p. 607, D2. Underground: Bank, Moorgate, St Paul's.

Guildhall is the ceremonial and administrative centre of the City of London Corporation. It is built over the largest Roman amphitheatre discovered in the UK, part of which is on view beneath the Guildhall Art Gallery (*see below*). The complex has many entrances but is best approached from Gresham Street through to Guildhall Yard. Stand with the church of St Lawrence Jewry behind you and the entrance to the Guildhall Art Gallery on your right, to admire the façade of the Great Hall, which dates from 1411 with a 'Hindoo Gothic' porch added in 1788 by George Dance the Younger. Surmounting the porch is the City coat of arms, with the motto *Domine dirige nos*: Lord, direct us. Much damage was sustained in the Great Fire in 1666 and again during World War Two. In the 1860s Sir Horace Jones restored its Gothic splendour and restoration in the 1950s was undertaken by Sir Giles Gilbert Scott and later by his son Richard. This is the only secular pre-Fire stone building in the City.

GREAT HALL AND CRYPT

Entry to the Great Hall and Crypt is free although both may be closed to visitors at short notice if an event is taking place. Access is via the modern west wing extension, where the City of London Corporation's offices are and which also houses the Library and the Clockmaker's Museum (see below). Your bags will be put through a security check.

The **Great Hall** is approached down a glass and concrete ambulatory—a 1970s' interpretation of a medieval cloister by Richard Gilbert Scott. The Great Hall (151.5ft long, 48ft wide and 89ft high) was built in 1411–29 by John Croxton as the third guildhall on this site, and the largest. The huge tracery windows are in essence 15th-century but much restored. The 19th-century hammerbeam roof was destroyed in 1940 and has been replaced by stone arches with a panelled ceiling (1954). The hall is used for Court of Common Council meetings, for City ceremonies such as the election of the Lord Mayor and sheriffs, and state banquets hosted by the Corporation. The most important of these is the banquet given in November, by the new Lord Mayor and sheriffs, for the members of the Cabinet, when the Prime Minister makes an important speech. At an earlier period the hall was used also for major trials (recorded on a panel).

Against the walls are a statue of Winston Churchill sprawled in an armchair (by Oscar Nemon) and monuments to Nelson (inscription by Sheridan), Wellington, Chatham (inscription by Burke), William Pitt (inscription by Canning) and Lord Mayor Beckford; the famous giants Gog and Magog, by David Evans (above the entrance at the west end), replace those burned in 1940. Gog and Magog have been regarded as guardians of the City since the reign of Henry V and played a traditional role in welcoming kings and queens to London. Two wicker effigies of them feature in the Lord Mayor's Show (*see p. 554*).

In the basement, the **Crypt** is an important survival of the buildings of 1411 and is the largest medieval crypt in London. The East Crypt is borne by clustered columns of Purbeck marble (restored in 1961). The West Crypt (restored 1973) has octagonal stone columns supporting a plain vault.

CLOCKMAKERS' MUSEUM

The Clock Room, Guildhall Library. Entrance on Aldermanbury. Map p. 607, D2. Open Mon–Sat 9.30–4.30. Free. T: 020 7332 1868; www.clockmakers.org.
This small museum houses the collection of the Worshipful Company of Clockmakers, a livery company established in 1631. On display are timepieces and chronometers dating from the 15th century to the present, including the work of leading makers such as Thomas Tompion and John Harrison (his H5 is here; H1 to H4 are in Greenwich; *see p. 453*). A silver skull watch said to have belonged to Mary, Queen of Scots, and the Smiths Deluxe wristwatch worn by Sir Edmund Hillary on his ascent of Everest in 1953, are other highlights. The room is filled with the gentle sound of ticking.

GUILDHALL ART GALLERY AND ROMAN AMPHITHEATRE

Guildhall Yard. Map p. 607, D2. Open Mon–Sat 10–5, Sun 12–4. Free (except for temporary exhibitions). T: 020 7332 3700; cityoflondon.gov.uk.
Housed in a building designed by Richard Gilbert Scott (with D.Y. Associates), with rather clownish statues of London notables, including Dick Whittington and his cat, under the porch, the **Guildhall Art Gallery** displays around 250 pictures at any one time from the Corporation of London's collection of over 4,000 works. During construction work in 1987, the astonishing discovery was made of London's Roman amphitheatre. The remains have been preserved and can be visited.

The gallery has display spaces on two floors, smaller rooms on the ground floor, and an open balcony gallery on the floor above. The interesting and varied collection includes works commissioned and collected by the Corporation since the 16th century and others presented or bequeathed to it. Among the portraits are eminent City office-holders, such as John Michael Wright's full-length portraits of two of the Fire Judges appointed to assess property claims following the Great Fire of 1666. Topographical views of London include Jan Griffier the Younger's *The Thames during the Great Frost*; Samuel Scott's *Entrance to the Fleet River*; and views of City landmarks such as St Paul's Cathedral and Smithfield Market. Works celebrating national victories and events include John Singleton Copley's enormous *Siege of Gibraltar*, commissioned by the Corporation in 1783 and completed in 1791. It is one of the largest pictures in the country and a particular requirement of this building was that it should have a wall large enough to accommodate it.

Other works include Constable's full-size sketch for *Salisbury Cathedral from the Meadows* and many fine Victorian pictures, in which the collection is particularly rich. Well known Pre-Raphaelite works include Millais' *My First Sermon*, *My Second Sermon* and *The Woodman's Daughter*; Holman Hunt's *The Eve of St Agnes*; and Rossetti's *La Ghirlandata*. Other notable works are Landseer's *The First Leap* and Tissot's popular *Too Early* (1873). Neil Simmons' larger-than-life-size Carrara marble statue of Margaret Thatcher, famously decapitated in 2002 and since repaired, is also on show, in a strong perspex box.

The dark, spot-lit **Amphitheatre Chamber** is on the lower ground floor. Do not expect Capua or the Colosseum: the remains are extremely scanty, consisting of parts of the stone-built eastern entrance and some well-preserved sections of wooden sump drains and water conduits. The theatre was first constructed c. AD 70, with a timber superstructure, and was capable of seating some 6,000 spectators at a time when the population of Londinium would have been only around four times that number. Elliptical in shape, more than 100 yards long and 90 yards wide, it would have been used mainly for animal fights and public executions, rarely for expensive gladiatorial contests. In the 2nd century it was improved with stone, and abandoned at some time in the 4th century. Curious luminous green silhouettes of pugilists evoke the atmosphere of the ring in full cry.

ST LAWRENCE JEWRY AND ALDERMANBURY

On the corner of Aldermanbury and Gresham Street stands **St Lawrence Jewry** (*map p. 607, D2; open Mon–Fri 8–6*), rebuilt by Wren in 1671–7 and well restored after war damage. It is the official church of the City Corporation and has a fine white and gold interior. The Trumpeter's Gallery is used on ceremonial occasions. Pepys records a visit to the church 'for curiosity' and his disappointment with the sermon. Sir Thomas More delivered a series of lectures here. The 'Spital' sermon is preached here in Feb or March, attended by the Lord Mayor, sheriffs and aldermen, who cross Guildhall Yard in a colourful procession. The service was originally preached to the governors of the Royal Hospitals. Note the weather vane in the shape of a gridiron, the attribute of St Lawrence, who was roasted alive on one in Rome in 258.

In Aldermanbury Square is a small garden on the **site of Elsing Spital**, an Augustinian priory founded in 1329 'for the sustentation of a hundred blind men' and dissolved in 1536. The statue here is *The Gardener* by Karin Jonzen (1972).

South across Aldermanbury, a pleasant garden surrounds the **site of St Mary**, a Wren church bombed in 1940 and removed in 1968 to the campus of Westminster College, Fulton, Missouri as a memorial to Winston Churchill (who made his famous Iron Curtain speech at the College). The memorial is to the actors John Heminge and Henry Condell, editors of Shakespeare's First Folio (of which the Guildhall Library has a copy). Judge Jeffreys was buried here, having died in the Tower in 1689.

At no. 20 Aldermanbury is the **Chartered Insurance Institute** (*map p. 607, D2; open weekdays; T: 020 7417 4425*), which preserves some items of early firefighting equipment, including fire-marks of the early fire brigades, which were operated by insurance companies and who would only fight fires in properties which bore the company's mark.

MOORGATE & THE NORTHERN CITY LIMITS

Map p. 607, D2–D1. Underground: Bank, Moorgate.

Moorgate is a street of mainly banks and offices, leading north towards Islington and Hackney. Some of the buildings date from the late 19th century, some from the early 20th century and many from the 1980s. In Great Swan Alley, on the east side, is the **Institute of Chartered Accountants**, a Renaissance-style building by John Belcher (1890–3; extended 1930 by J.J. Joass), in part inspired by Genoese *palazzi*. The carving is by Harry Bates and the sculpted frieze, deliberately placed above the first-floor windows so as to be comprehensible from the ground, is by Hamo Thornycroft. The 1970s' extension is by William Whitfield. At 36 Moorgate, next to Lloyds Bank on the east side, is the **former Ocean Accident building** (1928) by Aston Webb & Son (currently Habib Bank AG Zurich). Note the capitals designed as ships' prows and the sculpture of a lighthouse in an alcove on the corner of Moorfields Place.

The Moor Gate itself, from which the street takes its name, was a 15th-century postern in the City Wall. It was pulled down in 1762. Next to the pub on the corner, at 118 London Wall, is the **Fox umbrella shop** (1934) in black Vitrolite with two stainless steel foxes cavorting either side of the pink neon sign. To the east, where Heron Tower rises in the distance, is Bishopsgate (*see p. 81*). The Neoclassical church of **All Hallows-on-the-Wall** (1765–7; *map p. 607, E2*) was completed when the architect, George Dance the Younger, was in his mid-20s. It was admired by his pupil, John Soane. The church, although still consecrated, is now the offices of the Urban Youth Charity XLP and viewing of the unusual interior is by appointment only (*T: 020 7256 6240 or email: info@xlp.org.uk*). Part of the medieval City Wall may be seen in the churchyard.

Back on Moorgate, on the east side, just past the junction with London Wall, is **Electra House**, home of London Metropolitan University. This seeming monolith of a building, with bronze dome, was built c. 1902 by Belcher and Joass for the Eastern Telegraph and Allied Companies. Beyond opens Finsbury Circus.

FINSBURY CIRCUS

Finsbury Circus (*map p. 607, E2*) was laid out in 1815–17. None of the original gentlemen's houses remains. The fine gardens in the centre were closed at the time of writing for Crossrail construction. **Britannic House**, with a façade on Moorgate, was built by Lutyens in 1924 for the Anglo-Persian Oil Company (later BP). With its Corinthian order and sculpture (including Britannia with her trident by Derwent Wood), it was the first of his grand City buildings.

Moorfields, today commemorated in the name of a small street running parallel with Moorgate on the west side behind Moorgate Underground station (*map p. 607, D2*; leading into Ropemaker Street, where Daniel Defoe died in 1731), was once marshy open land, the resort of beggars, highwaymen and prostitutes. In Thackeray's *Vanity Fair*, Becky Sharpe is recommended to read *The Blind Washerwoman of Moorfields*. Here the Royal London Ophthalmic Hospital was established in buildings by Robert Smirke in 1821. In 1899, Moorfields, as the hospital came to be known, outgrew its premises and moved to its current headquarters on City Road. The poet John Keats, the son of an ostler, was born in 1795 in a house in this area.

St Mary Moorfields, at 4–5 Eldon St, is the only Roman Catholic church in the City. Until the Catholic Relief Act of 1791, public Catholic worship was illegal. Completed in 1903 by George Sherrin, the architect of the dome of the London Oratory, the building is easily missed but the sculpture of the *Virgin and Child* above the entrance points the way to a flight of steps leading down to the candlelit sanctuary below street level.

Moorgate becomes Finsbury Pavement (left at junction with Chiswell Street are the Barbican and The Brewery, an events venue on the site of the former Whitbread beer brewery) and leads north to **Finsbury Square** (*map p. 607, E1*), where City Road leads down to old London from the north. The square was laid out by George Dance the Younger in 1777, in an area formerly notorious as a cruising ground. The road that runs along the south side of the square replaces a pathway which in the early 18th century acquired the name of 'Sodomites' Walk'. No original buildings survive from Dance's design. One was Lackington's bookshop, the 'Temple of Muses', established in 1778 and known as a sight of London. Its memory survives in the name of nearby Lackington Street. On the north side of the square, at nos 22–25, is **Royal London House** (Belcher/Joass, 1928), with a skyrocketing tower.

ARMOURY HOUSE AND THE HAC

City Road continues northwards, away from the official boundaries of the City, past the entrance to the drill-ground and headquarters (**Armoury House**; Thomas Stibbs, 1735; *map p. 607, D1*) of the Honourable Artillery Company of the City of London (HAC), the oldest military body in the country and the second oldest in the world. A private museum tells the history of the HAC and can be viewed by appointment with the archivist (*T: 020 7382 1541, hac.org.uk*). The HAC is now a registered charity dedicated to 'military exercise and training and better defence of the realm'.

HAC was incorporated by Henry VIII in 1537 under the title of the Guild or Fraternity of St George. It has been established at its present home since 1642, and since 1660 the captain-general has usually been the Sovereign or the Prince of Wales. Officers for the Trained Bands of London were supplied by this company, in whose ranks Milton, Wren and Pepys served. The HAC has the rare privilege of marching through the City of London with fixed bayonets. On 15th September 1784, Vincent Lunardi made a balloon ascent from the HAC ground and travelled 24 miles, becoming the first aerial traveller in the English atmosphere and spawning a fad for ballooning. With him in the basket were a cat, a dog and a pigeon in a cage. The cat apparently became airsick and needed to be set down.

BUNHILL FIELDS AND WESLEY'S CHAPEL

Immediately to the north, between City Road and Bunhill Row (formerly Artillery Walk), lies **Bunhill Fields** (*map p. 607, D1*), the famous cemetery of the Nonconformists. Approximately 123,000 people were buried here until its closure in 1854, among them Daniel Defoe (d. 1731; obelisk), John Bunyan (d. 1688; worn recumbent effigy), Susannah Wesley (mother of the Methodists John and Charles) and William Blake (exact location unknown but a gravestone beside the Defoe obelisk commemorates him). Two tombs commemorate descendants of Oliver Cromwell. There has probably been a burial ground here since Saxon times and the name probably derives from 'Bone-Hill' Fields. Today the quiet graveyard is a sanctuary from the surrounding inner-city sprawl and the mature trees of plane, oak, lime and ash provide shelter and a haven for birds, bats and ground fauna. Fenced plots surround grids of 18th- and 19th-century gravestones and underground vaults in varying stages of deterioration (*for this reason the monuments may only be visited with a City Warden; see Attendant's Office in the centre of the grounds or T: 020 7374 4127*).

Milton wrote *Paradise Regained* and died in 1674 at a house in Bunhill Row (no. 125; demolished). In the **Quaker Gardens**, across Bunhill Row, laid out as a garden in 1952 and surrounded by flats, is the grave of George Fox (1624–91), founder of the Society of Friends (Quakers).

On the opposite side of City Road, at no. 49, stands **Wesley's Chapel**, built in 1778 by George Dance the Younger. A statue of John Wesley (1703–91), the founder of Methodism, is at the front and his grave is at the rear. Wesley's House adjoins the chapel and includes the Museum of Methodism, with a collection of Wesleyana and Methodist art. Wesley moved here in 1779 and it is furnished with many of his belongings. His small prayer room is on view (*open Mon–Sat 10–4, closed at service times: Sun and Thur at 12.45–1.30; free; T: 020 7253 2262, wesleyschapel.org.uk*).

A little further on, City Road crosses Old Street (busy roundabout), which leads right (east) to Shoreditch and left (west) to Clerkenwell, passing the **deconsecrated church of St Luke** (*map p. 604, C1*) by John James, with an extraordinary fluted obelisk steeple by Hawksmoor (1727–33), a sort of proto-Shard. William Caslon (d. 1766), the typeface designer, is buried here, as is the architect George Dance the Elder (d. 1768). The church is now a music centre for the London Symphony Orchestra and is known as LSO St Luke's.

City Road continues past Moorfields Eye Hospital and the Eagle tavern, immortalised in the nursery rhyme 'Pop goes the Weasel', to the Angel (a busy road junction named after a long-demolished but once famous coaching tavern) and Islington.

THE BANK OF ENGLAND, ROYAL EXCHANGE, LOMBARD STREET & CORNHILL

Map p. 607, D3–E3. Underground: Bank.

THE BANK OF ENGLAND

The Bank of England building covers a three-acre quadrilateral area between Lothbury, Bartholomew Lane, Threadneedle Street and Princes Street. It is the central bank of the United Kingdom.

The Bank was founded in 1694 by William Paterson, backed by powerful City men to regulate monetary policy. The bank became state-owned in 1946 and in 1997 gained operational independence. Its affairs are managed by a board consisting of a Governor, Deputy Governors and a Court of Directors appointed by the Crown. The Bank is the banker to the Government and on its behalf manages the National Debt and the UK's gold reserves, sets interest rates and has the sole right to issue banknotes in England and Wales. After the Gordon Riots (1780), the Bank was protected nightly until 1973 by a detachment of armed guards.

The building

The first building on this site was in Palladian style by George Sampson (1732–4 and 1745–51), with additions by Sir Robert Taylor from 1765. It was replaced by a curtain-walled Neoclassical building, with top-lit banking halls, by Sir John Soane (1788–1833). It was rebuilt by Sir Herbert Baker in 1925–39; only the sheer, unseeing outer wall remains from Soane's design, although this too did not escape Baker's modifications. The loss of Soane's masterpiece is now considered an architectural tragedy and drawings of his interiors are held at the Sir John Soane Museum in Lincoln's Inn Fields. The bank's façade is best viewed across Threadneedle Street, from the steps of the Royal Exchange. The wall, decorated with a Greek key motif, is punctuated by Corinthian columns and forbidding bronze doors with caducei, the attribute of Hermes, the god of trade and protector of trade routes (his symbol also peppers the exterior of the Royal Exchange). From within, Baker's building rises seven storeys above ground and descends three levels below (the Bank secures the gold reserves of the UK and other countries in an immense vault which takes a 3ft long key to open; it is the outline of this vault which determines the curvature of Bank Underground station, necessitating the famous admonitions to 'Mind the Gap'). The six huge sculptures are by Sir Charles Wheeler (who executed all the external sculpture as well as the bronze doors) and in the pediment appears the 'Old Lady' of Threadneedle Street, as the bank is popularly termed. From Threadneedle Street, walk clockwise around the bank to admire **Tivoli Corner**, at the junction of Princes Street and Lothbury. This survivor from Soane's bank, modelled on the Temple of Vesta at Tivoli, near Rome, was retained and 'improved' by Baker. The gilded figure of Ariel that surmounts it is by Wheeler.

The Bank of England Museum

The Bank of England Museum (*entrance on Bartholomew Lane; open Mon–Fri 10–5; free; shop*) illustrates the Bank's history. Displays include the Bank Stock Office modelled on Sir John Soane's hall of 1793, an iron chest-safe dating from 1700, goldsmith's receipts (the earliest form of banknote) and the Royal Charter of 1694. In Sir Herbert Baker's Rotunda (1930s) is the world's finest collection of Bank of England notes. A 13kg gold bar, which one may handle, is part of the eye-popping gold display. Interactive exhibits cover topics such as inflation, decimalisation, the Euro and the Bank's role today.

LOTHBURY, THROGMORTON STREET AND OLD BROAD STREET

Lothbury (*map p. 607, D2*) is a short street connecting Gresham and Throgmorton streets. Its name probably derives from 'Lattenbury', a place where copper- and tinsmiths worked, and the church of **St Margaret Lothbury** (*open lunchtimes Mon–Fri*), re-built by Wren in 1683–92, displays the armorial bearings of the Worshipful Company of Plate Makers. Its medieval foundations demonstrate that it once stood on the banks of the Walbrook stream (*see p. 73*). The obelisk lead spire, attributed to Robert Hooke, was completed in 1698–1700. The church is notable for its fine 17th-century fittings, including an exquisite font carved with biblical scenes (previously attributed to Grinling Gibbons due to its similarity to the one at St James's Piccadilly) and a rare chancel screen of an eagle with outstretched wings, carved by Woodruffe and Thornton in 1683–4 (the only other surviving chancel screen in a Wren church is at St Peter-upon-Cornhill; *see p. 69*). Most of these furnishings are not original to the church but are re-housed refugees from All Hallows the Great and St Olave Jewry, Wren churches torn down by the Victorians.

Opposite the church, in an alcove in the wall of the Bank, is a **statue of Sir John Soane**. Next to the church, at no. 7 Lothbury, is the Venetian Gothic **former Overseas Bankers' Club** (now flats), by George Somers Clarke Sr (1866). In Portland stone and pink sandstone, with carved reliefs and inflected arches, it appears transplanted from the canals of Venice, or at the very least from the pages of Ruskin's *Stones of Venice*. Next door again, at 41 Lothbury, the former headquarters of NatWest Bank (Mewès & Davis, 1921–32), redeveloped as offices, curves gently onto Throgmorton Street.

THROGMORTON STREET

Throgmorton Street (*map p. 607, E2*) is named after Sir Nicholas Throckmorton, a courtier of Elizabeth I. On your left, past Angel Court and Throgmorton Avenue, is **Drapers' Hall**, with two huge atlantes flanking the entrance. The hall, dating in part from 1667 though practically rebuilt in 1866–70 and restored in 1949, stands on the site of Thomas Cromwell's mansion and preserves his courtyard plan. After his execution, Henry VIII sold it to the Drapers.

In Austin Friars, a snaking alleyway (*entrance on the corner of Throgmorton St and Old Broad St*), stands the **Dutch Church** (Arthur Bailey, 1950–4; *open Mon–Thur 11–3*). This lofty church, with its graceful flèche, replaces the 13th-century building—originally the nave of a priory of Augustinian friars—that was assigned by Edward VI in 1550 to Protestant refugees and was ultimately left exclusively to the Dutch. The old church was completely destroyed in 1941 and the great west window, by Max Nauta, shows Edward VI and Princess Irene of the Netherlands. The latter laid the foundation stone of the new church. Beneath the Communion table is the altar stone of the priory church of 1253.

OLD BROAD STREET

Old Broad Street (*map p. 607, E2*) runs from Threadneedle Street to Liverpool Street. At no. 19 is the elegant, cream-coloured **City of London Club** (Philip Hardwick, 1833–4), which narrowly escaped demolition in the 1970s to make way for **Tower 42**, next door at no. 25. Tower 42 (formerly the NatWest Tower; R.Seifert & Partners, 1970–81), was the tallest office block in Europe until One Canada Square in Docklands was completed in 1990. The Tower, severely damaged by the Bishopsgate bomb in 1993 (*see p. 82*) and by then considered outdated in any case, was recommended for demolition. When this was deemed too expensive, it was refurbished instead and now houses offices, a restaurant and top-floor bar, Vertigo, which has excellent views.

At no. 125 (back towards Threadneedle Street) is the **former London Stock Exchange**. Built in 1972 as a seven-sided concrete tower, it was completely remodelled in glass in 2004–8 for office and retail use. A sculpture of an angel's wing is outside. The current Stock Exchange is at Paternoster Square (*map p. 606, C3*)

THREADNEEDLE STREET

Threadneedle Street (*map p. 607, D3–E3*) runs from the Bank of England and Royal Exchange all the way to Bishopsgate. At no. 30 is the **Merchant Taylors' Hall**, the largest of the livery company halls, on this site since 1347 (*for the livery companies, see p. 21*). It was damaged by the Great Fire, gutted in the Blitz and re-opened in 1959. The 14th-century crypt survives. The activity of the Merchant Taylors and the Needlemakers (whose hall was nearby) probably gave Threadneedle Street its name.

At nos 37–8, in rusticated Palladian style, is the **former British Linen Bank** (1902–3), by Macvicar Anderson, currently a restaurant, Jamie's Italian (one of several 'Jamie's Italian' restaurants in the capital, part of the culinary imperium of celebrity chef Jamie Oliver). It is built on the site of South Sea House, the South Sea Company's headquarters, where the 'South Sea Bubble' speculation scandal burst in 1720. Note the carved stone relief of two sailors over the archway. Next door, curving onto Bishopsgate, is the splendid single-storey **Gibson Hall** (John Gibson, 1864–5), built as the National Provincial Bank's headquarters and now a private events venue. The exterior is rich in sculptural ornament. The reliefs by Hancock represent Industry and the statues ranging on the top of the building, covered with netting to deter London's omnipresent pigeons, from left to right, represent Manchester, England, Wales, Birmingham, Newcastle and the potteries, Dover, the shipbuilding towns, the mining towns and London.

Opposite is the building site for the **Pinnacle**, a skyscraper designed to look like a fairground helter skelter. At the time of writing construction had been suspended owing to funding difficulties.

THE ROYAL EXCHANGE

Standing at the entrance to the Royal Exchange (*map p. 607, E3*), you are in the most ancient part of the City and at the centre of Roman London. The steps afford a fine view of the Mansion House (*see p. 72*), NatWest and the Bank of England (*see p. 63*), as well as straight ahead to No 1 Poultry, by James Stirling (1998).

The forecourt features twelve Victorian-style lamps, donated by the twelve great livery companies (*see p. 21*), each with a brass plate and company motto and surmounted by a spiky dragon rampant. The equestrian statue of Wellington (Chantrey and Weekes, 1844) was cast from French cannon. The war memorial commemorates Londoners who fell in both world wars. The statue on a traffic island on Cornhill is of Sir Henry Greathead (1844–96), chief engineer of the City and South London Railway and inventor of the travelling shield that enabled the deep-level cutting of the Tube system. His plinth is positioned over a ventilation shaft for Bank Underground station. At the rear is a granite column topped by a statue of Baron Paul Julius Reuter, who founded the Reuter's News Agency at the Royal Exchange in 1851 (Michael Black, 1976); a seated figure of George Peabody, founder of the charitable Peabody Trust (1869) and a fountain-group, *La Maternité*, by Dalou (1877–9).

The first Royal Exchange, inspired by the Bourse at Antwerp, was built in 1566 by Sir Thomas Gresham, a rich merchant and valued royal agent instrumental in reducing the royal debt, as a commercial forum for merchants to meet and do business in convivial surroundings. It was destroyed in the Great Fire in 1666 and rebuilt in 1669. This second building burned down in 1838 but some of the sculptures survived the fire. The current building, designed in classical style by Sir William Tite, was opened by Queen Victoria in 1844. It ceased operating as a bourse in 1939. The Royal Exchange was used by the London International Financial Futures until the late 1990s, its trading floor constructed as a separate shell within the existing building. In 2002, the Royal Exchange was remodelled as a luxury shopping and dining mall (*open Mon–Fri*).

Inside, the Grand Café occupies the central mosaic courtyard and offers all-day dining and fine surroundings from which to eat, drink and people-watch. The courtyard was enclosed by Charles Barry Jr in 1883–4; the current glazed roof dates from 1991. Panels originally commissioned to line the walls of the courtyard are now in the first-floor gallery. They include one of Lord Leighton's few murals, *Phoenicians Bartering with Ancient Britons* (1894–5).

The richly decorated exterior of the building, essentially a Victorian classical pastiche with caducei (symbol of Hermes, patron of trade), is well worth inspecting. The impressive tympanum group above the Corinthian portico, by Sir Richard Westmacott (1844), represents *Commerce holding the Charter of the Exchange*, attended by the Lord Mayor, British merchants and natives of various foreign nations. The Wren-like campanile has a statue of Gresham on its east face and a large golden grass-hopper vane (Gresham's badge), said to be from the post-Fire building. On the wall along Threadneedle Street are statues to Sir Hugh Myddleton (1844) and Richard Whittington (1844).

LOMBARD STREET

Lombard Street, Cornhill and King William Street (*map p. 607, D3*) fan out towards Gracechurch Street in an area that for centuries has been one of the chief banking and financial centres of London. Between them, a meandering network of narrow passages and alleys evokes the old, densely-packed City where coffee houses, taverns and chop houses were located and where today one still chances upon hidden pubs and shops. They are particularly lively at lunchtime on weekdays, when crowds of suited City men fill them, loudly chatting and laughing, clutching their prandial pints.

CITY ALLEYS

Change Alley (*entrances on both Cornhill and Lombard St*) saw scenes of wild speculation during the South Sea Bubble excitement in 1720. Jonathan's Coffee House, the principal meeting place of stockbrokers, was located here from 1680–1778. At the entrance to Ball Court (from Cornhill) is Simpson's, 'London's oldest chop house', founded 1757 (*see p. 89*). In Castle Court is The George and Vulture pub, founded 1600 and known to readers of Dickens's *Pickwick Papers*: 'Mr Pickwick and Sam took up their present abode in very good, old-fashioned, and comfortable quarters, to wit, the George and Vulture Tavern and Hotel, George Yard, Lombard Street'. A good view of the back of building is from Bengal Court, where once can also view the back of the former Barclays Bank HQ. Set in a wall in Corbet Court is a stone carving of the Mercers' Maiden, the earliest surviving property mark of the Mercers' Company dating from 1669 and installed here in 2004. In St Michael's Alley is St Michael's churchyard and the Jamaica Wine House (1885; *see p. 89*), on the site of London's first coffee house, the Pasqua Rossee's Head, founded 1652 (plaque).

Lombard Street, once a street of banks, derives its name from the 'Lombard' money-lenders from Genoa and Florence, who held financial sway here from the 13th–16th centuries. The first Lloyd's Coffee House (1691–1785) was founded on Lombard Street and during the 1930s, the street was paved in rubber from British Malaya to muffle the sound of traffic so as not to disturb its moneymen. The phrase 'Lombard Street to a China orange' means heavily-weighted odds, with 'Lombard Street' being taken to signify value and the 'China orange', a trifle. Since de-regularisation, the banks have deserted Lombard Street in favour of Canary Wharf and elsewhere. However, a number of colourful hanging signs commemorate the historic institutions once based here: note the enormous **gilded grasshopper**, the badge of the great financier Sir

LOMBARD STREET
The Gresham grasshopper.

Thomas Gresham, with the initials TG and the date 1563, hanging outside no. 68.

Number 1 Lombard St, part of the curving building overlooking the Bank of England and Mansion House, stands on the site of the Smith, Payne & Smith bank, where the father of Charles Dickens's first love, Maria Beadnell, worked. It is now a smart restaurant and brasserie (*see p. 88*).

At the end of the street, **no. 54 Lombard St**, on the corner of Gracechurch Street, with Post-modern curved glass rooftops (GMW Partnership 1986–94), is the former headquarters of Barclays Bank. The church of **St Edmund the King**, rebuilt by Wren, and possibly Hooke, during the 1670s, is now home to the London Centre for Spirituality and the Centre Bookshop. The spacious interior houses excellent carved woodwork including a font cover topped with gilded apostles, and has a fine display of Church silver.

ST MARY WOOLNOTH

The church of St Mary Woolnoth (*map p. 607, D3*), which forms a monumental bastion between King William Street and Lombard Street, is a building of great originality. It is Nicholas Hawksmoor's only City church, erected in 1716–27 and restored and altered in 1875–6 by William Butterfield. It was the only City church to remain intact throughout the air raids of 1940–5. The interior contains an elaborate reredos and ornamental woodwork. From the pulpit John Newton (d. 1807, author of the hymn *Amazing Grace*; tablet on north wall) helped to set William Wilberforce and Hannah More on their abolitionist and philanthropical paths. On the south wall is a memorial to Edward Lloyd, founder of the first Lloyd's coffee house (*see Lloyd's of London, overleaf*).

CORNHILL

Cornhill (*map p. 607, E3*) is named after a long-extinct grain market. It is a low eminence, standing at 58ft above sea level: together with Ludgate Hill it is the highest point in the City. At no. 39, the former Union Discount Company of London building (c.

1890) occupies the site of the house (burned down in 1748) in which the poet Thomas Gray was born in 1716. **St Michael's Church**, with an unexpectedly tall tower (a survivor of the Great Fire), was rebuilt by Wren and Hawksmoor in 1670–1724 and restored by Sir George Gilbert Scott in Gothic style in 1857–60. It stands on one of the oldest Christian sites in Britain, dating back to the Roman occupation, and today offers a traditional Anglican service following the Book of Common Prayer (*choral Eucharist on Sun at 11am*). The sky-blue and gold interior houses a sculpture of a terrifying-looking pelican in her piety.

St Peter-upon-Cornhill, on the corner with Gracechurch Street and visible behind 19th-century shopfronts, was rebuilt by Wren in 1677–84. A good view of the façade may be had from Gracechurch Street. It contains a carved wooden choir screen, one of only two such screens in Wren churches (the other being in St Margaret Lothbury; *see p. 64*). Wren is known to have been reluctant to divide the interior space in this way; this screen was installed at the insistence of rector William Beveridge, a fervent believer in the sanctity of Communion. The church (*closed to the public*) is used by the benefice of St Helen's Bishopsgate as a Bible study centre and youth group meeting point, and there is a service for Mandarin-speaking Christians on Sun. Otherwise the interior must be viewed by appointment (*T: 020 7283 2231*). Behind, in St Peter's Alley, the small garden is the old burial ground alleged to have been founded by the British early Christian ruler Lucius in AD 179 (the historical existence of Lucius is contested by scholars, though Bede mentions him).

Back on Cornhill, opposite St Peter's, stands the neo-Venetian Gothic **Shanghai Commercial Bank**, built by Edward I'Anson (1870). In an earlier building on this site were the offices of Smith, Elder & Co., publishers of Thackeray and the Brontës.

The junction of Cornhill with Gracechurch Street (*map p. 607, E3*) is a good place to pause to get one's bearings. If you stand with Leadenhall Street ahead of you, the Monument (*see p. 77*) is to your right. The skyscraper nicknamed the Walkie-Talkie, on Fenchurch Street (*see p. 87*), looms over this part of town. On your left is Bishopsgate (*see p. 81*). Leadenhall Street leads to Aldgate, with the Aviva Tower, Lloyd's and the Cheesegrater (*see p. 70*).

ON & AROUND LEADENHALL STREET

Map p. 607, E3. Underground: Bank.

LEADENHALL MARKET AND LLOYD'S
Leadenhall Market is the work of Sir Horace Jones (1880–1), architect of Smithfield and Billingsgate markets. A meat and game market existed on the site from medieval times and in 1663 Pepys bought 'a leg of beef, a good one, for sixpence' here. Jones retained the medieval street plan when the elaborate arcaded buildings of glass and steel were erected. They were built over part of a Roman basilica and forum of AD 150,

one of the largest buildings of its kind in the Roman Empire, and a column reputedly survives in the basement of no. 90 Gracechurch St. Today the market, open 24hrs a day as a thoroughfare, houses shops, bars and restaurants (*open Mon–Fri*) and nearby office workers are its clientèle.

Walk straight through the market to come out onto Lime Street. Here, on your left (at no. 1), is the main entrance to the stainless steel, glass and concrete tubular edifice of **Lloyd's of London**, designed by Richard Rogers and opened by HM The Queen in 1986. A building of 1928, designed by Sir Edwin Cooper and which Lloyd's had long outgrown, was demolished to make way for the new tower in 1979.

Lloyd's, the great international association of underwriters and insurance brokers, transacting most kinds of insurance, began in 1688 as a gathering of merchants in Edward Lloyd's coffee house in Tower Street (later in Lombard Street and in the Royal Exchange); its original business was marine insurance. Rogers's building was designed with a dealing room that could expand or contract according to market conditions by means of a series of galleries around a central space. The Lloyd's Building is considered one of the greatest buildings of the 1980s and has achieved listed status. It is a leading exponent of what is sometimes termed 'Bowellism', architecture that places functional elements such as elevators and air-conditioning pipes on the exterior so as to maximise space inside.

The East India Company was founded on Leadenhall Street in 1600. The old East India House (demolished 1862) stood on part of the site where the Lloyd's Building is now: the essayist Charles Lamb and economists James Mill and his son John Stuart Mill once worked as East India clerks in its halls.

AVIVA TOWER AND THE CHEESEGRATER

The 28-storey **Aviva Tower** (1 Undershaft; *map p. 607, E3*) is set back from the road in an open piazza. The block, of tinted brown glass, was built in the 1960s as the Commercial Union Insurance building, influenced by similar office blocks in midtown Manhattan. The adjacent skyscraper, officially the Leadenhall Building but known as the '**Cheesegrater**' due to its wedge shape, is to a design by Richard Rogers. The nickname was coined after the City of London's chief planner saw a model and commented that it was the sort of thing his wife would use to grate parmesan. The glass and steel building, of 48 storeys, is, unusually, designed not rely on concrete foundations. Instead the glass and steel megaframe, by Arup, will provide stability. At the time of writing, it was the world's tallest building of this kind.

ST ANDREW UNDERSHAFT

At the corner of Leadenhall Street and St Mary Axe stands the church of St Andrew Undershaft (*map p. 607, E3*), dominated by the Gherkin rising directly behind it. It was built in Perpendicular style in 1520–32, though a church has stood on this site since the 12th century. The name is derived from the ancient practice (discontinued in 1517) of erecting a 'shaft' or maypole, taller than the tower, in front of the south door. The last maypole survived, slung under the eaves of a neighbouring cottage, until 1549, when a zealous cleric declared it to be idolatrous, and it was taken down and burned.

The church survived both the Fire and the Blitz but was grievously damaged in the Bishopsgate bombing (*see p. 82*) and its rare surviving 17th-century stained-glass window of portraits of monarchs was blown out. The church falls under the jurisdiction of St Helen's Bishopsgate: to visit the interior you must make an appointment (*T: 020 7283 2231*). Inside, the alabaster monument to historian and antiquary John Stow, author of the *Survey of London* of 1598, holds a quill pen which is ceremonially renewed every three years by the Lord Mayor. The organ was installed by Renatus Harris (*see p. 204*) in 1696.

THE GHERKIN AND HOLLAND HOUSE

In St Mary Axe, on the site of the former Baltic Exchange (1903), the headquarters of a body of merchants and brokers dealing in air and sea cargoes which was severely damaged by the IRA bomb attack of 1992 and not rebuilt, stands one of London's architectural icons, 30 St Mary Axe, fondly known as the **Gherkin** (*map p. 607, E2–F2*). It was built in 2004 to the designs of Foster & Partners. This distinctive structure, covered in diamond-shaped panes of glass, lends itself to an environmentally-friendly spiralling ventilation system. During construction, the grave of an unknown Roman girl was discovered on the site and this is commemorated on the low wall surrounding the piazza (plaque in the pavement opposite Holland House).

Holland House, on Bury Street, with its western façade facing the Gherkin, was built in 1914–16 by pre-eminent Dutch architect Hendrik Petrus Berlage. A Modernist symphony in black granite and green Delft ceramic tiling, it is the architect's only London building and very unusual. Commissioned by the Muller shipping company, it features a large ship's prow in granite on the southeast side. Peer through the entrance on the west (Gherkin) side to see the mosaic De Stijl interior.

ST KATHARINE CREE

On the corner of Creechurch Lane and Leadenhall Street is the church of St Katharine Cree (*map p. 607, F3*). The name is a corruption of Christchurch, a priory of the Holy Trinity, founded by Matilda, queen of Henry I, in 1108. The church was rebuilt in 1628–30, retaining the medieval tower of 1504. It is the only surviving Jacobean church in London. William Laud, bishop of London, consecrated the church in 1631 and the form of service he used was later judged heretical and popish by the Puritans at his trial in 1644. A chapel commemorates both Laud and his patron, Charles I, and contains the tomb of Sir Nicholas Throckmorton (d. 1570), the Elizabethan statesman after whom Throgmorton Street is named.

The stained-glass rose window at the east end incorporates glass from the 1630s and is said to have been modelled on the one in Old St Paul's Cathedral (destroyed in the Fire). The font dates from c. 1631 and the restored organ has 17th-century pipes by Father Smith (*see p. 204*). Both Handel and Purcell played on the original instrument. An unverified tradition has it that Hans Holbein the Younger (d. 1543) was buried in the earlier church.

The annual lunchtime 'Lion Sermon', held around 16th Oct, commemorates the escape from a desert lion of fishmonger Sir John Gayer, Lord Mayor of London and founder of the Levant Company, who held office in Charles I's time. The church, restored in 1962, is now a guild church with a weekly lunchtime Eucharist. Each Sunday it is used by a Syrian Orthodox congregation.

SIR JOHN CASS PRIMARY SCHOOL AND BEVIS MARKS

In Duke's Place, just north of Aldgate, stood the Great Synagogue of London, established in 1690 and destroyed during the Blitz. Here is the **Sir John Cass Foundation Primary School**, founded in 1710 by a charitable alderman (d. 1718; memorial in St Botolph's Aldgate) and rebuilt in 1908 by A.W. Cooksey. A playground is on the roof. The two figures of a charity boy and girl (1710–11) are from the original school. On the annual Founder's Day, children and guests wear red feathers in honour of Sir John Cass, who suffered a fatal haemorrhage whilst writing the will by which he funded the school, staining his white goose quill red with blood.

Off Bevis Marks, in a little gated courtyard facing Heneage Lane, is the Spanish and Portuguese Synagogue or **Bevis Marks Synagogue** (*map p. 607, F2; open Mon, Wed, Thur 10.30–2, Tues and Fri 10.30–1, Sun 10.30–12.30; closed bank holidays, Sat and Jewish holidays; bevismarks.org.uk*), a handsome building in red brick looking rather like a Wren church or Nonconformist chapel but also bearing resemblance to the Spanish and Portuguese Great Synagogue of 1675 in Amsterdam. Built in 1699–1701, it is probably by Joseph Avis, a carpenter who worked for Wren. The interior is very fine, with seven brass chandeliers representing the seven days of the week, 18th-century wooden seating and an elaborate oak Torah Ark (Ehal) at the east end. The twelve columns that support the women's gallery symbolise the Twelve Tribes of Israel and are painted to resemble marble. This is the oldest synagogue in Great Britain and was founded by Sephardic Jews who had fled Spain and Portugal to escape the Inquisition. It was the synagogue of Isaac d'Israeli, a talented poet and essayist of Italian Jewish ancestry, who quarrelled with the synagogue in 1817 and baptised his sons as Christians. The eldest of those sons was Benjamin, who later rose to become Prime Minister and Earl of Beaconsfield. The building was damaged in the 1993 IRA bombing but has been faithfully restored.

MANSION HOUSE & WALBROOK

Map p. 607, D3. Underground: Bank.

Mansion House (*guided tours every Tues at 2pm; entrance by the door in Walbrook*) is the official residence of the Lord Mayor. A Palladian edifice, with an imposing Corinthian portico, it was erected by George Dance the Elder in 1739–52, with alterations by Dance the Younger from 1795. The pediment, depicting the City of London receiving gifts of Plenty, was sculpted by Sir Robert Taylor. The splendid Egyptian Hall on the first floor is the scene of banquets, balls and other functions. Dance modelled it after the so-called 'Egyptian Hall' as described by Vitruvius, taken to mean a large central space surrounded by colonnaded walkways. It contains some 19th-century sculptures. Also included in the tour are the Long Parlour, with a remarkable coffered ceiling; the Saloon, adorned with plasterwork, tapestry and sculpture; and the State Drawing Room.

ST STEPHEN WALBROOK

In Walbrook, just behind the Mansion House, is the church of St Stephen Walbrook (*map p. 607, D3*), which takes its name from the Walbrook stream that flows beneath it, from Finsbury to the Thames. The church was rebuilt by Wren in 1672–80 but is now ignominiously dwarfed by the monstrous bulgy office block, Walbrook House, next door. The noble interior, with its circular dome supported on eight arches, is one of the architect's masterpieces, his dress rehearsal for St Paul's Cathedral. It was carefully restored after its partial destruction in 1941. The church's later restoration in 1978–87 was led by the property developer and arts patron Peter Palumbo (later Baron Palumbo of Walbrook), a churchwarden, who also commissioned the central altar, of travertine, by Henry Moore (1972–83). It is the only piece of church furniture Moore designed and its installation caused controversy because it contradicted Wren's Restoration vision, whereby the altar was placed at the east end and not in the centre of the church. After a hearing at the Court of Ecclesiastical Causes Reserved, Moore's altar was finally allowed to remain, though it is still not universally liked and has been compared to a ripe camembert cheese.

The 17th-century stone font is by Thomas Strong, with a fine wood cover by William Newman, and the wooden reredos and pulpit (also 17th-century) are by Thomas Creecher, William Newman and Thomas Maine. A glass mosaic memorial on the south wall commemorates the composer John Dunstable (d. 1453), 'the father of English harmony'. Sir John Vanbrugh (d. 1726), playwright and architect of Blenheim Palace, is interred here without a monument. The famous couplet by Abel Evans:

Lie heavy on him, Earth! for he
Laid many heavy loads on thee...

was published as an epigrammatical epitaph in verse.

ROMAN FINDS: THE 'POMPEII OF THE NORTH'

The triangle between Queen Victoria Street, Cannon Street and Walbrook was, at the time of writing, a cacophonous building site from which the Bloomberg media headquarters will rise as part of a new plaza development. The area is rich in Roman remains. In 1954 a Temple of Mithras, dedicated to the ancient mystery cult and built shortly before AD 200 on the banks of the Walbrook stream, was unearthed. In 2013, contractors digging foundations for the new Bloomberg building stumbled upon one of the most important archaeological finds of modern times. The discovery, dubbed the 'Pompeii of the North', included timber structures and over 10,000 objects including writing tablets, coins and a gladiator's amber amulet, all preserved in layers of Walbrook mud. Archaeologists from the Museum of London are now working with the construction team and an on-site museum is planned as part of Bloomberg's completed headquarters.

ON & AROUND CANNON STREET

Map p. 607, D3. Underground: Cannon Street, Mansion House.

Cannon Street takes its name from the wax chandlers who worked here; its name is a corruption of Candlewick Street. To the west (10 Cannon St) is the former Financial Times building, **Bracken House** (Sir Albert Richardson, 1955–9, redeveloped by Hopkins & Partners, 1988–91), a striking construction in dark pinkish stone and sandstone with an interesting astrological clock by Philip Bentham: at its centre is the face of Winston Churchill (a friend of Brendan Bracken, Chairman of the *FT*) in a sunburst motif. It is said that pink sandstone was chosen for the building because of the famous salmon pink colour of the *Financial Times* newsprint.

At 30 Cannon Street and 84–94 Queen Victoria Street, the **former Crédit Lyonnais building**, built in the 1970s by Whinney, Son & Austen Hall, fills the triangular space. Each floor is wider than the one below and clad in cast sections of glass-fibre-reinforced concrete, giving the impression of a flaring tiered confection dripping in icing. Viewed from certain angles, it looks like a hybrid of the Flatiron Building in Manhattan, a cruise liner and the Leaning Tower of Pisa.

Opposite, in Queen Victoria Street, is the church of **St Mary Aldermary** (so called, according to Stow, because it is 'elder than any church of St Marie in the City'). It was rebuilt by Wren's office after 1679 (tower 1704) and is an important surviving example of 17th-century neo-Gothic architecture. Inside, the elaborate white plaster fan-vaulted ceiling is especially noteworthy. Milton married his third wife, Elizabeth Minshull, here in 1663.

ST JAMES GARLICKHYTHE AND VINTNERS' HALL

In Garlick Hill is the church of **St James Garlickhythe** (*map p. 607, D3*), so called because this was once an important Roman or Saxon harbour (hithe) where garlic was traded. Wren rebuilt the church after the Fire in 1672–82 and the complex steeple (1713–17) is thought to be after a design by Hawksmoor. The use of clear glass clerestory windows and high ceilings gave the church its nickname, 'Wren's Lantern'. It is a traditional Anglican church, noted for its music. The interior has fine 17th-century wood-carving and ironwork. The organ, of 1718–19, is probably by Knopple but has previously been attributed to Father Smith (*see p. 204*).

The church looks down over the relentless traffic of Upper Thames Street, and opposite, to the Neoclassical façade of **Vintners' Hall**. This is one of the larger livery halls and has occupied this site since 1446. It was rebuilt in the 1670s, after the Great Fire, and escaped World War Two bombing with superficial damage. Its collections include fine tapestries and paintings. The company, one of the original Great Twelve (*see p. 21*), is still linked to the UK wine trade; in 2013 it celebrated its 650th anniversary. The Vintners share ancient custody, with the Crown and the Worshipful Company of Dyers, of Britain's Mute swan population and take part in the annual Swan Upping ceremony, which is a census of the swan population on the Thames (*see p. 533*). The custom dates from the 12th century, when swans were considered a tasty and exclusive delicacy and the Crown claimed possession of them to ensure that the royal banquet table was duly provisioned.

THE THAMES RIVER WALK AROUND CANNON STREET

Cross over Upper Thames Street, via the pedestrian bridge. The river walk stretching east and west is highly recommended. Wharves and warehouses may have gone, but narrow lanes bearing historic names run down to the Thames. Queenhithe dates from the re-colonisation of the Roman City by Alfred the Great in AD 886. The area became an important medieval dock, named after Queen Matilda, wife of Henry I. Henry III decreed that all grain ships should discharge here. Look left (west) and you will see the Millennium Bridge. Head right (east) and the walk takes you all the way to the Tower of London, with interesting detours back into the City along the way. Southwark Bridge, with its green and yellow colour scheme, was originally the work of John Rennie, designer of Waterloo Bridge (1813–19), but was entirely rebuilt in 1912–21 by Sir Ernest George. Excavations in the vicinity unearthed evidence of the Roman quay and remains of three Saxon ships and other Roman and Saxon finds. In Walbrook Wharf, with the Banker Pub on the river, is the entrance to Steelyard Passage, a shadowy route beneath the Victorian turrets of Cannon Street Station, with glowing circular floor lights and echoing with the clanging and clinking sound effects of metal being forged. The Hanseatic League's trading colony had their base here from the 13th century.

UPPER THAMES STREET AND DOWGATE HILL

Leave the river and head up Cousin Lane. On Upper Thames Street, the small patch of green on your left is **Whittington Garden** (*map p. 607, D3*), commemorating Sir Richard Whittington (1354–1423), merchant, politician, philanthropist, four times Mayor of London and the inspiration for the folk tale of 'Dick Whittington and his Cat'. Here is the church of **St Michael Paternoster Royal**, rebuilt by Whittington in 1409 and also his burial place. The name derives from the rosary (paternoster) sellers who used to live in the area. Destroyed in the Fire, it was rebuilt by Wren in 1685–94, one of the last of the 51 City churches to be rebuilt. The fine steeple (1713–17) is possibly by Hawksmoor. It was also one of the last churches to be restored after the Blitz and in 1968 was re-dedicated as the chapel and headquarters of the Mission to Seafarers, an Anglican charity serving merchant sailors around the world. Inside are vivid stained-glass windows by John Hayward, including one of Dick Whittington and his cat. In College Hill a blue plaque records the site of Whittington's house in 1423.

Three more livery halls are in Dowgate Hill just before Cannon Street: note the decorative entrances to the halls of the **Tallow Chandlers** (no. 4), the **Skinners** (no. 8) and the **Dyers** (nos 11–13). Excavations in this area in 1965 revealed traces of a Roman governor's palace of AD 80–100, overlooking the Thames beside the mouth of the Walbrook stream, which entered the Thames at Dowgate. At a lower level, timber foundations suggested that this was the earlier site of a Roman fort. Further excavations in 1988–9 revealed a late Roman building.

MONUMENT
King Charles II, in Roman guise, directs the resuscitation of London, while Fire,
an aged hag, breathes brimstone from below.

THE LONDON STONE AND A GROPIUS SHOPFRONT

At no. 111 Cannon St, on the site of St Swithin's Church (rebuilt by Wren but so badly damaged during the Blitz that it was demolished in 1962), is the **London Stone**, an unremarkable-looking lump of limestone immured in the wall at ground level behind a wire grille. The stone is of ancient yet contradictory provenance. Some believe it to have been the *miliarium* of Roman London, from which all distances on the Roman high roads were measured. Others claim it as the stone from which King Arthur drew *Excalibur*. In 1450, rebel leader Jack Cade, who marched 5,000 men to London in revolt against King Henry VI, struck the stone with his staff, exclaiming 'Now is Mortimer Lord of this City'. The building where the stone is currently encased was due for demolition at the time of writing and the Stone will be moved to a new location in Cannon Street.

Just before no. 111, the narrow Salter's Hall Court leads to **St Swithin's Church Garden**, nestled in the lee of the bulbous backside of Walbrook House.

Just past the London Stone, on the corner of St Swithin's Lane, is a building dated 1870 and with painted wrought-iron ram's heads at pavement level. The Founders' Hall was in this lane, before its removal to Cloth Fair in the 1980s.

At no. **115 Cannon St**, the Art Deco shopfront in black Vitrolite (1936) is by the great 20th-century modern architect and founder of the Bauhaus School, Walter Gropius. German-born Gropius sought refuge from the Nazis in London in 1934–7, where he worked with Maxwell Fry before emigrating to America.

Laurence Pountney Hill (right off Cannon Street off Abchurch Lane) boasts two fine houses built in 1703 (nos 1 and 2). Round the corner at no. 7a, past Vestry House, is the dark-brick post-Fire Rectory House (1678–70), within a fenced garden.

ST MARY ABCHURCH

St Mary Abchurch on Abchurch Lane (*map p. 607, D3*) was rebuilt by Wren in 1681–6 and restored by Godfrey Allen (1945–57). In the interior, the **dome**, with its four oval windows is an architectural *tour de force*. The painted decoration that adorns it is by William Snow (1708): it shows angels adoring the name of God, which appears in Hebrew in a burst of golden sunlight. The splendid **limewood reredos**, with a gilded pelican in her piety (1686), is a superb work by Grinling Gibbons. The City churches are rich in fittings either traditionally or hopefully attributed to the great wood carver, but not many are actually confirmed as being by his hand. Gibbons was greatly admired for his exquisite and realistic limewood carvings, often of fruit and flowers: he was the unsurpassed master of this medium. Other examples of his work may be seen in St Paul's Cathedral, Hampton Court Palace and St James's Piccadilly. The V&A has several pieces, including a wooden 'filigree' cravat resembling Venetian lace, which was one of Horace Walpole's prize possessions (he would wear it on occasion at his home, Strawberry Hill).

THE MONUMENT & LONDON BRIDGE

Map p. 607, E3–E4. Underground: Monument.

The busy crossroads where King William Street converges with Gracechurch Street and Eastcheap is the site believed to have been occupied by the Boar's Head Tavern, where Falstaff and Prince Hal (in Shakespeare's *Henry IV*) caroused. **St Clement Eastcheap**, left off Clement's Lane (*map p. 607, E3*), was rebuilt by Wren in 1683–7. It contains handsome 17th-century wood furnishings, including a carved and gilded font cover depicting a dove with an olive branch (not always on display), and a fine organ case of c. 1695. Samuel Pepys and John Evelyn worshipped here. The church claims to be the St Clement's in the nursery rhyme 'Oranges and Lemons'.

Eastcheap itself was once the medieval City's chief meat market. Animal puddings (entrails) were carried down **Pudding Lane**, on the right, to be disposed of in the river. Some interesting mid-Victorian former storehouses survive. The building at nos 33–35, in extravagant Victorian Gothic style (R.L. Roumieu, 1868), was the London base for Hill & Evans, makers of vinegar.

THE MONUMENT

Map p. 607, E3. Open April–Sept daily 9.30–6, Oct–March 9.30–5; last tickets 30mins before closing. Large bags must be deposited; themonument.info.

At the junction of Monument Street and Fish Street Hill stands the Monument, a colossal Doric column, 202ft high, erected from the designs of Wren and Hooke in 1671–7 to commemorate the Great Fire of London. It is the tallest free-standing column in the world.

The Great Fire started on 2nd September 1666 in Pudding Lane, at a point exactly 202ft from the Monument. The fire raged for three days and was reported to have covered 373 acres inside the walls and 63 acres outside, destroying 13,200 houses, 44 livery halls and 86 churches; only nine people died. The Monument stands on the site of St Margaret's Church, New Fish Street, the first to perish in the Fire.

The Monument is built of Portland stone with a pedestal 21ft square and 40ft high and a fluted shaft 120ft high and 15ft in diameter. Latin inscriptions record the Fire. The bas-relief by Cibber represents the King consoling the City—the female figure in the ruins—while Fire, a ghastly crone, breathes smoke from below. The four dragons are by Edward Pierce. Inside the column, a winding staircase of 311 steps leads to the caged gallery, which commands wide and striking views. The gallery was first enclosed in 1842 to prevent suicides. The flaming gilt urn surmounting the Monument is 42ft high and has recently been re-gilded.

LONDON BRIDGE

London Bridge (*map p. 607, D4–E4*) divides the Thames into 'above' and 'below' bridge. Downstream is the Port of London. The reach immediately adjacent to the bridge is known as the Pool of London, while upstream is the King's Reach. The present bridge (Mott, Hay & Anderson with Lord Holford, 1967–72) is a box girder bridge borne on three shallow arches of pre-stressed concrete faced with granite. It is 105ft wide. The former bridge, designed by John Rennie before his death and completed by his son in 1832, was sold in 1967 to an American oil tycoon for £1,025,000. It was dismantled into 10,000 granite slabs which were numbered and shipped to Lake Havasu City, Arizona, where the bridge was re-erected over an artificial lake.

OLD LONDON BRIDGE

A wooden bridge across the Thames existed by the 1st century AD. This probably survived until 1176, having been repaired by the Saxons. The popular rhyme 'London Bridge is Falling Down' may date from this time, when it was resolved to 'build it up with stone so strong'. The new bridge, about 100ft west of the old, was begun in 1176 by Peter of Colechurch, at the instance of Henry II, but it was not completed until 1209 in the reign of King John. It stood close to the west end of the church of St Magnus. Rows of wooden houses sprang up on each side, and in the middle was a chapel dedicated to St Thomas à Becket. At each end stood a fortified gate, on the spikes of which the heads of traitors were exposed. The Thames under the bridge was notoriously difficult to navigate because of the narrow passage between the starlings and the force of the ebb tide. After a fire in 1758, the last houses were demolished and the bridge was partly reconstructed and opened in 1763. It was the only bridge over the Thames until the opening of Putney Bridge in 1729. Most Thames crossings were made in wherries rowed by watermen. Old London Bridge was removed after the completion of Rennie's bridge 100ft upstream (*see above*).

On the west side of London Bridge is **Fishmongers' Hall**, commonly known as Fish Hall, one of the grandest livery halls. The present hall, with a fine Neoclassical façade on the river, was built in 1831–5 by Henry Roberts and George Gilbert Scott. It was badly damaged in 1940 (an earlier hall was also burnt down in the Great Fire). The Fishmongers' Company is one of the richest as well as one of the oldest of the twelve great livery companies (*see p. 21*). Its origin is lost in antiquity though it certainly pre-dates the reign of Henry II. The fine interior has been restored in its former style. It contains the Annigoni portrait (1955) of Queen Elizabeth II (the model for stamps and banknotes) and a fine portrait of Sir William Walworth, the Mayor who killed Wat Tyler in 1381, as well as the dagger with which he is supposed to have done the deed.

From London Bridge, look down onto Lower Thames Street, once cobbled and now a roaring modern highway. Geoffrey Chaucer is said to have lived in this street from 1379–85, during part of which period he was Comptroller of the Petty Customs in the Port of London. Left of the bridge is Adelaide House, a 1920s' office block, and next to it the church of **St Magnus-the-Martyr** (*map p. 607, E4*). The church stands on the site of the old approach to London Bridge: a hunk of blackened timber, part of the old Roman wharf, is placed just outside the entrance and stone portions from earlier London bridges are in the churchyard. Inside is a wooden model of Old London Bridge. The church was reconstructed after the Fire, the rebuilding completed by Wren in 1671–4; the steeple, 185ft high, is considered one of his masterpieces, built in 1703–6. The church has been much altered over the centuries and today the grand interior, with fine woodwork, continues an Anglo-Catholic tradition assumed between the two World Wars. Miles Coverdale (d. 1569), translator of the first complete English version of the Bible (1535), was rector of St Magnus in 1563–6 and is commemorated by a neo-Gothic tablet of 1837, right of the altar. On the west side is a sculpture of St Magnus himself, a horned-helmeted Viking jarl, and a stained-glass window commemorating him.

OLD BILLINGSGATE AND CUSTOM HOUSE

The former Billingsgate Fish Market (Old Billingsgate; *map p. 607, E4*) was designed in 1874–8 by Sir Horace Jones. It took its name, according to Stow, from an old gate supposedly named after Belin, a legendary king of the Britons, first built here in 870. Billingsgate Wharf, said to be the oldest on the river, was used from very early times (perhaps indeed from the 9th century) as a landing-place for fishing boats and other small vessels. The free fish market was established in 1699. Anyone could land their fish here and sell it in the market. Old Billingsgate Walk, down the side of the mar-ket building, joins the Thames Path and from the spacious waterfront terrace you have a good view of the river façade, with fishy wrought ironwork and twin gilded fish weather vanes. In its heyday, Billingsgate claimed to be the only market in which every variety of fish was sold—'wet, dried, and shell'. The porters wore 'bobbing hats', round, hard-topped leather hats for carrying loads of fish. The market moved to West India Docks in 1982 and the old building is now an events venue.

The large Neoclassical edifice behind an avenue of plane trees next to the old market is **Custom House**, by David Laing (1812–17) and Sir Robert Smirke, who redesigned the central section after subsidence in 1825–8. The first custom house was established here in the 14th century to collect duty on trade on the river. Wren designed the replacement building after the Great Fire, but it burnt down in 1715.

ST MARY-AT-HILL

On the narrow Lovat Lane, approached from opposite Billingsgate, is the entrance to the church of **St Mary-at-Hill** (*map p. 607, E3*), rebuilt by Wren and Hooke in 1670–4 from the medieval church destroyed in the Great Fire. Fires in 1848 and 1988 damaged the noteworthy woodwork, the box pews and other interior features, including the organ by William Hill (deemed one of the ten most important organs in the history of British organ building). The church has a distinguished musical tradition: Tallis and Mundy sang in the church choir in the 16th century. Today, the church is the venue for the annual Harvest Festival of the Sea, which celebrates the fish harvest.

Exit via the small churchyard garden (note the 17th-century relief carving of the *Last Judgment* on your way out), which emerges onto St Mary at Hill. Continue down the hill and on your right is the charming **Hall of the Watermen and Lightermen**, built in 1780, the only Georgian hall in the City. Note the morose-looking carving of Old Father Thames above the entrance and the fish in the Ionic pilasters. The Company of Watermen and Lightermen of the River Thames, without livery for historic reasons, was founded in 1514 to regulate the trade of watermen, wherrymen and bargemen. The Company still examines and approves all apprentices who wish to work on the river.

At the corner of St Mary at Hill and Lower Thames Street, a Roman bath house was discovered in 1969, part of a private residence of c. AD 200. Finds on the site showed the house to have been occupied until the second half of the 5th century.

ST DUNSTAN-IN-THE-EAST

A narrow alley leads from St Mary at Hill to Idol Lane and the ruined church of **St Dunstan-in-the-East**, on St Dunstan's Hill (*map p. 607, E3*). The medieval church, damaged in the Fire, was restored and a fine tower added by Wren in 1695–1701. The body of the church was then rebuilt by Laing, architect of the Custom House, in 1817. The tower escaped the Blitz and now houses the Wren Centre for Natural Health and Calm, offering complementary therapies and counselling sessions for stressed-out City workers. The rest of the church was severely damaged in 1941 and has been turned into a wonderfully peaceful public garden with vines and creepers twining over the walls and windows; flowers and exotic plants and a pair of splendid oak trees adorn the ruined shell. Winter's bark (*Drimys winteri*), of which there is an example in the lower garden, was once eaten to prevent scurvy as its leaves are high in Vitamin C. Here also is a fig tree commemorating the coronation of George VI in 1937.

In Harp Lane, a little further east, is the **Bakers' Hall** (no. 9; 1963) with windows by John Piper commemorating the burning of the former hall.

ST MARGARET PATTENS

At the corner of Rood Lane, where Eastcheap becomes Great Tower Street, is the church of St Margaret Pattens (*map p. 607, E3*), with the fritted glass office block of

OLD BILLINGSGATE
Motifs of fish and the City of London motto on the exterior of the old market hall.

Plantation Place, Fenchurch Street, rising behind. Destroyed in the Fire, rebuilt by Wren in 1684–7, the soaring, medieval–style, lead-covered spire (1698–1702), possibly by Hawksmoor, is the third highest in the City after St Bride's and St Mary-le-Bow. A guild church since 1954, it is home to the Busoga Trust charity and maintains close links with the Worshipful Company of Pattenmakers and the Worshipful Company of Basketmakers. It is thought to be named from the pattens (shoes raised on iron struts attached to the soles to protect the wearer from muddy roads) once made and sold in the lane. The carved wooden reredos is a fine work; the altarpiece is attributed to Carlo Maratta, a classically-inspired artist of the Roman school. The two 17th-century churchwardens' canopied pews on either side of the entrance to the nave are unique survivors in London. Left of the altar is the original enclosed Beadle's pew. The church owns a rare silver gilt Communion cup of 1545, reputed to be the oldest in the City. A copy of the cup is used at a special service held on 30th Jan each year (or nearest Thur) in memory of King Charles I, the Martyr.

BISHOPSGATE

Map p. 607, E2–F2. Underground: Liverpool Street.

Bishopsgate is the main commercial artery on the eastern side of the City, running north over the old Roman road that led from London to York, later known as the Old North Road or Ermine Street. Now choked with traffic, it was once threaded by a network of small alleys and courts with coaching inns and merchants' houses. Since the 1960s the area has been developed for office blocks and today a knot of skyscrapers lies at its western end. Only the fabric of the medieval churches and a few small streets survive from its historic past.

In April 1993, an IRA bomb exploded in Bishopsgate. One person was killed and 44 were injured and the blast and shockwaves caused £350 million worth of damage, especially to historic buildings and churches. The attack followed an earlier bombing the previous year in St Mary Axe, which had not only undermined the structure of the old Baltic Exchange but had caused £800 million worth of damage and cost three lives. The wealth of new building and clusters of high-rises in this area is in part due to the fabric of many buildings having been damaged by these terrorist attacks.

ST HELEN'S BISHOPSGATE

Just beyond the building site of the Pinnacle (*see p. 66*), the church of St Helen's Bishopsgate (*map p. 607, E2*) nestles in front of the bulk of the Gherkin and the Aviva Tower. The small square in front, with a tomb chest in the centre, is sheltered by plane trees. The church is a relic of a Benedictine nunnery founded c. 1210. The nunnery and its church were built alongside an existing parish church, hence the peculiar arrangement of the present structure, which has two parallel naves (one the former nuns' choir). The south transept and two chapels were added in the 14th century, the church remodelled in the 15th and 17th centuries and restored by Pearson in 1891–3, in the Gothic style. The church was badly damaged by both the 1992 and 1993 bombs and to accommodate a larger, evangelical congregation, the architect Quinlan Terry re-arranged the interior as part of the restoration, including controversially raising the floors to one level.

Nonetheless, the medieval interior houses an important plethora of surviving pre-Fire monuments, including the altar-tomb of Sir Thomas Gresham (d. 1579). In the north wall is the nuns' night staircase, an Easter Sepulchre and a 'squint' (peephole). In the chancel are some fine 15th-century stalls brought from the nuns' choir and a rare wooden sword rest (1665). Beyond the tomb chest of Sir John Crosby and his wife (d. 1475; of Crosby Hall; *see Chelsea p. 313*), the Chapel of the Holy Ghost contains fragments of 15th–17th-century glass. The fine brasses (15th–16th centuries) include a lady in a heraldic mantle (c. 1535). Beside the south entrance is the fine restored monument of Sir John Spencer (d. 1609). The Jacobean font, pulpit, poor box and door-cases (west end) are noteworthy.

Back on Bishopsgate, in the middle of the curving Palladian façade, nos 52–68 (Mewès & Davis, 1926–8), is the iron-gated entrance to St Helen's Place and the **hall of the Leathersellers' Company**, incorporated in 1444. The surrounding area is currently a building site for 100 Broadgate, a 40-storey glass high-rise. Next door, in the midst of heavy construction work, bravely stands the small ragstone façade of **St Ethelburga**. This 15th-century church escaped the Great Fire but was almost completely destroyed by the 1993 bomb. The exterior has been faithfully restructured and the church is now a centre for peace and reconciliation.

The old Bishop's Gate (pulled down in 1761) stood at the point where Camomile Street leads east and Wormwood Street leads west. It is commemorated with a bishop's mitre fixed on the wall of a building at the junction of Bishopsgate and Wormwood Street, facing the Heron Tower. The **Heron Tower** (2011), by KFP architects, stands 46 storeys tall, the tallest building in the City. It incorporates offices and a restaurant and sky bar. At ground level, Heron Piazza forms a new network of public squares and gardens on Houndsditch.

ST BOTOLPH-WITHOUT-BISHOPSGATE

Facing the Heron Tower is the church of **St Botolph-without-Bishopsgate** (*map p. 607, E2*). First mentioned in 1213, it was rebuilt in 1725–8 by James Gould and a team of masons, including his son-in-law George Dance the Elder, and then restored by the Roman Catholic architect J.F. Bentley in 1890–4. It was much damaged by both Bishopsgate bombs. Keats was baptised here in 1795 in the present font.

The churchyard has been a public garden since 1863 and was the first churchyard to be so transformed. It backs onto the line of the old City wall. The church hall, formerly a primary school, is c. 1861 and the two Coade Stone (*see p. 415*) statues of charity children on either side of the entrance date from 1821.

Continue down Bishopsgate Churchyard until you come to the Victorian **Turkish Baths** (1895), nestled in front of glass office blocks. Owned by Henry and James Forder Nevill, who owned other Turkish baths in London, and designed by Harold Elphick, the Moorish kiosk is really the tip of the Turkish iceberg, as the rooms extend below ground. It is in part modelled on the shrine at the Church of the Holy Sepulchre, Jerusalem, and is richly decorated with terracotta, faïence, mosaic and stained glass. The onion dome with star and crescent finial housed the water tanks. Until relatively recently, the baths housed a Turkish restaurant and underground belly-dancing venue.

LIVERPOOL STREET STATION AND BROADGATE

Liverpool Street Station (*map p. 607, E2*) stands on the site of the first hospital of St Mary Bethlehem (1247–1676). A *tour de force* of Victorian Gothic cast iron and brick by Edward Wilson (1875), it was modernised and expanded in 1985–91. It is the busiest transport hub in the City, gateway to Essex and a major part of the Crossrail urban transport development. The adjoining hotel, formerly the Great Eastern (Charles Barry, 1884), is now the Andaz, part of the Hyatt chain, re-opened in 2000 after a £70-million refurbishment. Inside, the opulent interior retains many original features, including a Masonic temple of 1912 on the first floor.

The massive 30-acre **Broadgate development** surrounding Liverpool Street was conceived to provide modern office space for financial companies following the deregulation of the stock markets known as the 'Big Bang', which took place during Margaret Thatcher's government in 1986. In a major property deal, Broadgate was built over the former Broad Street Station (demolished 1985), which had opened in the mid-19th century to transport goods from the East End Docks to the Midlands. Built in phases, this vast office city has plenty of public spaces, overhung with green-

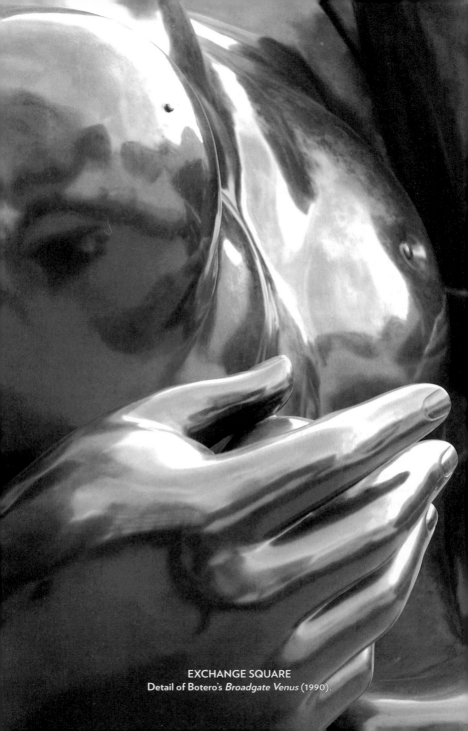

EXCHANGE SQUARE
Detail of Botero's *Broadgate Venus* (1990).

ery, where one can eat, drink and shop. It is built in a mixture of architectural styles, in particular American Post-modern, and is the work of several architects including Arup Associates and latterly Skidmore, Owings and Merrill. At the centre is Broadgate Circle, an arena used for displays and performances in summer and for ice-skating in winter. Much has been invested in public art: among the works are *Rush Hour*, influenced by T.S. Eliot's *The Waste Land* (George Segal, 1987), in Finsbury Avenue Square; *Fulcrum*, colossal sheets of rusting steel (Richard Serra, 1987), at the western entrance to Liverpool Street; the *Broadgate Venus*, overlooking Exchange Square (Fernando Botero, 1990) and the illuminated pavement, *Finsbury Avenue Lit Floor* (2004, by SOM and Maurice Brill Lighting Design). The most recent phase of development was the 35-storey Broadgate Tower (2004–8), north along Bishopsgate. A Welcome Centre in Finsbury Avenue Square displays an interactive model of the complex.

Off Bishopsgate, opposite Liverpool Street, is Devonshire Row, leading to Devonshire Square, with pleached lime trees and two fine 18th-century houses: Osborne House at no. 12 and **Coopers' Hall** at no. 13. Further down is the Cutlers Gardens/Devonshire Square office, residential and retail development in former warehouses of the East India Company and Port of London Authority.

At no. 202 Bishopsgate, opposite Liverpool Street station, is **Dirty Dick's** pub of c. 1870. The pub is named after 18th-century City merchant Nathaniel Bentley, who on the death of his fiancée became a recluse with questionable personal hygiene. It is said that Bentley inspired Dickens's character of Miss Havisham in *Great Expectations*.

At no. 230 Bishopsgate is the **Bishopsgate Institute**, opened in 1895 to bring educational and cultural opportunities to the people of this once-deprived area. The driving force was the Rev. William Rogers, the rector of St Botolph for 30 years. Charles Harrison Townsend designed the building in Art Nouveau style with a terracotta exterior of meandering trees and foliage, topped by twin turrets. The library (*free admission*) has important collections relating to the history of London and lectures, concerts and events are usually held in the Great Hall.

The City now merges imperceptibly with the area traditionally known as the East End of London. However, the local authority boundary is quite clearly marked with dragons, emblems of the City of London, and roughly coincides with a line linking Liverpool Street Station, Aldgate, Fenchurch Street Station and Tower Hill.

FENCHURCH STREET & ALDGATE

Map p. 607, E3–F3. Underground: Monument, Aldgate.

Until the Reformation, numerous religious orders were based in this area of London. **Minories** (*map p. 607, F3*), the main thoroughfare leading south from Aldgate, derives its name from an old convent of Minoresses (*Sorores Minores*), or nuns of the Franciscan Order of St Clare. On Minories is the 1930s' Ibex House, an example of late Art Deco office Modernism on the fringes of the City.

HART STREET

St Olave Hart Street (*map p. 607, F3*) dates from the 13th century and is a rare surviving medieval parish church in the City. Small and humble, it is immensely atmospheric. It is dedicated to King Olaf II of Norway, who fought with King Ethelred against the Danes at the Battle of London Bridge in 1014. In 1666 the Great Fire came within 100m of the church before the wind changed direction, thereby saving it from being engulfed in flames. The church was not so lucky during World War Two and sustained two direct hits during bombing raids. Although 90 percent of the façade was reduced to rubble, enough of the original masonry survived and it was rebuilt and the interior restored in the 1950s. King Haakon VII of Norway laid a stone from Trondheim Cathedral in the sanctuary during its re-dedication. The original stained-glass windows were all destroyed except for the 19th-century window on the north side with coats of arms; it was away having another coat of arms added when the church was bombed. Monuments include a wall tablet, right of the southeast window, commemorating William Turner (d. 1568), Dean of Wells, militant Protestant and father of English botany. Left of the southeast window is an early 17th-century painted alabaster portrait bust of Turner's son, Peter, 'Doctor in Physick', who attended Sir Walter Raleigh in the Tower. Peter Turner also wrote a treatise on plague cakes: little phials of arsenic to wear around the neck in order to combat infection. His effigy (c. 1614) disappeared from the church during the confusion of the Blitz and resurfaced in 2010 at public auction. In 2013 it was reinstalled after a 70-year absence, in a partial recreation of the original monument. The vestry, where Samuel Pepys paid his poll tax, has a 17th-century plaster ceiling depicting an angel.

Samuel Pepys lived and worked in this area and worshipped in this church. Both he and his wife are buried here: high up on the north chancel wall, left of the altar, is a bust of Elizabeth Pepys (d. 1669). A memorial service dedicated to the great diarist is held here annually. The 17th-century stone skulls in the pediment of the churchyard gate, overlooking **Seething Lane**, captured Pepys's imagination and later that of Charles Dickens. Pepys is purported to have safeguarded his parmesan cheese from the ravages of the Fire by burying it on or near Seething Lane gardens.

When Pepys was Secretary of the Admiralty, the Navy Office stood in **Crutched Friars** (i.e. 'Crossed Friars', from the Franciscan emblem of crossed stigmatic hands), the prolongation of Hart Street to the east.

MINCING LANE

Mincing Lane, from the Old English *mynecen*, a nun, once led to the Benedictine priory of St Helen's Bishopsgate. Later it became the headquarters of the wholesale tea trade and was also a centre of the opium trade. Reginald Wilfer, in Dickens's *Our Mutual Friend*, was a clerk here, 'in the drug-house of Chicksey, Veneering, and Stobbles.' The marble and granite giant known as Minster Court, in surging Post-modern Gothic style (GMW Partnership, 1987–91), links Great Tower and Fenchurch streets.

The **Clothworkers' Hall** in Dunster Court was rebuilt in 1956 after its destruction in 1941. It is the sixth hall on this site since 1456. The archives and the plate, among which is a loving cup presented by Samuel Pepys, Master of the Company in 1677, were saved. A small oasis of greenery to the west, in Fen Court, marks the churchyard of St Gabriel Fenchurch (destroyed 1666; not rebuilt). The sculpture celebrating the abolition of slavery was unveiled by Archbishop Desmond Tutu in 2008. Nearby is the surviving 14th-century **tower of All Hallows Staining** (Mark Lane), which is maintained by the Clothworkers' Company.

FENCHURCH STREET

Number 20 Fenchurch St is the site of one of London's newest and most controversial skyscrapers: the £200 million, 37-storey **Walkie-Talkie** (Rafael Viñoly; *map p. 607, E3*). The enormous building, with its unique shape, bulging in different directions depending on your angle of view, utterly dominates the City skyline; a leviathan on the landscape. At the time of writing it was unfinished but the 'sky gardens' on the roof were due to open to the public. In the summer of 2013, sunlight reflected down from the skyscraper's curved glass surface caused the panels of a car parked in Eastcheap to melt. Even while under construction it attracted cynical comments about its shape: flaring upwards to allow larger surface areas on the upper floors, where higher rents can be charged for the premium of a splendid view.

At no. 71 Fenchurch St, on the corner with Lloyd's Avenue (*map p. 607, F3*), is the **Lloyd's Register of Shipping building**, a society founded in 1760 (distinct from Lloyd's of London; *see p. 70*). The late Victorian building, its roof surmounted by an appropriate gilt weather vane, has been extended by Richard Rogers.

Fenchurch Street Station was the first station to be built in the City, in 1841. The current façade dates from the 1850s, with 20th-century modifications and extension.

ALDGATE

Aldgate (*map p. 607, F3*) takes its name from the 'old gate' which guarded the road out of London to the east. A 'draught (draft) on Aldgate Pump' (still standing at the beginning of the street) was once a cant expression for a worthless bill. Geoffrey Chaucer leased the house above the Aldgate from the City of London in 1374 (tablet). Among massive new office blocks and a complicated traffic system, only the Hoop and Grapes pub on the south shows the former scale of the buildings. The pub has foundations going back to the 13th century and the building itself is probably late 17th-century.

Opposite is the church of **St Botolph-without-Aldgate** (*map p. 607, F3*), first built over 1,000 years ago outside the old City gate so that travellers could pray on arrival and departure (Botolph is the patron saint of wayfarers; relics of his were kept at four churches dedicated to him at London city gates: Aldersgate, Aldgate, Bishopsgate and Billingsgate. The last of the four is no longer extant, having perished in the Fire). The current building is by George Dance the Elder (1744) with an interior by John Francis Bentley (1888–95). In the octagonal vestibule beneath the tower is a handsome font and cover. There are memorials to Sir John Cass (d. 1718), the founder of the Sir John Cass School (*see p. 72*) and Robert Dow (d. 1612), a benefactor, with anxious-looking portrait bust, his arms clamped upon a complacently grinning skull. Thomas Darcy and Sir Nicholas Carew, beheaded on Tower Hill in 1538, are buried in the churchyard.

The organ, one of the oldest in the country, was a gift from Thomas Whiting in 1676 and is attributed to Renatus Harris (*see p. 204*). Thomas Bray, founder of the SPCK and SPG, was vicar here from 1708–22. William Symington, pioneer of steam navigation who built the *Charlotte Dundas*, died here 'in want' in 1831 and is buried in the church (tablet on west wall). In the south aisle is a finely-carved panel of David playing the harp which, together with the lectern, dates from the early 18th century. Jeremy Bentham was christened here in 1747. The fine peal of eight bells was cast in the 18th century at Whitechapel bell foundry (*see p. 115*). Daniel Defoe was married here in 1683: he mentions Aldagte and its church frequently in his *Journal of the Plague Year*.

EATING AND DRINKING IN THE CITY

During the working week, the City is a hubbub of activity. Bars and restaurants are crowded and lively at lunchtime and the streets are filled with cafés and sandwich bars. Getting fed is not a problem. The situation is less easy at weekends: the streets are more tranquil and better for sightseeing, but the weekday workers' watering holes are shut. The list below includes traditional weekday haunts as well as a handful of places that cater to weekenders.

£££ **1 Lombard Street**. Bar and brasserie in the heart of the City, popular with bankers at lunchtime but a hearty greeting is extended to all. Superb food (modern European). Closed weekends *1 Lombard St. T: 020 7929 6611, www.1lombardstreet.com. Map p. 607, D3.*

£ **Black Friar**. A member of the Nicholson's group of pubs. Wonderful Arts and Crafts interior (*see p. 28*). Pub food. Open daily. Some outdoor seating. *174 Queen Victoria St. T: 020 7236 5474. Map p. 606, B3.*

£££ **Bonds**. Bar and restaurant in an old banking hall serving modern, award-winning cuisine (ingredients combined in previously unthought-of ways). Good wine list. Restaurant open Mon–Fri, bar open daily, serving sandwiches and snacks at weekends from 3pm. *5 Threadneedle St. T: 020*

7657 8090, bonds-restaurant.co.uk. Map p. 607, D3.

££–£££ **Duck and Waffle**. Brasserie with excellent views. Open almost round the clock (6am–5am). *40th Floor, Heron Tower, 110 Bishopsgate. T: 020 3640 7310, duckandwaffle.com. Map p. 607, E2.*

££–£££ **Grand Café**. Occupying the courtyard and upper level of the old Royal Exchange are the Grand Café, with brasserie-style food, and the Restaurant Sauterelle ('Grasshopper', named after the Gresham emblem; *see p. 68*), offering a Provençal-influenced menu midday and evening. Closed weekends. *Royal Exchange. T: 020 7618 2480, royalexchange-grandcafe. co.uk. Map p. 607, E3.*

££ **Imperial City**. Good Chinese restaurant under the Royal Exchange. Closed weekends. *Cornhill. T: 020*

7626 3437, orientalrestaurantgroup. co.uk. Map p. 607, E3.

£–££ Jamaica Wine House. Originally a coffee house, now a pub known familiarly as the 'Jampot', a popular City lunch spot. Downstairs at Todd's Wine Bar you can sit over a full meal or a trencher of tapas. Good wine list. Closed weekends. St Michael's Alley (off Lombard St). T: 020 7929 6922. Map p. 607, E3.

££ The Mercer. Angels on horseback, bubble and squeak and spotted dick? If your mouth begins to water, then the Mercer is for you. Large, airy space serving good old British scran. Lunch and dinner. Closed weekends. 34 Threadneedle St. T: 020 7628 0001, themercer.co.uk. Map p. 607, E3.

£–££ New Street Wine Shop. A wine 'shop', technically, but with big wooden tables, dozens of great wines by the glass, and simple charcuterie and sandwiches for sale. Closed weekends. 16 New Street (off Bishopsgate). T: 020 3503 0795, newstreetwineshop.co.uk. Map p. 607, F2.

£–£££ One New Change. Plenty of places to eat and drink in this shopping centre, and all are open daily, which makes it a possible solution if you are visiting the City at a weekend. Among the many options are Searcy's Champagne Bar (also offers snacks and lunch), Gordon Ramsay's Bread Street Kitchen, which serves ceviche (perhaps the 21st-century East Ender's equivalent of the jellied eel) and Jamie Oliver's Barbecoa, where meat is seared and grilled in a variety of ways. 1 New Change. onenewchange. com. Map p. 606, C3.

£ Pizza Express. Better than acceptable pizza, salads and pasta dishes. Swift, efficient service. Decent wine. Open at weekends. Close to the Barbican. 125 Alban Gate, London Wall. T: 020 7600 8880, pizzaexpress. com. Map pp. 606, C2–607, D2.

The Ship. Tiny old pub in Hart St (see p. 104 for details). Map p. 607, F3.

£ Simpson's Tavern. 'The oldest chop house in London', in business since 1757 and still serving traditional English food (roast beef and Yorkshire pudding, Lancashire hot pot, ham with parsley sauce). Open Tues–Fri for breakfast and lunch, Mon lunch only; closed weekends. Ball Court (off Cornhill). T: 020 7626 9985, www. simpsonstavern.co.uk. Map p. 607, E3.

££ Sweetings. Classic fish restaurant, in business since 1889. Delicious potted shrimps. Lunchtimes only, closed weekends. 39 Queen Victoria St. No reservations. sweetingsrestaurant.com. Map p. 607, D3.

£ Viaduct. Historic tavern close to St Paul's and Smithfield Market. Bar food served at lunchtimes (they are proud of their roast beef sandwiches). Open for drinks until 11pm. Closed weekends. 126 Newgate St. T: 020 7600 1863, viaducttavern.co.uk. Map p. 606, B2.

£ Ye Old Cheshire Cheese. Historic pub on Fleet Street (see p. 24) offering atmosphere, good cheer and edible pub food. Open Mon–Fri lunchtime and evenings. 145 Fleet St (entrance on Wine Office Ct). T: 020 7353 6170. Map p. 606, B3.

TOWER OF LONDON
'En Dieu est mon espérance': prisoner graffiti.

The Tower of London, & St Katharine Docks

The Tower of London is built on the easternmost of the City's three hills.
Spanning the Thames to the east is Tower Bridge, a tourist attraction in its
own right, and just beyond are St Katharine Docks—a foretaste of Docklands.

Historic **Tower Hill** (*map p. 607, F3*), encompassing Trinity Square, was until 1747 a place of high-profile public execution. Among those put to death here were Sir Thomas More, George Boleyn (brother of the unfortunate Anne), Bishop John Fisher and Archbishop Laud.

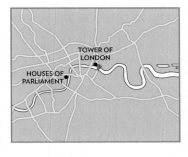

Just outside Tower Hill Underground station, an impressively large section of **Roman and medieval wall** has been preserved. It acts as a backdrop for a bronze statue of the emperor Trajan (d. AD 117; statue believed to be 18th century), shown in the act of addressing his troops. Another stretch of the wall, with windows and a sentry walk along the top, may be seen in a courtyard off Cooper's Row (the street leading north towards Aldgate; *map p. 607, F3*). The remains of the wall's medieval postern gate can be seen before the underpass from Tower Hill station to the Tower of London. From here you start the London Wall Walk (*see p. 57*).

TRINITY SQUARE

Trinity Square Gardens (*map p. 607, F3*) are filled with memorials to mariners of the Merchant Navy who died with 'no grave but the sea'. Lutyens's **Mercantile Marine Memorial** (1928), designed as a Greek temple, honours those who perished during World War One. The peaceful sunken garden extension, which commemorates the merchant seamen lost in World War Two, is by Sir Edward Maufe, with reliefs by Sir Charles Wheeler.

Behind, on Trinity Square itself, is the elegant **Trinity House** (Samuel Wyatt, 1793–5; *not open to the public*). It is the headquarters of the General Lighthouse Authority of England, Wales, the Channel Islands and Gibraltar, founded in 1514 when Henry VIII granted a Royal Charter to a fraternity of mariners called the Guild of the Holy Trinity,

TRINITY GARDENS

Plaque from the Mercantile Marine Memorial commemorating the loss of MV *Swedru*, destroyed off the Irish coast in 1941. During the early part of World War Two, millions of tons of merchant shipping and many human lives were lost to U-boat torpedoes and air attack.

to 'regulate the pilotage of ships in the King's streams.' Pepys was Master as, later, was the Duke of Wellington.

Just beyond, the dominating Neoclassical edifice with a tower and sculpture, stretching onto Muscovy Street, is the **former Port of London Authority building** (Sir Edwin Cooper, 1922). At the time of writing it was due to be redeveloped as a luxury hotel.

ALL HALLOWS BY THE TOWER

The church of All Hallows by the Tower (*map p. 607, F4; open every day*) is the oldest surviving church in the City, founded in 675 for the tenants of the Saxon Barking Abbey. It survived the Great Fire when Admiral Sir William Penn and his sailors blew up houses around the church to create a firebreak, but it was largely destroyed in the Second World War (although the tower and the exterior walls survived). The brick tower is thus the same one from which Pepys watched the progress of the Great Fire: it is an important surviving example of Cromwellian church architecture in London. Pepys wrote, 'I up to the top of Barkeing steeple and there saw the saddest sight of desolation that I ever saw. Everywhere great fires, the fire being spread as far as I could see it.' Today's copper spire, in the manner of Wren, dates from post-war restoration work. Also during restoration, a large Saxon arch, with Roman masonry, was fully uncovered at the west end.

William Penn, son of the firefighting Admiral Penn, was born on Tower Hill in 1664 and was baptised in All Hallows. Here also John Quincy Adams, sixth president of the United States, was married to Louisa Johnson in 1797.

All Hallows is the guild church of Toc H, a Christian organisation founded in 1922 by a former Army chaplain, the Rev. Philip ('Tubby') Clayton, whose effigy can be seen in the north aisle. In the south aisle, in the Mariners' Chapel, the 16th-century Spanish corpus on the Crucifix is said be from the flagship of the Spanish Armada. The font is of Gibraltar limestone and the fine font-cover of limewood is attributed to Grinling Gibbons. The tombs and brasses in the Sanctuary and Lady Chapel survived the bomb damage. In the Sanctuary is the Resurrection Brass (c. 1500), showing Christ rising from the tomb; in the Lady Chapel the Toc H Lamp of Maintenance still burns.

The Undercroft

The Oratory of St Clare, in a former burial vault, is dedicated to the Toc H Women's Association. The St Francis Chapel has a 13th-century barrel-vaulted roof. The Undercroft Chapel contains the ashes of members of Toc H. The plain crusading altar is from Richard I's castle at Athlit in Palestine. The remains of Archbishop Laud were temporarily laid here after his beheading in 1645 (they were removed to St John's College, Oxford in 1663). In the Crypt Museum there is a tessellated Roman pavement—probably the floor of a Roman house—as well as many other Roman remains, including fragments of pottery and ashes from the city burned by Boudica in AD 61.

THE TOWER OF LONDON

Map p. 607, F4. Underground: Tower Hill. DLR: Tower Gateway. Open March–Oct Tues–Sat 9–5.30, Sun–Mon 10–5.30; closes 1hr earlier in Nov–Feb. Advance tickets available online (hrp.org.uk) or on T: 0844 482 7799 (+44 20 3166 6000 from outside the UK).

Her Majesty's Royal Palace and Fortress, the Tower of London, has been at the centre of English national life and consciousness for over 900 years, not only as a palace and stronghold but also as a prison, treasury, mint, records office, menagerie and wharf. Today it attracts over two million visitors a year: be prepared for queues and crowds at all times but especially during high season and school holidays. It is one of London's four World Heritage Sites: the eruption of plate-glass and steel skyscrapers in the vicinity is perceived by some as careless city planning, having recently threatened the Tower's World Heritage status.

The distinguishing 11th-century keep known as the White Tower rises at the centre of the 18-acre complex and is a superb—and complete—example of Norman castle-building. It is one of the most important and largest of William the Conqueror's castles and was purpose-built both to subjugate and to defend London following the Norman Conquest of 1066. The massive stone edifice would have towered over the city's low-rise timber buildings, visible for miles from land and water.

A programme of enlargement and reinforcement was initiated in the 12th century during the reign of the great warrior king Richard I (The Lionheart); by 1350 the Tower

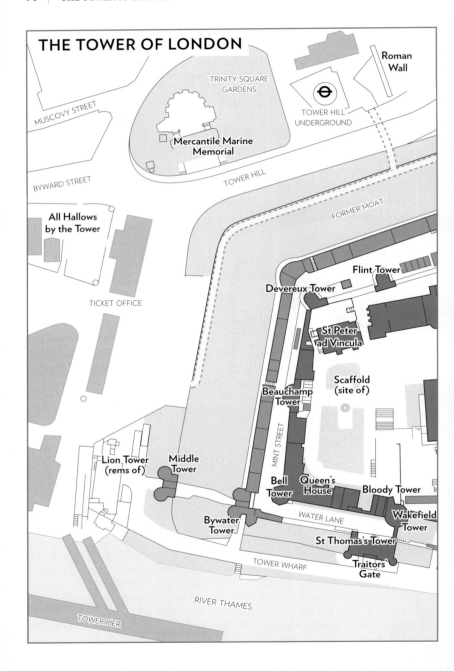

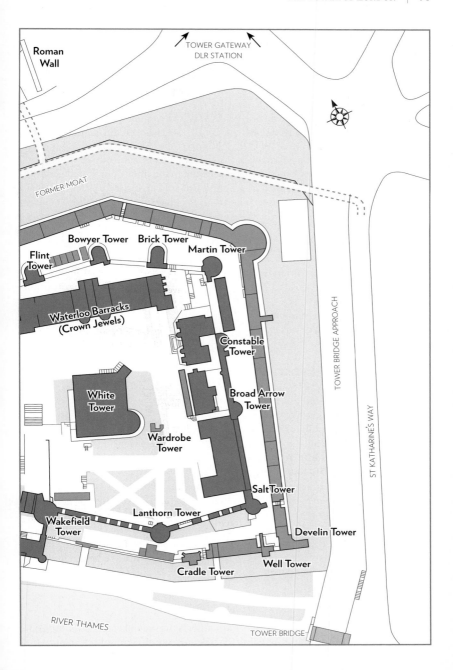

had become a mighty citadel. Framing the White Tower are the 13th-century concentric curtain walls built by Henry III and Edward I. The wall around the Inner Ward has 13 towers; the wall of the Outer Ward has six. From their names, one may deduce what some of them were used for. The rolling turf surrounding these fortifications was once a deep moat. This was not only the Tower's outermost defence system but also served as a fishpond, millpond and rubbish dump for those living within its precincts. It was drained in the 19th century and during World War Two was planted as an allotment.

Although never seriously assaulted, the Tower was besieged during the Peasants' Revolt of 1381. A detachment of rebels gained entry, abused the King's mother (Joan, the 'Fair Maid of Kent') and put to death the Archbishop of Canterbury.

Under the Tudors, when it was used as an armoury and munitions store and less as a royal residence, the Tower gained its reputation as a terrifying state prison and place of torture. Anne Boleyn was both crowned and executed here; her daughter, Princess Elizabeth, was held captive; and a later wife of Henry VIII, Catherine Howard, was also beheaded here.

Charles I lost control of the Tower at the beginning of the Civil War in 1642. In 1661 Charles II (the last monarch to sleep in the Tower) processed from here to Westminster Abbey to be crowned, a tradition that had obtained since the 14th century.

During the 19th century, after the relocation of many of the Tower's institutions (such as the Royal Mint), the Gothic Revival architects Anthony Salvin and John Taylor undertook a programme of re-medievalisation. Buildings were pulled down and rebuilt and the Tower was restored to its 'authentic' former glory. It was during the 19th century that the Tower became a thriving tourist attraction.

ENTRANCE AND OUTER WARD

The western entrance was built in the 13th century by Edward I. The barbican known as the **Lion Tower**, where the Tower's beasts were kept (*see Royal Beasts Exhibition, p. 100*), no longer exists but its excavated remains can be seen on the left, with Kendra Haste's life-size wire sculptures of lions on top of them (more sculptures of former animal inmates, including a polar bear, are dotted around inside).

Pass through the **Middle Tower** (1280, partially rebuilt 1717): on this causeway the Yeoman Warders' guided tours start. Moving on, **Byward Tower** (1280) has one surviving portcullis. Inside are rare surviving fragments of 14th-century wall paintings, and though it is not open to the public, a touch-screen interactive tour is available next to the ravens' cages (*for the ravens, see opposite*).

Once in the Outer Ward, **Water Lane** continues straight ahead, running parallel with the Thames. It is so called because Edward I successfully reclaimed it from the river. In the Beefeaters' shop, on the right, audio guides are available. On the left is **Mint Street**, where the Yeoman Warders and their families live. The Mint was in operation here until 1810.

SOUTH WALL WALK

The 12th-century **Bell Tower** (*closed to the public*) is the second oldest building in the complex after the White Tower; it is here that the curfew bell is rung. Sir Thomas More and Bishop Fisher were confined here for refusing to recognise Henry VIII as head of the Church. As a princess, Elizabeth I was held captive in the Bell Tower by her half-sister Mary I.

CUSTODIANS OF THE TOWER AND THE TOWER RAVENS

Today the Tower is cared for by Historic Royal Palaces but because it is home to the Crown Jewels, it is also a high-security garrison looked after by a unit of the Queen's Guard. Once the tourists have departed, the night watch is reputed to be an eerie duty and numerous ghostly sightings have been reported by the Tower's small resident community. Distinct from the Queen's Guard are the ceremonial custodians of the Tower, the Yeoman Warders, a body of about 40 men—and at the time of writing one woman—chosen from retired warrant and non-commissioned officers of the Army. They wear historic costume, said to date from the time of Henry VII or Edward VI, and are familiarly known as 'Beefeaters', probably derived from the rations once served to them. The Yeoman Warders provide free guided tours in English during the day and participate in the Ceremony of the Keys each evening, a ceremony dating from the 14th century that secures the Tower for the night.

Black ravens have always lived at the Tower and are attended by the Yeoman Warder Ravenmaster, who feeds them fresh butcher's meat and other treats. According to legend, the kingdom will fall should the ravens leave the Tower, so their flight wings are clipped. The longest-lived raven, Jim Crow, died aged 44 in 1924.

St Thomas's, Wakefield and Lanthorn towers were once royal lodgings and together they form the Medieval Palace Exhibition. St Thomas's Tower (1275–9) and the water entrance known as Traitors' Gate, were built by Edward I. The name **Traitors' Gate** was coined because Tudor prisoners accused of treason arrived here by barge, having first passed under London Bridge, where the heads of recently executed prisoners were displayed on pikes. Inside **St Thomas's Tower**, Edward I's bedchamber has been reconstructed, complete with royal bed and crackling faux fire. The peaceful oratory would have overlooked the Thames. A 19th-century covered bridge leads from St Thomas's Tower to **Wakefield Tower**, which was built by Henry III and which he could have entered via private stairs from his water-gate. Inside is a replica throne, a restored fireplace and a chapel. In 1471, at the end of the Wars of the Roses, Henry VI was murdered here whilst at prayer and a plaque on the chapel floor commemorates this. **Lanthorn Tower** was built as lodgings for Henry III's queen and later housed a lantern by which boats could navigate the Thames by night. It was gutted by fire in the 18th century and the present building dates from the 19th century.

THE WHITE TOWER

The White Tower, begun c. 1078, once dominated the London skyline. It is one of the most important surviving 11th-century buildings in Europe. Standing 90ft high, with walls 15ft thick in places, it was built using London labour to the Norman specifications of Gundulf, Bishop of Rochester. Caen limestone was imported from France and Kentish ragstone came up river by barge. Originally it incorporated parts of the

Roman city wall in its defences (the ruined Wardrobe Tower outside the entrance was built on a Roman bastion). It received its name after Henry III limewashed the façade in 1240. The leaden onion tops to the turrets were added by Henry VIII in the 1530s. Of the four turrets, the round one was once an observatory. The windows were enlarged in the 17th–18th centuries.

The tower was a military storehouse from the 14th century and since the reign of Henry VIII a showcase for armour and weapons. Today it is home to important items from the collections of the Royal Armouries, the national museum of arms and armour. The roofs of the upper floors were created during the reign of Henry VII and are constructed from massive load-bearing beams—some of the largest single timbers ever used in wooden roof construction in England.

Entry is via a wooden staircase on the south façade (probably how the Tower was originally entered, the idea being that if under attack, the staircase could easily be destroyed and the stone keep secured).

Entrance floor: The display covers 500 years in an exhibition entitled 'Fit for a King'. On show is Henry VIII's skirted field armour (including horse armour) in silvered steel (1515). The engraved Tudor rose and Spanish pomegranate motifs, with the initials H and K, celebrate his union with Katherine of Aragon, whom he married here at the Tower. Also here is the tournament armour that Henry wore as an older and bulkier king in 1540. Both suits were probably made at Henry's Greenwich workshop. The exquisitely tooled and gilded armour of Charles I is probably of Netherlandish origin, made c. 1612 for his older brother Henry, Prince of Wales, the promising heir to the throne who died aged 18. The Japanese Samurai armour (1610) was a diplomatic gift to James I. The 'Line of Kings' is an exhibition of life-size models of carved and painted horses together with surviving sculpted heads and hands of England's monarchs, some by Grinling Gibbons. The exhibition was conceived by Charles II at the Restoration and this is a partial re-creation of the original 17th-century display. There are plans to re-unite the kings with their horses and to create a new line as magnificent as its predecessor once was.

First floor: The Norman chamber in the eastern room has one of the earliest fireplaces in the country and early indoor lavatories (garderobes) built into the thickness of the walls. This room would originally have been open to the rafters but an additional floor was added in the 15th century.

St John's Chapel is one of the most beautiful and complete examples of Anglo-Norman church architecture in England. Henry VI lay in state here in 1471 as did Elizabeth of York, mother of Henry VIII, in 1503.

The Great Hall next door would have been used for ceremonies and receptions. It exhibits further treasures from the Royal Armouries. Tiny armour, once believed to have been made for Queen Henrietta Maria's dwarf, stands next to a giant steel suit made for a man of 6′8″, thought to be from Brunswick.

Second floor: The interactive exhibition 'Power House' tells the history of the White Tower's institutions, including the Ordnance Office, Ordnance Survey, the Royal Mint, Record Office, the Jewel House, Menagerie and Royal Observatory. Don't miss the executioner's block, complete with axe.

Basement: The spiral staircase in the round tower takes you down to the basement, where there is a collection of 17th–18th-century weaponry.

THE CROWN JEWELS

The Crown Jewels are housed in the Waterloo Barracks, a building conceived by the Duke of Wellington around the time of the Chartist riots in 1848. There is nothing understated about this priceless collection of diamonds, historic gems and plate; the quantity and sheer size of the gemstones are astonishing. Unlike most other European crown jewels (notably the fabled French and Russian treasures, which were broken up and sold off following the revolutions of the 19th and 20th centuries), the British gems are still in use as important elements of an ancient Christian ceremony that can be traced back to the crowning of King Edgar at Bath in 973. The tradition of being crowned at Westminster Abbey was begun by William the Conqueror in 1066.

The exhibition, created in 2012 in honour of Queen Elizabeth II's Diamond Jubilee, explains the coronation ceremony and the jewels' sanctity as symbols of divine kingship, whereby the Sovereign undertakes to rule according to law, to exercise justice with mercy and to maintain the Church of England. The Sovereign is 'anointed, blessed and consecrated' by the Archbishop of Canterbury. A video of Queen Elizabeth II's coronation in 1953 is shown on large screens. This was the first coronation to be televised but no cameras were allowed to film the anointing because it is the most sacred part of the ritual. The sovereign is crowned with the 1661 St Edward's Crown, modelled on Edward the Confessor's medieval diadem. Once crowned, the Sovereign receives the Imperial State Crown, which is worn each year at the State Opening of Parliament.

Only four pieces of pre-Civil War regalia survive: the three swords (of Temporal Justice, Spiritual Justice and Mercy) made for Charles I's coronation in 1626 and the 12th-century silver gilt Coronation Spoon, used to anoint the Sovereign with holy oil from the Golden Ampulla. Oliver Cromwell melted down and sold the rest during his calculated disposal of the late king's goods. The Coronation Spoon was bought in 1649 by a Royalist sympathiser and returned after the Restoration. The rest of the collection—the orb, sceptres, crown, spurs and armills—dates from the reign of Charles II and was later supplemented with the spoils of Empire.

The jewels are viewed from slow-moving travelators which pass along the glass cases. It is worth taking several turns in order to absorb the magnificence. The great diamond, Cullinan I, the First Star of Africa, was set in the Sovereign's Sceptre with Cross in 1911. At 530 carats, it is the largest top-quality white diamond in the world. It was one of several large diamonds cut by the Asscher Diamond Company from the Cullinan crystal, which weighed a colossal 3106 carats (Joseph Asscher supposedly fainted in relief once the successful cleaving strike was made). Cullinan II is in the Imperial State Crown and Cullinans III–VIII are in the jewel collection of Queen Elizabeth II. The Imperial State Crown of India, made in 1911 for George V's coronation as Emperor of India, has over 6,000 gems and has only been worn once. The Crown of Queen Elizabeth, the Queen Mother is set with the luminous Koh-i-Noor ('Mountain of Light') diamond, a historic 15th-century Mughal gem said to have been owned by Emperor Shah Jahan in the 17th century. The Mughals deliberately left the diamond in as natural a state as possible so as to retain its magical-religious properties. However, after it was presented to Queen Victoria, it was re-cut (in 1852) according to 19th-century European ideals and lost over 40 percent of its weight. A replica of how the diamond looked before re-cutting is set in an Indian armlet. In the same case is the miniature diamond crown that Queen Victoria wore as a grieving widow.

The Imperial State Crown stands alone at the end of the exhibition. It was made for George VI's coronation in 1937 and incorporates gems of thrilling provenance: St Edward's Sapphire, in the centre of the Maltese Cross, was removed from a ring found in the tomb of Edward the Confessor in Westminster Abbey; the large uncut spinel, known as the Black Prince's Ruby, was given to the Black Prince by Pedro the Cruel in 1367 and was worn by Henry V in his helmet at the Battle of Agincourt; some of the natural pearls are believed to have belonged to Mary, Queen of Scots, Catherine de Medici and Elizabeth I. The massive 317-carat Cullinan II or Second Star of Africa sits at the front of the crown. The Stuart Sapphire is at the back.

The **Fusilier Museum**, in the headquarters of the Royal Regiment of Fusiliers, has uniforms, medals, equipment and relics relating to the history of the regiment from 1685 to the present.

EAST WALL WALK
Salt Tower contains interesting prisoner graffiti, including Hew Draper's astrological sphere of 1561 (Draper had been imprisoned for sorcery). **Broad Arrow Tower** is where Sir Everard Digby, one of the conspirators in the Gunpowder Plot, was held. **Constable Tower**, rebuilt in the 19th century on the site of one of Henry III's mural towers, has a display relating to the Peasants' Revolt of 1381. **Martin Tower** was the scene of Colonel Blood's bold and nearly successful attempt to carry off the State Crown in 1671. In the 19th century the Crown Jewels were displayed in a cage and the public were allowed to reach through the grille to touch them. Security was heightened in 1815 after the arches of the State Crown were crushed by overzealous fondling. The 'Crowns Through History' exhibition shows a rare collection of royal crown frames, including the Imperial State Crown of George I, the Coronation Crown of King George IV, Queen Victoria's crown of 1838 and the Coronation Crown of Queen Alexandra.

ROYAL BEASTS EXHIBITION AND BOWYER TOWER
The Beasts Exhibition is housed in **Brick Tower**. The Tower Menagerie originated during the reign of Henry III, when he received diplomatic gifts of exotic animals, including leopards, a lion, an elephant and, in 1252, a polar bear from Haakon IV of Norway. The bear was tethered to a long rope and allowed to swim and fish in the Thames. By the early 19th century, the menagerie of over 60 species had outgrown the Tower and in 1830 was given to the Zoological Society, who used it to form London Zoo.

Bowyer Tower, with a medieval vaulted ceiling, is where George, Duke of Clarence drowned in a butt of Malmsey wine in 1478. A plasma video screen fitted into the top of a large wooden keg ghoulishly reconstructs his misadventure.

TOWER GREEN, BEAUCHAMP TOWER AND THE QUEEN'S HOUSE

Seven executions took place on Tower Green: those of William Hastings, 1st Baron Hastings (1483); Queen Anne Boleyn (1536); Margaret Pole, Countess of Salisbury (1541); Queen Catherine Howard (1542); Jane Boleyn, Viscountess Rochford (1542); Lady Jane Grey (1554) and Robert Devereux, Earl of Essex (1601). A modern memorial marks the site of the scaffold. To the north is the Chapel Royal of **St Peter ad Vincula**, rebuilt in 1307 and again by Henry VIII in 1520. Within are buried Anne Boleyn, Catherine Howard, Lady Jane Grey, Essex, Monmouth and other illustrious victims. The chapel holds services for the Tower's resident community and may be visited outside these times as part of a Yeoman Warder tour.

Across Tower Green is **Beauchamp Tower**, notable for its 13th-century brick interior. The walls are covered with the inscriptions and carvings of former prisoners. Guildford Dudley, husband of Lady Jane Grey, was imprisoned here by Mary I and is believed to be the author of the engraving 'JANE'. Philip Howard, Earl of Arundel, was incarcerated here for ten years under Elizabeth I.

In the southwest corner of the Green is the **Queen's House** (*no admission*), built in 1530 and one of the few houses to have survived the Fire of London. Reputed to be the most haunted of the Tower's buildings, it is the residence of the Resident Governor and incorporates the Bell Tower. The Tower's last state prisoner, Rudolf Hess, Deputy Führer, was held here in May 1941.

BLOODY TOWER

The Bloody Tower, begun by Henry III as a water-gate and completed by Edward I, was the prison of Cranmer, Raleigh, Laud and Judge Jeffreys. Sir Walter Raleigh's room has been reconstructed. During his interment, he wrote his *History of the World* (Vol. I of the 1614 edition is on display). Up a short but steep spiral staircase, the 'Princes in the Tower' exhibition is designed as a medieval whodunnit.

TOWER BRIDGE

Map p. 607, F4. Underground: Tower Hill; DLR: Tower Gateway.

Tower Bridge is one of the most famous bridges in the world and an ingenious feat of late Victorian engineering. Completed in 1894, it fulfilled the urgent contemporary need for a Thames crossing east of London Bridge in order to counter heavy traffic and congestion. It was decided that its appearance should be in keeping with its neighbour, the Tower of London, and although not without its critics, this fanciful neo-Gothic design (by architect Horace Jones and civil engineer John Wolfe Barry) was chosen.

TOWER BRIDGE

The resulting combined suspension and bascule bridge took eight years to build and its 11,000-ton steel core is clad in Cornish granite and Portland stone. The carriageway between the towers is composed of two bascules (or drawbridges), which are raised to allow tall ships to pass through. The original steam pumping engines used to provide hydraulic power to raise the bascules were replaced in 1976 by electric motors. The two high walkways between the towers were constructed to allow pedestrians to cross uninterrupted when the bascules were in operation. However, pedestrians preferred to cross at road level and the walkways became the haunt of unsavoury characters, leading to their closure in 1910. Although river traffic in this part of the Thames has diminished since its 19th-century heyday, the raising of the bascules is still an impressive sight (*a timetable of bridge lifts may be found on towerbridge.org.uk*).

VISITING TOWER BRIDGE

Entry to the Tower Bridge Exhibition (*open April–Sept 10–6, Oct–March 9.30–5.30; admission charge; shop; T: 020 7403 3761, towerbridge.org.uk*) is via the North Tower and visitors are taken up by lift. The two walkways (now covered, and which also serve as exhibition space) afford impressive panoramic views of London; worth the entry fee alone. London's historic landmarks increasingly jockey for position with its new skyscrapers. UNESCO and English Heritage are concerned that these giant edifices are unsympathetic and recently the World Heritage status of the Tower of London and Westminster was called into question. After a short film in the South Tower about the bridge's construction, you are transported down by stairs and lift to road level. Follow the blue line on the pavement to the final part of the tour, the Victorian Engine Rooms, which are situated on the south side of the river (Shad Thames). Here one can see the enormous pumping engines, accumulators and boilers that were originally used to raise the bascules. An interactive model of the bridge allows you to raise the bascules via both steam and modern hydraulic methods. Exit via the gift shop. You can either explore the south side of the river from here, where there are plenty of riverside places to eat (*see p. 435*) or return across the bridge to St Katharine Docks.

ST KATHARINE DOCKS

Map p. 605, E3. Underground: Tower Hill; DLR: Tower Gateway.

Since the 1990s, the area of the Thames known as the Upper Pool, which stretches from London Bridge to just below Tower Bridge on both sides of the bank, has been enjoying a revival and the area thrives once more, albeit in a 21st-century guise. The riverside walk has been opened up, new buildings have been built and old warehouses and wharves have been converted into living units, offices, shops and riverside eating and drinking establishments.

St Katharine Docks were the first of London's docks to be regenerated into commercial and leisure space after the demise of London's shipping industry. Today the serene waterside expanse houses accommodation, offices, restaurants, shops and an exclusive marina: it makes a good place to go for a drink or a bite to eat after visiting the Tower.

HISTORY OF ST KATHARINE DOCKS

A dock has existed here since 1125. In 1147–8, a hospital and priory were founded on the land under the patronage of Queen Matilda, wife of King Stephen, who referred to it as 'my hospital by the Tower'. The priory escaped dissolution thanks to Katherine of Aragon, by then its patron. She remained in the role, even after her divorce from Henry VIII, until her death. By the end of the 18th century some 3,000 people lived and worked in the precincts of the ancient hospital and church and thousands more continued to settle here, turning the area into a densely-built slum. In 1825 the area was taken over for development as a dock and the inhabitants were unceremoniously evicted.

St Katharine Docks as they exist today opened in 1828. They were built by Telford as two connected basins accessed via a lock at the entrance to the Thames. A range of warehouses by Philip Hardwick lined the quays so goods could be unloaded straight into them; the docks specialised in wine, brandy, tea, rubber, marble, ivory, sugar and other valuable commodities. After fire damage in the Second World War, and also because modern steam and container ships were unable to enter the docks, they finally closed as a commercial enterprise in 1968. Their redevelopment is seen as a model for urban regeneration.

VISITING ST KATHARINE DOCKS

The surviving original buildings include Ivory House with its clock-tower (1852; listed), a large warehouse converted into apartments, boutiques and a restaurant (which hosts all-inclusive medieval banquet extravaganzas) and the Dickens Inn, another warehouse, moved from its original site and converted into a pub and restaurant. The Dockmaster's House by Philip Hardwick was demolished to make way for Devon House, an office building with views over the Thames. The gates towards East Smithfield, adorned with two elephants raising their trunks, remain, while Hardwick's other warehouses were destroyed by fire during the War and during the redevelopment.

The luxury Guoman Tower Hotel, on St Katharine's Way, was built during the first phase of the docks' restoration. This 1970s' concrete bastion, probably once considered a perfect foil for the Tower, has been voted the second ugliest building in Britain. However, the interior affords excellent river panoramas and the view of Tower Bridge when illuminated at night is especially good seen from the Xi Bar, which has huge picture windows.

EATING AND DRINKING NEAR THE TOWER

The **Good Food Market** at St Katharine Docks takes place every Friday between 11am and 5pm. Stalls sell food from around the globe. The ££ **Dickens Inn** grill and pizzeria is popular (*Marble Quay, St Katharine's Way; T. 020 7488 2208, dickensinn. co.uk; map p. 605, E3*). The Xi Bar and Lounge in the Guoman Hotel on St Katharine's Way is a fun place for drinks. Snacks are also served (*open daily, T: 0871 376 9036*).

Northwest of Trinity Square is the tiny £ **Ship Inn**, an old-fashioned pub with a wonderful painted stucco exterior, mainly of 1914, showing fat bunches of grapes glistening amid foliage. Above the window a scallop shell with the entwined numbers 1897 commemorates Queen Victoria's Diamond Jubilee (*3 Hart St, map p. 607, F3; for a description of St Olave's church, see p. 86*).

Restaurants where one may sit and admire the views of this part of London and watch the river traffic are particularly good on the south side (across Tower Bridge) around **Shad Thames and Butler's Wharf** (*map p. 605, E3; see p. 435*).

The East End & Docklands

The City merges almost imperceptibly with the area traditionally known as the East End of London: Whitechapel, Spitalfields, Shoreditch, Bethnal Green and Bow. Lining the waterfront are the famous Docklands, once receivers of tangible cargoes and now home to trading of another kind.

London's East End is a concept as much as a geographical location. Tough, poor, densely populated and vividly alive, it is traditionally the heartland of London's Cockneys, born within earshot of Bow Bells. But few Cockneys live in the East End today: most of the old families have moved further east, to Essex, and their place has been taken by newer arrivals. The East End has long played host to immigrant groups. Huguenots came here in the 17th century, escaping persecution in France. In

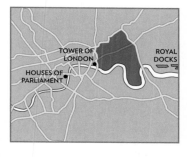

the 19th century, thousands of Polish Jews fleeing Russian oppression settled here. Most of the descendants of those families have now migrated to other parts of London and today the area around Whitechapel Road, most particularly on and around Brick Lane, is known as Banglatown. The borough of Tower Hamlets, of which this is a part, has the largest Bengali community in the United Kingdom, many of them from the Sylhet region of Bangladesh. While at the end of the 19th century there were 80 synagogues here, now the East London Mosque lifts its minaret over Whitechapel Road.

Spitalfields and Whitechapel have long been centres of the rag trade. Huguenot weavers set up looms in their attics. Then came the Jewish tailors (in 1897 the social researcher Charles Booth noted the presence of Welsh cowmen who supplied them with kosher milk). In the 20th century the tailors were supplanted by Bangladeshi sweatshops. Political refugees have found sanctuary in the East End too. Whitechapel prides itself on being the place where Lenin first met Trotsky. The 5th Congress of the Russian Social Democratic Labour Party was held here in 1907.

Brick Lane is often regarded through rose-coloured glasses, as a 'vibrant' example of triumphant diversity. It is not as easy as that. Somewhere in a refuse-blown street on the borderlands of Spitalfields, Shoreditch and Bethnal Green, a spraypaint sloganist has called for 'Death to hipsters!' London's East End is a place where economic migrants struggle to make a living and then move on from. It does not aim to be a place for aspirant arts-sector professionals to move into, pushing up property prices. Jack the Ripper may no longer stalk the streets and the Kray Twins are no longer at large; but hardship, poverty and a kind of latent turbulence are still to be felt here.

BANGLATOWN

Map p. 605, E2. Underground: Liverpool Street, Aldgate, Aldgate East.

Houndsditch follows the course of the old moat outside London's city wall. It leads to the site of the Aldgate, at the top of Aldgate High Street, signalled now by a timber tower. The church of St Botolph-without-Aldgate (*see p. 87*) stands on a traffic island. Outside it, built into its churchyard wall, is an old Metropolitan Drinking Fountain of 1906, with the iron cup still attached by a chain.

PETTICOAT LANE
The association of the East End with cloth and clothing began in the 16th century, when traders moved here from London Bridge. A map of 1603 refers to 'Petticoat Lane', named thus because of its clothes stalls. The official name of the road is Middlesex Street (*map p. 607, F2*), and it is still lined with textile emporia. The market survives under the name Petticoat Lane, operating in the side streets to the east, notably Bell Lane and Wentworth Street. Vans arrive in the morning to unload their merchandise: mainly clothing, but other items as well (*Sun 9–2; limited market Mon–Fri*). Middlesex Street once offered lodging to the West African prince Ukawsaw Gronniosaw, who was captured and sold into slavery and afterwards made his way to Britain, where he married and struggled to make ends meet as a free citizen. His short autobiographical *Narrative* was published in 1772. Here he describes his arrival in London and his first meeting with his future bride:

> *Mr Whitefield receiv'd me very friendly, was heartily glad to see me, and directed me to a proper place to board and lodge in Petticoat Lane, till he could think of some way to settle me in, and paid for my lodging, and all my expenses. The morning after I came to my new lodging, as I was at breakfast with the gentlewoman of the house, I heard the noise of some looms over our heads: I enquir'd what it was; she told me a person was weaving silk. I express'd a great desire to see it, and ask'd if I might. She told me she would go up with me; she was sure I should be very welcome. She was as good as her word, and as soon as we enter'd the room, the person that was weaving look'd about, and smiled upon us, and I loved her from that moment. She ask'd me many questions, and I in turn talk'd a great deal to her. I found she was a member of Mr Allen's Meeting, and I begun to entertain a good opinion of her, though I was almost afraid to indulge this inclination, lest she should prove like all the rest I had*

WHITECHAPEL ART GALLERY
Weather vane by Rodney Graham (2009).

met with at Portsmouth etc. and which had almost given me a dislike to all white women. But after a short acquaintance I had the happiness to find she was very different, and quite sincere, and I was not without hope that she entertain'd some esteem for me...

On Old Castle Street, **Calcutta House** is an old East India tea warehouse, now housing London Metropolitan University.

WHITECHAPEL ART GALLERY

77–82 Whitechapel High St. Map p. 605, E2. Open Tues–Sun 11–6 (until 9pm Thur). Free. Café/Restaurant. T: 020 7522 7888, whitechapelgallery.org.

The Whitechapel Art Gallery has been hosting exhibitions of work by established and aspiring artists for over a century. It was founded in 1901 and the striking main building, with its Arts and Crafts façade of falling golden foliage, is by Charles Harrison Townsend. The adjacent wing, with its decorative frieze of rams' heads and putti, is the former Whitechapel Library, founded by the philanthropist John Passmore Edwards (the library has moved to the Whitechapel Idea Store; *321 Whitechapel Rd*). A plaque commemorates the poet Isaac Rosenberg, who came to study at the library and wrote 'A Ballad of Whitechapel':

> *The traffic rolled,*
> *A gliding chaos populous of din,*
> *A steaming wail at doom the Lord had scrawled*
> *For perilous loads of sin.*
>
> *And my soul thought:*
> *'What fearful land have my steps wandered to?*
> *God's love is everywhere, but here is naught*
> *Save love His anger slew.'*

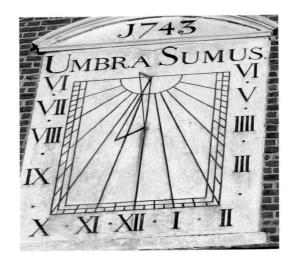

BRICK LANE
Admonitory motto on the building that has successively been a Huguenot church,
a Methodist meeting house and a synagogue, and which is now a mosque: the Jamme Masjid.

The weather vane (Rodney Graham, 2009) is a self-portrait of the artist as Erasmus, seated backwards on a horse reading *In Praise of Folly*.

Diagonally opposite the gallery, on the corner of Whitechurch Lane, is the site of St Mary's church, the eponymous 'White Chapel', which was destroyed in the Blitz. The churchyard is now the **Altab Ali Park**, entered under an ironwork arch commemorating a young Bengali who was fatally stabbed by three teenage boys in a racially-motivated assault in 1978.

BRICK LANE

Brick Lane (*map p. 605, E1*), the street whose name became the title of a famous novel by Monica Ali, is the heart of Banglatown. In its aspect it resembles, more closely than most other London streets, a traditional old-fashioned high street, with small individual shopfronts advertising owner-run businesses. There are no chain stores, no franchises, no Prêt, no Patisserie Valerie, no Costa Coffee. In the 19th century and for the first part of the 20th, the businesses would all have been Jewish: the name KATZ, in black paint over the door of a former twine merchant, is the only surviving reminder. Today the shops are Bengali. Where Osborne Street ends and Brick Lane begins, Ye Frying Pan tavern still thrusts its crumbling brick crest into the sky—but the premises now house the Sheraz Balti House and Bangla Lounge. Street signs here are all bilingual, written in English and Bengali.

At no. 59, on the corner of Fournier Street, is the London **Jamme Masjid**, the congregational mosque, with a tall, cylindrical steel minaret. The building dates from 1743, when it was built as a church by the Huguenots, who adorned it with the sundial reminding passers-by of mortality: '*Umbra sumus*; We are but a shadow'. Methodists took over the building in early 19th century; then, in 1898, it was converted for use as a synagogue. Since 1976 it has been a mosque.

Further up Brick Lane, straddling Hanbury Street, is the former **Truman Brewery**. Under Brick Lane is an artesian-fed well, a good source of water, and a brewery was established here in the 17th century. Beer was still brewed here up until 1989. The site has now been redeveloped as offices, workshops and nightclubs. Vibe, with its plane-shaded courtyard, is on one side, and 93 Feet East on the other. The Backyard Market operates here at weekends (*10am–5pm*).

On Sundays Brick Lane comes alive with its famous **street market**. It developed during the 18th century, with farmers selling livestock and produce outside the City boundary. However, the main impetus came from the Jewish population, who were permitted to trade on Sundays. Stalls offer a mix of fruit and vegetables, clothes, household goods, books, bric-à-brac and antiques (be aware: provenance uncertain).

SPITALFIELDS

Map p. 607, F1–F2. Underground: Liverpool Street.

The area known as Spitalfields was once occupied by silk-weavers, largely descended from Huguenot refugees who arrived after the Edict of Nantes was revoked in 1685. The name comes from the priory of St Mary Spital, founded in 1197, where the 'Spital Sermon' (now delivered at St Lawrence Jewry; *see p. 59*) was first preached. Some fine Georgian buildings, with tall windows and handsome doorways, survive on **Fournier Street**. **Tenter Ground** (*map p. 607, F2*) takes its name from the frames on which weavers stretched their cloth (hence the phrase 'on tenterhooks'). The **Sandys Row Synagogue** was the first—and is now the last—fully-functioning Ashkenazi temple of worship in London's East End.

CHRIST CHURCH

When Christopher Wren surveyed Brick Lane in the 17th century, he found it 'unpassable for coach, adjoining to dirty lands of mean habitations, and far from any church.' That circumstance has now been rectified: at the corner of Fournier and Commercial streets is Hawksmoor's masterpiece: Christ Church, Spitalfields (*map p. 607, F2; open weekdays 10–4, Sun 1–4; ccspitalfields.org*), recently restored thanks to the largest sum ever made over to a church restoration project by the Heritage Lottery Fund. It triumphantly and gloriously closes the vista down Brushfield Street, a truly spectacular sight. The massive portico with its paired Tuscan columns takes the form of a vast Serlian window giving onto an eccentric, sandwich-board tower, surmounted by

CHRIST CHURCH, SPITALFIELDS

a tapering spire. The 1720 interior features a flat coffered ceiling with stucco decoration, all painted bright white. On either side of the altar are monuments by Thomas Dunn (right) and John Flaxman (left), both signed. In the entranceway are tablets commemorating ten evangelisers of the Jews, originally in the Episcopal Jews' Chapel in Bethnal Green but moved here in 1897.

OLD SPITALFIELDS MARKET

The fruit and vegetable market on this site was first established under Charles II in 1682. The present covered market building (*map p. 607, F1*) dates from 1928. It closed as a wholesale market in 1992 and has found a new role as an arts, fashion and antiques market (*open daily until 4 or 5pm; antiques on Thur, fashion and art on Fri; oldspitalfieldsmarket.com*).

DENNIS SEVERS' HOUSE

18 Folgate St. Map p. 607, F1. Open Sun and selected Mondays 12–4, 'Silent Night' visits must be booked: T: 020 7247 4013, dennissevershouse.co.uk.

The extraordinary experience offered by this 1724 Georgian terrace house is, in the words of its creator, Dennis Severs (d. 1999), 'a collection of atmospheres, moods that harbour the light and the spirit of various ages.' Unenamoured of the 20th-century world in which he lived, the US-born Severs sought to evoke the past through a collage of the senses and an assortment of locally-sourced objects (the emphasis is on atmosphere rather than precise historical accuracy). In 1979 he bought a dilapidated house on Folgate Street with a wonderful conceit in mind: to transform it into the living home of a fictional family of Huguenot silk weavers, the Jervises, spanning the years from 1724 to 1914. The tour includes ten rooms or 'spells', beginning with the Cellar and ending with the Back Parlour and following the history of Spitalfields from its origins to the Great War, taking in Hogarthian London along the way (The Smoking Room). The candlelit itinerary is a sensory imaginarium, with open fires, chiming clocks, half-eaten plates of food and unfinished glasses of port, the smell of freshly-baked scones, rumpled and still-warm beds, and even a full chamber pot.

THE HUGUENOT CONTRIBUTION

Throughout the 16th and 17th centuries, large numbers of French Calvinist refugees found a safe haven in England. Many came to escape the French Wars of Religion and the 1572 Massacre of St Bartholomew, and numbers peaked sharply following the 1685 revocation of the Edict of Nantes, which removed Protestant freedom of worship. Huguenot communities were established in East Anglia, Kent and along the south coast, as well as in London. By 1700 Spitalfields, Leicester Fields and Soho had become distinct Huguenot areas. Spitalfields, being beyond the jurisdiction of the Weavers' Company in the City, became increasingly identified with the silk industry.

Many Huguenots were prosperous merchants who were able to escape with their goods intact. Their investments in London banking and insurance houses (several Huguenots were foundation subscribers to the Bank of England) contributed substantially to the capital's wealth, whilst marriage alliances created powerful trading and financial dynasties. A great many more Huguenots were skilled craftsmen, whose expertise and innovatory techniques had a profound impact on London's luxury trades. One such figure was Daniel Marot, a pupil of Louis XIV's *maître ornemaniste*, who worked at Hampton Court in the 1690s. Important carvers and gilders included the Pelletier family, who made furniture for Kensington Palace and Hampton Court, and a leading upholsterer was Francis Lapiere, based in Pall Mall. Many of London's finest 18th-century goldsmiths, such as Paul Crespin, Paul de Lamerie and the Rococo master Nicolas Sprimont, were second-generation Huguenots, while native masters such as George Wickes and Thomas Heming were Huguenot-trained.

Elder Street (*map p. 607, F1*) leads out of Folgate Street. The house at no. 32 was once the home of the artist Mark Gertler, born in Spitalfields to Polish Jewish parents. He became the protégé of Lady Ottoline Morrell, who introduced him to members of the Bloomsbury group (Virginia Woolf found him a 'forcible young man' and egocentric). He committed suicide in 1939. The coal-hole cover outside the house is decorated with a detail from his famous anti-war painting *Merry-go-Round* (original in Tate Britain). The house is now the atelier of 'bespoke casual' tailor Timothy Everest, whose clients have included David Beckham, Mick Jagger and Tom Cruise.

SHOREDITCH & HOXTON

Map p. 597. Underground: Old Street. Overground: Shoreditch High Street, Hoxton.

Shoreditch is an area once famous for its cobblers and furniture makers, a place of wishful thinking, whose bells in the old nursery rhyme promise to pay 'when I grow rich'. Perhaps that is happening, slowly—at least if the arty cafés, galleries, artisans' boutiques and furniture stores on Redchurch Street and Calvert Avenue are anything to go by. One of the oldest monuments is **St Leonard's Church** (*map p. 597, D2; usually open noon–2*) on Shoreditch High Street, which stands above the source of the Walbrook stream. The current building, with its plain Tuscan Doric porch, was built c. 1740 by George Dance the Younger. James Burbage and his sons Cuthbert and Richard (the friend of Shakespeare) are buried in the crypt, as is Gabriel Spencer, the actor whom Ben Jonson killed in a duel in Hoxton Fields in 1598.

Further south, opening off the High Street, is **New Inn Yard** (*map p. 605, E1*) once an insalubrious area bounded by a sewer and a horsepond, where James Burbage built his octagonal wooden Theatre in 1576. The site lay just outside the City, which had recently banned 'play-acting'. In 1597, after a dispute over the lease, the structure is said to have been pulled down overnight by Cuthbert Burbage, who used the salvaged planks to construct the Globe Theatre in Southwark. Further south again was another wooden playhouse, the Curtain, also for a time managed by Burbage. Shakespeare's *Henry V* was first performed here and the theatre's circular structure is alluded to in the play's Prologue: 'May we cram within this wooden O the very casques that did affright the air at Agincourt?' In 2012 the foundations of the Curtain were discovered in Hewett Street, east off Curtain Road.

The **Prince's Foundation for Building Community**, a charity set up by Prince Charles with a focus on architecture and design, is based on Charlotte Road (*princes-foundation.org*).

GEFFRYE MUSEUM
136 Kingsland Rd. Map p. 597, D2. Underground: Liverpool Street, then bus 242 or 149; Old Street then bus 243; Overground: Hoxton. Open Tues–Sun and bank holidays 10–5, garden open April–Oct. Free. Restaurant and Shop. T: 020 7739 9893, geffrye-museum.org.uk.

Kingsland Road leads north from Shoreditch High Street to (c. 450yds) the iron railings, tall trees and low-lying buildings of the former Geffrye almshouses, now a museum of the English domestic interior. It is one of London's hidden treasures.

The almshouses were the charitable foundation of Sir Robert Geffrye (1613–1704), a merchant with interests in India and the Far East, a Master of the Ironmongers' Company, a member of the Court of Aldermen, and Lord Mayor of London in 1685. In his will he left a sum of money for the establishment of almshouses. In 1712 a plot of land was purchased on the Kingsland Road, then an area of market gardens and plant nurseries, and a simple but dignified building was constructed. Externally, the building is little altered. The statue of Sir Robert Geffrye in the niche above the central door is a copy after the 1723 original by John van Nost the Elder (now at the new almshouses in Hampshire; *see below*). The pensioners, 43 of them when the almshouses opened, received £6 each per year. Each pensioner had one room, where he would eat, sleep and live, with a fireplace and two windows overlooking the front gardens, with a small closet off it. With the decline of the local area, in 1911 the almshouses moved to Mottingham, Kent, and in 1974 to Hook, Hampshire.

The Geffrye Museum displays a chronological succession of period rooms, furnished and decorated to reflect the domestic living arrangements of the urban middle classes through the ages, from Jacobean oak panelling to the minimalist loft conversions of the late 1990s. The old Great Room, converted into a chapel in 1716, has been restored and contains a fine marble monument to Geffrye and his wife, removed from Geffrye's local parish church of St Dionis Backchurch on its demolition in 1881. A particularly good time to visit the museum is in December, when the rooms are dressed for Christmas in the traditions of the times.

HOXTON

The district of Hoxton (*map p. 597, D2*) enjoyed a blazing, comet-like surge of glory for the twelve years that it was home to Jay Jopling's White Cube Gallery. The gallery closed in 2012 (though it still operates in St James's and Bermondsey; *see pp. 219 and 433*), but its legacy is still felt: Hoxton has self-confidence and style. On Pitfield Street is the 'Waterloo' (*see p. 419*) church of **St John the Baptist** (1826), with a vast Edwardian ceiling painting of the *Apocalypse*. The architect was Francis Edwards, pupil of Sir John Soane. A Pakistani Christian congregation gathers here on Sun afternoons. **Hoxton Hall**, at 130 Hoxton St, is an old Victorian music hall still used for live performances (*hoxtonhall.co.uk*).

BETHNAL GREEN & WHITECHAPEL ROAD

Map pp. 597 and 605. Underground: Bethnal Green, Whitechapel.

Bethnal Green was one of London's most crowded and poorest areas during the 19th century. On Charles Booth's famous Poverty Maps, it features large and black, denoting 'Lowest class: vicious, semi-criminal'. Since then it has attracted Victorian social reformers, slum clearers, optimistic post-war planners, estate housing and a famous pugilist.

The Boundary Estate stands on the border of Bethnal Green and Shoreditch. Its centrepiece is **Arnold Circus** (*map p. 605, E1*), surrounded by red-brick mansion houses constructed from 1890 onwards on the site of the notorious Old Nichol slum. Rubble from the slum clearance was used to construct the high mound in the centre of the circus, which now supports a bandstand. Arthur Morrison, in his 1896 novel *A Child of the Jago*, calls the old slum 'the blackest pit in London'.

Another housing project, much later, is the **Cranbrook Estate** (Skinner, Bailey and Lubetkin, 1964), north of Roman Road. In its day it was a utopian dream; today it is somewhat wan and run down, but it is home to Dame Elizabeth Frink's sculpture *The Blind Beggar*, which immortalises a famous fictional character of Bethnal Green (*see p. 116*). The lively **Columbia Road Flower Market** (*Sun 8–2; map p. 597, D2*) sells plants, bulbs, seeds, pots and garden tools and is worth a visit just for the atmosphere. On this site was the huge Columbia Market built in 1869 by the philanthropist Baroness Burdett-Coutts to provide a place to buy cheap and nourishing food. It failed and the building was finally pulled down in 1960. As Charles Booth dryly noted, philanthropy and well-meaning alone are not enough: 'a market must grow by natural causes.'

Very close to Bethnal Green Tube station, at the corner of Cambridge Heath Road and Roman Road, is the Anglo-Catholic church of **St John**, designed by Soane (1826–8), with an eccentric squat tower (*open Mon–Thur 12–2, Sat 10–1, stjohnbethnalgreen. org*). It contains a series of Stations of the Cross by contemporary artist Chris Gollon (2000). On the opposite side of the Green, a plaque on no. 3 Paradise Row commemorates Daniel Mendoza, English heavyweight boxing champion in the late 1790s, who lived here and wrote his *Art of Boxing*. Despite his many wins and his great fame, he died penniless in 1836.

V&A MUSEUM OF CHILDHOOD

Map p. 597, E2. Cambridge Heath Road. Underground: Bethnal Green. Open daily 10–5.45. Free. Café and shop. T: 020 8983 5200, museumofchildhood.org.uk.

The Museum of Childhood, a branch of the V&A, opened in 1872 as the Bethnal Green Museum, satisfying a desire first raised in 1851, in the wake of the Great Exhibition, to establish a museum in the East End. The framework of the building is in fact a section of the Iron Building erected in 1857 as part of the South Kensington Museum, as the V&A was then known. In 1866 it was partially dismantled and re-erected here, with an outer façade of red brick designed by J.W. Wild. A series of mosaic panels decorates its two long sides, with scenes representing Agriculture on one side, and Art and Science on the other, all to the designs of Frank Moody. They were made by female students of the South Kensington Museum Mosaic Class under the supervision of Minton's. Inside, the museum reveals its delicate iron framework, its spacious central hall overlooked on either side by upper-level balconies. The monochrome mosaic floor was laid by female prisoners. The focus on children dates from the 1920s and the museum now

BETHNAL GREEN
Mosaic designed by Frank Moody (1857) on the V&A Museum of Childhood.

contains the national collection of childhood-related objects, dating from the 17th century to the present. It is, unsurprisingly, popular with school parties.

WHITECHAPEL ROAD

Map p. 605, E2–F1. Underground: Aldgate East, Whitechapel.

At no. 34 Whitechapel Road, on the corner of Fieldgate Street, is the charming old **Whitechapel Bell Foundry** (*map p. 605, F2*), established in 1570. It moved here in 1738 and occupies part of an inn building of c. 1670. Here bells have been made since 1583, from tiny hand chimes to great clangers such as Big Ben (1858) and the Liberty Bell (1752). A small museum is housed in the front office (*museum open Mon–Fri 9–5, free; tours of the foundry on Sat, approx. 90mins, can be booked on T: 020 7247 2599, whitechapelbellfoundry.co.uk*).

Further along, at no. 46, is the London Muslim Centre, next door to which stands the huge, yellow-brick **East London Mosque** (1985) with its towering minaret (*entrance to men's prayer hall from the main façade; women's prayer hall around the corner*). The East London Bookshop, diagonally opposite, sells, as well as books, thobes and burkas and prayer mat-and-compass sets (the compass to locate the direction of Mecca).

Whitechapel Market occupies the northern side of the street between Vallance Road and Cambridge Heath Road. There are stalls of all kinds, selling dresses and scarves, pots and pans, fresh fish and excellent fruit and vegetables, including okra and other staples of Bengali cooking.

Opposite Whitechapel Tube station is the Royal London Hospital, founded in 1759. Behind the main buildings, in Newark Street, in the crypt of the hospital's former church of SS Philip and Augustine, is the **Royal London Museum** (*open Tues–Fri 10–4.30; free; T: 020 7377 7608, bartshealth.nhs.uk*) featuring sections on early surgery, Dr Barnardo, the Jack the Ripper murders, Joseph Merrick (the Elephant Man), the last letter of Edith Cavell—the nurse executed by the Germans in 1915 for helping Allied soldiers to escape occupied Belgium—and, last but not least, a fragment of George Washington's false teeth. Whitechapel achieved notoriety in 1888, with the Jack the Ripper murders of several prostitutes. The first body was found just off Whitechapel Road in Durward Street, and others in alleyways in the area. The murderer was never identified.

Off Brady Street is an **Ashkenazi burial ground**, one of two in this area, kept locked, though you can see the graves through the gate (*map p. 605, F1; entrance behind the new houses at nos 43–47; to visit, contact Bushey Burial Office, T: 020 8950 7767*). It dates from 1761 and was closed to burials in 1858. Nathan Rothschild (d. 1836), founder of the family bank in London, is buried here.

Back on Whitechapel Road, the impressive main entrance to the old Watney Mann Brewery, next to the Idea Store (and Whitechapel Library), dates from 1902. Beside it is the **Blind Beggar pub**, named after the central character in a long traditional ballad, the blind beggar of Bethnal Green, who providentially manages to find a large dowry for his daughter. The pub has several claims to both fame and notoriety: William Booth, founder of the Salvation Army, preached his first sermon outside the pub doors; the Blind Beggar Gang was a posse of pickpockets who operated in the nearby streets at the turn of the 20th century; Ronnie Kray shot a man in the head with a Mauser here in 1966; the pub garden has been voted 'best outdoor smoking area in London'.

MILE END ROAD, STEPNEY & BOW

Map p. 597, E2. Underground: Mile End, Stepney Green, Bow Road, Stratford.

Mile End Road begins one mile from the old City Wall and leads through the area known as Stepney to the south and Globe Town to the north. Just beyond the junction with Cambridge Heath Road, facing the traffic, is a bronze **bust of William Booth**, from whose open-air services in this neighbourhood in 1865 sprang the Salvation Army. A replica of the statue of him at Denmark Hill (*see p. 464*) was added in 1979, a little further along the road, to mark the 150th anniversary of his birth.

The picturesque **Trinity Almshouses** were established in 1695 for '28 decay'd masters and commanders of ships or ye widows of such', a reminder that the docks are not far away. Look up to see the models of fully-rigged ships on either ends of the gables.

On Alderney Street is a second **Ashkenazi burial ground**. Prominent rabbis and founders of the community are buried here (*visits as for Brady St; see above*).

There are two **Sephardic cemeteries** in Mile End Road. Behind Albert Stern House at no. 253 is the old cemetery, the Velho, founded in 1657. The much larger Nuevo Beth Chaim cemetery was established to the east in 1733. It is now within the grounds of Queen Mary, University of London. Some of the remains, including those of the boxer Daniel Mendoza (*see p. 114*), were moved to Brentwood. In both cemeteries the tombstones are laid flat, a symbol of the levelling power of death.

ALDERNEY STREET
Tombstone in the Ashkenazi burial ground.

STEPNEY GREEN TO BOW AND STRATFORD

Stepney Green, a wide street with handsome houses (c. 1700), ends at the large churchyard of **St Dunstan and All Saints** (*open Thur 10–12*), mostly of the 15th century, though there has been a church on the site for much longer. A Saxon rood panel (early 11th century) decorates the chancel. In the wall of the south aisle is a stone with an inscription (1663) stating that it was brought from Carthage.

At the corner of Ben Jonson and Aston streets, the 19th-century gasholders of the former Stepney Gas Works fill the sky. Take the bridge over the Regent's Canal and then turn left into Copperfield Road for the **Ragged School Museum** (*open Wed and Thur 10–5, first Sun of the month 10–2; free; T: 020 8980 6405, raggedschoolmuseum. org.uk*). The museum is housed in the warehouse where Dr Barnardo opened his 'Ragged School' in 1877, providing free schooling and meals for the poorest children in the area. The main feature is the Victorian classroom, complete with serried ranks of desks, slate writing boards and dunce's hats.

Further north, the Mile End Road crosses the Regent's Canal and becomes Bow Road. **Bow** takes its name from the original stone bridge, shaped like a bow, across the River Lea. There was a flourishing porcelain manufactory here in the mid-18th century. In **Stratford** is the Olympic Park, built for the 2012 Olympic Games. The swimming pool at the Aquatics Centre, designed by Zaha Hadid, is open to the public (*for prices and times, see queenelizabetholympicpark.co.uk*), as is the velodrome, for cycling.

DOCKLANDS

NB: This section covers Wapping, Shadwell, Limehouse and the Isle of Dogs (Canary Wharf). For St Katharine Docks, see p. 103; for the area from London Bridge to Bermondsey, including Butler's Wharf, see p. 432 and for Surrey Quays, see p. 439.

The London Docklands share geography as well as history with the East End. At one time, these docks were the largest and most impressive in the world, the nucleus of the British Empire, employing thousands in trade and the manufacturing industries. By the 1960s, however, the docks were in decline: modern container shipping requires deep-water harbours and the industry moved out and buildings were either demolished or abandoned.

HISTORY OF THE DOCKS

London's prosperity during the 16th and 17th centuries depended on its growing port, based on quays along the Thames such as Billingsgate and Queenhithe, and some deep-water moorings at the Tower, Wapping and Puddle Dock. Most moorings were in the Pool of London itself, the area of water below (east of) London Bridge, with sufferance wharves on both banks to take the overflow from the legal docks. The first commercial dock was the Great Howland (*see p. 439*). Enclosed docks began to be the norm in the 19th century, when trade—and pilfering—had increased and high-security berths and warehouses became a necessity to prevent ships lying idle in the Thames, waiting to unload and declare their cargoes. The City Corporation, which operated the Pool, resisted the building of docks which instead were developed piecemeal by private companies in the marshy land below Tower Bridge.

The first to be completed was West India Dock (1802). London Docks at Wapping followed in 1805, then the East India (1806), the Surrey Docks on the south bank (1807), St Katharine in 1828, Royal Victoria (1855), Millwall (1868), Royal Albert (1880) and King George V (1921). Each dock specialised in a particular type of trade and security was tight, with high walls, gates and even a drawbridge at West India Docks. The formation of the Port of London Authority in 1909 removed some of the destructive competition between each dock.

During World War Two, Hitler strenuously attempted to disable Britain's economy by bombing the entire densely-populated area: though rich in infrastructure, it was where the poorest communities in London lived and worked. For 57 consecutive nights incendiary bombs rained down, causing destruction and loss of life. Post-war revival was stifled by new container shipping. By the 1960s trade had declined to such a low level that docks began to close. The increasingly titanic container vessels were better served at Tilbury and Felixstowe, which offered more up-to-date facilities and deep-water harbours. Thirty years ago this whole area was in decay; now, thanks to the London Docklands Development Corporation (LDDC), over 8.5 square miles of land and water-filled docks on both sides of the river, from Tower Bridge in the west to past the Thames Barrier at Woolwich in the east, form an upmarket and desirable business and residential area. When the LDDC was set up in 1981 it was heralded as 'the most important inner-city development in Europe', a description that today seems largely justified. The London Docks (Wapping; north side) and part of Surrey Docks (now Surrey Quays; south side) have been filled in, but in the main, redevelopment has incorporated the large expanses of water of the original docks.

Travelling around Docklands

The Docklands Light Railway (DLR), an automated light metro system, rather like a toy train, runs on an elevated track to and from Tower Gateway, Lewisham, Stratford, Bank, Beckton, London City Airport and Woolwich Arsenal and is a good way to travel and see the area. The best view is looking out from the front carriage (there is no driver)—although in doing so you might have to disappoint numerous children whose parents have promised their offspring that they can 'drive the train'. The area is also well served by the Jubilee Line (London Underground).

WAPPING

Wapping (*map p. 605, F3*) once thronged with sailors, dockworkers and all manner of people connected with boats; former residents include Captain Cook and Vice Admiral William Bligh. London Docks opened here in 1805, covering 90 acres and specialising in wine, tobacco, rice and brandy; the bodies of water have been filled in except for Hermitage Basin near St Katharine Docks and Shadwell Basin. In 1986 Rupert Murdoch controversially moved his newspaper publishing company News UK (formerly News International) here from Fleet Street; the multi-million pound plant, 'Fortress Wapping', stands over part of the former western dock. Wapping's main attraction is probably the riverside stretch with its remaining historic pubs. It is possible to walk all the way from Wapping to Canary Wharf, taking in Shadwell and Limehouse along the way.

ALONG THE RIVER

At Wapping Underground Station, plaques and sound effects of rushing water commemorate the tunnel, the first public traffic tunnel to be built beneath a river, designed by Marc and Isambard Kingdom Brunel and completed in 1843. It was used by pedestrians until the late 1860s, when its present use as a railway tunnel began (the East London Line takes you through the tunnel to Rotherhithe, where there is a small museum; *see p. 439*).

Wapping High Street (left out of the Tube station) winds its way along the narrow river-front, bounded by former wharves and warehouses now converted into offices and flats. In the 19th century, this stretch was known as Sailor Town; a rough, frenetic neighbourhood of 36 taverns where sailors from all corners of the globe could quench their thirst and slake their ardour and where press gangs roamed. The **Captain Kidd pub**, a converted coffee warehouse, has good views from the riverside terrace and shares a claim with Wapping Old Stairs to be the site of the notorious Execution Dock (*see below*).

Wapping Old Stairs of the eponymous ballad ('Your Molly has never been false, she declares, Since last time we parted at Wapping Old Stairs, When I swore that I still would continue the same, And gave you the 'bacco box, marked with your name...') are accessed via a small alley next to the **Town of Ramsgate pub**, which lays claim to be the oldest pub on the Thames. Here Judge Jeffreys was arrested in 1688, disguised as a sailor, attempting to flee the country, and was brought to the Tower. **Execution Dock**, which may have been at the bottom of this slippery flight of steps, was where Captain Kidd (executed 1701) and other notorious pirates were hanged and their bodies left until three tides had covered them. Slaves were also unloaded here.

Further along, opposite the surviving tower of St John (1760; the church was destroyed in the Second World War and the tower converted into flats), is **Wapping Pier Head**, where desirable Georgian residences, built in 1811–13 for senior dock officials, flank the infilled Wapping Basin (formerly the entrance to Western Dock; now a garden).

TOBACCO DOCK

Head away from the river up Scandrett Street. Follow Tench Street right, which turns into Watts Street, where the **Turner's Old Star pub** is reputed to have been owned by the painter J.M.W. Turner. At the end of Watts Street turn left into Wapping Lane and continue until you reach Reardon Street and, behind forbidding walls, the expansive **Tobacco Dock** (D.A. Alexander, 1811–14; *map p. 605, F2–F3*). Tobacco Dock linked Western Dock and Eastern Dock and was used to house tobacco, wool, wine and spirits. After the docks closed in the 1960s, Tobacco Dock's buildings stood empty until redevelopment in the 1990s into a shopping and restaurant complex by Terry Farrell, utilising the original vaults, cast-iron columns and timber trusses. The development did not take off and after another decade of lying empty, the site is now an events venue.

SHADWELL

At the end of Wapping Lane is The Highway (*map p. 605, F2*). This relentless road is now technically Shadwell, once a hamlet in its own right, a seafaring community and then a slum. Excavations in the 1970s and again in 2002–3 uncovered Roman remains including a bath house, quarry, tower, drains, tanks, plots and a leather bikini.

Across The Highway is Hawksmoor's **St George-in-the-East**, with a massive 160ft 'pepperpot' tower. Gutted in 1941, it has a modern interior. It is one of the churches built after the New Churches Act of 1710–11, a scheme for 50 new churches to be built to spread the Word to new communities, often where immigrants were settling. When Charles Booth drew his portrait of East London in 1897, he noted that 'Each [district] has its charm except St George's, which has a squalor peculiar to itself.' Today, the neighbourhood remains one of the most disadvantaged in the city.

Cable Street further north, running parallel with The Highway, is where the **Battle of Cable Street** took place (on Sunday 4th October 1936) between policemen and forces opposed to Oswald Mosley's fascist Blackshirts, who planned to stage a march through the East End. A mural commemorating the event was painted in the 1980s

SHADWELL
Mural commemorating the Battle of Cable Street of 1936.

on St George's Town Hall (*236 Cable St*), which faces St George's Gardens, the former churchyard.

To the east, the large expanse of water is **Shadwell Basin** (*map p. 597, E2*), formerly part of London Docks and now a popular boating and water sports area with housing on three sides. Garnet Street leads south to Wapping Wall and the Wapping Project Gallery, in the building formerly belonging to the London Hydraulic Power Company, providers of power to manipulate the docks' cranes. Opposite, the ever-popular and picturesque **Prospect of Whitby pub** overlooks the river. Built in 1520, it was formerly called the Devil's Tavern because of the smugglers and thieves who drank here. The 'hanging' Judge Jeffreys was a customer, as were Samuel Pepys and later Dickens and Turner. Its current name was taken from a ship in 1777.

Glamis Road leads back to The Highway. On your left, overlooking Shadwell Basin, is **St Paul's church** (the current building dates from 1820). It was known as the Church of the Sea Captains because over 70 were buried in the graveyard. Captain Cook and Thomas Jefferson's mother were both parishioners; John Wesley preached his last sermon here.

King Edward VII Memorial Park, on the opposite (east) side of Glamis Road, marks the site of the old Shadwell fish market; it was landscaped in 1922 over slum dwellings. Back on the Thames Path, note the ventilation shaft (circular red-brick building) for the Rotherhithe Tunnel and the memorial to Willoughby, Frobisher and other 16th-century navigators who 'set sail from this reach of the River Thames near Ratcliff Cross'. Further along on your left, the massive **Free Trade Wharf**, originally built by the East India Company in the 18th century, retains two of the original saltpetre warehouses in a mixed residential/commercial development.

North from Narrow Street, at 2 Butcher's Row (*map p. 597, E2*), is one of England's oldest charities, the **Royal Foundation of St Katharine**. St Katharine's Royal Hospital was originally founded near the Tower in 1147 by Queen Matilda; in 1273 Queen Eleanor, wife of Henry III, took the wardenship into her own hands and reserved the patronage for ever for the queens of England personally. However, after Queen Caroline's death in 1821, George IV took over and allowed the controversial bill for destruction of the ancient church and precincts to go through, in order for St Katharine Docks to be excavated in 1825. The Foundation removed to Regent's Park, only returning to the East End in 1950. The 18th Warden's House occupies the former rectory of St James's church, which was destroyed in the Second World War. The Foundation offers accommodation for those on retreat, business or just on holiday.

LIMEHOUSE

Limehouse (*map p. 593, A1; DLR: Limehouse, Westferry*) takes its name from the lime kilns which manufactured quicklime for the building industry; from the 16th century it was one of London's main shipbuilding centres. Later the area became populous with labourers serving the West and East India Docks. A Chinese community established itself here in the 1890s, and the area gained a reputation for vice and opium dens which was enhanced and romanticised by writers including Oscar Wilde and Sir Arthur Conan Doyle, the books and films of Dr Fu-Manchu, and the press. The area was immortalised by Gertrude Lawrence in the popular song 'Limehouse Blues' (1922). London's Chinese community is now centred in Soho but there is still a small Chinese population in this area. Limehouse was also historically known for its lascars, sailors mainly from the Indian subcontinent who served on British ships and either failed to find a passage back or chose to stay and settle.

The church of **St Anne's Limehouse** (1730) on Newell Street is considered one of Hawksmoor's masterpieces. It is another of the twelve churches built in this area as a result of the 1711 Act of Parliament (*see p. 120*). Badly damaged by fire in 1850, the church was restored by Philip Hardwick. Its clock is the highest church clock in London: designed as a special maritime clock, it used to chime every 15mins. The curious pyramid in the churchyard, contemporary with the church, is carved with 'The Wisdom of Solomon'. It is not known what the pyramid was for but some believe Hawksmoor intended it to be installed on top of the church.

Back on Newell Street, opposite the church, the straight stretch of water ahead is the **Limehouse Cut**, London's oldest canal, built in 1770. Bear left down the canal path to reach **Limehouse Basin**, formerly Regent's Canal Dock. Built in 1820, the dock was constructed to allow ships to unload cargoes onto barges for onward transport along the Regent's Canal. In this way, coal was supplied to the power plants along the canal and until the coming of the railway, the dock was the major entrance from the Thames to England's inland waterway network. The dock is also linked to the River Lee (also spelled Lea) via the Limehouse Cut. Continuing left, the path skirts the revitalised

Limehouse Basin, a marina with houses, shops and leisure facilities, and eventually comes out onto the Thames Path, where the Narrow pub is in a former dockmaster's house. Follow the Thames Path east (left) along Narrow Street, with its fine 18th-century merchant's houses. The historic **Grapes pub** at no. 76 was immortalised by Dickens as The Six Jolly Fellowship Porters in *Our Mutual Friend*. There is a good view up and down the river, including the glittering towers of Canary Wharf.

THE ISLE OF DOGS

The Isle of Dogs (*map p. 593, B2–B3; DLR: West India Quay, Canary Wharf, Heron Quays; Underground: Canary Wharf*), once a boggy peninsula known as Stepney Marsh, remained relatively unpopulated until the docks were constructed here in the 19th century, bringing employment and industrialisation. Row upon row of Victorian terraces were built, such as at Poplar and the purpose-built estate called Cubitt Town, to shelter the humble dock- and ship-workers and their families. The name 'Isle of Dogs' may derive from the hunting hounds of Henry VIII, who came here for some sport from Placentia Palace across the river in Greenwich. However, this tongue of land was never really an island until the docks and canals were excavated. The West India Docks opened in 1802 as two rectangular basins, one for import and one for export. A shipping canal was cut across the peninsula in 1805 and was later incorporated as the South West India Dock. The huge L-shaped Millwall Dock, now a watersports and sailing centre, followed in 1868. All this caused the peninsula to become largely cut off from the rest of London. Only with the opening of the DLR and the Underground Jubilee Line extension in the late 20th century did getting here became relatively quick and easy.

CANARY WHARF

The gleaming towers of Canary Wharf (*map p. 593, A1–B1*), London's Wall Street-on-Water, stand on the northern part of the Isle of Dogs, on a narrow piece of land between two of the West India Docks which once handled trade with the Canary Islands. After the last dock closed in 1980, the area became a wasteland. Today, the colossal development, with some of the tallest buildings in the UK and Europe, comprises 14 million square feet of offices, flats, hotels, restaurants and shops. The expanses of water that formed the docks are now mainly ornamental, the redundant cranes that used to hoist heavy cargoes frozen into pieces of public art.

All the major names in international finance are represented at Canary Wharf and over 60,000 employees make the Monday–Friday commute. Weekends are increasingly busy as newly-built waterside apartment blocks are filled and as people choose to come here for recreation. The view from Canary Wharf Pier takes in the skyscrapers of London's other financial hub: the City. But it was not an easy transformation. After the 'Big Bang' deregulation of the City in 1986, Docklands was expected to become the stock-trading centre of London. Manhattan-style buildings soon began to fill the sky, but Paul Reichmann, the Canadian property tycoon who staked so much on the development, famously lost millions when the buildings failed to find tenants. Poor transport infrastructure was blamed (the Jubilee Line extension arrived too late and the Docklands Light Railway offered only a rickety, fairground ride). It was not until after 1999 that Canary Wharf began to take off.

At the heart of Canary Wharf rises Cesar Pelli's 50-storey steel tower, known as 'Canary Wharf' but officially **One Canada Square**. Completed in 1991, it was then the tallest building in Europe and at 800ft high it dominates the East London skyline (it was the tallest building in London until 2010, when it was surpassed by the Shard). The winking light at the apex of the pyramidal roof is a warning to aircraft passing by on their way to City Airport. Shops and cafés fill the arcades which lead from the DLR station, built into the base of the Tower, to Cabot Square. Here, as with the rest of Canary Wharf, a high standard of landscaping has been achieved with trees, sculpture and street furniture.

The glass arc of **Canary Wharf Underground Station** (Jubilee Line) was designed by Sir Norman Foster. The vast interior, over 70ft below ground, features platforms that are as long as One Canada Square is high.

WEST INDIA QUAY

A footbridge links Canary Wharf with West India Quay. Overlooking the old import dock (North Dock), in a listed Georgian sugar warehouse, is the **Museum of London Docklands** (*map p. 593, A1; open daily 10–6; free; T: 020 7001 9822, museumoflondon. org.uk/docklands*) which charts the history of the Docklands over three floors, from Roman settlement up to present-day regeneration. Start on the third floor and work your way down. Among the items on display are an excavated Viking axe, fragments of Venetian glass and a model of old London Bridge. An exhibition on slavery explores London's part in the slave trade. The galleries devoted to the building of the 19th-century docks are aided by many interesting contemporary maps and prints. The excellent ground-floor galleries tell the story of the Docklands at War during the Blitz and the destruction wreaked on 'Black Saturday', 7th September 1940, when the bombing began. The final displays tell the story of the docks' rebuilding as a financial centre.

OTHER PLACES OF INTEREST

The **new Billingsgate Market** (*map p. 593, B1*), which moved here in 1982, is London's main wholesale fish market, originally established at Billingsgate wharf (*see p. 79*). The new market building offers modern freezing and storage facilities.

In Coldharbour (*map p. 593, B2*) is **The Gun pub**, in a street of mainly 19th-century houses overlooking the river. Lord Nelson and Lady Hamilton are said to have had assignations here in an upstairs room (the pub's lavatories are named after them). The pub serves good food and has a large riverside terrace overlooking the O2 Arena, formerly the Millennium Dome.

Burrell's Wharf (*map p. 593, A3–B3*) is where the iron plates for the *Great Eastern*—the wonder and failure of her age—were manufactured. Isambard Kingdom Brunel and John Scott Russell designed the 629ft-long ironship, which was built between 1853 and 1858. It took three months to float her sideways into the Thames. As a cargo and passenger ship she proved of little use (too slow) and she was put to work laying

CANARY WHARF

Atlantic cables before being broken up in 1888. Some of the original buildings of the wharf survive (Plate House) and have been incorporated in the residential Burrell's Wharf complex. Further south, the Great Eastern Slipway, Napier Avenue, is the original timber slipway from which the *Great Eastern* was launched; Charles Dickens was among the crowd who came to enjoy the spectacle.

Mudchute (*map p. 593, B3*), so called from the artificial landscape created by the silted mud dredged and dumped here from excavating Millwall Dock, is now a 32-acre park and farm in the middle of the Isle of Dogs (*open every day; free; mudchute.org*).

From **Island Gardens**, first laid out in 1895, there are good views of Greenwich and Deptford. The Greenwich Foot Tunnel under the river here opened in 1902 and replaced the ferry. The walk to Greenwich takes less than 10mins.

EAST INDIA DOCK AND ROYAL DOCKS

The old basin of **East India Dock** (*map p. 593, C1*) is now a wildlife sanctuary, home to newts and kingfishers. Further east, the **Royal Docks** (Royal Victoria, Royal Albert and George V docks; *map p. 597, F2*), the largest enclosed docks in the world with the largest man-made body of water), are undergoing development and landscaping as residential areas, business parks, convention centres, shopping malls and entertainment venues. The **Emirates Air Line** is a cable car service operating between Emirates Royal Docks (*Royal Victoria station on the DLR*) and Emirates Greenwich Peninsula (*North Greenwich on the Jubilee Line*). The experience is unique in London and there is a splendid prospect of the Thames Barrier (*cable car runs daily until 9pm, emiratesairline.co.uk*).

EATING AND DRINKING IN THE EAST END

BETHNAL GREEN, SHOREDITCH

£ E. Pellicci. Old-fashioned 'greasy spoon' or 'caff', run by the same family since 1900 and an East End institution. The décor (Vitrolite outside and Formica within) has earned it Grade II listed status. Come here for carbs: fry-ups, mixed grills, puds. Closed Sun. *332 Bethnal Green Rd. Last food served 4pm. Map p. 597, E2.*

£ Geffrye Museum. Glass-walled, light-filled space overlooking the museum gardens. Soups, sandwiches, filled bagels, lunches and tea. Closed evenings. *Kingsland Rd. T: 020 7739 9893, geffrye-museum.org.uk. Map p. 597, D2.*

££ Merchant's Tavern. Cosy, convivial place close to the site of the old Curtain Theatre. Good-value set lunches. Closed Mon. No dinner Sun. *36 Charlotte Rd. T: 020 7060 5335, merchantstavern.co.uk. Map p. 605, D1.*

BRICK LANE, WHITECHAPEL

Brick Lane is known for its curry houses (Nazrul at no. 130 is the oldest). Recommendations are difficult to make, as everyone has their favourite. Universally admired for its Pakistani Punjabi cooking is **£ Tayyabs** in Whitechapel. Like most restaurants of its type, it has no alcohol licence. You can bring your own—or drink delicious mango lassi instead. Booking ahead almost always essential. Open every day (*83–89 Fieldgate St, T: 020 7247 9543 or 6400 or 8521, tayyabs. co.uk; map p. 605, F2*).

Beigel Bake is a traditional Jewish bakery producing bagels around the clock, available with a variety of fillings (*159 Brick Lane; map p. 605, E1*). **Indo** is a popular pub (*133 Whitechapel Rd; map p. 605, F1*).

DOCKLANDS

On the Isle of Dogs there is no shortage of places to eat lunch, as a sizeable weekday workforce has to be catered for. The most historic places to eat in this area are the surviving waterside pubs, which include the following: The **£ Captain Kidd**: Named after the pirate of the same name who was hanged at Execution Dock in 1701. It was a bungled affair: the rope snapped on the first attempt and Kidd had to be hauled up again. He spotted a former lover laughing amongst the crowd. The pub is right on the river with an adjacent beer garden. A good place for a drink. *108 Wapping High St. Map p. 605, F3.*

£ The Grapes: A pub where Dickens is reputed to have danced on the tables. Bar food is served or you can eat in the restaurant (devilled whitebait, grilled haddock). *76 Narrow St. T: 020 7987 4396, thegrapes.co.uk. Map p. 593, A1.*

£ The Gun: Pub with Nelson associations (*see p. 124*) serving good food on the Isle of Dogs. Open every day. *27 Coldharbour. T: 020 7515 5222, the-gundocklands.com. Map p. 593, B2.*

££ The Narrow: Not really a pub. This is a Gordon Ramsay bar and restaurant overlooking the river and

Limehouse dock. Pleasant location. Open every day. *44 Narrow St. T: 020 7592 7950, gordonramsay.com. Map p. 593, A1.*

£ Prospect of Whitby: Early 16th-century smugglers' den preserving its pewter-topped bar. It was patronised by the usual suspects, Pepys and Dickens (where did those *bon viveurs* not drink?). Pub food served daily. *57 Wapping Wall. T: 020 7481 1095. Map. p. 597, E3.*

£ Town of Ramsgate: Another 16th-century inn, named after the Kent town whose fishermen landed their catches at Wapping Old Stairs (*for the story of Judge Jeffreys, see p. 120*). Pub food, but better than average. The whitebait is a good starter. Open daily. *62 Wapping High St. T: 020 7481 8000, townoframsgate.co.uk. Map p. 605, F3.*

£ Turner's Old Star: Allegedly bought by Turner for his mistress Sophia Booth, a widow from Margate, this pub prides itself on being a true old-fashioned East End 'local', complete with darts board, pool table and Sky Sports. Open daily (closes 8pm Sun). *14 Watts St. T: 020 7702 9199, turnersoldstar.co.uk. Map p. 605, F3.*

SPITALFIELDS

£–££ Canteen. A mini chain (also in Canary Wharf, South Bank, Baker St) serving good British food, including bubble and squeak, fish pie, steak and chips. Open every day. *2 Crispin Place, off Brushfield St, north of Crispin St. T: 0845 686 1122, canteen.co.uk. Map p. 607, F2.*

£££ Galvin La Chapelle. One of a collection of restaurants run by the Galvin brothers. Michelin-starred French cooking. *Prix-fixe* lunches. *35 Spital Square. T: 020 7299 0400, galvinrestaurants.com. Map p. 607, F1.*

££–£££ Hawksmoor. Another small chain famed for its 'dude food': steak and burgers. Prime British meat. Roast Sunday lunches. Bar food only on Sun eve. *157a Commercial St. T: 020 7426 4850, thehawksmoor.com. Map p. 607, F1.*

££ St John Bread and Wine. Proper old-style English food. Eccles cake and Lancashire cheese for pud. Soused herring to start. Open every day. *94–96 Commercial St. T: 020 7251 0848, stjohnbreadandwine.com. Map p. 607, F1.*

££ Ten Bells. Historic pub downstairs (famous for its possible connections with the Jack the Ripper murders) and a restaurant above, catered by young British chefs. Restaurant closed Mon and on Sun eve. *Corner of Fournier St and Commercial St. T: 07530 492986, tenbells.com. Map p. 607, F1.*

£–££ The Water Poet. Attractive pub on one of the best-preserved streets in Spitalfields with bar, dining room and garden (barbecues served in summer). Open every day. *9–11 Folgate St. T: 020 7426 0495, waterpoet.co.uk. Map p. 607, F1.*

In **Spitalfields Market** (*map p. 607, F1*) there are plenty of snack counters, as well as the Androuet cheese and wine bar, for cheese soufflés and fondue; and Square Pie, offering genuinely good pies to eat in or take away.

HOUSES OF PARLIAMENT
Statue of Richard the Lionheart by Carlo Marochetti (1856).

Westminster
& Royal London

'Earth hath not anything to show more fair.' Thus wrote William Wordsworth
of the view from Westminster Bridge in 1802. Standing here, one surveys
the seat of British government, the famous Houses of Parliament.
Whitehall, with its government buildings, leads north, while to the west lies
Buckingham Palace,the London residence of the British sovereign.

As you stand with Westminster Bridge behind you, the magnificent 940ft façade of the Houses of Parliament sweeps away to your left. These buildings, collectively known as the Palace of Westminster, are a UNESCO World Heritage site and cover eight acres, with 11 courtyards, 100 staircases, 1,100 apartments and two miles of passages. The instantly recognisable gilded Elizabeth Tower, with the Great Clock of Westminster, houses the famous bell known as Big Ben (the tower itself is

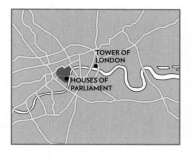

often erroneously referred to by that name). Head straight down Bridge Street, with Elizabeth Tower on your left, to reach Parliament Square.

PARLIAMENT SQUARE

Map p. 603, F2. Underground: Westminster.

The area here was once a desolate, marshy place known as Thorney Island. The first Palace of Westminster (palace, monastery and church) was built for Edward the Confessor (r. 1042–66) between the Thames and the Benedictine church of St Peter, founded AD 900, which later became Westminster Abbey. William the Conqueror made the palace his home and in 1097–9 his son, William Rufus (William II), added the magnificent Westminster Hall, one of the largest Norman halls in Europe. It remained the main residence of the kings of England until Henry VIII removed the court to

Whitehall Palace after a fire in 1512. In 1547 the House of Commons transferred its meetings here from the Chapter House of Westminster Abbey. In 1834 the entire complex, by then a mix of Norman, medieval and later buildings, was burned down, with the exception of Westminster Hall, the crypt of St Stephen's Chapel and part of the cloisters and the Jewel Tower, which was a separate entity in any case. Reconstruction, in prescribed neo-Gothic style, began c. 1840 and lasted about 30 years. The building, which incorporates the ancient Westminster Hall and the crypt and cloisters of St Stephen's Chapel, was designed by Sir Charles Barry, at heart an Italian classicist, aided by Augustus Pugin, a zealous Gothicist. The result is a triumphant fusion of symmetry and asymmetry, rich in external decoration including oriels, pinnacles, turrets and statues of former kings and queens. World War Two damage completely destroyed the House of Commons but the building has been faithfully restored.

Besides the **House of Commons** in the north half and the **House of Lords** in the south half, the palace contains the homes of various parliamentary officials. Of the three towers, the huge, square **Victoria Tower** at the south end (right) is the highest; at its base is the Sovereign's Entrance to the House of Lords. The octagonal **Central Tower** rises above the Central Lobby and serves as a ventilating shaft. The other tower, the **Elizabeth Tower**, houses the Westminster Clock (still wound by hand), an authoritative time-keeper. It has four dials, each 23ft square; the Roman numerals are 2ft high and the minute-hands are 14ft long. Big Ben, the enormous bell which famously strikes the hour on an E note, was installed in 1858; it took 30 hours to winch the 9ft bell up the tower.

Parliament Square was laid out in 1868 as London's first traffic roundabout. Today three lanes of traffic swirl around it and it is crowded with tourists. In the central space are statues of eminent statesmen, including Winston Churchill and Benjamin Disraeli (d. 1881), whose statue is decorated with primroses (his favourite flower) each year on 19th April, the anniversary of his death.

Turn left onto Abingdon Street, once an ancient lane. Here the west façade of the Houses of Parliament, with Thornycroft's statue of Oliver Cromwell in front, is interrupted by the long line of **Westminster Hall**, a splendid and rare Norman survivor from the original Palace of Westminster. It is shown as part of the official guided tour (*see below*).

Guided tours of the Houses of Parliament

Although security around the Palace of Westminster is tight and visible, there are guided tours on Saturdays throughout the year and on selected weekdays during parliamentary recesses. The tours are led by 'Blue Badge' guides and take approx. 75mins. For details, see parliament.uk/visiting. Buy/collect tickets at the kiosk adjacent to the Jewel Tower or from officials wearing jackets with the Houses of Parliament portcullis insignia. Only UK residents are admitted to the Elizabeth Tower and Big Ben; tickets may be requested through your local MP.

The tours include The Queen's Robing Room, Lords' Chamber, Central Lobby, Members' Lobby and Westminster Hall.

THE WESTMINSTER SYSTEM

The Palace of Westminster gives its name to the 'Westminster system' of parliamentary democracy, variations of which operate in many countries of the world. Such countries are led by a legal and constitutional head of state (in the case of the UK, the sovereign). Answerable to him or her is the leader of the democratically elected government (the Prime Minister), whose cabinet of senior officials holds executive power and devises and implements government policy. In the UK, the Queen performs a mainly ceremonial role. Officially she has reserve powers of veto but she seldom if ever exercises them.

The Westminster system is bicameral, consisting of an upper house, the House of Lords, whose members, Lords Temporal (secular) and Lords Spiritual (Church leaders), are partly appointed and partly made up of hereditary peers; and a lower house, the House of Commons, whose members (MPs) are chosen by national election. The official Opposition to the government is made up of 'Shadow' ministers.

JEWEL TOWER, VICTORIA TOWER GARDENS, ST JOHN'S SMITH SQUARE

The small, ragstone **Jewel Tower**, opposite the House of Lords and now dwarfed by its surroundings, is a rare survival of the medieval Palace of Westminster. It was built by the king's mason, Henry Yevele, for Edward III in 1356–66, as a royal treasure house. From 1621 to 1864 it served as the Record Office of the Lords and thereafter (until 1938) as an assay office of weights and measures. Around the tower you can see the excavated remains of its moat and behind it part of the 10ft ragstone wall built in the 14th century to surround the precincts of Westminster Abbey. The Tower is maintained by English Heritage and the interior may be viewed for an entry fee (*open Nov–March Sat–Sun 10–4, April–Oct daily 10–6; english-heritage.org.uk*).

Next to the Jewel Tower, in Abingdon Street Gardens, stands *Knife Edge*, a sculpture by Henry Moore (1967). Opposite, next to the majestic Victoria Tower of the House of Lords, is the entrance to **Victoria Tower Gardens**. Just inside is a statue of the leader of the suffragettes, Emmeline Pankhurst (1858–1928), and a memorial to her daughter Christabel, by A.G. Walker (1930). Dominating the centre of the gardens is a bronze cast of Auguste Rodin's famous group of 1889, *The Burghers of Calais*, depicting the six who surrendered themselves to Edward III in 1340 to save their city from destruction during the Hundred Years' War. This cast is dated 1908 and was installed in 1915; it is one of the official twelve casts the French Government allowed to be taken after Rodin's death. Continue through the gardens (there is a good view of the river and of Lambeth on the opposite bank) until you reach the Buxton Memorial Fountain. Exit here onto Millbank, cross over and walk up Dean Stanley Street to Smith Square, at the centre of which is the eccentric Baroque church of St John the Evangelist, known as **St John's Smith Square**, with four massive towers topped by pineapples.

The square was laid out by the Smith family, who owned the land, in 1726; the houses at nos 3–5 and 6–9 are original Georgian survivors. The church, now a noted Classical music and lecture venue, was completed in 1728 by Thomas Archer and has been much derided over the years: Dickens, in *Our Mutual Friend*, likened it to 'a petrified monster on its back with its legs in the air'; some say the four angle towers were designed to ensure that the swampy foundations settled uniformly. There is a good café/restaurant in the crypt, which stays open until after the evening performance on concert days (*sjss.org.uk; box office open Mon–Fri 10–5*).

Continue back towards the precincts of Westminster Abbey through the quiet Georgian streets. Lord North Street is particularly pleasing and dates from the 1720s (look out for the faded signs to World War Two air raid shelters). At 14 Barton St lived T.E. Lawrence (Lawrence of Arabia).

WESTMINSTER ABBEY PRECINCTS

Map p. 603, F2–F3. Underground: Westminster, St James's Park.

At the end of Great College Street an archway (right) leads into Dean's Yard, once a portion of the Abbey Gardens. On the right are entrances to the cloisters and to **Westminster School**, one of the UK's great public (independent) schools, founded by Benedictine monks in 1179 and re-founded by Elizabeth I in 1560. The school is built around Little Dean's Yard on the site of the monks' quarters, relics of which remain (*visitors are admitted on written application to the bursar*). The College Hall, with a fine hammerbeam roof, dates from the time of Edward III and was formerly the abbey refectory. The main hall was the monks' dormitory. Ashburnham House, the library, dates from 1400 but was rebuilt in 1660 as the home of the Earls of Ashburnham, probably to a design by John Webb, pupil of Inigo Jones. Westminster School now educates over 750 boys and girls. They enjoy certain privileges, such as shouting the 'Vivats' at coronations in the abbey, where they attend twice-weekly services. On Shrove Tuesday the 'Greaze' takes place in the main hall: a horsehair-reinforced pancake is tossed over a bar and the pupil securing the largest fragment is symbolically rewarded with a gold sovereign. On the long list of famous alumni are the names of Ben Jonson, Dryden, Purcell, Wren, Judge Jeffreys, Charles Wesley, Gibbon, A.A. Milne, six prime ministers and two deputy prime ministers.

On the south side of Dean's Yard is **Church House** by Sir Herbert Baker (1937–40), the headquarters of the Archbishops' Council, the Church Commissioners and all its Boards and Councils as well as of the Church of England Pensions Board and the National Society. It is the meeting place, twice each year, of the General Synod of the Church of England. It is now used as a conference centre and events venue in addition to its Church functions. To the west is the **Abbey Choir School**, whose boys share the central green with Westminster School.

BROAD SANCTUARY

Broad Sanctuary, the road in front of Westminster Abbey, recalls the sanctuary where refugees were protected from civil power by the Church; a privilege abolished by James I. The neo-Gothic red granite **Westminster Column**, opposite the west end of the abbey, by Sir George Gilbert Scott (1861), was erected in memory of Westminster School alumni who fell in the Crimean War and the Indian Mutiny (the Uprising).

At the corner of Tothill Street rises the former **Methodist Central Hall**, with a huge lead dome, built in 1911 (Lanchester and Richards) as the headquarters of the Methodist Church and now also used for concerts and public meetings. In January 1946 it became the first home of the General Assembly of the United Nations. Despite its neo-Renaissance appearance, it has a steel frame and is one of the earliest examples of this method of construction in London.

Opposite Westminster Abbey is the **Queen Elizabeth II Conference Centre**, opened by HM The Queen in June 1986, built on an empty site occupied until 1936 by the old Westminster Hospital. Architects Powell, Moya and Partners have achieved an unobtrusive building on a potentially contentious site. The **UK Supreme Court** is in Edwardian neo-Gothic buildings overlooking Parliament Square.

ST MARGARET'S CHURCH

In the shadow of the great abbey stands the picturesque St Margaret's Church (*open Mon–Fri 9.30–3.30, Sat 9.30–1.30, Sun 2–4.30; T: 020 7654 4840*), dating from 1485–1523. It has been repeatedly altered and restored and the interior is adorned with Elizabethan and Jacobean wall monuments. It provides a welcome sanctuary from the traffic of people and vehicles outside.

It was founded before 1189 as the parish church of Westminster, and is also (since 1621) the 'national church for the House of Commons'. Samuel Pepys was married here in 1655; John Milton (for the second time) in 1656 and Winston Churchill in 1908. Sir Walter Raleigh, who was executed in 1618 in front of the Palace of Westminster, is buried in the chancel; and in the church or churchyard also rest William Caxton (1422–?91) and Wenceslaus Hollar, the Bohemian etcher who depicted London before the Great Fire.

At the east end of the south aisle is the notable chest tomb of Lady Dudley (d. 1600), and on the east wall, memorials to Caxton (whose first printing press was next to the Chapter House from 1476) and Raleigh, to whom the large west window is also dedicated. The window at the west end of the north aisle, with an inscription by Whittier, commemorates Milton. The richly-coloured east window, made in Holland before 1509, celebrates the betrothal of Katherine of Aragon to Prince Arthur, Henry VII's eldest son, in 1501. On the external east wall is a lead bust of Charles I (c. 1800).

WESTMINSTER ABBEY

Map p. 603, F3. Underground: Westminster. Open to visitors Mon–Sat 9.30–3.30 and for worship on Sun. Opening times are subject to frequent change and are different for the abbey itself, the cloisters, Chapter House and museum. T: 020 7222 5152, westminster-abbey.org. Hefty admission charge.

Westminster Abbey, officially the Collegiate Church of St Peter in Westminster, holds a unique position in English history as the site of both the coronation and the burial of most English sovereigns. Though built at different periods, it is mainly (with the exception of Henry VII's magnificent Perpendicular chapel at the east end and the 18th-century west towers) in the Early English style, of which it constitutes one of the most impressive and best-preserved examples.

Special services are held in the abbey throughout the year and include the opening of the Law Courts in October, when judges in their robes walk in procession from the House of Lords.

HISTORY OF WESTMINSTER ABBEY

According to tradition, a church on Thorney Island or the Isle of Thorns was built by the East Saxons and consecrated by Mellitus, first Bishop of London, in 616; but there is no authentic record of any earlier church than that of the Benedictine Abbey, founded here in the 10th century and dedicated to St Peter. It received the name 'West Minster', or western monastery, probably from its position to the west of the City of London and its great cathedral of St Paul. King Edward the Confessor (d. 1066) rebuilt the abbey on a larger scale, using money that he had originally set aside for a pilgrimage to Rome. His Romanesque church was consecrated in 1065, and when he died the following year, his body was laid to rest here while his throne was contested by both the Saxon Harold and the Norman William. At the famous Battle of Hastings, William defeated Harold, and the long years of Norman rule began. Edward was canonised in 1161, after cures began to be reported at his tomb. He received the epithet 'Confessor' (to denote a devout man who had not died a martyr's death) and his body was placed in a new shrine. The abbey became a place of pilgrimage. Within this church, or its successor, every English sovereign since Harold (with the exceptions only of Edward V and Edward VIII) has been crowned. In 1220 the Lady Chapel was added at the east end, and in 1245 Henry III decided to honour Edward the Confessor by rebuilding the entire church in a more magnificent style, as it appears today. The architects were Henry de Reyns (1245–53), John of Gloucester (1253–60) and Robert of Beverley (1260–84). The influence of French cathedrals such as Rheims and Amiens and of the Sainte Chapelle in Paris can be seen in the height of the nave and the arrangement of the radial chapels at the east end.

In 1269 the new church was consecrated. From this time until the reign of George III the abbey became the royal burial church. In about 1388 Henry Yevele began to rebuild the nave for Archbishop Langham, and the work was continued after 1400 by William of Colchester; the design of Henry III's time was followed, with even the details little changed. The nave vault was completed by Abbot Islip in 1504–6. The new nave was hardly finished when the Lady Chapel was pulled down to make way for the magnificent Chapel of Henry VII (1503–19), attributed to Robert Vertue.

At the Dissolution, the abbey's community of Benedictine monks surrendered all their possessions, in perpetuity, to the king and his heirs. A new cathedral church was founded. Elizabeth I made the church a 'Royal peculiar' (directly responsible to the monarch) under an independent Dean and Chapter, whose successors administer it today. The extant monastic buildings date mainly from the 13th and 14th centuries, but there is Norman work in the Pyx Chamber and adjoining Undercroft.

The lower part of the west façade dates from c. 1390, but was altered by Hawksmoor; the towers (225ft high) were added by him in 1745. Sir Christopher Wren was appointed Surveyor in 1698. Since his day there have been several programmes of restoration.

INTERIOR OF THE ABBEY

The abbey is 513ft in length (including Henry VII's Lady Chapel), 200ft wide across the transepts and 75ft wide across the nave and aisles. The Chapel of Henry VII itself is 104.5ft long and 70ft wide.

Visitors enter from the north door and once in the north transept are encouraged to take a free audio guide to see the abbey in a designated order. As with all London's major historic attractions, the abbey is crowded all the time (three million tourists pass through its precincts each year) and in order to deal with the numbers, each visit is designed to be simple and quick, to make sense of the daunting and important number of funerary and commemorative monuments by outlining only the essential. It is not easy to wander at will around the abbey; 'The Way' is clearly delineated and potential avenues for deviation are cordoned off. The description below therefore follows the trail of the audio tour and attempts to flesh out the information along the way. Remain patient: a visit to the abbey is rewarding and should not be missed. If the audio guide appeals, the English-language version features the liquid diction of actor Jeremy Irons.

Once through the north door, head straight to the nave at the west end. The tour starts and finishes here.

The nave: centre and north: The nave appears to be homogenously of the 13th century but is actually a mixture of dates: the east part is the earliest; the western section dates from the 14th–16th centuries. Its height is striking: separated from the aisles by a tall arcade supported on circular columns, around each of which are grouped eight slender shafts of grey Purbeck marble, it is the loftiest Gothic nave in England. Above the arches runs the double triforium with exquisite tracery and diaperwork and, still higher, the tall clerestory.

Burials in the nave took place only after the Reformation. Many monuments throughout the church commemorate people who are not buried in the abbey; not all are mentioned here.

A few paces from the west door, in the centre of the nave, a slab of green marble is simply inscribed 'Remember Winston Churchill' **(1)**. It was placed here 'in accordance with the wishes of the Queen and Parliament' on the 25th anniversary of the Battle of Britain. Churchill's body lies at Bladon, Oxfordshire. Isolated by paper poppies in the centre of the floor is the **Tomb of the Unknown Warrior (2)**: the body of an unidentified soldier from Flanders interred on 11th November 1920, representing all the nameless British dead in the First World War. 'They buried him among the kings because he had done good toward God and toward his House.' He rests in earth brought from the battlefields.

The great benefactress Baroness

Burdett-Coutts is commemorated near the west door. In the centre of the nave, further east, is the grave of David Livingstone (d. 1873) **(3)**, traveller and missionary in Africa. Across the front of the Belfry Tower is a bronze effigy of Lord Salisbury (d. 1903) **(4)**. On the west wall is a bust of General Gordon (d. 1885), the defender of Khartoum, by Onslow Ford. Among the crowded monuments is one (east side) to Viscount Howe (d. 1758) by Scheemakers, erected by the Province of Massachusetts while it was a British colony.

North aisle: Across the head of the aisle is a large monument to Charles James Fox (d. 1806) **(5)**. Floor slabs commemorate Ramsay MacDonald (d. 1937), Lloyd George (d. 1945), Ernest Bevin (d. 1951), Clement Attlee (d. 1967) and the noted Fabians and admirers of Soviet Russia Sidney and Beatrice Webb (d. 1947 and 1943), who were buried here at the behest of George Bernard Shaw. On the wall is a monument to Campbell-Bannerman (d. 1908). Dean Stanley (Arthur Stanley, the liberal churchman who was Dean of Westminster from 1864–81) called this part of the abbey 'Whigs' Corner'.

In the third bay, a small stone upright in the wall at the bottom, inscribed 'O Rare Ben Johnson' [sic], marks the grave of the dramatist and poet Ben Jonson (d. 1637) **(6)**. The memorial was made, according to John Aubrey, 'at the charge of Jack Young (afterwards knighted) who, walking there when the grave was covering, gave the fellow eighteen pence to cut it.'

The north choir aisle has fine examples of early heraldry on the wall. A series of medallions under the organ (right) commemorate famous scientists, among them Charles Darwin (d. 1882; tomb in north nave aisle) and Lord Lister (d. 1912). Matching lozenges in the pavement honour men associated with music, including Elgar, Vaughan Williams, Britten, William Walton, Adrian Boult and C.V. Stanford. In the next bay William Wilberforce (d. 1833) **(7)**, one of the chief opponents of the slave trade, and Sir Stamford Raffles (1759–1833), founder of Singapore, sit pensive in effigy above the tomb of Henry Purcell (d. 1695) **(8)**, composer and organist at the abbey.

Choir and sanctuary: The choir screen (1834, with medieval masonry) is the work of Edward Blore. Set into it are two impressive works by Rysbrack and Kent commemorating Sir Isaac Newton (d. 1727) **(9)** and Earl Stanhope (d. 1721) **(10)**, faithful public servant of George I.

It is in the **sanctuary (11)**, the raised space within the altar rails, that coronations take place. The altar screen is by Sir George Gilbert Scott (1867). In front is a beautiful Cosmatesque pavement of 1268, signed 'Odoricus'; it is thought to be by the hand of a member of the Roman Oderisi family. The original brass inlaid letters specified its intended cosmological significance: '*Sphaericus archetypum globus hic monstrat macrocosmum*' (This round sphere represents a model of the universe): an appropriate place for the coronation and anointing of a temporal sovereign. On the left are three beautiful architectural tombs, dating from between c. 1298 and 1325. Buried within them are Edmund 'Crouchback' Plantagenet, Earl of Lancaster (d. 1296) **(12)**, second son of Henry III and founder of the House

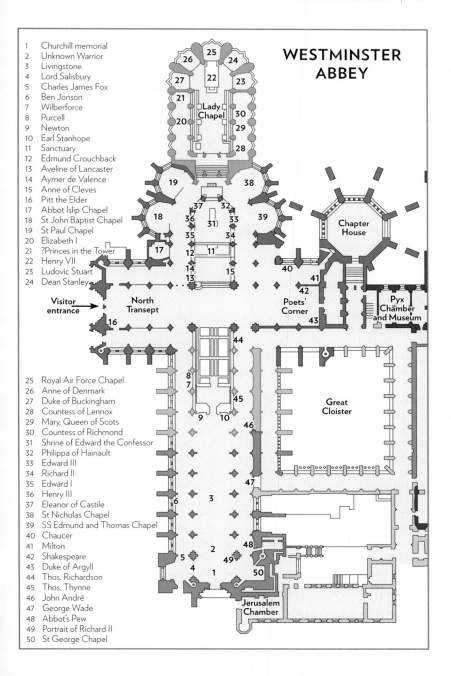

1 Churchill memorial
2 Unknown Warrior
3 Livingstone
4 Lord Salisbury
5 Charles James Fox
6 Ben Jonson
7 Wilberforce
8 Purcell
9 Newton
10 Earl Stanhope
11 Sanctuary
12 Edmund Crouchback
13 Aveline of Lancaster
14 Aymer de Valence
15 Anne of Cleves
16 Pitt the Elder
17 Abbot Islip Chapel
18 St John Baptist Chapel
19 St Paul Chapel
20 Elizabeth I
21 ?Princes in the Tower
22 Henry VII
23 Ludovic Stuart
24 Dean Stanley

25 Royal Air Force Chapel
26 Anne of Denmark
27 Duke of Buckingham
28 Countess of Lennox
29 Mary, Queen of Scots
30 Countess of Richmond
31 Shrine of Edward the Confessor
32 Philippa of Hainault
33 Edward III
34 Richard II
35 Edward I
36 Henry III
37 Eleanor of Castile
38 St Nicholas Chapel
39 SS Edmund and Thomas Chapel
40 Chaucer
41 Milton
42 Shakespeare
43 Duke of Argyll
44 Thos. Richardson
45 Thos. Thynne
46 John André
47 George Wade
48 Abbot's Pew
49 Portrait of Richard II
50 St George Chapel

WESTMINSTER
ABBEY

Lady Chapel

Chapter House

Visitor entrance

North Transept

Poets' Corner

Pyx Chamber and Museum

Great Cloister

Jerusalem Chamber

of Lancaster; his first wife Aveline, who died aged 15 in 1274 **(13)**; and Aymer de Valence, Earl of Pembroke (d. 1324) **(14)**.

On the right side of the sanctuary are sedilia dating from the time of Edward I, with a 15th-century Florentine altarpiece of the *Madonna and Child* by Bicci di Lorenzo. Below is the tomb of Anne of Cleves **(15)**, fourth wife of Henry VIII (d. 1557). The choir fittings were designed by Edward Blore in 1830.

North transept: The uniformity and proportions of the architecture in both transepts have been altered by the host of monuments and closures. Each transept is lit by a large rose window: the glass in the north transept is the oldest in the abbey, to a design of 1722 by Thornhill; below it on either side are exquisitely carved censing angels, sculpted by Master John of St Albans c. 1250.

Several eminent statesmen are commemorated here, including Richard Cobden, famous opponent of the Corn Laws (d. 1865; bust); Warren Hastings, Governor General of India (d. 1818); William Pitt, Earl of Chatham (d. 1778; huge monument) **(16)**; Lord Palmerston (d. 1865; statue) and Lord Castlereagh (d. 1821; statue). Towards the east wall are statues of George Canning (d. 1827) by Chantrey; Benjamin Disraeli (d. 1881) by Boehm; Gladstone (d. 1898) by Brock; and Sir Robert Peel (d. 1850) by Gibson.

North ambulatory: The backs of the tombs of Aymer de Valence and Edmund Crouchback are well seen from here. Opposite the former, on the left-hand pier, is a plaque to Aymer's wife, Countess of Pembroke, who founded Pembroke College, Cambridge. Also on the left is an overwhelming monument to General Wolfe in bas-relief by Joseph Wilton, commissioned by William Pitt to commemorate Wolfe's victory and death at Quebec in 1759. Behind are many monuments. To the left is a bust of Sir John Franklin, lost in the search for the Northwest Passage in 1847, with a noble verse by Tennyson: 'Not here: the white North has thy bones; and thou, heroic sailor-soul, art passing on thine happier voyage now toward no earthly pole...' To the right lies Sir Francis Vere (d. 1609), a distinguished soldier of Queen Elizabeth I. His magnificent Renaissance tomb is modelled on that of Engelbert II of Nassau (d. 1504) at Breda, where kneeling knights also bear a canopy strewn with accoutrements. The tomb of Lady Elizabeth Nightingale (d. 1731), with a menacing figure of Death emerging from below to threaten the lady with a spear, is by Roubiliac, clearly inspired by Bernini's monument to Pope Alexander VII in St Peter's in Rome. Other memorials are to the actress Mrs Siddons (d. 1831), in her celebrated pose as the Tragic Muse, a bust by Chantrey after Reynolds; the actor John Kemble (d. 1823), designed by Flaxman; and the engineer and bridge-builder Thomas Telford (d. 1834).

The **Chapel of Abbot Islip (17)** is of two storeys: the lower chapel, seen through a screen, is where Islip is buried. Islip was one of the last abbots of Westminster before the Reformation (1500–32). The ceiling is decorated with his rebus of a boy falling from a tree and the motto 'I slip'. The upper chapel is now the Florence Nightingale Chapel. Next door, the **Chapel of St John the Baptist (18)** is entered through the tiny Chapel of Our Lady of the Pew. Above the entrance is a delicately carved alabaster niche from the demolished Chapel of St Erasmus (15th century); just inside is a modern alabaster carving of the Virgin. Traces of the painted vault remain from the late 14th century. The large monument to Thomas Cecil, Earl of Exeter (d. 1623), son of Lord Burghley, features his effigy and that of his first wife. His second wife refused to accept the less honourable position on his left hand and was buried in Winchester Cathedral.

Opposite outside is a staircase leading to the **Chapel of St Edward the Confessor (31)**, east of the high altar. Access is restricted but you can glimpse the Confessor's shrine at the centre and see the tombs surrounding it from the ambulatory (*a fuller description of the chapel is given on p. 142*); note the grate of Queen Eleanor's tomb, an admirable specimen of English wrought-iron work by Thomas of Leighton (1294). The back of Henry III's tomb is visible from the ambulatory.

The **Chapel of St Paul (19)** has the restored, brightly-coloured tomb of Sir Lewis Robbesart, Lord Bourgchier (d. 1430), acting as a reminder that the medieval abbey would have been brightly painted. The chapel also contains a monument to Frances Sidney, Countess of Sussex (d. 1589), founder of Sidney Sussex College, Cambridge. The fine monument to Dudley Carleton (d. 1632) is by Nicholas Stone.

Henry VII's Lady Chapel: A flight of steps leads to the Lady Chapel or Chapel of Henry VII. Built in 1503–19, this chapel is the finest example in England of late Perpendicular or Tudor Gothic. Henry ordered it to be 'painted, garnished and adorned in as goodly and rich a manner as such work requireth and as to a king's work apperteyneth'. The culminating glory of its profuse decoration is the superb fan vaulting, hung with pendants in the nave, and stretched as a canopy to accommodate the bay windows in the aisles. The beautiful tall windows, curved in the aisles and angular in the apse, are particularly ingenious. The carving throughout is of the highest quality, and includes a series of 94 (originally 107) statues of saints popular at the time, with a frieze of angels and badges below. The chapel was begun as a shrine for Henry VI, and carved stalls of the Knights of the Bath separate the nave from the aisles. In 1725, it became the chapel of the Order of the Bath (reconstituted by George I), with the Dean of Westminster its perpetual dean.

A doorway (left) leads to the north aisle, in the centre of which is the tall canopied **tomb of Elizabeth I** (d. 1603) **(20)**, erected by James I. Elizabeth rests here in the same grave as her half-sister Mary I (d. 1558); the Latin inscription translates: 'Partners in realm and tomb, here we sisters rest, Elizabeth and Mary, in hope of resurrection'. The marble figure is the work of Cornelius Cure (1605–7); Elizabeth's jewels are by the 20th-century British jeweller Sah Oved. The east end of this aisle was called 'Innocents' Corner' by Dean Stanley, for here are commemorated two small daughters of James I (d. 1607) **(21)**, one represented in a cradle which is the actual tomb (the infant's effigy is seen in the mirror which has been placed opposite). In the marble urn between them, made to a design by Sir Christopher

WESTMINSTER ABBEY
Early 15th-century fan vaulting in the Lady Chapel.

Wren, are some bones, claimed as those of Edward V and his brother Richard, Duke of York, the young sons of Edward IV, who disappeared from the Tower c. 1483. Edward V had been born in the abbey sanctuary, where his mother had sought refuge from the Lancastrian faction. The Latin inscription on the urn expresses no doubt that the boys were suffocated in the Tower by order of their perfidious and usurping uncle Richard III. The jury is still out on this case.

Now proceed through oak and plated bronze doors to the nave of the Lady Chapel. The doors date from the 16th century and the heraldic devices that appear on them and recur elsewhere in the decoration of the chapel refer to Henry VII's ancestry and to his claims to the throne. The Welsh dragon indicates his Tudor father; the daisy (marguerite) plant and the portcullis refer to his Lancastrian mother, Margaret Beaufort; the falcon was the badge of Edward IV, father of Elizabeth of York, whom Henry married; the greyhound is that of the Nevilles, from whom she was descended. The crown on a bush recalls Henry's first coronation on Bosworth Field, when the defeated Richard's crown was plucked from a thorn tree; while the roses are those of Lancaster and York united by his marriage. Other emblems are the lions of England and the fleur-de-lys of France. On each side are the beautiful carved stalls of the Knights of the Bath, with the arms of its successive holders emblazoned on small copper plates and the banner of the current holder suspended above. The lower seats are those of the esquires (no longer used as such) with their coats of arms. Beneath the seats are a number of carved misericords. A certain Thomas Rixon has carved his name on one of the seats on the south side.

The altar dates from 1935 but is a reconstruction of the original; the painting of the *Virgin and Child* is by the 15th-century Venetian artist Bartolomeo Vivarini. Beneath the pavement, lozenges with faded inscriptions mark the resting place of several Hanoverians, including George II (d. 1760; the last king buried in the abbey). Below the altar is the grave of Edward VI (d. 1553). Behind it, surrounded by a bronze screen, is the magnificent **tomb of Henry VII (22)** (d. 1509) and Elizabeth of York (d. 1503), an important work in marble and gilt-bronze by Pietro Torrigiano, completed c. 1518. The noble effigies of the king and queen lie on a black marble sarcophagus, with a carved frieze of white marble and adorned with gilt medallions of saints. James I (d. 1625) is buried in the same vault as Henry VII and his queen. The first apse chapel on the south is filled by Le Sueur's gilt-canopied monument to Ludovic Stuart **(23)**, Duke of Lennox and Richmond (d. 1624), coloniser of Ulster and of Maine in the United States; in the next is buried Dean Stanley (d. 1881) **(24)**, with a fine effigy by Boehm.

The east chapel is the **Royal Air Force Chapel (25)**. The window, by Hugh Easton, commemorating the Battle of Britain (July–Oct 1940), incorporates in the design the badges of the 63 fighter squadrons that took part. The chapel keeps the Roll of Honour (facsimile in adjoining chapel) of the 1,497 airmen of Britain and her allies who fell in the battle. Nearby is the grave of Lord Dowding (d. 1970), who commanded the air defence of Great Britain, and on the south side that of Lord Trenchard (d. 1956), 'father' of the RAF. In this chapel

Oliver Cromwell (d. 1658) was buried (stone at entrance), only to be exhumed after the Restoration and symbolically hung at Tyburn. His head was struck off and afterwards exposed on Westminster Hall (*see also Red Lion Square, p. 353*).

In the next chapel is a vault (usually covered with an organ) with the graves of Anne of Denmark (d. 1619) **(26)**, queen of James I, and Anne Mowbray, the child wife of Richard, Duke of York, the younger of the Princes in the Tower. Anne died at the age of eight; her remains were reburied here in 1965. In the last chapel is the large tomb by Le Sueur of George, Duke of Buckingham (assassinated in 1628) **(27)**, the favourite of James I and Charles I, with statues of his children by Nicholas Stone.

In the south aisle is the tomb of Margaret, Countess of Lennox (d. 1578) **(28)**. Her son, Henry Darnley, was the second husband of Mary, Queen of Scots and father of James I of England, and his figure among the effigies of her children on the sides of the tomb may be identified by the (restored) crown over his head (as Henry I of Scotland). Under a tall canopy is the recumbent figure of **Mary, Queen of Scots** (1542–87) **(29)**, whose remains were removed here from Peterborough Cathedral in 1612 by order of her son, James I. The work of Cornelius and William Cure (1605–10), this was the last royal tomb erected in Westminster Abbey.

The tomb of Margaret Beaufort, Countess of Richmond (d. 1509) **(30)**, mother of Henry VII, patron of Wynkyn de Worde and founder of Christ's and St John's colleges at Cambridge, has a beautiful gilded effigy, a masterpiece by Pietro Torrigiano of Florence, noted for the delicate modelling of the hands.

Chapel of Edward the Confessor:
The Chapel of St Edward the Confessor is the most ancient, the most gorgeous and the most sacred part of the church. Visiting it is therefore restricted but from the north and south ambulatories one can peep in and recognise the monuments. In the middle stands the mutilated Cosmatesque **Shrine of St Edward the Confessor** (d. 1066) **(31)**, erected in the late 13th century by 'Peter of Rome', possibly the son of Odoricus, and showing traces of the original mosaics. The upper part, now of wood (1557), was originally a golden shrine decorated with jewels and gold images of saints, all of which disappeared at the Dissolution. In the recesses of the base, sick people used to spend the night in hope of a cure.

On the south side of the shrine is the tomb of Philippa of Hainault (d. 1369) **(32)**, wife of Edward III, with an alabaster effigy by Hennequin de Liège, sculptor to the King of France. The elaborate **tomb of Edward III** (d. 1377) **(33)** has niches in which were statuettes of his 14 children, six of which remain (seen from south ambulatory). The last tomb on this side is that of **Richard II** (d. 1400) **(34)** and his first wife Anne of Bohemia (d. 1394), which is in the same style as that of Edward III. It is profusely decorated with delicately engraved patterns, among which may be distinguished the broom-pods of the Plantagenets, the white hart, the rising sun, etc.; the beautiful paintings in the canopy represent the *Trinity*, the *Coronation of the Virgin*, and Anne of Bohemia's coat of arms.

At the west end is a beautiful screen (mid-15th century) with 14 scenes of the life of Edward the Confessor. In front are remains of the Cosmati pavement.

On the north side is the plain altar-tomb, without effigy, of **Edward I** (d. 1307) **(35)**; in 1744 his body (6ft 2in long) was found to be in good preservation, dressed in royal robes with a gilt crown. Beyond are the Gothic tombs of **Henry III** (d. 1272) **(36)** and his daughter-in-law, Eleanor of Castile (d. 1290) **(37)**, wife of Edward I. Both the bronze effigies, the earliest cast in England, are by William Torel, a London goldsmith.

South ambulatory: The **Chapel of St Nicholas (38)**, off the south ambulatory, is the vault of the dukes of Northumberland, the only family with right of sepulture in the abbey.

The **Chapel of SS Edmund and Thomas the Martyr (39)** is separated from the ambulatory by an ancient oak screen and entered across a very worn threshhold. Inside to the right lies William de Valence, 1st Earl of Pembroke (d. 1296), half-brother of Henry III. This is the only example of champlevé Limoges enamel in England. The seated figure of Lady Elizabeth Russell (d. 1601), showing her with her eyes closed and her foot upon a skull, is the earliest non-recumbent statue in the abbey. Beside the door is the tomb of John of Eltham (1316–37), second son of Edward II. This is the earliest alabaster effigy in the abbey and is interesting for the careful representation of the prince's armour. Opposite the entrance to this chapel is the outer side of Edward III's tomb, with finely worked little brass statuettes of his children, with enamelled coats of arms. The back of Richard II's tomb is also well seen.

South transept: The south transept is known as **Poets' Corner**, taking its name originally from the tombs of Chaucer and Spenser. More than 100 writers and other creative artists are now commemorated here, on the walls and in the floor. Poets' Corner is officially full and the abbey has further memorials in the two windows of the transept. The first to be unveiled (in 1996) commemorates the poet A.E. Housman (d. 1936). Memorials have also overflowed into the south end of the central aisle and John Betjeman (d. 1984), former Poet Laureate, was in 1996 squeezed in with a small silver tablet on a pillar. On the end wall of the transept are two magnificent wall-paintings of *St Christopher* and the *Incredulity of St Thomas*. Uncovered in 1936, they are ascribed to Walter of Durham (c. 1280) and are outstanding examples of the Westminster school of painting.

There are too many memorials to enumerate. Those mentioned below are either actual burials or monuments of artistic importance: the bust of John Dryden (d. 1700; buried here) is by Scheemakers and that of William Blake (d. 1827) by Epstein. The Gothic **tomb of Geoffrey Chaucer** (d. 1400) **(40)**, the poet of the *Canterbury Tales*, was erected 155 years after his death. In front of Chaucer's tomb is the grave of Robert Browning (d. 1889) and a bust of Tennyson (d. 1892; also buried here).

Rysbrack's memorial to John Milton (d. 1674) **(41)** was only placed here in 1737, having been delayed by political feeling for over 60 years after the poet's death. Dr Samuel Johnson (d. 1784; buried here) is commemorated with a bust by Nollekens. The actors David Garrick and Henry Irving are also buried here, as are the ashes of Sir Laurence Olivier.

William Shakespeare (d. 1616) **(42)** is commemorated with a statue by

Scheemakers, erected in 1740 with lines from *The Tempest*. At the corners of the pedestal are carved heads representing Elizabeth I, Henry V and Richard III. James Thomson (d. 1748), who wrote the words of 'Rule Britannia', is commemorated in a fine monument designed by Robert Adam. Above the door to the Chapel of St Faith is a portrait medallion by Nollekens of Oliver Goldsmith (1728–74; date of birth given wrongly in the epitaph), with an epitaph by Johnson.

The roster of famous names continues to the right of the chapel and includes John Ruskin (d. 1900), with a memorial roundel by Onslow Ford. Ruskin declined the offer of a Westminster Abbey funeral and was buried at his home at Coniston in the Lake District. The monument to John Campbell, 2nd Duke of Argyll (d. 1743) **(43)** is an exceptionally fine work by Roubiliac. Above on the west wall is Handel (d. 1759), also by Roubiliac, holding the script of *Messiah* (a slab in the floor marks his grave, and one beside it that of Charles Dickens). Also in the floor is a tablet commemorating Thomas Hardy (d. 1928), whose ashes are interred here, and the grave of Rudyard Kipling (d. 1936).

South aisle: Opposite the east door into the cloisters are good monuments to William Thynne (d. 1584) and to Sir Thomas Richardson (d. 1635) **(44)**, in black marble, by Le Sueur. In his capacity as Chief Justice, Richardson refused to allow the assassin of the Duke of Buckingham (also buried here; no 27) to be tortured on the rack. Further on is a monument by Rysbrack to Sir Godfrey Kneller (d. 1723), the only painter commemorated in the abbey. In the third bay

is a tablet to William Tyndale (d. 1536), translator of the Bible. Under the organ loft is a monument to Thomas Thynne (d. 1682) **(45)**, with a bas-relief depicting his murder (he was shot in Haymarket in a love feud). Commemorated further on is Major John André (d. 1780) **(46)**, hanged by Washington as a spy during the War of American Independence; the bas-relief shows Washington receiving André's vain petition for a soldier's death. Floor-slabs in front of the next bay mark the graves of Andrew Bonar Law (d. 1923) and Neville Chamberlain (d. 1944), prime ministers.

Above the West Cloister door is a dramatic monument by Roubiliac to Field-Marshal George Wade (d. 1748) **(47)**, who provided the Scottish Highlands with roads and bridges in 1720–30. In the last bay is a small gallery of oak called the Abbot's Pew **(48)**, erected by Abbot Islip (16th century), and below, a memorial to the dramatist William Congreve (d. 1729).

On the first nave pier hangs a **portrait of Richard II (49)**, the oldest contemporary portrait of an English monarch. **St George's Chapel (50)** (*no entry*) is dedicated to all who gave their lives in the World Wars and containing a tablet to the million British dead. Here is the **Coronation Chair**, made in oak by Walter of Durham c. 1300–1. It has left the abbey only three times—when Cromwell was installed as Lord Protector in Westminster Hall, and for safety during the two World Wars. It enclosed the famous Stone of Scone (*see below*), carried off from Scotland by Edward I in 1297 and used for all subsequent coronations of English monarchs.

THE STONE OF SCONE

This historic block of sandstone, on which all kings of Scotland were crowned from time immemorial down to John Balliol (1292), was traditionally identified with Jacob's pillow, upon which he rested his head when he had his famous dream, afterwards transported to Ireland, where it became the *Lia Fail* or 'Stone of Destiny' on the sacred hill of Tara. Historically it is recorded as being used for the enthronement of Macbeth's stepson at Scone in 1057, and was certainly in use there earlier. It was seized by Edward I, 'Hammer of the Scots', in 1297, and taken to London, where it was built into the Coronation Chair. Its sacred property as the *palladium*, or safeguard, of Scottish independence was supposed to have been vindicated when James VI of Scotland became James I of England in 1603. In 1996, the British Government ordered the stone's removal to Edinburgh Castle, with the provision that it should return to Westminster Abbey for future coronations.

CHAPTER HOUSE AND PYX CHAMBER

Entrance to the cloisters is by two doors from the south aisle. From them you have good views of the abbey's flying buttresses. The East Walk leads to the Chapter House, Pyx Chamber and Abbey Museum. The **Chapter House** is an impressive octagonal room, 56ft in diameter, built c. 1245–55 above the crypt of the Confessor's chapter house. The lofty roof is supported by a single central shaft, 35ft high, and it is lit by six huge windows. The tracery, like the roof, is modern, though copied from the blank window which escaped mutilation in the Reformation. The tiling at the centre is original. The arcading on the walls is adorned with medieval paintings (partly restored) of the life of St John and of the Apocalypse, with a frieze of animals below, presented by John of Northampton (1372–1404), a Westminster monk. The beautiful *Angel Gabriel* and *Virgin Annunciate* above the door date from 1250–3. The Chapter House is especially memorable as the 'cradle of representative and constitutional government throughout the world', for here the early House of Commons, separated from the House of Lords in the reign of Edward III, held its meetings until 1547, when it moved to St Stephen's Chapel at the Palace of Westminster. On your return to the cloister, note the wooden door on your left (c. 1050); the oldest door in London.

The **Pyx Chamber** is entered through a Norman archway and massive double door; each door has three locks. It was part of the 11th-century undercroft beneath the monks' dormitory and became the royal treasury in the 13th century. The altar is the oldest in the abbey.

ABBEY MUSEUM

The vaulted Abbey Museum (*usually open daily 10.30–4*) houses the famous royal effigies. The earliest effigies date from the 14th century, when wooden images—instead of the actual corpse—were used during state funeral procedures: the effigy would have been used for the lying-in-state, would have been placed on top of the coffin for the journey to the abbey and for the duration of the funeral, and sometimes marked the place of burial in the abbey prior to the erection of the monument. Westminster Abbey has 21 effigies, which can be divided into three groups: medieval wooden effigies of monarchs and members of the royal family; later 17th-century wax figures of royal and noble persons, not used during the funeral ceremonial but placed in the abbey as reminders of the deceased, probably near to the place of burial; and later wax figures of 'celebrities', tourist attractions which boosted the meagre incomes of the monument guides.

The earliest of the **wooden effigies** is that of Edward III, which was used at his funeral in 1377, placed on his coffin within a magnificent hearse. The body, which would have been clothed in costly robes provided by the Great Wardrobe, is of carved wood. The head is based on a death mask and is the earliest known likeness of an English monarch. Anne of Bohemia's carved wooden head, long and thin, is all that remains of her effigy (queen of Richard II, she died at the palace of Sheen in 1394). Also head-only is Elizabeth of York's effigy, which contemporary accounts indicate was incredibly life-like. Henry VII's bust, a painted gesso death mask applied over wood, is a powerfully realistic and skilled likeness (the death mask was the source for Pietro Torrigiano's celebrated terracotta sculpture of the king at the V&A; *see p. 329*). Mary I's wooden head is also here, and the body of the original effigy of Elizabeth I, still with its under-garments and corset. The wax effigy beside it was made in the 18th century.

After the Restoration in 1660 **wax effigies** were introduced, wax being a medium which offered a more startling likeness. The effigies have wax heads and hands, with painted complexions, wigs of real hair and eyelashes of bristle or canine hair. The bodies are of stuffed canvas, clothed in contemporary or near-contemporary dress and jewels, sometimes in garments which had belonged to the deceased. Charles II stands tall and realistic, in his own Garter Robes and monogrammed undergarments. Queen Anne is represented seated. Frances Theresa Stuart, Duchess of Richmond and Lennox, 'La Belle Stuart', was a court beauty who in the 1660s resisted the advances of Charles II. By her side is her pet of 40 years, an African parrot, which died a few days after her. If original, it is one of the earliest examples of taxidermy in the country.

The figures of Nelson and Pitt are not funeral effigies but were added to attract visitors. They are outstanding as portraits. Nelson wears his own clothes and the shoe buckles he wore at Trafalgar.

Also on display is one of the abbey's finest treasures: the **Westminster Retable**. This richly painted and decorated altarpiece is the oldest altarpiece in England (c. 1270). The surviving exquisite paintings depict St Peter, the Virgin, St John the Evangelist and some of the miracles of Christ.

VICTORIA EMBANKMENT

Map p. 603, F2. Underground: Westminster.

Victoria Embankment, which runs from Westminster Bridge to Blackfriars Bridge, was completed in 1870 to a design by civil engineer Sir Joseph Bazalgette. Bazalgette reclaimed 37½ acres of land to construct a road with a dual purpose: to relieve traffic congestion in the Strand and Fleet Street and to carry sewage beneath it. Previously all waste and effluent ran into the Thames and cholera was rife. Crisis was reached in 1858 when a scorching summer caused the unspeakable 'Great Stink', which was suffered acutely in Central London. The smell of the polluted Thames was so disgusting that MPs were driven from the House of Commons. From 1859 construction started and after completion around 1875, London's drinking water and riverscape were purified. Bazalgette's subterranean sewer network was a true wonder of the Victorian age and still serves London today, thanks to his deliberately extravagant pipe widths. As he rightly predicted, 'there's always the unseen.'

The section of Victoria Embankment described here is the stretch from Westminster Bridge to Hungerford Bridge and Charing Cross station.

Westminster Bridge was designed by Thomas Page in 1862. On the left-hand side of it is Thornycroft's **statue of Boudica** and her two daughters, driving her chariot (without reins) to victory against the Romans. Below is Westminster Pier, with boat services up and down river. Down by the water is the **Battle of Britain monument**, commemorating all those who took to the skies in defence of Britain from the Luftwaffe. Overlooking the Thames at Whitehall Stairs is the **RAF Memorial**, a large gilded eagle poised to fly ('I bear you on eagle's wings and brought you unto myself'), by William Reid Dick with a stone pedestal by R. Blomfield (1923).

Lining the Embankment above the road are government office buildings. The corner site is occupied by **Portcullis House** (2001) on top of Westminster Underground station, its great bronze chimneys giving it the air of a neo-Tudor parliamentary factory. Next door, the pair of neo-Gothic buildings in red and white banded brick, the Norman Shaw Buildings (1887–1906), are named after the architect who built them. Outside the Modernist Ministry of Defence building, the **Chindit Badge** commemorates those who fought in North Burma during World War Two. Surmounting the plinth is a mythical *chinthe*, the beast that guards Burmese temples. On the further corner are the fragmentary remains (reconstructed) of **Queen Mary's Steps**, part of a river terrace built for Mary II by Wren in 1691–3. In the 17th century, the steps would have provided direct access from the royal barge to Whitehall Palace.

The green stretch beyond Horse Guards is **Whitehall Gardens**, laid out in 1875 by Vulliamy. Overlooking the gardens is the elaborate, late 19th-century neo-Gothic façade of **Whitehall Court** (when viewed from the Blue Bridge in St James's Park it looks like every little girl's embodiment of a fairytale castle), with Waterhouse's National Liberal Club (1887) at one end. The major part, by Archer & Green (1892), was built as luxury flats and includes the former Horseguards Hotel (being refurbished at the time of writing and due to reopen as the luxurious Clermont). In front of Whitehall Gardens is a monument to Samuel Plimsoll (d. 1898), inventor of the Plimsoll Line, erected 'in grateful recognition of his services to the men of the sea of all nations'. Over the road, in the river wall, the Embankment engineer Sir Joseph Bazalgette is commemorated in a bust by George Simonds (1899). Moored here are the *Tattersall Castle*, a Clyde paddle-steamer, now a pub, and the *Hispaniola*, a restaurant.

WHITEHALL

Map p. 603, F2. Underground: Westminster.

Whitehall, which has become a figure of speech denoting British governmental administration, is the wide boulevard that stretches for half a mile from Parliament Square to Charing Cross, where government offices and ministries are based. On this site, from the river to St James's Park, stretched Henry VIII's Palace of Whitehall, which burned down in 1698; today only archaeological fragments and Inigo Jones's Banqueting House remain from the great complex.

OLD WHITEHALL PALACE

Whitehall Palace originated in a mansion purchased in 1240 by Walter de Grey, Archbishop of York, which for nearly 300 years became the London residence of his successors. When Cardinal Wolsey became archbishop, he embellished the palace (on the river side) with characteristic extravagance and Henry VIII seized the desirable property in 1529. He changed its name from York Place to Whitehall (a name then generally applied to any centre of festivities) and acquired more land towards St James's Park, on which he erected a tiltyard, cockpit and tennis courts. Whitehall became the chief residence of the court in London. Anne Boleyn was brought here on the day of her marriage to Henry in 1533 and in 1536 it was the scene of Henry's marriage to Jane Seymour. Henry died in the palace in 1547.

Masques by Ben Jonson, with sets by Inigo Jones and James Shirley, were frequently presented at the court in the time of James I and Charles I. Plans for a huge and sumptuous new palace for James I, drawn up by Inigo Jones and John Webb, were never carried out although the new Banqueting House (*described on p. 150*) was completed in 1622. Charles I was executed in front of it in 1649. Oliver Cromwell died in the palace in 1658. Under Charles II, Whitehall became the centre of revelry and intrigue described by Pepys, and James II fled into exile from here in 1688. The offering of the Crown to William and Mary provided the last great ceremonial function here in 1689. In 1698 the palace was accidentally burned to the ground and the royal residence was transferred to St James's Palace (*see p. 159*).

Start from Parliament Street—where younger generations of tourists fall over themselves to photograph each other posing in old-fashioned red telephone boxes, historic London relics in their own right—and walk up towards Nelson's Column.

On your left are grandiose government complexes; the corner building overlooking Parliament Street and Parliament Square is the **Treasury** (Brydon, 1917), which connects via a bridge over King Charles Street to Sir George Gilbert Scott's **Foreign Office** of 1868. The building, in Inigo Jones style, covers 5.5 acres. When the British Empire was at its height, it incorporated the Foreign Office, the India Office, the Colonial Office and the Home Office. During World War Two, a sprawling underground network of concrete reinforced, bomb-proof rooms was built for Churchill's War Cabinet underneath the portion of these buildings that overlooks St James's Park. These now form an exhibition called the **Churchill War Rooms**, where you can see the transatlantic telephone from which Churchill spoke to President Roosevelt in the White House. Access is from Horse Guards Road by the Clive Steps, which has a statue of Clive of India (*open daily 9.30–6, admission charge; T: 020 7930 6961, iwm.org.uk*).

CHURCHILL WAR ROOMS

Map p. 603, F2. Open daily 9.30–6 (last admission at 5). Admission charge. Café and shop. T: 020 7930 6961, iwm.org.uk/visits/churchill-war-rooms.

'This is the room from which I will direct the war,' announced Churchill on first visiting the Cabinet War Rooms, which are located 10ft underground, with reinforced concrete above, hence the nickname, 'The Slab'. Constructed between June 1938 and August 1939, and only completed a week before Britain's declaration of war, they were the operations headquarters from which Britain's Second World War effort was directed during air raids. Much is still as it was during the War. The wall maps in the Map Room, for example, are punctured with pin marks representing the movements of the Allied convoys; and on a desk sit the variously coloured phones known as the 'beauty chorus', which connected the bunker to control rooms around the country. The Transatlantic Telephone Room was where Churchill spoke in private to President Roosevelt. The small permanent exhibition entitled 'Undercover: Life in Churchill's Bunker', tells of the day-to-day life of the people who often worked 16-hour shifts here. Through oral histories and filmed interviews there are reminiscences, for example from Elizabeth Layton, one of Churchill's personal private secretaries and author of the memoir *Mr Churchill's Secretary* (1958), who recalls the wartime leader's character flaws and towering greatness in equal measure.

In the middle of Whitehall rises the **Cenotaph** (1920), Lutyens's monument to the Glorious Dead of the First World War. In its dignified simplicity it now commemorates the dead from all wars and is the UK's national war memorial. Every year the Remembrance Day ceremony takes place on the Sunday nearest to the 11th Nov (Armistice Day). Members of the Royal Family, the Government and Opposition and other representatives lay poppy wreaths around the Cenotaph, and two minutes' silence are observed. Just beyond is the national monument to the Women of World War II, unveiled in 2005.

At 70 Whitehall, the 19th-century building with Corinthian order and ornamental frieze is the **Cabinet Office** and former old Treasury by Sir Charles Barry (1844–7), incorporating earlier parts by Sir John Soane and William Kent as well as excavated relics of Whitehall Palace, including Henry VIII's tennis courts. Next door, the Palladian **Dover House** is used by the Scotland Office. Designed in 1758 by James Paine for Sir Matthew Featherstonhaugh, it was remodelled by Henry Holland (portico and dome) for Prince Frederick, Duke of York in 1792, then belonged to the Melbourne family until 1830. Opposite, in the middle of the road, is an equestrian statue of the First World War commander Earl Haig (d. 1928), erected in 1937. The colossal **Ministry of Defence building**, headquarters of the British Armed Forces (E. Vincent Harris,

1939–59), dominates the east side of Whitehall as well as the river view. Inside are the remains of Cardinal Wolsey's wine cellar, later appropriated by Henry VIII. In front are statues of Field Marshals Montgomery (Oscar Nemon, 1980), Alanbrooke (Ivor Roberts-Jones, 1993) and Slim (with binoculars; Ivor Roberts-Jones, 1990). The main entrance is in Horse Guards Avenue (behind Banqueting House) flanked by colossal sculptures, *Earth* and *Water* (Sir Charles Wheeler, 1949–52).

Next door is the attractive **Gwydyr House** (1772), the Welsh Office, and then the only surviving part of Whitehall Palace: the Banqueting House (*described below*). Beyond Banqueting House are more vast government complexes. The huge building with façades on Whitehall and Horse Guards Avenue is the former War Office (William Young, 1906). The building just before Great Scotland Yard is the former Ministry of Agriculture and Fisheries (John Murray, 1909). **Great Scotland Yard** itself was the location of the headquarters of the Metropolitan Police until 1891. The street name originates from a mansion occupied before the 15th century by the kings of Scotland and their ambassadors when in London. Members of the retinue of James I are thought to have had their first kirk here (*see p. 251*). In popular parlance and crime fiction, Scotland Yard stands for anything connected with London policing and detective work.

DOWNING STREET

Tucked away behind wrought-iron gates and a police presence, this narrow street (*map p. 603, F2*), built in the 1680s by Sir George Downing (a member of the first class to graduate from Harvard in 1642; later a profiteering soldier and diplomat who served both Cromwell and Charles II), is famous out of all proportion to its appearance as the residence of the British Prime Ministers since 1735. No. 10 Downing St became the property of the Crown in 1732 and George II offered it as a gift to Sir Robert Walpole, who accepted it for his office as First Lord of the Treasury. From that day it became the official residence of Prime Ministers, although many in the early years preferred to live on their own—often far grander—houses. William Kent redesigned the interior in 1732 and further alterations were made by Sir John Soane, who designed the impressive State Dining Room. The narrow front of the building belies its size; it is really two amalgamated houses containing 160 rooms and offices as well as the Prime Minister's private apartments. No. 11 Downing St became the residence of the Second Lord of the Treasury, the Chancellor of the Exchequer, in 1805.

Before Downing Street became the official residence of the Prime Minister, other well-known people lived in it, including James Boswell, who took lodgings here in 1762, and Tobias Smollett, who set up a doctor's practice here c. 1745–8.

BANQUETING HOUSE

Map p. 603, F2. Open daily 10–5 (but often closed for official functions; details are posted on the website). Admission charge. Small shop. T: 0844 482 7777 (from within UK); hrp.org.uk.

The Banqueting House, on the corner of Whitehall and Horse Guards Avenue, is the most complete remnant of the old Whitehall Palace, the principal residence and seat of government of the Tudor and Stuart monarchy. The residential part was almost totally destroyed in a fire in 1698, but the Banqueting House was saved.

Erected in 1619–22, the building was conceived as a setting for formal spectacles and grand court ceremonies. The design was entrusted to the great architect Inigo Jones, whose approach to architecture, based on Classical Roman models, the mathematical principles of Vitruvius and the geometrically proportioned designs of Palladio, was revolutionary in Britain. Jones's strict use of the orders, Ionic below and Corinthian above, and of alternate triangular and segmental window pediments, produced a rational, measured and dignified building of tremendous impact. Externally the building has been altered: sash windows were installed in 1713 and in the 19th century it was given a Portland stone façade. Internally, however, it has been restored to how it would have appeared in early Stuart times, the double cube proportions of its main hall upstairs providing a fitting stage for state occasions. It was here that the sovereign touched for the King's Evil, an ancient ceremony performed for those with scrofula (last performed by Queen Anne; Samuel Johnson was a beneficiary); and it was also where the Maundy Thursday ritual of the washing of the feet of the poor and distribution of money was performed by the monarch. After the 1698 fire, William III had the building converted into the Chapel Royal, a function it retained until the 1890s. It is now used for formal royal and state occasions and banquets.

The main hall

The hall is approached by the main stairway, added in 1808–9 by James Wyatt to replace the original timber structure. Though the stairs are not the same as in Stuart days, the window aperture is the very one through which, on 30th January 1649, King Charles I was led out to the scaffold, built up against the exterior wall.

The king and court would enter the main hall at the north end, where the throne, under its symbolic canopy of state, was erected. The public was admitted from the south (still the case today). Beanbags are scattered on the floor and you are invited to sprawl on them to admire the magnificent painted ceiling.

Peter Paul Rubens, an artist already fêted by the courts of Europe, and whom the Stuart monarchy was eager to engage, was commissioned in 1629–30. He presented to Charles I his great painting *Peace and War* (now in the National Gallery), was knighted, and then set to work on the nine Banqueting House canvases on his return to Antwerp. The completed works were installed by 1636 (Rubens was paid the princely sum of £3,000 and never saw them *in situ*). Their theme was the glorification of the peaceful rule of James I: the canvases are filled with the kind of heavy allegory of wise and beneficent rule that was so popular at the courts of France, Italy and the Vatican but had yet to be seen in Britain. As you enter from the south, you are immediately struck by the central oval, the *Apotheosis of James I*, the king borne heavenwards by Religion and Justice, his temporal crown carried by putti while Minerva (Wisdom) holds out a wreath of laurel. Above the throne, visible the right way round to the visitor entering from the south, is the *Benefits of the Government of James I*. Peace and Plenty embrace, Minerva defends the throne against Mars (War). On either side are ovals with the *Triumph of Reason over Discord* and *Triumph of Abundance over Avarice*.

At the north end, visible to the king seated on his throne, is the *Union of England and Scotland*, showing James I gesturing towards a child, the new-born fruit of the two countries' union, while Britannia holds the joined crowns above his head. To left and right are *Minerva driving Rebellion to Hell* and *Hercules beating down Envy*.

On the installation of the canvases, the Banqueting House ceased to stage court masques or theatrical spectacles which involved flaming or smoking torches.

HORSE GUARDS PARADE

Opposite Banqueting House is **Horse Guards**, a white stone Palladian building with a central arch surmounted by a clock tower, built in the 1750s by William Robinson and John Vardy, influenced by the designs of William Kent. It is the official entrance from Whitehall to St James's Palace, via St James's Park, and the headquarters of the London District of the British Army and of the Household Cavalry; the Household Cavalry Museum is located here too. Two mounted troopers of the Life Guards or Royal Horse Guards (or Blues and Royals) are posted here daily and there are two dismounted sentries within the archway. The former are relieved hourly, the latter every two hours (no doubt a welcome relief, as they are nearly always surrounded by tourists taking photos). During the Changing of the Guard, the guard on duty is relieved by a new guard of twelve men who troop in via the Mall.

The passage beneath the clock tower is the entrance to **Horse Guards Parade**, a wide parade ground on the fringes of St James's Park, formerly Henry VIII's tiltyard and where Elizabeth I's birthday was celebrated. In May and June the Parade Ground is used for the ceremonies of Beating the Retreat, when military music and parades are performed under floodlights in the early evening, and Trooping the Colour, the Queen's Official Birthday parade on the second or third Saturday in June. The Trooping the Colour ceremony is preceded by a parade along the Mall, when the Queen and other members of the royal household ride on horseback or by royal coach to Horse Guards.

Straight ahead is the Guards' Monument (1925–6). On the right-hand side, the vast neo-Wren wing in red brick and white stone with green copper domes is the Admiralty extension (1888–1905), connected to Admiralty Arch (*see below*). On your left are the high-walled gardens of Downing Street and statues of Kitchener by John Tweed and Earl Mountbatten of Burma by Franta Belsky.

In front of the Horse Guards archway are two equestrian statues and the **Cadiz Memorial**, a huge mortar from Cadiz presented by the Spanish Government in 1814, mounted on the back of a winged dragon.

THE MALL

Map p. 603, F2–E2. Underground: Embankment, Charing Cross.

The Mall is the spacious avenue lined with double rows of plane trees that skirts St James's Park on the north. It is London's only parade route (on official occasions barriers go up along the pavements) and it also provides an impressive finish for the London Marathon each spring. At the weekend this area is quiet, though full of visitors strolling in the park and along The Mall.

The sweeping curve of **Admiralty Arch** forms an impressive entrance to The Mall. From it there is a striking view down the 'triumphal avenue' to the Victoria Memorial and Buckingham Palace, which close the vista. This massive triumphal arch was designed by Sir Aston Webb as part of the national memorial to Queen Victoria. On the left is the startling red brick of the Admiralty extension block. On the right, in front of the modern British Council headquarters, is the gentle life-size *White Horse*, by Mark Wallinger (2013).

The dirty-looking concrete building on the left, covered in Virginia creeper, is the 'Citadel'. This 'Cubist fortress' was built in 1941–2 as an extension to the Admiralty to provide bomb-proof protection for the communications room.

Overhanging The Mall on the right is the honeysuckle-coloured stucco façade of Nash's Carlton House Terrace (*see p. 224*), once the smartest, most aristocratic address in London. Here is the entrance to the **Mall Galleries**, the exhibition space of the Federation of British Artists (*mallgalleries.org.uk*). Beyond, just before Duke of York Steps, at Nash House (no. 12), is the **ICA** (Institute of Contemporary Arts). Founded in 1946, this organisation has a proud history of supporting living artists and launching their careers through its programme of exhibitions and films (*ica.org.uk*).

At the end of Carlton House Terrace, a double flight of steps (by De Soissons) leads to Carlton Gardens. At the top is a statue of George VI (W. McMillan, 1955) and below is a statue of Queen Elizabeth, the Queen Mother (Philip Jackson, 2009). Bronze friezes on either side of the steps (Paul Day, 2009) depict scenes from the life of the Queen Mother: on the left she and George VI are shown visiting the East End during the Blitz; on the right are vignettes of the Queen Mother as a widow, greeting members of the public, attending race meetings, and petting a beloved corgi.

MARLBOROUGH HOUSE

The Mall continues past the gardens of **Marlborough House** (*map p. 603, E2*). Built of Dutch red brick, it was designed by Christopher Wren in 1709–11 for Queen Anne's intimate friend and Mistress of the Robes, Sarah, Duchess of Marlborough, wife of the victor of Blenheim. Inside the house, on the staircase, are murals of the battles of Ramillies and Malplaquet, and in the Saloon, wall paintings of the Battle of Blenheim by Louis Laguerre. Also in the Saloon, about the cupola, is the ceiling painting *An Allegory of Peace and the Arts* (1635–8) by Orazio Gentlieschi, removed from the Great Hall of the Queen's House at Greenwich. In the 19th century, Marlborough House was the home of dowager queens: Queen Adelaide (widow of William IV), Queen Alexandra (Edward VII) and Queen Mary (George V) all lived here. From 1965 it has been home to the Commonwealth Secretariat (*tours lasting 2hrs can be arranged on weekdays by appointment, T: 020 7747 6491, secretariat.thecommonwealth.org*).

At Marlborough Gate, turn left into Marlborough Road to see the Symbolist **Queen Alexandra Memorial Fountain** (1932), in memory of the consort of Edward VII. It was completed by Sir Alfred Gilbert (who also made the famous '*Eros*' at Piccadilly Circus). The bronze sculpture portrays *Faith*, *Hope* and *Love* supporting an adolescent girl and leading her through the 'River of Life'; on the plinth one can read the words: 'Faith, Hope and Love: the Guiding Virtues of Queen Alexandra'.

CLARENCE HOUSE AND LANCASTER HOUSE

Back on The Mall are the entrances to two impressive mansions. **Clarence House**, in pale stucco, was built in 1825 by Nash for William IV when Duke of Clarence. It was formerly the residence of Queen Elizabeth, the Queen Mother and is now the official London home of the Prince of Wales and the Duchess of Cornwall, and Prince Harry. Next door, **Lancaster House**, dressed in Bath stone with a Corinthian portico, was built for the Duke of York by the Wyatt brothers from 1825. After the Duke's death, it was completed in the 1830s by Smirke for the Marquess of Stafford, later 1st Duke of Sutherland. Here the Sutherlands entertained lavishly until 1913 when it was bought for the nation by Lord Leverhulme. It is now an events venue managed by the Foreign and Commonwealth Office.

The Mall's grand parade route culminates in a landscaped circus; at the centre is Aston Webb's **Victoria Memorial**. The backdrop is Buckingham Palace. The Memorial, executed by Sir Thomas Brock in 1911, shows Queen Victoria seated on the east side with groups representing *Truth*, *Motherhood* and *Justice* on the other sides, and is crowned by a gilt bronze figure of *Victory*. The tree-lined road on the right is **Constitution Hill**, said to be named after the 'constitutional' walks that Charles II used to take here in the company of his spaniels. It leads due west to Hyde Park Corner, with a sand-track for riders skirting Green Park. Here three attempts on the life of Queen Victoria were made (in 1840, 1842 and 1849), and here too, in 1850, Prime Minister Sir Robert Peel was fatally injured by a fall from his horse.

BUCKINGHAM PALACE, THE QUEEN'S GALLERY & ROYAL MEWS

Map p. 603, E2–E3. Underground: St James's Park, Victoria. Ticket office (with tensile fabric roof) on Buckingham Palace Road. Tours from late July to end Sept each year, and sometimes in Dec and Jan—dates and details vary; T: 020 7766 7300, royalcollection.org. uk. Admission charge. Combined ticket with Queen's Gallery and Royal Mews available. Shop. Garden café.

Buckingham Palace, impressively situated at the west end of the Mall, is the official residence of the British monarch (when the Queen is in residence the Royal Standard flies from the roof). It is the Mall façade, from the balcony of which the Queen waves on great public occasions, that is best known to the world. A picturesque view of it, framed by trees, can be had from the bridge over the lake in nearby St James's Park. The façade dates from 1913 and was designed by Sir Aston Webb, who was also responsible for the spacious circus in front of the palace and the Victoria Memorial at its centre (*see above*). On the wide palace forecourt, behind the ornamental railings, the **Changing of the Guard** ceremony takes place (*11.30am, daily May–July, otherwise alternate days, weather permitting, see royal.gov.uk; a Changing the Guard app is also available*). The new guard, accompanied by a band with pipes and drums, marches from the nearby Wellington Barracks to relieve the old guard assembled on the forecourt. When the officers of the old and new guards advance and touch left hands, symbolising the handing over of the keys, the guard is 'changed'.

BUCKINGHAM PALACE: MALL FAÇADE

Buckingham Palace was originally Buckingham House, a private mansion built by John Sheffield, 1st Duke of Buckingham, in 1702–5. In 1762 the house was purchased by George III and it became the chief residence of Queen Charlotte, who had it enlarged and altered by Sir William Chambers. It was for George IV that the building was transformed into a palace; on his accession the new king signalled his intention to vacate his magnificent home, Carlton House, and to rebuild Buckingham House on a grand and regal scale. Parliament voted £250,000 for the project, John Nash was the chosen architect and building work began in 1825. On the king's death in 1830, with the palace still unfinished and costs having more than doubled, Nash was dismissed and Edward Blore, considered a safe pair of hands, was appointed in his place. Blore removed Nash's insubstantial and much criticised dome, added an attic storey, and in 1846–50 created the east wing across the forecourt, now hidden behind Webb's 1913 refacing. The new wing necessitated the removal of Nash's Marble Arch, designed as a ceremonial gateway to be topped by a statue of the monarch (*for its story, see p. 287*).

TOUR OF THE PALACE

Tours of the State Rooms last approx. 1hr. Visitors are free to tour the rooms at leisure, with an audio guide.
The tour takes in the main State Rooms, the majority of them opulently conceived by Nash in the 1820s and completed by Blore. Nash's inventive interiors, with their

gilded plaster ceilings, heavily decorated coves, wall hangings in richly-coloured silks and use of expensive materials (Carrara marble, gilt bronze), offered the unsurpassed grandeur sought by George IV. Many of the rooms were partially designed around the king's magnificent collection of pictures, furniture and porcelain from Carlton House, several items from which, together with other items from the Royal Collection, still furnish them.

Visitors enter the palace via the **Ambassador's Entrance** on Buckingham Gate, which leads to the courtyard behind the east wing. Here, Nash's building, in warm Bath stone, with Blore's alterations, is revealed. The sculptural theme is British sea power: in the pediment is *Britannia Acclaimed by Neptune*, designed by Flaxman, and inside Nash's two-storey columned portico is J.E. Carew's *The Progress of Navigation*. The friezes in the attic storey, *The Death of Nelson* and *The Meeting of Blücher and Wellington*, both by Westmacott, were added by Blore and were originally intended for the Marble Arch.

The portico entrance leads into the **Grand Hall**, with mahogany furniture from Carlton House and Brighton Pavilion. From here, you approach the magnificent **Grand Staircase**, one straight flight leading to a landing and branching into two to the upper floor. The stairs are of Carrara marble, the intricate balustrade of gilt bronze, the work of Samuel Parker, who also made the gilt metal mounts for the mirror-plated doors which occur throughout the State Rooms.

The **Green Drawing Room**, with its deeply coved and bracketed ceiling, set off by silk hangings, is Nash's. It contains items from George IV's collection of Sèvres porcelain, the finest in the world, much of which was purchased from the French Royal Collection during the French Revolution. The **Throne Room** itself, with red silk wall hangings, was intended for investitures and ceremonial receptions. The throne (the chairs were made for Queen Elizabeth II's Coronation Ceremony of 1953) is divided from the rest of the room by a proscenium with two winged Victories holding garlands, modelled by Francis Bernasconi, the chief plasterer employed at the palace. The classical sculptural frieze, designed by Stothard, has a medieval theme: the Wars of the Roses. The **Picture Gallery**, 155ft long, is hung with works from the Royal Collection.

The **East Gallery** is the first of the rooms in the new block added by Queen Victoria in 1853–5 to designs by James Pennethorne. The interior decoration was overseen by the Prince Consort, although it is now much altered. Of the pictures usually on show, the most important is the familiar Franz Xaver Winterhalter's *Family of Queen Victoria* (1846). The **Ballroom**, 123ft long, is where present-day investitures and other official receptions take place. The **State Dining Room** is hung with a series of full-length Hanoverian royal portraits. The room is used for official luncheons and dinners. Examples from George IV's magnificent silver-gilt service by Rundell, Bridge & Rundell are on show. The **Blue Drawing Room** is a magnificent, pure Nash interior, one of the finest in the Palace, with wide, flaring ceiling coves and coupled columns painted in imitation onyx. The delicate plasterwork reliefs show the apotheoses of Shakespeare, Spenser and Milton. The gilt sofas and armchairs are from Carlton House and the 'Table of the Grand Commanders', commissioned by Napoleon in 1806–12, with a top of hard-paste Sèvres porcelain with the head of Alexander the

Great in the centre, was presented to George IV by Louis XVIII.

The **Music Room** is the most beautiful interior in the palace. Completed by Nash in 1831 and not much altered, it occupies the bow window, the central feature of Nash's west front, with views over the palace's private gardens. The large plate glass windows were an innovation of the 1820s. The magnificent early 19th-century cut glass and gilt bronze chandeliers are from Carlton House.

The **Gardens** were landscaped by Nash and William Aiton of Kew Gardens, and include an ornamental lake, fed by the Serpentine. It is on these spacious lawns that the Queen's famous garden parties take place. Nash's garden façade, a hidden and less familiar view of the palace, is worth a backward glance. Above the central bow is Westmacott's *Fame Displaying Britain's Triumphs*. The 'King Alfred' frieze, designed by Flaxman, is also by Westmacott.

JOHN NASH

'His style lacks grandeur, and great monotony is produced by his persistent use of stucco.' Thus the *Dictionary of National Biography* dismisses John Nash (1752–1835), the millwright's son who became one of the most distinctive of all British architects, whose grand, aspirational creations add character to much of London. There is more behind the portentous façades than meets the eye. Nash was a brilliant engineer and gifted town planner. He was chosen by the Prince Regent as architect of an ambitious project: developing a tract of former farmland into a graceful 'garden city', with a ceremonial avenue linking it with the prince's residence at Carlton House. Regent's Park, the layout of Trafalgar Square, and the graceful sweep of Regent Street (though altered since) are all legacies of this splendid scheme. When George became king, he retained Nash to transform Buckingham House into a palace of a splendour to rival Napoleon's Paris. Napoleon, by his own account, approved of what he saw, remarking that Nash had made London appear 'for the first time like a royal residence, no longer a sprawling city for shopkeepers'. Though Nash longed for a knighthood, he never received one. Wellington, the prime minister, refused to grant it so long as Buckingham Palace remained unfinished. And Nash never completed it.

THE QUEEN'S GALLERY

Map p. 603, E2. Open daily 10–5.30 (last admission 4.30). Admission charge. Combined ticket with Buckingham Palace and Royal Mews available. Shop (free entry). T: 020 7766 7301, royalcollection.org.uk.

Winner of the Georgian Group Award for Best New Classical Building 2003 and described as 'high camp' by *The Guardian*, this grammatical Classical Revival gallery, partly inspired by the Greek temples at Paestum (the Doric portico and entrance hall) and the Temple of Isis in Pompeii (the garden pavilion elevation), as well as the work of Soane and Nash, is a permanent space for changing displays of objects taken from the outstanding and eclectic Royal Collection. At the behest of Queen Elizabeth II and the Duke of Edinburgh, the original gallery was built in 1962 on the site of the bomb-damaged private chapel once used by Queen Victoria. The subsequent £20-million redevelopment (John Simpson & Partners, 1998–2002), commissioned to mark the Queen's Golden Jubilee, tripled the exhibition space, which is now dominated by three principal galleries, all named after celebrated Neoclassical architects: the Pennethorne Gallery (decorated in green), the Nash Gallery (red) and the Chambers Gallery (blue). Of particular note in the double-height entrance hall are the two winged genii bearing torches, which evidence the strong influence of Canova, and 70-ft long Homeric friezes which include allegorical representations of the Cold War (the *Iliad* panel) and the benevolent reign of Queen Elizabeth II (the *Odyssey* panel). They are all the work of the Sculptor in Ordinary to The Queen in Scotland, Alexander Stoddart.

THE ROYAL COLLECTION

Formed through acquisitions and gifts, and held in trust for the nation by the British monarch, the Royal Collection is one of the most exquisite assemblages of fine and decorative arts in the world, and numbers over one million objects: paintings, sculpture, furniture, textiles, porcelain, clocks, miniatures, jewellery and Fabergé, books and manuscripts, maps and prints and arms and armour. Besides the Queen's Gallery, where some 450 objects are on display at any one time, works from the Royal Collection are also displayed at other royal palaces and residences, national museums and galleries, on domestic touring exhibitions and on international loan exhibitions.

Though a few items date back to the reign of Henry VIII, the real origins of the collection began with Charles I, celebrated connoisseur and patron of art, who purchased part of the renowned Gonzaga collection of pictures and secured Anthony van Dyck as his court painter. Charles I's collection included works by Giulio Romano, Tintoretto, Titian, Raphael and Rubens, among many others. He acquired Raphael's important 'Acts of the Apostles' cartoons (*see p. 519*) as well as Mantegna's *Triumphs of Caesar* (now at Hampton Court; *see p. 522*). Following Charles I's execution, his collection was dispersed by the Commonwealth government. However, many works were either bought back or returned to the restored Charles II by loyal supporters and constitute the core of the royal picture collection today.

The wider collection of objects is as diverse as it is large: Guido Mazzoni's *Henry VIII* (c. 1498), a terracotta bust of the boy-prince Henry; the armour of Henry VIII for the field and tilt (1539); Hans Holbein the Younger's chalk drawing of Sir Thomas More (c. 1526–7); Van Dyck's magnificent equestrian portrait of Charles I with M. de St-Antoine (1633); Vermeer's *A Lady at the Virginal with a Gentleman, 'The Music Lesson'* (c. 1662–5) and Queen Charlotte's tortoiseshell, gold and diamond notebook (c. 1765). The collection also contains gifts from Commonwealth countries, such as the Maori feather capes (*kahu kiwi*) and the 203-carat 'Andamooka' opal, presented to Queen Elizabeth II and the Duke of Edinburgh on the 1954 Royal Tour of New Zealand and Australia respectively.

THE ROYAL MEWS

Map p. 603, E3. Open Feb–March and Nov Mon–Sat 10–4, April–Oct daily 10–5. Admission charge. Combined ticket with the Queen's Gallery available. Shop (free entry). T: 020 7766 7324, royalcollection.org.uk.

The Royal Mews is a working department of the Royal Household, responsible for the maintenance of the sovereign's horse-drawn carriages and other official conveyances. Designed by Sir William Chambers in 1765–6, it was one of George III's early improvements to his new purchase, Buckingham House. The pediment was adorned in 1859 with a relief of *Hercules and the Thracian Horses*, the man-eating mares whom Hercules tamed by feeding them their master's flesh. Queen Victoria watched her nine children learn to ride here, and here royal horses are still trained to become accustomed to the sight and sounds of marching bands, crowds and flag-waving.

The Irish State Coach (1851) conveys the monarch to State Openings of Parliament. The Glass State Coach (1910) is used for royal weddings. The Australian State Coach (1988) is the most comfortable equipage, with electric windows, hydraulic suspension and heating. Also on display are some of the five royal Rolls-Royce Phantoms IV to VI. In place of the marque's 'Spirit of Ecstasy', a silver statuette depicts St George and the Dragon, designed by Edward Seago. The extraordinary Gold State Coach was built for George III in 1762 to a design approved by William Chambers. A fantastic showpiece designed to trumpet British sea power, the gilded body framework carved by Joseph Wilton comprises eight palm trees, each of the four corner trees rising from a lion's head and supporting trophies symbolising British victories against France in the Seven Years' War (1756–63). The body is slung on braces of morocco leather held by four gilded tritons, the front pair blowing conch shells, the winged pair behind holding trident fasces, symbols of maritime authority. Putti symbolising England, Scotland and Ireland stand at the centre of the roof, supporting the royal crown. The design of the wheels is based on those of an ancient triumphal chariot. It weighs almost four tons, requires eight horses to pull it, and has been used at every coronation since that of George IV in 1821. William IV likened the ride in it to 'a ship tossing in a rough sea'. After the death of Prince Albert, Queen Victoria refused to use it, complaining of the 'distressing oscillations'.

ST JAMES'S PALACE

Map p. 603, E2. Underground: Green Park. The public may attend services at the Chapel Royal and Queen's Chapel between Oct and Good Friday, 8.30am and 11.15am. The palace is not otherwise open to visitors. Switchboard T: 020 7839 1377, royal.gov.uk.

The irregular brick building of St James's Palace was built by Henry VIII from 1531 on the site of a hospital for female lepers, St James-in-the-Field. The modest palace was perhaps never meant for the king himself, rather his illegitimate son Henry Fitzroy (d. 1536); however, it became the main London residence of the sovereign after Whitehall Palace burned down in 1698 and it was here that all official court functions were held. The current crenellated fabric is essentially 19th-century, but the distinctive Tudor Gatehouse overlooking St James's Street, with its polygonal towers, survives from Henry's reign, as does the Chapel Royal.

It is here that Queen Elizabeth I lodged during the crisis of the Spanish Armada and here that the marriages of George III to Charlotte of Mecklenburg-Strelitz and of Queen Victoria to Prince Albert took place. Queen Elizabeth II gave her first official speech here in 1952. Today it is the senior royal palace of the monarchy and although the sovereign has not lived here since Queen Victoria moved the royal family to Buckingham Palace, the British court is officially known as the Court of St James's; the title transfers to wherever the sovereign is located. All ambassadors and high commissioners to the UK are officially received at the Court and are grandly styled Ambassador to the Court of St James's. Members of the Royal Family and Royal Household live and have offices here.

THE CHAPEL ROYAL

The Chapel Royal has been greatly altered since it was built for Henry VIII. However, it preserves its fine painted timber ceiling (1540) by Hans Holbein the Younger, which incorporates the mottoes and badges of Anne of Cleves, whose short-lived marriage to Henry VIII it honours. In 1836 the ciphers of William IV and his consort Queen Adelaide were added.

ORIGINS OF THE CHAPEL ROYAL

In origin the Chapel Royal was not, as it is now, a building, but a group of people, essentially the spiritual retinue of the monarch: a group of clergymen, lay clerks and choristers headed by a dean and sub-dean, who formed part of the Royal Household and travelled with the sovereign (in c. 1509, there were nine chaplains, 20 clerks and ten choristers; and in c. 1700 around ten men in orders and ten singers). The first explicit reference to this body of men as a 'portable chapel' came in a petition of 1295 from English prelates seeking to clarify who had jurisdiction of appointment to the Chapel.

The itinerant tradition continued right up to the Tudor period, with the monarch frequently on royal progresses during the winter months. It was only in the 17th century that the nature of the Chapel Royal changed, alternating between the palaces of Whitehall and St James's before finally coming to be based permanently at the latter in 1698.

At the core of the history of the Chapel is sacred music, which was at its zenith between the 16th and 18th centuries. Thomas Tallis (d. 1585), William Byrd (d. 1623), Orlando Gibbons (d. 1625) and Henry Purcell (d. 1695) all worked as organists here. Handel was appointed 'Composer of Musick of His Majesty's Chappel Royal' in 1723. In 1727 he composed his famous setting of 'Zadok the Priest' for the coronation of George II.

The Chapel Royal has witnessed many intimate spiritual struggles: it was here that Elizabeth I prayed on the eve of the Spanish Armada in 1588 and here that the martyr-king Charles I received his last Holy Communion on the morning of 30th January 1649, before his execution at Whitehall. In 1997, the coffin of Diana, Princess of Wales, lay for private respects to be paid by her family before her funeral at Westminster Abbey. The heart of Mary I, who died here, is buried under the choir stalls.

QUEEN'S CHAPEL

This second Chapel Royal (*map p. 603, E2; for service times see p. 159*), projected by Inigo Jones, was begun in 1623 for the Infanta of Spain, the intended wife of King Charles I, and was completed for Henrietta Maria of France, his eventual bride. Palladian in style, of yellow brick and edged with white quoins, it utilises a double-cube space like the Banqueting House at Whitehall. Its main architectural features are its barrel-vaulted ceiling and Venetian window. In 1642 it was used as a barracks by Cromwell's army. After the Restoration, it was refurbished by Wren for Catherine of Braganza, consort of Charles II.

To the west of St James's Palace is **Cleveland Row** (*map p. 603, E2*), where three mansions (now offices) overlook Green Park. The Reform Bill of 1832 was drafted in Stornoway House (Wyatt, 1794–6; rebuilt in 1959), which became the residence of Lord Beaverbrook in 1924 and housed his Ministry of Aircraft Production in 1940–1. Beyond the bow-fronted Selwyn House (1895) is Barry's huge and elaborate Italianate Bridgwater House (1849), built for the 1st Earl of Ellesmere on the site of a house presented by Charles II to his mistress Barbara Villiers, Duchess of Cleveland, who lived here in 1668–77.

ST JAMES'S PARK

Map p. 603, E2–F2. Underground: St James's Park.

South of the Mall is St James's Park, the oldest of the royal parks, which extends over 57 acres from Horse Guards Parade on the east to Buckingham Palace on the west, and is bounded on the north by The Mall, on the south by Birdcage Walk. Laid out in English naturalistic style in a patrician environment of palaces and government offices, and commanding a famous view of Buckingham Palace, Horse Guards and Whitehall Court from the Blue Bridge, this park is one of the most picturesque in London and in warm weather, the perfect spot to while a way a few hours in a deck chair (*available for hire*).

Henry VIII laid out the watermeadows between his palaces at Whitehall and St James's in 1532 as a park in which to hunt deer. Under the early Stuarts it was the resort of the court and other privileged persons. One of these, during the Commonwealth, was Milton, who lived in a house in Petty France overlooking the park from 1652 until the Reformation in 1660. In 1649, Charles I had walked across the park from St James's

Palace to Whitehall, on the morning of his execution, and here in 1660 Pepys had his first view of Charles II on his return to London: 'Found the King in the parke. There walked. Gallantry great.'

After the Restoration, the French landscaper André Mollet was employed to make 'great and very noble alteracions', and the scattered ponds were united to form a 'canal'. The park was then opened to the public, and remains the only large park in London which has not been enclosed by railings. It became a fashionable resort, where the King was frequently to be seen strolling unattended and feeding the waterfowl. The lake in the centre is still patronised by numerous water birds, for which Duck Island at the east end is reserved. Among the 'great variety of fowle' described by Pepys are the famous resident pelicans, descendants of those first presented by the Russian ambassador in the 17th century. For the Restoration poet Rochester, the park was little more than a profligate pimping ground, an 'all-sin-sheltering grove' where he is mortified to see his beloved Corinna skip away into a hackney coach with three suitors: a 'Whitehall blade', a 'Gray's Inn wit' and a 'lady's eldest son' not yet of age. Until 1905, a dairy herd was grazed at St James's Park and milkmaids sold mugs of fresh milk, warm from the cow, to passers-by.

BIRDCAGE WALK AND THE GUARDS' MUSEUM

Birdcage Walk (*map p. 603, E2*) skirts the south side of the park; its name recalls the royal aviary established here in the reign of James I. Overlooking it are the bow-fronted Georgian houses of Queen Anne's Gate (*see below*). Near the end of Birdcage Walk are the **Wellington Barracks**, the headquarters of the Household Regiments, spaciously laid out around a parade ground. The **Guards' Chapel**, or Royal Military Chapel (*open Mon–Thur 10–4, until 3 on Fri, unless service in progress; army.mod.uk*), is approached by a memorial cloister (1956) by H.S. Goodhart-Rendel, in honour of the Household Brigade in the Second World War. The chapel was wrecked by a flying bomb in 1944, during morning service, with the loss of 121 lives, including that of the chaplain. The altar candles remained burning, and the same candlesticks are used today. The present chapel, opened in 1963, is by George, Trew and Dunn; its austerity sets off the surviving ornate mosaic apse by G.E. Street.

Opposite is the **Guards' Museum** (*open daily 10–4, T: 020 7414 3428, theguardsmuseum.com*), with artefacts pertaining to the five regiments of Foot Guards (Grenadier, Coldstream, Scots, Irish and Welsh), who furnish the troops that can usually be seen on parade, here and in front of Buckingham Palace, at the Changing of the Guard. Along with the cavalry regiments, the Blues and Royals and the Queen's Life Guards, they form the Household Division. Their duties are not merely ceremonial: all seven regiments of the Division are composed of fighting soldiers who have seen, or will at some time see, active service. The museum displays an annotated collection of uniforms, medals, silverware, weapons, colours, trophies and memorabilia. It also has a shop, the **Toy Soldier Centre**.

NEW SCOTLAND YARD AND QUEEN ANNE'S GATE

On the corner of Broadway and Dacre Street (*map p. 603, F3*) is the famous revolving sign of **New Scotland Yard**, the headquarters of the Metropolitan Police since 1967 (in 2013, plans were announced for the Met to return to a building on Victoria Embankment which will be called Scotland Yard). The former **Blewcoat School** on Caxton Street (1709) features a charming sculpture of a pupil in his uniform blue coat and yellow stockings.

At the north end of Broadway (no. 55), **St James's Park Underground station** occupies a massive and imposing building by Adam, Holden & Pearson with a lofty tower and relief sculptures by Jacob Epstein, Henry Moore and Eric Gill. At the corner of Petty France and Queen Anne's Gate is an ugly concrete turret by Sir Basil Spence (1976), housing the Ministry of Justice. **Queen Anne's Gate** itself is a lovely enclave, its brown brick and stone-banded houses built in 1704 with the money of Charles Shales (who lived at no. 15) and probably also of William Paterson, 'founder' of the Bank of England (who lived at no. 19 in 1705–18). The houses have carved mascarons on the keystones and elaborate door cases with richly carved hoods, unique in London. There is an unfinished statue of Queen Anne at no. 13. The larger houses overlooking St James's Park are later, from about 1780. Lord Palmerston was born at no. 20 in 1784. No. 14, possibly designed by Adam, was home to the collector and early trustee of the British Museum Charles Townley; here he entertained friends, including the painters Reynolds and Zoffany, to excellent Sunday dinners.

EATING AND DRINKING IN WESTMINSTER

It is not easy in this part of London to find dinners as excellent as those given by Townley. There is a good café/restaurant in St James's Park: £ **Inn The Park** (*open daily for breakfast and lunch; booking required for afternoon tea, T: 020 7451 9999; map p. 603, F2*). Westminster Abbey itself has the £ **Cellarium Café** in its old buttery (*entrance from Dean's Yard; open daily for breakfast, lunch and afternoon tea; map p. 603, F3*).

At the ££–£££ **Caxton Grill** in the sleek St Ermin's Hotel you will find Trimalchio-like levels of extravagance on the menu: 'hand-dived scallops' and belly not merely of pig, but of 'piglet'. Club sandwiches and other simpler meals are available in the Bar (*Bar open all day, Grill evenings only;*

2 Caxton St; T: 0800 652 1498, caxton-grill.co.uk; map p. 603, E3).

£££ **Quilon** (*41 Buckingham Gate; T: 020 7821 1899, quilon.co.uk; map p. 603, E3*) is a Michelin-starred restaurant serving cuisine from India's southwestern coast. The Q Bar serves 'qojito' cocktails: vodka, mint and green chilli. The ££–£££ **Cinnamon Club** is an excellent modern Indian restaurant occupying the old Westminster Library (*30–32 Great Smith St; T: 020 3355 1167, cinnamon-club.com; map p. 603, F3*).

The café in the crypt of £ **St John's Smith Square** serves snacks, lunch and tea Mon–Fri 8–5 and on concert evenings (*T: 020 7222 2779, sjjs.org.uk; map p. 603, F3*). The **Goring Hotel** also offers a fine tea (*see p. 546*).

TRAFALGAR SQUARE
Close-up view of the monument to Admiral Lord Nelson (1840–?)

Trafalgar Square & The Strand

From Trafalgar Square, Nelson surveys London from the top of his column. Behind him is the National Gallery, with one of the finest collections of European paintings in the world. To the east, the Strand and Victoria Embankment lead to Somerset House and the Courtauld Gallery.

Trafalgar Square (*map p. 603, F2*) is one of the focal points of London, always busy with traffic and tourists, with crowds who gather to watch the performance artists in the piazza before the National Gallery, and at Christmas time to sing carols beneath the tree (which is donated by the people of Norway in recognition of Britain's help during the Second World War), and to see in each new year. The square was once well-known—even infamous— for the feral pigeons which flocked here in their

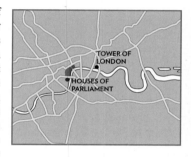

hundreds. In the last decade measures such as banning the sale of birdseed and the use of trained birds of prey have successfully reduced their numbers and it is now just the tourists who flock here.

MONUMENTS IN TRAFALGAR SQUARE

Trafalgar Square was described by Sir Robert Peel as 'the finest site in Europe'. The layout is by Sir Charles Barry and it takes its name from the naval battle of Trafalgar, Nelson's great victory over the French in 1805, at which the British hero lost his life. The **Nelson Monument**, popularly known as Nelson's Column, 172ft high, by William Railton (1841), carries a colossal 17ft statue of Nelson by E.H. Baily (1840–3). The fluted granite column rises from a base guarded by four huge bronze lions couchant, popular with children. These were modelled by Sir Edwin Landseer and cast by Marochetti in 1867. The four bronze reliefs are cast from French cannon captured at the naval battles they depict: Cape St Vincent, The Nile, Copenhagen, Trafalgar.

The two fountains in the square were designed by Lutyens in 1939. At the four corners are tall plinths topped by statues of two servants of the Empire, Sir Henry Havelock (by Behnes) and Sir Charles James Napier (by G.G. Adams); and by a monarch, George IV (by Chantrey; originally intended to surmount Marble Arch). An equestrian statue of William IV was intended for the fourth plinth but it was never installed due to insufficient funds. For 150 years the plinth stayed bare and now it is used for a changing series of contemporary sculpture and installations. Against the north wall are bronze busts of admirals. The wall is interrupted by a flight of steps up to the piazza. There is a café with outside seating (and also public lavatories).

Around Trafalgar Square are several large buildings: when facing the National Gallery, to the left (west) is **Canada House** (Smirke, 1824–7; remodelled) and on the right (east) **South Africa House** (Sir Herbert Baker, 1933), where another Nelson, the late Mr Mandela, addressed a crowd of thousands from the balcony in August 1996.

OLD CHARING CROSS

At the top of Whitehall are the **Admiralty buildings**: the former Paymaster General's Office (John Lane, 1733) and, set back behind a wall and railing, the flank of Admiralty House (S.P. Cockerell, 1786–8). The Old Admiralty, now the Ripley Building (Thomas Ripley, 1723–8), with a tall classical portico, stands in a small courtyard masked from the street by a Tuscan colonnaded screen with two seahorses (Robert Adam, 1760–1). This was the Admiralty of Nelson's time and it is here that his body lay in state in 1805. On the corner is Drummond's Bank, founded as a private bank in 1717. Former account holders include George III, Alexander Pope, Robert Adam, Thomas Gainsborough and Beau Brummell.

Charing Cross is officially the circular traffic island just south of Trafalgar Square (it is not the open space in front of Charing Cross Station). It was here, in 1291, that Edward I erected the last of the series of 13 crosses that marked the stages in the funeral procession of his wife Eleanor to Westminster Abbey the previous year. The cross, which gave its name to the ancient road junction, was destroyed in 1647 (a replica was later erected in front of Charing Cross Station). A plaque in the ground marks the spot from which all distances to and from Central London are measured. The traffic island is now the site of a fine bronze **equestrian statue of Charles I** by Hubert Le Sueur (1633), which amazingly survived the Civil War. The pedestal is by Joshua Marshall, from a design by Wren. Every year on the Sunday closest to 30th January, the anniversary of the execution of Charles I, the English Civil War Society organises a march down The Mall in full period costume and the statue is adorned with wreaths. At all times of year a single rose is often to be seen attached to the side of the plinth. At the restoration of the monarchy in 1660, Charles II's triumphal procession was greeted here by 600 pikemen and later in the same year it was the scene of the execution of Thomas Harrison and seven other regicides, witnessed by Pepys, who wrote, 'I went out to Charing Cross, to see Major-general Harrison hanged, drawn, and quartered; which was done there, he looking as cheerful as any man could do in that condition. He was presently cut down, and his head and heart shown to the people, at which there was great shouts of joy...Thus it was my chance to see the King beheaded at White Hall, and to see the first blood shed in revenge for the blood of the King at Charing Cross.' (*Diary, 13th Oct 1660.*)

ST MARTIN-IN-THE-FIELDS

Map p. 603, F1. Open Mon, Tues, Fri 8.30–1 & 2–6, Wed 8.30–1.15 & 2–5, Thur 8.30–1.15 & 2–6, Sat 9.30–6, Sun 3.30–5. T: 020 7766 1100, stmartin-in-the-fields.org.

The large church of St Martin-in-the-Fields, at the northeast corner of Trafalgar Square, is the work of James Gibbs (1722–6), modelled on a Classical temple with a hexastyle porch, behind which protrude the traditional tower and steeple. The church's design has been imitated across the USA and in India (St Andrew's Church, Edgmore, Chennai, built in 1821, is directly modelled on it). Inside, the ceiling is richly decorated by Artari and Bagutti. There is a font (1689) from the previous church on this site, and a handsome 18th-century pulpit brought here after 1858. The side aisles, with canted walls and 'closet' pews, are particularly attractive. A bust of James Gibbs by Rysbrack is preserved in the Vestry Hall.

In this church Charles II was christened and Nell Gwyn was buried. The burials of Roubiliac, Chippendale and John Hunter are also recorded. The first broadcast religious service took place here in 1924. The church is the regular venue for the memorial services of actors, actresses and politicians and it is also the parish church of the Royal Family and of no. 10 Downing Street.

The church provided the first home for the now world-famous Academy of St Martin-in-the-Fields orchestra. The musical tradition continues, with regular Classical music concerts; jazz concerts are held in the crypt. Also in the crypt is a café, bookshop, gift shop, brass-rubbing centre, art gallery and visitor centre. A life-size statue of London's first Pearly King, Henry Croft (d. 1930; *see p. 50*) was brought here in 2002 from St Pancras. The statue, commissioned in 1931 after Croft's death, shows him wearing the pearly tail coat which he donned in order to raise money for various hospitals and charities. Also in the crypt is the Dick Sheppard Chapel (1954), a memorial to the vicar who began the church's tradition of social service by giving refuge to soldiers on their way to fight in the First World War trenches. The church holds over 20 services a week and is known as the 'Church of the Ever Open Door', offering sanctuary to all. It is particularly known for its work with the homeless.

THE NATIONAL GALLERY

Map p. 603, F1–F2. Underground: Charing Cross. Open daily 10–6 (Fri until 9pm). Free. 'Love Art' app. Restaurant, café. Shop. T: 020 7747 2885, nationalgallery.org.uk.

The National Gallery's collection of Western European art, spanning the period c. 1250–1900, is one of the finest in the world. The Italian early and high Renaissance collection is particularly rich, with numerous works of international significance. There are also important early Netherlandish works; major holdings of 17th-century Dutch and Flemish masters, including Rembrandt, Rubens and Van Dyck; notable works by the French masters Claude and Poussin; as well as a significant collection of French Impressionist pictures. Although Tate Britain is the official home of British art, the

National Gallery also has some seminal masterpieces of the British School.

Entrance to the National Gallery has always been free. Even during World War Two, when the collection was removed for safety to old mining caves in Wales (*see p. 176*), one masterpiece per month was shown at the gallery, at risk in the capital alongside Londoners. During its evacuation, much scholarly study of the collection was undertaken, resulting in published catalogues which set the international standard.

HISTORY OF THE GALLERY

Compared with other European national galleries, London's was established relatively late, in 1824, when the artist and collector Sir George Beaumont offered his collection to the nation with two provisos: that the government purchase the collection of the wealthy banker John Julius Angerstein, one of the finest private collections in London, and that suitable accommodation be found for it. Angerstein's 38 Italian, Dutch, Flemish and British works form the core of the National Gallery's holding. Sebastiano del Piombo's magnificent *Raising of Lazarus* was officially the first work to enter the collection (it has the accession number NG1). In 1826 those first works were joined by Beaumont's own 16 pictures, which included several masterpieces: Canaletto's *The Stonemason's Yard*; Rubens' *View of Het Steen* (Beaumont considered Rubens 'the Shakespeare of painting'); and Beaumont's personal favourite, Claude's *Landscape with Hagar and the Angel*, which travelled with him whenever he left London for his country home.

In 1851 came J.M.W. Turner's overwhelming bequest of over 1,000 of his own watercolours, drawings and oils. In 1871 the collection of the late Prime Minister, Sir Robert Peel, came to the gallery, a distinguished assembly of mainly Dutch and Flemish pictures, including Hobbema's supreme *Avenue at Middelharnis* and Rubens' *Chapeau de Paille*. Since its foundation—and particularly from 1855, with the appointment of Sir Charles Eastlake as Director—the gallery had also been making acquisitions of its own. Eastlake travelled throughout Italy purchasing important works, mainly early Italian 'Primitives'. Acquisitions continue—no longer solely of European art.

THE BUILDING

Built between 1833 and 1838 by William Wilkins, the building is dignified but somehow not imposing, its long façade punctuated with a central portico with Corinthian columns, and a dome and further porticoes to east and west, with column bases and capitals salvaged from the recently demolished Carlton House. A new east wing extension, designed by E.M. Barry, was completed in 1876. Its central octagonal **Rotunda** (Room 36) has green Genoa marble columns, white and gilded plasterwork and a domed ceiling of etched glass panels. Between 1885 and 1887 Sir John Taylor added further architecturally important spaces: the **Central Hall**, with richly-coloured Venetian wall fabric; and the grand **Staircase Hall**. The gallery is adorned by four **mosaic pavements by Boris Anrep**, commissioned in 1928–33. The foremost mosaicist working in Britain, Anrep's themes were *The Labours of Life* (west vestibule, 1928), *The Pleasures of Life* (east vestibule, 1929) and *The Awakening of the Muses* (portico entrance landing, 1933). *Modern Virtues* (north vestibule) followed later, in 1952.

Anrep included many portraits of famous people (and also of his friends): Augustus John appears as Neptune; Margot Fonteyn (Delectation); Edith Sitwell (Sixth Sense); Bertrand Russell (Lucidity); Churchill (Defiance); Greta Garbo (Tragic Muse) and Virginia Woolf (Muse of History).

The building was further added to in 1907–11, with new galleries behind Wilkins' west wing. The Northern Extension was built in 1970–5. More recently, in 1991, the Sainsbury Wing was completed to designs by Venturi, Rauch and Scott, who won the commission after the original scheme, the winner of an architectural competition, was famously denounced by the Prince of Wales as a 'monstrous carbuncle on the face of a much-loved friend'. In a modern classical style which acknowledges Wilkins' building, the new wing's main feature is a giant, broad and tall staircase which rises from the entrance foyer up to the main gallery level, with views over Trafalgar Square. The Getty entrance and foyer (Dixon/Jones 2004) allows entry directly from Trafalgar Square, rather than up the main portico stairs.

THE COLLECTION

NB: The National Gallery is too large to see in full at one visit. Below, ordered by date and school, are the major highlights, many of which are long-established favourites. The information was correct at the time of going to press, but paintings are frequently moved, sent out on loan, or taken in for restoration. To locate a work of art, ask at one of the information desks.

Early Italy (13th–15th centuries)

The classic illustration of the development of art in Italy from the hieratic Middle Ages to the human focus of the Renaissance is furnished by Margarito of Arezzo's 1260s Byzantine icon-like **Virgin and Child** (Room 51), the earliest Italian work in the collection, then Duccio's *Annunciation, Jesus Opens the Eyes of a Blind Man* and *Transfiguration*, predella panels from his masterwork, the *Maestà*, the high altarpiece of Siena Cathedral (1311), and lastly Giotto's *Pentecost*. Leonardo da Vinci's large cartoon, **The Virgin and Child with St Anne and St John the Baptist** (c. 1499–1500), a large-scale preparatory drawing for a painting commissioned by Louis XII of France, is also displayed in this room.

Not Italian, but displayed in this section, is the outstanding **Wilton Diptych** (c. 1395; Room 53), the highpoint of painting to survive from medieval England. Possibly of French authorship, it shows Richard II being presented to the Virgin and Child, accompanied by St John, St Edmund and St Edward the Confessor. Early Florentine works in Room 53 include Lorenzo Monaco's brilliantly coloured *Coronation of the Virgin* (c. 1414); the only documented painting by Masaccio (a 1426 *Virgin and Child*, part of the altarpiece for the chapel of Santa Maria del Carmine, Pisa); and Fra' Angelico's *Christ Glorified in the Court of Heaven* (before 1435), with its ranks of angels.

Sienese art (Room 54) includes works by Sassetta, one of the city's leading artists of the early 15th century; and Giovanni di Paolo's *Scenes from the Life of St John the Baptist*, the desert realised as tall, craggy mountains. Uccello's *Battle of San Romano*, from Palazzo Medici, also in Room 54, shows the mercenary general Niccolò da

THE NATIONAL GALLERY

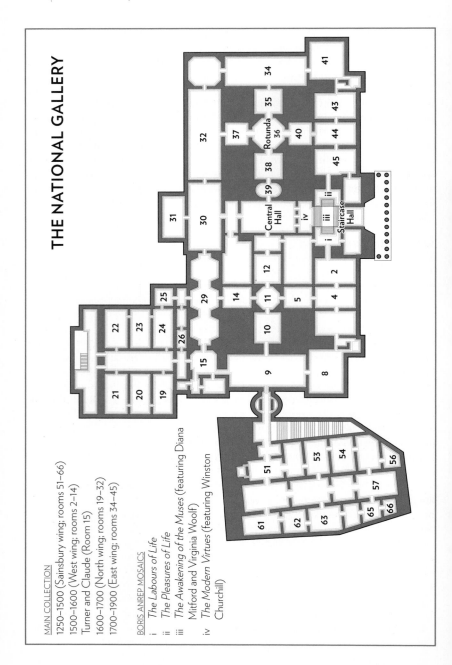

MAIN COLLECTION
1250–1500 (Sainsbury wing: rooms 51–66)
1500–1600 (West wing: rooms 2–14)
Turner and Claude (Room 15)
1600–1700 (North wing; rooms 19–32)
1700–1900 (East wing: rooms 34–45)

BORIS ANREP MOSAICS
i   *The Labours of Life*
ii   *The Pleasures of Life*
iii *The Awakening of the Muses* (featuring Diana Mitford and Virginia Woolf)
iv   *The Modern Virtues* (featuring Winston Churchill)

Tolentino in a magnificent headdress on a rearing white charger (the other two parts of this painting are in the Uffizi and the Louvre).

Works by **Botticelli** include the *Mystic Nativity* (Room 57), one of the gallery's best-known works, showing the Virgin kneeling in adoration, with a circle of dancing angels above the stable. Leonardo da Vinci's great ***Virgin of the Rocks*** (c. 1508), the central panel for the altarpiece of the oratory of the Milanese Confraternity of the Immaculate Conception, and one of the gallery's most renowned works, is also here.

From **Venice and the Veneto**, 1450–1500, are important works by Mantegna, including the *Agony in the Garden* (Room 62), the slumbering Apostles in the foreground with rabbits hopping on the road along which Judas conducts the Roman soldiers; and works by the great Giovanni Bellini, Mantegna's brother-in-law (Rooms 61–62), including the *Madonna of the Meadow* and his famous portrait of Doge Leonardo Loredan, in an expensive gold and silver damask robe, prominent against a blue background.

In a separate gallery (Room 66) are outstanding masterpieces by **Piero della Francesca**, who worked chiefly in his native Borgo Sansepolcro, Tuscany, and was recognised as a rare and extraordinary talent in the second half of the 20th century. The National Gallery has exceptional works by him, including the *Baptism of Christ*, a work of great delicacy, and *The Nativity*, an unfinished work allowing insight into his working methods.

Early Netherlands and Germany (13th–15th centuries)

Unlike early Italian works, which are painted in egg tempera, early Netherlandish and German works are in oil on panel. The technique, in fact, is thought to have been brought from the Netherlands to Italy by **Antonello da Messina** (whose *St Jerome in his Study*, with splendid architectural perspectives, is in Room 62).

One of the greatest artists of his day was **Jan van Eyck**, who worked for Philip, Duke of Burgundy at Bruges. One of the most important of the National Gallery's pictures is his remarkable ***Arnolfini Portrait*** (Room 56), probably a marriage portrait, the couple standing in a well-furnished room, their reflections seen in the round mirror in the background.

The outstanding Netherlandish painter of his time was **Rogier van der Weyden**, who worked in Brussels and probably for the Burgundian court. His beautiful *Magdalen Reading* (c. 1440–50; Room 56) has been cut down from a once large altarpiece. There are also works by Dieric Bouts, Memling (Room 63) and the leading Antwerp painter Quinten Massys (or Metsys).

Southern German painting includes *The Painter's Father* (1497), by one of the greatest European artists of his age, **Albrecht Dürer** (Room 65).

Italian Renaissance works (16th century)

The National Gallery's Italian Renaissance collection is extensive and excellent. In Room 2 are **Correggio**'s *Madonna of the Basket*, in excellent condition, and his well known *School of Love* (c. 1525), purchased in 1824. Room 8 contains major works by Florentine and Roman artists: **Michelangelo**'s unfinished *Entombment*; **Bronzino**'s outstanding *Allegory with Venus and Cupid*, the 'picture of singular beauty' mentioned by Vasari in 1568; **Raphael**'s large *Ansidei Madonna*; his beautiful *Mond Crucifixion* and *St Catherine of Alexandria*, twisted towards the sky in a position of holy rapture; his important and influential portrait of Pope Julius II, an 1824 Angerstein foundation work; and the small and gentle *Madonna of the Pinks*, which caused controversy when it was acquired for £22m in 2004. Here also is **Sebastiano del Piombo**'s *Raising of Lazarus*.

Rooms 9–12 host the Gallery's magnificent works by **Venetian artists**, 1530–1600: Veronese's enormous and impressive *Family of Darius before Alexander*; and *The Rape of Europa*, which came to the gallery in 1831 and was highly esteemed in the 18th and 19th centuries. Tintoretto, Jacopo Bassano, Palma Vecchio and Giorgione are also represented.

The Netherlands and Germany (16th century)

The fine collection of 16th-century Netherlandish pictures can be seen in Rooms 5 and 14 including, in the latter, **Jan Gossaert**'s meticulous, tightly handled *Adoration of the Kings* (c. 1500–15), with angels hovering above the Virgin and Child, the kings bearing their costly gifts and dogs wandering across minutely observed cracked paving invaded by weeds. **Jan Brueghel the Elder**'s later depiction of the same subject (1598) is in the same room and provides an interesting contrast. The collapsing stable roof, raised above the meagre hovel from which crowds bathed in holy light flock from all directions, is intensely memorable.

The collection of 16th-century Northern painting from the Protestant states of what are now Germany and Switzerland is of particular note for its works by **Holbein**: ***The Ambassadors*** (Room 4), one of the National Gallery's major masterpieces, dominates one wall. Painted in 1533 for Jean de Dinteville, French Ambassador at the court of Henry VIII, it shows Dinteville standing with Georges de Selve surrounded by objects symbolic of Humanist learning. The perspective of the distorted skull, bottom centre, is corrected when viewed from the right. *Christina of Denmark* (1538), depicting a prospective bride of Henry VIII, is a rare, early example of full-length portraiture.

Dutch pictures (17th century)

Of the only 30 works known by **Vermeer**, the National Gallery has two, including the outstanding *Young Woman Standing at a Virginal* (c. 1670; Room 25). Nearby is Pieter de Hooch's *Courtyard of a House in Delft* (1658), with its carefully observed brickwork. Also on show is Hoogstraten's *Peepshow* (c. 1655–60), a painted box with two viewing holes, through which the illusion of a three-dimensional Dutch interior can be seen. From a black and white tiled floor a dog stares up at you, and through a doorway further rooms recede into the distance. On the other side a sleeping figure can be glimpsed in bed. Of such boxes to survive, this is the finest and most elaborate. Numerous works by **Gerrit Dou**, the principal artist of the Leiden *fijnschilders* (literally 'fine painters'), are on show, including his *Poulterer's Shop* (c. 1670; Room 26), seen through a stone window, its produce of gamebirds and a hanging hare shown in a virtuoso performance of meticulous detail.

In Room 21–23 are works by **Cuyp** and the Dutch Italianate landscapists. Cuyp's brilliant *River Landscape with a Horseman and Peasants* (c. 1658–60), suffused with a beautiful golden light, was bought by the Earl of Bute in the 1760s and is supposedly the picture that stimulated the admiration of Cuyp (and his landscapes populated by cows) among British collectors. **Hobbema's *Avenue at Middelharnis*** (1689), with its central avenues of trees receding into the distance, was formerly owned by Robert Peel and is one of the gallery's best-loved works. In Room 22 are works by **Jacob van Ruisdael**, the most famous landscapist of his day, including *Landscape with a Ruined Castle and a Church* (c. 1665–70), a famous work with light playing on the fields below scudding clouds.

The National Gallery has a large collection of **Rembrandt**'s works, both portraits and large-scale biblical pictures (Rooms 23–24). The *Woman Taken in Adultery* (1644) was one of Angerstein's 1824 foundation works; the *Lamentation over the Dead Christ* was Beaumont's; and the famous *A Woman Bathing in a Stream* (1654), probably Hendrickje Stoffels, who lived in Rembrandt's household, came to the gallery in 1831. The important *Belshazzar's Feast* (c. 1635) is an early attempt by Rembrandt to establish himself as a large-scale history painter. He shows the moment when, having served wine in sacred vessels looted from the Temple in Jerusalem, Belshazzar observes the appearance of Hebrew script on a wall predicting the fall of his kingdom.

Flemish pictures (17th century)

The large and impressive collection of works by the great Baroque artist **Rubens** is in Room 29. Many arrived at the gallery in the 19th century, including the *Rape of the Sabine Women* (1635–40), acquired in 1824; *A View of Het Steen in the Early Morning*, showing Rubens' country estate purchased in 1635 (part of the Beaumont bequest); and the important *Peace and War*, painted when Rubens was in England on a diplomatic mission to negotiate peace with Spain (presented by the Duke of Sutherland in 1828). Other works produced for English patrons include the portrait of the celebrated art connoisseur Thomas Howard, Earl of Arundel (*see p. 365*). One of the most famous pictures in the National Gallery is ***Le Chapeau de Paille***, part of the Peel collection purchased in 1871, the name of the picture dating back to the 18th century. Other important works include *The Watering Place*, a landscape which inspired Constable's work of the same name.

Works by Rubens' most famous pupil, **Van Dyck**, the most celebrated and influential artist working in Britain in the 17th century, are in Room 31. The most important is the enormous *Equestrian Portrait of Charles I* (c. 1637–38), painted for the King whose official painter Van Dyck was, and by whom he was knighted for his services.

ITALIAN PICTURES (17th century)

Rooms 32 and 37 contains Italian works of the 17th century: by **Caravaggio** is the early *Supper at Emmaus* (1601) as well as his late *Salome Receives the Head of St John the Baptist*, with theatrical, dramatic lighting and intense passion. Works by the **Bolognese school** (Annibale Carracci, Guido Reni and Guercino) are also on display. Orazio Gentileschi's large and imposing *Finding of Moses* is an important work executed in England in the 1630s when the artist was in the service of Charles I and his queen, Henrietta Maria.

French pictures (17th century)

Rooms 19 and 20 are dedicated to the two great French landscape artists **Poussin** and **Claude**. Both the foundation Angerstein and Beaumont collections contained Claude, reflecting the high esteem in which British collectors held his work. *Landscape with Hagar and the Angel* was Beaumont's favourite picture. The gallery's collection of his hugely influential, poetic classical landscapes, peopled by figures from Classical mythology and the Bible, includes *The Enchanted Castle* (1664), which influenced Keats's 'Ode to a Nightingale'. When J.M.W. Turner bequeathed his pictures to the nation he stipulated that two of them, *Dido Building Carthage* and *Sun Rising through Vapour*, were to be shown alongside two of Angerstein's Claudes, *Seaport with the Embarkation of the Queen of Sheba* and *Landscape with the Marriage of Isaac and Rebekah*. They hang together in Room 15, the modern genius alongside the influential predecessor.

Spanish pictures (17th century)

Religious works created in the service of the Counter Reformation, and other 17th-century Spanish pictures, are displayed in Room 30: the highly individual works of **El Greco**, including *Christ Driving the Traders from the Temple* (c. 1600); important works by **Velázquez**, expressing the dignity of the court of Philip IV, including the majestic 1630s full-length of the king, in a splendid costume with sparkling silver embroidery; and the exceptional *Toilet of Venus* ('*The Rokeby Venus*'; c. 1647–51), the only surviving female nude by the artist, famously slashed by a suffragette in 1914. Zurbarán's *St Francis in Meditation* shows the kneeling saint with uncompromising realism, in a stark interior, his face partially hidden by the dramatic shadow cast by his hood. **Murillo**'s more gentle works, with their soft style and colouring (known as *estilo vaporoso*), include his self-portrait, *Peasant Boy Leaning on a Sill* and the sweet and gentle *The Two Trinities* (1681–2).

Italy (18th–early 20th centuries)

Rooms 38–40 show 18th-century Spanish and Italian works, including many by the Italian *vedutisti*, such as **Canaletto**'s excellent *Stonemason's Yard* (Room 38). There are further Venetian views by Canaletto and **Guardi**, and two English works by Canaletto: *The Rotunda at Ranelagh* and *Eton College*. **Goya**'s *Doña Isabel de Porcel* is in Room 39. **Tiepolo** is well represented in Room 40 with a good range of works, including the lovely and very characteristic *Allegory with Venus and Time*.

British School (18th–early 20th centuries)

In the Rotunda (Room 36) are important full-length works including Sir Thomas Lawrence's *Queen Charlotte* (1789–90), shown seated at Windsor Castle in expensive pearls, with a view of Eton College chapel through the window. Sargent's excellent *Lord Ribblesdale* (1902) is a likeness of a former trustee of the National Gallery.

Rooms 34 and 35 display the bulk of the British pictures: **Hogarth's *Marriage à la Mode*** series (Room 35), a moralising commentary on contemporary life, was part of Angerstein's collection; **Gainsborough**'s early *Mr and Mrs Andrews*, a genteel couple outdoors in their park; **Joseph Wright of Derby**'s full-length *Mrs and Mrs William Coltman*; **Constable**'s well-known *Hay-Wain* (Room 34), the quintessential image of the English countryside, as well as *The Cornfield* (1826) and *The Cenotaph to Reynolds' Memory, Coleorton*. The latter had been erected in the grounds at Coleorton, Sir George Beaumont's country home, in 1812. Also here is Gainsborough's portrait of the actress Mrs Siddons, of whom he is said to have complained while painting it: 'Confound her nose, there's no end to it!' **Stubbs**' monumental *Whistlejacket* shows a great rearing, riderless horse against a stark background. Other pictures include Joseph Wright of Derby's famous *An Experiment on a Bird in the Air Pump* (1768); **Turner**'s celebrated *The Fighting 'Temeraire', tugged to her Last Berth to be broken up* (1839) in Room 34; and his *Rain, Steam and Speed—The Great Western Railway* (before 1844).

France (18th–early 20th centuries)

French 19th-century Academy painting (Room 41) includes works by Géricault and **Delacroix**; and **Ingres**' *Mme Moitessier* (1844–56), the wife of a wealthy banker, shown seated in her finery. The picture, with its extraordinary porcelain finish, took Ingres twelve years to complete.

The gallery has an excellent Impressionist collection which includes several outstanding masterpieces: **Manet**'s *Music in the Tuileries Gardens* and his *Execution of Maximilian* (1867–68), the latter the second version he painted of the execution by firing squad of Archduke Maximilian, younger brother of the Emperor Franz Joseph of Austria, who had been installed as Emperor of Mexico by Napoleon III but was captured and executed by Mexican forces after the withdrawal of French troops. The mutilated fragments of the picture were rescued and pieced together by Degas. **Monet**'s work (Room 43) includes *Gare St-Lazare*, (1877); *The Water-Lily Pond* (1879); *The Beach at Trouville* (1870) and *The Thames below Westminster* (1871). **Seurat**'s *Bathers at Asnières* (Room 44) is partly executed in his 'pointillism' technique. **Renoir**'s supreme *Les Parapluies* is also here.

The final decades of the 19th century are represented with works by **Cézanne** (Room 45), including his well-known *Bathers, 'Les Grandes Baigneuses'*, one of three large works of the same theme. Of **Van Gogh**'s work (also Room 45), the gallery has one of the versions of his famous *Sunflowers* (1888) as well as *Van Gogh's Chair*, painted at Arles in November 1888 when he was working in the company of Gauguin, and *A Wheatfield with Cypresses*, painted in September 1889 at the mental asylum at St-Rémy. **Henri Rousseau**'s *Tiger in a Tropical Storm* (*'Surprised!'*), the first of his over 20 jungle pictures (1891), is also in this room.

In 2014 it was announced that the National Gallery was to purchase George Bellows' 1912 *Men of the Docks*, showing shipyard workers in Manhattan: small labouring figures dwarfed by skyscrapers and a transatlantic steamer. This represents an important new departure for an institution hitherto known for its Western European art collection.

LONDON MUSEUMS IN THE SECOND WORLD WAR

Shortly before the outbreak of the World War Two, on 23rd August 1939, the government ordered the evacuation of all major London collections. The British Museum moved the Elgin Marbles into a disused Tube tunnel at Aldwych. Unable to remove Stanley Spencer's large-scale *The Resurrection, Cookham* (1924–7), the Tate protected it on site behind a purpose-built brick wall. Most of the National Gallery's paintings were removed to north Wales. Initially many were housed at Penrhyn Castle, where the owner's drunken behaviour gave the gallery staff serious misgivings about the collection's safety. Other institutions also relied on country houses—the V&A sent some of their collection to Montacute House in Somerset, the Wallace Collection to Hellens in Herefordshire—until the fall of France brought the Luftwaffe within range of these more remote areas and suggestions arose in the press that home-owners were keen to store artefacts in order to dodge army billets and avoid working-class evacuees. In September 1940, five large chambers in the Manod slate quarries near Blaenau Ffestiniog, north Wales, were identified by the National Gallery as a suitable bomb-proof repository for its pictures. Meanwhile, back in London, the almost empty gallery building hosted lunchtime charity concerts. Organised by the great pianist Dame Myra Hess, the first of more than 1,500 consecutive recitals was given on 10th October 1939. Another popular morale-boosting initiative began in early 1942, in response to a letter to *The Times* from the sculptor Charles Wheeler, when the first 'Picture of the Month' (Rembrandt's *Margaretha de Geer*) was displayed in the gallery. Forty-three pictures were transported to and from Manod on a three-week cycle for the duration of the war. The 'Picture of the Month' scheme is still going strong.

NATIONAL PORTRAIT GALLERY

Map p. 603, F1. Open daily 10–6 (Thur and Fri until 9pm). Free. National Portrait Gallery app. Restaurant (reservations essential; T: 020 7312 2490), café and bar. Shop. T: 020 7306 0055, npg.org.uk.

The National Portrait Gallery was founded in 1856, the first establishment of its type in the world. The three men responsible for its foundation, the 5th Earl Stanhope, Thomas Macaulay and Thomas Carlyle, were all historians and biographers keenly interested in Britain's past. Stanhope was the author of a seven-volume history of Georgian Britain, Macaulay of a monumental *History of England*, and Carlyle of the famous *On Heroes* (1841), in which he argued that 'the history of the world is but the biography of great men'. All three agreed that a National Portrait Gallery should not only illustrate British history but should celebrate the individuals who had contributed to Britain's pre-eminence, a view reflective of mid-19th-century British optimism. The gallery was to be a historical resource where images of the great and good could be venerated and could inspire emulation.

The foundations of the collection were laid by the etcher and illustrator George Scharf. Beginning with the 'Chandos' portrait of Shakespeare, the gallery's first acquisition, the collection steadily grew from an original 57 pictures to over 1,000. Scharf's profound study of portraiture enabled him to authenticate as genuine or dismiss images, and his meticulous manuscript notebooks of portraits in private collections, with lively sketches and annotations, now in the gallery's archive, remain a valuable resource.

THE BUILDING

The building (1890–5) was designed by Ewan Christian. The north block is in Florentine Renaissance *palazzo* style while the principal entrance, on St Martin's Place, is inspired by the delicate terracotta façade of Santo Spirito, Bologna. The three portrait busts (by Frederick Thomas) on the entrance façade are of the significant figures in the museum's history: Stanhope, Macaulay and Carlyle. Continuing round the building are images of artists, sculptors and historians.

In 1998–2000 came alterations and improvements by Dixon/Jones. Straight ahead of the entrance lobby, with its original mosaic floor, is the bright, white hall of the Ondaatje wing. From here, the contemporary collections are to the right; the long escalator takes visitors straight up to the second-floor Tudor and Stuart galleries (and off them, the 18th- and early 19th-century collection); and stairs lead to the first-floor Victorian and 20th-century pictures. On the third floor is the Portrait Restaurant, with its famous bird's-eye panorama of Nelson on his column, with the Palace of Westminster and Big Ben beyond.

THE COLLECTION

The National Portrait Gallery holds many iconic images of famous figures from British history and visitors will inevitably have their own interests and specialisms. Nevertheless, an attempt to outline some of the highlights may be helpful. The collection is arranged in reverse chronological order, with the latest works on the ground floor and the earliest on the second.

NB: Not all the collection can be shown at once. To minimise their exposure to light, miniatures, works on paper and photographs are shown in selected rotations. The entire collection can be viewed at the terminals in the IT mezzanine gallery.

Tudor and Stuart portraits (2nd floor)

The collection of 16th- and 17th-century British pictures is one of the best in the world. The earliest portrait in the collection is the finely painted *Henry VII* (1505), his hand resting on a stone ledge, a composition taken from early Flemish portraiture. The most important early work, probably the most important work in the gallery, is Holbein's famous 'cartoon' for a mural in Whitehall Palace (since destroyed) celebrating the Tudor dynasty. King Henry VIII's commanding full-length pose served as the prototype for other images of him. Other Tudor figures include Thomas More, shown surrounded by his family in a copy after Holbein's lost portrait; Thomas Cranmer; and the curious anamorphic portrait of Edward VI, a distorted image which comes into line at one visual point. The full-length 'Ditchley Portrait' of Elizabeth I, by Marcus Gheeraerts the Younger, is an exceptionally fine image of the deliberately ageless queen (c. 1592). It was painted to commemorate her stay at Ditchley, in Oxfordshire, as the guest of Sir Henry Lee. She stands on a globe, her feet on Oxfordshire, with lightning flashes behind her (banished by her radiance) and sunshine before, all typical of the symbolic portraiture so loved by the Elizabethans.

By James I's reign canvas had become the most common support for painting, allowing for larger pictures. As well as James himself, by Daniel Mytens, are beautiful full-lengths by Robert Peake of Frederick, Prince of Wales and his sister Princess Elizabeth, in an intricately embroidered gown of gold and silver thread. From Charles I's reign are images of Charles himself, Queen Henrietta Maria and Lord George Stuart, Seigneur d'Aubigny (c. 1638), a young royalist killed at the battle of Edgehill, an excellent late work by Van Dyck, who was Charles I's official painter.

One of the best works from the mid-17th century is Walker's *John Evelyn*, a wonderful study of intellectual melancholia. The later 17th-century collection is particularly rich, with several portraits by Sir Peter Lely, official painter to Charles II. There are also portraits of the king's mistresses, of court wits such as the Earl of Rochester and of Samuel Pepys: the portrait by John Hayls that he mentions in his diary.

The later Stuart collection includes the ruthless Judge Jeffreys by John Michael Wright; a particularly beautiful Lely of Mary II, as Princess of Orange; a very fine full-length of Queen Anne by Michael Dahl; Anne's close friend, and later enemy, the powerful Duchess of Marlborough, shown with her gold key of office around her waist; and Sir Godfrey Kneller's small allegorical oil sketch of the Duke of Marlborough, the famous victor of Blenheim, shown on a rearing horse.

18th- and early 19th-century portraits (2nd floor)

The 18th-century collection includes portraits of Sir Christopher Wren, of Hogarth (a terracotta bust by Roubiliac), and of men of letters such as the satirist and author of *Gulliver's Travels*, Jonathan Swift. Hung together are Kneller's important Kit-cat portraits, with their uniform frames, showing the politically Whig-minded members of the convivial drinking and dining club. Later Georgians include the great painter Sir Joshua Reynolds and the famous Dr Johnson, author of the Dictionary.

There are portraits of George III and Queen Charlotte by Allan Ramsay. The expanding East India Company is the subject of Francis Hayman's important image *Robert Clive Receiving the Homage of Mir Jaffir after the Battle of Plassey*. The gallery also possesses Sir Thomas Lawrence's autocratic profile oil sketch of George, the Prince Regent, with his hair brushed forward, Roman style; as well as the great military and naval heroes of the day, the Duke of Wellington and Lord Nelson. Romantic poets and novelists include Lord Byron (in 'magnifique' Albanian costume), Benjamin Robert Haydon's portrait of the 72-year-old Wordsworth, as well as Coleridge, Keats and Sir Walter Scott. Also in the collection is the delicate sketch of Jane Austen by her sister, Cassandra. Sir George Hayter's enormous *The Reformed House of Commons* (1833) was painted to commemorate the passing of the 1832 Great Reform Act, which widened the country's electorate.

Victorian collection (1st floor)

The Victorian displays include portraits, both painted and sculpted, of Victorian statesmen, writers, artists, travellers, inventors and politicians. The British Empire's self-confidence and evangelising spirit is summed up well in Sir George Strong Nares' *The Secret of England's Greatness*, showing Queen Victoria presenting a Bible to a kneeling African convert. Large historical portraits include Jenny Barret's *The Mission of Mercy: Florence Nightingale Receiving the Wounded at Scutari* (c. 1856–8). As well as these ponderous pieces is James Tissot's wonderful *Frederick Gustavus Burnaby* (1870), a cavalry officer and explorer who died of a spear wound on an expedition to Khartoum. He is shown in uniform, relaxing on a sofa, with an elegantly twirled moustache.

Famous portraits include Branwell Brontë's painting of his sisters, Charlotte, Emily and Anne, a naïve work discovered folded up on top of a cupboard by the second wife of Charlotte Brontë's widower. John Ballantyne's 1865 image of Landseer shows the great artist at work modelling the stone lions for the base of Nelson's column in Trafalgar Square. Also here is Robert Howlett's well-known 1858 photograph of Isambard Kingdom Brunel, standing before the massive anchor chains of his steamship *Leviathan* (later the *Great Eastern*). Shown together are G.F. Watts' 'Hall of Fame' portraits of the great men of his day, which Watts bequeathed to the gallery. His belief in the importance to history of men of intellectual power and vision, close to Carlyle's theory of the Hero, coincided with the founding mission of the gallery. Carlyle, of course, is included (he hated his portrait). The gallery also owns Watts' famous image of his wife for one year, the actress Ellen Terry, shown at the age of 17 'choosing' (the title of the work) between the worldly camellia and the innocence of violets. Terry—who was 30 years younger than Watts—left her husband and returned to the stage.

John Singer Sargent's powerful and brilliant 1908 portrait of the Earl of Balfour, a pivotal figure in British politics from the 1880s, was thought by G.K. Chesterton to sum up not only the man but also the vague pessimism of the age. The gallery's other late Victorian and turn-of-the-century images include the Italian Boldini's exuberant *Lady Colin Campbell*, socialite and journalist, shown in black chiffon with an impossible wasp waist; Napoleon Savory's photograph of his 'picturesque subject', Oscar Wilde, taken in New York in 1882; and portraits of such leaders of the avant garde as Walter Sickert, Philip Wilson Steer and Augustus John.

20th-century collection (1st floor)

Figures from the period of the First World War include the suffragette Emmeline Pankhurst. There are many portraits of politicians. Graham Sutherland's oil sketch of Sir Winston Churchill is a reminder of the original, disliked by Churchill and destroyed by his wife. Post-war images include Sir James Gunn's elegant *Conversation Piece at Royal Lodge, Windsor*, showing George VI and his family taking tea. Later works include a self-portrait by Lucian Freud and famous faces of stage and screen.

Photography (shown throughout the gallery)

Photography is a growing part of the collection. There are over 100 images by the early Victorian photographer Julia Margaret Cameron, dating from the 1860s and '70s, as well as famous images such as Frederick Henry Evans' 1893 portrait of Aubrey Beardsley and George Charles Beresford's 1902 portraits of Virginia Woolf. The gallery also owns over 1,000 works by Cecil Beaton and images by, among others, Norman Parkinson, Bill Brandt, Henri Cartier-Bresson and Helmut Newton.

PORTRAIT AWARDS

Since 1987 the National Portrait Gallery has hosted the Portrait Award (first sponsored by John Player, now BP), the world's most important open portrait competition, which receives around 2,000 entries each year from across the globe. Fifty-five are selected for display (in summer) and compete for a first prize of £30,000 and a commission worth £5,000. The exhibition is one of the most popular in London each year. The Taylor Wessing Photographic Portrait Award (inaugurated in 2003) seeks to celebrate contemporary photographers, professional and amateur alike.

VICTORIA EMBANKMENT

Map p. 604, A3. Underground: Embankment. NB: The description below takes in the section of the Embankment between Hungerford and Waterloo bridges. For the section north from Westminster Bridge, see p. 146.

Victoria Embankment runs from Westminster Bridge to Blackfriars Bridge. The idea of creating an embankment along the Thames had been first suggested by Christopher Wren after the Great Fire but the ambitious piece of planning did not take shape until the mid-19th century, when it was carried out to a design by civil engineer Sir Joseph Bazalgette (*for the history, including the 'Great Stink', see pp. 146–7*). In Carting Lane, a narrow side street bordering the Savoy Hotel (*map p. 604, A2–A3*), a lone Victorian streetlamp survives from Bazalgette's time, ingeniously powered by methane gas rising from the hotel's sewers.

Opposite Embankment Underground station, over the busy lanes of traffic, is **Embankment Pier**, from which river cruises depart (*see p. 541*). From here, as you look across at the South Bank, Hungerford Bridge and the Palace of Westminster are on your right, while on your left is Waterloo Bridge with the towers of the City beyond (the dome of St Paul's can still just be seen amongst the skyscrapers). Built into the river wall is a bronze portrait medallion of W.S. Gilbert (d. 1911), one half of the comedy-opera duo Gilbert and Sullivan, whose operettas were performed at the nearby Savoy Theatre. 'His foe was folly and his weapon wit'; the small sculptures represent *Tragedy* and *Comedy*.

Further along on the river stands London's oldest monument: the so-called **Cleopatra's Needle**, an ancient Egyptian obelisk, erected in 1878 and now much weathered by acid rain and pollution. It is flanked by two large bronze sphinxes, c. 1882.

The obelisk dates from 1450 BC and consists of a single piece of Aswan granite, quarried by Thutmose III. It was originally one of a pair at Heliopolis; the other now stands in New York's Central Park. The hieroglyphs were added by Ramesses II, 200 years later. Emperor Augustus had the obelisks moved to Alexandria, Cleopatra's city, in 12 BC. In 1819, Mohammed Ali, Viceroy of Egypt, presented the Needle to the British people in memory of Nelson and Abercromby and their successful Egyptian campaigns. However, it lay unclaimed in the desert until Prince Albert pressed for it to brought to London (Paris had been similarly presented with an obelisk and had already erected theirs). Eventually it cost £10,000 and six sailors' lives to tow the obelisk across the treacherous seas in a floating iron cylinder: at one point it was abandoned to the waves in the Bay of Biscay, but eventually recovered. It arrived in 1878 and after much disagreement, the site on the Embankment was chosen. The names of the sailors who died bringing the Needle to London are commemorated on a plaque at its base; beneath it is buried an 1878 time capsule, which includes photographs of beauties of the day.

Opposite, across the road, in front of **Victoria Embankment Gardens**, is a concave monument 'to the British nation from the grateful people of Belgium, 1914–18'. Victoria Embankment Gardens is an elongated banana-shaped stretch of greenery planted with shrubs, trees, a small lily pond and flowerbeds amongst which are several statues. The façades of several of the Strand buildings overlook the gardens, including the Savoy Hotel (*see p. 184*). From the Waterloo Bridge entrance, walking back towards the Embankment, statues and monuments include Robert Raikes, founder of Sunday Schools; a bronze medallion of the blind campaigner for women's rights, Henry Fawcett (his blindness indicated by his closed eyes); and a bronze bust of Arthur Sullivan (the other half of Gilbert and Sullivan, d. 1900) by William Goscombe John (a topless maiden weeps against his plinth). In front of the Savoy is a small seating area and the D'Oyly Carte memorial. A stone tablet on the grass beneath trees commemorates those who died in the 2005 London Bombings; former Mayor of London Ken Livingstone is quoted: 'the City will endure, it is the future of our world.' The *pièce de résistance*, the last relic of the Strand's historic past, when it was lined with courtly mansions, is the **water-gate of York House**. Built in 1626 by Nicholas Stone for George Villiers, 1st Duke of Buckingham, its rusticated Italianate façade, much eroded, is surmounted by two lions on either side of the Buckingham coat of arms. Before the Embankment was built, the Thames reached this point.

THE STRAND

Map p. 604, A3–B2. Underground: Charing Cross.

The Strand is a major thoroughfare, curving east for nearly three quarters of a mile, between Trafalgar Square and Temple Bar, the junction with Fleet Street that marks the official boundary between Westminster and the City of London. It is the ancient link between the City and the Palace of Westminster. Originally it ran along the banks of the Thames—hence its name—and from the 12th and 13th centuries bishops and royal courtiers built grand residences that led down to the water. Today, since the building of Victoria Embankment, the Strand is no longer on the river but it is still the official processional route from the City of London to Westminster. The boundary between Westminster and the City is marked by two dragons, painted silver and red, who rear up on either side of the Embankment proffering the City's coat of arms. The aforementioned grand residences are today mainly referenced by street names, and the road is lined with offices, shops and restaurants, as well as one or two fine buildings such as Somerset House and the Savoy Hotel. There are also several theatres here; this was Victorian London's bustling theatre district. At its eastern side, just before Fleet Street, are two churches marooned on traffic islands: St Mary-le-Strand and St Clement Danes. Victoria Embankment, Joseph Bazalgette's feat of engineering (*see p. 146*), runs below along the Thames, and in between are quiet streets of fine surviving Georgian terraced housing. Northumberland Avenue, a wide boulevard lined with imposing buildings over land anciently owned by the Dukes of Northumberland, was created to connect the Strand with the new Embankment.

CHARING CROSS STATION AND VILLIERS STREET

This busy commuter station (*map p. 604, A3*) brings passengers from southeast London and the south coast across the Thames via Hungerford Bridge. When built it provided a train-boat service to Europe; the popular music hall song 'Let's All Go Down The Strand' tells of a group of tourists on their way to the Rhineland. The station (John Hawkshaw, 1863–5) occupies the site of Hungerford Market (1682). The townhouse of Walter, 1st Baron Hungerford (d. 1449), a knight who fought at the Battle of Agincourt, stood here from 1425. The adjoining **Charing Cross Hotel**, with painted white, red and green decorative ironwork, was designed by E.M. Barry—it was one of the first buildings to be faced with artificial stone; in this case pale painted terracotta. In the paved forecourt, in front of the cab rank, stands an elaborate **neo-Gothic Cross** (E.M. Barry, 1865; restored) based on the original cross dedicated to Eleanor of Castile (wife of Edward I) which stood at the top of Whitehall to mark the last resting place of her bier on its journey from Nottinghamshire to Westminster Abbey for burial in 1290. The cross was demolished in 1647 during the English Civil War and in its place is a statue of Charles I, erected after the Restoration (*see p. 166*). Behind the station frontage, Terry Farrell's huge Post-modern office and shopping complex, **Embankment Place** (1986–91), stretches over the tracks and arches, down Villiers Street and all the way to Hungerford Bridge. The river façade, all curves and towers, is best observed from the Embankment (better still from the South Bank); it looks like a giant locomotive bursting out onto the Thames.

The part-pedestrianised **Villiers Street** was once the site of York House, the residence of the Archbishop of York, owned from the 1620s by the royal favourite George Villiers, 1st Duke of Buckingham, and after the Civil War by his son, the 2nd Duke. At no. 47 is **Gordon's**, London's oldest wine bar, famous for its schooners of sherry and range of fortified wines sold by the glass. Continue along its outdoor seating area, the narrow Watergate Passage overlooking Victoria Embankment Gardens, until you come to the back of York Gate (the old water-gate of York House; *see p. 181*) and a small flight of steps leading up to Buckingham Street, built on the site of York House. Here is an enclave of houses dating from the late 17th and early 18th centuries, many with fine doorcases. Samuel Pepys lived at no. 12 in 1679–88. Charles Dickens lived on the site of no. 15.

CRAVEN STREET

South of Charing Cross Station is Craven Street, where at no. 36 is **Benjamin Franklin House** (*T: 020 7925 1405; benjaminfranklinhouse.org*), an elegant Georgian townhouse of 1730 and the only surviving London home of Benjamin Franklin, the great American statesman and scientist, who lived here from 1757–75. It was here that he sat at the windows 'air bathing', learnt to play the harp, guitar and violin, and conducted political negotiations with William Pitt the Elder on the eve of the American Revolution. While in London, Franklin forged friendships with many leading intellectuals and continued with his many writings and experiments, including the invention of the lightning conductor (it is also said that he performed alarming demonstrations of electricity at dinner parties). The house is open for a 'historical experience blending drama and technology' (*Wed–Sun at 12, 1, 2, 3.15 and 4.15; tours last 40mins*). The staircase and much of the panelling is original. During restoration, a pit with human remains was discovered in the basement—probably connected to the anatomy school run by Franklin's friend William Hewson. Hewson is said to have died of blood poisoning after cutting himself during a dissection. The German poet and essayist Heinrich Heine (d. 1856) lived at no. 32 and no. 25 was home to Herman Melville, author of *Moby Dick*. On the same street at no. 42 is the **British Optical Association Museum** (*open Mon–Fri by appointment only; T: 020 7766 4353, college-optometrists.org*), with displays of over 2,000 pairs of spectacles from the 17th century to the present and a portrait of Benjamin Franklin sporting a pair of *pince-nez*. Franklin is usually credited with the invention of bifocals.

On the other side of the Strand, the cream stucco turreted façade with shops at ground level is Nash's **West Strand Improvements** of 1830–2. At the centre, behind a modern glass screen, is Coutts' Bank (established 1692), traditionally bankers to Britain's aristocracy although today, if you have at least £1 million in liquid funds, you might be considered as a client. Behind, in the triangle between William IV Street and Agar Street, is the former Charing Cross Hospital, the foundation stone laid in 1831 (now a police station). **Zimbabwe House** on Agar Street opposite was designed by Charles Holden as the British Medical Association in 1907–8; nude statues above the second-floor windows are by Epstein, apparently carved *in situ*. In 1937 their eroded parts were taken off, giving them their current maimed appearance.

JOHN ADAM STREET AND THE ADELPHI

John Adam Street (*map p. 604, A3*) runs parallel with the Strand. On the site of no. 16 lived the caricaturist Thomas Rowlandson, who along with Cruikshank and the bitingly satirical Gillray, lampooned English social and political life from the 1790s. Further on, the quadrangle made up of John Adam Street, Robert Street, Adelphi Terrace and

Adam Street, is what remains of the **Adelphi**, an ambitious residential project built by the four Adam brothers, John, Robert, James and William, from 1768 (Adelphi means 'brothers' in Greek). The development, on the site of Durham House, former residence of the Bishop of Durham, where Anne Boleyn had lived for a time, involved the building of high-quality residential streets, houses and terraces, all of uniform design, supported on an embankment of arches and subterranean vaults which were to be leased to river trade. Adelphi Terrace is the site of Royal Terrace, where 24 houses overlooked the river, their design inspired by the Palace of Diocletian at Split in Croatia. Directly behind and on either side were similar streets of quality housing. The project was a financial disaster, bringing near-bankruptcy on the brothers, and in 1774 a lottery was authorised by Parliament to rescue the enterprise. Among those who did come to live here, apart from the architects and builders themselves, were Sir Richard Arkwright, Charles Booth, Richard d'Oyly Carte, David Garrick, Charles Dickens (the Adelphi features in *David Copperfield*), George Bernard Shaw, J.M. Barrie, H.G. Wells and John Galsworthy. In 1936–8 the entire central part was demolished and replaced by the **New Adelphi**, the current colossal Art Moderne office block, by Colcutt and Hemp, in brick, Portland stone and bronze, with much carved ornament (busy putti, signs of the zodiac, etc.) and over the river terrace, huge sculptures representing *Dawn, Contemplation, Inspiration* and *Night*. Today, in the surrounding side streets, a few of the fine original houses survive; note those with stucco pilasters covered in Robert Adam's repeating anthemion motifs. Below, Lower Robert Street is one of the surviving vaults, now a narrow, winding cut-through and part of a London cab driver's 'Knowledge'. It is said to be haunted by a Victorian prostitute, 'Poor Jenny'.

The **Royal Society of Arts** (RSA) occupies a fine Adam building (no. 8 John Adam St) with an Ionic portico, Venetian window and statuary on the roof. The Society was established in 1754 to foster art, manufacture and trade. The equally fine interior may be visited by appointment or on designated open days (*T: 020 7930 5115, thersa.org*). The Great Room features James Barry's *The Progress of Human Knowledge* painting cycle, hung below the cornice.

Adam Street leads back to the Strand. Opposite are two popular theatres: the Adelphi (1806; rebuilt twice) and the Vaudeville (1870). In between, a narrow ceramic-tiled passage, Old Bull Yard, leads to the tiny Nell Gwynne pub (*cash only*). At no. 339 is Stanley Gibbons, 'the home of stamp collecting since 1856'. Opposite, at nos 77–86, the enormous building in red granite is what remains of the **former Cecil Hotel**, the largest hotel in Europe when it opened in 1885. The archway leads through to the 1930s' **Shell Mex House**, with its distinctive, monumental façade and giant clock face, overlooking the Embankment.

THE SAVOY HOTEL

The Savoy Hotel (*map p. 604, A2–A3*), which immediately eclipsed the nearby Cecil in grandeur when it opened in 1889, is still one of the most luxurious hotels in the world, today managed by the Fairmont group. It has recently undergone a multi-million pound refurbishment: all the original contents were sold at auction and many of the interior spaces have traded elegance for a hard, brash aesthetic aimed at evoking the

NEW ADELPHI
Busy putto.

'decadent' chic of the 1930s. The hotel, built on the site of the Savoy Palace (*see below*), was conceived by the theatre impresario Richard d'Oyly Carte, renowned for his collaboration with the comic opera duo Gilbert and Sullivan; adjacent is D'Oyly Carte's earlier Savoy Theatre (1881; the first theatre to have electricity), built explicitly for the 'Savoy Operas' as they were then called (*The Mikado, The Pirates of Penzance, Iolanthe,* etc.).

The Savoy was one of the first hotels to have private bathrooms with hot and cold running water, electric lifts and 24-hour room service. César Ritz was the first manager and Auguste Escoffier the first chef. On either side of the recessed forecourt entrance, above which are the famous green neon sign and the gilded statue of Count Peter of Savoy, are the Art Nouveau shopfronts for the Savoy Taylors Guild and Coal Hole pub (right) and the restaurant Simpsons (left), founded in 1848, a bastion of English cuisine and still famous for its roast beef with Yorkshire pudding. A plaque in an elaborate cartouche nearby confirms the site of the 18th-century Fountain Tavern, where members of the Fountain Club, political opponents of Sir Robert Walpole, met (*for the lamp post in Carting Lane, the narrow street, leading down past the Coal Hole pub, see p. 180*).

SAVOY PALACE AND CHAPEL

Savoy Palace, built in 1246, was given by Henry III to Peter II of Savoy, 1st Earl of Richmond (d. 1268) and uncle of Eleanor of Provence, Henry III's consort. The palace later passed into the possession of John of Gaunt, Duke of Lancaster, and was known for its magnificence until it burned down and was systematically destroyed in its entirety during the Peasants' Revolt of 1381. John of Gaunt was the patron of Geoffrey Chaucer and part of *The Canterbury Tales* was written in the palace. John of Valois, King of France, taken prisoner at the Battle of Poitiers by the Black Prince, died here in 1364. On part of the site in 1640 was built Worcester House, home of Edward, 2nd Marquess of Worcester, where in 1660, James II (then Duke of York) married Anne

CARTING LANE
Street lamp behind the Savoy Hotel powered by methane from the sewers beneath.

Hyde. Their daughters Mary and Anne would later become Queens of England. In the house in 1658, Oliver Cromwell drew up the Confession of Faith; in 1661 Charles II ordered the Savoy Conference.

Savoy Street leads south to the **Queen's Chapel of the Savoy**, entered from Savoy Hill (*map p. 604, A2; open Mon–Thur 9–4, Sun 9–1*), a royal peculiar, belonging to the Queen in her right as Duke of Lancaster. After Savoy Palace was destroyed in 1381, and following John of Gaunt's death in 1399, the manor was made over to the Crown. Henry VII built a hospital for the poor and homeless on the land in 1512. The chapel is all that remains of that hospital and was restored after a fire in the 19th century. It is the Chapel of the Royal Victorian Order and the stalls of the knights are marked by small copper plates emblazoned with the arms of the holder. A stained-glass window commemorates Richard d'Oyly Carte (1844–1901).

ST MARY-LE-STRAND AND TEMPLE PLACE

Next door to Somerset House (*described on p. 188*) is **King's College London**, one of the incorporated colleges of the University of London, founded in 1829 by George IV and the Duke of Wellington in response to theological objections to the 'godless' London University (now UCL), founded in 1827. The 1971 façade conceals the interior buildings, built in the 1830s by Robert Smirke.

In the middle of the Strand stands the church of **St Mary-le-Strand** (*map p. 604, A2; open Tues–Thur 11–4, Sun 10–1; stmarylestrand.org*), with a classical portico and a steeple decorated with flaming urns. This was the first of the 'Queen Anne' churches

erected under the 1711 New Churches Act, built by James Gibbs from 1714 and consecrated in 1723. The windows were designed deliberately high up so as to mitigate the
noise of traffic. It is now the church of the Women's Royal Naval Service.

The names of the three side streets that lead south to the Embankment, Essex,
Arundel and Surrey, commemorate the sites of the town houses of the Earls of Arundel
and Essex. In Temple Place stands Marochetti's statue of Isambard Kingdom Brunel.
On the corner of Milford Lane, at **2 Temple Place**, the richly ornamented neo-Eliza-
bethan building is the former estate office of William Waldorf Astor, built in 1895 by
Pearson. It is owned by the Bulldog Trust and viewing of the opulent interior is limited
(*twotempleplace.org*). Exterior features include the bronze lamp posts, by Frith, outside the main entrance; one depicts a cherub on the telephone. The large gilded ship
weather vane is of the *Santa Maria*, in which Columbus discovered America.

In the Temple section of Victoria Embankment Gardens is a statue to John Stuart
Mill and a memorial fountain to Lady Mary Somerset, President of the National British
Temperance Association. From the river are fine views west (right) of the Palace of
Westminster and the gables of Whitehall Place. Opposite is the Oxo Tower (*see p. 420*).
Moored here is HQS *Wellington*, the last surviving wartime escort ship (she served in
the Battle of the Atlantic and is now the headquarters of the Honourable Company of
Master Mariners). The gate in the river wall, with a sombre *Old Father Thames*, com-
memorates the naming of this stretch of water as King's Reach, on the 25th anniversary of George V's accession.

ALDWYCH AND ST CLEMENT DANES

The semicircular street looping south off the Strand and lined with grand, imperial
buildings is **Aldwych** (*map p. 604, A2*), a piece of Edwardian town planning. It takes
its name from an old colony (*ald wych*) of Danes who settled here before the Conquest.
The church of **St Clement Danes** (*map p. 604, B2; open daily 9–4 except bank holidays;
sometimes closed for special events, T: 020 7242 8282*), a castaway on a traffic island,
was designed by Wren and built in 1679–82 on the site of a much earlier building. It is
traditionally believed to be the burial place of Harold Harefoot (Harold I; d. 1040), son
of Canute. The tower, added by James Gibbs in 1719–20, contains a famous peal of bells
('Oranges and lemons, say the bells of St Clement's'). In 1941, the church was gutted by
fire and it has been restored as the church of the Royal Air Force. William Webb Ellis,
the inventor of rugby football in 1823, was rector here (memorial tablet). Dr Johnson
was a worshipper and is commemorated by a statue by Percy Fitzgerald (1910) outside
the back (east end). His sculpted book was stolen by vandals and replaced in 1996 by
the sculptor Faith Winter. Before the entrance to the church are three sculptures. One
is Hamo Thornycroft's 1905 memorial to William Gladstone, the liberal politician who
was four times Prime Minister. His statue is surrounded by four groups of women and
children representing *Education*, *Brotherhood*, *Aspiration* and *Courage*. The other two
statues are by Faith Winter: Lord Dowding, commander of the RAF Fighter Command
during the Battle of Britain, who was also a spiritualist, campaigner for the humane
killing of animals and a believer in fairies and ghosts; and fighter pilot Sir Arthur
'Bomber' Harris, in charge of Bomber Command during World War Two, who said of

the Luftwaffe, 'they sowed the wind, now they are going to reap the whirlwind.'

At time of writing, most of the huge buildings on the inner Aldwych island were under hoardings, being renovated by their Japanese owners Kato Kagaku. The complex will be renamed the Aldwych Quarter. On the east corner, overlooking St Clement Danes, is **Australia House**, built in 1911–18 as the office of the Commonwealth of Australia, utilising building materials especially imported from Australia. High above, Phoebus drives the Horses of the Sun, who leap headlong out of the pediment. The buildings along the inner curve include the Waldorf Hilton Hotel, the Aldwych Theatre and buildings belonging to the London School of Economics (LSE). Kingsway, at the centre, is the boulevard leading north to Holborn and Bloomsbury.

SOMERSET HOUSE & THE COURTAULD GALLERY

Map p. 604, A2. Underground: Temple. Open daily 10–6 (Drawing and Prints collections by appointment). Admission charge. Café (light meals also available) and shop. T: 020 7872 0220, courtauld.ac.uk.

Somerset House, built largely between 1776 and 1801, is the masterpiece of the architect Sir William Chambers, former architectural tutor to George III and from 1769 Comptroller of the King's Office of Works. The complex was designed to house various government offices, in particular the Navy Office (which occupied the river block), as well as three learned societies under royal patronage: the Royal Society, the Society of Antiquaries and the Royal Academy of Arts. They moved out in the 19th century and the Courtauld Institute moved in in 1989–90. Their gallery has one of the finest collections in London, highly enjoyable to visit. Installed in elegantly decorated 18th-century interiors, some of the greatest masterpieces of French Impressionist and Post-Impressionist art can be appreciated in an atmosphere of calm and restrained luxury.

THE BUILDING

Chambers intended Somerset House as a public showcase for English architectural and sculptural design. Its façades are enriched with the work of leading Royal Academician sculptors, exploring themes of maritime glory and royal patronage, symbolic of the building's function. The **Strand façade**, for instance, is surmounted by the arms of the British Empire, supported by *Fame* and the *Genius of Britain*, by John Bacon Sr (renewed in 1896); below this stand *Prudence, Justice, Moderation* and *Valour* (by Agostino Carlini and Giuseppe Ceracchi), the qualities, according to a 1781 description, upon which dominion is built; and the bearded heads on the keystones of the arcade, mainly by Joseph Wilton, represent Ocean and the great rivers of England.

Chambers' building was built on a site originally occupied by the townhouse of the Duke of Somerset (hence the name Somerset House), brother of Henry VIII's third wife, Jane Seymour. He became Lord Protector during the minority of his nephew Edward VI. His position was usurped by a rival and in 1552 he was executed on Tower Hill and his property was ceded to the Crown. In the 17th century Somerset House served as the official residence of successive Queen Consorts. Following the Restoration in 1660, the palace was refurbished for Henrietta Maria, the Queen Dowager, and included a Catholic chapel. Samuel Pepys was a frequent visitor to Somerset House and found the new works 'might fine and costly'. Although probably by John Webb, Chambers believed the gallery, which along with the rest of the palace was demolished to make way for the new building, to have been the work of the revered Inigo Jones, and its pure Classicism inspired his Strand façade. Under Catherine of Braganza, Portuguese consort of Charles II, Somerset House and its chapel remained a gravitational centre for Roman Catholics. Steep steps in front of the west wing lead down to a subterranean passage under the courtyard, the **Deadhouse**, where funerary tablets, the only remnants of the palace's religious past, can be seen (*guided tours only, on Thur and Sat; free; tickets from the Seamen's Hall*).

The central **courtyard** is one of the most elegant public spaces in London, with café tables from which one can enjoy Chambers' dignified architecture as well as the rectangular 55-jet fountain (Dixon/Jones 1999–2000). Over Christmas and New Year the latter is covered with a temporary ice rink which, on a dusky winter afternoon with its lighted flambeaux and Palladian surroundings, is extremely atmospheric.

THE COURTAULD GALLERY

Part of the Courtauld Institute of Art, a leading college of art history and conservation, the Courtauld Gallery comprises a series of private collections, the foremost of which is the superlative Impressionist and Post-Impressionist collection of its founder, Samuel Courtauld.

Descended from a Huguenot family of silversmiths, silk weavers and textile manufacturers, Courtauld (1876–1947) was chairman of the multinational company which in the early 20th century had become a leading producer of the artificial textile rayon (the company still operates but the Courtauld name has been subsumed by mergers and acquisitions). As well as giving £50,000 to the nation for the purchase of works of art for the National Gallery and the Tate (among them Van Gogh's *Sunflowers* and Seurat's *Bathing Party*), Courtauld also built up a private collection, concentrating mainly on the 'modern' French school. Manet's *A Bar at the Folies-Bergère* (1881–2), Monet's *Antibes* (1888), Renoir's *The Theatre Box* ('*La Loge*', 1874) and Cézanne's *The Montagne Sainte-Victoire* (c. 1887) are just a handful of the now internationally famous works which can be admired here.

After the death of his wife in 1931, Courtauld gave over the majority of his collection (the rest was bequeathed on his death) to a new art history teaching school (there was no other in the country), which opened its doors as the Courtauld Institute of Art in 1932. Viscount Lee of Fareham was another of the founding fathers. As well as donating Chequers to the nation, for the use of Prime Ministers, he also gave his personal collection to the Courtauld. Wide-ranging, it included the richly carved and painted 1472 Morelli-Nerli *cassoni* (marriage chests for household linen); masterpieces such as Rubens' sketch for *The Descent from the Cross*, the great altarpiece for Antwerp Cathedral; and Cranach's *Adam and Eve*. Although Gainsborough's *Portrait of Mrs Gainsborough* (1778–9) came through Courtauld, most of the gallery's important British pictures are part of the Lee collection, including Hans Eworth's extraordinary allegorical portrait of Sir John Luttrell, rising half naked out of the sea with a shipwreck behind him, and Sir Peter Lely's *The Concert*, one of the rare landscapes he painted when he first came to England in the 1640s.

The collections were further enhanced by the painter and art critic Roger Fry, who had advised Courtauld on his Impressionist purchases. As well as a number of his own works, he bequeathed Bloomsbury Group paintings and Omega Workshops ceramics, as well as works by other artists including Walter Sickert. Sir Robert Witt, the third player in the institute's foundation, gave over 4,000 Old Master drawings as well as his important photographic archive. Further gifts followed: the Mark Gambier-Parry bequest of 1966, consisting mainly of early Italian works; Dr Alistair Hunter's collection of British artists, including Ben Nicholson's *Painting 1937*; and in the late 1970s came the major benefaction of the Anglo-Austrian connoisseur Count Antoine Seilern, known as the Prince's Gate Collection (from Seilern's London address). Astutely advised by curators, scholars and dealers, Seilern built up an exceptional collection of Old Master Dutch, Flemish and Italian paintings, extremely rich in works by Rubens and Tiepolo, but also including Oskar Kokoschka's 1950 *Prometheus* triptych, the artist's largest work, commissioned by Seilern for the ceiling of his Prince's Gate house.

The collection is displayed in the **Fine Rooms**, designed by Chambers, with beautifully ornamented plasterwork ceilings. When the Royal Academy vacated the building, they took with them many of the works of art by Academicians, though Chambers' original colour scheme, with ceilings of pale green, pink and lilac, is preserved. On the upper floor is the **Great Room**, where the famous Royal Academy Summer Exhibition took place from 1780–1836. The precipitous climb was wittily satirised by Thomas Rowlandson in his c. 1800 image *The Exhibition Stare-case*, showing eager exhibition visitors tumbling down it, with the billowing hindquarters of Albacini's completed *Venus Callipygos* in a niche, an amusing symbol of both exhibitionism and voyeurism. The empty plaster frame once housed Cipriani's *Minerva with the Muses on Mount Parnassus*. Above the door of the Great Room is the Greek inscription 'Let no one uninspired by the Muses enter here'.

EATING AND DRINKING AROUND TRAFALGAR SQUARE

££ Albannach. Restaurant and lounge bar decorated with faux antlers and known for its outstanding range of Scotch whiskies. Closed Sun. *66 Trafalgar Square (Cockspur St). T: 020 7930 0066, albannach.co.uk. Map p. 603, F2.*

£ Coal Hole. Historic pub. Its cellars are said to have been the coal store for the Savoy Hotel. Gilbert and Sullivan, of the Savoy Operas fame, performed here. Pub food and a lively after-work crowd. Open daily. *91–92 Strand. T: 020 7379 9883. Map p. 604, A2.*

£ Courtauld Gallery Café. A pleasant place, with both indoor and outdoor seating, serving light lunches, drinks and pastries. Open daily 10–5.30. *Strand. T: 020 7848 2527, courtauld.ak.uk. Map p. 604, A2.*

Corinthia Hotel. The Northall Bar, with a big central counter with stools to perch on and seating at small tables around the sides, is usually not crowded and is good for a drink and a place to sit down. The cocktails are excellent. Choose gin- or vodka-based: both house spirits are distilled in London. *10 Whitehall Pl. Map p. 603, F2.*

£ Gordon's Wine Bar. Family-run wine bar which prides itself on being the oldest in London. Plenty of wines, plus sherry, port and madeira, and food to accompany it: platters of cheese and cold cuts, simple hot dishes, roasts on Sunday. Open every day. *47 Villiers St. No bookings by phone, gordonswinebar.com. Map p. 603, F2.*

££ Joe Allen. Technically in Covent Garden, but very handy for the Strand and Trafalgar Square, this is something of an institution and it stays open late. Patronised by a lively post-theatre crowd, including the actors in current West End shows. Live piano. One doesn't come for food or service but for atmosphere and fun. Those in the know order the hamburger, which is never listed on the menu but is available if you ask for it. *13 Exeter St. T: 020 7836 0651, joeallen.co.uk. Map p. 604, A2.*

££ National Dining Rooms. In the Sainsbury Wing of the National Gallery. Modern British cooking. Also serves afternoon tea. Open daily until 5.30, until 8.30 on Fri. *Trafalgar Square. T: 020 7747 2525, nationalgallery.org.uk. Map p. 603, F1–F2.*

££ Portrait Restaurant. In the National Portrait Gallery, famed especially for its views of Trafalgar Square. Open daily for lunch, dinner also on Thur, Fri, Sat (last orders 8.30). *Trafalgar Square/Orange St. T: 020 7312 2490, www.npg.org.uk. Map p. 603, F1.*

££ Simpson's in the Strand. Traditional British restaurant in business for 170 years. It boasts a long list of famous guests, including both Gladstone and Disraeli—aged Scotch beef and bread and butter pud will break down all political barriers. Open daily. *100 Strand. T: 020 7836 9112, simpsonsinthestrand.com. Map p. 604, A2.*

££ Terroirs. ■ Wine bar which does food. The terroirs in question are those of Italy, France and Spain. Organised on two floors: wines, cold cuts, cheeses and a small menu of *plats du jour* on the ground floor; slightly more leisured dining in the cellar. Closed Sun. *5 William IV St. T: 020 7037 0660, terroirswinebar.com. Map p. 603, F1.*

£–££ The Vista Bar. At the top of the Trafalgar Hotel, a good place to come in spring and summer, either to eat (they do light bites and burgers) or just for drinks. *2 Spring Gardens. T: 020 7870 2900, thetrafalgar.com. Map p. 603, F2.*

TEMPLE BAR
Detail of the heraldic dragon and the Royal Courts of Justice.

Legal London

*The area around Chancery Lane, including Lincoln's Inn, Gray's Inn
and the Inner and Middle Temples, can fairly be described as
'Legal London'. The Royal Courts of Justice are here as well as solicitors'
offices and barristers' chambers. A good way of exploring the area is to join a
Legal London walking tour (see www.discovering-legal-london.com).*

The **Royal Courts of Justice**, or Law Courts, where the Strand meets Fleet Street (*map p. 606, A3*), is an imposing Victorian-Gothic building faced in Portland stone. Here civil cases are heard (criminal cases are heard at the Old Bailey; *see p. 42*). Built in 1873–82, the sole architect was G.E. Street, responsible for both the exterior and the interior of the vast pile (so vast that a person was once found living in its basements—it has a thousand rooms and over three miles of corridors).

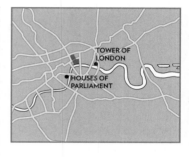

Street's untimely death, about a year before completion, was brought on by the strain of the monumental project and it was finished by his son, A.E. Street, and Sir Arthur Blomfield. Queen Victoria opened it in December 1882. The total cost for building was £1 million, excluding the £1,452,000 paid for the six-acre site and the demolition of 450 houses before work began. Members of the public are allowed free entry and may observe the courts when they are in session (*Mon–Fri 9–4.30 unless otherwise stated*). Once past the airport-style security system at the entrance, you are in the lofty Great Hall, which has a fine mosaic pavement designed by G.E. Street. Official tours (*every Tues at 10.30 and 11.45; approx. 1hr; fee*) include the history of the art collection, a view of Guy Fawkes's court documents from 1605 and observing a High Court case from the public gallery.

Behind the Law Courts, north of the Strand, is **Carey Street**, its name synonymous with bankruptcy proceedings. The term 'in Queer Street', meaning in financial trouble, is thought to be a corruption of Carey. The small Seven Stars Pub (1602), one of the oldest in London, serves real ale and has an eccentric window display of dusty curios, including an animal skull sporting a barrister's horsehair wig and a lump of coprolite, a 'cretaceous turd from 146–66.4 million years ago'.

Next door (nos 51 and 52), an attractive archway admits to the dignified 17th-century quadrangle of New Square, part of Lincoln's Inn.

INNS OF COURT AND INNS OF CHANCERY

The four great Inns of Court (Lincoln's Inn, Inner Temple, Middle Temple and Gray's Inn) provide education and training for barristers at law and reserve the exclusive right of calling persons to the Bar (the railing that enclosed the judge), in other words, granting them the qualification to argue cases in court. The Inns originated in the 13th century, when the clergy ceased to practise in the courts of justice, giving place to professional students of Law. The members of the Inns comprise Students, Barristers and Benchers. Senior barristers appointed as Queen's Counsel (QCs) wear silk gowns; others wear 'stuff' gowns. Each Inn has a dining hall, library and chapel. The Inns provide lectures for students and examine candidates for admission to the Bar. Students may pursue their legal studies elsewhere, but in order to qualify they must become a member of an Inn. *(Visitors are usually admitted freely to the quaint and quiet precincts of the Inns on Mon–Fri. The gates are usually closed at weekends.)*

The nine Inns of Chancery are completely different. It was originally the custom for students of Law to enter first an Inn of Chancery and then graduate to an Inn of Court, but this practice had become obsolete by the beginning of the 17th century. Instead, the Inns of Chancery became associations and offices for solicitors. By the middle of the 18th century they had practically ceased to have any legal character and after the founding of the Law Society of England and Wales in 1825, they ceased to have any legal purpose. Clement's Inn, Thavie's Inn and Furnival's Inn now exist merely as names of modern buildings. Lyon's Inn, New Inn and Strand Inn have completely disappeared. The entrance and only surviving part of Clifford's Inn may be seen off Chancery Lane. The buildings of Staple Inn (c. 1585) survive on High Holborn (*see p. 200*). Barnard's Inn is now home to Gresham College (*see p. 201*).

LINCOLN'S INN

Map p. 606, A2. Underground: Temple, Holborn, Chancery Lane. Precincts open Mon–Fri 7am–7pm. The Inn's buildings are open for organised tours only, except for the chapel, which is open Mon–Fri 9–5. For details of tours, see lincolnsinn.org.uk.

Lincoln's Inn may derive its name from Henry de Lacy, Earl of Lincoln (1251–1311), adviser to Edward I in matters of law and a proponent of legal education; the Inn is near the site of his London mansion. It is more likely, though, that the name derives from Thomas de Lincoln, a serjeant at law during the 14th century. Formal records of the Inn date from 1422, although a body of lawyers is known to have practised here prior to this.

Between New Square and the Old Buildings to the east, is the **Old Hall** (c. 1489–90). It served as the Court of Chancery from 1733 to 1873 and is famously mentioned in the opening scene of Dickens's *Bleak House*.

The **Chapel** (1623) has been subsequently restored and enlarged. Its foundation stone was laid by Jonne Donne in 1620. The old tradition of ringing the chapel bell at midday to signify the death of a bencher of the Inn is thought to have inspired Donne's famous *Meditation XVII*:

> *No man is an island, entire of itself; every man is a piece of the continent, a part of the main. If a clod be washed away by the sea, Europe is the less, as well as if a promontory were, as well as a manor of thy friends or of thine own were. Any man's death diminishes me, because I am involved in mankind. And therefore never send to know for whom the bell tolls: it tolls for thee.*

The chapel is built on a series of pillars and entry is via the double staircase. Thus the arcaded, open space below is in fact the crypt—and careful inspection of the flagstones reveals them to be the weathered tombs of interred members of the Inn. In the 18th and 19th centuries, unwanted babies were often left here and if adopted by the Inn were given the surname Lincoln. Today this is where the guided tours meet.

The **Gate House**, which leads into Chancery Lane (*see below*), was commissioned in 1517–21 by Sir Thomas Lovell, Chancellor of the Exchequer to both Henry VII and Henry VIII. On the Chancery Lane side, it bears Lovell's arms as well as those of Henry VIII and Henry de Lacy. It was rebuilt in the 1960s but the oak doors are from the 16th century.

To the west is the **Great Hall** (or New Hall), in red-brick Tudor style by Philip and P.C. Hardwick (1845). At the north end is the **Library**, extended in 1872 by Sir George Gilbert Scott.

An archway with a second porter's lodge at the northwest corner of New Square leads into Lincoln's Inn Fields, with tall plane trees (*described below*).

CHANCERY LANE

Chancery Lane (*map p. 606, A2–A3*) skirts the east side of Lincoln's Inn and in addition to the Law Society houses a number of shops selling legal books and legal dress. Ede & Ravenscroft at no. 97 sells horsehair wigs. At nos 53–64 are the **London Silver Vaults**, with an Aladdin's Cave of antique and modern silver on sale in the basement (*open Mon–Fri 9–5.30, Sat 9–1*). In Star Yard is a rare surviving double-door **Victorian urinal** in green-painted cast iron. According to John Aubrey in his *Brief Lives*, the young Ben Jonson built a wall here, on the Lincoln's Inn side:

> *[Jonson's] mother, after his father's death, married a bricklayer; and 'tis generally said that he wrought sometime with his father-in-law (and particularly on the garden-wall of Lincoln's Inn next to Chancery Lane, and that a knight, a bencher, walking thro' and hearing him repeat some Greek verses out of Homer, discoursing with him, and finding him to have a wit extraordinary, gave him some exhibition to maintain him at Trinity College in Cambridge.*

The **former Public Record Office**, the fortress-like Gothic Revival building by Sir James Pennethorne and Sir John Taylor, on the east side of Chancery Lane, was built in slow stages 1851–96. It was the first major neo-Gothic public building to be constructed after the Houses of Parliament and was conceived as 'the strongbox of the Empire' to secure the National Archives. It is built on the estate of the Master of the Rolls, including the Rolls Chapel, founded in 1253 by Henry III, originally as a Domus Conversorum (House of Converts) for Jews who had renounced their worldly goods in order to convert to Christianity. After the Archives' removal to Kew in 1997, the building was bought by King's College, London and after restoration reopened as the Maughan Library. In the Western Room are remnants from the chapel; a 13th-century archway, three funerary monuments, stained glass and a mosaic floor. The monument to Dr John Yonge (d. 1516) is credited as the earliest Renaissance funerary monument in England and is attributed to Pietro Torrigiano, who was also responsible for Henry VII's tomb in Westminster Abbey. The 19th-century sculptures on the clock-tower are of four queens: Victoria, Elizabeth I, Anne and Maud (Matilda).

Almost opposite the former Public Record Office is the **Law Society**, a Neoclassical building dating from 1832, which represents the interests of solicitors in England and Wales.

LINCOLN'S INN FIELDS

Map p. 604, A2. Underground: Holborn, Chancery Lane.

This large, grassy expanse, just outside the City boundary, takes its name from Lincoln's Inn but was previously three fields called Cup, Purse and Fickett's, originally belonging to the Crown. In 1586 the Babington Plotters, who conspired against Elizabeth I in favour of Mary, Queen of Scots, were hung, drawn and quartered here. The site was laid out and developed in the 1630s by William Newton, with 32 houses surrounding a public open space, but the original plan is thought to have been by Inigo Jones. In 1666, the possessions of City inhabitants displaced by the Great Fire were secured at Lincoln's Inn Fields. In 1683 Lord William Russell was beheaded here for his part in the Rye House Plot, an attempt to assassinate Charles II. Charles' mistress Nell Gwyn lived here until 1687. By 1735, according to a government report, Lincoln's Inn Fields had become a favourite duelling-ground as well as a 'receptacle for rubbish, dirt and nastiness of all sorts' where vagabonds and beggars committed 'robberies, assaults, outrages and enormities', and the inhabitants had them enclosed. They remained under private stewardship until a campaign to restore public access was successful in 1894. Today it is the largest public square in central London, cruciform in layout and covering twelve acres, with lawns and tennis courts. Once a fashionable place to live, the buildings surrounding it are now mainly offices and chambers, with solicitors taking advantage of the proximity to the Inns of Court. The LSE (London School of Economics) also occupies buildings here.

On the south side, the **Royal College of Surgeons** (nos 35–43) occupies a large building with an Ionic portico. The first building, erected in 1805–13, was by George Dance the Younger and Nathaniel Lewis. It was redesigned by Sir Charles Barry and rebuilt from 1834. The building was badly bombed during World War Two and only the library and portico survive. Within the college is the **Hunterian Museum** (*open Mon–Sat 10–5; free; a visitor's pass must be obtained from main reception to allow entry through the barriers; T: 020 7405 3474*). The museum is upstairs on the first floor and displays what was once the greatest medical museum in the world, founded by the celebrated surgeon John Hunter (1728–93). The state-of-the-art Crystal Gallery, displaying thousands of Hunter's antique pickled specimens, is arranged as an illuminated multi-storey arena. The effect is strangely soothing, even though the blanched contents of the jars range from curious to freakish. In front of the cabinets at ground level is the skeleton of the wretched Charles Byrne, a 7′7″ Irish giant (d. 1783). Byrne, who made an unhappy living from his excessive height and who drank himself to death, wished to be buried at sea so his mortal remains could not be exploited. Against his wishes, surgeons vied for his body and 'surrounded his house just as harpooners would an enormous whale'. The Evelyn Tables, mounted on the wall at the entrance, are a set of four anatomical preparations on 6ft wooden boards on which dissected human nerves, arteries and veins are glued and varnished. Thought to be the oldest in Europe, they were acquired by the diarist John Evelyn in Padua in 1646 and subsequently used as teaching boards. The museum also displays the collections of the Wellcome Museum of Anatomy and Pathology and the Odontological Museum and is a valuable resource for medical students as well as for artists who wish to settle knotty anatomical and biological questions.

The southwest corner of the square extends into Portsmouth Street where an old shop survives, a short way down on the left, claiming to be Dickens's **Old Curiosity Shop**, though it was named after the novel's publication. Nonetheless, this may well be the oldest shop in London, dating back to 1567. It now sells handmade shoes.

On the west side of Lincoln's Inn Fields, **Lindsey House** (nos 59–60, c. 1640) is one of the few original buildings from the 17th century and was previously attributed to Inigo Jones. **Newcastle House** (no. 66 at the northwest corner) is a brick building of 1684–9 and was where the charter for the Bank of England was sealed. It was remodelled by Sir John Vanbrugh in the 18th century and again by Lutyens in 1930s. Since 1790 is has been the offices of Farrer & Co., solicitors to the Queen.

On the north side is Sir John Soane's Museum.

SIR JOHN SOANE'S MUSEUM

Map p. 604, A2. 13 Lincoln's Inn Fields. Nearest Tube: Holborn. Open Tues–Sat 10–5 (first Tues of the month 6pm–9pm by candlelight, though this is often oversubscribed and only 200 tickets are issued, no advance booking). Free. There is limited capacity in the house and queues can form outside. You are asked to turn off your telephone and large bags must be left in the cloakroom. T: 020 7405 2107, soane.org.

This extraordinary house was the home of Sir John Soane (1753–1837), one of England's most important and original architects. The façade, of Portland stone and red brick, with its projecting loggia and incised lines representing pilasters, was daringly modern in its day, considered by many a 'palpable eyesore'. The two large Coade Stone caryatids, based on those from the Erechtheion in Athens, give a foretaste of what can be expected within, in one of the most unusual interiors in London. The house was designed by Soane to house his ever-growing collection of antiquities and paintings, and the unusually-shaped rooms are crowded with works of art. Cunning use is made of surprise vistas and changes of level. Carefully positioned mirrors reflect light and judiciously-placed possessions; ceilings are punched through to admit shafts of light at desired angles, dramatically falling on walls encrusted with sculpture and architectural fragments. Windows of rooms overlook courtyards packed with sculpture, and in the basement are solemn Gothic cloisters and cells, originally lit by light faintly penetrating through stained glass. The whole creates an overwhelming labyrinthine effect.

Soane's home is in fact spread over three houses, largely pulled to pieces and reconstructed to his own designs. He and his wife Eliza and their two children lived in the house and Soane also had his architect's office here. Here he was able to continue and perfect architectural ideas he had used elsewhere: at the Bank of England (*see p. 63*), his country villa at Ealing, Pitzhanger Manor (*see p. 490*) and at Dulwich Picture Gallery (*see p. 457*). Today the collection of Greek, Roman and Egyptian antiquities, casts, bronzes, gems and medals, ceramics, oil paintings and watercolours, 8,000 books, 30,000 architectural drawings (including many by Adam) and 150 architectural models, displayed in astonishing surroundings, is one of Soane's most extraordinary legacies. By the end of his life Soane was already referring to the ground floor of Lincoln's Inn Fields as 'the Museum'. He bequeathed it to the nation by Act of Parliament in 1833.

Tour of the house

To the right as you enter is the **Library and Dining Room**, conceived as one space: the Library at the front of the property, the Dining Room at the rear. Painted a rich, glossy Pompeian red, an arcaded division, suspended from the ceiling, articulates the two spaces, its two mirrored piers on either side of the room arranged with objects, including a model of the Soane Monument. Made in 1816 after the death of Soane's wife Eliza, the actual monument stands in the burial ground of St Giles-in-the-Fields (now St Pancras Gardens, near St Pancras Station; *see p. 367*). Elizabeth Soane, Soane himself and their son John are buried there. Mirrors in the recesses above the bookcases, made for the room by John Robins, give an impression of a room beyond. The mythological ceiling paintings, with scenes from the story of Pandora, were commissioned from Henry Holland and positioned in 1834. Over the Dining Room chimneypiece is Sir Thomas Lawrence's portrait of Soane (1828–9), one of his last works, and below it a model of the Board of Trade offices which Soane designed at the entrance to Downing Street. Convex mirrors, canted forward, reflect the entrance from the Hall, and mirror-backed niches contain sculpture. It was in this room that Soane exhibited his large collection of antique vases, or 'Grecian urns', the most celebrated being the large 'Cawdor Vase', an Apulian volute krater of the late 4th century BC.

Approached from the Dining Room is Soane's **Study**, a tiny room also painted Pompeian red, crammed with marble fragments displayed on shelves and brackets of 'bronzed' green. Above the door to the Dining Room is a large cast of the *Apotheosis of*

Homer, taken from the marble relief purchased by the British Museum in 1819, originally in Palazzo Colonna, Rome. The oak-grained **Dressing Room**, with an elaborate ceiling in Soane's late manner, leads through into the **Corridor**, a forest of architectural plaster casts lit by a long skylight filled with tinted yellow glass, admitting a mellow light. The **Dome** continues the overwhelming assemblage of architecture and sculpture. Large and dominating is a cast of the *Apollo Belvedere* (formerly in the collection of Lord Burlington at Chiswick House), of which Soane was exceedingly proud, not least because of its provenance. Lined up on the balustrade, with a view down onto the Egyptian sarcophagus (*see below*), are antique vases and urns and Sir Francis Chantrey's bust of Soane. The **Ante-Room**, off the Corridor, contains a cast of the Michelangelo tondo now in the Royal Academy (*see p. 215*). The **Breakfast Parlour** remains almost unaltered from Soane's day. The ceiling is a beautiful flattened dome, almost floating in the air; to either side, openings rise to skylights with coloured glass. In the four corners of the ceiling are convex mirrors, and nearly 100 more punctuate the surfaces of the room, some merely small glittering orbs. On the north wall is a large watercolour of Mrs Soane's tomb, Flaxman's figure of *Victory* having been positioned in front of it by Soane just ten days before he died in 1837.

The **Picture Room**, its suspended ceiling a curious mix of Classical and Gothic forms, is where Soane displayed his best paintings, hung on an ingenious method of hinged panels which swing out, revealing different layers. Prized by Soane were his original ink-and-wash views of Paestum by Piranesi (1720–78) but the chief pictures are those by Hogarth: the celebrated eight-canvas *Rake's Progress* series (1732–3) and the magnificent four-canvas *Election* series (c. 1745). In addition Soane possessed watercolours by Turner; an oil sketch for Sir James Thornhill's Baroque ceiling for the Queen's State Bedchamber at Hampton Court; and a fragment of a tapestry cartoon, from the studio of Raphael, for the 'Life of Christ' tapestries for the Vatican. In the inner recess of the south wall is a plaster nymph by Sir Richard Westmacott, a friend of Soane's, who was invited to dinner to admire the placement of his sculpture.

In the basement is the **Monk's Parlour**, or the 'Parloir of Padre Giovanni' as Soane was amused to called it, the first of a series of theatrical spaces for his medieval and Gothic treasures, inspired by, and satirising, the taste for gothic novels and medieval antiquarianism, an elaboration of the sombre reclusive hermit theme begun at Pitzhanger. Ancient stained glass and coloured glazing was set into windows and doors, rearranged in the 1890s for its greater protection, with yellow light filtering down from the Picture Room recess. The walls are covered with casts and genuine Gothic fragments, many from the old Palace of Westminster. In this odd, tenebrous environment, Soane would entertain close friends to tea.

The **Sepulchral Chamber**, where light floods down from the dome above, bouncing off the walls encrusted with marbles, sculpture and architectural fragments, is dominated by the colossal bulk of the alabaster **sarcophagus of Seti I** (d. 1279 BC; father of Ramesses the Great). This was Soane's most expensive and triumphant purchase, made in 1825. Huge and translucent, covered in hieroglyphs, it had been discovered by the Italian strongman and hydraulic engineer Giovanni Belzoni and offered to the British Museum by the British Consul-General in Egypt, Henry Salt, but was turned down on grounds of cost. In March 1825 Soane threw a three-day party to celebrate his purchase. Eight hundred and ninety guests, among them Turner, Coleridge and Sir Thomas Lawrence, viewed his home-cum-museum by lamp and candlelight, the flickering light shimmering in the mirrors and illuminating the spaces with dramatic chiaroscuro. The drama of the presentation was, of course, deliberate.

Returning to the inner hall, the stairs lead up to the Drawing Rooms, passing on the way the **Shakespeare Recess** and other niches with sculpture busts.

GRAY'S INN

Map p. 606, A1–A2. Underground: Chancery Lane. Walks and Chapel open Mon–Fri noon–2.30.

Known to have been occupied by lawyers by 1388, Gray's Inn stands on or near the ancient manor of Purpoole or Portpool, owned by Sir Reginald de Grey, Chief Justice of Chester, Constable and Sheriff of Nottingham (d. 1308). The Inn was seriously damaged by Luftwaffe bombing in 1941 and the Hall, Chapel and Library were burned out, along with 30,000 books. It was restored in a harmonious style in the 1950s.

Enter through **South Square**, which has a statue of Francis Bacon, one of the great names of Gray's Inn. Empiricist philosopher, statesman, lawyer and writer, he rose to become Treasurer of the Inn, retaining chambers here from 1577 until his death. From here continue north into **Gray's Inn Square**. In the Hall here (1566, rebuilt 1951), Shakespeare staged the first performance of *The Comedy of Errors* in 1594. Luckily, during the Blitz, the stained glass had been taken to a place of safety, so much of it is original. The Chapel next door likewise preserves its original glass.

The gardens, known as **Gray's Inn Walks**, or simply the Walks, entered from Field Court, were laid out by Francis Bacon in 1606 and altered in the 18th century. They consist of two sweeping parallel gravel drives bordered by plane trees, shrubs and sloping lawns. Many office workers choose to enjoy their lunch breaks here in fine weather. Raymond Buildings (1825) and Verulam Buildings (1811) skirt the gardens on the west and east in long terraces.

STAPLE, FURNIVAL'S & BARNARD'S INNS

Map p. 606, A2. Underground: Chancery Lane.

The western limits of the City (Holborn Bars) are indicated by stone obelisks near Chancery Lane Underground station and opposite Staple Inn. In the roadway stands the War Memorial of the Royal Fusiliers (City of London Regiment), by Albert Toft (1924). On the south side is **Staple Inn**, the gabled and timbered façade of which, dating from 1586 (restored), is one of the oldest surviving buildings in London. The inn, which seems to have been a hostel of the wool staplers in the 14th century, was an Inn of Chancery (*see p. 194*) from the reign of Henry V until it was sold in 1884. It was severely damaged in 1944, when the fine 16th-century hall was demolished. This has now been rebuilt (with much of the old material) and is occupied by the Institute of Actuaries; the courtyard can be entered. Dr Johnson lived here for a time in 1759–60 and here he is said to have written *Rasselas* in the evenings of a single week, to pay for his mother's funeral. The second court now contains a pleasant garden.

At **39 Brooke St**, to the north, the poet Thomas Chatterton, the 'sleepless soul that perished in his pride' (Wordsworth's tribute), poisoned himself in 1770. He was 17.

The huge, neo-Gothic complex now known as **Holborn Bars** (clad in terracotta by the same tiling firm that supplied the National History Museum) occupies the site between Brooke Street and Leather Lane. It was built as the headquarters of the Prudential Assurance Company (Alfred Waterhouse, 1879–1906; altered in the 1930s) and incorporated state-of-the-art Victorian gadgetry such as electric lighting and hot running water as well as a company chapel, restaurant, library and rooftop promenade for employees. It occupies the **site of Furnival's Inn**, in which Charles Dickens was lodging when he wrote the first part of *The Pickwick Papers* (memorial tablet and bust by Percy Fitzgerald, 1907, in the central courtyard).

Leather Lane Market (*Mon–Fri 10–2*) sells clothes, accessories, flowers and food. A market has traded here for 400 years. The name has nothing to do with leather; it is probably a 14th-century derivative of the name of a local merchant.

On the opposite side of the road, near the corner of Fetter Lane, is the entrance to **Barnard's Inn**, with a device of the Mercers' Company ('Mercers' Maiden') in the pediment above the gateway. From 1894–1959 the defunct inn was occupied by the Mercers' School. The school was founded about 1450 and had Sir Thomas Gresham among its pupils. Since 1991, Barnard's Inn has been home to Gresham College, the institute of higher learning founded by Sir Thomas Gresham in 1579 for the delivery of lectures in Latin and English on 'divynitye, astronomy, musicke, geometry, law, physicke, and rhetoricke' by seven professors. The Chair of Commerce, funded by the Mercers' School Memorial Trust, has now been added to these seven ancient professorships. Gresham Professors and visiting guests still deliver free City lectures, (*see gresham.ac.uk for upcoming events*), which are held in the Inn's old hall on a first come, first served basis. The restored hall dates from the late 14th century and has 16th-century linenfold panelling. At no. 80 Fetter Lane is the Art Nouveau facade of the **former Buchanan's Distillery** by Henry J. Treadwell and Leonard Martin (1902).

INNER & MIDDLE TEMPLE

Map p. 606, A3. Underground: Temple. Guided tours of Middle Temple can be booked on T: 020 7427 4820, middletemple.org.uk. Inner Temple Garden open weekdays 12.30–3. For the Temple Church, see p. 203.

TEMPLE CHURCH
Effigy of Gilbert Marshal, 4th Earl of Pembroke (d. 1241).

The quiet enclave shared by the Inns of Inner and Middle Temple lies south of Fleet Street near the Temple Bar, which marks the boundary between the City of London and the City of Westminster. Here elegant chambers and courtyards, and the beautiful, historic church, lie within several acres of gardens that lead towards the Embankment. Widespread destruction in 1940–1 has been repaired, and new buildings in the traditional style have been erected by Sir Edward Maufe, Sir Hubert Worthington and T.W. Sutcliffe. Buildings belonging to the Inner Temple bear the device of the Winged Horse (Pegasus), those of the Middle Temple the Lamb and Flag.

The Temple was originally the seat in England of the Knights Templar, the famous order of soldier-monks formed in 1118, originally to protect pilgrims to the Holy Land, but who went on to amass impressive property holdings and to become the Christian world's first powerful bankers. On the dissolution of the Order from 1307, the Temple passed to the Crown and later into the possession of the Knights Hospitaller of the Order of St John, who continued at their priory in Clerkenwell (*see . 373*) and leased the land to lawyers looking for premises near the courts of Westminster. In 1604,

James I granted the land to the Inns of Inner and Middle Temple on the understanding that they provide accommodation and education for their members and share the maintenance of Temple Church. A neo-Gothic column topped by a horse and two knight-riders (emblem of the Templars) stands today at what was once the heart of the Templars' monastery. It was erected in 2000 and also marks the point at which the Great Fire of 1666 finally ceased to spread.

TEMPLE CHURCH

The Temple Church, or Church of St Mary the Virgin, belonging to the Middle and Inner Temples in common, is a 'peculiar', i.e. exempt from episcopal jurisdiction. The circular nave is modelled on the Church of the Holy Sepulchre in Jerusalem, the holiest of sites where Jesus is believed to have been buried. It was consecrated in 1185 by Heraclius, Patriarch of Jerusalem, probably in the presence of King Henry II, and is in a transitional style between Norman and Gothic. The chancel was added in 1240. Henry III declared his intention to be buried here, although he was in fact buried in Westminster Abbey. The whole building was restored several times in the 19th century and then very seriously damaged in 1941, and has since been restored once again. The church is noted for its music and holds services according to the Book of Common Prayer (*for details of concerts, and of opening times, which are not standard and which are subject to change at short notice, see templechurch.com*).

Entry, via a new south porch (where a fee is payable), is to the **chancel**, borne by clustered piers of Purbeck marble, from the same quarry as the originals. The reredos, designed under Wren's supervision in 1682, was removed in 1840 and so escaped damage. The stained glass dates from the 1950s; Bradley notes that it is some of the best post-war glass in London.

In the **south aisle** is a noble effigy of a 13th-century bishop. When his coffin was opened in 1810, a child's skeleton was found at his feet; perhaps the remains of William Plantagenet, the fifth son of Henry III, who died in infancy. Near the south door (beneath a glass slab) is the gravestone of John Selden (1584–1654), the Middle Temple jurist who dryly complained that 'Few men make themselves masters of the things they write or speak.'

In the **Round Church** is a series of 12th–13th-century recumbent marble effigies of knights in full armour, some with crossed legs, an attitude popularly—though probably erroneously—believed to signify that the deceased was a Crusader. They include the effigy of William Marshal (feet resting on a lion), 1st Earl of Pembroke, soldier, statesman and Lord Protector of England during Henry III's minority (d. 1219) and the effigy of his son, Gilbert Marshal, 4th Earl of Pembroke (d. 1241), who is in the act of drawing his sword, his feet on a winged dragon. The effigies were heavily restored, some reattributed, and rearranged in 1841 by Edward Richardson and casts of some of them were taken for display at the Great Exhibition of 1851. In 1941 an incendiary bomb caused the roof of the church to fall inwards and the effigies were caught up in the molten firestorm and badly damaged. They have since been restored and four of them lie next to their Victorian plaster casts (on long-term loan from the V&A), giving an idea of what they looked like prior to the war damage but after 19th-century restoration. As the church's website notes: the effigies may appear to be stiff and lifeless, frozen in martial attitudes which no longer have any relevance. But the knights are all shown with open eyes. They are all portrayed in the vigour of youth. 'The effigies are not memorials of what has long since been and gone; they speak of what is yet to come, of these once and future knights who are poised to hear Christ's summons and to spring again to war.' The arcading was replaced in the 19th century; the waggish carved heads (note the man having his ear chewed off by a creature) are copies of the originals.

The two coloured monuments between the chancel and Round Church are to Richard Martin, Recorder of London, kneeling at his desk (1615; south side) and Edmund Plowden, Treasurer of the Middle Temple (1584; north side).

> ### THE BATTLE OF THE ORGANS
> In 1683, two organs were commissioned by the Inns of the Temple from the two finest organ makers of the day: Bernard ('Father') Smith and Renatus Harris. The plan was to erect them in the halls of the Inner and Middle Temples, where each was to be tested and a judgement formed as to which produced the finer sound. Both masters were irritated by the commission, each feeling that the contract should have been awarded to him alone: and each separately secured permission for his instrument to be set up in the Temple Church instead of in one of the halls. Smith's was placed between the Round Church and chancel and Harris's at the opposite end. Such was the fury of the contest that acts of sabotage were even reported. The final verdict was passed in 1688, by Judge Jeffreys (of Bloody Assizes fame). Smith's instrument was deemed the winner and Harris's was removed. The Smith organ remained in the church until it was destroyed in the Second World War.

The **Master's House**, the home of the incumbent of the Temple Church, northeast of the church, was re-erected after the Great Fire and totally destroyed in 1941, but has been rebuilt in its 17th-century form.

INNER AND MIDDLE TEMPLE HALLS
Inner Temple Hall and Library, by Worthington (1952–6), replaces the 19th-century range destroyed in 1941. The refaced buttery at the west end and the crypt below it date from the 14th century (*not open to the public*). To the east is **King's Bench Walk**, with two houses ascribed to Wren (nos 4 and 5), popular locations for film companies. Towards the river lies the tranquil expanse of **Inner Temple Gardens**. Tudor Gate leads east onto Tudor Street towards Blackfriars; until the 18th century this was a lawless area known as 'Alsatia'.

On the west side of Middle Temple Lane are Middle Temple Gardens. **Middle Temple Hall**, a fine example of an Elizabethan chamber with double hammerbeam roof, was begun in 1562 under Edmund Plowden (commemorated in the Temple Church). The interior, heavily damaged in 1941–4, has been rebuilt and restored. The High Table, at which benchers still dine, consists of three enormous planks cut from a single oak cut down in Windsor Forest and floated down the Thames, reputedly a gift from Elizabeth I. Sir Francis Drake was welcomed in this hall after returning from one of his expeditions; Shakespeare is said to have taken part in the première of *Twelfth Night* here in 1602 (*entry via pre-booked guided tour only, subject to availability; fee payable, contact Middle Temple Events Team, T: 020 7427 4820, events@middletemple. org.uk*).

EATING AND DRINKING IN LEGAL LONDON

££ 113 Restaurant and Bar. Modern, rather uncompromising décor in the stately, porticoed headquarters of the Law Society, but the food is good. The restaurant and bar are open to the public, offering a seasonally changing menu of mainly British cuisine: classic recipes with a contemporary slant. Lunch only. *113 Chancery Lane. T: 020 7320 9555. www.113chancerylane. co.uk. Map p. 606, A2.*

££ Bountiful Cow. North of High Holborn and west of Gray's Inn, this pub is devoted to beef, as its name suggests. Come here for burgers and steaks. The owner is Roxy Beaujolais, of the Seven Stars (*see below*). Open daily but closes 6pm on Sun. *51 Eagle St. T: 020 7404 0200. thebountifulcow. co.uk. Map p. 604, A1–A2.*

£–££ Cigalon. Named after the symbol of Provence, the cicada, this restaurant offers the evocative scents and tastes of the south of France. *Salade niçoise*, olive *tapénade* and red mullet carpaccio. Closed weekends.

115 Chancery Lane. T: 020 7242 8373, cigalon.co.uk. Map p. 606, A2.

£ Seven Stars. Chef and proprietress Roxy Beaujolais serves good food and creates a fine atmosphere in this ancient pub behind the Royal Courts of Justice. Open daily. *53 Carey St. T: 020 7242 8531. Map p. 606, A3.*

£ Fields Bar and Kitchen. Right in Lincoln's Inn Fields, this light and airy wood-and-glass restaurant, with copious outdoor seating, has a wood-fired pizza oven and serves good light meals and snacks. A percentage of all earnings goes to the Sir John Soane's Museum. Open daily, daylight hours (to coincide with the park). *T: 020 7242 5351. Map p. 604, A2.*

£ Old Bank of England. Occupying a magnificent former banking hall, just opposite Inner Temple Lane: beer and pies in an opulent setting. Open Mon–Fri. *194 Fleet St. T: 020 7430 2255, oldbankofengland.co.uk. Map p. 606, A3.*

PICCADILLY CIRCUS
Anteros (detail) by Alfred Gilbert (1893).

Piccadilly, St James's & Mayfair

Piccadilly, a wide and busy thoroughfare, home to the Royal Academy and the Ritz, divides two of central London's most patrician districts, St James's and Mayfair. St James's is old-fashioned and sedate, with its peppering of gentlemen's clubs. Mayfair attracts newer money.

Piccadilly Circus (*map p. 603, E1*), on which seven streets converge, is one of the most traffic-congested and animated intersections in London. Its most famous landmark, polythene-wrapped in winter, is the **statue of '*Eros*'** (1893), which stands at the centre of the fountain. In reality, the precariously balanced archer represents Anteros, the twin of Eros, who is 'love requited'. Made of aluminium (a novelty at the time), it was designed by Sir Alfred Gilbert to commemorate the philan-

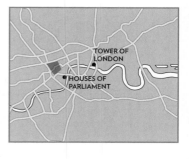

thropic work of Anthony Ashley Cooper, 7th Earl of Shaftesbury, reformer of working conditions in factories, promoter of Ragged Schools and campaigner for clean drinking water for the poor. The statue was condemned by contemporary critics but has since been taken to the public's heart.

The thoroughfare of Piccadilly itself, which leads southwest from the Circus to Hyde Park Corner, began life in 1612, when a certain Robert Baker bought a plot of land for £50 on the east side of the present-day Great Windmill Street. He built what was most likely a lodging-house, which became known locally as 'Pickadilly Hall', a nickname which may have originated as a joke, for Baker was by trade a tailor who made 'pickadils', the scalloped frills at the armholes and necks of dresses, which were very fashionable at the time. The name caught on, and in 1627, for the first time, 'Pecadilly' was used to refer to the district to the north of Haymarket

The nobility began to move to the area in increasing numbers, building mansions such as Burlington House (*see p. 213*). But Piccadilly's real rise to importance began in the 19th century, with John Nash's 1811–13 Regent Street Plan, which aimed to create a *Via Triumphalis* by linking Carlton House (residence of the Prince Regent; since demolished) and St James's Park with Regent's Park. In the late 1870s and

1880s, Shaftesbury Avenue was created by cutting through Tichbourne Street into the Circus. The Circus quickly became a busy traffic nexus as well as a public space—somewhere to rest, drink (metal cups were provided, chained to the fountain), buy flowers, meet friends and lovers, pick up prostitutes (notably the 'Dilly Boys'; *see below*) or get a shoe-shine.

THE DILLY BOYS AND 'PICCADILLY POLARI'

Piccadilly was the heartland of London's 'queer culture' at the beginning of the 20th century. The most notorious denizens of the district were the so-called 'Dilly Boys', effeminate or 'painted' (largely) working-class teenage boys who plied their trade up and down Piccadilly, in its shopping arcades and at the gates of the Royal Academy (the favoured spot of an infamous 'rouged rogue' named 'Gertie'). The distinguished homosexual Quentin Crisp (1908–99), author of *The Naked Civil Servant* (1968), was a Dilly Boy in the 1920s.

Dilly Boys had their own cant slang known as 'Piccadilly polari' (or 'parlare'), in which they communicated with their well-to-do customers. Part-Italian, part-Romany in origin, it was spoken in a sing-song manner as a 'vocal embodiment of their sexual character'. It also owed a lot to cockney slang, sailors' patois and the world of the theatre and the circus. While its heyday was in the 1920s, it underwent a public revival in the 1960s with the popular BBC radio comedy *Round the Horne*, in which two characters named Julian and Sandy spoke exclusively in this outrageous vernacular. Many words which were once the preserve of pre-Second World War underground gay culture are now common in everyday English: 'barney'=a fight, 'camp'=effeminate, 'clobber'=clothes, 'naff'=cheesily awful, 'rozzer'=policeman, 'scarper'=run, to name a few.

THE PICCADILLY LIGHTS

A central feature of Piccadilly is its world-famous Lights, the digital and LED video displays with the names of Hyundai, TDK, Samsung, McDonalds's and Coca-Cola emblazoned up on high for all to see. As far back as 1928, *The Times* referred to the then electric advertisements as a 'hideous eyesore which no civilised community ought to tolerate'. Nevertheless, they are perfectly in keeping with the commercial and consumerist idiom of the place.

The first electric sign went up in 1890. In 1897 the New London Pavilion music hall (on the northeast corner, where the Trocadero amusement arcade is now) began advertising Spaten beer; and display space was being leased to anyone willing to pay for the privilege from around 1910 onwards. In 1922 illuminated signs went up advertising such household names as Bovril yeast extract, Schweppes drinks, Glaxo baby food and Pirelli tyres. Finally, in 1955, came the most famous advertising hoarding of all: the first Coca-Cola sign.

The advertising space has not only been used to sell products: the 1964 general election results were put up on the front of the Criterion Theatre building and, in 2002, the artist Yoko Ono paid £150,000 to erect a banner for three months with the words 'Imagine all the people living in peace' on it.

PICCADILLY

Map p. 603, E1–D2. Underground: Piccadilly Circus, Green Park.

As you stand with your back to Piccadilly Circus, the left-hand side of Piccadilly is the south and the right hand side the north. A short way down on the north is Le Méridien Piccadilly (Norman Shaw, 1908), with a colonnade on the upper storey. On the south is the flagship branch of **Waterstones**, the largest bookshop in Europe. The building (Joseph Emberton, 1936) is a triumphant piece of Modernism, dynamically bringing together a Chicago steel frame, Art Deco and Bauhaus, faced in Portland stone. On the top floor is the 5th View cocktail bar and grill (*see p. 237*).

Just beyond Waterstones is St James's Piccadilly (*see below*), usually with a street market in its courtyard. Further up on the right, beyond Sackville Street, is Albany Close. The three-storey house, **Albany** (1771–4), in dark Flemish-bond brick with a Tuscan porch, was designed by Sir William Chambers as a town mansion for Peniston Lamb, 1st Viscount Melbourne (his son was the Whig prime minister, buried in St Paul's Cathedral, who gave his name to Melbourne in Australia). The house takes its name from Frederick, Duke of York and Albany, second son of George III, who used it as his residence from 1792. In 1803 the Whig architect Henry Holland, who was also responsible for Brooks's club in St James's (*see p. 221*), converted the building into a series of bachelor pads—known as Sets and still in use today—by adding two apartment ranges to the sides of the building. The covered walkway (where troughs of communal herbs are grown for residents and which you can glimpse through the open doorway) is known as the Ropewalk. Gladstone liked to stay here after a late-night House of Commons sitting. The poet Macaulay was another resident, as was the Conservative Prime Minister Sir Edward Heath.

On the other side of the street is **Hatchard's**, the oldest bookseller's in London (though now owned by Waterstones). It is a five-storey building with a wooden shop front. Four tall Corinthian columns unite the central bays of the third and fourth floors. On 30th June 1797, John Hatchard wrote in his diary: 'This day, by the grace of God, the good will of my friends and £5 in my pocket, I have opened a bookshop in Piccadilly [sic].' He need not have fretted. Hatchard's soon established itself as a supplier of books, pamphlets, magazines and newspapers to aristocrats and politicians of all persuasions; the Tory Robert Peel and the Liberal William Gladstone among them. It is certainly worth going in, if only to take a sweep up and down the central wooden staircase.

FORTNUM & MASON

Fortnum & Mason (*181 Piccadilly; open every day, fortnumandmason.com*) was founded c. 1707 by William Fortnum, footman to Queen Anne, and his landlord Hugh Mason, a shop-owner in St James's. By 1756, Charles Fortnum, also a royal footman, had premises in Piccadilly supplying foodstuffs to kings, queens and aristocrats (hence the royal coat of arms and Prince of Wales feathers on the façade). Every hour on the hour the clock (1964) reveals the figures of William Fortnum and Hugh Mason, who emerge to salute one another in fine gentlemanly fashion.

The present exterior is mainly of the 1920s by the Scottish firm of architects Wimperis, Simpson & Guthrie. In 2007 it was refurbished by Jestico + Whiles and David Collins, among others, who added a four-storey atrium space, an elegant white volute staircase and a domed roof-light.

Throughout its history Fortnum & Mason has responded to customer needs and the demands of world crises: it trail-blazed the selling of teas and spices brought into the country through the East India Company in the mid-18th century; it innovated its own line of preserves for use by British soldiers during the Peninsular War (1808–14); a line in ready-to-eat dishes was developed for the Great Exhibition of 1851; and a huge quantity of concentrated beef tea for the troops was sent to Florence Nightingale in the Crimea. It is also Fortnum & Mason who historically supplied the gentlemen's clubs in Pall Mall and St James's with their food parcels; they created 'concentrated luncheons' for shooting and fishing parties (the forebears of the modern-day hampers). In 1922 George Mallory took 60 tins of quail in foie gras and four cases of Montebello 1915 champagne from Fortnum's on his second (failed) attempt to scale Everest.

As a department store from the 1920s onwards, Fortnum's has also played an important role in encouraging the art of the window display. Its themed *montages* are famous. Today the store sells an array of goods from food, wines and spirits, tea and coffee, to gifts, household items and fashion and beauty products. There are also a number of restaurants and a wine bar in the basement.

ST JAMES'S PICCADILLY

Map p. 603, E2. Open daily. Food market Mon 11–5; antiques market Tues 10–6; arts and crafts market Wed–Sat 10–6. Frequent music recitals lunchtime and evening. T: 020 7734 4511, st-james-piccadilly.org.

The church of St James's was one of approximately 50 churches projected from 1670 onwards by Wren's office as part of the scheme of rebuilding after the Great Fire of London: according to a paper written in relation to the scheme in 1711, Wren regarded it as the model church of its kind. Though devastated by bombing in 1940, it has been well restored.

A plain-looking building of brick with Portland stone quoins, St James's is based on a basilica plan. It is five bays wide, with a tunnel-vaulted nave but no chancel, with galleried aisles supported by Corinthian columns resting on square piers. The contrast between the simple exterior and rich interior is immensely rewarding. Central to the design was the aim of ensuring that the preacher and the celebrant be both audible and visible to the whole congregation, hence the spaciousness of the church, the large glass windows and the near absence of internal supports. Note the white marble **font** by Grinling Gibbons showing Adam and Eve standing by the Tree of Life, which is represented by the stem of the font itself, the snake curled lasciviously around it proffering an apple while the tree obligingly sprouts a branch to cover Adam's nakedness. The bas-reliefs on the bowl are, in a clockwise direction, the *Baptism of Christ, Noah's Ark* and the *Baptism of the Treasurer of Queen Candace of the Ethiopians by St Philip.*

Gibbons was also responsible for the organ case (made for the Catholic chapel of King James II at Whitehall in 1685; it was transferred here in 1691) and for the outstandingly beautiful **limewood reredos**, which so moved John Evelyn (*see below*), carved with flowers and fruit and acanthus whorls (the acanthus leaf is a symbol of rebirth and eternal life).

As parish church of the Royal Academy, St James's has many artistic associations: William Blake was baptised in the font, and buried at the church are the caricaturist James Gillray (d. 1815) and the auctioneer James Christie (d. 1803), a close friend of Gainsborough. In the central vestibule are memorials to the father-and-son painters of sea battles, the Elder and Younger Willem van de Velde, who both worked for Charles II and James II.

Today, St James's is much engaged with the local community, with outreach programmes providing help for the homeless (it is customary to find people sleeping in the pews). It is also home to the William Blake Society (*blakesociety.org.uk*).

JOHN EVELYN ON ST JAMES'S CHURCH

'I went to see the new church at St James', elegantly built, especially adorned was the altar, the white marble enclosure curiously and richly carved, the flowers and garlands about the walls by Mr Gibbons in wood, a Pelican with her young at her breast just over the altar in the carved compartments environing the purple velvet fringed with I.H.S richly embroidered. And most noble plate were given by Sir R. Geere to the value (as was said) of £200. Such an altar was nowhere in any church in England, nor have I seen any abroad more handsomely adorned.'

Diary, 7th December 1684

BURLINGTON ARCADE

The Piccadilly Arcade leads off the south side of Piccadilly. Opposite it is the more famous Burlington Arcade (*map p. 603, E1–E2*). Its heavy Mannerist façade (c. 1930–1) is by Arthur Beresford Pite. There is nothing heavy about the interior: a narrow passage under a glass roof, leading right through to Burlington Gardens and sheltering bow-fronted shops on both sides. It boasts a regal red carpet for visitors to walk on; you can also get a shoe-shine.

Built in 1819 by Samuel Ware under the patronage of Lord George Cavendish, son of William Cavendish, 4th Duke of Devonshire, Burlington Arcade was almost certainly designed to be a shopping centre, to provide a snug and bespoke experience. In 1925, the author of 'A Discourse on Shopping for the Elite' was moved to remark that: 'Whosoever finds in shopping a delight, whosoever is fastidious in his taste, whosoever values quality, distinction and style, will turn aside a moment from the roar of Piccadilly and saunter along the Burlington Arcade, for here is the shopping place of the true epicurean.'

From the first day until now a beadle in splendid yellow-and-black livery has patrolled the arcade, to keep a watchful eye on the behaviour of the shoppers. Originally the beadles were all members of the 10th Hussars (now The King's Royal Hussars), George Cavendish's own regiment, but are now ex-servicemen of all kinds.

THE ROYAL ACADEMY OF ARTS

Map p. 603, E1. Underground: Green Park, Piccadilly Circus. Open daily 10–6 (until 10pm on Fri). Free guided tours of the Fine Rooms Tues–Fri 1pm. T: 020 7300 8000; royalacademy.org.uk. Admission charge. Restaurant/café.

Founded in 1768 under the patronage of George III, with the distinguished portraitist Sir Joshua Reynolds as its first President, the Royal Academy's aim was—and still is—the promotion of art and design through its teaching Schools, its Summer Exhibition of contemporary British work (an annual event since 1769) and via the staging of international loan exhibitions. It is for the last that the Royal Academy (RA) is perhaps best known today, being one of the principal venues in London for major national and international shows.

The RA has always been a self-governing institution, its President elected from its body of Academicians (RAs) composed, since the 18th century, of leading painters, sculptors and architects and, from the 19th century, engravers. As well as Reynolds, past Presidents include great figures such as Benjamin West, Sir Thomas Lawrence, Lord Leighton, Sir Edwin Lutyens and Sir Hugh Casson.

SIR JOSHUA REYNOLDS

Joshua Reynolds (1723–92), the son of a Devon schoolmaster, was one of the pre-eminent society portraitists of his generation, first President of the Royal Academy of Arts and 'founder of the British School of Painting'. While on a tour of Italy as a young man, he had beheld with awe the works of Michelangelo, Raphael and Titian and returned home with the aim of raising the status of the artist in Britain.

Reynolds had a competitive relationship with other painters. He was more at home with men from outside his field, the lexicographer Samuel Johnson and actor David Garrick among them. Indeed, he belonged, along with Johnson, to The Club, a group of a dozen or so men who met for supper and conversation at the Turk's Head Tavern in Gerrard Street, Soho.

Apart from his prolific output of pictures, Reynolds has left us his *Discourses on Art* (15 in total), which were mostly given by him at the annual prize-giving ceremony at the RA. They are more a series of occasional essays than a coherent theory, touching on subjects ranging from colouring and the life model to art education and the work of Gainsborough. Not a good speaker, he was inaudible to many who attended his lectures, and those who could understand him did not always like what they heard—or read: William Blake notoriously wrote on his copy of the *Discourses*, 'This Man was Hired to Depress Art'.

Reynolds's chief inspiration came from the Old Masters of Italy. His final remark to the RA was: 'And I should desire that the last words which I should pronounce to this Academy, and from this place, might be the name—Michael Angelo.' Suffering from loss of sight and acute deafness (a silver ear-trumpet was never far from his side), he died at the age of 69. He is buried in St Paul's Cathedral.

BURLINGTON HOUSE

BURLINGTON HOUSE

The present building, largely the work of Sydney Smirke (1866–76), encases a much older one, begun c. 1664 by Sir John Denham, then bought and completed in 1668 by the 1st Earl of Burlington. It was one of London's foremost private mansions. In the early 18th century it underwent radical alterations: first by James Gibbs for Juliana, Duchess of Burlington; and in 1717–20 by Colen Campbell for the Duchess' son, the famous promoter of Palladianism, the 3rd Earl of Burlington (*see Chiswick House, p. 476*). The current façade, which faces you as you pass through the central archway, has Campbell's Palladian ground and first storeys and Smirke's third storey, a heavy addition with niches containing statues of British and Italian Renaissance painters and sculptors. The wings creating the courtyard, by Banks and Barry in Italian Renaissance style (1868–73), house learned societies: to the left, the Linnaean Society, Royal Astronomical Society and Society of Antiquaries; to the right, the Royal Society of Chemistry and the Geological Society. The pleasant fountain jets in the centre of the courtyard are placed, apparently, according to Reynolds' horoscope.

Entrance hall

The low-ceilinged entrance hall (ticket office), remodelled in 1899, contains ceiling paintings by West (in the centre, *The Graces Unveiling Nature*, with the *Four Elements* around it) and roundels by Angelica Kauffmann (*Composition, Design, Painting* and *Invention*) removed from the RA's old meeting room in Somerset House on the Strand. The central grand staircase by Samuel Ware (1815–18) leads to the Main Galleries. Behind, past Sebastiano Ricci's grand Baroque paintings (*The Triumph of Galatea* and *Diana and her Nymphs*; c. 1712–15) and Kent's ceiling roundel of *Architecture* with the portrait of Inigo Jones (c. 1720), are the Fine Rooms (*see below*).

The Main Galleries and Fine Rooms

Smirke's **Main Galleries** consist of a central octagonal hall giving onto a succession of large, grand spaces. These galleries have witnessed spectacular crowds, especially in the 1880s and '90s during Leighton's successful presidency, when 350–400,000 visitors flocked to see popular masterpieces such as Sargent's *Carnation, Lily, Lily, Rose* and Anna Lea Merritt's *Love Locked Out* (both now owned by the Tate). In was also here, in the octagonal hall in 1896, that Leighton's body lay in state. The Summer Exhibition (working hard to shake off its reputation as a bastion of conservatism) still takes place here, as do the RA's excellent major loan exhibitions.

Overlooking the courtyard are the **John Madejski Fine Rooms** (*viewed by guided tour*), the principal apartments of old Burlington House, which display the RA's permanent collection. Originally decorated—and perhaps designed—by William Kent for the 3rd Earl of Burlington, some were altered by John Carr for the 3rd Duke of Portland in 1771–5 and then remodelled again by Samuel Ware in 1815–18 for Lord George Cavendish. The Saloon, with its pedimented doorcases, rich gilding and a ceiling by Kent (*The Marriage Feast of Cupid and Psyche*), is the most intact. The Secretary's Room has another Kent ceiling but others are by Ricci, taken, like the Riccis on the current central stairway, from Gibbs's old staircase decorated for Juliana, Duchess of Burlington. The Council Room has Ricci's old staircase ceiling while the General Assembly Room has his *Triumph of Bacchus*, originally on the staircase wall.

The RA's permanent collection includes diploma works presented by RAs on their election as members (a requirement since 1768); plaster casts after the antique (used for teaching in the RA Schools); portraits of RAs; and other works either collected or bequeathed. Among them is Reynolds' *Self-portrait with a bust of Michelangelo*.

The Sackler Galleries

Norman Foster's Sackler Galleries on the third floor (1985–91) have created additional exhibition space, dramatically approached via a glass capsule lift (or staircase) slotted into the narrow space between the back of Burlington House and Smirke's Main Galleries, affording an extraordinary close-up view of the architecture. Displayed outside the galleries is the Academy's greatest treasure, Michelangelo's unfinished marble *Madonna and Child with the Infant St John*, the so-called '**Taddei Tondo**' (1504–5), a work of great beauty and spirituality, bequeathed to the RA in 1830.

Behind the main building, at **no. 6 Burlington Gardens**, the neo-Renaissance building festooned with statues of scientists and philosophers was built in 1866–70 by Pennethorne as the seat of London University. It now belongs to the RA and is used for temporary exhibitions.

WESTERN PICCADILLY

THE RITZ

150 Piccadilly. Map p. 603, E2. To reserve afternoon tea in the Palm Court, T: 020 7300 2345 or book online (see website for toll-free number from the US). Rivoli Bar open until midnight Mon–Sat, until 10pm on Sun. T: 020 7493 8181, theritzlondon.com.
The most famous hotel in London, the Ritz opened its doors on 25th May 1906 and immediately established itself as the best of the best. It was founded by the Swiss-born César Ritz, who worked himself up from (unsuccessful) wine waiter through manager

ROYAL ACADEMY
Michelangelo's Taddei Tondo (1504–5).

of the Savoy in London to international hotelier with a chain of luxury establishments in Paris, London, New York and Budapest. He was dubbed, by no less a figure than King Edward VII, 'hotelier to kings and king of hoteliers'.

The hotel itself was designed by the Parisian architect Charles Mewès and his London-born pupil Arthur Joseph Davis, who had already worked together on the Paris Ritz and would later plan the Royal Automobile Club in Pall Mall. The Ritz is both modern and classical: it is actually constructed on a steel frame from Chicago, and while Portland stone was used on much of the façade, as was the fashion at the time, the ground-floor level is, more unusually, faced with Norwegian granite. The style of the interior is decidedly French, with its framed vista, grand enfilade and tribune and a grand staircase which sweeps down majestically into the vestibule.

The interior decoration can be appreciated in the **Palm Court** (*no sports clothing; men must wear a jacket and tie*). Inspired by an 18th-century French garden, it has a glass roof in a wrought-iron framework, hanging wrought-iron lamps, trellis-work painted in gold and exquisite French Neoclassical oval-backed armchairs, all separated from the vaulted corridor by a screen and two Ionic columns. In a central niche stands the gilded lead sculpture *La Source*, above which tritons blow caressingly into conch shells. In *A Dance to the Music of Time*, Anthony Powell describes the female figure thus: 'Although stark naked, the nymph looked immensely respectable; less provocative, indeed, than some of the fully-dressed young women seated below her.' The Art Deco-inspired **Rivoli Bar**, with glass panels, soft underlighting and scalloped ceiling domes, is recommended for a cocktail.

Hotel guests have included King Edward VII and his mistress Mrs Keppel, the Aga Khan (always dined at Table 1), Charlie Chaplin, Winston Churchill, Noël Coward, King Zog of Albania (and his eight bodyguards), Mahatma Gandhi, Nancy Mitford,

Evelyn Waugh, Graham Greene, Tallulah Bankhead (who was famously photographed drinking champagne from a slipper at a reception party in 1951), Jackie Onassis (Table 9 by the window), Bill Clinton, and Prince Charles, the Prince of Wales with Camilla, Duchess of Cornwall (they made their first public outing together at the Ritz).

Piccadilly continues to Hyde Park Corner (*see p. 234*), with buildings, mainly offices and hotels, facing Green Park. The enormous **Devonshire House**, built in the 1920s with New York-inspired architectural touches, replaced the original Devonshire House, built by William Kent for William Cavendish, 3rd Duke of Devonshire. When the 9th Duke found himself dogged by death duties, the house was abandoned and finally demolished in 1924. Its magnificent former entrance gates, hung between sphinx-topped pillars, are now preserved across the road as an entrance to Green Park.

At no. 94 is the Neoclassical **Cambridge House** (1758), built for the Earl of Egremont. Formerly home to the Naval and Military Club (now in St James's Square), the instructions on the gateposts IN and OUT gave the club its nickname, 'The In and Out'. It has since been purchased as a private mansion. Further along is the Park Lane Hotel (1927). At the very end is the original **Hard Rock Café**, in a former car show-room of 1905.

GREEN PARK

Green Park (*map p. 603, E2*), a triangular, 40-acre oasis of grassland and trees, without formal flowerbeds, extends from Buckingham Palace and Constitution Hill towards Piccadilly. Straight ahead is The Broadwalk, under which flows the ancient Tyburn river. On your left, the Canada Memorial (1994), a slanting sculpture with water gently lapping over bronze maple leaves and a central walkway, commemorates those in the Canadian forces who lost their lives during both World Wars. It is said that Thomas Wyatt's 1544 rebellion against Mary I's marriage to Philip II of Spain crossed this land. Charles II enclosed the park in 1668, constructing ice houses from which chilled drinks were served at royal picnics. By the 18th century Green Park was a fashionable pleasure garden: high society promenaded along Queen's Walk (named after Queen Caroline, wife of George II), which skirts the mansions of St James's on the eastern side. In the 1820s Nash landscaped the park and in 1826 it was opened to the public. In early spring, it is carpeted with daffodils.

ST JAMES'S

Map p. 603, E2. Underground: Green Park, Piccadilly Circus.

The street layout of St James's has remained virtually as it was planned in the 1670s by Henry Jermyn, 1st Earl of St Albans, favourite of Queen Henrietta Maria (it was he who broke the news to her of Charles I's execution) and described by Pepys as 'a fine civil gentleman'. Established as a residential district near the court of St James's (*see p. 159*), the area became famous in the late 18th century for its bachelor lodgings. From the reign of William III, the coffee and chocolate houses (the forerunners of today's clubs) were the rendezvous of aristocratic and learned London society, and specialist shops sprang up to serve both the club members and the courtiers. A number of such shops still survive: the area is well-stocked with purveyors of tobacco, shirts, hats, hand-made shoes, perfumes and fine foods as well as shooting and fishing accessories. Also here are many specialist art galleries and antique dealers.

ON AND AROUND ST JAMES'S STREET

Berry Bros & Rudd, wine merchants, have traded at no. 3 St James's St since 1699; the shopfront retains a late 18th-century design. Today they run excellent wine courses (*bbr.com*). **Lock & Co. Ltd.**, hatters, were established at no. 6 in 1676. Nelson's hat (on his wax effigy in Westminster Abbey Museum) was made here. Further along, Byron House occupies the site where in 1812, after the publication of the third Canto of *Childe Harold*, Lord Byron 'awoke one morning to find himself famous'.

On the opposite side of the road, at no. 74, is the former Conservative Club in Palladian style (Basevi and Smirke, 1845). At nos 69–70 is the Carlton Club (*for this and the other gentlemen's clubs on St James's Street, see p. 220*).

King Street is pre-eminent among the art dealers and galleries in the area, with **Christie's** at no. 8, fine art auctioneers since 1766 (and in King Street since 1823). At no. 28 the modern Almack House stands on the site of the now defunct **Almack's** (1765–1871), the first club to admit both men and women. It was famous in Regency London for its aristocratic assemblies. Entry was by exclusive voucher and to qualify one was selected by the Club's formidable patronesses, who included Princess Esterhazy, Sally Villiers, Lady Jersey and Emily Lamb, Lady Cowper. To be barred from attending Almack's was the ultimate social disgrace. The small 17th-century **Crown Passage**, with cafés, sandwich bars, a tailor and a pub, links King Street with Pall Mall.

Back on St James's, on the west side is St James's Place, where two luxury hotels are discreetly located. **Dukes Hotel** is renowned for its Martinis; the **American Bar at the Stafford** has been serving cocktails since the 1930s (bar entrance at the back, in the tiny cobbled Blue Bell Yard, which has remains of 18th-century stables).

At the end of St James's Place, at no. 27, is **Spencer House**, a fine Palladian mansion built in 1756–7 by John Vardy, a pupil of William Kent, for John, 1st Earl Spencer. The interiors were completed by James 'Athenian' Stuart in 1766. It was considered one of the finest houses in 18th-century London and is the only 18th-century private mansion to survive intact. Today it operates mainly as a hospitality venue and the interior, notable for Stuart's Greek detailing, is open to the public on Sun by guided tour (*spencerhouse.co.uk*). The narrow passage past no. 23 leads to Green Park and a good view of the fine Neoclassical façade, with a palm-wreathed oculus and statuary over the pediment.

JERMYN STREET

Jermyn Street (*map p. 603, E2*) was one of the first streets to be laid out according to Henry Jermyn's plan. Historically it was a street of shirt-makers, hat-makers and bootmakers to the courtiers of the Restoration period. On the corner with St James's Street is Beretta, gunmakers since 1526 and also selling sporting accessories. The rest of the street is filled with **gentlemen's outfitters**, old-fashioned shops which stock the kind of clothing that has apparelled the English gentleman for generations: Hilditch & Key (founded 1899), Charles Tyrwhitt, Thomas Pink, Hawes & Curtis (famous for introducing to the world the Duke of Windsor spread-collar) and T.M. Lewin & Sons. New & Lingwood Ltd at no. 53 began life in 1865, serving scholars at Eton College. Next door at no. 55 is Favourbrook, which specialises in dinner jackets and other evening attire. Opposite at no. 67 is Tricker's shoe shop, where you can still get a pair of bench-made brogues made to measure. The company was founded by a master shoemaker in 1829 and still operates its manufactory in Northampton, the traditional heartland of the English leatherworking industry.

Next to New & Lingwood is the entrance to the neo-Georgian **Piccadilly Arcade** (G. Thrale Jell, 1909). There are 16 shops in total, selling shirts, waistcoats, art books, watches, china and glassware. The Armoury of St James's at no. 17 has specialised for 30 years in regimental brooches. On the Jermyn Street side of the arcade there is a bronze statue (2002) of Beau Brummell, arbiter of St James's fashion.

BEAU BRUMMELL

The sculpture of George Bryan 'Beau' Brummell (1778–1840), based on a caricature of 1805 by Richard Dighton, shows the great dandy with artfully windswept hair, wearing fitted coat and trousers, top boots and an elaborate cravat. Brummell advocated simple but perfectly tailored clothing; it allegedly took him five hours each day to achieve sartorial perfection and his boots were polished with champagne. According to the *New Oxford Dictionary of National Biography*, 'His principal achievement while at Oxford was to perfect the "cut", the English art of ignoring people though conscious of their presence.' No one was his social inferior, not even a member of royalty. Promenading in St James's one day, he came across his one-time friend the—by then corpulent—Prince Regent, accompanied by Lord Monie. Ignoring the former, while acknowledging the latter, Brummell wondered aloud, 'Pray, who is your fat friend?' Alas, White's (*see p. 220*) proved his downfall: after losing £10,000 in a card game he was ruined financially and had to flee to France, where he remained for the rest of his life.

The **Princes Arcade** (opposite the Piccadilly Arcade) contains 22 bow-fronted shops. Other shops of note in Jermyn Street include **Paxton & Whitfield** (no. 93), 200-year old cheesemongers; **Floris** (no. 89), which has been selling fragrances, combs and shaving accessories on this site since 1730; **Geo. F. Trumper** (no. 20; corner of Duke of York St), traditional gentleman's barber and perfumer, selling all kinds of male grooming products (the main shop is on Curzon Street; *map p. 603, D2*).

THE WHITE CUBE

Opening off Duke Street St James's is Mason's Yard (*map p. 603, E2*), named after Hugh Mason of Fortnum's (*see p. 209*), who ran a stabling and ostling business here. Today it is home to the White Cube gallery (*open Tues–Sat 10–6; free; T: 020 7930 5373, whitecube.com*). Founded in 1993 and run by the artworld impresario Jay Jopling, the White Cube has played an important role in exhibiting and publicising the work of a generation of British artists, most notably the 'YBAs' (Young British Artists), among them Tracey Emin and Damien Hirst. The original site of the White Cube was on Duke Street, a simple room within a room, hence the name. It moved here in 2006, to a purpose-built building on the site of an electricity substation (MRJ Rundell & Associates). The gallery has another exhibition space in Bermondsey (*see p. 433*).

ST JAMES'S SQUARE

This pleasant open space (*map p. 603, E2*), London's first West End square, was laid out in the 1670s as part of Henry Jermyn's development of the area. The original plan was to make it a piazza in the Italian and French style: symmetrical, 60ft wide, with four wide streets converging on the centre. In practice, three of the streets (Charles II Street, King Street and Duke of York Street) were shortened and one was eliminated completely and replaced by two smaller entrances which connect to Pall Mall, thus giving the square its slightly irregular shape and feeling of seclusion.

For the first 150 years of its life, the square—once known as the Place Royal—was a fashionable residential enclave. Today, none of the houses from the 17th century survives. From the mid-19th century, many private residences were taken over by businesses and institutions and in the 1930s new office blocks completely replaced some of the houses. Nonetheless, architecturally speaking, those that remain form an important group.

Shrouded by trees and bushes, in the garden at the centre of the square, is an equestrian statue of William III (John and Thomas Bacon, 1809). The king's death was precipitated after a fall from his horse, when the horse tripped over a molehill—'the little gentleman in black velvet', as the Jacobites toasted the innocuous culprit thereafter. In fact, on falling King William only broke a collarbone; he died a few weeks later of pulmonary fever. Behind, is a seat by Nash (1822). The garden is open to all by day during the week and is a pleasant place to sit.

At no. 16 on the west side of the square is the **East India Club** (*male members only, women as guests*), in a handsome building of 1865. The club was formed by members of the East India Company in 1849. Over the years the club has incorporated a number of other smaller clubs, including the Sports Club, the Public Schools Club, the Devonshire Club and the Eccentric Club—once the favoured home-from-home of music hall stars. Next door is the **London Library** (*members only; T: 020 7766 4720, londonlibrary. co.uk*), founded in 1841 by Thomas Carlyle (*see p. 311*) and based here since 1845. The house was remodelled as a steel-framed building in 1896–8. Deceptively small from the outside, it is a labyrinth within, with a unique and charmingly simple cataloguing system. It houses over a million books and has over 8,000 members, many of whom are writers. Past members include George Eliot, Charles Dickens, Sir Arthur Conan Doyle,

George Bernard Shaw, Henry James, T.S. Eliot, Virginia Woolf and Agatha Christie. The current president is the playwright Sir Tom Stoppard.

At no. 12 is a blue plaque to Ada Byron (Lovelace), the mathematician who devised one of the earliest computer programs. Across Duke of York Street at no. 4, on the front of the Naval & Military Club building (familiarly known as the 'In and Out' after a building it formerly occupied on Piccadilly, with the entrance and exit gates thus boldly marked), is a plaque to the Virginia-born Nancy Astor, who in 1919 became the first woman to be elected a member of parliament in the UK. This is the Lady Astor who, so the story goes, once said to Winston Churchill: 'Winston, if I were married to you, I'd put poison in your coffee'; Churchill replied: 'Nancy, if I were married to you, I'd drink it.'

THE CLUBS OF ST JAMES'S

St James's is home to that peculiarly British institution: the gentleman's club. These elitist bodies (literally so: you have to be elected to join), discreet in the extreme—there are no name plates on the front doors and the very traditional ones have no website—have a venerable history. Inspired by Athenian symposia, the first recognisable 'club' in the metropolis was established at the Mermaid Tavern in Bread Street (*see p. 49*). Gentlemen's clubs in the 18th century evolved out of those taverns, supper houses and coffee houses, developing into the exclusive, polished and shuttered institutions of the 19th century and today. In spite of their misogynistic reputations, many clubs now admit women. The first to do so (after Almack's; *see p. 217*) was the aptly-named Reform Club in the 1980s. Today the clubs are valued for providing their members with affordable accommodation and dining in central London, and with comfortable rooms in which to meet, relax and entertain.

White's: White's is the oldest surviving London club. Jonathan Swift called it 'the common rendezvous of infamous sharpers and noble cullies.' Indeed, it has been the area's chief gambling den (and a bolt-hole for prime ministers) for centuries. Politically, it has always been Conservative. The club rules date from 1736, the earliest extant of their kind.

White's began life in 1698 as a chocolate-house owned by Francis White (d. 1711), his name probably anglicised from Francesco Bianco or Bianchi (he is buried in St James's, Piccadilly). The original building burnt down in 1733 and in 1755 it moved to its present site in St James's. James Wyatt may have been the original architect; the bow window dates from c. 1811 and the façade is a mid-Victorian alteration.

Here poor George Harley Drummond of Drummond's Bank lost £20,000 to the professional dandy Beau Brummell (*see p. 218*). A later game proved Brummell's own ruin. White's is also the club where Prince Charles had his stag night before his marriage to Lady Diana Spencer. *37–38 St James's St. Map p. 603, E2. Male members only.*

Boodle's: Established in 1762 in Pall Mall, this club, named after its former head waiter, Edward Boodle, is London's second oldest. It moved here in 1782.

The building is of yellow brick, designed by John Crunden in the style of Robert Adam. Notice the beautiful fan-sur-rounded Venetian window.

This was the club of choice of Ian Fleming, author of the James Bond novels. Although it began life as a political club—an early member was the economist Adam Smith—its character soon became shaped by the comfortable country gentlemen who formed the bulk of its membership. *28 St James's St. Map p. 603, E2. Men and women members.*

Brooks's: Founded in 1764, Brooks's moved to Henry Holland's purpose-built Palladian building in 1778.

Brooks's was a hotbed of Whig intrigue. Its founding members were all young Regency dandies who had been on the Grand Tour. It became a second home to Charles James Fox, who taught lessons in governance to the Prince Regent, the future King George IV, much to the chagrin of his father, George III. The tutorials were given, so it is recorded, with Fox dishevelled, in his night-gown and open-breasted, still recovering from a heavy night of whist and piquet. A number of prime ministers have been members of Brooks's, as well as Gibbon, Macaulay, Reynolds, Garrick and Sheridan. It was bombed in 1974 by the Provisional IRA: Edward Heath, who was Prime Minister at the time, was dining nearby at Pratt's. *60 St James's St. Map p. 603, E2. Male members only (women as guests).*

Pratt's: Tiny men's dining club founded in 1857 and named after William Pratt, who was attached to the household of the Duke of Beaufort. *14 Park Place. Map p. 603, E2. Male members only.*

The Carlton Club: The Carlton Club was formed in 1832 in direct opposition to the Reform Bill and remains to this day the club home of the Conservative Party. It began life in Pall Mall in a building designed by Sir Robert Smirke which was destroyed by bombing in 1940. The club then moved to its present location, a five-bay neo-Palladian build-ing (1826) with a rusticated ground floor and first floor decorated with Corinthian columns. It was designed by Thomas Hopper (who would be defeated by Sir Charles Barry in the competi-tion for the design of the Houses of Parliament). Despite being a bastion of conservatism, the Carlton Club could hardly have refused membership to Margaret Thatcher on her election as Conservative party leader in 1975; thus she 'joined the lads' as the BBC put it and became the first honorary woman member, the only woman afforded such a privilege until 2008, when women were permitted to become ordinary members. *69 St James's St. Map p. 603, E2. Men and women members.*

The Athenaeum: The Greek Revival exterior (1827–30) was conceived by Decimus Burton, who had worked with Nash on Regent's Park and Regent Street. The processional frieze (sculpted by John Henning) is copied from the Parthenon Marbles and the presiding figure of Pallas Athene (by E.H. Baily), goddess and patroness of learning, makes clear the club's intellectual bent. The Athenaeum was founded in 1824 as a club for artists, scientists and writers. Three of its founder members were Sir Thomas Lawrence RA, Sir Humphrey Davy (the wheelchair in which he died is still kept in the club) and Sir Walter

Scott. The president of the RA has always been an *ex-officio* member, and the club has had many other RA members in its long history, including J.M.W. Turner and Decimus Burton himself, as well as writers such as Dickens, Trollope and Macaulay. It has the best library of any club in London: Thackeray wrote some of his books here. *107 Pall Mall (facing Waterloo Place); Map p. 603, F2. Men and women members.*

Travellers Club: The club was established in 1814 by Robert Stewart, Lord Castlereagh, Marquess of Londonderry, the British Foreign Secretary who helped forge the European alliance against Napoleon. In the beginning membership was open to all men but those who 'shall not have travelled out of the British Islands to a distance of at least 500 miles from London in a direct line'. For most of its history it has been home to diplomats and explorers.

The premises were built in 1829 by Sir Charles Barry in the style of a Florentine palace. *106 Pall Mall. Map p. 603, F2. Male members only; women, even if much-travelled, may only come here as a member's guest.*

Reform Club: It was at this club that Jules Verne had Phileas Fogg accept the wager to attempt to travel around the world in 80 days. Built in 1841 by

Sir Charles Barry, the Reform Club, like the Travellers Club next door, takes its inspiration from Italian *palazzi* and is perhaps Barry's masterpiece. As an institution, its origins lie in the Reform Bill of 1830–2. The Liberal prime ministers Palmerston and Gladstone were members, as was Isambard Kingdom Brunel. It was the first club to provide its members with bedrooms. *104–105 Pall Mall. Map p. 603, F2. Men and women members. Tours can be arranged for individuals and small groups on weekdays and large groups on Sat (reformclub.com). Formal attire–jacket and tie–required. Donation recommended. The club also participates in Open House London (see openhouse.org.uk for details).*

Royal Automobile Club: Founded in 1897, the Royal Automobile Club moved to this sumptuous French Renaissance-style building in 1911. It was built by Charles Mewès and Arthur Joseph Davis (who also collaborated on the Ritz), based, probably, on Ange-Jacques Gabriel's twin palaces of 1748 in the Place de la Concorde, Paris. There is a splendid two-storey domed, oval entrance hall in Louis XVI style, which can just about be spied through the main door. General Charles de Gaulle used the club regularly during the Second World War. *89 Pall Mall. Map p. 603, E2. Men and women members.*

PALL MALL

Pall Mall (*map p. 603, E2–F2*) is named after a croquet-style game called *palla a maglio* ('ball to mallet') which was popular in the area during the 17th century (The Mall has the same derivation). Pall Mall is famous, like St James's, for its gentlemen's clubs, as well as for being the street in London where gas lighting was first demonstrated, by Frederick Winsor in 1807. The elaborate flambeaux which survive outside some of the buildings are still lit by gas on special occasions and for film shoots. By 1820 the whole of St James's was lit by gas; the area retains some of the oldest and most closely-spaced lamp posts in the city.

From 1774 until his death in 1788, Gainsborough lived in the west wing (no. 80) of **Schomberg House**, a 17th-century building of red brick with stone dressings (restored in 1956, when the rest of the house was rebuilt). The house at no. 79 (rebuilt) was given to Nell Gwyn by Charles II, with whom, according to Evelyn, she used to talk over the garden wall.

THOMAS GAINSBOROUGH

Born in Sudbury, Suffolk, the son of a cloth merchant, Gainsborough (1727–88) painted landscapes, portraits and genre scenes. Predominantly self-taught, he may have been apprenticed to a silversmith in London. His influences were less the Old Masters of Italy (as Reynolds's had been) and more 17th-century Northern European painters such as Rubens and Van Dyck. He frequently used models to draw from: coal for rocks and broccoli for trees were especial favourites. He did not enjoy being, as he put it, a 'phizmonger' (portrait-painter). Perhaps as a reaction to this, out of his landscapes he developed his so-called 'fancy pictures' (a term first applied to them by Reynolds), rustic genre paintings of peasant children and the deserving poor, which sought to evoke emotion and sympathy in the viewer. In this he was much influenced by Murillo. Tate Britain has several representative works. Shortly before his death he was visited by his rival Reynolds, to whom his last words are reputed to have been: 'We are all going to Heaven–and Van Dyck is of the company.' (*For Reynolds's own last words to the Royal Academy, see p. 212.*)

WATERLOO PLACE

On the corner of Pall Mall and Waterloo Place is the former United Service and Royal Aero Club, once the favourite haunt of the Duke of Wellington. It is now the head-quarters of the **Institute of Directors**. The building, by Nash (1828), incorporates the main staircase from the demolished Carlton House. It was remodelled by Decimus Burton to match the Athenaeum opposite.

On Waterloo Place itself is the **Crimean War Memorial**, at the centre of which stands a female personification of *Victory* (1915). The memorial, by John Bell, was first unveiled in 1859 to commemorate the Crimean War (1853–6) and consisted of the central figure—then known as *Honour*—and the three guardsmen cast from three Russian cannons used during the Siege of Sebastopol. John Henry Foley (who also fashioned the sculptural group *Asia* and the figure of Prince Albert for the Albert Memorial; *see p. 318*) and Arthur George Walker were responsible for the additions to the ensemble, with the dominant statue of the Secretary at War Lord Sidney Herbert of Lea (1867) and his close ally Florence Nightingale (1915). The gas lamp with gilded finial dates from 1830.

To the south of this, on the other side of Waterloo Place, is a group of fine bronze statues of kings, soldiers and explorers, including Matthew Noble's sculpture of Sir John Franklin (d. 1847), the Arctic explorer who discovered the Northwest Passage.

Just beyond are the Duke of York Steps, which lead down to St James's Park. At the top of the steps stands the Tuscan granite **Duke of York Column** (1831–4), which commemorates Frederick, Duke of York and Albany, the 'grand old Duke of York', second and favourite son of George III. The column is by Benjamin Wyatt and the bronze statue by Sir Richard Westmacott. The Duke was Commander-in-Chief of the British Army until his death in 1827. Every officer and soldier in the Army forfeited a day's pay to provide funds for the monument to 'the soldier's friend'.

CARLTON HOUSE TERRACE

On either side of the Duke of York Steps stretches Carlton House Terrace (*map p. 603, F2*), once one of the most aristocratic places of residence in London, overlooking the Mall. Carlton House, which stood on this site, was a mansion built in 1709. It was the town residence of the Prince Regent, later George IV, from 1783. The Prince engaged Henry Holland to remodel the house in sufficiently opulent manner and it was here that he celebrated the news of his accession. Nash laid out Regent Street as a processional route to link the house with Regent's Park to the north, but the plan was never realised. Carlton House was demolished in 1827 and Nash's Carlton House Terrace (1827–33), with the Duke of York's column between, was built in its stead.

Under a tree on the right (west side) of the Duke of York Column is a small tombstone (behind glass) marking the grave of the German ambassador's terrier, Giro (d. 1934). The Prussian and later German Embassy was at nos 7–9 from 1849 until 1939.

The **Royal Society**, one of the most famous scientific bodies in the world, has occupied nos 6–9 (entrance at no. 6) since 1967. It originated from a group of eminent scholars who began to meet informally in London and Oxford in 1645. No. 5 was formerly the residence of Lady Cunard and no. 2 was the home (in 1906–25) of eminent statesman and Viceroy of India, Lord Curzon, a statue of whom stands opposite.

Further west in Carlton Gardens, Lord Palmerston and Lord Balfour lived at no. 4 (rebuilt in 1933 by Sir Reginald Blomfield), where a tablet marks this as General de Gaulle's Free French headquarters from 18th June 1940. A statue of De Gaulle has been erected opposite (Angela Conner, 1993). A small square opens behind a statue of George VI, and stairs descend to The Mall. Lord Kitchener lived at no. 2 in 1914–15. No. 1 was occupied by Napoleon III in 1840–1; it is now the official residence of the Foreign Secretary.

MAYFAIR

Map p. 603, D2–D1. Underground: Hyde Park Corner, Green Park, Marble Arch, Bond Street.

Exclusive Mayfair, bounded by Oxford Street, Regent Street, Piccadilly and Park Lane, vies with Belgravia as the most prestigious address in London. The area offers a profusion of luxury boutiques, high-end jewellers, antique shops, art galleries and picture dealers. And after an extravagant retail spree, one can indulge in stylish drinking and fine dining in the area's smart hotels, bars, restaurants and clubs. Mayfair boasts more Michelin-starred restaurants than any other area of London (*see p. 238*).

Mayfair takes its name from the annual May Fair which was held around present-day Curzon Street and Shepherd Market from the late 17th century until 1764, when the area's well-to-do residents finally suppressed what was in reality fifteen days of rowdy and debauched revelry.

Mayfair's transformation into an elegant residential enclave then began. By the end of the 18th century it was largely complete. The streets and squares were laid out by wealthy landowners, among them Sir Richard Grosvenor (Grosvenor Square), the Lords Berkeley of Stratton (Berkeley Square) and the Earl of Scarborough (Hanover Square). The present Duke of Westminster, one of Britain's richest land and property owners, still owns large tracts of Mayfair.

Right up until the late 1930s, it was customary for members of the nobility and landed gentry to keep townhouses in Mayfair for use during the London Season. The 'season' was the annual period of several months (roughly Jan–June) in which the 'Ton', the fashionable *beau monde*, converged in 'Town' for an unremitting round of socialising and lavish entertainments. Daughters of marriageable age were presented at Court, thereby launching them into Society and into the paths of suitable husbands. Two world wars and subsequent shifts in society sounded the Season's death knell. The heads of the noble houses could no longer keep up their grand lifestyle and their magnificent town residences have now mostly been demolished. Many other former private houses have been converted into embassies, clubs or the offices of estate agents and hedge fund managers. The area commands some of the highest rents in London and ultra-rich foreign residents and 'new money' now tend to make up the population. Much interesting architecture survives, including original mews. Behind a discreetly elegant Georgian façade, you might catch a glimpse of an opulent private interior and in the narrower streets, large pockets of less grand houses, often in individual architectural styles, are to be found.

PARK LANE

Park Lane, overlooking Hyde Park, was at its fashionable zenith in the 1820s and '30s, when private mansions lined the street. Today most of the great houses have gone, replaced by modern blocks, hotels and luxury car dealerships. In 1963 Park Lane was widened, turning it into the relentless dual carriageway that it is now. There is nothing like thundering, deafening traffic to extinguish any lingering pretensions to aristocratic grandeur.

Hamilton Place and Old Park Lane run parallel to Park Lane and converge at the 30-storey **London Hilton** (1961–3; *map p. 603, D2*), Mayfair's tallest point, where the rooftop bar and restaurant have good views. Nearby, the Four Seasons Hotel opened in 1970 and the Inter-Continental in 1975. At no. 5 Hamilton Place, the 19th-century building in French classical style is **Les Ambassadeurs**, a private-members' casino which featured in The Beatles' film *A Hard Day's Night* and in the James Bond film *Dr No*. The Metropolitan Hotel, formerly the Londonderry, on the corner of Hertford Street, opened in 1967 on the site of Londonderry House, designed in the 1760s by James Stuart and reconstructed by Wyatt in the 1820s for the Marquess of Londonderry. Its grand staircase, magnificent ballroom and fine collection of statues all succumbed to the wrecking ball in 1962.

Set back from the road, at 47 Park Lane, the grey stone neo-Gothic building with elaborate tracery is **Stanhope House**, built for the soap magnate R.W. Hudson by Romaine-Walker in 1901. It is now a branch of Barclays Bank. In contrast is the smooth, white, relatively unadorned façade of the **Dorchester Hotel** (Owen Williams and William Curtis Green, 1931) on the site of Dorchester House, later Hertford House. The Dorchester is constructed from incredibly strong reinforced concrete, allowing for clean lines and spaciousness: when it opened it was considered dazzlingly modern. During the Blitz, it was one to the safest places to shelter and many of Mayfair's aristocratic residents took refuge at 'The Dorch'. In 1942 General Eisenhower moved in on a semi-permanent basis until the end of the War.

The huge **Grosvenor House Hotel**, conceived as serviced apartments and a hotel in four connected blocks (A.O. Edwards, 1929), stands on the site of the London house of the Grosvenor family (later the Dukes of Westminster). The Grosvenors' 19th-century residence was the first of the grand houses to be demolished to make way for a hotel; Lutyens was consultant architect. The Great Room—London's biggest hotel banqueting venue—was used as a skating rink in 1929–34 and served as an American officers' mess in 1943. This was the first hotel to offer *en suite* bathrooms.

Benjamin Disraeli lived at no. 93 Park Lane from his marriage in 1839 until the death of his wife (to whom the house belonged) in 1872. The charming row of bowfronted houses with 'Chinese' balconies (nos 93–99) survives from the 1820s. At no. 100 is **Dudley House**, a nine-bay, three-storey Neoclassical mansion with later castiron conservatory, built for the 1st Earl of Dudley in 1828 by William Atkinson. It is now owned by the Emir of Qatar (whose lavish renovations may have mollified the angry lady who reputedly haunts it).

GROSVENOR SQUARE

Upper Brook Street leads to Grosvenor Square (*map p. 603, D1*), laid out, with adjoining streets, in 1725–31 by Sir Richard Grosvenor. It covers six acres and is one of the largest of London's squares. The surrounding monumental terraces are mostly neo-Georgian blocks of apartments, offices and hotels built between the 1920s and 1960s; however no. 9 in the northeast corner survives from c. 1725.

At the time of writing, the square was dominated on the west side by the **American Embassy** (Eero Saarinen, 1957–60), with statues of two former American Presidents in front of it: a 10ft Ronald Reagan with a fine head of hair (unveiled 2011) and Dwight D. Eisenhower, with his hands on his hips. The square's garden was re-planned in the 1940s as a memorial to Franklin D. Roosevelt, President of the United States in 1932–44, and includes his statue by Reid Dick (1948). Opposite is a memorial to the Royal Air Force American Eagle Squadron: a Portland stone pillar crowned by a bronze American bald eagle by Elizabeth Frink, unveiled in 1986. There is also a memorial garden commemorating those who lost their lives in the terrorist attacks on the USA on 11th September 2001. It is partly the threat of terrorist attack that has prompted the Embassy to leave Grosvenor Square. At the time of writing they were set to remove to a purpose-designed moated building in Vauxhall.

At no. 13 Carlos Place, **Hamiltons Gallery** occupies an unusual brick building with an open attic sporting lion's head roof blocks. This was Major Stephen Courtauld's racquets court (E. Vincent Harris, 1924). Originally the Carlos Place façade was without door or windows because the building extended back and adjoined Courtauld's residence at 47 Grosvenor Square. The large central niche, which has been extended into a door, formerly housed a bronze figure of St George, known to residents as 'Old George'.

North Audley Street leads out of the northwest corner of the square to Oxford Street. On the right is the atmospherically decaying neo-Grecian **church of St Mark** (J.P. Gandy Deering, 1824–8), with an Ionic porch and pierced stone tower. The church has been redundant for many years and a campaign to save the building may yet see it turned into an events venue.

THE LONDON SQUARE

By the middle of the 19th century, London had upwards of a hundred squares. Some were fashionable, some were not, but all had a sward of green in the centre and were planted with trees and flowers, even adorned with statuary. The London square, claimed the writer, reformer and social researcher Henry Mayhew, was 'utterly unlike your foreign "*platz*", that bare paved or gravelled space with nothing but a fountain, a statue or a column in the centre of it.'

According to Todd Longstaffe-Gowan in *The London Square* (Yale, 2012), two main factors contributed to the development of the London square as it exists today: the aim to enclose and safeguard common ground which people were in the habit of using for pasture and recreation; and the desire to create unified architectural ensembles to enhance the appearance of the city. Early prints show squares laid out with buildings of harmonious similitude surrounding a central area bounded by post-and-rail palisades. The apparent exclusivity of the square, however, was soon to be seen as a problem. Commentators complained that the common man was kept at bay while squares became the preserve of genteel children and their nurserymaids. Yet when private landlords were not in charge, the spaces often degenerated into squalor. Leicester Square was a famous example: it rapidly became a 'depository of refuse'.

Trafalgar Square remained an exception. No garden was ever planted there and old prints show it looking decidedly 'foreign', with not a shrub in sight yet plentifully supplied with pavement, fountains, statues and of course its column. It quickly became—and still remains—a place of public congregation, often for leisure but also for political protest.

Today London's squares are sometimes private (Cadogan Square), sometimes public (Lincoln's Inn Fields) and sometimes a mixture of the two (St James's Square, open to all by day but locked at night, when the key is given to residents only).

During the Second World War, many of the squares were dug up and planted with vegetables to feed the civilian population.

DUKE STREET, BROOK STREET AND SOUTH MOLTON STREET

Brown Hart Gardens, on Duke Street (*map p. 603, D1*), is a public square laid out on the roof of an eccentric-looking neo-Baroque electricity substation in Portland stone (C. Stanley Peach, c. 1905). The gardens offer a café, spacious wooden seats, tubs of ornamental plants (including cabbages) and a good view of the Ukrainian church (*see below*). The substation replaced existing gardens at street level and after its completion, the Duke of Westminster ordered the creation of a public square to recompense the local, mainly working-class, residents who had lost their green space. Opposite the gardens is the red-brick **Cathedral of the Holy Family in Exile**, the mother church of the Ukrainian Greek Catholic Apostolic Exarchate of Great Britain, in a building of c. 1890 by Alfred Waterhouse.

Brook Street leads east. **Claridge's**, in red brick on the corner of Davies Street, is one of London's most exclusive hotels (built 1898, enlarged 1931) and frequently the choice of visiting heads of state and royalty. No. 41 is a 1720s' building Italianised by Barry. Jimi Hendrix lived at no. 23 for about 18 months in 1968–9. At no. 25 (plaque) Handel lived from 1725 until his death in 1759. It is now the **Handel House Museum** (*map p. 603, E1; open Tues–Sat 10–6, until 8pm on Thur; Sun noon–6; closed bank holidays; admission charge; T: 020 7495 1685, handelhouse.org*). Handel ran his opera company from here, giving the first rehearsal of *Alcina* in 1735. His dining habits in these rooms are the subject of the following anecdote, reported by Charles Burney in 1785: 'During the repast, Handel cried out "Oh—I have de taught"...the company begged he would retire and write it down, with which request he so frequently complied that, at last, one of the most suspicious had the ill-bred curiosity to peep through the key-hole into the adjoining room, where he perceived that "dese taughts" were only bestowed on a fresh hamper of Burgundy.'

HANDEL ON BROOK STREET

From 1723, when he was appointed Composer to the Chapel Royal, until his death in 1759, Handel lived and worked in this Mayfair townhouse. Born in Saxony, Handel came to London in 1710, having been Kapellmeister to the Elector of Hanover, later King George I. What attracted him was the opportunity to stage Italian operas. In the next year his *Rinaldo*, at the Haymarket, proved a huge success. Naturalised a British citizen by Act of Parliament in 1727, he composed *Zadok the Priest* for the coronation of George II later in the same year. The words had been used at every coronation since that of King Edgar in 973; Handel's musical setting of them has been used at every coronation since that of George II. Concentrating increasingly on the composition of oratorios, Handel's work often drew parallels between British history and the Old Testament: they were patriotic pieces extolling by association the glories of the new Hanoverian dynasty. The most popular remains the *Messiah* (1741), of which regular Christmas charity performances in aid of the Foundling Hospital (*see p. 351*) were given after 1750. After 1751, unsuccessful operations on his cataracts left Handel completely blind. Until that time, he was exceptionally prolific, composing some 50 operas and over 20 oratorios, as well as cantatas, concerti and instrumental pieces—the majority of them while he was living in the rooms that can be seen here.

On either side of the street here are the entrances to Haunch of Venison Yard and a view of the Bonhams Auctioneers building (main entrance on New Bond Street) and Avery Row and Lancashire Court, where boutiques, bars and restaurants jostle along the compact connecting streets.

South Molton Street is a pedestrianised street of shops. In the triangular site behind Bond Street Underground, on Davies Street and South Molton Lane, is **Grays Antique Centre**. Inside the late 19th-century terracotta building, previously the headquarters of water closet manufacturers John Bolding & Son, is a warren of 200 antique dealers. It is built over a tributary of the River Tyburn and in the basement a raised canal full of goldfish is fed with running water from the now underground source.

HANOVER SQUARE

Hanover Square (*map p. 603, E1*) is adorned with a bronze statue of William Pitt the Younger (Chantrey, 1831). The house at no. 21 was occupied by Talleyrand in 1835 (plaque). The church of **St George's, Hanover Square**, with a Corinthian portico, was built in 1724 to designs by John James, as part of the New Churches Act of 1711. Concerts are held regularly and a Handel Festival takes place each year (Handel worshipped here, being a neighbourhood resident; *see above*). The register contains entries of the marriages of Sir William Hamilton and Emma Lyon or Hart (1791), Benjamin Disraeli and Mrs Wyndham Lewis (1839), 'George Eliot' and Mr J.W. Cross (1880), Theodore Roosevelt and Edith Carrow (1886) and H.H. Asquith and Margaret Tennant (1894); also of the remarriage of Shelley and Harriet Westbrook in 1814, legalising their Scottish elopement of 1811.

BOND STREET

Bond Street (*map p. 603, D1–E2*), divided into New Bond Street to the north and Old Bond Street to the south, was laid out by Sir Thomas Bond in 1686. Its name has been synonymous with fashion and shopping since the 18th century. Here was the place for dandies—known as 'Bond Street Loungers'—to be seen and it is here that they ogled promenading ladies through their quizzing glasses. Weston, famously the tailor to the leader of fashion himself, Beau Brummell (*see p. 213*), was located in Old Bond Street. Former residents include Jonathan Swift, James Boswell and Admiral Lord Nelson. Thereafter it became known as the centre of the London fine art world: long-established auctioneers **Sotheby's** and **Bonhams** both still have their flagship salerooms here. Today, this street of mainly 19th- and 20th-century façades is home to major international luxury brands. Gucci, Prada, Chanel, Versace and Louis Vuitton rub shoulders with traditional British brands such as upmarket stationer **Smythson** (no. 40). A relative newcomer to the street is the lingerie giant Victoria's Secret, whose shopfront draws large crowds, often of teenage boys. This is also the **jewellers'** street, where the most famous names in fine jewellery—Tiffany, Boucheron, Boodles, Cartier, Van Cleef & Arpels, Graff, Leviev, De Beers—are represented one after the other and along the side streets. This is the only place in the world where dealers in the largest and rarest diamonds congregate in high concentration, giving the false impression that these extraordinary multi-million-pound gems exist in abundance.

ALBEMARLE STREET
Building by Ernő Goldfinger (1956).

Allies, at the junction of Old and New Bond Street, is a popular sculpture of Roosevelt and Churchill sitting casually on a bench (Lawrence Holofcener, 1995). It was unveiled to mark the 50th anniversary of the end of the Second World War. Further down on the right, the Royal Arcade (1879) links Old Bond Street with Albemarle Street.

SAVILE ROW

Savile Row (*map p. 603, E1*) has been the home of British bespoke tailoring since the 1850s and it is here that the term 'bespoke' (used to signify when a particular cloth was already spoken for by a customer) was coined. Among the illustrious outfitters located here are Henry Poole, Gieves & Hawkes, Hunstman and Hardy Amies. Napoleon III and Winston Churchill (to name but two) were outfitted in Savile Row; the tuxedo was invented here in the 1860s. Sheridan lived at no. 14 (tablet) and died in 1816 in the front bedroom of no. 17. Nearby **Cork Street** is a centre for the contemporary arts world, with many commercial galleries.

ALBEMARLE STREET

Behind an impressive rank of Corinthian columns, modelled on the Temple of Antoninus and Faustina in the Roman Forum, is the **Royal Institution of Great Britain,** founded in 1799 to promote 'the application of Science to the common purposes of life'. A fascinating themed museum on three floors is devoted to the scientific discoveries of Michael Faraday (1791–1867), whose laboratory occupied the basement here (*21 Albemarle St; map p. 603, E1; open Mon–Fri 10–6; free; bar/restaurant; T: 020 7409 2992, rigb.org*). Born the son of a blacksmith and initially apprenticed as a bookbinder, Faraday discovered electromagnetic rotation (the principle behind the electric motor) and—even more importantly for 19th-century industry—electromagnetic induction (the principle behind transformers and generators), as well as benzene, the magneto-optical effect, diamagnetism and field theory. The museum includes his restored laboratory as well as displays on Humphry Davy, whose assistant Faraday became, and Ada Lovelace, the mathematician and computer pioneer (and daughter of Lord Byron).

Brown's Hotel, at 33 Albemarle St, was founded by James Brown, former valet to Lord Byron, in 1837; it is famous for its afternoon tea (*served daily noon–6.30; T: 020 7518 4155, brownshotel.com*) and for the fact that Alexander Graham Bell made the first UK demonstration of his new invention, the telephone, from the lobby in 1876.

Also on Albemarle Street, at no. 50, is the early 18th-century building that used to be the premises of John Murray, publishers of Byron, Jane Austen, Darwin and Sir Arthur Conan Doyle. It was in this building that Byron's memoirs were burned after his death because they were thought too salacious. The late 1950s building at nos. 45–46 is notable for being by Ernő Goldfinger, architect of Trellick Tower (*see p. 281*) as well as of his own home in Willow Road, Hampstead (*see p. 397*).

BERKELEY SQUARE

Berkeley Square (*map p. 603, D1–E1*) was once one of the most elegant of London squares, laid out by William Kent c. 1739 on part of the gardens of Berkeley House. In the famous war song, Vera Lynn was 'perfectly willing to swear' that a nightingale sang here. It might have had its nest in one of the beautiful plane trees in the open garden in the centre (planted 1789).

On the southwest corner is the **Lansdowne Club**, begun in 1762 by Robert Adam for the Earl of Bute and sold in 1765 to the Earl of Shelburne, later 1st Marquess of Lansdowne. It became a club in the '30s; the façade is by Charles W. Fox. Blue plaques on either side of the entrance commemorate that the Marquess of Lansdowne lived here as well as Harry Gordon Selfridge, founder of the eponymous department store on Oxford Street.

On the west side of Berkeley Square, past Charles Street, the row of **fine Georgian buildings** dates from the 1740s. No. 50, previously the home of George Canning (plaque) and now the offices of antiquarian booksellers Maggs Bros Ltd, is the so-called 'haunted house', which remained empty for long periods in the 19th century following numerous different sightings. Winston Churchill lived as a child at no. 48, and at no. 47 (now the exclusive J. Safra Sarasin Bank) William Pitt resided for a time with his brother, the 2nd Earl of Chatham. No. 45 was redecorated by Chambers for Clive of India in 1763 and was also the scene of Clive's suicide in 1774; in the 19th century Lady Dorothy Nevill received Gladstone and Disraeli and other celebrities of the day here. No. 44 (now the **Clermont Club**) is a survivor of Kent's original square, built in 1742–5 for Lady Isabella Finch; this 'finest terrace house in London' (Pevsner) possesses a beautiful interior with a Baroque-style staircase leading to a graceful drawing room. In the basement is the famous members-only nightclub **Annabel's**, founded by Mark Birley and the haunt of the 1960s' jet-set. It is now owned by rag-trade tycoon

Richard Caring, whose multi-million property portfolio includes other clubs and fashionable restaurants. Of particular note outside these buildings are the wrought-iron lamp holders, many of them complete with **original candle snuffers**; further examples may be seen in Charles Street. Charles Street, Hill Street and Hays Mews all lead west to Waverton Street. Along the way are more attractive Georgian and Edwardian houses.

MOUNT STREET AND SOUTH AUDLEY STREET

The **Connaught Hotel** on Carlos Place (*map p. 603, D1*) dates to 1896, when it was known as the Coburg. It was the headquarters of General de Gaulle in the Second World War. It has a fine bar and an acclaimed restaurant.

Mount Street takes its name from 'Oliver's Mount', the defensive earthwork that was hastily thrown up in 1643 during the English Civil War when news spread that Charles I was approaching London after the Battle of Edgehill. Today it is fronted mainly by late 19th-century pink terracotta buildings housing shops and restaurants, including an unexpected butcher's shop with fresh meat and game hanging in the window. Further along on the other side of the road is Scott's, Mayfair's fashionable fish restaurant (*see p. 238*). At the end, on the corner of South Audley Street, is a good Victorian pub, The Audley. In Mount Street Gardens, a pleasant oasis, is the back of the neo-Gothic Jesuit **Church of the Immaculate Conception** (J.J. Scoles, 1849). The church's main entrance is on Farm Street (it is possible to walk through the church), hence its familiar name of Farm Street Church. Evelyn Waugh mentions it in *Brideshead Revisited*. The high altar is by A.W.N. Pugin, who designed the interiors of the Houses of Parliament.

Mount Street Gardens lead straight onto South Audley Street, where, on the left, you will see the **Grosvenor Chapel**, in plain brick with a quoin-edged tower (1730–1). The foundation stone was laid by the landowner Sir Richard Grosvenor; it was used by US armed forces during the Second World War. At no. 19 South Audley St, Thomas Goode, china and glass specialists, occupy an elaborate building of 1875–90. Opposite, no. 71 has a fine doorway and porch of 1737. At no. 72 lived Charles X, last King of the Bourbons (r. 1824–30).

CHARLES STREET AND QUEEN STREET

Charles Street (*map p. 603, D2*) preserves its original wrought-iron lamp holders and snuffers. Dartmouth House (no. 37) is home to the **English Speaking Union**, itself in the former home of Lord Revelstoke, of the Baring banking family and great-great-grandfather of the late Diana, Princess of Wales. From 1885, Revelstoke joined two 18th-century houses behind the present unified Anglo-French façade. The fine interiors were designed to show Revelstoke's art and furniture collection to advantage. Next door is the traditional **Chesterfield Hotel**, on the site of a house once occupied by the noted Regency dandy Lord Petersham, who owned a vast collection of snuff boxes and used a different one on every day of the year.

The Regency courtesan Harriette Wilson lived in **Queen Street**. She was born in Mayfair in 1786, the daughter of a Swiss clockmaker. Her announcement in 1825 that

BERKELEY SQUARE
Snuffer on the 'haunted house' once occupied by Lord Canning.

she planned to write her memoirs prompted Wellington's famous reaction 'publish and be damned'. Harriette's response was that 'old frights like himself, who cannot be contented with amiable wives, but must run about to old procuresses, bribing them to decoy young girls, ought to pay us for the sacrifice they tempt us to make, as well as for our secrecy.' The memoirs are still in print. Wellington, we learn, was a dull companion, with whom conversation was 'very uphill work'. Queen Street today is home to two Michelin-starred restaurants (*see p. 238*)

CURZON STREET AND SHEPHERD MARKET

Curzon Street (*map p. 603, D2*) has fine older houses on the south side. Disraeli died at no. 19 in 1881. No. 30, an Adam house (c. 1771), is home to the exclusive Crockford's private gambling club. The Curzon Cinema (1933, rebuilt in 1963) is almost opposite Crewe House (now the Saudi Embassy), a preserved stucco mansion set back from the road in its own grounds, designed by Edward Shepherd (c. 1740s, altered in 1810s) and occupied by the Marquess of Crewe from 1899. Opposite Half Moon Street is the large portico of the extraordinary **Third Church of Christ Scientist** (1910–12, tower c. 1932). Next door is **Geo F. Trumper**, barbers since 1875, still selling 'unique preparations for the hair and scalp, shaving creams and soaps of the purest qualities and all manner of toilet requisites'. Two archways lead south from Curzon Street into secret **Shepherd Market**, established by Edward Shepherd, builder and entrepreneur, and still retaining its 'village' atmosphere and 18th-century layout. It is filled with restaurants, pubs and a few small shops.

HYDE PARK CORNER

Map p. 603, D2. Underground: Hyde Park Corner.

Hyde Park Corner is a busy road junction at the point where Piccadilly meets Park Lane. It is so busy, noisy and congested, undermined by a confusing array of pedestrian subways, that it is neither easy nor pleasant to stop and look around. Isolated in its centre is the triumphal **Wellington Arch**, formerly erected opposite the main entrance to Hyde Park but moved in 1883 to align with Constitution Hill. It now forms part of a processional route from Buckingham Palace to Kensington Palace (the massive gates are occasionally opened to allow horses and ceremonial cars through). Designed by Decimus Burton in 1828, in conjunction with the tripartite **Hyde Park Corner Screen**, it was at first topped with M. Cotes Wyatt's much derided over-sized equestrian statue of Wellington (1838). Described as 'a gigantic triumph of bad taste' (*Punch*) and 'a perfect disgrace' (Queen Victoria), it was in fact liked by Wellington, who was upset at plans to remove it. In 1883 it was finally taken down and replaced with Adrian Jones' magnificently animated *Peace Descending on the Quadriga of War* (1912). The arch can be visited (*joint ticket with Apsley House; see below*). The equestrian statue of Wellington that now stands on the island is by Boehm (1888). It faces Apsley House, Wellington's former London home.

On the western side of Hyde Park Corner (junction of Knightsbridge and Grosvenor Place) is the luxurious **Lanesborough Hotel** (formerly St George's Hospital; William Wilkins, 1827, with later extensions).

APSLEY HOUSE

Map p. 603, D2. 149 Piccadilly (Hyde Park Corner). Open April–Oct Wed–Sun 11–5. Admission charge. Joint ticket with Wellington Arch. T: 020 7499 5676, english-heritage.org.uk.

Apsley House, once known as 'No. 1 London' since it was the first house after the turnpike from Kensington and Knightsbridge, was the town residence of Arthur Wellesley, 1st Duke of Wellington, the famous 'Iron Duke', victor of Waterloo and Prime Minister from 1828–30. It was built by Robert Adam in 1771–8 for Lord Apsley, later 2nd Earl Bathurst. In 1807 it was leased by the 1st Marquess Wellesley, Wellington's elder brother. Wellington himself bought it in 1817 and two years later commissioned Benjamin D. Wyatt to remodel some of the interiors. Further improvements were carried out in 1826–30 by Wyatt and his brother Philip. It was during this phase that the 90ft Waterloo Gallery was constructed, where, from 1830, the magnificent annual Waterloo Banquets took place to mark the anniversary of the great victory. By 1831 the Duke had apparently spent £64,000 on improvements and Wyatt's bill was three times over the original estimate, for which he was 'abused furiously'. Apsley House is the only historic London mansion to retain the majority of its contents, a circumstance which creates a unique opportunity: much trouble has been taken to restore the interiors to the aspect they would have worn in Wellington's day.

Ground floor

A large part of Wellington's magnificent collection of silver and porcelain is displayed in the **Plate and China Room**. Elaborate dinner services decorated with depictions of the Duke's exploits were presented to him by grateful crowned heads, including Franz I of Austria, Frederick Augustus of Saxony and Frederick William III of Prussia. Also here is the famous Sèvres 'Egyptian Service' (1809–12), its astonishing centrepiece based on the Temples of Karnak, Dendera and Philae, commissioned by Napoleon as a divorce present for the Empress Josephine, rejected, and presented to Wellington by Louis XVIII in 1818. Wall frames contain the 'Wellington Shield' (c. 1822), designed by Thomas Stothard and made by Benjamin Smith; and gold and silver swords and daggers, including the sabre that Wellington carried at Waterloo and the c. 1790 Indian sword of Tipu Sultan, ruler of Mysore, a relic of Wellington's military career in India, taken after the siege of Seringapatam.

Beyond the Inner Hall (the old entrance hall of the original Adam house) is the **Staircase**, remodelled by Wyatt after 1826. Its cast-iron stair-rail curves round Canova's celebrated larger-than-lifesize **sculpture of Napoleon**, naked except for a figleaf and a draped cloak, and holding a small winged Victory in his right hand. Carved in 1802–6 from a single block of Carrara marble, it was disliked by Napoleon (allegedly because the Victory appeared to be flying away) and remained in storage in the Louvre until 1816, when it was purchased by the British Government and presented to Wellington by the Prince Regent.

Upper floor

Lawrence's very fine full-length **portrait of Wellington** is seen to full advantage as you mount the stairs to the first floor. As a pendant to it, on the other side of the door, is a (much less imposing) portrait of Napoleon. The main showpiece apartments are here, some of which retain Adam features such as stucco grotesques (though these were all gilded by Wyatt when he remodelled the apartments in 18th-century French taste). The carpeting is a modern reweaving based on a fragment of the original discovered in the attics of the Duke's country house, Stratfield Saye, and some of the wall hangings reproduce the original fabrics. The paintings are very numerous. Many were purchased by the Duke himself, though some of the finest are from the Spanish royal collection, including works by Correggio, Murillo, Rubens and Velázquez. They were discovered rolled up in Joseph Bonaparte's captured baggage train following the French defeat at the Battle of Vitoria in 1808 and presented to the Duke in 1816 by Ferdinand VII of Spain.

The **Piccadilly Drawing Room** contains some of the finest pictures, including David Wilkie's *Chelsea Pensioners reading the Waterloo Despatch*, commissioned by Wellington in 1816 and completed in 1822. The scene is set in the King's Road, Chelsea, with the Royal Hospital to the left. When exhibited at the Royal Academy it created a massive stir and a protective barrier had to be erected. The **Portico Drawing Room** has a collection of personal items, including the Duke's false teeth and walking-stick-cum-hearing-trumpet.

The grand **Waterloo Gallery**, in Louis XVIII style with heavy gilding, was designed by Wyatt. It was here, from 1830–52, that the magnificent Waterloo Banquets took place. The east windows have mirrored shutters which, when drawn, transform the room into a supposed *Galerie des Glaces*: with the lighted candles and richly-adorned table, it must have been a sumptuous spectacle. Today slightly over half the paintings remain of the 130 that hung here in Wellington's day. According to the artist William Frith, it was the Duke's 'small weakness' when he had guests to identify the pictures in turn without consulting the catalogue. His favourite was the small *Agony in the Garden* by Correggio, showing Christ consoled by an angel while the disciples lie slumped asleep behind him. Goya's large equestrian portrait of Wellington is a rather hasty work painted in 1812, the likeness based on a chalk sketch Goya made of the Duke soon after the British army entered Madrid after the Battle of Salamanca. X-rays show that the head is painted over that of another sitter.

Wyatt's **Striped Drawing Room** contains Lawrence's famous half-length portrait of Wellington (1815) and Sir William Allan's *Battle of Waterloo* (1815), seen from the French side as it stood at 7.30pm on 18th June 1815, when Napoleon, on the right, was making his last desperate efforts to turn the allied armies. Wellington found it 'Good—very good; not too much smoke'. The **Dining Room** was where the Waterloo Banquets were held before 1830. On the table is the 26ft silver parcel gilt centrepiece of the 'Portuguese Service', presented to Wellington by the Portuguese Council of Regency in 1816. On the walls are full-length portraits of European monarchs (many of them the same ones who donated all the dinner services downstairs), including Wilkie's kilt-clad *George IV*.

Basement

Here are displayed Wellington's death mask as well as his magnificent collection of 47 orders, decorations and medals. There are caricatures of Wellington when Prime Minister by William Heath (including the famous 'Wellington Boot') and items that the Duke took with him on campaign, among them his tongue scraper and pots of rhubarb pills (a remedy against both constipation and diarrhoea).

Behind Apsley House in Hyde Park (just inside Queen Elizabeth Gate to the right) is Westmacott's 18ft bronze ***Achilles***, cast from cannon captured at the battles of Salamanca, Vitoria, Toulouse and Waterloo. It cost £10,000 and was paid for by 'the women of England'.

EATING AND DRINKING IN PICCADILLY AND MAYFAIR

This is an area of London amply stocked with places to eat and drink. There are good places to have cocktails too. The **Ritz Rivoli bar** ▬ is a supreme example: your drink will be shaken to perfection by the hotel's superior mixologists. Also on the list are Dukes Hotel on St James's Place, where the **Dukes Bar** prides itself on mixing some of the finest Martini cocktails in the world. At the Stafford, also on St James's Place, the **American Bar** has been known for its cocktails since they were first brought across the Atlantic by sophisticated US visitors to foggy Albion. A short selection of restaurants is given below.

PICCADILLY, ST JAMES'S

£– ££ 5th View. Café, cocktail bar and restaurant well placed as a meeting point, on the top floor of the big Waterstones bookshop on Piccadilly. The outer area, with rooftop views, is good for dining. Behind it is a snug where people retreat with books and laptops. No dinner Sun. *203–205 Piccadilly. T: 020 7851 2433, 5thview. co.uk. Map p. 603, E1.*

££ Le Caprice. Excellent, unfussy food (try the fish cakes). A firm favourite with many, including a fair few famous faces. Professional, understated excellence. Open daily. *Arlington St. T: 020 7629 2239, le-caprice.co.uk. Map p. 603, E2.*

£–££ Fortnum's. The ground-floor Gallery is informal and popular with shoppers. Good lunches with fresh ingredients from the Food Hall. Call ahead to book, or find a place at one of the communal tables. Closed evenings. *181 Piccadilly. T: 020 7734 8040, fortnumandmason.com. Map p. 603, E2.*

££ Franco's. Old-established restaurant catering to shoppers, office workers and visitors. Breakfast, lunch, tea and supper every day. Modern Italian with a good wine list. A St James's stalwart. *61 Jermyn St. T: 020 7499 2211, francoslondon.com. Map p. 603, E2.*

££ Greens Restaurant and Oyster Bar. 'Consistently excellent', Greens is renowned for its extensive fresh fish and seafood as well as for its British classics, grills and meat dishes. It also serves a properly good green salad as a side dish. Closed Sun. *36 Duke St. T: 020 7930 4566, www.greens.org.uk. Map p. 603, E2.*

£ The Red Lion. Atmospheric old pub with a Victorian engraved mirrored interior, popular with after-work drinkers. Lunch served Mon–Sat, drinks only in the evening. *2 Duke of York St, T: 020 7321 0782, redlionmayfair.co.uk. Map p. 603, E2.*

££ Rowley's. Old-established steak house. Much loved. *113 Jermyn St. Open daily. T: 020 7930 2707, rowleys. co.uk. Map p. 603, E2.*

£££ Seven Park Place. Michelin-starred restaurant in the St James's Hotel. *7–8 Park Pl. Map p. 603, E2.*

££ The Wolseley. ▬ Grand, *belle-époque*-style café-restaurant. Good, affordable food and wine. Usually humming. Open daily. *160 Piccadilly (next to the Ritz). T: 020 7499 6996, thewolseley.com. Map p. 603, E2.*

MAYFAIR

Mayfair has a plethora of Michelin-starred restaurants (all £££). At the time of writing, they were as follows (NB: Some have dress codes): **Alain Ducasse at the Dorchester** (*Park Lane; map p. 603, D2*); **Benares** (*12A Berkeley St; map p. 603, E2*); **Galvin at Windows** (*London Hilton; map p. 603, D2*); **Le Gavroche** (*43 Upper Brook St; map p. 603, D1*); **The Greenhouse** (*27A Hays Mews; map p. 603, D2*); **Hakkasan Mayfair** (*17 Bruton St; map p. 603, E1*); **Hélène Darroze at The Connaught** (*16 Carlos Place; map p. 603, D1*); **Hibiscus** (*29 Maddox St; map p. 603, E1*); **Kai Mayfair** (*65 South Audley St; map p. 603, D2*); **Maze** (*10–13 Grosvenor St; map p. 603, D1*); **Murano** (*20 Queen St; map p. 603, D2*); **Nobu** (*19 Old Park Lane; map p. 603, D2*); **Nobu Berkeley** (*15 Berkeley St; map p. 603, E2*); **Pollen Street Social** (*8–10 Pollen St; map p. 603, E1*); **The Square** (*6 Bruton St; map p. 603, E1*); **Tamarind** (*20 Queen St; map p. 603, D2*); **Umu** (*14–16 Bruton St; map p. 603, E1*); **Wild Honey** (*12 St George St; map p. 603, E1*).

Good restaurants without a Michelin star also abound:

££ **28°–50°**. One of a small chain of restaurants from the team behind Texture in Marylebone (there are also branches in Fetter Lane in the City and on Marylebone Lane. Informal, relaxed and popular, serving good food and with an emphasis on wine. Closed Sun. *17–19 Maddox St. T: 0207 495 1505, 2850.co.uk. Map p. 603, E1.*

£ **The Audley**. Pub food. *41–43 Mount St (corner of South Audley St). Open daily. T: 020 7499 1843. Map p. 603, D1–D2.*

££–£££ **Brown's**. The English Tea Room for champagne and cucumber sandwiches (*open daily noon–6, T: 020 7518 4155*) or the Hix Mayfair restaurant for modern British cuisine (hay-baked lamb and the like). Open daily. *33 Albemarle St. T: 020 7518 4004, hixmayfair.co.uk. Map p. 603, E2.*

££ **Cecconi's**. Ritzy sort of place originally founded by a former manager of Cipriani in Venice. Modern Italian cuisine. *5A Burlington Gardens. Open daily. T: 020 7434 1500, cecconis.co.uk. Map p. 603, E1.*

£ **Garden Café**. Catered by the Benugo chain, an outdoor and indoor raised space (*see p. 228*) offering simple lunches. Very pleasant on a fine day. Open daily until 5pm. *Brown Hart Gardens. Map p. 603, D1.*

£££ **Scott's**. Smart seafood restaurant with a loyal following. Perch at the bar with oysters and champagne or book a table for fine *à la carte* dining. Open daily. *20 Mount St. T: 020 7495 7309, scotts-restaurant.com. Map p. 603, D1.*

Shepherd Market. There are plenty of places to eat in this lively little enclave (*for its history, see p. 233*), from pubs and sandwich bars to more formal restaurants. The Turkish restaurant £ **Sofra** has been in business for many years (*T: 020 7493 3320, sofra.co.uk*). ££ **Le Boudin Blanc** is an acclaimed French bistrot: *tian de crabe, moules marinières* and other authentic dishes (*T: 020 7499 3292, leboudinblanc.co.uk*). *Map p. 603, D2.*

Soho & Covent Garden

London's 'West End', centred on Leicester Square, Soho and Covent Garden, is the city's entertainment heartland, home to theatres, clubs, restaurants and nightspots.

On the northeast corner of Piccadilly Circus (*map p. 603, E1*) is Ripley's Believe It or Not!, an 'odditorium' of bizarre curiosities housed in the former London Pavilion music hall. On the south side is the **Criterion Theatre and restaurant**, designed by Thomas Verity in a French Renaissance style, with the frontage clad in Portland stone. The theatre opened in 1873 and the restaurant (formerly known as the Criterion Long Bar) a year later. During the Second World War the

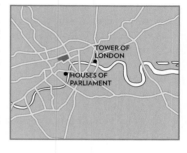

Criterion Theatre was used by the BBC to broadcast live light entertainment shows to keep up the morale of the nation. The core of the original premises, including the basement theatre, restaurant and central staircase, has been beautifully preserved.

On the corner, and part of the Criterion building, is the sporting department store Lillywhites, which opened in 1925. On the Haymarket corner, poised as though diving down into the multitudes below, are the slender aluminium and gold-leaf figures of the **Three Graces** by Rudy Weller. Below, at street level, is the **Horses of Helios fountain** (1992), also by Weller.

HAYMARKET

Map p. 603, F1–F2. Underground: Piccadilly Circus.

Historically, the Haymarket had an unsavoury reputation. In *Piccadilly in Three Centuries* (1920), Arthur Irwin Dasent remarked that 'Other and less innocent wares than hay were openly bought and sold in it until it became, in process of time, a recognised mart for human frailty.' Today the street is an adjunct to theatre-land.

Theatre Royal Haymarket (*trh.co.uk*) was built in 1821 by John Nash as part of his Regent Street development. Its stuccoed Neoclassical façade, with a portico and six

Corinthian columns, is best viewed from Charles II Street. The great actor-manager Sir Herbert Beerbohm Tree, founder (in 1904) of the Royal Academy of Dramatic Art (RADA), leased the theatre and managed it from 1887–97, establishing it as a centre for Shakespearian drama. In its distinguished history it has staged some important productions: in 1893, the premières of Oscar Wilde's *A Woman of No Importance* and *An Ideal Husband* were held here; in 1914, Ibsen's *Ghosts* was seen on the English stage for the first time.

Almost directly opposite the Haymarket Theatre stands **Her Majesty's Theatre** (*hermajestystheatre.co.uk*), conceived by Charles J. Phipps in French Renaissance style (1897). George Bernard Shaw's *Pygmalion* premièred here in 1914. Today the musical is the staple fare: Andrew Lloyd Webber's *The Phantom of the Opera* has been running since 1987. Just behind the theatre, leading from Charles II Street through to Pall Mall, is the **Royal Opera Arcade**, the earliest covered shopping arcade of its kind in London (1816–18). Originally part of the Royal Opera House, it was designed by Nash in collaboration with his pupil George Stanley Repton. At the time of writing, the arcade was home to art galleries, a florist, a café and a wine bar.

Suffolk Street (*map p. 603, F1–F2*) remains (largely) unadulterated Nash, a sumptuous clotted-cream-coloured stucco enclave of Classicism. The north side remains completely intact. Conceived as one architectural body, it has a three-storey façade, the lower part of which is decorated with fluted Doric columns resting on corbels, an iron balcony railing running along the top.

The blue plaque at no. XIV commemorates Richard Dadd (1817–86), the famous 'fairy painter' whose febrile imagination eventually broke down into schizophrenia, leading him to obey his 'voices' and stab his father to death in 1843, spending the rest of his days in the mental institutions of Bethlem and Broadmoor.

In Panton Street is the **Harold Pinter Theatre** (Thomas Verity, 1881), where the Watergate Club was established in 1956, allowing controversial plays to be performed to a 'club' audience as a way of circumventing censorship regulations.

LEICESTER SQUARE & CHINATOWN

Map p. 603, F1. Underground: Leicester Square.

Leicester Square, at the heart of the West End, had already begun to take on its present raucous flavour by the mid-18th century. It was laid out in the 1670s and named after Leicester House, built for the 2nd Earl of Leicester in 1635, which had stood on the north side. With the demise of Leicester House, fashion and respectability fled the area and it became popular with artists and entertainers. Victorian music halls came and went, replaced by vast picture palaces. First to be repurposed, in 1920, was the Empire (rebuilt 1927). The site of Daly's Theatre on Cranbourn Street is now occupied by the Vue cinema. The Odeon occupies the site of the Alhambra, which had

NOTRE-DAME DE FRANCE
Crucifixion by Jean Cocteau (1960; detail).

hosted the distinguished Diaghilev season in 1921. A second, smaller Odeon occupies the building of the old Leicester Square Theatre (1930). The centre of the square is filled by a garden with a statue of Shakespeare (a 19th-century copy of the monument by Scheemakers in Westminster Abbey). TKTS operates the Half Price and Discount Theatre Ticket Booth in The Lodge, a pavilion on the south side of the garden (*tkts. co.uk*).

From 1753 until his death in 1764 Hogarth had his town house at the southeast corner (no. 30, where Capital Radio is now), Sir Joshua Reynolds lived at no. 47 (on the opposite side) from 1760 until his death in 1792; this was the first house to acquire an official commemorative plaque (1875).

Irving Street, leading out of the southeast corner of the square, has cafés and restaurants in its cream-and-stucco row of buildings. St Martin's Street leads to the National Gallery (*see p. 167*) past the **Westminster Reference Library** (*free; open Mon–Sat 10–8, until 5 on Sat*) on the site of a house occupied by Sir Isaac Newton (1710–27) and Charles Burney (1774–94). Here Fanny Burney wrote *Evelina*.

In Leicester Place, off the northeast corner of the square, is the French church of **Notre-Dame de France**, burned in 1940 and completely rebuilt in 1955. Over the altar is an Aubusson tapestry of the *Bride of Christ*, shown in a Paradise garden with a very fluffy, pompom-headed Lamb. In the chapel on the north side, the altar is decorated with a mosaic of the *Nativity* by Boris Anrep and the walls with frescoes by Jean Cocteau (1960). On the left is the *Annunciation*; on the right the *Ascension*; and in the centre a very original *Crucifixion*, showing only the lower register of the scene, with just the bleeding feet of Christ and the bottom of the Cross, the focus of attention being on the faces of the mourners and the gesticulating of the Roman centurions.

CHINATOWN

The area to the north of Leicester Square is London's Chinatown, where many settlers from Hong Kong set up businesses: restaurants, bakeries and supermarkets and places offering massage, acupuncture and Chinese medicine. **Gerrard Street** (*map p. 603, F1*) is a pedestrianised Chinese avenue with large entrance gates, lion sculptures and signs in Chinese. At Chinese New Year (Jan/Feb) there are lion and dragon dances and entertainment.

CHARING CROSS ROAD

Charing Cross Road (*map p. 603, F1*) was known in the past for its bookshops, and a good few still survive. In **Great Newport Street** to the east is the small Arts Theatre, established in 1927 as a club theatre with a reputation for 'avant-garde' plays. The Covent Garden Cocktail Club now occupies the basement. At no. 62 Charing Cross Road is Caffè Vergnano, with a gleaming chrome replica coffee machine. It's part of a chain, but the coffee is good.

The busy **Cambridge Circus**, with the Cambridge pub on one corner, is named after the 2nd Duke of Cambridge, who made the land over for development in 1887. The circus is dominated by the ruddy terracotta façade of the Palace Theatre (T.E. Colcutt, 1888). Built for Richard D'Oyly Carte (who was born in nearby Greek Street), it opened as the English Opera House in 1891 with Sir Arthur Sullivan's *Ivanhoe*. The great Russian ballerina Anna Pavlova made her first London appearance here. Today it is the home of the musical.

Opposite the Cambridge pub is the site of the former Marks second-hand bookshop, made famous by Helene Hanff in *84 Charing Cross Road* (plaque).

Beyond the circus, on the left, is **Foyles**, once known as 'the world's largest bookshop'. It was founded in 1906 by two brothers who sold off their textbooks after failing their civil service exams and realised they had the start of a good business. The elegant Phoenix Theatre opposite opened in 1930 with Coward's *Private Lives*. The Licensed Sex Shop on the corner of Manette Street tells you that Soho is near.

ST MARTIN'S LANE

West Street (*map p. 603, F1*) is home to a chapel where Wesley preached, to the Ambassadors Theatre and the Ivy restaurant (*see p. 254*). The St Martin's Theatre has been staging *The Mousetrap* for over 60 years: it is the world's longest-running play. West Street leads right into **St Martin's Lane**, where there are more theatres, including the Coliseum, topped by its prominent globe. It was built in 1904 as a music hall and Ellen Terry, Lillie Langtry and Sarah Bernhardt all appeared on its elaborate stage. The English National Opera (*eno.org*) is now based here. The Duke of York's Theatre (1892) saw the first performance of Barrie's *Peter Pan*. Opposite the Noel Coward Theatre is the St Martin's Lane Hotel, an Ian Schrager/Philippe Starck 'urban resort'.

A tablet on no. 60 marks the **site of Chippendale's workshop** from 1753; in St Martin's Court is Sheekey's fish restaurant and oyster bar, dating from 1896; opposite is New Row, with Hardy's traditional sweetshop. A little further down is the narrow Goodwin's Court, which leads through to Covent Garden. It has some charming early

CHINATOWN
Bilingual street sign.

Georgian bow-windowed shop-fronts preserved as homes and offices. In 1764 Mozart lodged in **Cecil Court** (opposite), now lined with print and second-hand book shops. The street was known as 'Flicker Alley' during the early 20th century, when the pioneers of newsreel film-making set up offices here.

SOHO

Map p. 603, E1–F1. Underground: Leicester Square, Tottenham Court Road, Oxford Circus.

Soho, the epicentre of London's entertainment scene, buzzing until the small hours, is a cramped, lively district, bounded by Regent Street, Oxford Street, Charing Cross Road and Shaftesbury Avenue. The grids of small streets—some scruffy, some seedy, always crowded—are lined with bars, pubs, restaurants, cafés, delicatessens, clubs and other venues. Soho caters for everyone: rich or poor, gay or straight, local or tourist; and nearly every nationality is represented here. If you are looking for cheap eats, international cuisine or serious gastronomy, cocktails, pints of beer, comedy, jazz, theatre or dancing, to purchase vintage vinyl or to take part in the annual Chinese New Year festivities, Soho has it all, plus a few stylish hotels and private members' clubs. Plans to pedestrianise parts of Soho are cyclically shelved and the narrow roads hum with traffic and cycle rickshaws, usually propelled by young antipodeans paying their way around Europe rather than residents of nearby Chinatown.

HISTORY OF SOHO

Originally hunting grounds belonging to Henry VIII, the name is said to derive from an old hare-coursing cry of 'So-ho!' From the 1670s the land, along with the rest of the West End, began to be built up by wealthy landowners, who laid out streets and squares. Soho was mostly conceived by the bricklayer Richard Frith (a street is named after him) but unlike in neighbouring Mayfair and Bloomsbury, the rich and aristocratic did not stay long. Artists and writers settled here from the 18th century; an outbreak of cholera in the mid-19th century finally drove the better-off residents away. Soho is well-known for its immigrant communities, who have given the area its distinctive feel. Huguenots escaping persecution after the revocation of the Edict of Nantes at the end of the 17th century were the first to arrive, founding the French church in Soho Square. Then came Greeks, escaping the Turks (Greek Street commemorates them). Italians, Hungarians and Jews all came here after being exiled by revolution and to escape persecution. A large Chinese community, in part displaced from Limehouse (*see p. 122*), forms the area known as Chinatown.

By the mid-20th century, Soho stood for all things bohemian, alternative and edgy, a place frequented by intellectuals, artists, writers, actors and musicians, who congregated here in search of inspiration, and while waiting for it to descend, consumed copious quantities of liquor. Dean Street's recently defunct Colony Rooms was Soho's famous and eccentric drinking den. It was founded in 1948 by Muriel Belcher, described by *bon viveur* jazz musician George Melly as 'a benevolent witch, who managed to draw in all London's talent up those filthy stairs'; she 'adopted' the artist Francis Bacon to tout for punters in exchange for free drinks. The exhaustive list of famous members and regulars, who crowded into the ghastly-coloured green bar (perfumed by alcohol with undertones of drains and vomit), included E.M. Forster, Lucian Freud, Peter O'Toole, Dylan Thomas, Tracy Emin and Damien Hirst as well as Colin MacInnes, famed for his 1959 Soho novel *Absolute Beginners*. Princess Margaret, London's original It girl, once went for a pink gin.

Soho was also London's red light district and centre of the sex trade, acquiring a sleazy and sordid reputation that still lingers. Today, the area has been cleaned up considerably and prostitution is no longer overt, even though some strip clubs and clip joints still survive alongside the many bars and excellent restaurants. The gay sex shop Prowler on Brewer Street sells not only hard-core accessories but also a good range of non-salacious greeting cards and gifts. Those in the media, film, fashion and the arts tend to work and socialise here. For the most part, Soho is a place to eat, drink and have a good time.

WHAT TO SEE IN SOHO

Golden Square (*map p. 603, E1*), one of Soho's two squares, is home to a number of film, TV and radio companies. The artist Angelica Kauffmann lived at no. 1. The statue of George II in Roman costume in the centre is by John Nost (1753). In **Warwick Street**, a peaceful Roman Catholic chapel, Our Lady of the Assumption and St Gregory, survives from 1788.

Kingly Street and **Carnaby Street** (*map p. 603, E1*) lie parallel behind Liberty's department store and are the main shopping streets of Soho, although independent boutiques are dotted around elsewhere. Carnaby Street was famous for its cutting-edge fashions in the Swinging Sixties and British designers such as Mary Quant set themselves up here. Today it a pale shadow of its former self, with generic brands and a branch of the sandwich franchise Prêt-à-Manger. Kingly Street has a new shopping mall with interior court. In **Marshall Street** is a late 1920s/early 1930s public swimming bath. It was also in this street that the poet and visionary artist William Blake was born in 1757; he later lived in Poland Street. Shelley took lodgings at **15 Poland St** in 1811 after his expulsion from Oxford; one night he was found to have sleep-walked from Poland Street all the way to Leicester Square. The building is now home to excellent and long-established Umbrian restaurant Vasco & Piero's. The street to the west is **Ramillies Street**, with the **Photographers' Gallery** (*16–18 Ramillies St; open Mon–Sat 10–6, Thur 10–8, Sun 11.30–6; free; T: 020 7087 9300, thephotographersgallery.org. uk*), the first exhibition space in the UK devoted entirely to photography and still the largest public gallery of its kind in the country. It is also home to the annual Deutsche Börse Photography Prize (established 1996).

Wardour Street (*map p. 603, E1*) was once the home of furniture makers, including Thomas Sheraton in 1793–5. The Marquee Club was based here in the 1960s, encouraging many new bands (The Who, The Rolling Stones) who have since become household names. The church of St Anne's (*entrance at 55 Dean St*) only has a tower (1685, partly by Wren); the rest was destroyed in 1940. A garden has been laid out around it (*entrance in Wardour St*). The heavy steeple (1801–3) is by S.P. Cockerell and below is a monument to William Hazlitt (d. 1830). Dorothy L. Sayers, mystery writer and translator of Dante's *Inferno*, was a churchwarden here.

   Old Compton Street is the centre of gay Soho. A plaque at no. 59 commemorates the 2i's ('two eyes') coffee shop, hailed as the birthplace of British rock 'n' roll, where many stars once performed.

   Karl Marx lived in **Dean Street** in c. 1850 (at no. 28, above the restaurant Quo Vadis), in two cramped rooms with his wife, a growing family and their housekeeper Helene Demuth. He walked daily to the British Museum Reading Room to write. The **French House** at no. 49 is a Soho institution. The pub has served emigré French since 1914 and was the meeting place for the Free French during World War Two. Photographs of previous patrons—artists, writers, poets and journalists—line the walls. Beer is served by the half pint; mobile phones are banned. Die-hard regulars and professional soaks still frequent the bar, although the modern clientèle is more mixed in terms of age, sex and profession. Also here is good hotel and restaurant, the Dean Street Townhouse.

Soho Square (*map p. 603, F1*) was laid out from 1677. In 1764 Mozart (then lodging at no. 20 Frith St) taught music in the house (no. 22) of Lord Mayor William Beckford, brother of Richard (*see below*). The statue in the garden of Charles II is by Cibber (c. 1681). On the east side of the square, the Italianate St Patrick's church (RC) was opened in 1793 (rebuilt 1891–3). The dark red-brick French Protestant Church, a reminder of Soho's Huguenot past, dates from 1893 and is by Sir Aston Webb. Services are conducted in French. The square was first surrounded by large mansions, including one belonging to the Duke of Monmouth, who chose 'Soho' as his password at the Battle of Sedgemoor (1685). It soon became a fashionable area, and Sir Roger de Coverley had his town quarters here. In the 18th century it was a favourite residence of ambassadors. In 1777 Sir Joseph Banks came to live at no. 32 (rebuilt), which became the centre in London for the scientists of the time: the inaugural meeting of the Royal Institution was held here. In the southeast corner of the square, on the corner with Greek Street, is the **House of St Barnabas**, a Grade I listed Georgian mansion built in the late 1740s. Richard Beckford, wealthy Member of Parliament, lived here during the 1750s and was probably responsible for the fine Rococo plasterwork, wood carving and ironwork interior, one of the finest in London. The cantilevered staircase is particularly noteworthy. The Council Room on the first floor features an outstanding ceiling and a copy of the original fireplace. The Chapel dates from 1862. Since 1862, it has been occupied by a charity for the destitute and homeless, founded by Dr Henry Monroe in 1846. The building now operates as a private members' club with donations and subscription fees going towards the charity's outreach programmes.

Greek Street (*map p. 603, F1*) is named after a colony of Greeks from the island of Milos whose church, founded c. 1680, was in the nearby Charing Cross Road. The fine restaurant L'Escargot was established in 1927 by George Gaudin, who came up with the idea of farming his own colony of snails below stairs, thereby becoming the only English restaurant serving fresh snails. A bust of him riding a snail is above the main entrance—'slow but sure' was his motto. In 1754 the relentless Latin lover Giacomo Casanova lived in Greek Street; Thomas de Quincey, author of *Confessions of an English Opium Eater* (1821) lived here too for a time. At no. 28 is Maison Bertaux, founded in 1871 and still serving mouth-watering French *patisserie*.

In **Frith Street**—which has many buildings dating from the late 17th and early 18th centuries—is the famous jazz club **Ronnie Scott's**, founded by the eponymous tenor saxophonist in 1959. At no. 6 (1718; partly rebuilt) Hazlitt died in 1830 (it is now a comfortable hotel of the same name). On the site of no. 20, Mozart stayed in the 1760s. Barrafina, at no. 54, is an excellent tapas bar. Bar Italia, another Soho classic, founded by Italian emigrants in 1949, is still going strong serving good coffee, but is now very touristy. John Logie Baird demonstrated his television here in 1926.

Shaftesbury Avenue (*map p 603, F1*) forms the eastern border of Soho. It was laid out in 1886 and quickly superseded the Strand as London's theatre district. Today it is still home to a number of theatres. At the western end are four in quick succession: the Lyric (C.J. Phipps, 1889; refurbished in the 1930s), the Apollo (1901, in ornate French Renaissance style; part of its ceiling collapsed in 2013, causing multiple injuries); the Gielgud (W.G.R. Sprague, 1906) and the Queen's Theatre (1907; also by Sprague but given a new exterior by Sir Hugh Casson following bomb damage).

COVENT GARDEN

Map pp. 603, F1–604, A2. Underground: Leicester Square, Covent Garden. NB: There are no escalators at Covent Garden station, only lifts. At busy times of year it is quicker to walk from Leicester Square.

Covent Garden was once a thriving fruit and vegetable market; it is now a tourist attraction drawing crowds at most times of the year, both to the old covered market hall itself and to the streets that surround it, which are filled with shops, theatres and restaurants, and lined by human statues, performers, hawkers and touts of all kinds. Much of the retail space in the market hall is now occupied by global brands, not dissimilar from the departure terminal of an international airport. But there is a handful of surviving individual stores.

HISTORY OF COVENT GARDEN

The name 'Covent Garden' comes from the area's origin as the kitchen garden of the 'convent' of Westminster Abbey. After the Dissolution of the Monasteries, the first Earl of Bedford, John Russell, received the land from Henry VIII and the gardens of Bedford House, on the site of the present Covent Garden Piazza, continued to produce fruit and vegetables. In the 17th century the 4th Earl decided to take advantage of the growing demand for property and appointed Inigo Jones as architect to plan a new square. The resulting Piazza became one of the first and finest of its kind in London, focused on the portico of St Paul's Church on the west side. The north and east sides comprised porticoed houses with an arcaded walk underneath—the present buildings are a modern imitation. The south side was bounded by Bedford House gardens. Traders set up fruit and vegetable stalls against the south wall and later, when Bedford House was demolished, market stalls began to appear in the centre of the Piazza.

During the 18th and 19th centuries, Covent Garden became known for its coffee houses, attracting the writers and artists of the day. One well-known establishment was Bedford's in the northeast corner of the Piazza and others were Will's, Button's and Tom's. Tom's quickly gained a reputation for being little more than a brothel, and as the area began to be a place of scandal and ill repute, so fashionable residents began to trickle away.

The 6th Duke of Bedford decided that the market needed a permanent hall and commissioned Charles Fowler to design the Central Market Building. This Neoclassical structure, supported on Doric columns, transformed the open square when it was completed in 1830. The iron and glass roofs were added by Cubitt between 1875 and 1889. By the middle of the 20th century the market activities had grown to such proportions that they were causing appalling congestion. In 1974, the market moved to a new site at Battersea, where it remains (*see p. 467*). The congestion here in central London is as bad as ever.

THE PIAZZA AND ST PAUL'S CHURCH

The Piazza—the area between the portico of St Paul's Church and the Central Market—is the setting for street entertainment continuing a long tradition, recorded by Samuel Pepys who watched a Punch and Judy performance here in 1662. Performances are generally of a high quality; an excellent view is afforded by the Balcony Bar of the Punch and Judy pub. The annual May Fayre still hosts traditional (and alternative) Punch and Judy shows.

The wide Tuscan portico of **St Paul's Church** is just a false front: the entrance is from the other side (you can walk through the churchyard, where you are likely to come upon a juggler or some such, limbering up for a performance). Inigo Jones was given a very small budget for this church. When asked to keep costs down, he promised, undaunted, to build 'the handsomest barn in England'. It is not an unfitting description. And although most of the building was destroyed by fire in 1795, it was reconstructed by Thomas Hardwick to the original design.

Today it is known as the 'Actors' Church' (*actorschurch.org*) and inside the walls are covered with memorials: Vivien Leigh, Boris Karloff, Terence Rattigan, Charlie Chaplin and Noel Coward are all commemorated here, to name but a few. On the north wall is a plaque to Thomas Arne, composer of 'Rule Britannia', who was baptised and buried here. A silver casket mounted on the south wall of the chancel holds the ashes of Ellen Terry. At the west end, on the entrance screen, is a carved limewood wreath from St Paul's Cathedral by Grinling Gibbons. It was placed here as a memorial in 1965 (Gibbons is buried here).

THE MARKET

Shops and stalls are open daily. There are large map boards on site and an information office. At the time of writing, the antiques market was held on Mon. For details, see coventgardenlondonuk.com.

The Central Market Hall is divided into three parts: a main central building and two lateral halls. The stalls in the Apple Market on the west side of the central building originate from the old Flower Market. They are fixed but the traders change, bringing a range of original British crafts and jewellery design, with antiques on Mon.

The **Jubilee Hall** at the southwest corner of the Piazza was built in 1908 to house the imported fruit market. It has now been redeveloped behind its original façade, offering a general market on weekdays, antiques on Mon, and art and crafts at the weekends. The **Flower Market** building in the southeast corner of the Piazza dates from 1872. It now houses the **London Transport Museum** (*map p. 604, A2; open Sat–Thur 10–6, Fri 11–6; admission charge; café and shop; T: 020 7379 6344, ltmuseum.co.uk*). The collection began to be formed in the 1920s by the London General Omnibus Company and constitutes a unique record of public transport from c. 1830 to the present day. Exhibits include splendid old buses, omnibuses, taxis and trains; a display on art and design, including the history of the London Transport 'roundel' (its logo) from its inception in 1908 to the present; Harry Beck's famous map of the London Underground; the Johnston typeface; and some superb London Transport posters, which incorporate the work of leading British graphic artists of the 20th century. There is also a display on how the Underground was dug, with rotary excavators and tunnelling shields.

ROYAL OPERA HOUSE

Map p. 603, F1. Public areas open Mon–Sat 10–3 except when there is a performance. Box office open Mon–Sat 10–8. For details of Backstage Tours, see roh.org.uk or T: 020 7304 4000; tours last approx. 75mins.

ROYAL OPERA HOUSE
Foundation stone of the second theatre on the site, laid in 1808.

Bow Street, which takes its name from its shape of a bent bow, is fronted by the impressive portico of the **Royal Opera House**, home of the Royal Ballet and Opera companies. The first Royal Opera House was designed by Edward Shepherd (of Shepherd Market fame) and opened in 1732. The actor and manager John Rich had a triumphant opening with a revival of Congreve's *The Way of the World*. There was lively rivalry with the Theatre Royal, Drury Lane (*see below*) over the next 150 years until the Opera House became the place for Italian opera. In the 18th century a disastrous fire destroyed the theatre and Handel's organ. The second theatre on the same site, by Robert Smirke, was modelled on the Parthenon. The *Annual Register* for 1809 describes the opening: 'The New Theatre opened on Monday night, with the Tragedy of *Macbeth*... It was crowded the instant the doors were open, and though on the steps of the portico the mob were exclaiming against the advance of prices, yet when they got into the theatre, they were silenced by the beauty of the spectacle they beheld.' The silence did not last, and the price riots continued for two months, until prices were reduced. Another fire followed in 1856, leaving only Flaxman's frieze undamaged. The present theatre, the third on the site, was designed by E.M. Barry and completed in 1860. It is dominated by the Corinthian-style portico and the sculptural embellishments by Flaxman and Rossi salvaged from its predecessor. Also salvaged was the foundation stone of the second theatre, laid by the Prince of Wales (the future George IV). It is now on display in the foyer and reads: 'LONG LIVE GEORGE PRINCE OF WALES'.

To the left of the Opera House's main façade is the graceful cream ironwork **Paul Hamlyn Hall**, built in 1860 as a market hall for exotic flowers. Further to the left again is the Linbury Studio Theatre. Archaeological excavations here in 1996 revealed parts of Saxon Ludenwic, the settlement which covered much of Westminster from the mid-7th century.

FLORAL STREET
The 'Bridge of Aspiration', linking the Royal Opera House to the Royal Ballet School.

The Royal Opera House is linked to the Royal Ballet School by the accordion-like **Bridge of Aspiration**, which stretches across Floral Street (WilkinsonEyre, 2003).

Opposite the Royal Opera House is the **former Bow Street Magistrates Court**, completed in 1880 but representing a link with law and order that dates back to the first courthouse on the site in 1740. Here in 1749 the Fielding brothers (Henry and John) established the Bow Street Runners to catch thieves and villains; forerunners of the Metropolitan Police which followed less than 100 years later. The Magistrates Court, at which Emmeline Pankhurst, Oscar Wilde, Casanova and the Kray twins were all at one time defendants, closed in 2006. At the time of writing there were plans to convert some of the old cells into a museum.

DRURY LANE

In Catherine Street (*map p. 604, A2*) is the entrance to the large **Theatre Royal, Drury Lane** (*reallyusefultheatres.co.uk*). On the wall near the entrance is a bronze bust and stone plaque commemorating Sir Augustus Harris, owner-manager from 1879–97, set in an elaborate fountain by Thomas Brock. The present theatre was designed by Benjamin Wyatt in 1811–12; the portico was added ten years later and the colonnade in 1830. The pillars came from Nash's Quadrant in Regent Street. A ghost is said to haunt the Upper Circle. The theatre has an illustrious 300-year history; the first playhouse on the site was opened in 1663 for Thomas Killigrew's 'King's Company', under the first royal patent to be granted after the Restoration. Charles II was frequently in the audience and here he met and became enamoured of the actress Nell Gwyn, who had lodgings in Drury Lane (she is commemorated by the pub opposite: Nell of Old Drury). The theatre burnt down in 1671 and was rebuilt in 1674 to a design by Wren. The theatre's stormy history includes riots and attempted assassinations, including those of the future George II in 1716 and of George III in 1800 (after his assailant had been removed, the King calmly gave orders for the play to continue). From 1747 the great actor-manager David Garrick revived the works of Shakespeare here—though when Sheridan took over in 1776, it became a theatre of comedy, including his own *School for Scandal*. In 1809, despite its possession of the world's first ever safety curtain, the theatre burned to the ground. Sheridan watched the flames while sipping a glass of port in a coffee house across the road and said, 'Surely a man may take a glass of wine by his own fireside'. Brave words: he was ruined by the fire and died in want. In the Victorian era the theatre was known for its melodrama. Today it is famous for musicals.

Catherine Street is filled with places to eat and drink. On Russell Street, opposite the lateral flank of the Theatre Royal, is the Art Deco Fortune Theatre (1924). Beside it, in Crown Court, is the **Scottish Presbyterian kirk** (*crowncourtchurch.co.uk*), on this site since 1718. Scottish Presbyterians have had a place of worship in London since the early 17th century, when courtiers of James I established themselves in Scotland Yard (*see p. 150*). Drury Lane itself is named after the Drury family, who were courtiers to the Tudor monarchs. In the 18th century the area was known for its gin shops and by the end of the 19th century it was one of the worst slums in London. The Peabody Estate on the east side was one of the many developments built for the poor during the 1860s and '70s by the American-born philanthropist George Peabody.

LONG ACRE

Drury Lane leads north to Long Acre. Look up Great Queen Street to the right and you will see the huge **Freemasons' Hall** (*map p. 604, A2*), the second on the site (H.V. Ashley and F. Winton Smith, 1933). It is the headquarters of the United Grand Lodge of England, established in 1768, and houses an exhibition of the history of English Freemasonry (*open Mon–Fri 10.30–5.30, Sat 10–2.30 except summer, phone to check; T: 020 7395 9257, freemasonry.london.museum*). Adjoining it in Great Queen Street are the Grand Connaught Rooms, which incorporate some parts of the original Freemason's Hall, including the fine banqueting hall designed by F. Cockerell. They are named after the Duke of Connaught, who both laid the foundation stone of the new Hall and ceremonially opened it. He succeeded his brother Edward VII as Grand Master of the Lodge.

Historically **Long Acre** was known for the coach- and cabinet makers—including Chippendale—who settled here. Neal Street, which leads off it to the north (*map p. 603, F1*), is a long shopping street filled with shops in former warehouses. The buildings of **Neal's Yard**, off Short's Gardens, are painted in bright colours, as if in wishful imitation of La Boca, Buenos Aires. The yard has given its name to a commercial brand of herbal remedies and beauty products. At no. 31 Neal St, the vegetarian café Food For Thought is a survivor: it has been here, virtually unchanged, since 1974.

Continuing down Long Acre, at nos 12–14, is **Stanfords** (1852), a long-established and excellent travel bookshop. Covent Garden's acting tradition continues in **Garrick Street**, where the Garrick Club (the sombre building opposite the Floral Street corner) has attracted actors and writers since 1831. Rose Street runs through to the **Lamb and Flag pub**, which dates back to 1638 although the present building is 18th-century. The poet John Dryden was nearly assassinated here by opponents of his writings in 1679. At the corner of King Street is the huge Carluccio's restaurant and food store. Antonio Carluccio came to London as a wine merchant. He was appointed manager of Sir Terence Conran's restaurant in Neal Street (where Jamie Oliver also trained; the restaurant closed in 2006). Now he is a national brand.

SEVEN DIALS

The road junction known as Seven Dials (*map p. 603, F1*) was once a notorious thieves' quarter. A Doric pillar topped by six sundials was erected here in 1694. It was taken down in 1773, allegedly because of a rumour that treasure was buried beneath it, although it is more likely that its removal was an attempt to give undesirable loiterers nothing to loiter around. As Dickens noted in *Sketches by Boz*: 'It is odd enough that one class of men in London appear to have no enjoyment beyond leaning against posts.' The original pillar now stands on the green in Weybridge, Surrey. Its removal made no difference: 'Lounging at every corner, as if they came there to take a few gasps of such fresh air as has found its way so far, but is too much exhausted already, to be enabled to force itself into the narrow alleys around, are groups of people, whose appearance and dwellings would fill any mind but a regular Londoner's with astonishment.' Such was Seven Dials in the late 1830s. The new **Sundial Pillar**, made by trainee masons, was unveiled by Queen Beatrix of the Netherlands in 1989, when she was in London to celebrate the tercentenary of the accession of William of Orange. The seven wedge-shaped house frontages that face the pillar are all different and all interesting. One of them is the Cambridge Theatre (1930); another the Mercer Street Hotel (the land here once belonged to the Mercers' Company); and on another is a plaque with complicated instructions for converting the solar readings on the dials to Greenwich Mean Time.

Beside the Cambridge Theatre, Earlham Street leads to the **Donmar Warehouse** theatre (*donmarwarehouse.com*), known for its 'reimaginings' of classic plays. In the other direction on Earlham Street, there is a small street market.

EATING AND DRINKING IN SOHO AND COVENT GARDEN

HAYMARKET, LEICESTER SQUARE

££–£ **Assaggetti**. Prosecco bar on the corner of Haymarket and Charles II St. Snacks, salads, pasta. After or before the theatre. Open daily. *71 Haymarket. T: 020 7839 3939, assaggetti.co.uk. Map p. 603, F2.*

£ **Cork and Bottle**. Convivial little place tucked away in an alley off Cranbourn St near Leicester Square. Good food and wine. *44–46 Cranbourn Alley. T: 020 7734 7807, thecorkandbottle.co.uk. Map p. 603, F1.*

££ **Criterion Restaurant**. Modern European and British food in an opulent neo-Byzantine setting, complete with marble walls, mosaics, mirrors and a golden ceiling, true to the 1874 original. Open daily. *224 Piccadilly. T: 020 7930 0488; criterionrestaurant. com. Map p. 603, E1.*

££ **Le Troisième**. Old-fashioned French bistrot serving *bavette frites* and *tarte tatin*. Closed Sun. There are plenty of other places to eat on this street too. *3 Panton St. T: 020 7930 2777. Map p. 603, F1.*

Pall Mall Fine Wine. Tiny wine bar in Royal Opera Arcade, a secret nook to retreat to from the noise and crowds. *6–8 Royal Opera Arcade. Mon–Sat 11–9.30, Sat 4–8. T: 020 7321 2529, pallmallfinewine.co.uk. Map p. 603, F2.*

££ **Sheekey's**. Ever since the 1890s, when a Covent Garden stallholder named Joseph Sheekey obtained a licence from Lord Salisbury to serve fish and seafood in St Martin's Court (with an understanding that he also cater Lord Salisbury's post-theatre dinners), this restaurant and oyster bar has been serving fresh fish and *fruits de mer*. Now part of the group that includes the Ivy, Scott's and Le Caprice. *28–32 St Martin's Court. T: 020 7240 2565, j-sheekey.co.uk. Map p. 603, F1.*

COVENT GARDEN, SOHO

££ **Andrew Edmunds**. Plenty of people would swear by this place. Good, eclectic (though mainly British) food and some astounding wine bargains. In an 18th-century Soho townhouse. Open daily. *46 Lexington St. T: 020 7437 5708, andrewedmunds.com. Map p. 603, E1.*

£–££ **Barrafina**. Excellent tapas bar

serving fresh fish and seafood and delicious Spanish (including Galician) wines. The restaurant doesn't take bookings; space at the horseshoe-shaped ceramic bar is on a first-come, first-served basis but the conviviality of the queue, especially if one orders a chilled glass of *fino* and some olives, makes it worth the wait. Open daily. *54 Frith St. barrafina.co.uk. Map p. 603, F1.*

££ **Bar Shu**. Acclaimed Chinese restaurant. Ginger- and chilli-rich Sechuan cuisine. *28 Frith St. T: 020 7287 8822. Map p. 603, F1.*

£ **Bi bim Bap**. Korean restaurant. Cheap and good. *11 Greek St. T: 020 7287 3434, bibimbapsoho.co.uk. Map p. 603, F1.*

£–££ **Bocca di Lupo**. Italian restaurant aiming to cover the finest recipes from all 20 regions of the country. Excellent wine list. Open daily. *12 Archer St. T: 020 7734 2223, boccadi-lupo.com. Map p. 603, E1.*

£–££ **Brasserie Zédel**. Parisian-style brasserie with Art Deco American Bar attached. Begin with a Chrysler Cocktail and move on to breaded frogs' legs or beef tournedos. *20 Sherwood St (off Glasshouse St). T: 020 7734 4888, brasseriezedel.com. Map p. 603, E1.*

££ **Compagnie des Vins Surnaturels**. Just off Seven Dials. Wine bar serving dishes of the day, charcuterie and cheeses. Open daily. *8–10 Neal's Yd. T: 020 7734 7737, cvs-sevendials.com. Map p. 603, F1.*

Covent Garden Market. There are numerous opportunities for eating here. Fine pies, to eat in or take away, are available from the Pie Shop (Battersea Pie) on the lower ground floor (steps from the South Hall). Jamie's Union Jacks offers sit-down dining in the Central Hall; the Brasserie Blanc (also Central Hall) is on the upper level. Overlooking the performers in the Piazza is the Punch and Judy pub. *Map p. 603, F1.*

££ **Dean Street Townhouse**. Restaurant (and hotel) in the Georgian building of the former Gargoyle Club, open all day and serving wonderful comfort food such as macaroni cheese and scones and cream. *69–71 Dean St. T; 020 7434 1775, deanstreettownhouse.com. Map p. 603, E1.*

£–££ **Ember Yard**. Restaurant and bar on two storeys advertising charcuterie—but what it really does is get inventive with ways to cook on charcoal, inspired by the traditions of Italy and Spain. A place to come for a full meal or just tapas and wine. *60 Berwick St. T: 020 7439 8057, ember-yard.co.uk. Map p. 603, E1.*

£ **The French House**. Famous Soho pub (*see p. 245*), a haven for drinking and chatter, with a no-devices rule (no TV, no fruit machines, no mobile phones). Lunches served Mon–Fri, also bar snacks on Tues, Wed, Thur evening. *49 Dean St. T: 020 7437 2477, frenchhousesoho.com. Map p. 603, E1.*

££ **Green Man and French Horn**. Delicious French food and wine from the Loire. Friendly service, relaxed atmosphere. Menu changes daily. Closed Sun. *54 St Martin's Lane. T: 020 7836 2645, greenmanfrenchhorn. co. Map p. 603, F1.*

££ The Ivy. Well-known restaurant, popular with theatregoers, in business since 1917. Good fish, grilled meats, vegetable dishes. Open daily. *1–5 West St. T: 020 7836 4751, the-ivy.co.uk. Map p. 603, F1.*

Joe Allen. Popular place on Exeter St. *See listing on p. 191.*

££ Kettner's. Named after Auguste Kettner, chef to Napoleon III, who opened it in 1867. French-inspired and British menu. Previous customers include Oscar Wilde, Edward VII, Lillie Langtry, Agatha Christie and Bing Crosby. It is has an elegant champagne bar. *Open daily. 29 Romilly St. T: 020 7734 6112, kettners. com. Map p. 603, F1.*

££ L'Escargot. A Soho fixture (*for the history, see p. 246*). Trout rillette, *boeuf en daube* and other delights. Pre-theatre dinners from 5.30pm. Closed Sun evening. *48 Greek St. T: 020 7437 6828, lescargotrestaurant. co.uk. Map p. 603, F1.*

Maison Bertaux. Patisserie and café with truly delicious cakes, haphazard and eccentric and properly old school (loose-leaf tea, no styrofoam, no other Maison Bertaux on any other street anywhere). Open daily. *28 Greek St. T: 020 7437 6007, maisonbertaux.com. Map p. 603, F1.*

££ Mon Plaisir. Prides itself on being the oldest French restaurant in London. Traditional and authentic and much loved. Closed Sun. *19–21 Monmouth St. T: 020 7836 7243, mon-plaisir.co.uk. Map p. 603, F1.*

£ Polpo. If the drizzle of London gets too perpetual and you yearn for the sunny skies of the Venetian lagoon and a simple *bàcaro* serving *cicchetti* and Prosecco—come here. No dinner Sun. *41 Beak St. T: 020 7734 4479, polpo.co.uk. Map p. 603, E1.*

£ Polpetto. Sister establishment to the above, with the same opening hours. *11 Berwick St. T: 020 7439 8627, polpo.co.uk. Map p. 603, E1.*

£–££ Red Fort. Long-established Indian restaurant, named after the famous Red Fort in Delhi, serving Mughal cuisine. Closed Sat–Sun lunchtime. *77 Dean St. T: 020 7437 2525, redfort.co.uk. Map p. 603, E1.*

££ Rules. When Thomas Rule set up his restaurant in 1798, he may not have imagined that it would still be going over two centuries later, with a top-hatted doorman posted outside. London's oldest dining establishment serves unabashedly British fare: oysters, puddings and pies, and game from its own estate in the Pennines. Numerous luminaries have eaten here. It also features in several novels. Open daily. *35 Maiden Lane. T: 020 7836 5314, rules.co.uk. Map p. 603, F1.*

££ Vasco and Piero's Pavilion Restaurant. Cuisine from Umbria, home of the finest Italian pork. All ingredients carefully sourced. Closed Sun and Sat midday. *15 Poland St. T: 020 7437 8774, vascosfood.com. Map p. 603, E1.*

£–££ Yalla Yalla. Popular place serving 'Beirut street food'. Good mezes. There is another branch just north of Oxford Street, on Winsley St. *1 Green's Ct (south off Peter St). T: 020 7287 7663, yalla-yalla.co.uk. Map p. 603, E1.*

Oxford Street, Marylebone, Bayswater & Notting Hill

This chapter explores London's most celebrated shopping street and the adjacent district of Marylebone (with the excellent Wallace Collection). Close by are the expansive Regent's Park and modish Notting Hill, as well as the tranquil backwaters of Little Venice.

Oxford Street and Regent Street make up London's busiest shopping district, frenetic at times: some boast that it is the most intensive retail to be had in Europe. The shops are open late, seven days a week, and perpetually swarm with shoppers and tourists, becoming exceptionally crowded during holiday seasons. If it is the mix of architectural styles you have come to see, these are not the streets for ambling: enjoy the buildings from the top of a double-decker bus. As traffic often slows to a crawl, you will have ample time to look around you.

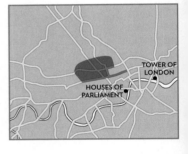

OXFORD STREET

Map p. 603, D1–E1. Underground: Marble Arch, Bond Street, Oxford Circus, Tottenham Court Road.

Oxford Street, London's most famous shopping street, stretches for about 1¼ miles between Marble Arch and Tottenham Court Road. Of the 300 shops that line it, all the major high street names in fashion are represented, some with more than one branch. The shopping here may not be as glamorous or exclusive as that in Mayfair and Knightsbridge, but what sets Oxford Street apart are its giant flagship department

PARK CRESCENT
Regency elegance by John Nash (1812–22).

stores: Selfridges, Debenhams, House of Fraser and John Lewis. These great emporia queue up along the north side of the street, vying with one another for public notice, and are constantly refurbished and upgraded to keep up with the contemporary thirst for disposable luxury and high-end brands. Perhaps paradoxically, a titanic branch of the throwaway clothing giant Primark has now opened towards Marble Arch. Another branch near Tottenham Court Road effectively bookends the street. The major stores cluster around Bond Street and Oxford Circus; towards Tottenham Court Road, the offering become increasingly bargain-basement.

HISTORY OF OXFORD STREET

Lying on the line of a Roman road and formerly known interchangeably as 'the road to Oxford', 'Tyburn Way' and 'Uxbridge and Worcester Road', Oxford Street, which is built over the River Tyburn, was properly established in the 18th century. It takes its name from the Earl of Oxford, Edward Harley, who married Lady Henrietta Cavendish Holles; their daughter married the Duke of Portland and the three families' names have lent themselves to streets throughout the area. Horse-buses arrived in 1833 and the Central Line in 1900, bringing carriage-loads of new customers to the shops. Every year in mid-November, the famous Christmas lights are switched on by a 'celebrity'.

THE DEPARTMENT STORES

Selfridges (*map p. 603, D1; selfridges.com*), the second largest department store in the UK after Harrods, was founded in 1909 by the innovative American businessman Harry Gordon Selfridge, who is credited with putting the 'fun' into shopping and who believed 'the customer is always right'. Setting up in London some 30 years after the first great department stores of Manhattan, Selfridge pulled in the crowds with the aid of several stunts, one of which was to exhibit Blériot's monoplane after his successful crossing of the English Channel in 1909. By the 1920s and '30s, the store was the last word in ultra-modern, Art Deco luxury: one of the original French lacquer lift panels of 1928 is in the V&A; an entire lift can be seen in the Museum of London. The grand Ionic façade that shadows Oxford Street was designed by another American, Daniel Burnham, in 1928. It features a giant Art Deco clock, 'Queen of Time', by Gilbert Bayes. The rooftop garden hosted fashion shows and was a popular place to relax, while the large windows at street level were—and still are—renowned for their innovative displays, especially at Christmas. Today, Selfridges continues to embrace the concept of luxury and in 2013 became the first department store to instal a champagne-vending machine.

Debenhams (*debenhams.com*) was founded as a draper's shop on Wigmore Street by one William Clark in 1778. On receipt of financial support from William Debenham, the store changed its name to Clark and Debenham. The company is no longer privately owned, but the Debenham name remains. The Oxford Street store occupies a building of 1968–71, which received a 'kinetic façade' in 2014.

House of Fraser (*houseoffraser.co.uk*) is a privately-owned chain of department stores first established in Glasgow in 1849. This is now the company's flagship store.

The Art Deco building (1935) was the first in Britain to introduce the novelty of escalators (rather than elevators) to every floor.

John Lewis (established 1864; *johnlewis.com; map p. 603, E1*), along with Peter Jones in Sloane Square, make up the John Lewis Partnership where the knowledgeable, admirably trained staff are partners in the business as well as employees. This quintessentially British emporium is the place to go when needing to choose fabric for new curtains, to chat to someone about the pitfalls of buying a new TV, to have an underwear fitting or to browse the latest fashions and skincare products. A huge Waitrose foodhall is in the basement. Here also, reassuringly, the merchandise is 'never knowingly undersold'. The current building dates from 1960; Barbara Hepworth's aluminium ***Winged Figure*** (1963) graces the façade overlooking Holles Street. At no. 16 Holles St (the site now engulfed by John Lewis), Lord Byron was born in 1788.

OTHER OXFORD STREET LANDMARKS

St Christopher's Place (*map p. 603, D1*) connects Oxford Street with Wigmore Street. Here are narrow Victorian passages and courts with shops, boutiques, cafés and restaurants, some with outside dining.

Opposite Bond Street Underground, set back from the street, is **Stratford Place**, all that remains of Oxford Street's 18th-century past. It was built in the 1770s by Richard Edwin for the Hon. Edward Stratford, who went on to become the 2nd Earl of Aldborough. His Neoclassical mansion, Stratford House, is now home to the Oriental Club, founded in 1824 for 'noblemen and gentlemen associated with the administration of our Eastern empire, or who have travelled or resided in Asia, at St Helena, in Egypt, at the Cape of Good Hope, the Mauritius, or at Constantinople.' In New Bond Street is **Fenwick** (recognised by its green flag), a family-run department store first set up in Newcastle-upon-Tyne in 1882 and now positioning itself at the upper end of department-store retail.

Oxford Street is interrupted by **Oxford Circus**, the junction with Regent Street and part of Nash's grand and uncompleted scheme for linking Regent's Park with Carlton House (*see p. 224*). The crossing is of the type known as a 'pedestrian scramble' or 'X-crossing'. It stops traffic completely and allows pedestrians to cross diagonally as well as laterally, in order to relieve congestion.

Marks & Spencer (*marksandspencer.com; map p. 603, E1*) occupies a black granite building of 1937–8, called The Pantheon. The store is built on the site of the original Pantheon, James Wyatt's assembly room of 1772 and 'the wonder of the 18th century'. Marks & Spencer (known as 'M&S', 'Marks and Sparks' or simply 'Marks') began in Leeds in 1884 when Michael Marks set up his famous bazaar with the slogan 'Don't ask the price, it's a penny.' Ten years later he went into partnership with Tom Spencer. The result is a British retailing phenomenon, selling everything from evening gowns to ready meals, with stores now occupying high streets, airports and railway concourses up and down the land (not to mention their strong online presence).

Attached to the façade of the **Plaza shopping centre** (*map p. 603, E1*), built in the 1920s, is a 1990s' sculpture of a girl gymnast, about to somersault onto the street below, twirling her ribbon.

REGENT STREET

Map p. 603, E1. Underground: Piccadilly Circus, Oxford Circus.

Regent Street, along with Oxford Street and Bond Street, make up central London's premier shopping district. But Regent Street's architecture gives it a stateliness that bustling Oxford Street lacks, despite sharing the same clientèle. It is named after the Prince Regent (later George IV) and was conceived by the architect John Nash from 1811–14 as a ceremonial route linking the Prince's residence, Carlton House (since demolished; *see p. 224*) with Regent's Park. It was completed in 1825 and soon attracted wealthy traders and shopkeepers. By the late 19th century, however, Nash's buildings had deteriorated and the arches and colonnades were the haunt of streetwalkers and undesirables. A plan was made to improve and modernise the vista, and from 1898 until about 1930, Nash's buildings were successively demolished and replaced by the current sweep of grandiose edifices in British Imperial style. Sir Reginald Blomfield is recognised as the principal architect but Arthur Joseph Davis, Sir John James Burnet, Henry Tanner, John Murray and Ernest Newton all had a hand. The apparent homogeneity of Regent Street's Portland stone emporia is belied upon close inspection: despite being on the same large scale, the buildings are not identical and there is a diffuse range of ornament here, from Classicist to French to Egyptian, the columns, balustrades and Dutch gables enhanced by Greek key patterns, palm leaves, swags, garlands and volutes. Regent Street remains a significant and historic example of town planning and the buildings along it have achieved listed status.

PICCADILLY CIRCUS TO LANGHAM PLACE

This first, curved section of Regent Street originally had colonnades protecting shoppers and above, balconies fronting lodging houses. The new façades omitted the colonnades. At no. 68 is the **Café Royal**, established in 1865 and now a luxury hotel (David Chipperfield Architects). It was formerly a meeting place for artists and writers including Beardsley, Oscar Wilde, Whistler, Max Beerbohm, Sickert, T.S. Eliot, J.B. Priestley and Compton Mackenzie. **Veeraswamy**, at nos 99–101, is London's oldest Indian restaurant, founded 1926 to serve Anglo-Indian cuisine (*entrance on Swallow St*). Heddon Street leads to a quieter backwater of restaurants now known as Regent Street's 'food quarter'.

Hamley's (*hamleys.com*) is London's largest and most famous toy store. **Liberty** (*liberty.co.uk*) was founded in 1875 by the draper Arthur Lazenby Liberty to sell his imported silks, fabrics and furnishings, capitalising on the contemporary taste for all things oriental. Ruskin and members of the Pre-Raphaelites all flocked here. Liberty then went on to develop its well-known 'Liberty Style', via collaboration with the best Art Nouveau and Arts and Crafts artists and designers of the day. Its mass-produced enamelled jewels and silverware were marketed under the inclusive banner 'Cymric'. The Edwardian stone building on Regent Street, with a concave, pillared frontage, is Liberty's original shop, now occupied by other retailers. The vast sculptural group above depicts *Britannia with the Wealth of East and West*, a reference to the founding concept of the store as a bazaar for Eastern merchandise. The mock Tudor extension of 1924, behind on Great Marlborough Street, is Liberty's current building. The wooden beams are from the hulls of two 19th-century Royal Navy ships: HMS *Impregnable* and HMS *Hindustan*.

Behind Regent Street, in Argyll Street, a pedestrianised shopping street, is the **London Palladium**, founded in 1910, a large-capacity theatre with a 19th-century Neoclassical facade.

Surrounding the 'pedestrian scramble' at Oxford Circus are four identical buildings making up the quadrant. North over the crossing, at 309 Regent St, the **University of Westminster**, formerly a polytechnic, was conceived in 1838 by British aeronautical engineer Sir George Cayley, to make scientific learning accessible. In 1882, the philanthropist Quintin Hogg continued its work providing 'mental, moral and physical development' for disadvantaged boys and young men. A statue of Hogg stands further on, in Great Portland Street.

At Langham Place (*map p. 600, C4*) is the only surviving Nash building from his *Via Triumphalis*, and also the only surviving Nash church: **All Souls** (1823; restored after World War Two; *T: 020 7580 3522, allsouls.org*). It is built in Bath stone and, with its circular Ionic porch resembles an Italian *tempietto*, though it is crowned by a soaring steeple instead of a dome. The design and placement is deliberate: Nash intended it to be a landmark uniting Regent Street with what is now Great Portland Street, the last run-up to the green expanse of Regent's Park. Today it has an active evangelical congregation. In the porch is a bust of Nash by Behnes (1831).

Looming behind All Souls, the steel-framed Art Deco building faced in Portland stone, with a copy of a short-wave radio antenna on the roof, is **BBC Broadcasting House**, the headquarters of the BBC from where news, radio, television and online services are produced and digitally broadcast. It was designed and purpose-built by Colonel Val Myer and opened in 1932. The main exterior sculpture of *Prospero and Ariel* (the spirit Ariel was chosen to personify broadcasting on radio waves) is by Eric Gill (1933), with a further three friezes of Ariel, also by Gill. The modern, curving glass extension and piazza, known as the Peel Wing, was completed in 2010. On the new roof, the ten-metre glass and steel sculpture entitled *Breathing* is by the Catalan artist Jaume Plensa. It is designed as a large listening glass, inscribed with the following poem: 'Life turns and turns on the crystal glass; breathing in our body; silence is a voice our voice; silence is a body our body', as a tribute to all journalists and technicians who have died carrying out their work. Each evening the glass is illuminated by a beam of light that travels through its centre, to coincide with the BBC's 10 o'clock News broadcast. The interior of the building may be seen as part of an official tour (*online pre-booking essential; bbc.co.uk/showsandtours*).

Diagonally opposite is the five-star **Langham Hotel**, by John James and Giles Murray, which opened in 1865 as the first purpose-built 'Grand Hotel' in London. The opulent interiors were decorated in marble with yards of silk, Persian tapestries and hand-printed wallpaper; it had the first hydraulic lifts in the world (known as 'rising rooms'), hot and cold running water, an early form of air conditioning and WCs in every bedroom. It had its own post office and travel agent (Thomas Cook & Son) and the corridors were wide enough for two women, when fashionably attired in the bouffant crinolines of the day, to pass each other with ease. Later in the 19th century the hotel kept abreast of modern developments by installing electric light and the telephone, and it proudly combined what it considered to be the best of English, French and American style, taste and service. Exiled emperors Napoleon III and Haile Selassie stayed here, as did poets and writers including Oscar Wilde, Mark Twain, Somerset Maugham, Sir Arthur Conan Doyle, Robert Browning and George Orwell. Wallis Simpson often stayed at the Langham while being courted by the Prince of Wales.

MARYLEBONE

Map pp. 603, D1–E1 and 600, B4–C4. Underground: Bond Street, Oxford Circus, Baker Street, Marylebone.

Marylebone is a well-to-do area bounded by Oxford Street, Great Portland Street, Marylebone Road and Edgware Road. In contrast to jostling Oxford Street, Marylebone has the feel of a genteel town, thanks to the orderly Georgian plan of its streets and squares, which retain remnants of elegant 18th-century terraces along with dignified late Victorian and Edwardian houses. The feeling is enhanced by the range of independent shops and boutiques, cafés and restaurants. The area is managed by its two principal landowners: the Howard de Waldens and the Portmans.

HISTORY OF THE HOWARD DE WALDEN ESTATE

The area known as the Manor of Tyburn was recorded in the Domesday Book in 1086. The name Marylebone is a derivation of 'St Mary by the Bourne', a reference to the parish church which lay next to the Tybourne—or Tyburn—river. By 1538, Henry VIII had created a royal hunting ground to the north (now Regent's Park). After a succession of tenants, John Holles, Duke of Newcastle, acquired some of the land in the early 18th century. It passed to his daughter, Lady Henrietta Cavendish Holles, whose husband, Edward Harley, 2nd Earl of Oxford, and the architect John Prince projected Cavendish Square and its surrounding grid of fashionable streets. After the 2nd Earl's death, the estate passed to his daughter, Margaret Cavendish Harley, who married the Duke of Portland. Building continued with Harley Street, Portland Place and Wimpole Street. In 1879, the 5th Duke of Portland died without issue and the estate passed to his sister, Lucy Joan Bentinck, widow of the 6th Baron Howard de Walden. Today the 90-acre estate is still managed and maintained by the de Walden family and is known as the Howard de Walden Estate. The streets, including Oxford Street, take their names from members of these families, their titles and possessions.

Cavendish Square (*map p. 603, E1*), behind the John Lewis department store on Oxford Street and near Oxford Circus, was the first of John Prince's developments for the 2nd Earl of Oxford, begun in 1717. The columned façades of two of the houses on the north side are relics of a noble mansion begun in the 1720s for James Brydges, 1st Duke of Chandos, politician and patron of the arts. It was never completed, though it has been suggested that the 'princely' Duke had plans to connect the proposed town mansion with Cannons, his grandiose Middlesex stately home (satirised by Pope as 'Timon's Villa') via a private road. The archway connecting the two wings is adorned with a lead *Madonna and Child* by Jacob Epstein (1953). No. 5 is now a hotel: previous tenants include the traveller and writer Lady Mary Wortley Montagu and Lord Nelson. No. 20, the Royal College of Nursing since 1926, is the former home of Liberal Prime Minister H.H. Asquith. In the central garden is a bronze statue of Lord George Bentinck, Conservative MP and horse-racing enthusiast, by Thomas Campbell (1851).

At the northeast corner of the square, Chandos Street leads to **Queen Anne Street**. On the corner, at no. 2, is Chandos House, built speculatively by Robert Adam in 1769–71 in a fine, grey stone (Craighleith, from a quarry near Edinburgh that the Adam brothers had interests in). It was leased by the 3rd Duke of Chandos in 1774 and from 1814–43 was the home of the Austro-Hungarian Embassy. Ambassador Prince Paul Anton III Esterhazy entertained here in lavish style. By the later part of the 20th century it had become grievously neglected and the Howard de Walden Estate purchased the lease in 2002. Now beautifully restored, with many original Adam interior features, it is owned by the Royal Society of Medicine and serves as a meeting and events venue as well as a place to stay (*see p. 544*). J.M.W. Turner lived at no. 47 Queen Anne Street and maintained it as his gallery space until his death. The property, famously squalid and known as 'Turner's Den', was purportedly infested with Manx cats and umbrellas were required indoors during wet weather. Mansfield Street, a continuation of Chandos Street to the north, has fine remaining Adam houses.

PORTLAND PLACE

The grand avenue known as Portland Place (*map p. 600, C4*), speculatively laid out in 1778 by Robert and James Adam for the Duke of Portland, stretches all the way to Regent's Park. It is very broad for a central London street because at the time of building, the southern end was taken up by Foley House, a large mansion within its own grounds, whose occupant, Lord Foley, insisted on retaining his uninterrupted view north. The completed street, over 100ft wide and lined on either side with elegant Adam houses, was splendid in proportion and scale, so splendid in fact that Nash would perceive it as the grand final section of his processional route from Regent's Street to the Park and he deliberately placed his church of All Souls at the bend with Langham Place to unite the vista. Today, the Adam terraces exist in fragment form and are interrupted by more modern buildings. No. 55 was presumably erected to fill a World War Two bombsite; note how the corner of the Adam pediment of the house next door, no. 61, looks as if it has been casually snipped off to accommodate it. At no. 63 lived the author Frances Hodgson Burnett, whose lesser-known adult novel *The Making of a Marchioness* (1901) was a great favourite of Nancy Mitford's.

The Art Deco building in Portland stone at no. 66 is the **headquarters of RIBA** (the Royal Institute of British Architects). It was a competition-winning design by C. Grey

Wornum and opened in 1934. The exterior sculpture and reliefs are by Bainbridge Copnall and James Woodford; the bronze doors depicting the River Thames and famous London buildings in relief are also by Woodford. The interior, open to all, houses a café/bar, restaurant, bookshop and library. Guided tours of the building are available on weekdays (*see architecture.com for details*).

In the middle of the boulevard are several monuments: Quintin Hogg, founder of Westminster Polytechnic (George Frampton, 1906), who sits reading to two boys; an equestrian statue of the Army officer Sir George White (John Tweed, 1922); General Wladyslaw Sikorski, Prime Minister of the Polish Government and Commander-in-Chief of the Polish Armed Forces, 1939–43 (erected 2000); and a bronze bust of Lord Lister, surgeon and founder of antiseptic medicine (by Thomas Brock).

Portland Place emerges into **Park Crescent**, where Nash's semicircular stucco composition of terraced houses (1812–22) is a fine prelude to Regent's Park itself. From the private garden, a statue of Prince Edward, Duke of Kent, 4th son of George III and father of Queen Victoria, surveys Portland Place.

HARLEY STREET, WIMPOLE STREET AND WIGMORE STREET

Harley Street (*map p. 600, C4*), running parallel with Portland Place to the west, has been synonymous with private healthcare since the 19th century. Here and in neighbouring Wimpole Street, doctors, surgeons and dentists have their practices. At nos 43–49 Harley St is Queen's College, an independent girls' school founded in 1848 by Frederick Denison Maurice, professor of English Literature and History at King's College London, to provide girls and young women with a serious education; it was the first institution in Great Britain where women could gain academic qualifications.

At no. 1 Wimpole St is the **Royal Society of Medicine**, in an Edwardian Baroque building (John Belcher, 1912), the entrance flanked by Rods of Asclepius in verdigris copper. At 64 Wimpole St is the **British Dental Association**, which has a small museum dedicated to the history of British dentistry. The museum was founded in 1919 by Lilian Lindsay, the first woman to qualify as a dentist, and entry is free (*bda.org/museum*). No. **50 Wimpole St** is the address from which the poet Elizabeth Barrett eloped in order to marry Robert Browning in 1846; the couple then left for Italy and lived in Florence until Elizabeth Barrett Browning's death in 1861. Note the many mews in this area, narrow streets parallel with the main thoroughfares, once providing stables for horses and coaches, then garages for cars, and now sought after as homes and offices. At no. 17 Wimpole Mews lived the fashionable osteopath Dr Stephen Ward (d. 1963), with whom the showgirl and model Christine Keeler lived for a time. Ward became famous for his part in the Profumo Affair: he introduced MP and Secretary of State for War John Profumo to Keeler and the ensuing scandal of their brief liaison brought down the Conservative government. At no. 94 Wimpole St, the former Abbatt Toyshop frontage is Ernő Goldfinger's earliest work in London (1936).

Wigmore Street runs parallel with Oxford Street. The terracotta building at no. 36 is the **Wigmore Hall**, a recital venue for Classical soloists and chamber musicians, hosting over 400 concerts a year. It was built as Bechstein Hall by the eponymous German piano-makers (who had showrooms next door) in 1901. The restored interior, celebrated for its intimacy coupled with near-perfect acoustics, was designed by Thomas Colcutt, who had previously collaborated with Richard d'Oyly Carte on various theatre projects as well as the public rooms of many P&O liners. It is richly decorated in mahogany, alabaster and marble. The Arts and Crafts mural in the cupola above the stage depicts the 'Soul of Music'. It is the work of Gerald Moira, whose other public commissions included artworks for Lloyd's Register of Shipping and the Central Criminal Court. During the First World War, anti-German feeling in England led to the affairs of many German firms being wound up by the Board of Trade (Dame Nellie Melba was vilified for singing 'Land of Hope of Glory' to the accompaniment of a Bechstein piano) and the hall was sold at auction to Debenhams the department store, who at the time occupied no. 33 opposite (the huge Edwardian Baroque building clad in white Doulton tiles). In 1917 it re-opened under a new name: Wigmore Hall.

The **chapel of St Peter**, Vere Street, of brick with stone quoins and with a Doric porch, is by James Gibbs (1721). Now, deconsecrated it houses the Institute of Contemporary Christianity (*interior may be visited during opening hours; ring the bell*).

Marylebone Lane winds north from Wigmore Street to join **Marylebone High Street** (*map p. 600, C4*), with restaurants, cafés, shops and boutiques selling a range of fashion, modern design, books and organic foods. This is the heart of old 'St Mary by the Bourne', where the Tyburn flowed (*see History, p. 262*). Today it is marketed as a niche shopping and eating destination, 'Marylebone Village'.

THE PORTMAN ESTATE

The western side of Marylebone extends for 110 acres from Marylebone High Street to Edgware Road, incorporating Manchester, Portman, Montagu and Bryanston squares. The land has been owned by the aristocratic Portman family since the 16th century and was built up from the 17th century. Today, the estate is run by Christopher Portman, 10th Viscount Portman.

Portman Square (*map p. 603, D1*) was built from 1764. On the site of the Radisson SAS Portman Hotel stood a fine townhouse of 1781, by James 'Athenian' Stuart. The house, destroyed during a World War Two bombing raid, was built for Mrs Elizabeth Montagu, wealthy widow, society hostess, bluestocking and close friend of Lady Margaret Harley, daughter of the 2nd Earl of Oxford and wife of 2nd Duke of Portland. She was careful never to invite 'idiots' to her literary soirées: guests included Joshua Reynolds, David Garrick, Samuel Johnson, Edmund Burke, George Lyttleton, Horace Walpole and William Wilberforce. Before her husband's death and prior to taking up residence in Portman Square, her salons were held at her home in Hill Street, Mayfair.

Home House (no. 20; 1773–7) is a fine surviving example of Robert Adam's work. It was sportingly commissioned by another wealthy widow, Elizabeth, Countess of Home, when she was in her 70s. From 1789–94 it served as the French Embassy. From 1932–90 it was home to the Courtauld Institute of Art (the Cambridge spy Anthony Blunt lived in a flat here during his tenure as Director). The splendid interior includes a flying staircase with glass dome, ceilings by James Wyatt (the architect originally commissioned) and walls decorated by Antonio Zucchi. It is now a private members' club, incorporating the Georgian townhouses on either side (nos 19 and 21).

The **Edward Lear Hotel** at no. 28–30 Seymour St is the former home of writer and artist Edward Lear. The area around New Quebec Street and Seymour Place has been revitalised as a small shopping district with select shops, boutique hotels, pubs and restaurants and is now promoted as 'Portman Village'. At 33 Seymour Place is the **West London Synagogue** (1872), with a Byzantine/Romanesque interior. Bryanston Court, on the corner with George Street and Seymour Place, was home to Mrs Wallis Simpson in 1933–6; she entertained the Prince of Wales here before moving to Cumberland Terrace, Regent's Park.

Montagu and Bryanston squares were built by David Porter, c. 1810–15; the architect was Joseph Parkinson. **Bryanston Square** (*map p. 600, B4*) is named after the Portland family estate in Dorset while **Montagu Square** takes its name from Elizabeth Montagu (*see Portman Square, p. 265*), Porter's former mistress who helped him become a builder. Anthony Trollope lived at no. 39. The Neoclassical church of St Mary's (*entrance on Wyndham Place*), with its Ionic stone portico and tower, is by Robert Smirke (1824) and was built to seal the view from Bryanston Square. Along with All Souls, Regent Street, it is one of the Commissioners' or 'Waterloo' churches (*see p. 419*). At no. 1 Dorset Street lived the computer pioneer Charles Babbage (1791–1871).

Chiltern Street was, at the time of writing, being transformed into a street of independent shops, with a hotel in the old fire station. Off Marylebone High Street, in **George Street**, Thomas Moore had his first lodgings in London (site of no. 85). The large Roman Catholic **church of St James's** on Spanish Place (*entrance at 22 George St*) is a pure example of Gothic Revivalism (1890). The architect, Edward Goldie, borrowed details from 13th-century English Gothic cathedrals at Lichfield and Salisbury, as well as from Westminster Abbey. Inside, the reredos in the Lady Chapel is by J.F. Bentley (architect of Westminster Cathedral). At no. 3 Spanish Place lived Captain Frederick Marryat, Royal Navy officer and novelist. His famous works include *Mr Midshipman Easy* and *The Children of the New Forest*.

Paddington Street Gardens, which in the 18th century was a burial ground for Old Marylebone Parish Church, were converted into formal gardens in the 1880s. The remaining Neoclassical Fitzpatrick mausoleum, in Portland Stone, dates from 1759.

THE WALLACE COLLECTION

Map p. 603, D1. Open daily 10–5. Free. Restaurant and shop. T: 020 7563 9500, wallacecollection.org.

The Wallace Collection, like the Frick in New York, is a supreme example of a private art collection displayed in the home of its collector. The museum is seldom crowded and a visit here is one of the great joys of London.

Built in 1776 for the 4th Duke of Manchester, Hertford House lies on the north side of the handsome Manchester Square. The collection that it contains was formed by successive members of the Seymour-Conway family, Marquesses of Hertford, and by Sir Richard Wallace, natural son of the 4th Marquess. Sir Richard Wallace's widow bequeathed the collection to the nation in 1897, on condition that nothing was added or removed from it, and thus the Wallace Collection remains: its mix of paintings, furniture and decorative arts retain much of the atmosphere of a grand aristocratic town mansion, as Hertford House was in its heyday.

The collection comprises important 18th- and 19th-century British portraits, mainly collected by the 1st and 2nd Marquesses, and a large collection of 17th-century Dutch and Flemish pictures, collected by the 3rd Marquess. Its chief importance and glory, however, is the exceptional collection of 18th-century French painting, sculpture, furniture, porcelain and *objets d'art*, amassed by the 4th Marquess and unparalleled in this country (in this area the Wallace Collection outdoes both the National Gallery and the V&A). It was the 4th Marquess who purchased two of the museum's greatest treasures: Fragonard's *The Swing* and Frans Hals's *Laughing Cavalier*. Sir Richard Wallace added an extensive collection of medieval and Renaissance works as well as the important collection of arms and armour, second only to that of the Royal Armouries.

Richard Seymour-Conway, 4th Marquess of Hertford (1800–70), spent much of his life in France, in Paris in an apartment on Rue Lafitte, and at the Château de Bagatelle in the Bois de Boulogne. Collecting was an obsession, made possible through the extraordinary works of art on the market following the French Revolution. He purchased works by the leading 18th-century painters Boucher, Watteau, Fragonard, Lancret and Greuze, as well as items by the finest French cabinet makers such as Boulle and Riesener. On his death in 1870 Hertford House was bought by his illegitimate son, Sir Richard Wallace, from his cousin, the 5th Marquess. To contain the collection, Sir Richard and his French wife altered and extended the house, most importantly adding to the rear the Great Gallery, designed by Thomas Ambler. More recent redevelopment (Rick Mather) has involved glazing the central courtyard, which is now home to the restaurant.

WALLACE FOUNTAINS

On the front lawn of Hertford House stands a Wallace Fountain, one of the type of 50 donated by Sir Richard Wallace in 1872 to the city of Paris, where they have become known simply as '*wallaces*'. Designed by Charles-Auguste Lebourg, the fountains provided a free supply of clean water, and were enthusiastically received by Parisians. The ornamental dome of the fountain is supported by four caryatids representing the gowned goddesses of Simplicity, Sobriety, Charity and Bounty, distinguishable by their knees, whether left or right, covered or bare. Eighty-two Wallace Fountains can now be found in different parts of Paris, with at least six in other French cities and towns, and others in more than 20 cities worldwide, including Macao and Tokyo.

Richard Wallace inherited the estate of his father the 4th Marquess in 1870, and found himself caught up in the Siege of Paris and the painful birth of the Second Republic. Staying on in the city, he paid for an ambulance and a hospital bearing the Hertford name. Beleaguered by the Prussians and forced to accept a humiliating peace, the city's violent suppression of the Paris Commune in the following year persuaded Wallace to remove his art collection to London for safe-keeping, offering the 50 fountains as a farewell gift.

Highlights of the collection: ground floor

The **Dining Room** has aristocratic French portraiture, including marble busts by Houdon of Madame Victoire, one of Louis XV's daughters, and Madame de Sérilly, maid of honour to Marie-Antoinette. The **Billiard Room** has a bronze bust (c. 1699) of Louis XIV by Antoine Coyzevox, the king's sculptor, and a wardrobe by Boulle (c. 1715), veneered with *contre-partie* marquetry (sheets of turtleshell and brass glued together and a design cut out). It is an exceptional example of the great cabinet maker's work.

Among the **medieval and Renaissance treasures** collected by Sir Richard Wallace is a marble bust of Christ by Pietro Torrigiano, from Westminster Abbey.

Wallace decorated his **Smoking Room** with Turkish-design Minton tiles and a mosaic floor. The large wine cooler (1574) is from the collection of Cosimo de' Medici.

The astonishing collection of **arms and armour** was built up by Sir Richard Wallace. There is an exceptionally fine 17th-century Indian dagger, made for either Jehangir or Shah Jahan, with a solid gold hilt set with diamonds and a floral design of rubies, with leaves of emeralds; Tipu Sultan's *tulwar*, a type of scimitar; and the gold and ivory sword of Ranjit Singh. Memorable in the European Armoury collection is the equestrian armour for horse and rider, the horse's breastplate equipped with a great ramming prong.

Highlights of the collection: first floor

The white marble **staircase**, rising grandly to the first floor, has a magnificent balustrade (1719–20) of cast and wrought iron and gilt brass, originally from the stairs leading to Louis XV's Cabinet de Médailles in the Palais Mazarin, Paris. One of the finest examples of French metalwork of the period, it was sold as scrap in the mid-19th century, bought by the 4th Marquess and, in 1847, altered to fit Hertford House and installed by Sir Richard Wallace. The **Small Drawing Room** contains fine views of Venice by Canaletto and Guardi. The **Large and Oval Drawing Rooms** were, at the time of the 2nd Marquess, magnificent ballrooms where, in 1814, a grand ball was held to celebrate the defeat of Napoleon. Among the objects in the former is a selection of Sèvres porcelain, including a cup with a portrait of Benjamin Franklin, who had visited Paris in 1776 to gain French support for American independence. In the Oval Drawing Room is a roll-top desk (c. 1770) by Jean-Henri Riesener, the leading cabinet maker under Louis XVI, decorated with marquetry still-life panels.

Sir Richard Wallace's **Study** displays more Sèvres, including an ice-cream cooler, part of a service made for Catherine the Great of Russia. Lady Wallace's **Boudoir** has 'fancy' pictures by Greuze (*The Broken Mirror*, 1763) and *Innocence* (a young girl holding a lamb), and by Reynolds (*The Strawberry Girl*). The **West Room**, Lady Wallace's bedroom, displays some of the 4th Marquess's exceptional collection of 18th-century French paintings and Louis XVI furniture. Boucher's portrait of Madame de Pompadour shows her in her garden at Bellevue (the statuary group in the background, *Friendship Consoling Love*, is a reflection of her now platonic relationship with the king). Also here is an elaborate perfume burner (1774–5) by Pierre Gouthière, which was formerly owned by Marie-Antoinette; and a delicate worktable (1786–90) by Adam Weisweiler, which belonged to the Empress Josephine.

MANCHESTER SQUARE
Detail of the Wallace Fountain outside Hertford House.

The full extent of the French 18th-century collection becomes apparent in the **West Gallery**, which has works by Watteau, including his well-known *Music Party* (c. 1718), with music-making on a palatial terrace. One of the Wallace's most famous paintings is Fragonard's *The Swing* (1767), a picture full of artful abandon, flirtation and innuendo, the graceful, provocative girl poised in the air, the action of the swing tossing her delicate slipper in the direction of her lover and allowing him a tantalising view up her frothing skirts. The *secrétaire* (1783) by Jean-Henri Riesener was supplied for Marie-Antoinette at the Petit Trianon, Versailles.

In the **East Drawing Room** Isabella, wife of the 3rd Marquess, would entertain the Prince Regent on his daily visits between 1807 and 1820. The **East Galleries** contain 17th-century Dutch and Flemish pictures, including Pieter de Hooch's *A Boy Bringing Bread* and Gerard ter Borch's *A Lady Reading a Letter*.

The **Great Gallery** extends the full length of the back of the house. It was purpose-built, with top-lighting, for the display of pictures as well as for glamorous entertaining. A water-powered lift provided additional access. Important works include Rubens' *The Rainbow Landscape* (c. 1636), a late summer afternoon scene on the artist's country estate (it is the pendant to *Het Steen* in the National Gallery, which the Gallery had wanted to acquire but was outbid by the 4th Marquess). Titian's *Perseus and Andromeda*, painted originally for Philip II of Spain and once owned by Van Dyck, was purchased by the 3rd Marquess in 1815. Poussin's exceptional *Dance to the Music of Time* is also here, as is Rembrandt's portrait of his teenage son Titus. Probably the best-known item in the Wallace Collection is Frans Hals's *Laughing Cavalier*. Painted in 1624, the identity of the man, neither a cavalier nor laughing, is unknown. Whichever angle you look at him from, his teasing eyes follow you. The 4th Marquess outbid

Baron de Rothschild for the picture, paying six times its auction estimate, which of course added to the picture's celebrity. Gainsborough's *Mrs Robinson as Perdita* (1781) was commissioned by the Prince of Wales after he had seen the actress perform the role from Shakespeare's *The Winter's Tale* at Drury Lane; she holds the miniature of him he sent to her. Reynolds's *Nelly O'Brien* shows the well-known beauty and courtesan seated with a pet dog in her lap, her face shaded by the brim of her hat. Lawrence's slick portrait of George IV (1822) was thought by the artist to be his best likeness of the king, and is mentioned in Thackeray's *Vanity Fair*.

BAKER STREET AND MARYLEBONE ROAD

Baker Street (*map p. 600, B4*), linking Oxford Street with Marylebone Road, is universally associated with Sir Arthur Conan Doyle's detective Sherlock Holmes and his assistant Dr Watson. A small museum in a Victorian house at no. 239 (north of Marylebone Road, near Regent's Park) tries hard to evoke the atmosphere of the novels by recreating the fictional detective's home based on descriptions in Conan Doyle's stories (*open daily 9.30–6; admission charge; shop; sherlock-holmes.co.uk*). Renumbered 221B (Sherlock Holmes's fictitious address), the detective's study and bedroom have been created and furnished with period memorabilia. The surreal experience is further enhanced on the upper floors, where die-hard fans video groups of waxworks on their smartphones.

On the south side of Marylebone Road (a roaring six-lane highway), at the junction with Gloucester Place, is Sir Edwin Cooper's **Old Marylebone Town Hall**, former headquarters of Westminster County Council (opened 1920), with a 1938 library extension next door. The huge building, with its giant Corinthian order, tower and pair of lion sculptures flanking the entrance steps, is to house the London Business School.

West (left) along Marylebone Road is the terracotta-clad **Landmark Hotel**, built by Robert Edis in 1899. Inside is an impressive palm atrium where one can take afternoon tea. Behind the hotel is Marylebone Station, of the same date. **Dorset Square**, originally part of the Portman Estate, was the site of Thomas Lord's first cricket ground in 1787–1811. The Georgian terraced houses were built after Lord moved the eponymous ground to St John's Wood (*see p. 276*). The square is named after the Duke of Dorset, an early cricketing enthusiast. George Grossmith, actor in several of Gilbert and Sullivan's operettas and co-author of *The Diary of a Nobody*, lived at no. 28; Dodie Smith lived at no. 18.

MADAME TUSSAUDS AND THE ROYAL ACADEMY OF MUSIC

The corner building on Marylebone Road with a huge, distinctive green copper dome, formerly the London Planetarium, is now part of the eternally-mobbed tourist attraction known as **Madame Tussauds**, a waxworks museum (*map p. 600, B4; madame-tussauds.com, T: 0871 222 0177*). It was founded by Marie Tussaud in 1835. Tussaud had been taught the art of wax-modelling by Dr Philippe Curtius, a physician and her mother's employer, who left her his collection of models after his death. At the court of Louis XVI she sculpted various famous personalities, including Voltaire, and during the French Revolution she famously took the death masks of guillotine victims in order to prove her allegiance to the Republic. After fleeing France, she toured Europe with her collection of waxworks, before coming to settle in England in 1802. Few waxworks from Tussaud's lifetime remain; a fire in 1925 and bombing during World War Two caused significant damage, although some of the casts still exist. The exhibition, now an international franchise and continually updated, focuses on waxworks of modern personalities: stars of film, stage, sport and music as well as royalty, politicians and comic-book superheroes.

Further along, on the corner with the York Gate entrance to Regent's Park, is the Royal Academy of Music, founded in 1822. The main building, in neo-Hampton Court style, is by Sir Ernest George (1912). The **Royal Academy of Music Museum** (*map p. 600, C4; open Mon–Fri 11.30–5.30, Sat 12–4, closed Sun and public holidays; free; restaurant and shop; T: 020 7873 7443, ram.ac.uk/museum*) is in a part of York Gate designed by Nash. The museum collections include scores, manuscripts, letters, art, photography, memorabilia, and three floors of musical instruments. Highlights include Sir Henry Wood's conducting batons (made of poplar wood, painted white) and a violin of 1709 by Stradivari, which was once owned by Giovanni Battista Viotti, violinist to Marie-Antoinette.

ST MARYLEBONE PARISH CHURCH

Directly opposite the Royal Academy of Music is Thomas Hardwick's St Marylebone parish church (1817; *map p. 600, C4*), with an impressive Corinthian portico and cylindrical tower; the domed bell chamber is supported by gilded angel caryatids. This is Marylebone's fourth parish church; the first was built near Oxford Street (probably where Debenhams now stands) c. 1200. This church, built on New Road (now Marylebone Road), faced towards open fields and was thought to be splendid enough for Nash to open up a view of it when he created York Gate opposite. Elizabeth Barrett and Robert Browning (*see p. 264*) were married here in 1846. Next to the church a small public garden serves as a cut-through to Marylebone High Street where, hard right, is the Memorial Garden of Rest, the site of the previous parish church where Byron was christened and where Nelson worshipped and had his daughter Horatia baptised in 1803. The small garden, planted with shrubs and trees, is lined with weathered, lichen-covered tombstones and dominated by a monument to Charles Wesley, parishioner and brother of John (d. 1788). Also buried here were James Gibbs, Allan Ramsay and George Stubbs.

REGENT'S PARK & LONDON ZOO

Map p. 600, B3. Underground: Regent's Park, Baker Street (Camden Town for London Zoo). Open daily 5am–dusk. Boats and pedalos can be hired at the boathouse (northwest end of the lake) from 10am. Deckchairs for hire March–Oct. There are numerous cafés. Performances are held in the Open-Air Theatre May–Sept.

Regent's Park is a roughly circular expanse of just under 500 acres, incorporating London Zoo. Originally known as Marylebone Park, it was appropriated by Henry VIII from the lands of Barking Abbey and turned into a royal hunting ground. It continued as such until Cromwell's day, when it was partially deforested. The Commonwealth government sold the timber to pay its debts from the Civil War. It was laid out in its present style as an aristocratic 'garden suburb' from 1812 by Nash, and it takes its name from the Prince Regent, who contemplated building a country house here. Of Nash's projected 56 villas, only eight were ever built, and today only two remain standing: St John's Lodge and The Holme.

The park is encircled by a carriage road known as the Outer Circle, much of which is flanked by fine monumental Regency terraces in the classical style, mainly by Nash. In the southwest part of the park is the Boating Lake (with many water birds), while to the north runs the Regent's Canal, laid out by Nash in the 1820s. It links the London docks with the Grand Union Canal and was once a significant waterway, used for shipments of building materials and of imported goods from the docks. The well-kept greensward covering the greater part of Regent's Park is used as sports pitches. Also here is Regent's University, a postgraduate college. In mid-October the park hosts the Frieze Art Fair, a leading contemporary art show (*friezelondon.com*).

QUEEN MARY'S GARDENS
Queen Mary's Gardens, perfectly round and bounded by the carriage drive known as the Inner Circle, were occupied from 1840 to 1932 by the Royal Botanic Society. Their main entrance is through the grand Jubilee Gates on York Bridge. The gates were set up to commemorate the Silver Jubilee of George V in 1935 and the gardens are named after Queen Mary, his consort. They contain a famous rose garden and the national collection of delphiniums. In the centre of the begonia garden is a statue of a boy with a frog by Sir William Reid Dick. The Open-Air Theatre is also here (*for information and to book, see openairtheatre.com or T: 0844 826 4242*).

West of the gardens, beyond the Inner Circle, is **The Holme**, one of the stately villas projected for the park by Nash. It was built by Nash's pupil Decimus Burton in 1818–19. **St John's Lodge** (1812), another Nash villa, is now a private residence.

WINFIELD HOUSE AND THE LONDON CENTRAL MOSQUE
Winfield House, on the Outer Circle to the west, stands on the site of Nash's Hertford Villa. In 1936 it was purchased by the American heiress Barbara Hutton, who pulled it down and commissioned Wimperis, Simpson and Guthrie (architects of Fortnum & Mason) to build this, which has the largest private garden in London after Buckingham Palace. It is now the residence of the American Ambassador. The Islamic Cultural Centre by Hanover Gate was opened by George VI in 1944. Adjoining it is the **London Central Mosque** (1978), with a spectacular golden dome. Its architect was Frederick Gibberd, who is known for a number of other visually striking buildings, including Liverpool Metropolitan Cathedral ('Paddy's Wigwam').

H.G. Wells (1866–1946) lived and died at no. 13 Hanover Terrace, and Ralph Vaughan Williams lived at no. 11 from 1953–8.

REGENT'S PARK
Deckchairs under the willow tree.

On the east side of the park, at the south end in St Andrew's Place, is the **Royal College of Physicians** (*rcplondon.ac.uk; guided tours at 2pm on first Fri of the month*), occupying a striking, top-heavy modern building by Denys Lasdun (1964), architect of the National Theatre. It stands on the site of a Nash villa that was demolished following bomb damage in the Second World War. Demolition proceeded 'on the condition that the new building would harmonise with its surroundings'—and *voilà*!

The neo-Gothic **St Katharine's church** (*map p. 600, C2*), has, since 1952, been the church of the Danish community in London (*danskekirke.org*). Before that it housed the St Katharine's Foundation, displaced from the East End (*see p. 122*).

LONDON ZOO

Map p. 600, B2. Underground: Camden Town and 15mins walk; bus 274 from Marble Arch or Baker Street station. Waterbus from Camden Lock or Little Venice (see p. 541 for details). Open daily from 10am; closing times vary, see website. Admission charge. Restaurant, snack kiosk and takeaway fish and chips. Shop. T: 020 7722 3333, zsl.org.

London Zoo, one of the oldest zoos in the world, occupies the northern end of Regent's Park and is officially the Zoological Society of London (ZSL). It is a thriving concern and has adapted well to changing attitudes to keeping wild animals in captivity. ZSL is a respected international scientific and educational body: it has bred and released into the wild animals from 650 species, 112 of which are threatened. ZSL also works to preserve fragile habitats. Its sister zoo, Whipsnade in Bedfordshire (opened 1928), has wide open spaces for the larger animals.

HISTORY OF LONDON ZOO

The Zoological Society of London was founded by Sir Stamford Raffles and Sir Humphry Davy in 1826; when the Zoological Gardens opened in five acres of Regent's Park in 1828, it was only Fellows of the Zoological Society who were admitted. In 1931, the menagerie of animals kept in the Tower of London was presented to the Society and re-housed here. The general public was admitted in 1847 and the Zoo became a fashionable and very popular day out. London Zoo pioneered the exhibiting of exotic animals; it had the world's first reptile house, the first hippo seen in Europe, the first aquarium and the first insect house. *London Zoo from old Photographs 1852–1914* (stocked in the gift shop) has 400 rare photos from ZSL's archive, from Victorian and Edwardian animal rides (llamas harnessed to carriages, Jumbo the Elephant, 1950s' schoolchildren walking with penguins) to all five-known photographs of a living quagga, a zebra sub-species native to South Africa that was ruthlessly hunted by white settlers. Several quaggas were sent to zoos but the creatures did not thrive and breeding programmes were unsuccessful: it was extinct in the wild by 1878 and extinct in captivity by 1883. London Zoo had three quaggas between 1831 and 1872; the photographs (all taken at the Zoo) are believed to be of the second animal (her skin is now in the National Museums of Scotland and her skeleton at Yale). The skin of the Zoo's first quagga (d. 1834) is in the National History Museum in London.

The Zoo has an interesting collection of animal buildings by leading architects, beginning with Decimus Burton, who laid out the original grounds. Surviving Burton buildings include the Clock Tower for the llama hut (1828, rebuilt; now a first aid centre), the raven's cage (1829; empty), the East Tunnel (1829–30; used as a bomb shelter during WW2). Burton's giraffe house (1836–7), with 16ft doors and 21ft ceilings, is the only animal building serving its original purpose. The Mappin Terraces (1913–14), a mountainous landscape in reinforced concrete for bears, by Sir Peter Chalmers Mitchell and J.J. Joass, currently have emus and kangaroos; underneath is the Aquarium (1923–4). The reptile house, with carved snake detail, dates from 1926–7. The Round House (1932–3) is a Modernist gorilla house by Berthold Lubetkin's practice, Tecton; it now houses nocturnal creatures. Also by Tecton is the Penguin Pool (1934), the Zoo's most celebrated piece of architecture, currently unused because the penguins enjoy a bigger, deeper pool and beach elsewhere. The aviaries, by Lord Snowdon (1962–4), pioneered the use of aluminium and tension support and are well seen from Regent's Canal. Sir Hugh Casson designed the Elephant and Rhino Pavilion (1962–5), heavy and solid in textured concrete with green lanterns; these animals are now kept at Whipsnade.

The Zoo has had numerous celebrated residents. Guy the Gorilla, who arrived clutching a hot water bottle in 1947 and died in 1978, is commemorated by a sculpture. Winnie, an American black bear, lived at the Zoo from 1914. She came to the Zoo when her Canadian soldier owner went to fight in the trenches in France. She became the inspiration for A.A. Milne's stories of Winnie the Pooh and Christopher Robin and was visited here by the author with his son.

PRIMROSE HILL & ST JOHN'S WOOD

Map p. 600, B2–A2. Underground: Camden Town, St John's Wood. For Lord's and Boundary Road in St John's Wood, also bus 189 from Oxford Circus.

Primrose Hill was once as bucolic as its name suggests. William Blake writes of 'FIELDS from Islington to Marybone, to Primrose Hill and Saint John's Wood.' Today the area is still well-endowed with parkland and is lovely to visit: from the top of the hill (250ft) there is a fine view of London. Every September, white-robed druids congregate here to celebrate the autumn equinox (they celebrate the vernal equinox on Tower Hill and the summer solstice at Stonehenge). Cecil Sharp House (*2 Regent's Park Rd*) is home to the English Folk Dance and Song Society and Vaughan Williams Memorial Library, the national collection of English folk music. In the 1990s the 'Primrose Hill Set' was a group of locally-resident actors who collaborated on various projects. The area has many residents from the fields of literature and the media.

ST JOHN'S WOOD

St John's Wood takes its name from the Knights of St John of Jerusalem, who owned the area when it was still thickly forested. Today it is residential, its streets lined with large and costly villas: the district's postcode (NW8) is one of the priciest in the city. The Beatles recorded their 1969 album *Abbey Road* (*map p. 596, C2*) at the eponymous studios; the pedestrian crossing on which the band were photographed for the album cover is a magnet for fans. Sir Paul McCartney still owns property in the area. At 108A Boundary Road is the **Ben Uri Gallery**, 'The Art Museum for Everyone', founded in Whitechapel in 1915 and home to a superb collection of art by European Jewish artists or artists of Jewish ancestry: Kitaj, Epstein, Chagall, Mark Gertler, Leon Bakst, Naum Gabo and many others (*open Mon 1–5.30; Tues–Fri 10–5.30, though Fri closure is at 3.30 in Nov–March; Sun 12–4; T: 020 7604 3991, benuri.org.uk*).

St John's Wood is also the home of the Marylebone Cricket Club (MCC), founded by Thomas Lord in 1787 (*see Dorset Square, p. 270*). **Lord's Cricket Ground** is here (*map p. 600, A3*) and has a museum with displays that all cricket fans will appreciate, such as gear worn by Donald Bradman. The famous Ashes Urn (the trophy that is battled over by England and Australia) is also housed here (*museum open 10–4.30 on days when there is no match; admission charge; T: 020 7616 8658, lords.org*). Tours of the cricket ground can also be booked (*see website for details*).

On the Lord's Roundabout is the **church of St John** (Thomas Hardwick, 1814). It was here that a fanatic named Joanna Southcott, prophet and writer (1750–1814), was buried. In the last year of her life she declared herself pregnant with the new Messiah (Shiloh), for which she was ridiculed in the popular press, prompting Rowlandson's vulgar cartoon 'A Medical Inspection, or, Miracles Will Never Cease' showing her lifting her skirts to be examined by doctors.

BAYSWATER

Map p. 602, A1–C1. Underground: Bayswater, Queensway.

The white stucco terraces of Bayswater, with their houses, flats, small hotels and serviced apartments, stretch behind the Bayswater Road towards Paddington. The neighbourhood was faded and unfashionable by the mid-20th century; today it is on the up and property here is tipped to be the next big thing. The triangle of streets, squares, crescents and mews bounded by the Edgware Road and Sussex Gardens is sometimes referred to as Tyburnia, in reference to the ancient tributary of the Thames which flowed past here to Westminster and the notorious gallows which once stood on the site of Marble Arch (*see p. 287*). Edgware Road itself leads north from Marble Arch, following the ancient Roman Watling Street.

A Middle Eastern community has settled in Bayswater, with associated shops, restaurants and cafés, some with opportunities for sheesha-smoking in cordoned off sections of the pavement. Off Harrowby Street, a turning to the east off Edgware Road, an archway leads into the narrow Cato Street, famed as the meeting-place of the 'Cato Street Conspirators' (hanged at Newgate in 1820), whose object was the wholesale extermination of the Ministers of the Crown at a Cabinet dinner in Grosvenor Square.

Bayswater was developed as a comfortable middle-class housing estate, on land belonging to the Bishop of London, by S.P. Cockerell, beginning around 1805 and attracting artists and writers. In 1885 its nickname 'Asia Minor' was due to the number of colonial officers who settled here on their return from secondment in Asia. The small cluster of independent shops and businesses around Connaught Square (*map p. 602, C1*) is now known as 'Connaught Village'.

Lancaster Gate (*map p. 602, B1*), built in the mid-19th century, is the smartest part of Bayswater. The grand stucco terraces overlooking Hyde Park were designed with a wide boulevard between them (now a busy road) and the neo-Gothic Christ Church sited in a square. The church has now been converted into housing; the tower and spire remain. The church of **St James, Sussex Gardens** (*map p. 602, B1*) is a late work of G.E. Street (1881–2), building on an earlier, smaller church from the original 1840s' estate, which he realigned, placing the altar at the west end. It was designed to form part of a vista, with a triangular garden in front and Sussex Gardens beyond, splitting into separate crescents behind the church.

PADDINGTON AND THE FLEMING MUSEUM

Paddington Station (*map p. 602, B1*), the former terminus of the old Great Western Railway, opened in 1854. Its engineer was the great Isambard Kingdom Brunel. The first underground railway in the world, operated by the Metropolitan Railway Company, was opened in 1863 between Paddington and Farringdon. The front of the station forms the Hilton London Paddington Hotel, formerly the Great Western Hotel, by P.C. Hardwick (the son of Philip, who designed the Euston Arch; *see p. 362*). The once proud stucco terraces tend to be peeling and soot-blackened today, although the area is undergoing redevelopment and regeneration around **Paddington Basin**, where new office, leisure and shopping complexes are being built as part of the Paddington Waterside Scheme (due for completion in 2018). Here is Thomas Heatherwick's **Rolling Bridge** (2004), a hinged truss bridge which curls and uncurls to allow pedestrians to cross and boats to pass.

In Praed Street is St Mary's Hospital and the **Fleming Museum**. The great scientist discovered penicillin at St Mary's in 1928, when he noticed that a mould had grown on some of his bacterial culture dishes and that colonies of staphylococcus could not survive near it. The museum includes a re-creation of Fleming's laboratory (*open Mon–Thur 10–1, other times by appointment; T: 020 3312 6528*).

PORCHESTER TERRACE AND QUEENSWAY

The Modernist 1950s' **Hallfield Estate** on Bishops Bridge Road (*map p. 602, A1*) was designed by the Tecton partnership and executed by Lindsay Drake and Denys Lasdun. The ten- and six-storey blocks, with landscaping in between, have chequered façades. At the western side is Lasdun's Hallfield School, also a landmark of its time.

In Leinster Gardens, nos 23 and 24 are sham fronts, built in the 1860s to hide the underground railway's steam condensers.

In **Porchester Terrace**, nos 3–5 are a pair of stucco houses designed as a 'double detached villa' by John Claudius Loudon, the gardening writer and architect. He built

PORCHESTER CENTRE
Detail of the Art Deco spa.

them for himself and his mother in 1823, a very early example of semi-detached housing (the glazed porch disguises the fact that the houses are a pair). In the **Porchester Centre** is an Art Deco spa (c. 1929), with original features including a series of Turkish hot rooms. It is open to the public (*weekdays 6.30–10, weekends 8–8*) and one can still have an authentic experience here: it is an old-fashioned Londoners' baths, not a wellness centre for trophy wives.

Queensway and Westbourne Grove are at the heart of Bayswater's lively multi-ethnic community and there are numerous shops, bars and restaurants catering to a wide variety of tastes. In Queensway is the **Whiteleys** shopping mall, with shops, restaurants and a cinema. Once this was London's premier department store, founded by William Whiteley in 1863, expanding to 17 departments and 6,000 staff by 1900. The building is by Belcher and Joass (1908). The atrium and sweeping staircase are surviving original features.

Down Ilchester Gardens and St Petersburgh Place are three places of worship, all built in the 1870s but in different styles and for different faiths and denominations. On the corner of Moscow Road is the neo-Byzantine **Greek Orthodox Cathedral** of St Sophia, built for the Greek merchants of Bayswater by John Oldrid Scott (1877), son of Sir George Gilbert Scott. **St Matthew's** was built for the Church of England (J. Johnson, 1881) in Gothic Revival style. Diagonally opposite is the **New West End Synagogue** (George Audsley, 1877–9), in a 'Gothick' mix of styles.

NOTTING HILL

Map p. 596. Underground: Notting Hill Gate, Ladbroke Grove.

Notting Hill is a fashionable, mixed-residential area famous for its Saturday antiques market (Portobello Market) and the annual Notting Hill Carnival (*see below*), which takes place during the last weekend in August.

NOTTING HILL CARNIVAL

First held in 1965 as a simple Caribbean street parade with music, the Carnival is now Europe's biggest street party and indeed the biggest street festival in the world outside Rio. During the 1950s many West Indian immigrants came to settle in Notting Hill and their arrival was greeted with suspicion by an indigenous white working-class population: hostility exploded in August 1958 into some of the worst rioting seen in the UK. The Carnival started as a way to promote cultural unity in an area fraught with racial tensions. Today over a million visitors descend on Notting Hill during late August (the weekend known as the 'August Bank Holiday') to join in the festivities and to take part in the processions of floats, costume parades, dancers and soca, calypso and steel bands.

Notting Hill began life in the 1840s when the main landowners, the Ladbroke family, developed their estate with the intention of turning the area into a fashionable suburb. Streets and crescents of large, handsome stuccoed terraced houses began to spring up, with private communal gardens; an aspect that appealed—and still does—to their wealthy, middle-class inhabitants. Artisans settled in streets of smaller, quainter cottages. By the end of World War Two, however, Notting Hill had become run-down. The big Victorian houses, now devoid of families and servants, were converted cheaply into multiple-occupancy tenements. Slum landlords, such as the infamous Peter Rackman, exploited tenants ruthlessly, moving entire West Indian immigrant families into substandard housing (stoking racial tensions) and coercing older tenants into giving up their properties by deliberately moving in noisy and intimidating neighbours.

In the late 1960s and '70s, Notting Hill began to attract an arty, bohemian community of writers, artists, journalists and actors. Musicians congregated around Ladbroke Grove (*map p. 596, B2*) and famous names who performed and recorded in the area include Van Morrison, Hawkwind, Nick Drake, Eric Clapton, The Clash and

Bob Marley. Jimi Hendrix died at no. 22 Lansdowne Crescent in 1970. From the 1980s Notting Hill experienced a renaissance and in the 1990s it was made famous by the eponymous film starring Hugh Grant and Julia Roberts.

Today, Notting Hill is a sought-after area to live in. It is also an area full of contrasts: attractive, designer, multi-ethnic, edgy, scruffy, where rich coexists with poor—although the artists, writers and musicians are increasingly being supplanted by moneyed bankers, celebrities and politicians. The main streets are now tenanted by upmarket shops and restaurants, including the ubiquitous international chains. The area around Ladbroke Grove station tenaciously resists gentrification.

EXPLORING FROM NOTTING HILL GATE STATION

Holland Park Avenue (*map p. 596, B3*), which leads west towards Shepherds Bush, was developed in the 1860s. It is lined with large, Italianate detached villas by Francis Radford (*for the Campden Hill area, see p. 320*). Pembridge Road leads north to **Portobello Road** (*map p. 596, B2*), which takes its name from the capture of Puerto Bello, in the Gulf of Mexico, by Admiral Vernon in 1739. On Saturdays this whole area plays host to the Portobello Market (*portobelloroad.co.uk*). Portobello Road, winding all the way to Ladbroke Grove, is crammed with stalls and with shoppers, who come to browse the antiques, jewellery, bric-à-brac, fruit, vegetables and fashion. There are plenty of interesting independent shops, cafés and pubs around here too, in particular along Westbourne Grove, Ledbury Road and Kensington Park Road. The **Electric Cinema** (*191 Portobello Rd, electriccinema.co.uk*) is one of the oldest cinemas in London and comprises an independent cinema, private-members' club and a popular bar/diner. In Colville Mews (off Lonsdale Road, *map p. 596, B2*) is the **Museum of Brands, Packaging and Advertising**, crammed with consumerist ephemera from Victorian days to the present (*open Tues–Sat 10–6, Sun 11–5, last entry 45mins before closing; admission charge; T: 020 7908 0880, museumofbrands.com*).

THE LADBROKE GROVE ESTATE

The smart, good-looking streets and crescents fanning out from Ladbroke Grove (*map p. 596, B2*) form the Ladbroke Grove Estate, laid out in the 1840s (and as you will see, Notting Hill is indeed a hill). From the 1730s the land was owned by the Ladbroke family, one of whom opened a race course called the Hippodrome (commemorated by Hippodrome Place) in 1837, erecting a circuit round the crest of the hill. It was not a success and closed in 1841. The subsequent housing development covered the hill with crescents in concentric circles, with St John's church slightly off-centre on the brow. The houses, by various developers, are large and impressive, some are attractively painted in pastel hues; they all have multi-million-pound price tags. There are private 'secret' gardens, for use by the residents, between the blocks. Around Clarendon Cross (off Clarendon Road) is an enclave of upmarket interior design shops; in Portland Road is Julie's wine bar and restaurant, with myriad small rooms and snugs. It has been catering to residents since 1969. Before development the area was filled with piggeries and potteries: in Walmer Road is a surviving 19th-century kiln that once fired bricks and tiles from Notting Hill clay. Further north, tucked just below the Westway, is Bartle Road, which stands on the site of the former Rillington Place, made infamous by John Christie, who murdered several women there between 1943 and 1953.

AROUND LADBROKE GROVE STATION AND GOLBORNE ROAD

The area stretching north from Ladbroke Grove station, also known as North Kensington, mutely resists gentrification. Under the Westway, an ugly elevated motorway, is Portobello's fashion market. **Golborne Road** (*map p. 596, B2*), which forks right off the northern reaches of Portobello Road, is worth a look for its small, more authentic, properly junky, market. It also has small independent shops and cafés. A Portuguese, Moroccan and Lebanese community lives around here. Excellent custard tarts are to be had in Café Lisboa.

At no. 5 Golborne Road, the forbidding **Trellick Tower** casts its shadow. This 31-storey concrete Brutalist skyscraper was designed by Ernő Goldfinger and completed in 1972. The lift and service shaft has walkways connecting it with the main block. The flats, designed as duplexes, each with its own balcony, were designed so that maximum light enters from both sides. Upon completion, the flats were given over to social housing and the Tower became a notorious hub for crime and anti-social behaviour in the 1980s. Today, the flats are mostly privately owned.

LITTLE VENICE, MAIDA VALE & KILBURN

Map p. 596. Underground: Paddington, Warwick Avenue, Maida Vale, Kilburn Park.

Little Venice and Maida Vale are prosperous, self-contained residential enclaves with 19th-century Italianate houses in their elegant, tree-lined boulevards.

On the edge of **Paddington Green** (underpass from Paddington Station; *map p. 600, A4*) is St Mary's church (1791), the successor of the church in which Hogarth was secretly married in 1729. The sculptors Thomas Banks (d. 1805) and Joseph Nollekens (d. 1823) and the painter Benjamin Robert Haydon (d. 1847), friend of Keats, have their tombs here. The actress Sarah Siddons is buried at the north end of the churchyard. In the adjoining recreation ground there is a statue (L.J. Chavalliaud, 1897), in a dramatic pose based on Reynolds' depiction of her as the Muse of Tragedy (a version of the portrait hangs in Dulwich Picture Gallery). In 1829, the first London horse-drawn omnibus service began between Paddington Green and the Bank of England.

LITTLE VENICE

Little Venice (*map p. 596, C2*) is where the Paddington arm of the Grand Union Canal meets the Regent's Canal. Brightly-painted houseboats are moored here; walking along the towpath is a good way to admire the picturesque villa architecture. Robert Browning lived in Warwick Crescent in the 1860s, overlooking the widest stretch of water, known as Browning's Pool, and it was he who coined the name Little Venice; the poet is said to have rowed over to the small island for poetry composition. Also here is the Waterway, a canal-side pub with a large terrace, crowded in fine weather. More restaurants, pubs and shops can be around Formosa Street. In Clifton Gardens (*Underground: Warwick Avenue*) is the church of St Saviour, with a fibreglass spire (it is a 1970s' replacement of a Victorian church on the site). Clifton Nurseries, through a narrow corridor between two stuccoed mansions in Clifton Villas, opens out into a small and charming garden centre with plants, gifts and books and a café/restaurant.

Canal cruises and events

At Blomfield Road, opposite no. 42, Jason's Trip offers rides in a 100-yr old canal boat to Camden Lock and back, passing through the Maida Hill Tunnel and Regent's Park (approx. 45mins; booking essential; jasons.co.uk). Other boat services are also available, services are most regular April–Oct. The Puppet Theatre Barge puts on popular marionette shows; it is moored in Little Venice all year and undertakes tours of the Thames during the summer. The annual Canalway Cavalcade, a festival when 100 narrow boats converge, takes place in May.

The part of Edgware Road known as **Maida Vale** is flanked by pleasant houses and large blocks of flats. The name (the pronunciation of which time and the southern English penchant for diphthongs have corrupted) recalls the Battle of Máida of 1806, when the British expelled the French from Calabria. To the east is St John's Wood (*see p. 275*) and to the north is **Kilburn** (*map p. 596, B2–C2*), once a predominantly Irish area, now multi-ethnic. The Anglo-Catholic **St Augustine's church** in Kilburn Park Road (east off Kilburn High Road) is one of London's finest neo-Gothic Victorian churches (J.L. Pearson, 1898; *saugustinekilburn.org.uk*). It is referred to as the 'cathedral of North London' due to its large size and elaborate architecture: the soaring 254ft tower is an architectural triumph. In the High Road itself are a couple of good renovated Victorian pubs, the Black Lion and the North London Tavern. There are also few lingering working-men's pubs: a bit intimidating; the kind of places where everyone falls silent when a stranger enters.

QUEEN'S PARK AND KENSAL GREEN

Queen's Park, between Kilburn and Kensal Green (*map p. 596, B2; Underground: Queen's Park*), is a pleasant public space which has given its name to the area more or less bookended by Salusbury Road and Chamberlayne Road. Originally this was a 19th-century working-class development, but recently young professionals and families who cannot afford to live in Notting Hill have started to move here and the area has altered enormously. There are some very good gastro pubs (*see p. 285*).

Kensal Green Cemetery (*map p. 596, B2; Underground: Kensal Green*) is one of London's oldest public burial places, opened in 1833. The design of the 72-acre grounds, with numerous listed monuments, is said to have been influenced by Père-Lachaise in Paris. Here are buried numerous famous people, including Marc Brunel (d. 1849), Isambard Kingdom Brunel (d. 1859), Thackeray (d. 1863), Trollope (d. 1882), Wilkie Collins (d. 1889) and the computer pioneer Charles Babbage (d. 1871).

EATING AND DRINKING IN REGENT STREET, MARYLEBONE AND NOTTING HILL

BAYSWATER

££ Le Café Anglais. Probably offers the cheapest and best-quality roast chicken in London. Open daily. *8 Porchester Gardens. T: 020 7221 1415, lecafeanglais.co.uk. Map p. 602, A1.*

MARYLEBONE, OXFORD STREET

££ Bistrot de Luxe. Modern French. The first restaurant opened by the Galvin brothers. *66 Baker St. T: 020 7935 4007, galvinrestaurants.com. Map p. 600, B4.*

£–££ Caffè Caldesi. Italian bar and restaurant. Very good, with some outside tables on the street for people who just want to stop by for a drink. Bar open daily, restaurant closed Sun. *118 Marylebone Lane. T: 020 7487 0753 (bar), 020 7487 0754 (restaurant), caldesi.com. Map p. 600, C4.*

££ Due Veneti. Cosily old-fashioned Italian restaurant serving Venetian specialities. No lunch Sat. Closed Sun. *10 Wigmore St. T: 020 7637 0789, 2veneti.com. Map p. 603, D1.*

££ The Grazing Goat. One of the many good places to eat in the area known as 'Portman Village'. Part of the popular Cubitt House chain of gastro pubs. Elegant interiors (also does rooms), succulent meat dishes and good fish (scallops, oysters, crab). The name is said to come from the flock of goats that Lady Portman kept on her estate (she was allergic to cow's milk). Open daily. *6 New Quebec St. T: 020 7724 7243, thegrazinggoat.co.uk. Map p. 602, C1.*

££ Hardy's. Tastefully old-style brasserie and wine bar: polished wood floors, bentwood chairs and a chef with impressive credentials. The menu ranges from classic fishcakes and shepherd's pie to roasted woodcock (in season). No dinner Sun. *53 Dorset St. T: 020 7935 5929, hardys-brasserie.co.uk. Map p. 600, B4.*

Landmark Hotel. The Winter Garden does a fine afternoon tea. Expensive as all London afternoon teas are, but elegant: silver teapots, dainty sandwiches, rattan sofas and palm trees. *222 Marylebone Rd. T: 020 7631 8188, landmarklondon.co.uk. Map p. 600, B4.*

£££ L'Autre Pied. Michelin-starred restaurant offering interesting taste combinations. No dinner Sun. *5–7 Blandford St. T: 020 7486 9696, lautrepied.co.uk. Map p. 600, B4.*

££–£££ Locanda Locatelli. When Giorgio Locatelli opened this restaurant it became so famous that it was impossible to get a table. Madonna loved it. Nowadays things are calmer, but the traditional Italian cooking is just as delicious. Open daily. *8 Seymour St. T: 020 7935 9088, locandalocatelli.com. Map p. 602, C1.*

£ Fishworks. One of the many restaurants in the eating-and-retail district known as 'Marylebone Village'. Fish and seafood restaurant and fishmonger's shop. Choose what you like either to take home and cook for yourself, or have it cooked for you. Scrubbed wooden tables, nice glassware, informal atmosphere. Other branches are in Richmond and Swallow St, Piccadilly. Open daily. *89 Marylebone High St. T: 020 7935 9796, marylebonevillage.com, fishworks.co.uk. Map p. 600, C4.*

£ Golden Hind. Excellent, long-established fish and chip restaurant. They have a corkage so you can bring your own wine. *73 Marylebone Lane. T: 020 7486 3644. Map p. 600, C4.*

£££ Texture. An Anglo-Icelandic co-production on the food front, supported by a talented French sommelier. Michelin-starred restaurant and champagne bar. Closed Sun and Mon. *34 Portman St. T: 020 7224 0028, texture-restaurant.co.uk. Map p. 603, D1.*

££ The Wallace Restaurant. In the roofed inner courtyard of the Wallace Collection. The menu is French, as befits the Wallace history: wild rabbit, nettle gnocchi and *madeleines à l'armagnac*. Open daily for lunch, dinner Fri and Sat. *Manchester Square. T: 020 7563 9505, wallacecollection.org. Map p. 603, D1.*

NOTTING HILL

£–££ The Cow. Pub and dining room, part of a small chain. The thing to eat here is not beef but oysters. And whelks and winkles, by the half-pint. *89 Westbourne Park Rd. T: 020 7221 5400 or 020 7221 0021 for the dining room, open daily for dinner, lunch on Sat–Sun), thecowlondon.co.uk. Map p. 596, B2.*

£££ The Ledbury. Recently voted one of the 100 best restaurants in the world. Australian chef Brett Graham has two Michelin stars. Reservations essential. No lunch Mon or Tues. *127 Ledbury Rd. T: 020 7792 9090, theledbury.com. Map p. 596, B2.*

£–££ Portobello Gold. Conservatory restaurant in the roofed back garden of the former Princess Alexandra pub. Open daily. *95–97 Portobello Rd. T: 020 7460 4910 or 4912, portobellogold.com. Map p. 596, B2.*

£ Walmer Castle. Tiny place offering an interesting synthesis: British pub meets Thai cuisine. Try a *Kha Nom Pang Na Goong* with your bitter shandy. Pub open daily all day, restaurant evenings only Mon–Fri, from noon at weekends. *58 Ledbury Rd. T: 020 7229 4620, thaipubs.co.uk. Map p. 596, B2.*

££ Prince Bonaparte. Gastro pub serving modern British cuisine and Sunday roasts. Open daily. *80 Chepstow Rd. T: 020 7313 9491, theprincebonapartew2.co.uk. Map p. 596, C2.*

£–££ Osteria Basilico. Popular Italian. Open daily. *29 Kensington Park Rd. T: 020 7727 9957, osteriabasilico.co.uk. Map p. 596, B2.*

£–££ E&O. Excellent dim sum. Open daily. *14 Blenheim Crescent. T: 020 7229 5454, rickerrestaurants.com. Map p. %96, B2.*

££ Julie's. Well-known restaurant and champagne bar, a temple to epicureanism (it features an old pulpit among its interior furnishings). Open daily from 10am for eggs benedict and other deliciousnesses. *135 Portland Rd. T: 020 7229 8331, juliesrestaurant.com. Map p. 596, B3.*

Lisboa. Portuguese café and delicatessen, famous for its custard tarts (*pastéis de nata*). If you are in this part of town, drop by. *54 and 57 Golborne Rd. Map p. 596, B2.*

QUEEN'S PARK, LITTLE VENICE

There are some good gastro pubs in the Queen's Park area (*map p. 596, B2*): the beef-focused ££ **Chamberlayne** (*no lunch Mon; 83 Chamberlayne Rd, T: 020 8960 4311, thechamberlayne.com*); ££ **The Salusbury** (*50–52 Salusbury Rd, T: 020 7328 3286, thesalusbury.co.uk*); £ **Hugo's** (*25 Lonsdale Rd, a small mews off Salusbury Rd; no dinner Mon; T: 020 7372 1232, hugosrestaurant.co.uk*); and the ££ **Paradise**, whose name makes reference to G.K. Chesterton's famous anti-Prohibition poem *The Rolling English Road*: 'For there is good news yet to hear and fine things to be seen, Before we go to Paradise by way of Kensal Green.' (*19 Kilburn Lane, T: 020 8969 0098*).

£ **Quince Tree Café**. In the palm house at Clifton Nurseries, Little Venice. Open for breakfast, lunch and tea. *5A Clifton Villas. T: 020 7432 1867. Map p. 596, C2.*

£–££ **The Waterway**. Restaurant with an eclectic menu and an outdoor terrace overlooking the canal in Maida Vale. Open daily. *54 Formosa St. T: 020 7266 3557, thewaterway. co.uk. Map p. 596, C2.*

PRIMROSE HILL

£ **Primrose Eatery**. Easy food (pizzas, falafel, salads) and a neighbourhood feel. *38 Primrose Hill Rd. T: 020 7483 3222, theprimroseeatery.co.uk. Map p. 600, B2.*

££ **The Engineer**. Good gastro pub with garden. Open daily. *65 Gloucester Ave. T: 020 7483 1830, theengineerprimrosehill.co.uk. Map p. 600, C2.*

££ **Odette's**. A Primrose Hill stalwart offering fine dining midday and evening. Open daily. *130 Regent's Park Rd. T: 020 7586 8569, odettesprimrosehill.com. Map p. 600, B2.*

££ **Lemonia**. Long-established family-run Greek taverna. *89 Regent's Park Rd. T: 020 7586 7454, lemonia.co.uk. Map p. 600, B2.*

REGENT STREET AND PARK

££ **Café Royal**. It was in the neo-Baroque opulence of the Oscar Wilde Bar (the former Grill Room) that the playwright lost his heart to Bosie. Come here for cocktails and light meals. Closed Sun. *68 Regent St. T: 020 7406 3310, hotelcaferoyal.com. Map p. 603, E1.*

Heddon Street 'food quarter'. Just off Regent St, with several Italian restaurants, a branch of the French chain £–££ **Aubaine** (*T: 020 7440 2510, aubaine.co.uk*), Swiss vegetarian buffet £ **Tibits** (*T: 020 7758 4112*) and popular Moroccan restaurant ££ **Momo** (*T: 020 7434 4040, momoresto.com*). *Map p. 603, E1.*

Regent's Park. You can find snacks and family-friendly meals at the Garden Café in Queen Mary's Gardens and the Boathouse Café by Hanover Bridges. *Map p. 600, B3.*

££ **Veeraswamy**. The oldest Indian restaurant in the UK and still a fine one. Open daily. *99 Regent St. T: 020 7734 1401, veeraswamy.com. Map p. 603, E1.*

NATURAL HISTORY MUSEUM
Climbing monkey (detail) by Brindley and Farmer.

Kensington, Knightsbridge & Chelsea

*Home to film stars and international billionaires; the London of Harrods,
Harvey Nichols and the King's Road; haunt of the once-famous
'Sloane Ranger'. The expansive Hyde Park and the voluminous collections
of the South Kensington Museums are also to be found here. Pimlico and
Tate Britain are likewise included in this chapter.*

At the time of writing, there was a website called 'bornrich.com' which nominated London as the world's most expensive city and, if you consulted a particular page, gave details of the parts of town responsible for this accolade. Welcome to Knightsbridge. On a summer's day in Hyde Park you will see Saudi women in full tented concealment manipulating pedalos on the Serpentine lake. In the depths of winter you will see eccentric Englishmen swim-ming in its glacial waters. London, in all its madness and its contrasts, is distilled in this district. Speakers' Corner is its sounding board.

Marble Arch (*map p. 602, C1*) gives its name to the point where Oxford Street, Park Lane, Edgware Road and Bayswater Road converge. At the centre of a busy traffic island, where pigeons flock and around which double-decker buses churn, stands the epony-mous sugar-white triumphal arch, projected by Nash as an entrance to Buckingham Palace. The architect modelled it on the 4th-century Arch of Constantine in Rome: it was to have been a celebration of the victories of Wellington and Nelson, topped by a statue of George IV. Marble was brought from Seravezza in Tuscany, a quarry favoured by Michelangelo—but the project was never completed. Sculpture and reliefs by E.H. Bailey, Sir Richard Westmacott and J.C.F. Rossi which were not installed now grace Buckingham Palace and the National Gallery instead and Chantrey's bronze eques-trian statue of George IV stands on one of the plinths in Trafalgar Square. When Buckingham Palace received a new east wing, the arch was brought here, in 1850–1, as a ceremonial entrance to Hyde Park. Road-widening in the 1960s cut if off completely.

Marble Arch stands close to the site of Tyburn, where stood the famous gallows, the 'Tyburn Tree' (a circular stone slab marks the spot), to which the tumbrils of Newgate dragged many a victim, both innocent and guilty. The last execution was that of the highwayman John Austin in 1783. Today the Tyburn Nuns, the 'Benedictine Adorers of the Sacred Heart of Jesus of Montmartre', pray ceaselessly (in shifts) in **Tyburn Chapel** on the Bayswater Road (no. 19; *tours daily at 10.30, 3.30 and 5.30; tyburnchapel.org.uk*) for the souls of Catholic martyrs executed here between 1535 and 1681. The body of one of those martyrs may be seen in Westminster Cathedral.

Very prominent close to Marble Arch is Nic Fiddian-Green's *Still Water* (2010), a colossal bronze horse's head, shown muzzle down as if drinking.

HYDE PARK

Map p. 602, C2. Underground: Hyde Park Corner, Knightsbridge, Marble Arch, Lancaster Gate. Park open daily 5am–midnight. For details on swimming and horse riding, see royalparks.org.uk and for boating, see solarshuttle.co.uk. Deckchair hire from March–Oct. The park is amply supplied with cafés. It is also an excellent place to picnic.

HISTORY OF HYDE PARK

Hyde Park stretches over 350 acres of land that once belonged to the monks of Westminster Abbey. After the Dissolution, Henry VIII appropriated it and turned it into a royal deer park. In the reign of Charles I, the carriage drive known as The Ring was built and the park was opened to the public in 1637. Queen Caroline, wife of George II, created the lake known as the Serpentine by damming the Westbourne stream. From Decimus Burton George IV commissioned the monumental entrance gate from Hyde Park Corner, and at this time too the West Carriage Drive was driven across the water, formally dividing Hyde Park from Kensington Gardens.

In 1851, for the first Great International Exhibition, Joseph Paxton's Crystal Palace was built between Rotten Row and Knightsbridge (it was afterwards re-erected at Sydenham; *see p. 461*). The forged steel and bronze Queen Elizabeth Gate (also known as the Queen Mother Gate; by Rogers, Wynne and Lund) was opened in 1993. In 2005, near the Hyde Park Corner entrance, the 7 July Memorial was set up to the 52 victims of the London Bombings. In the summer of 2013 (a particularly warm one) the park became home to an encampment of Romanian gypsies.

At the northeast tip of the park is the famous **Speakers' Corner**, where stars of the soap box address the assembled multitude (on Sun). The right to speak here has existed since 1872, although contrary to popular belief there is no allowance for complete freedom of speech: anyone may say what they please provided that it is lawful and does not incite violence. Orators here offer a glimpse into the following world views (a selection only): Marxist, Atheist, Post-Modernist, Black Supremacist; Independent Islamic; Sex and love; Free hugs.

Rotten Row, a sand-track for horse riders, leads east–west across the southern part of the park. Its name is possibly a corruption of *Route du Roi*, 'King's Road', from its creation by William III, who travelled along it between his new palace at Kensington (*see below*) and the court at St James's. Because the park at night was infested with footpads, he had 300 oil lamps installed along the length of Rotten Row, creating the first artificially illuminated street in England. East of The Dell, a green area watered by the now-underground Westbourne stream, is the **Holocaust Memorial** (1983). At Edinburgh Gate, outside the park on the other side of the road, is Jacob Epstein's sculptural group entitled ***Rush of Green*** (1959), showing a family and their dog joyfully racing towards the open space of the park, accompanied by Pan and his pipes. They might be fleeing in shock having just glimpsed the price tag for one of the apartments in One Hyde Park (Rogers Stirk Harbour + Partners), the most expensive on the planet. At the time of writing the complex's developer, Candy and Candy, had reportedly expressed an interest in acquiring and developing Sir Basil Spence's towering **Hyde Park Barracks** (1970), a 33-storey concrete block which (as yet) provides accommodation for the men of the Household Cavalry.

The artificial lake known as the **Serpentine** (*boats and pedalos for hire Easter–Oct; solarshuttle.co.uk, T: 0207 262 1330*) is home to a variety of water birds as well as to the **Lido**, set up in 1930 and still popular with swimmers (*open weekends in May, daily June–mid-Sept*). The Serpentine Swimming Club is the oldest swimming club in Britain: regulars come here for a dip at six o'clock in the morning, and every year on Christmas Day they hold a swimming race. The Lido Café Bar has tables on the water and is very pleasant in warm weather. The **Diana, Princess of Wales Memorial Fountain** (Kathryn Gustafson) was opened in 2004. The bridge over the Serpentine (1828) is the work of John Rennie the Younger and his brother George.

North of the Serpentine, just inside the railed-off bird sanctuary, is another work by Epstein: ***Rima***, a relief carved as a memorial to the writer and ornithologist W.H. Hudson. When it was unveiled in 1925 it drew 'gasps of horror' from the assembled crowd and was swiftly dubbed the 'Hyde Park Atrocity'.

KENSINGTON GARDENS & PALACE

Map p. 602, B2–A2. Underground: High Street Kensington, Lancaster Gate, Queensway.

Kensington Gardens, occupying an area of slightly under 300 acres, are separated from Hyde Park by the West Carriage Drive and by the portion of the Serpentine known as the Long Water. It was here, in 1816, that Harriet Westbrook, Shelley's first wife, drowned herself aged twenty-one.

THE SERPENTINE GALLERIES
Map p. 602, B2. Open Tues–Sun 10–6. T: 020 7402 6075; serpentinegalleries.org. Free. Shop. Restaurant.

The Serpentine Galleries (the Serpentine Gallery and the Serpentine Sackler Gallery) are set in pleasurable open surroundings on either side of the water. The original Serpentine Gallery (to the south), founded in 1970, occupies a Neoclassical tea pavilion (J. Grey West, chief architect for His Majesty's Office of Works, 1934; renovated by John Miller + Partners, 1998). Just north of it stands the Serpentine Sackler Gallery, a brick-built, Doric-colonnaded gunpowder store (1805) juxtaposed with a futuristic fly-away tensile structure (Zaha Hadid Architects, 2013) constructed of glass-fibre woven fabric, which seems to undulate in the wind ('a wedding marquee battling with a stiff breeze', as *The Guardian* put it). The former structure houses exhibition spaces; the latter the Magazine restaurant (named in honour of the old gunpowder store which yielded space to it). The Serpentine stages changing displays of modern and contemporary art, architecture, design and performance. The highlight is the annual Serpentine Summer Pavilion (June–Oct), which since 2000 has invited a different international architect or design team, who have never built in the UK previously, to create a temporary structure. The roll-call has included Zaha Hadid (2000), Daniel Libeskind (2001), Frank Gehry (2008) and Ai Weiwei and Herzog & de Meuron (2012).

Henry Moore's travertine **Arch** (1979), looking like a great palaeontological pelvis, stands on the north bank of the Long Water. Through it is a splendid framed view of Kensington Palace (*see below*), of which this park was once the private grounds. The **Italian Gardens**, with their urns and fountains, were laid out for Prince Albert by Sir James Pennethorne. The **Pet Cemetery**, with its diminutive memorials, can be glimpsed near Victoria Gate. It was opened in 1881 with the burial of a Maltese terrier named Cherry, but is now full and is closed to the public.

In the south part of the gardens is the Albert Memorial (*see p. 318*), behind which the charming Flower Walk leads west to the Broad Walk and Kensington Palace.

KENSINGTON PALACE

Map p. 602, A2. Open March–Oct daily 10–6, Nov–Feb daily 10–5; last entry 1hr before closing. Admission charge. Refreshments in Orangery. Shop. T: 0844 482 7777 (from within UK), hrp.org.uk.

The Jacobean mansion known as Kensington Palace was purchased by the Crown in 1689 and underwent a rapid architectural transformation under the supervision of Sir Christopher Wren, with Nicholas Hawksmoor as Clerk of the Works. William III and Mary II's new home was to be a winter retreat from the damp of Whitehall, a more suitable environment for the king, who suffered from asthma. It was always regarded as a private residence rather than a palace, though government business was conducted in the Council Chamber here in winter. Mary died at Kensington, of smallpox, in 1694, and it was to Kensington that William was carried following his fatal riding accident at Hampton Court. His successor, Queen Anne, spent much time at Kensington, apparently hating the 'stinking and close' air around St James's. It was here that she nursed her husband, Prince George of Denmark, whose death in 1708 'flung her into an unspeakable grief'; and it was also here that Anne herself died in 1714. Following the accession of George I, in 1718, an extensive new building programme saw the remodelling of the King's Apartments and their redecoration by William Kent. The apartments remain today as important early Hanoverian survivals.

After the death of George II in 1760, Kensington ceased to be a seat of the reigning monarch. Family members continued to use it, however. The lower floors were remodelled for Edward, Duke of Kent, the fourth son of George III, and it was here that his daughter, the future Queen Victoria, was born. She received the news of her accession here in 1837. From 1981 until her death in 1997, the palace was the home of Diana, Princess of Wales.

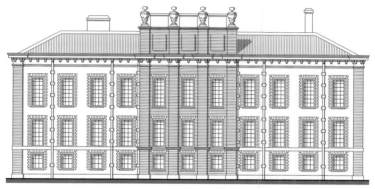

KENSINGTON PALACE: SOUTH FAÇADE

The main **south front** of the palace was added by William III in 1695: a handsome design in red brick, the four central Portland vases on the roofline were carved by Caius Gabriel Cibber. The **east façade**, part of George I's building campaign of 1718–21, is fronted by a seated marble statue of Queen Victoria, sculpted by her daughter Princess Louise (1893).

The King's Apartments

The sequence of rooms that are open for public visits begins with the **King's Staircase**, with painted decoration carried out by William Kent in 1725-7 for George I. The figures crowding against the *trompe l'oeil* balustrade, as if welcoming the king as he mounts the stairs, represent figures from his court, including his Polish page, his two Turkish Grooms of the Chamber, Mustapha and Mehmet, and 'Peter the Wild Boy', found living in the woods near Hanover and brought to England as a curiosity to be tamed. Kent himself appears on the ceiling. The **Presence Chamber**, used for formal receptions, has Italian 'grotesque' decoration on the ceiling, with Apollo in his chariot in the centre. The carved Grinling Gibbons overmantel was moved from William III's King's Gallery; its cupids, one cheerful, the other mournful, are apparently reflective of the death of Mary II in 1694. The **Privy Chamber**, used for more intimate and select audiences, retains its Kent ceiling, which shows Mars and Minerva resting on clouds, with symbols of the Arts and Sciences. The 1623–4 Mortlake tapestries (*see p. 495*) were made for Charles I when Prince of Wales.

The **Cupola Room** was one of the most important of the new rooms for George I. Lavishly decorated, it was the principal state apartment and a showcase for Kent, whose work at Kensington began here. Ionic pilasters with gilded fluting alternate with marble niches containing gilded lead statues of Roman deities. The bas-relief above the fireplace, by Rysbrack, depicts a Roman marriage. The blue and gold feigned coffering on the ceiling, giving an illusion of height, with the Garter Star in the centre, in fact follows an earlier design by the great Baroque artist Sir James Thornhill. As the king's official history painter, Thornhill may have expected to be awarded the Kensington commission, but the promotion of the new Palladianism saw Kent triumph. The **King's Drawing Room** was where the weekly court Drawing Rooms took place. Richly decorated with fine pictures from the Royal Collection hung against crimson damask, it has a fireplace and painted ceiling at its centre by Kent.

The **King's Gallery** retains its 1690s' carved cornice as well as the important wind-dial above the fireplace, made by Robert Morden in 1694. Points of the compass circle the map of the seas around Great Britain and a pointer, attached to the wind-vane on the roof, indicates the direction of the prevailing wind. Although not a great artist, Kent was a talented designer, and the entire decorative scheme, of white and gold woodwork and crimson wall-hangings and curtains, is his.

The Queen's Apartments

The apartments built for Queen Mary II in the early 1690s are the part of the palace which best retains its late 17th-century atmosphere. The **Queen's Staircase**, a plain and handsome space, was designed by Wren and retains some of its original sash windows. **Queen Mary's Gallery** was the richest and most grandly furnished of the queen's rooms. Her taste for oriental porcelain was given free rein here. It was massed in symmetrical, towering displays on lacquer cabinets placed between the windows, as well as above the doors and chimneypieces. The latter displays were set against looking glasses with elaborate carved surrounds, supplied by the royal cabinet maker Gerrit Jensen and by Grinling Gibbons. Displays of this nature were fashionable at the courts of Europe, and Mary was one of the chief promoters of the vogue in England. The richness of the room, with its expensive curtains (scarlet taffeta in winter and white flowered damask in summer), its porcelain and lacquerwork, would have been most apparent by candlelight.

The **Closet** contains portraits of Queen Anne in profile by Kneller, and George of Denmark by Michael Dahl (it was Anne's favourite image of her husband; she demanded to have it with her at St James's Palace after his death in 1708). It was in this room that Anne and her once-favourite, Sarah, Duchess of Marlborough, had their last, bitter quarrel in 1710.

Queen Mary's Drawing Room (hung with pictures from the Royal Collection) and her intimate **Bedchamber** (with original elm floorboards) complete the suite of apartments.

The Orangery

The gardens at Kensington were once very elaborate, but have long since disappeared. Queen Anne loved gardening and her most lasting achievement is the Orangery, designed by Hawksmoor (and altered by Sir John Vanbrugh), which housed plants in the winter and was used for entertainments in summer. It is now an elegant and airy restaurant (*see p. 336*) with, at either end, two magnificent carved vases by Cibber and Edward Pierce, originally from the gardens at Hampton Court but now placed here, safe from further weathering.

KENSINGTON PALACE GARDENS

The street which bounds the west side of Kensington Gardens (*map p. 602, A2*) is famed for having the highest house prices in London; indeed, they are some of the highest in the world. Some of the buildings are used as embassies; others have become homes for the international super-rich. At no. 8 was the London Cage, an interrogation centre for German prisoners of war set up in 1940. In 1863, Thackeray died at no. 2 Palace Green, a house that he had partly designed himself, in a style that Queen Victoria had been persuaded would not damage the prospect from Kensington Palace.

KNIGHTSBRIDGE & BELGRAVIA

Map pp. 602, C2–603, D3. Underground: Knightsbridge, Hyde Park Corner.

Knightsbridge extends from Sloane Street west to Exhibition Road and from that axis stretches south approximately to Cadogan Square. It is known chiefly as a shopping district: these are the purlieux of Harrods and Harvey Nichols, and residentially speaking, they harbour some of the most exclusive streets in the world.

SLOANE STREET

Harvey Nichols, on the corner of Knightsbridge and Sloane Street (*map p. 602, C2; harveynichols.com*), was founded on this site as a linen draper's by Benjamin Harvey in 1831. Today it is a luxury department store with branches around the world, including in Dubai, Riyadh and Kuwait. The present building dates from 1880. The Fifth Floor Foodmarket (with restaurant and café) is famous.

From here, Sloane Street extends south. Its upper part is lined with shops. At no. 55 is the **Danish Embassy**, designed by Arne Jacobsen (1978). The **Cadogan Hotel** at no. 75 (*cadogan.com*) was once the home of Lillie Langtry, mistress of Edward VII. After it became a hotel, it was patronised by Oscar Wilde, who was famously arrested here (from Room 118). The hotel is owned by Charles, 8th Earl Cadogan, whose family own much of this part of London (his heir is styled Viscount Chelsea) and have done since Elizabeth, daughter of Sir Hans Sloane (*see p. 354*) married the 2nd Baron Cadogan in 1717. The two families have lent their names to many of the streets in the area: Sloane Street, Cadogan Square, Hans Place. The building at no. 23 **Hans Place** stands on the site of the house where Jane Austen stayed with her brother Henry, while preparing *Emma* for publication. Hans Place today is entirely Victorian. It and the red-brick mansions of **Pont Street** (1870s) are built in a style for which Sir Osbert Lancaster coined the term 'Pont Street Dutch'. Strikingly positioned amid the gabled façades of Pont Street (corner of Lennox Street) is the Scottish church of **St Columba's** (*map p. 602, C3; stcolumbas.org.uk*), built by Sir Edward Maufe (1950–5) after the original church of 1884 was destroyed in the Blitz.

Beauchamp Place, leading into the Brompton Road, is lined with expensive boutiques. At no. 54 is the wonderful Map House, with an unrivalled collection of antiquarian maps, prints and globes (*themaphouse.com, T: 020 7589 4325*). The business was founded in 1907 and once supplied maps of Antarctica to Shackleton.

HARRODS

This (*map p. 602, C3; harrods.com*) is the largest department store in London, a place where historically it was claimed that anything could be bought from a pin to an elephant. It was first established on this site in 1849 by Charles Henry Harrod, grocer. Its present terracotta façade, strikingly picked out in lights at night, has become world-famous, as have the sage-green shopping bags with gold lettering. As Harrods developed into a department store, it began to aim at luxury: in 1898 the first 'moving staircase' in Britain was installed here and brandy and smelling salts were administered at the top to those for whom the automated journey had proved too gruelling. Harrods has remained at the top end of the market. The store is currently owned by the royal house of Qatar, who bought it from the Egyptian businessman Mohamed al-Fayed. Al-Fayed's son Dodi died in a car crash with Diana, Princess of Wales in 1997. The resulting froideur between Al-Fayed and the British royal family led to Harrods losing its royal warrant from the Duke of Edinburgh and renouncing the others, from the Queen, Queen Mother and Prince of Wales. The Egyptian Hall (with sculpted heads said to be modelled on the tycoon's own) was part of Al-Fayed's restoration and remodelling of the building. The beautiful Food Hall remains famous, not only for what it sells but for the environment in which the goods are displayed. The hall is adorned with faïence tiles designed by W.J. Neatby and made by Doulton (1902), depicting birds and flowers, fish and game. There are golden flying ducks on the ceiling.

HOLY TRINITY AND THE LONDON ORATORY

The church of the **Holy Trinity** stands end-on at the top of an avenue of trees (*map p. 602, C3*) Built in 1827 (chancel added by Blomfield in 1879), it was once the church of the rural parish of Brompton and is now known as the home of the evangelical Alpha course (*htb.org.uk*).

The imposing domed bulk of **Brompton Oratory** (*map p. 602, C3*), or the Church of the Immaculate Heart of Mary (1880–4, dome 1895–6), stands where Brompton Road meets Cromwell Road. It is one of the best-known Roman Catholic churches in the capital. It is served by the Community of Fathers, secular priests of the Congregation of the Oratory, which was founded in Rome by St Philip Neri in 1575. Oratorians came to England under the auspices of Cardinal Newman in 1848 and the church here was

HARRODS
A falconer, in Doulton tiles (1902), decorating the Food Hall.

founded by Father Wilfrid Faber, ancestor of Faber the publisher. The church both inside and out is in opulent (if rather tenebrous) Roman Counter-Reformation style, to designs by Herbert Gribble. It is remarkable in its solemnity, with a nave wider than that of St Paul's. The painting over the altar in the Chapel of St Philip Neri (north side) is a copy of the original by Guido Reni at Chiesa Nuova, Rome, where St Philip Neri is buried. The original Oratory in Rome (next to Chiesa Nuova) gave its name to the musical genre known as oratorio. Entirely appropriately, the London Oratory is known for its music (*bromptonoratory.com*).

BELGRAVIA

Belgravia began to be developed in the 1820s by Richard, 2nd Earl Grosvenor, later Marquess of Westminster. His surveyors were Thomas Cundy and his son, Thomas Cundy II, and his master builders were Thomas Cubitt, a former ship's carpenter who had already built speculative housing in other parts of London, and William Howard Seth-Smith. Cubitt lived at no. 3 Lyall St (*map p. 603, D3*) while building was in progress. The district survives remarkably intact and gives a vivid impression of London town life at the period, with wide streets lined by patrician residences backed by narrow cobbled carriage mews and stables. The centrepiece of the district is **Belgrave Square**, formed of white stucco terraces of a chilly hauteur (designed by George Basevi) with detached mansions at the corners and a central garden planted with shrubs and statuary. It is the home of ambassadors and oligarchs. At the top of the square (north) is a statue of Grosvenor, shown consulting an architect's plan, his foot on a milestone showing the distance to Chester (his country seat) and on the plinth a quotation from Ruskin intimating immortality. **Wilton Crescent** to the north was laid out by Cundy. In the mews behind, Wilton Row, where chauffeurs now nudge Bentleys into the old stables, is the Grenadier pub (*see p. 337*).

In **Motcomb Street**, lined with shops and restaurants, is the Doric colonnaded Pantechnicon, built in 1830 by Seth-Smith as fireproof warehouses and wine vaults (it burned down in 1874).

The Jumeirah Carlton Tower Hotel (1961, Michael Rosenauer) at no. 2 **Cadogan Place** incorporates copper panels, *Four Seasons*, on the south face by Elizabeth Frink, and artworks in the lobby and Rib Room restaurant by Feliks Topolski. William Wilberforce, the campaigner against slavery, died at no. 44 Cadogan Place in July 1833; the Slavery Abolition Act was passed in August of the same year.

At the corner of Upper Belgrave Street and **Eaton Square** is St Peter's (Henry Hakewill, 1827; enlarged by Blomfield, 1875; *map p. 603, D3*) with a tall and handsome Ionic portico. The church was gutted in an arson attack in 1987 and the interior (1990–1) is completely modern. Eaton Square itself, named after the Grosvenors' country seat of Eaton Hall, near Eccleston, Cheshire, is a long stretch of gardens flanked by white stucco terraces. Vivien Leigh and Laurence Olivier lived at no. 54 until their divorce in 1960. Leigh died here seven years later.

On the west corner of Eaton Place, a plaque at no. 99 records the first London concert given by Chopin (1848).

VICTORIA & PIMLICO

Map p. 603, E3–E4. Underground: Victoria, Pimlico.

Victoria lacks charm, but it is difficult to avoid it: it is a bustling and important transport hub. Victoria Station is one of London's busiest, serving Gatwick Airport, the south coast and the southeast suburbs. Victoria Coach Station on Buckingham Palace Road is the scene of incessant coming and going: the streets are choked with buses and coaches, thronged with people dragging wheelie luggage: there is an atmosphere of year-round transhumance.

North of Victoria Station, **Grosvenor Gardens** are two triangular patches of trees bisected by busy roads. In the southern triangle stands Georges Malissard's equestrian statue of Marshal Foch, supreme commander of the Allied Forces in 1918. Behind him is David Breuer-Weil's brobdingnagian *Alien* (2013), a colossal figure arranged as if apparently having plummeted head first to earth. Shell-adorned *cottages ornés* stand on either side. The northern triangle has a sculpture group of a lioness pursuing an antelope.

WESTMINSTER CATHEDRAL
Map p. 603, E3. Tower Viewing Gallery open Mon–Fri 9.30–5, Sat–Sun and bank holidays until 6. T: 020 7798 9055, westminstercathedral.org.uk.
Facing a broad modern piazza off the south side of Victoria Street is Westminster Cathedral, dedicated to the Most Precious Blood of Our Lord Jesus Christ. It is the seat of the Cardinal Archbishop of Westminster and the most important Roman Catholic

WESTMINSTER CATHEDRAL
Jesus Falls a Second Time (1917) by Eric Gill.

church in England. This extraordinary building—extraordinary, at least, in an English context—was completed in 1903 to designs by J.F. Bentley, who took his inspiration from early Christian basilicas, notably St Mark's in Venice and Haghia Sophia in Istanbul. The exterior of the church and its campanile are built in alternate courses of red brick and pale Portland stone. In the tympanum over the main entrance is a mosaic by Anning Bell (1916) showing Christ flanked by the Virgin and St Joseph with St Peter and Edward the Confessor. The Latin inscription is from John: 'I am the door: by me if any man enter in, he shall be saved.'

The vast and numinous interior is beautifully proportioned, and all the more atmospheric for being incomplete: the domes were to have been clad in mosaic and work is, in theory at least, ongoing. The walls and piers are revetted with coloured marbles supplied from Greece, Italy and North Africa by the Derbyshire-born marble merchant and stone carver William Brindley.

Nave: Two great **columns of red granite** (emblematic of the Precious Blood of Jesus to which the cathedral is dedicated) stand at the head of the nave. To the left is a bronze seated **statue of St Peter (1)**, modelled on that in St Peter's in Rome—and here, similarly, the faithful rub the saint's foot. The nave piers bear carvings in low relief by Eric Gill of the **Stations of the Cross**.

The **pulpit (2)** has fine Cosmati work. The **capitals of the nave pillars** are of many types, all of them based on the capitals in Haghia Sophia, with carved acanthus foliage deeply undercut so as to resemble lace.

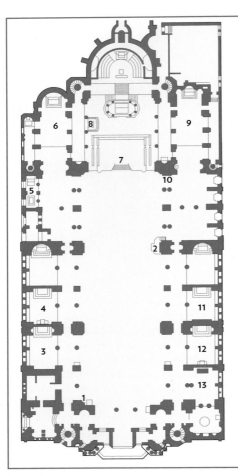

WESTMINSTER CATHEDRAL

1 Statue of St Peter
2 Pulpit
3 Holy Souls Chapel
4 Chapel of St George
5 Vaughan Chantry
6 Chapel of the Blessed Sacrament
7 Triumphal arch
8 Archbishop's throne
9 Lady Chapel
10 Alabaster *Madonna*
11 Chapel of St Andrew
12 Chapel of St Patrick
13 Chapel of SS Gregory and Augustine

North aisle: Though the architect Bentley died before the mosaic decoration could be carried out, he left instructions for it to be executed in a 'severe Greek style'. This is best seen in the **Holy Souls Chapel (3)**, where the scheme depicts the progress of the soul from the Fall (represented by Adam and the Tree) through the purifying fire of Purgatory (Shadrach, Meshach and Abednego in the Furnace) to the gift of eternal life (the Resurrected Christ). Here is displayed the body of John Southworth, a Catholic priest who was hung, drawn and quartered for his faith at Tyburn in 1654, during the Protectorate of Cromwell.

The next chapel, the **Chapel of St George (4)** has an altarpiece by Eric Gill showing *Christ Triumphant*, flanked by Thomas More (*see p. 313*) and Bishop John Fisher.

In the **Vaughan Chantry (5)** is the tomb of the founder of the Cathedral, Herbert Vaughan (d. 1903).

The **Chapel of the Blessed Sacrament** (**6**; *reserved for prayer*) is decorated with mosaics by Boris Anrep (1956–62): at either side of the entrance are a phoenix and a peacock, symbols of resurrection and eternal life.

East end: The great **rood** hanging from the triumphal arch **(7)** bears painted figures of Christ with the Evangelists in the terminals. The mosaic on the arch shows Christ seated on the rainbow with the Twelve Apostles and the symbols of the Evangelists. The high altar is surmounted by a white marble **baldachin** supported on eight monolithic columns of yellow Verona marble on pedestals of *verde antico*. The **Archbishop's throne**, to the left **(8)**, is a smaller-scale copy of the papal chair in St John Lateran at Rome.

South aisle: The **Lady Chapel (9)** contains a mosaic of the *Madonna* by Anning Bell. Above, in the conch, is a mosaic of the *Tree of Life* inspired by early mosaics in Rome.

Against the pier near the entrance is a much-venerated early 15th-century **Nottingham alabaster *Madonna* (10)**.

The **Chapel of St Andrew of Scotland (11)** is decorated with beautiful, shimmering Byzantinesque mosaics by Robert Schultz Weir showing cities associated with the saint: Patras, Constantinople and Bethsaida.

The **Chapel of St Patrick and the Saints of Ireland (12)** commemorates the Irishmen who fell in 1914–18. Each regiment has its own enamel plaque. The gilded bronze statue of the saint over the altar is by Arthur Pollen. The transenna that divides the chapel from the aisle features the shamrock of St Patrick and the oak leaves of St Bridget.

The **Chapel of SS Gregory and Augustine (13)** contains the tomb-slab of Cardinal Hume (d. 1999), who served as both Archbishop of Westminster and Cardinal-Priest in Rome from 1976. When a year before he death he applied to Pope John Paul II for permission to retire, his request was refused.

HORSEFERRY ROAD

South of Victoria Street, the cobbled **Strutton Ground** (*map p. 603, F3*) hosts a street-market selling clothes, flowers and food (*weekdays until 3pm*). To the west in Greycoat Place is the old Grey Coat Hospital, founded in 1698 and still a school for girls. On the pedimented façade below the clock tower, in niches, are statues of a boy and a girl pupil. Further south is **Vincent Square**, once a bear garden and now used as playing fields by Westminster School. On the north side of the square, at no. 80, are the Royal Horticultural Halls (1904 and 1928) belonging to the Royal Horticultural Society, founded in 1805 and well known for its flower shows. The halls are used as an events venue.

Horseferry Road leads from Strutton Ground towards the river, passing the Channel 4 headquarters at no. 124 (Richard Rogers, 1994), with an exterior lift and high tension steel cables supporting the glass atrium. Opposite, at no. 95, in the Territorial Army Centre, is the small **Museum of the London Scottish Regiment** (*open Tues, Wed and Thur by appointment only; archivistlsregt@aol.com, T: 020 7630 1639, london-*

scottishregt.org). At the end of Horseferry Road is **Lambeth Bridge** (Blomfield et al, 1932), replacing an earlier bridge of 1862, which in turn occupied the site of an ancient horse ferry to Lambeth. For many centuries there has been a busy river crossing here, between Lambeth Palace, the London home of the Archbishop of Canterbury, and the royal Palace of Westminster.

PIMLICO

The area hugged by the bend in the river between Lambeth Bridge and Chelsea Bridge is known as Pimlico (*map p. 603, F4–E4; Underground: Pimlico*), possibly named after a popular early 18th-century publican. Originally an area of marsh, it was developed from the mid-1820s for Richard Grosvenor by Thomas Cubitt, in a style less grand than that of Belgravia to the north, but perhaps less stand-offish and more pleasing. Many of Cubitt's porticoed and columned stucco houses and terraces have survived, and a **statue of Cubitt** himself (William Fawke, 1995) stands on the wedge-shaped corner where St George's Drive and Denbigh Street converge. He is shown in the attitude of surveying, rod in hand.

Mozart composed his first symphonies at **no. 180 Ebury St** in 1764 at the age of eight and a sculpture of the boy prodigy stands where Ebury Street meets Pimlico Road, at Orange Square (Philip Jackson, 1994). Close by is the neo-Gothic church of **St Barnabas** (*map p. 603, D4*), built in rusticated stone by Thomas Cundy in 1850 (spire rebuilt 2007). It was an early Anglo-Catholic foundation, which led to anxious mutterings about 'popery in Pimlico'. St Saviour's Church in Lupus Street and St Gabriel's in Warwick Square are also by Cundy.

Fronting the river in Grosvenor Road is **Dolphin Square** (*map p. 603, E4*), an early condominium built in 1937, when it was the largest block of flats in Europe, with over a thousand apartments and its own swimming pool and restaurant. To the west sprawls the housing estate of **Churchill Gardens** (Powell & Moya, 1946–62). In its day it aspired to be Utopia made manifest and was heated, via its tall, cylindrical accumulator tower, by hot water from Battersea Power Station.

MILLBANK

Millbank (*map p. 603, F4–F3*), the busy highway that skirts the Thames, takes its name from a former mill belonging to the monks of Westminster. In Riverside Walk Gardens, a short way downstream (north) of Vauxhall Bridge, is Henry Moore's ***Locking Piece*** (1963–4). A flight of steps between two huge bollards once led to the water here. Convicts from Millbank prison (on the site of Tate Britain; *see below*) were led down the steps onto ships bound for Australia. A plaque fixed to the surviving bollard (beside the riverside parapet) commemorates this.

On the opposite side of the road, on the corner building of Atterbury Street, a sculpted bronze figure impetuously springs forth amid a seemingly artless twist of drapery (which actually pins him to his plinth). This is ***Jeté***, by Enzo Plazzotta (1975), modelled on the great dancer David Wall, the youngest ever male lead in the Royal Ballet company (he was 21). Wall died in 2013.

TATE BRITAIN

Map p. 603, F3. Underground: Pimlico. Open daily 10–6, last admission 5.15. Free (except for special exhibitions). T: 020 7887 8888, tate.org.uk. Rex Whistler restaurant open daily for lunch and for afternoon tea Fri–Sun (to book, T: 020 7887 8825). Café and shop. Tate Britain and Tate Modern are linked by the Tate riverboat service (every 40mins during gallery opening hours; tickets can be bought online or T: 020 7887 8888). The exterior of the sleek catamaran (coloured spots) was designed by Damien Hirst.

Tate is in fact a family of galleries with a large collection displayed over four sites: two in London, Tate Britain and Tate Modern (*see p. 422*), as well as Tate Liverpool and Tate St Ives, in Cornwall. Tate has two roles: it houses the national collection of British art, from 1500 to the present day (at Tate Britain); and the national collection of post-1900 international art (at Tate Modern and outside London).

FOUNDATION, BUILDING AND GROWTH

Sir Henry Tate (1819–98), originally in the Liverpool grocery trade, began refining sugar in 1862 and was the pioneer producer, at his second refinery in London, of the new, patented commodity, cubed sugar. With the wealth this brought he began collecting modern British art and in 1889 he donated funds for the erection of a place to display it, as an annexe of the National Gallery. Work began in 1894 on the site of the old Millbank Penitentiary, formerly the largest prison in Europe, from where felons were dispatched to Australia. Sidney Smith's design, domed and temple-like, overlooks the river, its central portico surmounted by *Britannia*, flanked by the lion and the unicorn. This initial gallery has been added to many times to provide extra space for the expanding collection.

The gallery first opened in 1897 with displays of sentimental narrative pictures as well as Pre-Raphaelite works, including Millais' *Ophelia*. An increasing number of modern Continental works later came to be displayed here and in 1917 the Tate became the official home of modern foreign art as well as British. It was at the Tate that the great French Impressionist and Post-Impressionist pictures presented through the Hugh Lane Bequest and the Courtauld Fund were first shown. A conservative approach to modern art was, however, a defining feature of the Tate's early years. It was slow to acquire works by Cézanne; in the 1930s there was no German Expressionism and no Surrealism; and in the post-war years no Cubist works were purchased. This reluctance to engage with the avant garde hampered the formation of a modern art collection of weight and distinction.

Following the disastrous Thames flood of 1928, which engulfed the lower halls, damaged 18 works beyond repair and submerged J.M.W. Turner's portfolios and watercolours (which had to be spread out to dry on the upper floors), the art dealer Lord Duveen funded new exhibition rooms. Built in 1935–7 by the New York architect J. Russell Pope with Romaine-Walker and Jenkins, the imperious, monumental Duveens stretch like a great cathedral nave, vast and echoing, down the spine of the building.

Independence from the National Gallery came in 1955 and in the '60s and '70s the Tate became closely identified with contemporary art, staging live performance art and a succession of enthusiastically received exhibitions. The Turner Prize exhibition is held at Tate Britain every autumn (*see p. 306*). The building has recently undergone lavish refurbishment by Caruso St John Architects (completed 2013).

THE COLLECTION
The arrangement is chronological, devised as a 'Walk through British Art', with dates in the floors to orientate the visitor. The period rooms are interspersed with rooms devoted to single artists particularly associated with Tate.

Tudor and Stuart works
The earliest work in the collection is John Bettes' *A Man in a Black Cap* (1545), showing a plump man with an elaborately trimmed and parted beard. The fur around his neck is particularly well rendered. *The Cholmondeley Ladies* is a regional portrait of two women born, married and brought to bed on the same day: they sit in bed, stiffly painted in large starched ruffs, holding their tightly swaddled babies. The full-length *James Hamilton, 1st Duke of Hamilton*, standing in a deeply shadowed interior in fine red stockings, was painted by Daniel Mytens, who brought to England a new realism.

Anthony van Dyck, who became Chief Painter to Charles I, revolutionised portrait painting in Britain with his sophisticated handling of paint and the courtly swagger of his poses. The gallery also has a good collection of works by Sir Peter Lely, Chief Painter to Charles II; and an excellent collection of works by Sir Godfrey Kneller, the official painter of William and Mary, Anne and George I.

The second half of the 17th century witnessed a proliferation of new genres. *Monkeys and Dogs Playing* (1661) is by Francis Barlow, the first native-born landscape and animal artist; and there are still-life pieces by Edward Collier, collecting together objects symbolic of the transience of life.

The 18th century
One of the greatest painters of the Georgian age was William Hogarth, whose famous self-portrait, *The Painter and his Pug* (1745), has a palette in the foreground bearing the 'Line of Beauty', central to his ideas on harmony and beauty in art. Francis Hayman's portrait of the novelist Samuel Richardson, surrounded by his second wife and four daughters, is interesting for the clear influence it was to have on Gainsborough.

Grand Manner works from later in the century include portraits by Sir Joshua Reynolds, the Royal Academy's first President. Tate also has a large collection of works by Thomas Gainsborough, the other great portrait painter of the age (though his preferred inclination was landscape painting, of which the gallery has several important examples). Joseph Wright of Derby was another portraitist who turned his attention to other subjects, in his case the events and transformations of the Industrial Revolution and scientific invention. *An Iron Forge* (1772) is a superb example.

The lofty ideals of Neoclassical history painting are demonstrated in expansive images such as Benjamin West's *Pylades and Orestes brought as Victims before*

Iphigenia (1766). In John Singleton Copley's large and famous *The Death of Major Peirson, 6 January 1781*, the majesty of antiquity is applied to contemporary history.

There are also major works by the famous painter of horses, George Stubbs: *A Horse Frightened by a Lion* (1763) is among them, the horse's pose based on an antique sculpture. His *Haymakers* and its pendant *Reapers* show bucolic scenes in which the horse or horses are ancillary elements.

The Turner collection

Arguably the most famous of all British artists is J.M.W. Turner (1775–1851). His subjects were Classical mythology and history, contemporary events and natural disaster, painted with a concern for the changing atmospheric effects of light: golden sunsets, raging storms, tossing waves and enveloping mists. His early inspirations were Claude and Willem van de Velde the Younger: as his style developed, it became increasingly romantic and original, culminating in the great proto-Impressionist works for which he is so celebrated today. His brilliant image of the shadowy dome of the Salute looming out of the mist of the Venetian lagoon seems 'reminiscent' of Monet, even though it pre-dates Monet by almost half a century. Some of his work, where concrete forms are dissolved and diffused by the effects of light and colour, are almost abstract in feel. The Tate's vast collection incorporates all periods and aspects of Turner's art, as well as personal items such as his paintboxes. Highlights include his self-portrait of c. 1799; *Snow Storm: Hannibal and his Army Crossing the Alps*; *Norham Castle, Sunrise*; and the splendidly impressionistic *A Fire at the Tower of London*. There is also a wealth of watercolours and sketches demonstrating his evolution as an artist.

The Constable collection

John Constable (1776–1837) is one of Britain's most famous landscape artists. The collection ranges from early works painted in and around his native Suffolk to grander works, painted in London but based on previous sketches. Constable placed enormous emphasis on observation from nature, and on show are numerous rapidly executed and evocative sketches, of entire scenes or details such as scudding clouds. Highlights include *Flatford Mill*; *Fen Lane, East Bergholt*; *Hampstead Heath with a Rainbow*; *Stoke-by-Nayland*; *The Valley Farm*; and the *Sketch for 'Hadleigh Castle'*, a full-size sketch for a work exhibited at the Royal Academy in 1829, a working method Constable used when creating his famous 'six-footers'.

The Blake collection

Works by the visionary genius, artist and poet William Blake (1757–1827) have been an important component of the collection from its earliest years. Included are Blake's illustrations to Dante's *Divine Comedy* and other works which demonstrate Blake's very personal philosophy and iconography. Highlights include the large, colour-print *Newton* and *Elohim Creating Adam* (1795).

The 19th century

Landscape painting includes the Norwich School artists (John Sell Cotman's *Llanthony*

Abbey; 1801) as well as more monumental works such as James Ward's mighty *Gordale Scar*, a work of breathtaking proportions (sadly not on display at the time of writing). Not to be missed is Francis Danby's apocalyptic trio, *The Great Day of His Wrath, The Deluge* and *The Plains of Heaven* (1851–3). Richard Dadd's unfinished *The Fairy Feller's Master Stroke* was painted in Bethlem Hospital, where he was sent after murdering his father in 1843.

Tate's collection of Pre-Raphaelite works is outstanding. Among the many well-known major masterpieces are William Holman Hunt's *The Awakening Conscience* and Dante Gabriel Rossetti's *Ecce Ancilla Domini!, Beata Beatrix, Proserpine* and *Monna Vanna*. Sir John Everett Millais' *Ophelia* is one of the gallery's most popular pictures. Other familiar works are Henry Wallis's *Chatterton*, a romanticised view of the poet shortly after his suicide. Later works include Burne-Jones's extraordinary *Sisyphus* (c. 1870) and *The Golden Stairs* (1880), and Waterhouse's *Lady of Shalott* (1888).

The Tate's collection of late Victorian works includes paintings presented by G.F. Watts on the gallery's foundation and Frederic, Lord Leighton's heroic sculpture *An Athlete Wrestling with a Python*. William Powell Frith's *The Derby Day*, described by Ruskin as 'of the entirely popular manner of painting', created a sensation when exhibited at the Royal Academy in 1858 and was taken on a world tour. Sentimental narratives, ever popular at Royal Academy Summer Exhibitions, include Sir William Quiller Orchardson's *The First Cloud* (a married couple's first argument). Sir Frank Bramley's *A Hopeless Dawn*, a key work of the Newlyn School, shows the drama of ordinary lives as a young wife mourns her husband lost at sea.

James Abbott McNeill Whistler abandoned the Academy-led insistence on the importance of narrative and focused instead on the effects of light and atmosphere. His 'art for art's sake' aesthetic was fiercely attacked by Ruskin: *Nocturne in Blue and Gold: Old Battersea Bridge* (c. 1872–5) was painted as 'evidence' during the famous trial for libel after Ruskin had accused him of throwing a pot of paint in the face of the public—a case which Whistler won, but received damages of just one farthing. The Tate has an important collection of works by John Singer Sargent, including slick society portraits and the famous *Carnation, Lily, Lily, Rose* (1885–6), showing the pink glow of Chinese lanterns in the evening dusk.

Early 20th century

The response to Continental Post-Impressionism saw the emergence in England of a vigorous, innovative avant garde. The Camden Town Group, established in 1911 by Walter Sickert and others, produced sombre, realist, mainly urban scenes, including Sickert's own *La Hollandaise* (c. 1906), Harold Gilman's *Mrs Mounter at the Breakfast Table* (1916–17) and Charles Ginner's *From a Hampstead Window* (1923). Bloomsbury Group works, influenced by Cézanne and others, include paintings by Duncan Grant (*The Ass*, c. 1913) and Vanessa Bell (*Studland Beach*, c. 1912). Mark Gertler's highly original *Merry-go-Round* (1916) is a strident anti-war statement while Matthew Smith's *Nude, Fitzroy Street, No. 1* (1916), in its vivid use of colour, displays the influence of Matisse. Wyndham Lewis's *Workshop* (c .1914–15), David Bomberg's *The Mud Bath* (1914) and *In the Hold,* and works by Christopher Nevinson and other Vorticists, with their diagonals, fragmented geometry and emphasis on urban industrialism, display the influence of Cubism and Futurism.

The years following the First World War saw a return to more traditional, figurative painting. The dominant figure was Stanley Spencer, whose greatest work, *The Resurrection, Cookham* (1924–7), is a personal, religious vision of modern life. Also in the collection are sleepy views of rural England by John and Paul Nash, including *The Cornfield* and *Landscape at Iden*.

Mid-20th century

The great pioneers of modern sculpture in Britain were Jacob Epstein and Henri Gaudier-Brzeska. One of the most important and popular works is Epstein's massive *Jacob and the Angel* (1940–1), the angel's wings a great slab of alabaster.

Tate has an excellent collection of works by the outstanding figures of English abstraction, Barbara Hepworth, Henry Moore, Ben Nicholson and Paul Nash. Works include Nicholson's *1935 (white relief)* and *1956 (Val d'Orcia)*; Paul Nash's *Equivalents for the Megaliths* (1935); Edward Wadsworth's *Dux et Comes I* (1932), which is pure Surrealism; and Victor Pasmore's *Linear Motif in Black and White* (1960–1). Hepworth's *Three Forms* (1935), three white polished marble shapes of the utmost purity and simplicity, and *Pelagos* (1946) reflect her preoccupation with form. Henry Moore was the foremost British sculptor of the mid-20th century and one of the leaders in the revival of direct carving. Tate has a large collection of important works, including *Recumbent Figure* (1938). By 1939 Nicholson and Hepworth had moved to Cornwall, near St Ives, where a younger generation of artists was attracted. The St Ives School included Patrick Heron (*Azalea Garden: May 1956*) and Roger Hilton, whose *Oi Yoi Yoi* (1963) shows his naked wife jumping with rage during an argument.

The large collection of works by one of the most important 20th-century British artists, Francis Bacon, includes *Three Studies for Figures at the Base of a Crucifixion* (c. 1944).

British Pop artists of the late 1950s and '60s include Peter Blake (*On the Balcony*, 1955–7) and Richard Smith (*Piano*, 1963). A second phase of Pop was taken up by a group of artists trained at the Royal College of Art, including David Hockney (his witty Californian work *A Bigger Splash*; 1967) and Patrick Caulfield (*Greece Expiring on the Ruins of Missolonghi* and *Ruins* (1963 and 1964). The 'New Generation' of British sculptors, who moved from carved work to abstract constructions in industrial metals, brightly-painted steel, fibreglass and plastics, is represented by Sir Anthony Caro, Phillip King, Eduardo Paolozzi and William Turnbull.

Later 20th century

Works continuing the Realist or Figurative tradition include Graham Sutherland's landscapes and his portrait of Somerset Maugham; Lucian Freud's *Girl with a Kitten* (1947) and *Girl in a Striped Nightshirt* (1983–5); as well as works by Frank Auerbach, R.B. Kitaj and Leon Kossoff. The Tate has later important works by David Hockney, such as his enduringly popular *Mr and Mrs Clark and Percy* (showing the fashion designer Ossie Clark, a white cat on his lap, his toes buried in a hairy shagpile carpet, with his wife, the textile designer Celia Birtwell). Francis Bacon's *Triptych: August 1972* consists of three blurred and fused images of contemporary man based on the work of the pioneer stop-action photographer Eadweard Muybridge (*see p. 523*).

Since the 1970s, conceptual art and installations have been an important component of British modern art. Examples are Gilbert & George's 'sculpture on video tape' *In the Bush* (1972); Richard Long's sculptural interventions in the natural environment and indoor installations (*Slate Circle*, 1979; *South Bank Circle*, 1991); and Tony Cragg's *Stack* (1975). Sarah Lucas uses installation, sculpture and photography to explore self-perception and gender roles. In 2013 Tate stirred up controversy with its purchase of Martin Creed's *Work No. 227: The lights going on and off*, a Turner Prize-winner from 2001. It consists of an empty room where the lights flick on and off every few seconds.

THE TURNER PRIZE

The annual Turner Prize takes place at Tate Britain every autumn, with an exhibition of the work of four shortlisted artists (usually on show Oct–early Jan). The winner is usually announced in December. The genres of the entries are varied and include photomontage, sculpture, video, installation and painting (which tends to win least often). Recent winners include Rachel Whiteread, Antony Gormley, Grayson Perry (a ceramicist) and Susan Philipsz (the first sound artist to win). Turner Prize exhibitions have showcased the work of the Young British Artists, or YBAs, such as Damien Hirst and Tracey Emin, now household names (Hirst won in 1995 with his controversial cow in formaldehyde; Emin was a nominee in 1999, when she exhibited the equally controversial *My Bed*).

CHELSEA

Map pp. 603, D3–602, B4. Underground: Sloane Square.

Chelsea is an extremely attractive residential suburb extending for about one and a half miles along the bank of the Thames. Once a small fishing village, and until the 19th-century transport and housing boom, covered in gardens and orchards of fruit trees, it was relatively isolated from the rest of London. It has been the home of many eminent people, especially artists, who came here for the good light and the river-scape. Today it is a very pleasant—but also a very expensive—place to live.

SLOANE SQUARE

Sloane Square (*map p. 603, D3*) was laid out in the 1770s by Francis Holland and named after the lord of the manor, Sir Hans Sloane, the physician whose collections formed the nucleus of the British Museum (*see p. 354*). Sloane bought the manor in 1712 from Sir Charles Cheyne, though he did not take up residence in Chelsea until about 1742. In the centre, beneath plane trees, the **Venus fountain** is by Gilbert Ledward (1953).

The avant-garde Royal Court Theatre, next to the Underground, has been renowned for staging controversial and contemporary plays and works by new writers ever since its production of John Osborne's *Look Back in Anger* in 1956. On the north side of the square, a short way up Sloane Street, is the important Arts and Crafts **church of the Holy Trinity** (John Dando Sedding, 1888–90). The architect, who died just a year after the church's completion and who is commemorated within, wished to fill the building with painting and sculpture of a 'frank and fearless naturalism', celebrating the beauty of God's creation. The huge east window, with its stained-glass panels of saints, is by Burne-Jones and William Morris.

On the west corner of the square stands the department store **Peter Jones**, part of the John Lewis Partnership (*see p. 259*). The Modernist curtain-walled building, one of the first in the UK (1936), is by William Crabtree, of Slater, Crabtree and Moberly.

THE SLOANE RANGER

Sloane Square lends its name to the 'Sloane Ranger', or simply 'Sloane', a term invented in 1982 to describe a peculiarly British breed of person who was defined as young, upper middle class, privately educated, 'posh', not conspicuously bright, with a love of traditional country pursuits when not 'in Town', i.e. in Chelsea. Sloanes were educated together, lived, worked and socialised together and married within their class pack. The sexes each stuck to a separate uniform: Alice-bands and strings of cultured pearls for the girls, brogues and signet rings for the boys; both wore shirt collars turned up and sweaters and cardigans slung over the shoulders. Puffa and Barbour jackets were preferred outerwear; the Range Rovers they drove became known as Chelsea Tractors. Lady Diana Spencer, before her marriage to Prince Charles, was the Queen of Sloanes; in the 21st century, the Duchess of Cambridge is the 'Sloane on the throne'. Today's Sloane is leaner, better groomed and better educated, works in property or interior design and, due to escalating house prices, has been forced to colonise other areas of London, including Clapham, Battersea, Notting Hill and Chiswick. The Sloane epicentre is now Fulham (the White Horse pub in Parsons Green is popularly known as the Sloaney Pony). Further reading: *The Official Sloane Ranger Handbook: The First Guide to What Really Matters in Life* (Ann Barr and Peter York, 1982); *Cooler, Faster, More Expensive: The Return of the Sloane Ranger* (Peter York and Olivia Stewart-Liberty, 2007).

THE KING'S ROAD

Chelsea was once a fashionable resort, much patronised by Charles II and his court. King's Road, Chelsea's main artery (*map p. 602, C4*), was built as a private royal way linking Hampton Court with St James's. Three hundred years later, in the 1960s, it was at the cutting edge of fashion, rivalling Carnaby Street and frequented by the 'Chelsea Set', who came for the boutiques, clubs and bars. It is still Chelsea's main shopping street and in the small side streets are many attractive cottages and villas.

Opening out on the left-hand side is **Duke of York Square**, a public space surrounded by shops and cafés. The Neoclassical porticoed building known as the Duke of York's Headquarters was built in 1801 by John Sanders, a pupil of Soane, and used as a school for soldiers' orphans. It now houses the **Saatchi Gallery** (*saatchigallery.com; free*), a contemporary art space which exhibits pieces by artists whose work is rarely seen in the UK.

Set back from the King's Road at nos 152–154, behind an elaborate Georgian gateway with statues, is the former **Pheasantry**, so called because pheasants were once bred on the site for the royal household. The Russian ballet dancer Princess Seraphine Astafieva taught dance here from 1916; among her pupils were Alicia Markova and Dame Margot Fonteyn. Other famous residents have included Augustus John and Annigoni. A nightclub established in the basement was patronised by painters, writers and actors during the 1930s and '40s, and by Sloanes (*see above*) in the 1980s. The building is now a Pizza Express restaurant, ranged over three floors, with live jazz and cabaret in the basement.

Chelsea Old Town Hall, in neo-Baroque style, is by J.M. Brydon (1885–7) with later work by Leonard Stokes (1904–8). Sydney Street, which links the King's Road to the Fulham Road, is home to **Chelsea Farmers' Market**—with not a tiller of the soil in sight: this is an enclave of restaurants, cafés and shops focusing mainly on fashion. **St Luke's Church** (J. Savage, 1820–4), in warm yellow stone, is an early example of the Gothic Revival. Charles Dickens married Catherine Hogarth here in 1836. Twenty-two years and ten children later, the couple were to separate, after Catherine accidentally intercepted a piece of jewellery intended by Dickens for another, much younger, woman.

At 350 King's Road is the **Bluebird** (*see p. 338*), a 'gastrodome' opened in a former 1920s' garage in 1996 by Sir Terence Conran.

CHELSEA EMBANKMENT

From Sloane Square, Lower Sloane Street leads to Chelsea Bridge Road, passing on the right Royal Hospital Road, with an entrance to the Royal Hospital Chelsea (*see below*) and then the green expanse of Ranelagh Gardens, part of the Hospital grounds. On the left, just before Chelsea Bridge (1937), is the terracotta building of the former Lister Institute of Preventive Medicine, now a private hospital.

Chelsea Embankment (*map p. 603, D4*), built in 1874 to a design by Bazalgette, extends from Chelsea Bridge to Battersea Bridge, a distance of over a mile. This picturesque reach of the river, unfortunately marred by the incessant roaring traffic, is bordered on the south by new housing developments and Battersea Park, with its distinctive pagoda. Left of Chelsea Bridge, the Grosvenor Canal passes under the Embankment, near Bazalgette's attractive pumping station, with a tall chimney, looking like a French château. **Chelsea Bridge** itself was built in 1937, replacing an earlier structure which had become too narrow for the volume of traffic. Walk along the Embankment with the river on your left and the railings of Ranelagh Gardens on your right, until you come to an entrance to the Royal Hospital; here is a fine view of the beautiful brick buildings and gardens.

ROYAL HOSPITAL CHELSEA

Map p. 603, D4. Guided tours (approx. 90mins) can be booked Mon–Fri. Museum open

Mon–Fri 10–4 (closed bank holidays). Admission charge. Shop. T: 020 7881 5516, chelsea-pensioners.co.uk.

The Hospital was conceived by Charles II, possibly in emulation of Louis XIV's Les Invalides in Paris, as a retirement home for soldiers 'broken by age or war'. Sir Christopher Wren was appointed architect and Sir Stephen Fox was charged with coming up with the necessary funds. The buildings were completed in 1692 and later added to by Robert Adam and Sir John Soane; they have been restored since bomb damage during both world wars. The Hospital is home to around 400 pensioners, veterans of the British armed forces, who are boarded, lodged and nursed when ill, and who wear distinctive long scarlet coats. On Founder's Day, also known as Oak Apple Day, held around 29th May (as near to Charles II's birthday as possible), the Pensioners are reviewed by a member of the Royal Family. All participants wear sprigs of oak leaves in memory of Charles II, who hid in an oak tree after his escape from Parliamentarians at the Battle of Worcester in 1651; oak leaves are used to decorate Charles II's gilded statue (*see below*).

The central portion of the building, known as the **Figure Court**, dates from 1688. The Doric portico, flanked by a low colonnade with coupled columns, is surmounted by a small tower and cupola. The inscription along the colonnade commemorates the Hospital's foundation and establishment by Charles II and James II and its completion by William and Mary. In the projecting four-storey wings, known as **Long Wards**, are the pensioners' individual berths. The statue of Charles II as a Roman general is by Grinling Gibbons (1676); originally gilded, it was bronzed in the 18th century until re-gilding took place in 2002, in celebration of the Queen's Golden Jubilee.

The Figure Court leads to the **Chapel** (1681–7), with handsome oak carving by William Emmett, Grinling Gibbons's predecessor as royal carver. The organ case is by Renatus Harris. The painting of the *Resurrection* in the apse is by Sebastiano Ricci and his nephew Marco (1716, restored). The **Great Hall** is lined with portraits of monarchs and military heroes, including a huge equestrian portrait of Charles II, begun by Verrio and completed by Henry Cooke. The body of Wellington lay in state here in 1852.

The grounds are beautifully maintained: to the south, overlooking the river, they were severely truncated by the construction of the Chelsea Embankment in 1874. Before this, they were one of the Hospital's proudest features, laid out in the 1690s by George London and Henry Wise, the royal gardeners, with canals and avenues providing glorious settings for Wren's gazebos and summer houses. The gardens to the east, **Ranelagh Gardens**, were formerly those of Ranelagh House (Lord Ranelagh was the first Hospital treasurer and built himself a house on the site). During the 18th century they were fashionable pleasure gardens; in the centre was a huge rotunda (1742), long since disappeared. The area hosts the annual Chelsea Flower Show during the third week of May.

In the Secretary's Office Block is the **Museum**, which has photographs, prints, uniforms, medals, pewter, arms, etc., and a portrait of the pensioner William Hiseland, who served 80 years in the army and died in 1732 at the age of 112.

The East Walk emerges in Royal Hospital Road beside the **graveyard** (closed in 1854), where Dr Charles Burney, Hospital organist, is buried (d. 1814).

The **National Army Museum** occupies a purpose-built building (1971) further west (*map p. 602, C4*). Its collection illustrates, celebrates and records the history of the army from 1415 (the Battle of Agincourt) to the present day (*open daily 10–5.30; free; shop; T: 020 7730 0717, nam.ac.uk*).

Tite Street, whose enfilade of 19th-century mock-Queen Anne houses intersects Royal Hospital Road beyond the National Army Museum, was once home to a colony of writers and artists. It was the residence for 24 years of John Singer Sargent, who died at no. 31 in 1925. No. 34 was the home of Oscar Wilde from 1884–95. Opposite is the site of the White House, built for Whistler but occupied by him for a few months only in 1878–9; he lived also at no. 13 (in 1881–5) and at no. 46 (in 1888). Whistler is famous for his Thameside *Nocturnes*, painted in Chelsea in the 1870s (*for the famous libel case, see p. 304*). A tablet at no. 23 Tedworth Square, to the north, marks the London residence of Mark Twain.

CHELSEA PHYSIC GARDEN

66 Royal Hospital Rd. Map p. 602, C4. Open April–Oct 11–6 and during the winter 'snow-drop days'. Admission charge. Café. T: 020 7352 5656, chelseaphysicgarden.co.uk.

The entrance to this enchanting, secret garden is in Swan Walk. The Garden was founded in 1673 as the Apothecaries' Garden; the Society of Apothecaries used it to train apprentices in plant identification and it was sited near the river to create a microclimate favourable to the cultivation of non-native species from warmer climes. The apothecaries also used the river as a transport route, setting forth on their barge on 'herborising' expeditions. In 1685, John Evelyn noted the garden's heated green-house, probably the first in Europe. When the former apothecary student Sir Hans Sloane (a copy of whose 1733 statue by Rysbrack stands in the garden) purchased the Manor of Chelsea in 1714, he leased the four acres to the Society of Apothecaries for £5 a year in perpetuity, on condition that it was maintained as a physic garden forever. A deed of covenant of 1722 requested that 2,000 specimens of distinct plants grown in the garden should be sent to the Royal Society 'well dried and preserved', in annual instalments of 50—and the condition was amply fulfilled: by 1795 the Royal Society had received 3,700 specimens. Today the garden continues to publish an *Index Seminum* and exchanges seeds with several hundred botanic gardens around the world. Sloane appointed Philip Miller as Gardener (curator). Miller, whose *Gardener's Dictionary* became a seminal work, made the garden world famous and trained William Aiton, the first Gardener at Kew. In 1736 the Swedish botanist Linnaeus visited the garden to collect plants and specimens and Mrs Elizabeth Blackwell illustrated her *Curious Herbal* (1739) by drawing plants here.

Today, the garden is run as a charity and is open to the public. It follows a formal layout and the plants are grown according to their classification, with many rare speci-mens. Explore the rock garden, completed in 1733, and the herb garden and borders of perfumery plants. The Garden of World Medicine, in the northeast quadrant, includes 150 species from eight different cultures around the world. A research and environ-mental education centre opened in spring 1997. The garden's licensed café, Tangerine Dream, serves salads, steaks and fish, all London-sourced.

CHEYNE WALK AND CARLYLE'S HOUSE

Meandering along the Embankment is historic Cheyne Walk (*map p. 602, C4*), with early 18th-century houses separated by narrow public gardens. No. 4 was occupied by George Eliot (d. 1880) during the last three weeks of her life. No. 16, the Queen's House, is erroneously connected with Catherine of Braganza, Charles II's consort, though it was not built until 1717, twelve years after her death. The fine railings are by Thomas Robinson. Dante Gabriel Rossetti lived at no. 16 in 1862–82, keeping his menagerie in the garden; later residents were Swinburne and George Meredith. Known as Tudor House, it too was built in 1717 and later extended by Lutyens. A memorial fountain to Rossetti in the Embankment Gardens, with a medallion by Ford Madox Brown (1887), faces the house. At no. 18 was the celebrated 'Don Saltero's' coffee house, owned by a proprietor named Salter, who also exhibited a museum of curios here, some of them gifts from Sir Hans Sloane. On the site of nos 19–26 stood the manor house which Henry VIII gave to Catherine Parr, his sixth and final wife, as a wedding present (he acquired the Manor of Chelsea in 1536). Here Princess (afterwards Queen) Elizabeth seems to have spent the interval between the execution of her mother, Anne Boleyn, and the death of her father. Anne of Cleves, Henry's fourth wife, died here in 1557. A plaque records that the manor house was demolished in 1753, after the death of its last occupant, Sir Hans Sloane. The old manor house garden lies beyond the end wall of Cheyne Mews and is said to contain mulberry trees planted by Elizabeth I.

Cross over Oakley Street, with Albert Bridge (1873) on your left. Cheyne Walk continues west. Nos 38 and 39 are by C.R. Ashbee, designer of many Chelsea homes (though few survive). In the gardens is a statue of Thomas Carlyle (Boehm, 1882), honouring the writer and historian known as the 'Sage of Chelsea'. In Cheyne Row, a sedate Queen Anne terrace of 1708, is **Carlyle's House** (*open March–Oct; T: 020 7352 7087*). Carlyle and his wife Jane, known for her beauty, intelligence and wit, moved here from Scotland in 1834 and remained until their deaths. The house is largely unchanged and, though the couple's relationship was often tempestuous, an atmosphere of quiet simplicity remains. It was here that Carlyle wrote *The French Revolution* (1837) and *On Heroes, Hero Worship and the Heroic in History* (1841), in which he outlined his theories on the importance of powerful and conviction-led individuals. The house is run by the National Trust and the rooms contain many of the original furnishings. The Sitting Room/Parlour is furnished much as it appears in Robert Tait's painting, *A Chelsea Interior* (c. 1857), which hangs here. Mrs Carlyle was irritated that Tait had made her dog Nero look the size of a sheep (her death was caused by an attack of shock when Nero escaped from the carriage at Hyde Park Corner). Downstairs, the Kitchen is little altered. Here Carlyle would smoke with Tennyson, and it was also where Mrs Carlyle's domestic servant (she was a difficult woman to work for and got through several) slept. Upstairs is the Library/Drawing Room, where Carlyle wrote *The French Revolution*. The Attic Study was built for Carlyle by the firm of Cubitt in 1853 as a sound-proof retreat. Unfortunately it actually amplified noise from the Thames, but nevertheless Carlyle used it for twelve years, until his biography of Frederick the Great was complete. The garden, with its walnut and cherry trees and lilac bushes, is much as it would have been in Carlyle's day. Nero is buried about 5ft from the southeast corner.

Further north is Glebe Place. The house at no. 35 is by Philip Webb (1868). It was used as Uncle Monty's house in the 1987 film *Withnail and I*. No. 49 is by Charles Rennie Mackintosh (1920), his only London work.

CHELSEA OLD CHURCH

The red-brick Chelsea Old Church (*map p. 602, C4; normally open Tues–Thur 2–4; entrance round the far corner in Old Church St; chelseaoldchurch.org.uk*) preserves the tomb of Sir Hans Sloane (*see pp. 310 and 354*) in the corner plot, behind the railings. The church was probably founded in the 12th century; Sir Thomas More and his family worshipped here. More settled in Chelsea around 1520; the site of his large house, with extensive grounds stretching down to the river, is on Beaufort Street (*see below*). The church, along with its many fine funerary monuments, was badly damaged by a parachute-bomb in the Second World War and has been largely rebuilt and the monuments painstakingly restored.

By the first window on the right is a small **chained library** of books given to the church by Sir Hans Sloane, including two volumes of Foxe's *Book of Martyrs* (1684). Close by is a monument to Lord and Lady Dacre, with alabaster effigies (1595).

The South Chapel (or **More Chapel**) was almost undamaged by the bombing and dates from 1325; it was rebuilt by Sir Thomas More in 1528 for his private use. The archway between it and the chancel is a reproduction of the 14th-century one but the capitals were carved in More's lifetime, c. 1528, and are similar to those on Pietro Torrigiano's tomb of Henry VII in Westminster Abbey. In the corner by the altar, on the right, is the tomb of Jane, Duchess of Northumberland (d. 1555), mother of Robert Dudley, Earl of Leicester (the favourite of Elizabeth I), mother-in-law of Lady Jane Grey, and grandmother of the poet Sir Philip Sidney. The tomb, which resembles Chaucer's in Westminster Abbey, has been much mutilated.

On the south side of the chancel is the **More Monument** (1532), designed by Sir Thomas More while still in royal favour, with a long inscription composed by him in memory of his first wife. It is almost certainly a cenotaph: More's head is in Canterbury and the whereabouts of his body are unknown. On the north side of the chancel is the tomb of Sir Edmund Bray (1539). Above it is the late 16th-century monument of Thomas Hungerford and his family. There is a wall-tablet to the novelist Henry James, who died in Chelsea 1916 and 'who renounced a cherished citizenship to give his allegiance to England in the first year of the Great War'.

The North Chapel (or Lawrence Chapel; 1325 but rebuilt) is entered by an archway of 1563; the arch is itself a monument to Richard Jervoise. The **monument to Charles Cheyne**, Viscount Newhaven and his wife Jane (1672), is by Paolo Bernini, son of the famous Gian Lorenzo, with an effigy by Bernini's great assistant Antonio Raggi. Henry VIII is said to have been secretly married here to Jane Seymour, some days before their public marriage.

Outside the church, in the gardens overlooking the river, is a seated **statue of Sir Thomas More** in black and gold (L. Cubitt Bevis, 1969). Over the junction with Old Church Street, in Ropers Gardens (named after Thomas More's son-in-law William Roper), is an unfinished bas-relief by Jacob Epstein, on the site of his studio (1909–14).

SIR THOMAS MORE

Thomas More was born into a prosperous family in the City of London in 1478. He studied first at Oxford before returning to London to study Law at Lincoln's Inn. As an adolescent he began to experience profound religious leanings—but More was ambitious as well as ascetic and in the end he married and took up a political career, becoming under-sheriff of London in 1510. Meanwhile he had met and befriended the Dutch Humanist Erasmus, and the two were to remain firm friends, collaborating on translations of works from Latin as well as producing original works of their own (More's *Utopia* and Erasmus' *In Praise of Folly*). More's abilities were greatly appreciated by Henry VIII, who noted his reputation for fairness and firmness. When Henry went to France to meet François I on the Field of the Cloth of Gold to discuss a lasting peace, he took More with him, and More helped Henry to compose his repudiation of Luther (for which Pope Leo X was to reward him with the title Defender of the Faith, a title still held by the British sovereign). More was knighted and numerous honours were heaped upon him. He was appointed Speaker of the House of Commons in 1523 and, after the downfall of Cardinal Wolsey in 1529, Lord Chancellor. But the same thorny thicket as had trapped Wolsey was to prove More's own undoing. More had not supported Henry's divorce proceedings; in 1533 he refused to attend the coronation of Anne Boleyn. In the spring of 1534, More refused to agree to the Act of Succession, which debarred Katherine of Aragon's daughter Mary from acceding to the throne; nor would he swear the Oath of Supremacy, recognising Henry as head of the Church of England. He was committed to the Tower, found guilty of treason, and beheaded the following year, alongside Bishop Fisher. In 1935 he was canonised by Pope Pius XI. He is the patron saint of lawyers.

CROSBY HALL

Past the junction with Danvers Street (*map p. 602, B4*) stands Crosby Hall, the surviving part of a medieval mansion brought from the City in 1910 and re-erected as far as possible with the careful retention of its original features. Its original site was Crosby Place, Bishopsgate, where it was built in 1466–75 by Sir John Crosby, a rich textiles trader and freeman of the Grocers' Company. A later resident, in 1483, was Richard, Duke of Gloucester, soon to be Richard III. Around 1523 it was bought by Sir Thomas More—whose Chelsea garden coincidentally once included the plot on which the hall is sited today—and More's daughter and son-in-law Margaret and William Roper later occupied it. In the 16th century the mansion was considered sumptuous enough to be the abode of various ambassadors.

Though the hall escaped the Great Fire, its fate was a chequered one until its purchase in 1908 by the University and City Association of London and its removal here by the architect Walter Godfrey, who added a 1920s' neo-Tudor block when it was used as the college hall of the British Federation of University Women. The interior (*no admission*) retains a fine oriel window and the original scissor ceiling covered in gold bosses, and contains a copy of Holbein's lost group of *Sir Thomas More's family* (c. 1527). In 1989 it was bought by the millionaire Christopher Moran, who has recreated a Tudor palace around it.

WEST TO CHELSEA WHARF

Further west along the Embankment is **Beaufort Street** (*map p. 602, B4*), where Sir Thomas More's mansion once stood; fragments of his orchard wall border the gardens of the houses in Paulton's Square. **Battersea Bridge**, an iron structure (1890) spans the river at the end of Beaufort Street; it replaced a picturesque old wooden bridge of 1771–2, which was a favourite subject with Whistler and other artists. The river, with many new blocks of flats opposite, here bends south, and has offered moorings for brightly-painted house-boats since the 1930s.

Beyond Beaufort Street is the western part of Cheyne Walk. Mrs Gaskell was born at no. 93 in 1810. Nos 95–100 make up Lindsey House (1674), the only surviving 17th-century mansion in Chelsea; it is now subdivided and largely invisible behind the high riverside fences. Whistler lived at no. 96 in 1866–78, and no. 98 was the home of the Brunels, father and son. The painter P. Wilson Steer died at no. 109 in 1942. At no. 119 J.M.W. Turner lived anonymously, in retirement, from 1846. He died here in 1851.

At the end of Cheyne Walk is Lots Road (at no. 114, the Lots Road Pub and Dining Room is good for a pit stop; from here you can walk up to the King's Road). In the vicinity, the eight-acre site with its vast disused power station (1904; listed) is being redeveloped as Chelsea Waterfront, with over 700 new homes. **Chelsea Wharf** (*map p. 596, C3*) has been converted into workshops and design studios; the gates in the adjoining gardens are from Cremorne Gardens—a popular pleasure garden which closed in 1877. Chelsea Harbour, with the distinctive pagoda-like Belvedere Tower, was constructed on 20 acres of derelict land used as a coal depot. The development includes luxury homes, a marina, hotel, shops, restaurants and offices. Adjacent is a similar mixed-use modern development, Imperial Wharf (Imperial Wharf station operates train services across the river to Clapham Junction).

FULHAM

Map pp. 602, A4 and 596. Underground: West Brompton, Putney Bridge.

Fulham occupies a broad peninsula on the north bank of the Thames. Its riverside variously overlooks Battersea, Wandsworth, Putney and Barnes. Excavations near the river have revealed evidence of Neolithic and Roman settlements. In the 18th century, Fulham was a gentleman's retreat and several Georgian residences were built. From the late 19th century the area was built up with streets and terraces intended for the lower middle classes; by the mid-20th century Fulham was almost entirely a working-class community with a thriving river industry in the marshy district known as Sand's End, today occupied by Chelsea Harbour and Imperial Wharf. White earthenware vases—Fulham Vases—were made by the Fulham Pottery (established 1672) on the New King's Road until the 1970s. After World War Two, several council estates were built around West Kensington. Today, despite the congested and grimy character of some of the main roads, Fulham is ultra-respectable, especially popular with middle-class professionals. It is, in fact the Sloane epicentre (*see p. 307*). The small, former working-class terraces now command high prices and there are plenty of lively bars and restaurants.

Brompton Cemetery (*map p. 602, A4; Underground: West Brompton*), also known as the West London and Westminster Cemetery, opened in 1840. Surrounded by catacombs, it has a triumphal arch at the entrance. Many soldiers are buried here, due to the proximity of the Royal Hospital, Chelsea. Also here are Emmeline Pankhurst (d. 1928) and the master mason Thomas Cundy, who built so many of the streets and squares in this part of London.

The southern end of the cemetery leads into Fulham Road, lined with shops and restaurants. Left (over a barely-noticeable bridge which takes you over Chelsea Creek) is Stamford Bridge, the grounds of **Chelsea Football Club**. On match days this whole area is choked with barely-moving traffic. Fulham Broadway is the administrative centre of Fulham; the neo-Renaissance Town Hall was built in the 1880s.

PUTNEY BRIDGE AND FULHAM RIVERSIDE

The river is a short walk from Putney Bridge Station. The railway bridge was constructed for the London and South Western Railway in 1887–9; it is now used by the District Line. The curving grey **Putney Bridge** (*map p. 596, B3; see p. 496*) connects Fulham with Putney. Ranelagh Gardens on the left of the bridge leads to the **Hurlingham Club**, once famous for polo and now famed for the length of its waiting lists (*hurlinghamclub.org.uk*). On the right of the bridge, opposite Putney's boat clubs, stretches Bishops Park, home of Fulham Palace (*see below*). By Putney Bridge, tucked behind trees, is the parish church of **All Saints** (*allsaint-fulham.org.uk*), with a Kentish ragstone tower dating from the 1440s. The rest of the church was rebuilt in Gothic style in the 1840s and 1880s. Inside there is a fine collection of monuments from the earlier church. Ten Bishops of London are buried here.

Fulham Palace, overlooking the Thames in Bishop's Park (*map p. 596, B3*), was the official residence of the Bishop of London from 704 until 1973. The attractive red-brick Tudor quadrangle has Georgian additions and an adjoining Victorian chapel by William Butterfield, (1866–7). The buildings have been much restored and the early 19th-century wing, formerly the Bishop's dining room and library, houses the Museum of Fulham Palace (*open Sat–Wed 1–4; free; T: 020 7610 7165, fulhampalace.org*), which traces the history of the Bishops of London and Fulham Palace itself, with a small collection of pictures, stained glass and archaeological finds. The surrounding **botanical gardens** (*open daily dawn–dusk; free*) were made famous in the 17th century by Bishop Compton, who introduced many rare species, some never grown in Europe before. Originally the gardens covered 36 acres and were surrounded by a moat. Today, the remaining 13 acres are of 19th-century layout with relics of 18th-century landscaping and some rare trees, including an ancient oak which is estimated to be 450 years old. The Walled Garden has been replanted to its original 1830s' design, its derelict bothies restored and the curving wall of the Victorian vinery, where grapes and pineapples were once grown, reconstructed as a glasshouse.

KENSINGTON

Map p. 602, B2–B3. Underground: South Kensington, Gloucester Road, High Street Kensington.

Kensington is a largely residential area, leafy and well-mannered, containing some of the most desirable street addresses in London. It was made a royal borough after the death of Queen Victoria in 1901, in accordance with her express wish (she was born here; *see p. 291*). In 1965, it was amalgamated with Chelsea. During the 19th century, artists and writers settled in Kensington, around Holland Park and further west. Two artists' homes are preserved as museums—those of the painter Lord Leighton and the cartoonist Linley Sambourne—and many houses bear plaques commemorating famous literary residents: Macaulay, Browning, Henry James, Virginia Woolf, Newbolt, Galsworthy and Thackeray all either were born, died or resided here.

Brompton Road leads south through an area of stately squares and crescents (Alexander Place, Thurloe Square, Egerton Crescent) built in 1820–40. At Brompton Cross, where Brompton Road meets the Fulham Road, is the striking **Michelin House** (*map p. 602, C3*), previously headquarters for the Michelin Tyre Co., begun in 1909 and featuring colourful ceramic panels of racing cars and stained glass showing the Michelin Man himself, Bibendum. It now houses a well-known restaurant and oyster bar (*see p. 336*).

Cromwell Road further north is named from a vanished house of Henry Cromwell, fourth son of the Protector. On the south side, opposite a flank of the V&A, stands the striking **Ismaili Centre** (Casson Conder Partnership, 1985), its teak and bevelled glass windows a nod to the *mashrabiyah* screen. It is a meeting point for Shia Ismaili Muslims (whose spiritual leader is His Highness the Aga Khan).

ALBERTOPOLIS

The area of South Kensington around Exhibition Road (*map p. 602, B3*) is sometimes known as 'Albertopolis', after Albert, the Prince Consort, husband of Queen Victoria, who dreamed of bringing the Arts and Sciences together in a single, publicly-available cluster, inspired and in part financed by the Great Exhibition of 1851. His legacy includes the Royal Albert Hall, the V&A, the Natural History Museum, Science Museum and the Royal Colleges of Art and Music.

On Exhibition Road, which runs between the Natural History and Victoria & Albert museums, is the **Hyde Park Chapel** (1959–61), or Church of Jesus Christ of Latter-Day Saints (the Mormons), with a slim flèche covered in gold leaf. On either side of the road are buildings belonging to **Imperial College London** (The Imperial College of Science, Technology and Medicine), an independent university with a fine reputation. In Prince Consort Road is the **Royal College of Music**, occupying a building by Blomfield in 'French baronial' style (1884). The collection in their museum (*open during term time Tues–Fri 11.30–4.30; free; T: 020 7591 4842, rcm.ac.uk*) includes musical

ALBERT MEMORIAL
The bull, symbol of the continent of Europe (Patrick McDowell, 1876).

instruments from 1500 to the present day: the 'clavicytherium' of c. 1480 is the oldest surviving stringed keyboard instrument in the world.

Opposite the Royal College of Music, the Queen Elizabeth II Diamond Jubilee Steps lead up past a bronze statue of Prince Albert, commemorating the Great Exhibition of 1851, curated by Albert '*in pulcherrimis illis hortis*'. Behind the statue stands the Royal Albert Hall.

ROYAL ALBERT HALL AND ALBERT MEMORIAL

Map p. 602, B2–B3. Box office open daily 9–9; T: 0845 401 5045, royalalberthall.com. The Café Bar is open to non-ticket holders. Other restaurants are not.

A hybrid creation, part-Colosseum, part-Pantheon, the concert arena known as the **Royal Albert Hall** was clearly inspired by the architecture of ancient Rome. It was designed by two members of the Royal Engineers, Francis Fowke and Henry Scott, and opened in 1871 as the centrepiece of a cultural campus of the Arts and Sciences that had been planned by Prince Albert. Around the exterior drum of the shallow glass dome runs a continuous terracotta mosaic frieze depicting the continents of the Earth bringing forth the fruits of their labour, with an inscription proclaiming 'Glory be to God on high and on earth peace: this hall was erected for the advancement of the Arts and Sciences and works of Industry of all nations.' The interior auditorium has

KENSINGTON GORE

Ornamented brick gable end on the Royal Geographical Society building, the former Lowther Lodge, with the initials of its builder, the diplomat William Lowther, and his wife Alice.

a capacity of over 5,000 and a celebrated Willis organ, described by one of its hearers as possessing 'the voice of Jupiter'. The famous concert series known as the 'Proms' is held here annually from July–Sept. The name derives from the open-air 'promenade' concerts that took place in London's pleasure gardens. 'Proms in the Park' is still an important feature of the concert series.

Facing the Albert Hall is the **Albert Memorial** (*map p. 602, B3*), the national monument to Prince Albert of Saxe-Coburg Gotha, consort of Queen Victoria, who died in 1861 aged 42. The monument, unabashedly gaudy, was designed by Sir George Gilbert Scott in 1872 and unveiled by the Queen four years later. At the centre, beneath a canopy spire, is a seated statue of the prince (John Henry Foley, 1876), dazzlingly gilded and holding the catalogue of the Great Exhibition. The pedestal is decorated with a marble frieze of artists and scientists through the ages above which, at the four corners, are allegorical groups representing Agriculture, Engineering, Commerce and Manufacturing. The mosaics which decorate the canopy were designed by Clayton and Bell. Much of the decorative carving was carried out by William Brindley, who collaborated with George Gilbert Scott on St Pancras Station and whom the great architect described as 'the best carver I have met with and the one who best understands my views.' At the outer corners of the enclosure are further sculptural groups depicting the continents of Europe, Asia, Africa and America, each with a totem animal.

KENSINGTON GORE

Kensington Gore (*map p. 602, B2*) takes its name from Gore House, a property used as a restaurant by Alexis Soyer to feed visitors to the Great Exhibition. When the Exhibition closed, the building was pulled down to make way for the development of Albertopolis. Alexis Soyer took his culinary skills to the battlefields of the Crimea.

On the corner of Exhibition Road is the **Royal Geographical Society** (*rgs.org.uk*), in a red-brick Queen Anne-style building by Norman Shaw (1874), built as a town residence for William Lowther, diplomat and member of parliament, and his wife Alice (their initials adorn a brick gable end, with a huge sunflower growing between them). It was bought by the Society in 1912 and statues of Sir Ernest Shackleton and David Livingstone were added, on either side of the Exhibition Road corner. An old milestone is built into the wall at pavement level.

Across Exhibition Road, at no. 14 **Prince's Gate**, is a house once owned by John Pierpont Morgan, the New York banker and art collector. Many of the famous works acquired by him were once displayed here. Later, the young J.F. Kennedy lived here, while his father was ambassador to Britain (1937–40). The Iranian Embassy Siege of 1980 caused great damage to no. 16. At no. 20 is the **Polish Institute and Sikorski Museum**, with Polish art and archives (*open Tues–Fri 9.30–4 and first Sat of the month 10.30–4; T: 020 7589 9249, pism.co.uk*).

On the west side of the Albert Hall is the Royal College of Art's **Darwin Building**, designed in the 1960s by a group of RCA members of staff, including Hugh Casson. The college has a prestigious history and numbers many famous alumni on its rolls. Queen Victoria's sculptor daughter Louise was one of them, when the college was known as the National Art Training School. Further west is **Hyde Park Gate**, where at no. 18 Epstein had his studio (he died there in 1959). Sir Leslie Stephen, critic and scholar, lived at no. 22; his daughters Virginia Woolf and Vanessa Bell were born here. Winston Churchill died at no. 28 in 1965.

KENSINGTON HIGH STREET

Kensington High Street (*map p. 602, A2–A3; Underground: High Street Kensington*) is a busy and lively shopping street. Once home to three great department stores, Ponting's, Barker's and Derry and Tom's (and following the closure of the last in 1972, to the famous fashion store Biba), it now offers nothing more adventurous than the usual selection of chain stores. But the bustling atmosphere can be invigorating, and it is much less crowded than Oxford Street.

In **Young Street** (*map p. 602, A2*) Thackeray lived at no. 16 from 1846–53 and wrote *Vanity Fair*. Young Street leads to **Kensington Square**, established in the late 17th century to be close to the court at Kensington Palace. Talleyrand lived here after his escape from Paris in 1792. The artist Burne-Jones lived at no. 41 for a short period. At no. 23 on the opposite side is Heythrop College, a Theology school of Jesuit foundation. The sombre façade of the Maria Assumpta chapel is pierced by an enormous rose window. J.S. Mill lived at no. 18.

The monumental Art Deco building that once was Barker's department store now houses assorted shops. On Derry Street is the entrance to the **Roof Gardens**, owned by the Virgin Group (*roofgardens.virgin.com*) but once part of the Derry and Tom's department store (founded in 1862), which opened a six-storey emporium in 1930. There is public access to the Roof Gardens (*unless booked for a private function; to check, T: 0207 937 7994*), where flamingos wander among the full-grown oak trees.

On the corner of the attractive Kensington Church Street stands the parish church of **St Mary Abbots** (1869–81), a large church with a conspicuous spire. It was built on the site of the much earlier parish church of the village of Kensington. When that became too small for the congregation, Archdeacon Sinclair called for something 'exceedingly magnifical' and enlisted George Gilbert Scott to provide. **Holland Street**, north of the church, is a charming street of early 18th-century houses built for the ladies-in-waiting at Kensington Palace.

CAMPDEN HILL

The area around **Campden Hill** (*map p. 596, B3–C3*) was a favourite residential area in the 17th century. A few of the fine houses in spacious grounds survive, though the gardens of many have been absorbed by Holland Park School. Swift, Gray and Queen Anne (as Princess) were among its famous inhabitants. **Aubrey Walk**, a colony of artists in Edwardian days and more recently home to the singer Dusty Springfield, ends at the wooden gates of Aubrey House, built on the site of Kensington Wells, a spa established in the early 18th century and much esteemed for its curative waters. Aubrey Road leads downhill from here into **Campden Hill Square**, which slopes steeply away to the north. It was laid out in the 1820s by Joshua Hanson, who was a major developer of Regency Brighton. Here in the gardens, while staying at Hill Lodge (on the corner of Hillsleigh Road), Turner painted the sunset. Today, from some angles, you have a view of the infamous Trellick Tower: thus two very different kinds of London housing contemplate each other.

The Windsor Castle pub at no. 114 Campden Hill Road dates from 1835 and has a pleasant beer garden. Close by, on the corner of Bedford Gardens, is a Bauhaus building that looks as if it has been transposed from Stuttgart or Rationalist Italy: an incongruity amid the Victoriana. It is 'The Mount' (1962–4) by Douglas Stephen.

HOLLAND PARK

Holland Park (*map p. 596, B3*) is what remains of the grounds of a mansion built by John Thorpe in 1607 for Sir Walter Cope, Chancellor of the Exchequer under James I. The house passed by marriage to Henry Rich, created Earl of Holland (in Lincolnshire), who commissioned the surviving splendid **gateway** from Inigo Jones (executed by Nicholas Stone). Its piers of Portland stone are surmounted by worn griffins bearing the arms of Rich (the cross crosslets) and Cope (the rose). Lord Holland was executed by the Roundheads in 1649 and the house was occupied by the parliamentary general Fairfax, but was later restored to Holland's widow. Thereafter it was leased to a succession of tenants, among them William Penn and Joseph Addison. Eventually, the heir of the Rich family sold the house to Henry Fox (father of Charles James Fox), who was made Baron Holland in 1763. Under the 3rd Baron (and more particularly his imperious and strong-minded wife), the house became the centre of a Whiggish literary circle, the 'Holland House clique', to which Macaulay belonged. The house was badly damaged in World War Two and only the east wing remains (now a Youth Hostel).

The wooded park includes the former gardens. The Japanese Kyoto Garden was planted in 1991. The Orangery is used for exhibitions and other events and is popular for weddings. In the café are two sculptures of c. 1910: Eric Gill's *The Maid* and Epstein's *Sun God*. The area to the north is maintained as semi-natural woodland. The Open-Air Theatre stages opera performances and concerts in the summer. In 2013, cows were introduced into the park to graze down the woodland meadows.

At the south end of the park, approached from Kensington High Street, is the distinctive building of the former Commonwealth Institute. At the time of writing, the **Design Museum** was moving here from its old premises in a converted banana warehouse on the Thames bank in Bermondsey.

LEIGHTON HOUSE

At no. 12 Holland Park Rd (south of Melbury Road, where Holman Hunt died in 1910, at no. 18) is Leighton House, the home-cum-studio of the artist Frederic, Lord Leighton (*map p. 596, B3; open daily except Tues 10–5.30; admission charge; T: 020 7602 3316, 020 7471 9160 at weekends*). High Victorian painter *par excellence*, and the first British artist to be given a peerage, Leighton created for himself an exotic 'Palace of Art', where he lived and worked for the last 30 years of his life. Construction was planned in collaboration with the architect George Aitchison, who designed the extraordinary **Arab Hall**, a room richly evocative of the artist's fascination with the Ottoman world. In the centre, above a fountain trickling into a pool cut from a single block of black marble, hangs an ornate copper chandelier. The dome was purchased in Damascus and decorated with a mosaic frieze designed by Walter Crane. Upstairs is the **Great Studio**, where Leighton produced most of his work. Several of his larger paintings hang on the north wall, notably his *Clytemnestra*. There is also *The Uninterpreted Dream* by Burne-Jones and a bronze bust of the artist by Sir Thomas Brock, who also sculpted Leighton's memorial in St Paul's Cathedral. In the apse of the west wall is a tall door through which large canvases could be lowered. Right of the archway at the east end is a door leading to a staircase to the servants' quarters, which was also used by the artist's models and (indicating their status in Leighton's eyes) by art dealers.

At no. **18 Stafford Terrace** is the former home of the Punch cartoonist Edward Linley Sambourne, preserved in all its late Victorian detail (*admission by guided tour only, on Wed, Sat and Sun at scheduled times; booking advised, T: 020 7602 3316*).

Kensington High Street leads eventually to **Olympia**, with its trade fair centre. Further south is **Earl's Court**, with more exhibition halls.

VICTORIA & ALBERT MUSEUM

Map p. 602, B3. Underground: South Kensington. Open daily 10–5.45, until 10pm on Fri. Free except for special exhibitions. Café. Shops. T: 020 7942 2211 , vam.ac.uk.

The Victoria and Albert Museum (V&A) is one of the world's outstanding museums of applied arts. Its collection spans several centuries and encompasses sculpture, furniture, ceramics, glass, silver and metalwork, dress, textiles and jewellery. It is impossible to see even a tiny part of it on a single visit: but this is the joy of London's free museums. One can come again and again. The only scarce resource is time. Below is a brief outline of the V&A's history, its remarkable interiors and its collection highlights.

ORIGINS OF THE MUSEUM

The museum's origins lie in the School of Design, which opened in 1837 at Somerset House, established for the instruction of the application of art to industry. Works of ornamental art were collected by the school as instructional aids. In 1852 the school and its collection (now the Museum of Manufactures) had moved to Marlborough House and was under the control of the government Department of Science and Art, headed by the mighty figure of Henry Cole (1808–82). Cole, with the Prince Consort, had masterminded the Great Exhibition of 1851, a phenomenally popular success: almost 100,000 visitors mobbed it on one of the days, flocking to view the raw and manufactured products of the nations of the world, many of the chief exhibits being purchased for the museum. With the Exhibition's profits a plot of land was purchased in South Kensington and on the site of what is now the V&A, the South Kensington Museum was established. The School of Design and the Museum of Manufactures (which in 1853 had been renamed the Museum of Ornamental Art) moved to the site in 1857, partly accommodated in the Iron Building, nicknamed the 'Brompton Boilers'. (It was partially dismantled in 1866 and parts were re-erected for the Bethnal Green Museum; *see p. 114*). Thus were displayed the V&A's first objects, a miscellaneous collection of sculpture, architecture, 'animal products' (fur, feathers, bristles, human hair etc.), 'patented inventions' and construction and building materials, jostling for space alongside items of Ornamental Art, brought together to encourage excellence in contemporary British design and its application to industry, through a knowledge of the best examples.

THE BUILDING

Stretched over a twelve-acre site, the building itself is often said to be a work of art competing with the exhibits. The earliest permanent buildings were those that surround the central garden quadrangle, at the heart of the V&A. Built between 1857 and the early 1880s, they demonstrate what was to become known as the 'South Kensington style', its trademark being the use of ornamental terracotta. The museum's architect, Captain Fowke (architect of the Albert Hall), and Godfrey Sykes (who was responsible for much of the early interior embellishment), were assisted by a band of pupils from the museum's Art Schools (now the Royal College of Art). The first building was the 1857 Sheepshanks Gallery, half of the east range of the central quadrangle. Externally it had terracotta ornamentation with sgraffito medallion portraits of famous British artists. Internally it had gas illumination (South Kensington was the first museum in the world to be lit), which made evening opening possible—more convenient for working men and women. Attracting working people to visit was a cherished aim of Cole's, who saw museums as 'antidotes to brutality and vice'.

An arcaded corridor divided the South Court into two. On either side, below the roof, were balconies with large lunettes filled by frescoes by Leighton: *Industrial Arts as Applied to War* (1878–80; northeast) and *Industrial Arts as Applied to Peace* (1886; southeast). Today, the former magnificence of the South Court is hidden from view behind false walls but the Leighton frescoes, and the highly decorated soffits above them, can be viewed on Level 3 (*marked on the plan on p. 327*).

The museum's ornamentation reached a peak of elaboration in Fowke's Lecture Theatre range (north side of the central quadrangle), completed after Fowke's death in 1868. Internally and externally it is a showpiece of complex decoration. Its façade includes terracotta columns with figurative ornament, designed by Sykes and completed after his death by his former pupils and successors. A mosaic representation of the Great Exhibition (different countries presenting exhibits to a central Queen Victoria) fills the pediment. Inside, the Ceramic Staircase (*see plan on p. 326*) is an ornamental masterpiece, entirely encased in majolica and ceramic mosaic. Designed and modelled by Frank Moody, with students from the Art Schools, in Italian Renaissance style and executed by Minton in the new process of vitrified ceramic painting, its theme was the Arts, with stained-glass windows representing Art and Science. The mosaic portrait of Cole, in a majolica frame, marks his retirement from South Kensington in 1873. The Silver Galleries (Galleries 65–69, formerly the Ceramics Gallery), a long vista flanked by majolica-clad columns with elaborate ceilings designed by Moody, was once equally lavish; it has been restored to its former magnificence as far as possible.

On the ground floor of the wing are the old Refreshment Rooms (the museum was the first to have such a facility). The Morris Room (originally the Green Dining Room) was entirely decorated by Morris, Marshall and Faulkner, the firm established by William Morris in 1861, with painted panels by Burne-Jones, and stained glass designed by Burne-Jones and Philip Webb. The Gamble Room (the Centre Refreshment Room) has ceramic tiles, mirrors and stained-glass windows designed by Gamble (a pupil of Sykes). The upper ceramic frieze reads: 'There is nothing better for a man that he should eat and drink, and make his soul enjoy good in his labour' (*Ecclesiasticus 2:24*). The chimneypiece, from Dorchester House, Park Lane, is by Alfred Stevens.

In 1890 Aston Webb won an architectural competition to bring sense and order to the museum complex. Regular, grand façades along Cromwell Road and Exhibition Road would be the new public face of the museum, with additional gallery space behind, joined to the existing buildings. On 17th May 1899, Queen Victoria laid the foundation stone, at the same time announcing that henceforth the museum would be known as the Victoria & Albert Museum. This was her last official public ceremony and the occasion was captured on a moving picture device, the Mutocscope (in the photography collection). By 1906 the works were largely complete. The Cromwell Road central tower, in the shape of an Imperial crown, is topped by a statue of *Fame*. Queen Victoria stands above the great arched entrance, flanked by *St George* and *St Michael*. Prince Albert stands directly above the doors with representations of *Inspiration* and *Imagination* on either side. In a procession of niches along the façade, between the windows, are sculpture figures of great British artists. The new museum was officially opened by Edward VII in 1909.

THE COLLECTIONS

The museum's vast holdings are displayed in two types of gallery: those that focus on a particular material or technique and those that examine a geographical region and/or historical period. Many techniques, such as sculpture, are exhibited in more than one gallery. The plans on pp. 326 and 327 (overleaf) give an overview of the thematic dispersal on the principal levels. The description below highlights some of the artefacts not to be missed.

GALLERIES OF MATERIALS AND TECHNIQUES

Sculpture

The **Cast Courts** (46, Level 1) were intended for the display of large-scale casts of the most famous examples of sculpture in the world (Michelangelo's *David* is a notable example). These vast spaces were—and still are—one of the museum's most extraordinary sites.

The post-Classical sculpture collection includes outstanding masterpieces, from highly important medieval ivory carvings to large-scale monuments. The Italian Renaissance collection is the best outside Italy (star exhibits are shown in the Medieval and Renaissance Galleries; *see p. 329*). Pre-eminent examples of British sculpture include works of the 18th and 19th centuries by Rysbrack, Roubiliac (his *Handel* made for Vauxhall Gardens, shown seated, plucking a lyre), Flaxman, Wilton and Banks. Again, many of the principal items are shown in the Period Galleries (British Galleries; *see p. 329*). The **Gilbert Bayes Gallery** (111, Level 3), an open corridor with magnificent vistas over both the Cast Courts, has smaller pieces, the displays emphasising materials and techniques and the process of sculpting in general.

Metalwork: iron, silver and gold

The museum's fine collection of silver and gold objects is spread throughout the museum, but also in the sumptuous **Silver Galleries** (65–69, Level 3), one of the most lavish interiors of the 19th-century museum (*see p. 323*). As well as on contemporary *tour-de-force* works, 19th-century interest concentrated on heavily decorated 15th–17th-century European pieces. In the 20th century the museum started collecting English silver and its collection is now unrivalled (some key works are shown in the British Galleries). The displays include both ceremonial and domestic objects. Ceremonial salts are on show; a vast wine cistern by Thomas Jenkins (1677–8); elaborate candelabra; presentation cups and works by celebrated masters such as Paul de Lamerie, Charles Kandler and Matthew Boulton. The Ashburnham Centrepiece, or epergne, by Nicolas Sprimont (1747) is a major example of English Rococo silver. European silver 1400–1800 features an outstanding collection from Southern Germany, one of the greatest centres of European silversmithing.

As well as silver, the museum has a large collection of cutlery, brass, pewter and ironwork. The **Metalwork Gallery** (113–114e, Level 3) is famously described by H.G. Wells in his 1900 novel *Love and Mrs Lewisham*: 'The gallery is long and narrow...and set with iron gates, iron-bound chests, locks, bolts and bars, fantastic great keys, lamps and the like'. One of the major works is the 'Hereford Screen'. Designed by Sir George Gilbert Scott, it was hailed as 'the grandest, most triumphant achievement of modern architectural art' at the International Exhibition of 1862.

Ceramics

The Ceramics Galleries (136–146, Level 6) make immediately apparent the astonishing range, depth and sheer magnitude of the collection: the history of pottery and porcelain manufacture can be studied here uninterrupted. The collection ranges from the Far East and Imperial China to the Ottoman Empire and Europe. Among the outstanding examples are nine pieces of Medici porcelain, the first European attempts at copying Chinese ware, which reached Europe in the 16th century. Made in the Grand Duke of Tuscany's workshops in Florence, only 60 of these rare and precious pieces are known.

Italian majolica, French Renaissance pieces and Limoges are also represented, and there are comprehensive collections of the works from the great English potteries: Lowestoft, Coalport, Wedgwood, Chelsea, Worcester and Bow. Twentieth-century pieces include British studio pottery, works by Bernard Leach and Lucie Rie, and European works such as Picasso's 1954 vase showing an artist at his easel.

Glass

The excellent glass collection (Galleries 129 and 131, Level 4) ranges from ancient Egypt to the present, including commercial glass as well as works of art. On display are German goblets, Venetian and early English glass (including pieces by Jacopo Verzelini, who taught the art of glass-making in Elizabethan England), 18th-century drinking glasses, High Victorian pieces and modern items, including the rippling green stair and balcony balustrade by glass artist Danny Lane (1992). Of particular significance is the Luck of Edenhall, an exceptionally fine, pristinely preserved 14th-century Syrian beaker. In the main Rotunda Hall (Level 1) is Dale Chihuly's extraordinary lime green and turquoise Chandelier (2001): notoriously difficult to dust.

Jewellery

The Jewellery Gallery (91–93, Level 3) displays over 3,000 items tracing the history and development of Western jewellery from ancient times to the present day. It is one of the most comprehensive and important collections anywhere in the world. The wealth of antique jewels on display is particularly noteworthy. Before discoveries in the 19th century of seemingly inexhaustible supplies of precious metals, coloured gemstones and the South African diamond mines, fine or high jewellery was a much rarer commodity and was therefore not an experimental medium. When fashions changed, jewellery was usually dismantled and remodelled rather than a new item commissioned; gold was melted down and the gems were re-set into the new design. The collection of Renaissance jewels is thus remarkable: enamelled gold pendants which are really fanciful miniature sculptures decorated with gems and pearls are cleverly displayed in Perspex cases so you may walk around them—the backs of the jewels are as important as the front. The art of goldsmithing was an important part of

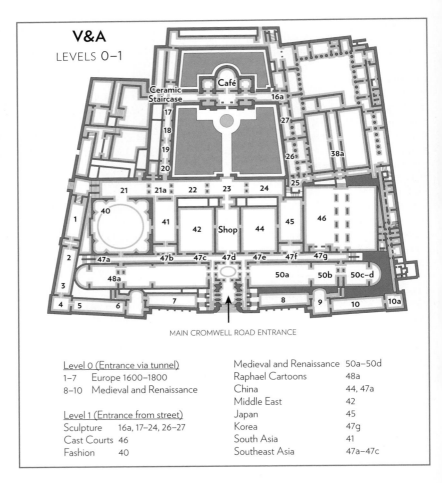

the Renaissance artist's training and there was a close relationship between sculptor and goldsmith. Note the Heneage Jewel (c. 1595), a gift from Elizabeth I to her loyal courtier Sir Thomas Heneage; it encloses a miniature of the Queen by Hilliard. Note also the jewels in frighteningly accurate Renaissance taste—but really the work of the 19th-century forger Reinhold Vasters. It is only in the last 30 years, since the discovery of vast numbers of design drawings, moulds, models and casts of Renaissance prototypes by known restorers and 'improvers' of antique jewellery, such as Vasters and Alfred André, that jewels with previously uncontested Renaissance attributions in both private and museum collections have had to be re-examined—to the consternation and shuddering of jewellery historians worldwide. The Canning Jewel (a gem-set merman with a baroque pearl body) was one such casualty.

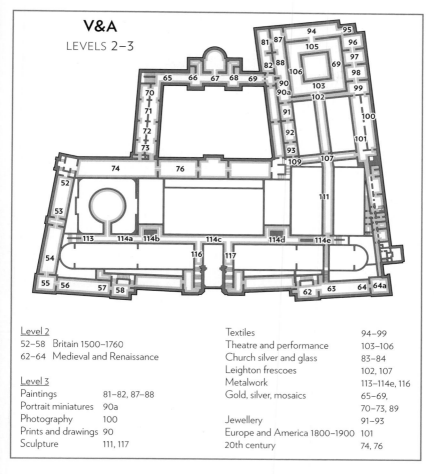

V&A

LEVELS 2–3

Level 2
52–58 Britain 1500–1760
62–64 Medieval and Renaissance

Level 3
Paintings 81–82, 87–88
Portrait miniatures 90a
Photography 100
Prints and drawings 90
Sculpture 111, 117

Textiles 94–99
Theatre and performance 103–106
Church silver and glass 83–84
Leighton frescoes 102, 107
Metalwork 113–114e, 116
Gold, silver, mosaics 65–69, 70–73, 89
Jewellery 91–93
Europe and America 1800–1900 101
20th century 74, 76

Also on show is a wide range of different types of jewel from the 19th century, including important Archaeological Revival pieces by Giuliano and Castellani, jewellers who worked from recently discovered Etruscan prototypes in order to rediscover the lost art of granulation. Here too are diamonds belonging to Catherine the Great and an emerald and diamond parure (1806 with 1820s' alterations) given by Napoleon to his adopted daughter. Also here are spectacular gem-set pieces from the greatest 20th-century jewellery houses and examples of work by 'artist' jewellers such as Lalique, whose innovative enamelling and use of non-precious materials defined Art Nouveau jewellery.

The V&A also invests in contemporary jewellery and there is a focus on works by living artists.

Fashion and textiles

The South Kensington Museum's collection of textiles (Spitalfields silks, Genoese velvets, upholstery fabrics etc.) was at first purely a learning resource. William Morris appears to have studied them, as elements of his designs are traceable to the specimens then exhibited. The serious collection of textiles began in the 1860s.

There are excellent examples of Indian and Persian **carpets**; an excellent **lace** collection (the largest in the world); and tapestries, including the **Devonshire Hunting Tapestries** (94, Level 3), a group of four magnificent and enormous mid-15th-century Flemish pieces formerly in the collection of the Dukes of Devonshire.

Items from the Dress Collection are displayed throughout the period galleries, as well as in the **Fashion Gallery** (40, Level 1). The European collection from Stuart times to the present day is particularly strong.

Paintings, Prints and Drawings

Among the V&A's most celebrated possessions are the **Raphael Cartoons** (48a, Level 1), seven of the ten executed by Raphael in 1515–16 for tapestries depicting Acts of the Apostles Peter and Paul to decorate the Sistine Chapel (*see p. 519*). They are among the most important surviving examples of High Renaissance art. Distemper on paper, they were originally cut into strips to enable the weavers to use them as guides. Purchased by Charles I in 1623, they were put back together in 1699, restored and displayed at Hampton Court. Still in royal ownership, they have been on loan to the museum since 1865.

The V&A's **Paintings Collection** (81–82, 87–88, Level 3) has at its core the Sheepshanks pictures, presented to the South Kensington Museum in 1857 and intended as the nucleus of a National Gallery of British Art. John Sheepshanks (1787–1863), a Leeds clothing manufacturer long settled in London, was acquainted with a wide circle of contemporary artists. His collection included fine works by Turner and Constable but his particular fondness was for early 19th-century genre pictures by Wilkie, Landseer and others, of which the collection has rich holdings (some are on show in the British Galleries). The V&A possesses a remarkable collection of oil sketches and works on paper by Constable, including a full-scale study for *The Haywain* (National Gallery).

The V&A houses the national collection of **portrait miniatures** (90a, Level 3 and the British Galleries). Among the many outstanding highlights by leading artists are Holbein's *Anne of Cleves*, with its carved ivory lid in the form of a rose; and pre-eminent works by Hilliard, including works with layered symbolism such as *Young Man Clasping a Hand from a Cloud*.

Changing displays are also shown from the **Prints, Drawings and Watercolours Collection** (90, Level 3), an enormous and important resource. The principal collections are of Italian Old Master drawings; Dutch and Flemish works; and the national collection of British watercolours. The bulk of the latter collection is of 18th- and 19th-century works, the 'golden age' of British watercolour (Sandby, Cozens, Girtin, Cotman). The **Prints and Drawings Study Room** (Level 4) has the bulk of the collection and a fine collection of photographs by Julia Margaret Cameron.

PERIOD GALLERIES

Medieval and Renaissance

Items from the collection, which spans the period c. 300–1600, are on display in various galleries on Levels 0, 1 and 2. Pre-eminent objects on Level 0 include glassware, stained glass and a collection of highly important ivory carvings, including the **'Basilewsky Situla'**, or Holy Water bucket (c. 980), probably presented to the Emperor Otto II on his visit to Milan in that year, an object of great rarity. The **Gloucester Candlestick** is an amazing survival of early 12th-century English medieval metalwork, a great masterpiece, with men and monkeys clambering through foliage, symbolic of the struggle between Good and Evil. Another major treasure is the **Becket Casket** (c. 1180), made to contain relics of St Thomas à Becket, the earliest, largest and best example in Limoges champlevé enamel showing Becket's martyrdom in shades of brilliant blue.

The silver-gilt **Burghley Nef** (62, Level 2) is a *tour de force* of Parisian goldsmiths' art of 1527. In the form of a ship, its body a nautilus shell balanced on the back of a mermaid, the tiny figures of Tristan and Isolde play chess at the foot of the main mast. Chief among the works of the Italian Renaissance are pieces by Donatello. His *Ascension with Christ Giving the Keys to St Peter* (64a, Level 2), from Palazzo Medici, Florence (c. 1428–30), is one of the finest surviving examples of *rilievo schiacciato* (very low relief carving).

British Galleries

The vast chronological scope of the British Galleries (52–58, Level 2 and 118–125c, Level 4) covers over 400 years of Britain's visual culture, bringing together the finest, most fashionable and most technically accomplished examples of sculpture, furniture, ceramics, silver, textiles and dress from the court of Henry VIII to the death of Queen Victoria. The incorporation of period interiors salvaged from important historic buildings lends the galleries particular authority and atmosphere.

One of the earliest objects on show is Pietro Torrigiano's famous painted terracotta **bust of Henry VII**, probably based on a death mask (*see Westminster Abbey Museum, p. 146*). Hilliard's famous *Young Man among Roses* is the quintessential image of the Elizabethan court, with its emphasis on complex emblems and symbolism. He is shown hand on heart, in devotion to the monarch, surrounded by eglantine roses (sweetbriar), the queen's symbol.

The celebrated **Great Bed of Ware** (1590–1600), from an inn in Ware, Hertfordshire, mentioned in Shakespeare's *Twelfth Night*, is twice the size of any bed of the period known and was famous for the numbers it could hold. A rare duo is the Jacobean **portrait of Margaret Layton** (c. 1620) and, usually displayed alongside it, the very jacket she wears in the painting, with elaborate floral embroidery. Another outstanding item is the **bust of Thomas Baker** (c. 1638) by the great Baroque sculptor Bernini. Baker was commissioned to deliver to Bernini in Rome Van Dyck's portrait of Charles I in three positions, from which Bernini would sculpt a bust; but he took the opportunity to commission a bust of himself. A famous later sculpture is **Roubiliac's *Handel*** (1738), commissioned by Jonathan Tyers for his pleasure gardens at Vauxhall, with Handel in the guise of Orpheus, shown seated and plucking at his lyre. **Horace Walpole's limewood cravat** (118a, Level 4) was carved by Grinling Gibbons c. 1690. Walpole famously once wore it when entertaining guests.

The 18th-century passion for Neoclassicism was stimulated by the young aristocrats, artists and connoisseurs who made Grand Tours and aesthetic pilgrimages to Italy to see Classical remains. There are many vases, including by **Wedgwood**, inspired by the antique, as well as candlestands and a mirror by **Robert Adam** adorned with Domus Aurea-inspired *grottesche*. Also by Adam is the plaster ceiling in delicate pastel shades from 5 Royal Terrace, part of the Adelphi development (*see p. 183*). When not in Edinburgh, Canova's magnificent *Three Graces* is on show, the famous marble sculpture commissioned by the Duke of Bedford for Woburn Abbey (it was purchased jointly with the National Museums and Galleries of Scotland after a national appeal in 1994). Examples of the new Regency taste for rich luxuriance—and for Greek, rather than Roman, sources—include an 1806 bookcase from the Prince Regent's luxurious Carlton House. The plaster model for Nash's Marble Arch (c. 1826) is also here.

Important items by A.W.N. Pugin, the seminal figure in the history of the **Gothic Revival**, include a candelabrum made for the House of Lords.

Arts and Crafts objects include items by William Morris (wallpaper designs, furniture, tiles and textiles), a Charles Rennie Mackintosh high-backed armchair and wallpaper designs by Walter Crane.

Europe and America

The European collection from 1600–1800 (1–7, Level 0) includes excellent examples of silver, glassware, porcelain and sculpture, with fine items of Meissen and Sèvres and distinguished pieces of French furniture by Riesener and Boulle. The exhibits continue in the Europe and America Gallery (101, Level 3).

Twentieth century

Twentieth-century art and design (74 and 76, Level 3) includes a chrome steel tubular lounger by Le Corbusier (1929), early 20th-century items from the Wiener Werkstätte, items of Art Deco household furniture (a radio, a teapot). Chairs by Charles and Ray Eames can be seen in the **Furniture Gallery** (Level 6).

Asia

The Asia Galleries (41–47g, Level 1) contain the museum's best examples of South and Southeast Asian, Japanese, Chinese, Korean and Middle Eastern art. **Southeast Asia** includes a 14th–15th-century standing crowned Buddha, from the workshops of Ayutthaya, then the Thai capital. It was cast in bronze using the lost wax method and then gilded.

The **Indian Collection** has its origins in the Asiatic Society of Bengal (established 1784) and the museum of the East India Company, housed at the Company's headquarters in the City. One of the most famous works, 'Tippoo's Tiger' (c. 1790), is a wooden organ made for Tipu Sultan, ruler of Mysore, in the form of a tiger mauling a British officer (shrieking sounds emanate from it when played). An important example of Hindu sculpture is the sandstone *Bodhisattva Avalokitesvara*, called the 'Sanchi Torso' (c. 900), beautifully carved and exceptionally elegant, from the ruined temple of Sanchi in Madhya Pradesh. Sixteenth–18th-century Mughal art includes early Indian painting, gold ornamental jewellery and Mughal textile designs. Shah Jahan's exquisite white jade wine cup (1657), in the form of a ram's head flaring to a wide bowl, is perhaps the finest known example of Mughal hardstone carving. There is also an exquisite portrait of Shah Jahan, shown wearing a diaphanous skirt, by the Persian artist Muhammad Abed (c. 1632). The golden throne of Maharajah Ranjit Singh (shown with other Indian Empire treasures at the 1851 Great Exhibition) was part of the state property taken by the British in 1849 on the annexation of the Punjab.

The **Islamic Near East**, covering the art of Egypt, Turkey, Iran, Iraq and Syria, contains the famous Ardabil carpet (1539–40), one of the largest and most magnificent Persian carpets in the world, from the shrine of the same name in northwest Iran. Purchased in 1893, to William Morris it was 'of singular perfection'.

Highlights in the **China Gallery** include the 206 BC–AD 220 large head and partial torso of a horse, the largest animal carving in jade known. A bronze incense burner in the shape of an angry goose, its neck outstretched, dates from the Song or Yuan dynasty (1200–1300). The Ming-dynasty lacquer table (1425–36) is one of the only surviving pieces from the Imperial lacquer workshop set up to the northwest of the Forbidden City in Beijing.

The **Korean Collection** includes beautiful examples of pale green celadon ware from the Koryo dynasty (935–1392) and fine examples of porcelain, furniture and decorative objects from the Choson dynasty (1392–1910), when Seoul became the capital. From **Japan** there is lacquerware, ceramics, ivory, textiles and netsuke.

NATURAL HISTORY MUSEUM

NATURAL HISTORY MUSEUM

Map p. 602, B3. Underground: South Kensington. Open daily 10–5.50 (last admissions 5.30), last Fri of the month until 10.30pm. Free (except for some temporary exhibitions). Cafés and shops. nhm.ac.uk; for Spirit Collection tours, T: 020 7942 6128.

NATURAL HISTORY MUSEUM
Greyhound: one of many of the motifs of living and extinct species which adorn the building.

The Natural History Museum's collection was originally a department of the British Museum, where the myriad stuffed animals, fish, skeletons, botanical specimens, rocks and fossils were first displayed. Lack of space prompted the move to South Kensington, which took place in 1881, when Alfred Waterhouse's astonishing new building finally opened to the public. Since then the collection has grown immeasurably. Between them the five departments of Botany, Entomology, Mineralogy, Palaeontology and Zoology contain over 70 million natural history specimens and the museum is—as it has always been—one of the world's leading centres of taxonomic research (the science of classifying species). The museum gained independence from the British Museum in 1963. At the core of the collection is the hoard of natural history 'curiosities' of the eminent botanist and physician Sir Hans Sloane (including his magnificently carved pearly nautilus shell). These items were joined by the eye-opening specimens brought back from Captain Cook's great voyages of discovery to the South Pacific. Objects from Darwin's revolutionary voyage to the Galapagos Islands in HMS *Beagle* in 1831–6 also came to the museum as did, in 1856, the entire collection of the Zoological Society, soon followed by that of the East India Company.

THE BUILDING
Waterhouse's magnificent building (1873–80), a great secular Romanesque cathedral clad in ornamental terracotta, incorporates in its design the ideas of Professor Richard Owen, a great comparative anatomist and palaeontologist and Superintendent of the Natural History Department from 1856. Owen was the prime agitator for a new museum and envisaged it as a great storehouse of divine creation. A broad flight of steps leads from the road up to the giant portal, centrally placed in the 680ft frontage, above which, surmounting the gable, Owen had placed a statue of Adam, man being creation's crowning glory (he fell off in the 1930s). Covering the façade and the interior is a veritable menagerie of birds and beasts cast in terracotta, symbolising the museum's function: to the west, where Zoology was displayed, designs of living animals; to the east, where Geology and Palaeontology were housed, extinct species. Extinct beasts line up on the entrance façade, monkeys scramble up arches in the entrance hall, fish

swim in rippling water around columns where further up lizards lurk, and on the stairs animals and birds—including a beautiful pair of demoiselle cranes—peep from twining plants. Waterhouse's dramatic entrance hall is conceived as a vast nave with a triforium above and, at the far end, the great staircase rising to the upper floors. Owen wished the Hall to be an 'Index' gallery, with displays of minerals, plants and invertebrates on one side and vertebrates on the other—a simple guide to the 'types' of the animal, plant and mineral kingdoms, carefully arranged according to the Linnaean system of classification. Owen's successor Sir William Flower introduced evolution to the display, a theory to which Owen had not wholly subscribed. In the centre were large mammals—whales, elephants and giraffes. Today the hall is dominated by the museum's most famous inhabitant, *Diplodocus carnegii*, 150 million years old and one of the largest land mammals which ever lived, cast from the original specimen at the Carnegie Museum, Pittsburgh and given to the museum in 1905. It is a fitting tribute to Owen, who coined the name 'dinosaur' in 1841.

TOUR OF THE MUSEUM

The museum today offers a very different visitor experience from the museum which opened its doors in 1881. Instead of carefully arranged classified specimens in mahogany cases there are now interactive audio-visual Life- and Earth-Science displays on Ecology, Evolution and Man. This popular staging of science, which sometimes fits uneasily in a building designed for the scientific knowledge of a different era, was introduced to the museum in 1977 with the opening of the Human Biology display. It outraged scholars, who believed that the Victorian founding ideal, both to educate and to amuse, had been pushed too far in the latter direction. Today we are more comfortable with the idea of interactive displays and the museum is enduringly popular.

Life Galleries (Blue and Green Zones): The most famous display on the ground floor is the ever-popular Dinosaurs, including a vast animatronic *Tyrannosaurus rex*. The Mammal Hall is almost completely filled by the vast 91ft Blue Whale suspended from the ceiling, with the White Whale, Sperm Whale and dolphins alongside it. Of particular note in the Bird Gallery (first floor) are the two Mauritius dodos. On the second floor is a cross-section of a giant sequoia tree from the Sierra Nevada, California, 1,335 years old when felled in 1892.

Earth Galleries (Red Zone): The entrance to the Earth Galleries is from Exhibition Road. 'The Power Within' explores volcanoes and has an immensely popular earthquake simulator. 'From the Beginning' takes you from the Big Bang, the formation of Earth 4,560 million years ago, to the creation and sustaining of life. 'Earth's Treasury' has a display of minerals and gemstones. The 'Earth Lab' explores the diversity of rocks and fossils, drawing on the museum's great mineralogy and palaeontology collections, which include 160,000 rocks and ocean bottom deposits, 3,000 meteorites and 30,000 ores, many collected on great expeditions such as Scott's second polar expedition (specimens brought back by the naturalist Edward Wilson proved that Antarctica had once been warm).

The Darwin Centre (Orange Zone):
The Darwin Centre is the storehouse for the museum's zoological 'Spirit Collection': 22 million jarred specimens preserved in alcohol. Standing in the atrium you can look up seven storeys and see the extent of the storage. A small section on the ground floor is available for viewing, although you can take behind-the-scenes tours of other storerooms and the laboratories where over 100 scientists carry out taxonomic research.

The 'Cocoon' on the seventh floor (C.F. Møller Architects, 2009) features extraordinary wall displays of plants and insects, including exquisite butterflies.

SCIENCE MUSEUM

Map p. 602, B3. Underground: South Kensington. Open daily 10–6 (last entry 5.15). Often crowded at weekends and during school holidays; to book (booking fee), T: 0870 870 4868. Free (except for some exhibitions and simulators). Cafés and shop. science-museum.org.uk.

Like the Victoria & Albert Museum, the origins of the Science Museum lie in the Great Exhibition of 1851. In the following year, the Museum of Manufactures was opened on the first floor of Marlborough House, maintaining a permanent collection of selected Exhibition items, later transferred to the South Kensington Museum. In 1870, the Scientific and Educational Department of the South Kensington Museum merged with it and with the Patent Office Museum collection, to form what became known as the 'Science Museum'. In 1924 the museum acquired the contents of James Watt's workshop (still on display) and four years later moved into its present site on Exhibition Road, where it has continued to grow, presenting the development of science, technology and medicine from the early 18th century to the present. The focus of acquisitions has been on artefacts that demonstrate developments in concepts and theory as well as practice, in the processes of discovery and invention, and in their relationship to economics and society. Artefacts associated with important historical events in science, individuals, groups of people and institutions have also found a home here. The exhibits cover an enormous range, from original items from the Great Exhibition to the latest in interactive technology; Charles Babbage and the earliest computers to the realms of 3D printing; Stephenson's *Rocket* to the *Apollo 10* command module. There is a also the chance to try out the RAF Typhoon Jet simulator.

On the fourth floor is a curiously fascinating series of tableaux and dioramas entitled 'Glimpses of Medical History', which show in great detail the development of medical practice from trepanning in Neolithic times to open heart surgery in our own day; amputations without anaesthetic in Nelson's time and early cataract operations. Curiosities in the museum's collection include Napoleon's silver-gilt toothbrush, Florence Nightingale's moccasins, Dr Livingstone's medicine chest and a microscope made for Lister.

LONDON CURIOSITIES

London is famous for its black taxicabs, its red double-decker buses and for a handful of distinctive articles of street furniture: its letter boxes, telephone kiosks and commemorative plaques attached to housefronts (of the latter, there are ever more to be seen; of the first two, ever fewer).

As the use of postage stamps became widespread during the reign of Queen Victoria, people began to post their own letters in handily-positioned boxes erected for the purpose by the Royal Mail. The best known types of letter box, of which numerous examples survive, are the wall box and the pillar box. The latter is a free-standing cast-iron cylinder, painted bright red, typically with a crimped lid, and with the cypher of the reigning monarch embossed on the stem. 'VR' boxes are rare because of their age; 'EVIIIR' examples even rarer because of the brevity of his reign.

The famous red telephone boxes, with their heavy and difficult-to-open doors, have been through several design permutations (models K1 to K6) since 1920. Enthusiasts can tell the difference between each model, though some are very rare. K2 was designed by Sir Giles Gilbert Scott in 1924. K6, designed in 1935, with a less articulated roof, is the most widespread. New plate-glass-sided designs introduced in the 1990s were never popular: many old red boxes were purchased by private buyers.

The notion that passersby will want to know who once resided in London's streets and squares is not a new one. The first commemorative plaque (to Sir Joshua Reynolds, in Leicester Square) went up in 1875. The most widespread type of plaque now seen, of glazed clay coloured blue with a white border, belongs to the scheme administered by English Heritage (*example illustrated*). But plenty of other London councils operate their own schemes, with plaques variously coloured brown, red, green, blue and black. The City of London Corporation plaques are rectangular, composed of glazed tiles. There is even a Blue Plaques app.

When people talk of the classic London double-decker bus, they are referring to the Routemaster, a model that first went into service in 1956. It was operated by a driver at the front, who had no contact with passengers, and a conductor in the bus itself, who went to and fro collecting fares. At the back was a hop-on hop-off platform, making it easy to board or jump off wherever you chose (particularly welcome in frustratingly slow-moving traffic). Most of today's buses stop only at designated bus stops and there are no conductors; fares are taken by the driver. A 'heritage' Routemaster service is maintained: no. 15 from Trafalgar Square to Tower Hill (though there are fears that it may not survive for long). The new Routemaster, designed by Thomas Heatherwick and his studio, was introduced in 2010. It has a back platform, but you can only board the bus this way if you have an oystercard (*see p. 538*). Otherwise you must show your ticket to the driver. The new Routemasters currently only run on selected routes, but more are promised.

EATING AND DRINKING IN KENSINGTON, KNIGHTSBRIDGE AND CHELSEA

HYDE PARK, KENSINGTON GARDENS

In Hyde Park, there are two good places for lunch: the £ **Lido Bar and Café** (*map p. 602, C2*) is lovely on a fine day, with tables out on the water (*T: 020 7706 7098*). At the eastern end of the lake is the £ **Serpentine Bar and Kitchen** (*map p. 602, C2*), serving unpretentious food: fish and chips, salads, pizza (*T: 020 7706 8114*). There are also plenty of 'refreshment points' dotted around the park, where you can get coffee and a sandwich (*open till 8pm in summer*).

In Kensington Gardens, in the annexe to the Serpentine Sackler Gallery, is ££ **Magazine**, where a Berlin-born chef with a love of sushi creates interesting results (*open Tues–Sun 10–6, Weds-Sat 10am–11pm; T: 020 7298 7552, serpentinegalleries. org; map p. 602, B2*). In Kensington Palace itself, the ££ **Kensington Palace Orangery** offers modern British cuisine in this former glasshouse, designed by Hawksmoor for Queen Anne. Open for breakfast, lunch and afternoon tea (*T: 020 3166 6133, orangerykensingtonpalace.co.uk; map p. 602, A2*).

When Heston Blumenthal, one of Britain's top chefs, offered to improve the menus of motorway service station diners, he met with frank dismay from motorists keen on their bangers and beans. £££ **Dinner by Heston Blumenthal** at the Mandarin Oriental Hotel on Hyde Park is another matter. Within minutes of opening, almost, the establishment had won a Michelin star and it routinely scoops a top spot in best-in-the-world dining lists. It offers extraordinary time-travel cuisine: when this guide went to press, the menu featured 'Rice and Flesh', a dish of c. 1390 (made with calf's tail) and spiced pigeon (in ale) from c. 1780. Reservations essential. No dinner jacket required. Open daily. *66 Knightsbridge (Mandarin Oriental Hotel). T: 020 7201 3833, dinnerbyheston.com. Map p. 602, C2.*

KENSINGTON

£–££ **Bibendum**. Named after the Michelin Man, who in turn takes his name from the slogan *Nunc est bibendum*, 'Now is the time to drink' (Horace). The Oyster Bar is recommended. *81 Fulham Rd. T: 020 7589 1480. Map p. 602, C3.*

££ **Babylon Restaurant**. Dine above the chimney pots in the extraordinary Roof Gardens (*see p. 319*). Open daily but phone ahead to check no private functions are being held. Dining here entitles you to reduced entry fee to The Club (also in the Roof Gardens). *99 Kensington High St (entrance on Derry St. T: 020 7368 3993, roofgardens.virgin.com. Map p. 602, A3.*

££–£££ **Clarke's**. Restaurant, bakery and shop in business for 30 years. Good cooking, using seasonal produce from southern England. Closed Sun. *122–124 Kensington Church St. T: 020 7221 9225, sallyclarke.com. Map p.*

Fitzrovia, Bloomsbury & The British Museum

Fitzrovia and Bloomsbury are both famed for their bohemian, artistic and literary associations. The latter is also home to two important institutions: University College London and the British Museum. Close by are the great railway hubs of Euston, King's Cross and St Pancras.

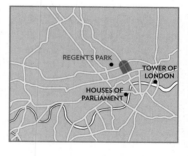

itzrovia (*map p. 601, D4*) lies between Portland Place and Tottenham Court Road. The northern part, including Fitzroy Square, was developed in the 18th century. Fitzrovia was later made famous by its avant-garde set (Virginal Woolf, Victor Pasmore, Augustus John, Dylan Thomas), who lived here from the 1920s and frequented its bars, notably the Fitzroy Tavern on Charlotte Street. Despite recent gentrification and increased rents, Fitzrovia manages to retain a diverse and scruffy charm. Several fashion wholesalers have their premises here, as do design studios and media companies.

FITZROY SQUARE

Fitzroy Square (*map p. 601, D4*) was built on land belonging to Charles FitzRoy, 1st Baron Southampton, who was a descendant of Henry FitzRoy, 1st Duke of Grafton, the illegitimate son of Charles II and his mistress Barbara Villiers. It was laid out speculatively in the 1790s; the elegant east and south sides, in Portland stone embellished with Venetian windows, medallions and anthemia, are by Robert Adam, continued after his death by his brothers James and William. The Adams never completed the square due to a property slump occasioned by the Napoleonic Wars. The stucco-fronted north and west sides were built in the 1820s–30s. Famous residents include Whistler (no. 8), the Bloomsbury Group artist Duncan Grant (no. 19), George Bernard Shaw and later Virginia Woolf (née Stephen; no. 29). Roger Fry established the Omega Workshops at no. 33 and Ford Madox Brown lived and entertained members of the Pre-Raphaelite Brotherhood at no. 37. On the corner of no. 40 is a statue of General Francisco de Miranda (1750–1816), Venezuelan soldier and campaigner for Spanish

American independence, who lived for a time on Grafton Way. Miranda died in gaol near Cadiz and his body was buried in a mass grave. Opposite at no. 41, on the corner with Fitzroy Street, is the YMCA Indian Student Hostel, founded in 1920 to foster Anglo-Indian relations by accommodating Indian students in London as well as giving them a place to entertain their British classmates. The building, by Ralph Tubbs (1953), has a very reasonably-priced Indian canteen, open to all and popular at lunch.

The **BT Tower**, south of Fitzroy Square, is surrounded by modern blocks. A strict sign in four languages says it is not open to the public. Commissioned by the General Post Office (GPO), it opened in 1964 as a telecommunications tower and at 627ft (including the aerial) was once the tallest building in London. Its narrow, cylindrical shape meant that it hardly moved in high winds and the tinted glass cladding prevented heat build-up. The revolving restaurant on the 34th floor closed after an IRA bomb attack in the 1970s. Plans to reopen it are perpetually put forward and then dropped.

ON AND AROUND CHARLOTTE STREET

Charlotte Street (*map p. 601, D4*), Fitzrovia's main thoroughfare, where Greeks and Italians settled after World War Two, is known for its mix of restaurants and pubs serving a wide variety of cuisine. At no. 16A is the famous **Fitzroy Tavern**, frequented by artists and writers such as Dylan Thomas, George Orwell and Augustus John from the 1920s until the 1940s. Opposite is the Charlotte Street Hotel. The range of restaurants continues round the corner in Goodge Street. Just before, the small pedestrianised Colville Street is filled with large tubs and planters of shrubs and flowers.

From Newman Street, the narrow Newman Passage leads to Rathbone Street. Here, the small pub on the corner, the **Newman Arms** (*see p. 369*), was frequented by George Orwell. Orwell, Thomas et al also drank in the Wheatsheaf pub in Rathbone Place.

Further north at no. 1 Scala St is **Pollock's Toy Museum** (*open Mon–Sat 10–5, closed Bank Holidays; admission charge; shop; T: 020 7636 3452; pollockstoymuseum.com*), which takes its name from Benjamin Pollock (d. 1937), one of the last of the Victorian printers and publishers of toy theatres. The museum occupies two interconnecting townhouses, whose upstairs rooms and staircases are crammed with displays of board games, mechanical toys, tin soldiers, marbles, wax dolls, puppets, toy theatres—and Eric, the museum's oldest teddy bear, dating from 1905. During the school holidays there are live toy theatre performances.

BERNERS STREET AND MORTIMER STREET

Coleridge lived briefly at no. 71 Berners St. At no. 50 is the **Sanderson Hotel**, with a Philippe Starck 'Cocteau-like dream-world' interior (white muslin curtains and red upholstered sofas designed to resemble pouting lips, etc.). The 230ft frontage, in International Modernist style, was built as Sanderson House in 1958–60 by Slater, Moberly & Uren, architects of the Peter Jones and John Lewis department stores; the central courtyard, with its Japanese-inspired garden (now adjoining the bar/restaurant), is by John Hicks. It was originally the showrooms for Sanderson & Sons, manufacturers of high-quality wallpaper, fabric and paint since 1860. The hotel is on the site of the house of a wealthy Mrs Tottenham, on whom a weird and unpleasant practical joke, the 'Berners Street Hoax', was allegedly played in or around 1810. Letters were sent out in her name to a wide variety of tradespeople and the ensuing traffic mayhem caused by horses and carts making endless attempts to deliver quantities of unwanted coal, fabric, pianofortes, jam tarts, meat, paintings, even a coffin, to her door, was widely reported in contemporary newspapers and alluded to in stage plays.

The site of the Middlesex Hospital on **Mortimer Street** is being redeveloped as offices, apartments and penthouses around a central green square. The complex, under the working title Fitzroy Place, will retain the hospital façade on Nassau Street. The site was previously owned by Candy and Candy (the property developers behind One Hyde Park), who demolished the hospital to make way for a ritzy housing and retail development. The scheme was abandoned in the 2008 Credit Crunch, to the relief of Fitzrovia's resident community. The sculptor Nollekens lived at no. 44.

ALL SAINTS MARGARET STREET

The church of **All Saints** (William Butterfield, 1850–9) at no. 7 Margaret St (*map p. 601, D4; allsaintsmargaretstreet.org.uk*) was built as a model church of the Oxford Movement, which sought within the Church of England a renewal of liturgical practice more in line with medieval traditions: in other words, less 'low church'. It is an important example of High Victorian Gothic Revival architecture and has hardly been altered since its consecration. The church, as well as a choir school and clergy house, is built on a confined site. The patterned red and black brick exterior with stone detailing and a slate roof, is dominated by a huge tower and spire, two feet taller than the western towers of Westminster Abbey; it can be seen from Primrose Hill. The interior is a riot of intense, brightly-coloured decoration: every available surface is adorned or revetted with stained glass, paintwork, tiling, inlaid hardstone and marble. The nave arches are of red Aberdeen granite. The multicoloured marble pulpit was installed in 1850 at huge expense, to accentuate the importance of preaching. The elaborate altarpiece (Ninian Comper, 1909) replaces the original by William Dyce, which had deteriorated; Comper also designed the Lady Chapel. The picture tiles running the length of the north wall were designed by Butterfield in 1873. The stained-glass west window was installed in 1877 under Butterfield's direction.

In **Foley Street**, Sir Edwin Landseer lived at no. 33 and the painter Henry Fuseli at no. 37. Great Portland Street (*map p. 600, C4*) is home to the **Central Synagogue**, founded in 1848 and rebuilt in 1958. James Boswell lived at no. 122.

BLOOMSBURY

Map p. 601, D4–E4. Underground: Tottenham Court Road, Goodge Street.

Bloomsbury, bounded by Tottenham Court Road, Euston Road, Grays Inn Road and High Holborn, is an area associated with the arts, literature and publishing. It is inextricably linked with the names of Virginia and Leonard Woolf, Clive and Vanessa

Bell, Lytton Strachey and others who, before the First World War, began here their unconventional association of intellectual and artistic interests later known as the Bloomsbury Group.

Today, Bloomsbury is the University of London's central precinct, home to its colleges, subsidiary departments and divisions as well as to several medical and healthcare institutions. In addition, Bloomsbury is home to the British Museum.

As was the case with so much of the West End, Bloomsbury was built up over fields and countryside by a succession of landlords; firstly by the Earl of Southampton in the 1660s and later by the Dukes of Bedford (the Russell family). The green squares date mainly from the 18th and early 19th centuries and handsome, well-proportioned terraced houses survive alongside newer buildings. Many smaller hotels and student residences occupy houses here. Bloomsbury's architecture is grander than that of adjoining Fitzrovia, but in common with its neighbour, its charm lies in its lack of pretension, in its smattering of interesting independent shops (concentrated particularly in northeast Bloomsbury) and in its modest, convivial pubs and restaurants (although the ubiquitous coffee and sandwich chains have sneaked in).

TOTTENHAM COURT ROAD

Tottenham Court Road (*map p. 601, D4*), known for its shops selling electronics and home furnishings, forms the western boundary of the area. Here, next to a large branch of Habitat between Chenies Street and Torrington Place, is **Heal's department store**, founded in 1810. The current building was designed by Smith and Brewer in 1917 with an extension by Sir Edward Maufe of 1938. Opposite, the **American International Church** (*amchurch.co.uk*) occupies the former Whitefield Memorial Chapel (E.C. Butler, 1956–8), which in turn was built on the site of a chapel erected for George Whitefield (1714–70), the cross-eyed evangelical preacher whose stentorian voice reportedly carried for miles and who preached many times in the American colonies and to American slaves. Further south at no. 46 (corner of Windmill St) is the Art Nouveau **Rising Sun pub**, by pub architects Treadwell and Martin (1896).

OLD ST GILES

The area known as St Giles, now bisected by New Oxford Street, was once a poverty-stricken and congested 'rookery' clustered around an old leper hospital that had been founded here in 1101 by Matilda, wife of Henry I. Disease long remained endemic in the area: one of the first cases of the Great Plague occurred among Flemish weavers in this parish in 1664. St Giles Circus, at the bottom of Tottenham Court Road, is dominated by the 1960s' concrete and glass tower of **Centre Point** (R. Seifert and Partners), which is built over a former gallows.

The church of **St Giles-in-the-Fields** (*map p. 603, F1*) was built in 1730–4 by Henry Flitcroft. Inside the entrance is a carved oak relief of the *Resurrection* (1687) and opposite, halfway up the stairs, a memorial to Flaxman (carved by the sculptor), placed here in 1930. Inside, the late 17th-century organ and pulpit survive from the earlier church. In the north aisle are memorials to Andrew Marvell and to George Chapman (d. 1634), the translator of Homer who occasioned Keats' 'wild surmise'. His memorial is in the form of a Roman stele, placed here by Inigo Jones. Also here is the upper part of a pulpit used by John and Charles Wesley in 1743–91 (formerly in West Street Chapel; *see p. 242*). Byron's daughter Allegra was baptised in the simple little font in 1818, as were Shelley's children William and Clara. Each of them died in Italy. Allegra, aged five when she died, lived longest.

ST GEORGE'S AND BLOOMSBURY SQUARE

At 53 New Oxford Street, at the junction of Bloomsbury Street and Shaftesbury Avenue, is **James Smith & Sons**, umbrella and walking stick merchants since 1830, still occupying their Victorian shop. North of New Oxford Street, in Little Russell Street, is the **Cartoon Museum** (*map p. 601, E4; open Mon–Sat 10.30–5.30, Sun 12–5.30; T: 020 7580 8155, cartoonmuseum.org*), which displays British comic art from the 18th century to the present day. **Museum Street** was once home to an extraordinary shop called Cameo Corner, which sold all manner of antiques, curios, watches, *objets d'art*, Fabergé and jewellery. It was run by its charismatic owner, Mosheh Oved, who typically appeared gowned in a velvet caftan with a huge cabochon amethyst pendant. In the shop's pre-World War Two heyday, its eclectic mix of customers included Nancy Cunard, Marghanita Laski, Jacob Epstein and Queen Mary (when her Daimler glided down the street, a moth-eaten red carpet would be rolled from the shop to the car door in homage). Oved was one of the founders of the Ben Uri Gallery (*see p. 276*).

In Bloomsbury Way is the church of **St George's Bloomsbury** (*map p. 601, E4*), with a grand Corinthian portico. It was built by Hawksmoor in 1716–31 as one of the new churches constructed after the 1711 New Churches Act (passed in reaction to the spread of Nonconformism). It is Hawksmoor's sixth and final London church. The steeple, inspired by Pliny's description of the Mausoleum at Halicarnassus (modern Bodrum, Turkey), is constructed to resemble a stepped pyramid: its base is borne by lions and unicorns and it is surmounted by a statue of George I. Its silhouette is clearly recognisable in Hogarth's famous satirical print *Gin Lane*. The church reopened after extensive restoration in 2006. An exhibition entitled 'Hawksmoor and Bloomsbury' occupies the undercroft (*usually open daily 1–4, though staffed by volunteers so subject to closures; call to check on T: 020 7242 1979, stgeorgesbloomsbury.org.uk*).

Bloomsbury Square (*map p. 601, E4*) was developed in the 1660s for the 4th Earl of Southampton; it was one of the earliest squares in London to be laid out, though none of the original buildings remains. The terraces on the north side (Great Russell Street/Bedford Place) date from c. 1800; at 3 Bloomsbury Place lived Sir Hans Sloane (*see p. 354*), physician and benefactor of the British Museum. In the garden, the bronze statue of Charles James Fox in Classical robes, holding a copy of the *Magna Carta*, is by Sir Richard Westmacott (1816).

BEDFORD SQUARE AND GOWER STREET

Bloomsbury Street leads to Bedford Square (*map p. 601, D4*), one of the first squares to be laid out on the Bedford Estate and built between 1775 and 1780 by Thomas Leverton and others. This is one of London's most complete 18th-century squares: each side is designed as a terrace of brick houses with a 'palace front' at the centre; the central

BLOOMSBURY
The distinctive spire of St George's church is seen in the background of Hogarth's *Gin Lane*.

houses on the north and east sides are stuccoed and made prominent with a pediment and Ionic pilasters. Each house has a distinctive doorcase of Coade Stone (*see p. 415*) with regular vermiculated blocks and a bearded head at the keystone. Look closely and you will see variations in the fanlights and the ironwork balconies and that the windows have an irregular rhythm; this is because London terraces were rarely the work of just one architect and builder. These were private houses and were sold or rented by lawyers, doctors and architects; today they are mainly offices and the square is in demand as a period film set. The Architectural Association is housed at nos 34–36. It has a reading room and exhibition space.

In Gower Street are the main entrances to UCL (*see below*), RADA (Royal Academy of Dramatic Arts) and the distinctive red-brick Cruciform Building (*also see below*). Former residents of the street include Charles Darwin. The Pre-Raphaelite Brotherhood was founded here in the home of John Everett Millais (no. 7 Gower St, corner of Gower Mews) in 1848.

SENATE HOUSE AND RUSSELL SQUARE

In Malet Street (*map p. 601, D4*) looms **Senate House**, the administrative centre of London University, holding the University archive and extensive central library. It was London's first skyscraper, built in 1933–6 by Charles Holden (designer of many Underground stations). It inspired George Orwell's Ministry of Truth in *1984*.

London was the last of the great European capitals to found a university. In 1836 a Royal Charter was granted constituting a University of London with the power of granting academic degrees, without religious tests, to students of University College (founded 1826; *for more on University College, see below*), King's College, (founded 1829) and certain other affiliated institutions. In 1858 the examinations were thrown open to all male students without restriction; 20 years later the University of London became the first academic body in the United Kingdom to admit women as candidates for degrees on equal terms with men. Hitherto purely an examining body, it was reconstituted in 1898–1900 as a teaching university, instruction being given in existing colleges and schools. Today, the University of London consists of 18 self-governing colleges and ten smaller research institutes.

Montague Place leads to **Russell Square** (*map p. 601, E4*), the largest of Bloomsbury's squares and one of the largest in London, laid out in 1800 by Humphrey Repton. There are some original houses on the west side by James Burton, father of Decimus Burton, who was the contractor during this period for the Bedford family estates. The central gardens have been restored, based on Repton's original plan. A blue plaque at no. 24, in the northwest corner, commemorates T.S. Eliot, who worked here as poetry editor for Faber & Faber. Opposite, on the corner with the central gardens, the green hut is one of London's 13 remaining cabmen's shelters, which were built between 1875 and 1914 as places were taxi drivers could take a break and share a meal. On the east side, the French chateau-inspired Hotel Russell, festooned in terracotta, is by Charles Fitzroy Doll (c. 1900), whose design for the dining room on RMS *Titanic* is said to have been based on the hotel's opulent restaurant. Doll had been appointed Surveyor to the Bedford Estate in the 1880s; Burton's houses on the north and west sides, with their terracotta cladding of the 1890s, were presumably 'dolled up' under his direction. On the north side, the Institute of Education, with anodised aluminium panels, is by Denys Lasdun (1965–76). The **Brunei Gallery**, a venue for exhibitions about Asia, Africa and the Middle East (*free admission*), opposite SOAS (School of Oriental and African Studies), is in Thornhaugh Street, northwest off the square. It has a Japanese roof garden.

GORDON SQUARE

Gordon Square (*map p. 601, D4*) was developed by Thomas Cubitt from the 1820s as a pair with neighbouring Tavistock Square. At no, 46, the Bloomsbury Group was born: here the siblings Virginia, Vanessa, Adrian and Thoby Stephen held their Thursday evening salons, which were attended by Leonard Woolf, Lytton Strachey, Clive Bell, Duncan Grant and John Maynard Keynes, among others. In Tavistock Square is a statue of Mahatma Gandhi by Fredda Brilliant (1966); he stayed near here when in London studying law at UCL. A cherry tree commemorates the victims of Hiroshima.

In the southwest corner of Gordon Square and Byng Place is the Catholic Apostolic Church known as the **Church of Christ the King**, a large Gothic Revival building in Bath stone and brick (Raphael Brandon, 1853). It was much admired by John Betjeman. The church revived apostolic beliefs and appointed twelve leaders—or 'Apostles'—to guide its followers. The Book of Revelation was at the centre of its teaching and its core belief was that Christ's Second Coming was imminent; this church was built as a fitting place to receive Him. However, the belief in imminence meant that Apostles were not replaced when they died; after the last one passed away in 1901, the church gradually ceased to function. From 1963–92 it served as the base for the University of London's Anglican chaplaincy; today it is home to the Anglo-Catholic Forward in Faith movement and is only open at certain times.

Opposite the church, in Torrington Place, is a neo-Gothic terracotta-clad terrace by Charles Fitzroy Doll (1907). It is interesting to compare it with his Russell Hotel (*see above*). The large branch of Waterstones here functions as the university bookshop.

UCL

Backing onto Gordon Street are the buildings of University College London, always known as UCL (*map p. 601, D4; main entrance round the corner in Gower St*). UCL was founded in 1826 with the title of University of London, with the object of affording 'at a moderate expense the means of education in literature, science and art' to students of any race, class or creed. King's College, on the Strand, was founded as an Anglican alternative to this 'Godless college on Gower Street'. Today is it proudly London's 'global' and 'multi-disciplinary' university, a centre of excellence with 25,000 students. Through the lodge gates on Gower Street, the central building, with its Corinthian portico and dome, was designed by William Wilkins in 1827–9; on all sides are extensions and additions. On your left (north) is the Slade School of Art (founded 1871), which produced Augustus and Gwen John, William Orpen, Stanley Spencer, David Bomberg and William Coldstream.

EXHIBITIONS AT UCL

UCL has several free exhibits that are open to the public during term time. Inside, under the dome, is the **Octagon Gallery**, a space for changing exhibitions; in the Library are **plaster casts by John Flaxman**. The college holds an extensive collection of drawings and casts by Flaxman and more are on display in the **UCL Art Museum** in the South Cloisters, which houses a collection of 10,000 prints, drawings, sculptures

PETRIE MUSEUM
Fragment of a colossal granite statue of Sesostris I from Armant. 12th Dynasty.

and paintings from the 1490s to the present day. At the end of the South Cloisters, follow the signs for 'Auto-Icon' to see the **embalmed body of Jeremy Bentham**, who sits fully clothed in a glass case. The philosopher and founder of Utilitarianism (d. 1830) asked that his body be dissected and preserved after his death; UCL has cared for it since 1850. The head is a wax version; the real one, deemed inappropriate for public display, is in safe storage. The **Geology Collection** of rocks, minerals and fossils is in the Rock Room in the South Wing.

'The present has its most serious duty to history in saving the past for the benefit of the future.' So believed the great Egyptologist Sir Flinders Petrie—and he saved a very great deal, much of it charmingly displayed in the **Petrie Museum of Egyptian Archaeology**, located on the first floor of the DMS Watson Building in Malet Place (*open Tues–Sat 1–5; free; T: 020 7679 2884, ucl.ac.uk/museums/petrie*). Here priceless pieces are crammed and crowded into old-fashioned display cabinets, some of them fitted with drawers which you can pull out to reveal yet more marvels. Jewellery, stelae, pottery, tools, ushabti figures, textiles, mummy portraits from the Fayyum: this is a real trove.

The **Grant Museum of Zoology** (*21 University Street; opposite the main entrance*) holds 67,000 specimens, including the bones of a dodo.

THE CRUCIFORM BUILDING

In Gower Street, opposite the main college gates, is the red-brick neo-Gothic building known as the Cruciform Building, the former University College Hospital, founded in 1834. The building (Alfred and Paul Waterhouse, 1896–1906) was designed in an X-shape so as to provide maximum light and ventilation by separating the wards via long, hygienic corridors. Here Robert Liston, UCH's first Professor of Clinical Surgery, known for his speed and dexterity with a knife (crucial in an age before anaesthetic), performed the first operation in Europe under ether, in December 1846 (the first such operation in the world had taken place in Massachusetts three months earlier). UCH's huge new hospital, white with tinted green glass, ranges along Euston Road behind Euston Square Underground station. (*For Euston Road, St Pancras and King's Cross, see p. 362.*)

At 5–7 Tavistock Place (*map p. 601, E3*), **Mary Ward House** was built by Passmore Edwards in 1898 as a teaching and care centre for Mary Ward (better known as Mrs Humphry Ward), novelist, social reformer and aunt of Aldous Huxley.

THE LONDON TOWNHOUSE

London is known for its terraces: street after street of contiguous houses stretching away to a distant vanishing point and thrusting myriad chimney pots into the sky. The continental European model, so familiar cities like Vienna, of a single main entrance giving onto a wide communal courtyard from which stairways lead up floor by floor to individual apartments, is entirely unknown. In London (as was also the case in early New York) there are rows of individual houses, all seamelssly joined but with separate entrances and hallways. The result is an arrangement of narrow abodes, side by side, sharing lateral walls, each accessed up a short flight of steps to an individual front door and with the interior rooms arranged steeply on multiple floors. The internal

arrangement would have included a ground-floor hall (with steep stairs leading straight up from it) and dining room, a drawing room and parlour above, bedrooms above that, and servants' rooms in the attic. A bathroom often opened off one of the landings. The kitchens of the well-to-do houses were in the basement, accessed by the servants' stairs from within and from the street by the 'area', a narrow light well beside and below the front-door steps, surrounded by railings and entered down a separate flight of steps: housemaids in Edwardian novels are perpetually to be seen scrubbing the area steps with chillblained hands and buckets of carbolic soap.

Further out in the workers' and artisans' districts, the arrangements of terraces is similar, but the doorways are less magnificent and there are no servants' attics and no areas: instead the kitchen is typically a narrow galley at the back of the ground floor, with a tiny yard leading off it.

EAST BLOOMSBURY

The northeast side of Bloomsbury, away from the University and the British Museum and within easy walking distance of St Pancras and King's Cross, lies off the main tourist trail. It is a good place to wander as there are plenty of interesting independent shops, honest eateries and watering holes, especially around Marchmont Street and Lamb's Conduit Street.

In **Marchmont Street** (*map p. 601, E3*), blue plaques dot the Georgian houses like patches on the face of a fashionable 18th-century beauty: no. 88 was the home of Kenneth Williams, star of the bawdy *Carry On* films; no. 47, a burger bar, was where one Mr Grey, manufacturer of artificial teeth, lived in 1817; at no. 43, Robert Dyas, ironmonger, first traded in the 1930s (shops bearing his name have swelled into a high-street chain). On the site of the Brunswick Centre lived Sir John Barbirolli (Giovanni Battista Barbirolli), conductor and cellist. The **Brunswick Centre**, between Marchmont and Hunter streets, incorporates flats, shops and the Renoir Cinema; it was built in 1968–72 by Patrick Hodgkinson. The flats, part private, part social housing, descend in two straight lines of terraces overlooking the shopping street; car parking is underneath.

CORAM'S FIELDS AND THE FOUNDLING MUSEUM

Brunswick Square (*map p. 601, E3*), named after Queen Caroline, the unloved wife of George IV, was laid out in 1800. At no. 40 is the **Foundling Museum** (*open Tues–Sat 10–5; Sun 11–5; admission charge; café and shop; T: 020 7841 3600, foundlingmuseum. org.uk*), a remarkable institution which records the foundation, history and continuing work of the Foundling Hospital, a charitable home for illegitimate children established in 1739 by Captain Thomas Coram. A humble Dorset man, Coram was a master mariner who had arrived back from the American colonies to be appalled by the plight of abandoned, orphaned and destitute children on the streets of London. In 1739, after 17 years of relentless campaigning, Coram persuaded George II to grant a Royal Charter to open 'A Hospital for the Maintenance and Education of Exposed and Deserted Young Children'. An entirely secular organisation, the first of its kind, it was funded through private donations and subscription. Coram was supported by Hogarth, Handel and other well-known figures of the day.

All Foundling children were baptised on admission. The first child was named Thomas Coram and the first girl Eunice Coram, after Captain Coram's wife. In 1742 new buildings were begun. In 1749 Handel, who became a Hospital governor, conducted a concert to raise funds for the completion of the Hospital chapel, for which he composed the 'Foundling Hospital Anthem'. Fundraising concerts became a feature of the Hospital's calendar, with Handel conducting annual performances of the *Messiah*. A terracotta bust of him by Roubiliac is in the collection. The original building has been demolished but several of the finer rooms were carefully salvaged and re-erected within the new headquarters, completed in 1938. The Hospital's old site, **Coram's Fields**, is now an enclosed seven-acre children's park where adults are not encouraged: a sign says adults may only enter if accompanied by a child under 16. Peer through the entrance gates and you can see remaining Georgian stucco colonnades.

The Hospital originally had official appointment days for receiving children, with desperate queues forming outside the gates with more children than could possibly be accommodated. A ballot method was introduced. On reception days mothers drew a ball from a bag, its colour deciding the fate of their child. Careful records were made of each child admitted, as well as of the identifying keepsakes which could be used to reclaim children. Several of these touching Foundling tokens are on now show: metal tags with names, ribbons, buttons, lockets and even a hazelnut shell. Also in the collection is Hogarth's great *March to Finchley*, the scene set in the Tottenham Court Road in the winter of 1745, where a band of guardsmen is moving off to Finchley before marching north against Bonnie Prince Charlie's rebels. The King's Head tavern has been commandeered by the notorious brothel-keeper Mother Douglas. Hogarth sold the picture by lottery: 167 of the unsold tickets were donated to the Hospital, which won the picture. By Hogarth also is the splendid *Captain Thomas Coram* (1740), a masterpiece of British art, which Hogarth presented to the Hospital. Coram is shown seated on a dais, with columns behind, holding the seal of the Hospital's Royal Charter: the composition is redolent of traditional Baroque pomp, and yet Coram appears wigless and ruddy-cheeked, a direct realism which gives the portrait its human appeal.

ST GEORGE'S GARDENS

Mecklenburgh Square (*map p. 601, E3*), with a private central garden, was named for Charlotte of Mecklenburg-Strelitz, wife of George III. It retains its elegant Georgian housing. Virginia Woolf lived on the site of no. 37 until her death by suicide in 1941.

In Heathcote Street, north of Mecklenburgh Square, is the entrance to **St George's Gardens**, which served as the burial grounds for St George the Martyr and St George's Bloomsbury from 1713. This atmospheric green space, with winding paths, mature plane trees and shrubs, is dotted with weathered monuments and tomb chests, one of which is to Anna Gibson (d. 1726), favourite daughter of Richard Cromwell and granddaughter of Oliver Cromwell. The terracotta figure of *Euterpe* (1898) was one of the nine Muses that decorated the Apollo Inn, which stood on the corner of Tottenham Court Road and Torrington Place.

THE CHARLES DICKENS MUSEUM

Doughty Street is a fine Georgian street leading to Gray's Inn; the writers Vera Brittain and Winifred Holtby lived at no. 52. At no. 48 is the Charles Dickens Museum (*map p. 601, F4; entrance through no. 49; open Mon–Sun 10–5, last admission at 4; pre-booked costumed tours on 3rd Sat of month; admission charge; shop and café; T: 020 7405 2127, dickensmuseum.com*), in the house where Dickens lived for £80 a year between 1837 and 1839. It is his only surviving London residence, arranged now to paint an intimate picture of his domestic life, showing us the young husband and father as well as the writer and man of the theatre. Dickens lived here with his wife Catherine and their infant son Charles; the house also witnessed the birth of his daughters Mary and Kate as well as the completion of *The Pickwick Papers*, *Oliver Twist* and *Nicholas Nickleby*, the trio of publications which established his literary reputation.

The house holds a vast collection of Dickens memorabilia, including portraits, personal items, furniture and autograph letters and manuscripts. A silhouette of Dickens on the stairs welcomes the visitor. The basement contains a re-creation of the **Kitchen, Scullery and Washhouse**, where one learns that the Victorians kept hedgehogs to control insects (the resident stuffed specimen is called Bill Spikes). The **Dining Room** plays host to a fictional dinner party: places are set for Thackeray and the painter Daniel Maclise. Note the grandfather clock which belonged to Moses Pickwick, a coach proprietor of Bath, whose name Dickens took for his famous character. The **Morning Room** was principally used by Catherine Dickens, whose double portrait with her husband hangs over the fireplace; on display, too, is the couple's marriage licence (though the great idealiser of hearth and home was later to jilt Catherine for a woman 24 years her junior).

On the first floor is the spacious **Drawing Room**, used by Dickens to entertain his frequent visitors; here is the reading desk Dickens designed and took on tour with him around England and North America. On the second floor is **Dickens's Bedroom**, where his wife Catherine gave birth to their two daughters. The **Mary Hogarth Room** is the bedroom where Dickens' 'young, beautiful and good' sister-in-law, Mary Hogarth, died in 1837, aged just 17, an event which affected him profoundly and provided him with much material (for example, the death of Little Nell in *The Old Curiosity Shop*). The sketch of Dickens on his deathbed is by John Everett Millais.

In the third-floor **Nursery and Servants' Bedroom** the display enters the world of workhouses and prisons, illustrated by a grille from the debtors' prison at Marshalsea, where Dickens' father languished for three months. There are also glass jars from Warren's boot-blacking factory, where Dickens pasted on labels to earn his keep.

AROUND THEOBALD'S ROAD

Lamb's Conduit Street (*map p. 601, E4*) is a pleasant, part-pedestrianised street. Here is Persephone Books, publishers of lesser-known female authors (where you will find *The Making of a Marchioness* by Frances Hodgson Burnett; *see p. 263*). The Lamb, a Victorian pub, is one of the many hostelries in London where Dickens drank.

To the west is **Great Ormond Street** and the well-known eponymous children's hospital, founded in 1852. J.M. Barrie donated the royalties of *Peter Pan* (1904) towards its funding. A small museum in the hospital (*visits Mon–Fri 9.30–5 by prior appointment only; T: 020 7405 9200*) holds archives, photographs and a collection of decorative and scientific objects as well as rare editions of *Peter Pan*. St Christopher's Chapel by E.M. Barry (1875) is in the hospital's Variety Club Building.

Queen Square was laid out in the early 18th century and named after Queen Anne. The church of St George the Martyr (1706) was part of the original plan; it survives today after merciless Victorianisation during the 19th century. In the garden is a statue (c. 1775) of Queen Charlotte, previously thought to represent Queen Anne.

South of Theobalds Road, on the site now occupied by **Red Lion Square** (*map p. 601, E4*; formally laid out in 1684 by Nicholas Barbon), the bodies of Cromwell, Ireton and Bradshaw were displayed in 1661 after being disinterred from Westminster Abbey. They were taken the next day to Tyburn where they were desecrated and the heads placed on poles at Westminster Hall. In the garden today is a bronze bust of Bertrand

Russell by Marcelle Quinton (1980) and a bronze statue of the international peace campaigner Lord Brockway (1985). Several Pre-Raphaelite artists lived here: Rossetti at no. 17 in 1851, and Morris and Burne-Jones in 1856–9. In the northeast corner is Conway Hall (F. Herbert Mansard, 1929), the seat of the South Place Ethical Society, a pioneering institution of religious-humanist thought, founded in 1793.

At the junction of Southampton Row and **Kingsway**, notice the entrance to the Kingsway Tram Tunnel (now defunct). Kingsway (opened 1905) was an impressive piece of Edwardian town planning: a wide boulevard with a tunnel for electric trams underneath it. Behind the gates, you can still see the tram tracks on the slope leading into this part of secret, subterranean London. On Bloomsbury Way, notice **Sicilian Avenue**, a pedestrianised shopping street with buildings faced in terracotta (Robert Worley, 1910); the Ionic entrance screen gives it an exclusive, Italianate feel.

THE BRITISH MUSEUM

Great Russell Street. Map p. 601, E4. Underground: Holborn, Tottenham Court Road, Russell Square. Open daily 10–5.30 (until 8.30 on Fri). Free. Restaurant, café and shop. T: 020 7323 8299, britishmuseum.org.

Founded in 1753, the British Museum is the oldest secular public museum in the world. Its vast collection spans over two million years of the world's cultural history and contains many objects of outstanding international importance. At the core of the collection are the curiosities of Sir Hans Sloane.

SIR HANS SLOANE AND THE EARLY BRITISH MUSEUM

Sir Hans Sloane (1650–1753), botanist and scientist, was President of the Royal College of Physicians and of the Royal Society. His terracotta bust by Rysbrack (1736) is placed to the right of the British Museum's main entrance. In his will Sloane offered for sale to the Crown, for £20,000, his enormous and renowned collection of 'curiosities': botanical and natural history specimens, coins and medals, shells, paintings, books and manuscripts, the accumulations of a man of the scientific revolution intent on discovering and ordering the products of God's creation. A state lottery raised funds for its purchase together with the important manuscript collection of Robert Harley, Earl of Oxford (1661–1724). These collections, joined by the Cottonian manuscripts in 1700, were displayed not in a purpose-built museum but in Montagu House, a mansion of 1686. It was here that early visitors, including the young Mozart in 1765, who composed a motet, 'God is our refuge', dedicated to the museum, came to marvel. Cases of stuffed animals, fish, fossils and minerals, Classical antiquities and the museum's first Egyptian mummy were incongruously placed amid late 17th-century grandeur. Watercolours exist of the majestic grand staircase rising to meet three giant stuffed giraffes on the landing.

THE BRITISH MUSEUM
The Arts and Sciences cluster around Athena in Westmacott's tympanum frieze.

EXPANSION OF THE COLLECTION AND THE NEW BUILDING

A wave of major acquisitions in the late 18th and early 19th centuries necessitated the provision of suitable accommodation. In 1772 the great Greek vase collection of Sir William Hamilton (diplomat and archaeologist, and husband of Nelson's lover Emma) was acquired; in 1802 came the first significant haul of Egyptian antiquities, including the Rosetta Stone, followed in 1805 by the Townley Marbles. Too heavy for the delicate floors of Montagu House, they were placed in the adjoining Townley Gallery, purpose-built to accommodate them. Then, in 1816, came the purchase of the 'Elgin' Marbles, the most significant acquisition in the museum's history. A temporary structure of brick and wood was erected in the garden to house them, and it was here that the romantic Keats felt a 'dizzy pain' as he gazed upon 'these mighty things'.

Between 1820 and 1823 Sir Robert Smirke produced plans for a vast new building. Greek Revivalist in style, austere and dignified, it reflected the purity and rationalism of ancient Greece so admired by the English Neoclassicists. The building was conceived as a large quadrangle, with an imposing Ionic colonnaded entrance front and a massive portico. It was built wing by wing, parts of Montagu House coming down as the new edifice went up. Richard Westmacott's frieze of sculptures, *The Progress of Civilisation*, showing man's 'emergence from a rude state' to his embracement of the Arts and Sciences, shown gathered around the goddess Athena, was hoisted into place in the pediment above the entrance in 1851. But by then the original ideal of a 'universal' museum containing all branches of learning under one roof was understood to be a physical impossibility. The pictures, the nucleus of the National Gallery, had already been diverted to Trafalgar Square even before the first floor of the west wing, which was to have housed them, was built. In the 1880s the natural history collections moved to South Kensington, where they became the Natural History Museum. In 1998, with the removal of the British Library to St Pancras, the museum expanded into large areas previously occupied by books.

Sydney Smirke's lofty **Reading Room** (1854–7), built in the centre of his brother Robert Smirke's quadrangle, is only 2ft smaller than the Pantheon in Rome. Many famous scholars have worked under its cream, blue and gold *papier mâché* dome. It retains its layout of reading desks and is now an exhibition space. The quadrangle itself, known as the **Great Court**, is covered by Norman Foster's vast glass roof.

It is not possible to view the museum's vast collections in a single visit, nor to give a comprehensive account of them. Below is an outline of the museum's highlights.

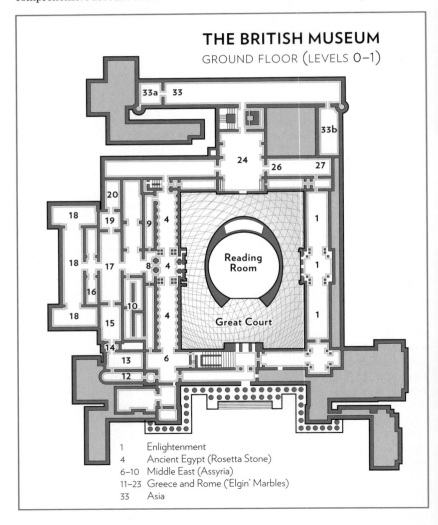

THE BRITISH MUSEUM

GROUND FLOOR (LEVELS 0–1)

Reading Room

Great Court

1	Enlightenment
4	Ancient Egypt (Rosetta Stone)
6–10	Middle East (Assyria)
11–23	Greece and Rome ('Elgin' Marbles)
33	Asia

Enlightenment (Room 1 on Level 0)

The restored King's Library, Smirke's magnificent Greek Revival space built to receive George III's library, donated to the museum by George IV in 1823, is the most imposing Neoclassical interior in London. It is 300ft long and decorated with an austere magnificence, with vast Corinthian columns of Aberdeen granite and a rich yet restrained plasterwork ceiling. Following the removal of the library to the British Library at St Pancras, the space has now been filled with a permanent exhibition looking at the age of the Enlightenment, the era of expanding knowledge, pioneering discovery and

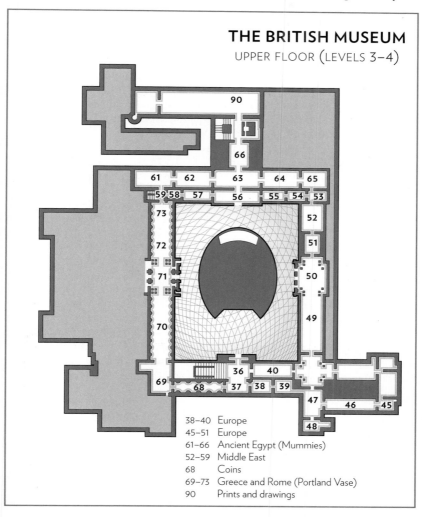

THE BRITISH MUSEUM
UPPER FLOOR (LEVELS 3–4)

38–40	Europe
45–51	Europe
61–66	Ancient Egypt (Mummies)
52–59	Middle East
68	Coins
69–73	Greece and Rome (Portland Vase)
90	Prints and drawings

rational observation in which the museum was founded. The displays contain objects from all aspects of the museum's collections, making it an ideal introduction to the museum as a whole. The development of methods for ordering, classifying and understanding man's growing experience of the world is explored.

Ancient Egypt, Nubia, Sudan and Ethiopia (Rooms 4 on Level 0; 61–66 on Level 3) The museum's famous Egyptian collection covers the cultures of the Nile Valley from the Neolithic age (c. 10th century BC) to Coptic times (12th century AD). Although Sloane's foundation collection had included some Egyptian material, it was not until 1802 that major items, ceded to the British under the terms of the 1801 Treaty of Alexandria, began to arrive. First and foremost among these was the famous **Rosetta Stone** (Room 4, Level 0), an object of unparalleled importance in the history of Egyptology. Originally discovered by French scholars who accompanied Napoleon's expeditionary force to Egypt, the stone, bearing an inscription in three scripts— hieroglyphic, demotic Egyptian and Greek—held the key to the decipherment of hieroglyphs. The code was finally cracked by the French Egyptologist Jean-François Champollion in 1822, thereby enabling the translation of texts and inscriptions which opened the door to the hitherto mysterious 'lost' civilisation of ancient Egypt.

The first great piece of Egyptian sculpture to arrive was the **bust of Ramesses II** (Room 4, Level 0), 'the Younger Memnon', a colossal seven-ton sculpture (actually only the head) carved from a single block of granite, excavated from the king's vast mortuary temple, the Ramesseum, in Thebes. Presented to the museum in 1817 by Henry Salt, British Consul-General in Cairo, and Jean Louis Burckhardt, a Swiss explorer, it had been physically removed from its site by Giovanni Belzoni, a former strongman and hydraulic engineer, whose team had taken twelve days to haul it to the river's edge.

The upstairs galleries house the museum's renowned collection of papyri, mummies, tomb sculpture and funerary objects. The mummies and their elaborate cases, including the Roman-period **mummy case of Artemidorus** (Room 62, Level 3) with its portrait of a young man from Hawara, are displayed alongside X-rays and CT scans, revealing amulets, scarabs and other sacred objects beneath the wrappings. Other grave goods such as jewellery, canopic jars and mummified animals are on show. There is a large collection of **Books of the Dead**, which offered spells to aid the dead in their passage through the underworld. The museum's most striking piece of tomb painting is the *Fowling in the Marshes* (Room 61, Level 3), a fragment from the tomb of Nebamun in Thebes (18th Dynasty, c. 1350 BC), showing Nebamun and his wife Hatshepsut in recreation in the afterlife.

Ancient Greece and Rome (Rooms 11–23 on Level 0; 69–73 on Level 3; 77–78 and 82–85 on Level -1)
The museum's collection of Greek and Roman antiquities is one of the finest in the world, ranging from the Bronze Age civilisations of the Cyclades and Minoan Crete to the late Roman Empire. The first major acquisition was the 1772 purchase of Sir William Hamilton's **Greek vase collection**, a large and valuable group mainly from southern Italy. In 1805 the Greek vases were joined by another major acquisition, the

Townley Marbles (Room 84, Level -1), a group of mainly Roman sculptures which Charles Townley began collecting in 1768 when in Rome on the Grand Tour. Interest in Classical sculpture was then at its zenith, fuelled by dealers who excavated sites such as Hadrian's Villa at Tivoli and restorers who worked alongside them. During his lifetime Townley's collection was displayed in his cluttered house in Queen Anne's Gate, Westminster, where it became a celebrated attraction visited by scholars and connoisseurs. Among the highlights was the bust of 'Clytie', Townley's favourite sculpture, which perhaps represents Antonia, daughter of Mark Antony and Octavia.

The Townley collection had an immense impact on 18th-century British taste, but its reputation was eclipsed by the arrival in the 19th century of several examples of Greek sculpture which cemented in people's minds the primacy of ancient Greek art and civilisation over Roman. The arrival which caused the greatest stir was that of the **'Elgin' Marbles** (Room 18, Level 0), acquired in 1816. Removed by Lord Elgin from the Parthenon, the 5th-century BC Temple of Athena Parthenos on the Acropolis, Athens, these sculptures have long been admired as the greatest achievement of Greek art. In the 19th century they became the benchmark against which all art was measured. The marbles include sculptures from the east pediment, originally a rhythmic succession of figurative groups illustrating the birth of Athena; slabs from the sculpted frieze showing the Panathenaic procession held to celebrate the birthday of Athena, carved with amazing skill and finesse; and sculpted panels once placed above the colonnade showing with great vividness the fight between the Lapiths and the Centaurs. Also removed by Elgin was the caryatid from the south porch of the Erechtheion, on the north side of the Acropolis. Although removed with full permission, and with the preservation of the marbles from the careless disregard of the Ottoman authorities in mind, even in the early 19th century Elgin was accused of robbery and plunder (by Byron). Visitors today cannot be unconscious of the arguments for the marbles' repatriation. The actor George Clooney recently added his voice to the chorus.

In 1845 slabs from the 4th-century BC **Mausoleum of Halicarnassus** (Room 21, Level 0), the tomb of Mausolus, King of Caria, and one of the Seven Wonders of the ancient world, arrived at the museum. Another of the Seven Wonders, the **Temple of Artemis at Ephesus**, from where St Paul preached to the Ephesians, is represented by a vast sculpted column drum (Room 22).

The well known **Portland Vase** (Room 70, Level 3), probably Roman (c. AD 5–25), was brought to England by Sir William Hamilton. It is a technical masterpiece of cobalt blue and white cameo glass decorated with a figurative frieze, famously copied by Josiah Wedgwood. In 1845 the vase was smashed into a hundred pieces by a drunken visitor, but successfully repaired.

Middle East (Rooms 6–10 on Level 0; 34 on Level -1; 52–59 on Level 3)
The museum's material from the ancient civilisations of the Near East includes art and artefacts from ancient Mesopotamia, Iran (Persia), the Levant, Anatolia and Urartu and southern Arabia, spanning the Neolithic period to the arrival of Islam in the 7th century AD. It has at its heart one of the finest collections of Assyrian sculpture in the world.

It was the great excavator Sir Austen Henry Layard (1817–94) who opened the West's eyes to the truly magnificent civilisation of the Assyrians. The sculptures arriving in London from the 1840s from Nimrud and Nineveh caused a sensation. They included the **Black Obelisk of Shalmaneser III** (r. 858–824 BC; Room 6, Level 0) with its carved representation of Jehu paying tribute to the king, a tantalising reference to a biblical figure; from the Northwest Palace of Ashurnasirpal II (r. 883–859 BC), a colossal **human-headed winged lion** (Room 6, Level 0) which guarded the entrance to the throne room; and carved slabs which lined the walls of the **Palace of Sennacherib** at Nineveh (Room 9, Level 0). Layard's local assistant, Hormuzd Rassam, continued to excavate on behalf of the museum, sending back astonishing discoveries from Ashurbanipal's North Palace at Nineveh, which he unearthed in 1852–4. From this richly-decorated palace came the famous Royal Lion Hunt slabs, in particular the **Dying Lion** (Room 55, Level 3), where the injured and bleeding animal is carved with incredible skill and observation. The discovery in 1872 that one of the cuneiform tablets (the **Flood Tablet**, 7th century BC; Room 55) contained a Babylonian version of the biblical deluge riveted Victorian minds.

Africa (Room 25 on Level -1)
Exhibits include the 12th–14th-century bronze head of a Yoruba ruler, probably Oni, King of Ife on the River Niger; sophisticated brass plaques from Benin, produced for the Oba rulers in the 16th century; and a collection of goldwork collected in 1817 by Thomas Boldwich on a journey to the Asante kingdom (present-day Ghana). Asante's great wealth was based on its vast gold deposits: at Kumasi, Boldwich noted the sun glinting off the massy gold ornaments of the people.

The Americas (Rooms 26–27 on Level -1)
The museum still has the great ceremonial cloak of feathers and mother of pearl, which is probably the one presented to Cook in Tahiti in 1774. **Hoa Hakananai'a**, the museum's monumental Easter Island statue brought back by the crew of HMS *Topaze* from its surveying expedition of 1868, is in the 'Living and Dying' exhibit in Room 24 (Level 0). These great human figures known as *moai*, part of the island's statue cult, which flourished up until the 17th century, originally stood upright on platforms, surveying the remote island scenery from under their heavy brows.

From Mexico come the three pieces of **Mixtec-Aztec turquoise mosaic**, possibly part of the tribute given by Emperor Moctezuma II to the Spanish conquistador Hernán Cortés in 1519.

Asia (Room 33 on Level 1; 67 and 95 on Level 2 and 92–94 on Level 5)
The large department covering the material remains of the Asian continent from Neolithic times to the present comprises the world's most comprehensive collection of sculpture from the Indian subcontinent; the best collection of Islamic pottery outside the Middle East; an outstanding collection of Chinese antiquities, including paintings, porcelain, lacquer and jade; the most important collection of Korean art in Europe; and, among the Japanese netsuke, samurai swords and ceramics (includ-

ing tea ceremony ware), the finest collection of Japanese paintings and prints in the West. The gilt-bronze 9th-century Sri Lankan **Bodhisattva Tara** (Room 33, Level 1) is one of the finest examples of Asian figural bronze-casting. The 133 1st–3rd-century delicately carved limestone **reliefs from the Great Stupa** (Room 33a), the Buddhist relic-house at Amaravati in Andhra Pradesh, southeast India, are one of the British Museum's greatest treasures.

The most important collection of Chinese artefacts was that of the Hungarian archaeologist and explorer of the Silk Route Sir Aurel Stein. Objects began to arrive from 1900, the most important of which was the group from the Tang period (AD 618–906): manuscripts, temple banners and paintings on silk and paper, including elaborate Paradise scenes, discovered in the **Valley of a Thousand Buddhas**, Dunhuang (Study Collection). Strategically placed on the Silk Route, the area had been an important centre for Buddhist pilgrims, who hollowed out over 1,000 cave shrines. In 1906, in Cave 17, closed since the early 12th century, Stein made his important discovery. In 1903 the museum purchased a major piece of Chinese art, the *Admonitions of the Instructress to the Court Ladies*, a painted scroll illustrating Zhang Hua's political parody attacking the excessive behaviour of the empress. The scroll is a valuable 6th–8th-century copy of the no-longer-extant original by the legendary artist Gu Kaizhi (AD 345–406), of whose work only a few not certainly attributed examples survive.

The excellent collection of **Japanese paintings and prints** includes fine pieces from the Kamakura period (1185–1333) and a great collection of Ukiyo-e (prints and paintings of the 'Floating World' school which flourished in the 17th–19th centuries), including the famous Mount Fuji woodblock print series by the leading artist of the late Edo period, Katsushika Hokusai (1760–1849).

The **Percival David Collection of Chinese ceramics** is in Room 95 on Level 2.

Europe (Rooms 38–40 and 45–51 on Level 3)
The department spans a vast expanse of time, from the Palaeolithic and Neolithic eras, through the Bronze and Iron Ages and Celtic Europe, to Roman Britain and the Christian cultures of the Medieval, Renaissance and Modern ages. Archaeological discovery and the ancient law of Treasure Trove, refined by the Treasure Act (1996), have benefited the collection enormously. Buried 'treasure', defined as any object containing ten percent silver or gold, over 300 years old and placed in the ground with the intention of retrieval, is administered by the museum. Through this route came the 12th-century **Lewis Chessmen** (Room 40, Level 3), discovered in 1831 in a stone chamber under a sandbank on the Isle of Lewis, Outer Hebrides; the exceptional **Mildenhall Treasure** (Room 49), a hoard of 34 pieces of superb Roman silver tableware of brilliant craftsmanship ploughed up in a field in Suffolk in the 1940s; and the great gold **Snettisham Torc** (Room 50), a magnificent 1st-century BC example of early Iron Age British craftsmanship. (Also in Room 50 is the extraordinarily well preserved **Lindow Man**, a 1st-century AD man of 25 who had been bludgeoned, garrotted and then had his throat cut, probably in a Druidic sacrifice.)

One of the greatest archaeological excavations in Britain was the 7th-century Anglo-Saxon **ship burial at Sutton Hoo**, Suffolk (Room 41), possibly the grave of Raedwald,

King of East Anglia. Discovered in 1939 under windswept heathland, the astonishing rich treasure of silver and gold set with garnets, includes a perfectly preserved and intricate gold buckle and a finely-crafted helmet.

Coins and Medals (Room 68 on Level 3 and throughout the galleries)
The British Museum has a fine numismatic collection spanning the history of coinage from its beginnings in the 7th century BC to the present day. Much of the collection is displayed in the Money Gallery (Room 68).

Prints and Drawings (Room 90 on Level 4)
The national collection of Western prints and drawings is one of the top three collections of its type in the world. At its heart are the pieces collected by Sloane, including volumes of Dürer's watercolours and drawings which are among the museum's most important possessions. Among the other highlights are over 90 works by Michelangelo, including studies for great commissions such as the Sistine Chapel ceiling; 80 sheets of sketches and drawings by Rembrandt, as well as a collection of his etchings; a large body of excellent works by Rubens; and British watercolours, including works by John Sell Cotman. There are also works by Thomas Girtin, a young artist of great promise, recognised as a genius by Turner. He died before he was 30. The collection is made available through a programme of temporary exhibitions in a room alongside the Print Room (which is open for research by appointment).

EUSTON ROAD, ST PANCRAS & KING'S CROSS

Map p. 601, D3–E3. Underground: Euston, Euston Square, King's Cross St Pancras.

Euston Road, the northern boundary of Bloomsbury, continues the line of Marylebone Road east to King's Cross. It forms part of the 'New Road' laid out in 1754–6 to connect Islington with Paddington, and now bears heavy traffic.

EUSTON STATION

Euston Station (*map p. 601, D3*), on the north side of the road, is the terminus of the London and Birmingham Railway, named after Euston Hall in Suffolk, the family seat of the Duke of Grafton. The railway engineer was Robert Stephenson: his statue, by Marochetti (1871), stands in the station forecourt. The station architect was Philip Hardwick and its builder Thomas Cubitt. It was one of the first—and perhaps the finest—of London's railway termini: at its entrance was Hardwick's colossal 70ft Doric propylaeum (1837; demolished), with lodges and bronze gates at either side, which became known as Euston Arch. It was so large that surviving drawings and photographs, show the people and carriages at its base looking tiny and ant-like. It was designed to be both a physical and symbolic grand gateway from London to the Midlands—on arrival in Birmingham, passengers passed through a complementary

EUSTON
The old Euston Arch, by E.B. Musman.

Ionic arch, also designed by Hardwick (1838; it still stands). In the station proper, the Great Hall, by Hardwick's son, Philip Charles Hardwick (1849), had a sweeping double staircase and coffered ceiling. By the 20th century, however, due to increased numbers of passengers and the electrification of the railway, the old station was overstretched and outdated. In the 1960s, the Euston Arch and the Great Hall were demolished, against considerable opposition: John Betjeman, Nikolaus Pevsner, Sir Charles Wheeler (director of the RA), the Society for the Protection of Ancient Buildings, the Georgian Group and the London Society all stepped in to try to save it. Their attempts were fruitless and the buildings were pulled down to make way for what stands here now. Although considered an act of philistinism, the loss of this monument to Britain's railway age (branded the 'Euston Murder' by the *Architectural Review* in 1962) did open up a wider debate about how other historic buildings in the capital were being treated and did prevent others from being torn down in similarly brutal fashion.

Currently, there is a campaign to rebuild the arch: much of its rubble was dumped in the Thames and some blocks of the hard Yorkshire stone have been retrieved. Time will tell. For more, visit the website of the Euston Arch Trust (*eustonarch.org*).

THE WELLCOME COLLECTION AND ST PANCRAS PARISH CHURCH

At no. 183 Euston Road, diagonally opposite the station, is the **Wellcome Collection** (*map p. 601, D3*), the 'destination for the incurably curious'. It is part of the Wellcome Trust, a charitable foundation devoted to medicine and medical science, established by Sir Henry Wellcome (1853–1936), and has a library, café and free exhibition galleries (*open Tues–Sat 10–6, until 8pm on Thur, Sun 11–6; wellcomecollection.org*). The Neoclassical building was built in 1932 to Wellcome's specifications.

Next door at no. 173 (on the other side of Gordon St) is the Neoclassical **Friends' House** (Hubert Lidbetter, 1926), the headquarters of the Society of Friends or Quakers (*entrance from the Friends' Gardens, leading to Endsleigh St*).

Continuing east, on the corner of Upper Woburn Place and Euston Road, rises **St Pancras Parish Church**, sometimes referred to as St Pancras New Church (St Pancras Old Church is north of St Pancras station; *see p. 367*), a distinctive landmark defined by the caryatid porch over the entrance to its crypt. It was built in neo-Greek style, in 1819–22, by William and Henry Inward, father and son, who borrowed features from the Erechtheion in Athens. The four robust caryatids, by J.C.F. Rossi, which face north over Euston Road (four more face south), are not of stone but terracotta, built around cast-iron columns. Unfortunately they were too tall to fit and had to be shortened in the middle, hence their stocky appearance. The church steeple was inspired by the Tower of the Winds in the Athens agora.

Woburn Walk, the charming street skirting the south of the churchyard, was built by Thomas Cubitt in 1822. It preserves quaint shopfronts, many of which are still in use by shops today. W.B. Yeats lived at no. 5 in 1895–1919.

In the **UNISON Centre** on the other side of the road (no. 130), on the ground floor of the former Hospital for Women founded by Elizabeth Garrett Anderson in 1872, is a small display on the life and work of the pioneering female doctor (*open Wed–Fri 9–6, third Sat of the month 9–4; free; egaforwomen.org.uk*).

THE BRITISH LIBRARY

96 Euston Rd; map p. 601, E3. T: 0843 208 1144, bl.uk. Exhibition galleries open Mon–Fri 9.30–6 (until 8pm on Tues), Sat 9.30–5, Sun and holidays 11–5. Free. Café and shop.
Formerly part of the British Museum, the British Library was housed until 1997 in the main museum building, with magnificent purpose-built reading rooms. Having outgrown those premises, it moved (in 1998) into this new building, originally designed by Colin St John Wilson in 1977. The unprepossessing red-brick exterior makes the interior a complete surprise: a wonderful white, tall, airy space flooded with light, with broad steps leading up to the reading rooms. In the centre, encased in a six-storey tower of bronze and glass and with their tooled leather and gold spines visible, are the 60,000 volumes of the King's Library, presented to the British Museum in 1823 by George IV. On the west wall is a tapestry woven after R.B. Kitaj's *If not, not*. At the core of the Library's collections are the three foundation collections of the British Museum: those of Sir Hans Sloane (*see p. 354*); Sir Robert Cotton (d. 1631); and Robert Harley, 1st Earl of Oxford (d. 1724). Their busts adorn the Entrance Hall. The Library is one of the largest and most comprehensive in the world and contains several treasures: two contemporary copies of *Magna Carta* (1215); the manuscript of the Anglo-Saxon epic *Beowulf*; the illuminated Northumbrian 'Lindisfarne Gospels' (c. 715–20); William Caxton's two editions of Chaucer's *Canterbury Tales* (1476 and 1483); the exceptional 'Sforza Hours' from Milan (c. 1490–1520); and the 'Codex Arundel' containing manuscript sheets of Leonardo da Vinci's mathematical notes and diagrams. The Codex was once owned by Thomas Howard, Earl of Arundel, who travelled to Italy with Inigo Jones (*see below*).

The large piazza outside the entrance has, crouching on one side, Eduardo Paolozzi's bronze, bespectacled *Newton* (1995), inspired by William Blake's image of the same. Surrounding the sunken 'amphitheatre' are the eight carved Swedish glacial boulders which make up Antony Gormley's *Planets*.

THOMAS, EARL OF ARUNDEL AND INIGO JONES

The friendship between Inigo Jones and Thomas Howard, Earl of Arundel began with Jones's court masques, in which Arundel's wife was a keen participant. When Henry, the gifted Prince of Wales who had been Arundel's friend and Jones's patron, died aged 18 in 1612, this seems to have prompted both men to travel overseas. Arundel had been to Italy before, and had been enthused by what he saw. In 1613 he and Jones travelled to Venice, where they spent time exploring its *palazzi*. Jones bought an edition of Palladio's *Quattro Libri* as well as a mass of Palladio's original drawings, acquired from Vincenzo Scamozzi, Palladio's pupil. From Venice the two went to Vicenza, where they spent a few days, visiting the Villa Rotonda, and eventually to Rome. Jones filled the margins of his copy of Palladio with notes on what he had seen and the two pored over the surviving ruins, spending hours gazing at antique sculpture and inscriptions. Both were repelled by the growing signs of the Baroque, Jones writing that he preferred his architecture to be austere and ordered. It was a second trip to Venice which fully consolidated Jones's ideas. He was appointed Surveyor of the King's Works in 1615.

ST PANCRAS
Detail of Paul Day's *The Meeting Place* (2007), a colossal sculpture on the station concourse.

ST PANCRAS AND KING'S CROSS STATIONS

Next to the British Library towers a Victorian Gothic masterpiece, **St Pancras Station** (properly, St Pancras International; *map p. 601, E3*), from where Eurostar trains serve continental Europe. It opened in 1868 as the terminus connecting London with the Midlands and Yorkshire. The richly ornamented station front, with its clock tower facing Euston Road, is the former Midland Grand Hotel, by George Gilbert Scott, which opened in 1873 and was described as one of the most sumptuous hotels in the Empire. It lay neglected and empty for many years until in 2011 it finally reopened as part of the luxury Renaissance hotel group, restored to its former glory. Inside is Gilbert Scott's grand staircase (guests only), which one may quickly peep at. The interior may be seen in proper detail on an official tour (*fee payable; contact the hotel for details; tours last approx. 90mins*). Behind the hotel façade stretches the Victorian train shed by William Henry Barlow, and the new Eurostar terminal with further platforms serving UK destinations as well as shops, restaurants and Europe's longest champagne bar. Barlow's shed was one of the wonders of Victorian engineering, a 100ft-high glass and iron structure, 20ft above ground level and spanning 240ft, which at the time was the largest single-span roof in the world.

Next door, in contrast, **King's Cross Station**, built in the 1850s in yellow stock brick with large twin arches, appears diminutive and purely functional.

The area around King's Cross and St Pancras has long been a deprived, run-down neighbourhood—London's red light district—notorious for its high levels of homelessness, prostitution and drugs. At the time of writing a regeneration programme was underway, involving new houses, new streets and new public areas covering 67 acres of land, anciently a crossing on the river Fleet known as Battlebridge, north of (behind) the two stations (it will have a new postcode upon completion). The *Guardian* and the *Observer* newspapers now occupy state-of-the-art multi-media suites and offices in King's Place, as do two of London's orchestras. A new arts university is also part of the project.

REGENT'S CANAL

North of St Pancras and King's Cross stations flows the Regent's Canal (*map p. 601, E2*), along which brightly-painted narrowboats, homes to their owners, are moored. The nine-mile canal, built in 1816–20, passes though Maida Vale, the Zoo at Regent's Park, Camden Town, Islington and Hackney to join the Thames at Limehouse. The **London Canal Museum** in New Wharf Road is housed in the former house of Carlo Gatti, the Victorian entrepreneur who sold ice cream to the masses. It tells the story of London's waterways (*open Tues–Sun and Bank Holidays 10–4.30; canalmuseum.org. uk*). There is good access for pedestrians and cyclists to the stretch of canal behind King's Cross and at the time of writing there were also plans for wider towpaths, more bridges, wall-gardens and restaurants and cafés. If you head northwest, you come to Camden; going east takes you towards Islington (although if going on foot, you have to leave the towpath when you reach the nearly 900m Islington Tunnel, and take the back streets). Also here is the **Camley Street Natural Park**, an extraordinary 2-acre inner-city nature reserve where you might spot kingfishers and warblers.

ST PANCRAS OLD CHURCH

On Pancras Road, the continuation of Midland Road that runs between the British Library and St Pancras International, on a small grassy hillock, a site of great antiquity, is the small and quaint St Pancras Old Church (*map p. 601, D2*). Photographed from a certain angle, it looks like the country chapel it once was in the 17th century. In reality, it bravely stands amongst new development, with high-speed Eurostar trains hurtling past its door; despite this, it is a very tranquil, soothing spot. Of ancient origin, and nearly derelict by the 19th century, it was rebuilt in Victorian fashion. During rebuilding, workmen stumbled upon Elizabethan and Jacobean silver (booty stashed by Cromwell's troops during the Civil War) as well as the church's missing 6th-century altar stone. In the churchyard is the **monument to Sir John Soane** (*see p. 198*). Also buried here is Mary Wollestonecraft (d. 1792), author of *A Vindication of the Rights of Woman* and mother of Mary Shelley (author of *Frankenstein*). Also here is the **'Hardy Tree'**. It is a curiously unsettling sight: a mass of tombstones, stuck in the earth at different depths, fan around the base of an ash tree, seemingly growing amidst its roots. In actual fact, the headstones were placed here during the 1860s, when the Midland Railway was being built over part of the churchyard. The tombs that were in the way were dismantled and their human remains exhumed under the direction of Arthur Blomfield. The tree is so named because Thomas Hardy was Blomfield's assistant at the time. Hardy's first career was as an architect; he turned to literature later.

EATING AND DRINKING IN BLOOMSBURY, FITZROVIA AND KING'S CROSS

The area around Charlotte Street, Goodge Street and Cleveland Street (*map p. 601, D4*) is amply stocked with places to eat, to suit all palates and pockets. You can find all manner of cuisines here: Japanese, Indian, Italian, Spanish, Middle Eastern and more. Or try one of the following:

BLOOMSBURY, FITZROVIA

£–££ Bam-Bou. In a rickety old townhouse, good Vietnamese food. Lively and popular. *1 Percy St. T: 020 7323 9130, bam-bou.co.uk. Map p. 601, D4.*

£ Barrica. Spanish-style tapas bar with a genuinely authentic feel. Good choice of wines and sherries. Closed Sun. *62 Goodge St. T: 020 7436 9448, barrica.co.uk. Map p. 601, D4.*

££ Berners Tavern. At the Edition Hotel, in a room fabulously adorned with stucco and as many paintings as the wall can handle. Mediterranean-British fusion cuisine. Worth a visit. *10 Berners St, T: 020 7908 7979, bernerstavern.com. Map p. 601, D4.*

£ Bubbledogs. Offers the unlikely combination of 'gourmet hotdogs': that is, hotdogs with champagne. They make quite a thing about not serving caviar. Closed Sun and Mon. *70 Charlotte St. T: 020 7637 7770, bubbledogs.co.uk. Map p. 601, D4.*

£ Byron. Burgers by St Giles church. Competent and convenient. They have branches all over town. *1A St Giles High St. T: 020 7240 2707, byronhamburgers.com. Map p. 603, F1.*

££ Charlotte Street Hotel. A good place for cocktails. They also serve afternoon tea. *15–17 Charlotte St. T: 020 7806 2000. Map p. 601, D4.*

£ Ciao Bella. Cheap, convivial and heartily recommendable for *spaghetti vongole* and a glass of wine. *86–90 Lamb's Conduit St. T: 020 7242 4119, ciaobellarestaurant.co.uk. Map p. 601, E4.*

£££ Dabbous. You couldn't get a table when this place opened in 2012, because chef Oliver Dabbous received so many plaudits. He is famed for his original presentations, using colour, texture and subtle flavour combinations. Closed Sun. *39 Whitfield St. T: 0207 323 1544, dabbous.co.uk. Map p. 601, D4.*

£–££ Fino. Contemporary Spanish with dishes from all over the Iberian peninsula. The chef hails from the Basque country. If you have never eaten goose barnacles, this is the place to do so. Dinner only on Sun. *33 Charlotte St. T: 020 7813 8010, finorestaurant.com. Map p. 601, D4.*

£–£££ Hakkasan. Michelin-starred Chinese cuisine. Now an international chain, but this was the original restaurant. Open daily. *8 Hanway Place. T: 020 7927 7000, hakkasan.com. Map p. 601, D4.*

£ Indian YMCA. The canteen here was set up some decades ago to provide a comforting taste of home to Indians newly arrived in London. It is now popular with all and sundry for a cheap and tasty lunch. *41 Fitzroy*

Square. Map p. 601, D4.

£ The Life Goddess. Greek deli with a superb array of tempting things, to take away or eat in at one of the café tables. Open daily. *29 Store St. T: 020 7637 2401, thelifegoddess.com. Map p. 601, D4.*

£ Newman Arms. George Orwell drank here. So did many others. The pub is known for its pies, freshly made with many fillings. Best to book. Open Mon–Fri. *23 Rathbone St. T: 020 7636 1127, newmanarms.co.uk. Map p. 601, D4.*

£££ Pied à Terre. Somewhat stark and angular décor, but the chef has a Michelin star and offers a good-value lunch menu. Or you can splash out on the full ten-course taster. Vegetarian menus also available. No lunch Sat, closed all day Sun. *34 Charlotte St. T: 020 7636 1178, pied-a-terre.co.uk. Map p. 601, D4.*

£££ Roka. Sister of Zuma (*see p. 338*). Contemporary Japanese. *37 Charlotte St. T: 020 7580 6464, rokarestaurant. com. Map p. 601, D4.*

££ Sardo. Sardinian cuisine. Their speciality is grated fish roe on spaghetti. No lunch Sat. *45 Grafton Way. T: 020 7387 2521, sardo-restaurant. com. Map p. 601, D4.*

£–££ Villandry. Food 'emporium', takeaway, bar/café for light meals and a formal restaurant with Mediterranean-inspired cuisine. *170 Great Portland St. T: 020 7631 3131, villandry.com. Map p. 600, C4.*

KING'S CROSS, ST PANCRAS

££ Booking Office. Open daily for cocktails at the long bar or a full meal (classic English cuisine). Atmospheric neo-Gothic interior of the old ticketing hall of St Pancras station. Lively and fun. *St Pancras Renaissance Hotel, Euston Rd. T: 020 7841 3566, bookingofficerestaurant.com. Map p. 601, E3.*

£ Caravan. Delicious small sharing plates and excellent breakfasts and coffee. Behind King's Cross on the far side of the Regent's Canal. *Granary Square. T: 020 7101 7661, caravankingscross.co.uk. Map p. 601, E2.*

££ The Gilbert Scott. Excellent (but pricey) cocktail bar in the St Pancras Hotel. Also a restaurant in a beautifully restored high-ceilinged room. Open daily. *St Pancras Renaissance Hotel, Euston Rd. T: 020 7278 3888, the gilbertscott.co.uk. Map p. 601, E3.*

££ Grain Store. By chef Bruno Loubet. There's an emphasis on seasonal produce and vegetables. Has an enthusiastic following. No dinner Sun. *Granary Square. T: 020 7324 4466, grainstore.com. Map p. 601, E2.*

£ Paolina. Very good value Thai café. Good fresh cooking and run by a friendly Thai family. *181 King's Cross Rd (south of Euston Rd). Map p. 601, E3–F3.*

£–££ Shrimpys. Very small but stylish restaurant/bar in a converted petrol station. American-style food and excellent cocktails. Open daily. *Goods Way. T: 020 8880 6111, shrimpys.co.uk. Map p. 601, E2.*

Simmons. Vintage, hipster-style evening-only bar with cheap cocktails served in tea cups and the like. *32 Caledonian Rd. T: 0207 278 5851, simmonsbar.co.uk. Map p. 601, E3.*

Holborn Circus, Clerkenwell, Islington & Camden

North of the City lie a number of lively areas. Camden is on the Regent's Canal and narrowboat trips can be made from here. Parts of Islington are residentially stylish. Holborn Circus makes a good starting point for exploration.

In the middle of Holborn Circus (*map p. 606, A2–B2*) stands the City's official monument to Prince Albert: an equestrian statue of him doffing his plumed hat, by Charles Bacon (1874). Northwest is what remains of Italian London. At Hatton Garden there are strong Jewish connections, while nearby Ely Place is a Catholic enclave.

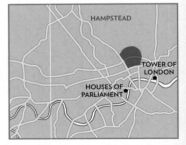

HATTON GARDEN AND ELY PLACE

Hatton Garden (*map p. 606, A1–A2*) is London's jewellery quarter. Diamond merchants, precious metal traders, jewellery wholesalers, retailers and dealers have clustered here since the 1870s. The street takes its name from the garden of a house made over to Sir Christopher Hatton, Lord Chancellor under Queen Elizabeth I. At no. 5, a tablet with a bas-relief portrait and a device of clasped hands commemorates the residence of Giuseppe Mazzini, Italian patriot, who lived here in exile 1836 and re-founded his 'Young Italy' movement, aimed at securing national independence for his country. While in London, he befriended Thomas Carlyle (*see p. 311*). In 1863 the Italian church of St Peter's was founded on Clerkenwell Road, just to the north, and the area came to be known as **'Little Italy'**. Caruso performed here and Garibaldi was a visitor in 1864. The Italian flavour of the district is now a thing of the past, though every year in mid-July a street procession in honour of Our Lady of Mount Carmel begins from St Peter's church. When it was first held in the 19th century, it was thought to be the first open-air Catholic celebration to take place in this country since the Reformation.

CAMDEN
Detail of the Stables Market, formerly a hospital for injured barge horses.

Ely Place (1772; *map p. 606, B2*) occupies the site of the townhouse of the bishops of Ely. Queen Elizabeth I forced them to cede part of the property to Sir Christopher Hatton (at the yearly 'rent' of ten loads of hay, £10 and a single rose) but they regained it at the Restoration. The gardens were famous for their strawberries, which are mentioned by Shakespeare in *Richard III*. Part of Shakespeare's *Richard II* is also set here: John of Gaunt (who died here in 1399) makes his famous 'sceptred isle' speech from Ely Place. The street still officially belongs to the diocese of Ely in Cambridgeshire and it is not under the jurisdiction of the Metropolitan Police. It is closed at night and is guarded by its own uniformed watchmen, whose small lodge stands between the two sets of gates. Ye Olde Mitre Tavern in Ely Court was built in the 18th century on the site of a 16th-century inn. It is known for its good beer.

St Etheldreda's Church (*stetheldreda.com; open Mon–Sat 8–5, Sun 8–12.30*), formerly the bishops' chapel, dates from 1290. The only surviving relic of the old bishops' house, it is the oldest Roman Catholic church in England (it returned to the Catholic rite in 1874) and has an atmosphere of serene and ancient sanctity. The arcaded statue-niches in the walls and the tracery of the east and west windows are superb. The bright stained glass and statues of English martyrs are by Charles and May Blakeman (1952–64). The west window shows the five 'proto-martyrs' of English Catholicism, executed at Tyburn in 1535. Among their number is the prior of the nearby Charterhouse (*see below*). The Blakemans also adorned the crypt with its fresco of the *Risen Christ*.

CLERKENWELL

Map p. 606, B1–C1. Underground: Farringdon.

Lively Clerkenwell, just north of Smithfield, is a fashionable and animated area, with designer offices and flats popular with those in the arts and the media. It is also a destination for serious foodies: delicious eating and fine-dining establishments abound. Former factories, warehouses and workshops have been converted into loft-style apartments, design studios, architects' practices, restaurants and bars. Many of these buildings have interesting façades, often featuring designs of livestock.

Historically Clerkenwell is also associated with watch-making as well as jewellery and printing. From the 17th century several fine houses were built for merchants and the well-to-do. Among former residents were Izaak Walton (1650–61), Christopher Pinchbeck, inventor of the brass alloy that bears his name (1721), the Swedish theologian Emanuel Swedenborg and Oliver Cromwell.

THE CLERKS' WELL

Clerkenwell was once a monastic settlement and takes its name from the Clerks' Well, mentioned as early as 1174, around which the clerks of the parish used to perform miracle plays. The well survives and is housed inside a 1980s' building, nos 14–16

ST ETHELDREDA'S CHURCH
Detail from the Window of the Catholic Martyrs, honouring the first men to die for their faith during the Reformation. Shown here are priors Lawrence, Houghton and Webster.

Farringdon Lane (*map p. 606, B1*). It is visible through the plate glass but may be also be visited, free of charge, by appointment (*Mon–Sat 9.30–1 & 2–5, closed Wed and Sun; contact Islington Local History Centre, Finsbury Library, 245 St John St; T: 020 7527 7988, local.history@islington.gov.uk*).

GATEHOUSE AND CHURCH OF ST JOHN

Another monument from Clerkenwell's monastic past is **St John's Gate**. This castellated gatehouse spanning St John's Lane (*map p. 606, B1*) once formed the main entrance of the Grand Priory of the Order of the Hospital of St John of Jerusalem (the Knights Hospitaller of the Crusades), founded in the early 12th century. Built shortly after that date, the priory was burnt down in Wat Tyler's Peasants' Revolt in the late 14th century, and rebuilt in something resembling its present form by Prior Thomas Docwra in 1504. The Order was one of the last to be suppressed by Henry VIII (in 1540) and the gatehouse was converted into the office of the Master of the Revels. Later it was variously the home of Hogarth; the offices of *The Gentleman's Magazine* (where Samuel Johnson worked); and the Old Jerusalem Tavern (where Dickens drank). In 1874 it was purchased by the British Order of St John (refounded as a Protestant Order in 1831) and now houses the **Museum of the Order of St John** (*open Mon–Sat 10–5; tours on Tues, Fri, Sat at 11 and 2.30; T: 020 7324 4005; museumstjohn.org.uk; free except tours*), exploring the history of the building, the Order of the Hospitallers and the work of St John's Ambulance.

In St John's Square, across Clerkenwell Road, lies the **Priory Church of St John**, with an adjacent small garden. It was rebuilt in the 18th century incorporating the choir walls of the ancient priory church and has been restored since its destruction in World War Two. In the well-preserved 12th-century crypt is a fine 16th-century alabaster effigy of a knight of the Order, brought from Valladolid.

From St John's Square, Jerusalem Passage cuts through to **Aylesbury Street** (*map p. 606, B1*). The corner building at the top of the passage on the right stands on the site of the home of Thomas Britton, the 'musical small-coal man', a charcoal vendor who fitted up his attic as a concert hall and held cramped but prestigious musical evenings every Thursday. It is rumoured that Handel was once among the company. Britton died in Clerkenwell in 1714, reputedly of fright after seeing a ventriloquist's act. His house is marked with a green plaque.

THE CHARTERHOUSE

The Charterhouse (*map p. 606, C1*), a charity and almshouse, occupies 16th–19th-century buildings behind a gatehouse off Charterhouse Square. A Carthusian priory was founded on the site in 1370 by Sir Walter de Manny, a distinguished soldier under Edward III. The monastery was brutally suppressed during the Dissolution and many monks were martyred at Tyburn (Marble Arch) before the priory surrendered. Sir Edward North, afterwards Lord North, to whom the property was granted in 1545, built a mansion on the site using material from the monastery buildings. It was sold to the Duke of Northumberland, who was executed in 1553 for his attempt to put Lady Jane Grey (his daughter-in-law) on the throne. Queen Elizabeth stayed here before her coronation in 1558. The property was considerably altered by a later owner, the 4th Duke of Norfolk, who was executed for complicity in a plot to put Mary, Queen of Scots on the throne. Elizabeth I paid further visits to the mansion (then known as Howard House). James I was entertained here by Thomas Howard, later Earl of Suffolk, to whom the property had passed in 1601. In 1611, the Charterhouse was bought for £13,000 by Thomas Sutton, a shrewd soldier, probably also a merchant-adventurer, who founded the 'Hospital of King James in Charterhouse'. This included a hospital for 80 poor brethren and a free school for 40 poor boys. The Charterhouse School rapidly developed into one of the best-known public schools in England and outgrew its premises. In 1872 it was transferred to Godalming in Surrey. Thackeray was a former, rather unhappy, pupil. From 1875 to 1933 the site of the school was occupied by the Merchant Taylors' School, founded in 1561 in Suffolk Lane, Upper Thames Street (this school is now at Moor Park, Hertfordshire).

One part of the Charterhouse is now let as private residences; the major part is used as a home for The Brothers, a community of retired gentlemen from various professions in need of financial and social support. The Brothers live privately but enjoy their meals together in the Great Hall.

Charterhouse may be visited on a private tour led by one of the Brothers. Tickets must be pre-booked (*see thecharterhouse.org or email tours@charterhouse.org*). Tours are usually available spring–autumn Mon–Sat. A per-person fee is charged.

RADICAL CLERKENWELL AND CLERKENWELL GREEN

Clerkenwell has also been associated with radicalism: during the 19th century Clerkenwell Green (*map p. 606, B1*), the old part of village Clerkenwell, became a political meeting place and the scene of Chartist marches. At No 37A Clerkenwell Green, built in 1738 by James Steer as a Welsh charity school, is the **Marx Memorial Library**

CLERKENWELL
Motifs of livestock adorn numerous Clerkenwell façades, buildings that once housed storage facilities and other accessory businesses to nearby Smithfield Market.

(red door). Visitors are admitted as part of a tour (*Mon–Thur 1–2 or by appointment, T: 020 7253 1485, marx-memorial-library.org*). The London Patriotic Society based itself here until the Twentieth Century Press took up the lease for its Socialist printing works. William Morris and Eleanor Marx spoke here, and Lenin edited *Iskra* (1902–3). The Marx Memorial Library was established in 1933 to commemorate the 50th anniversary of his death and contains well over 100,000 books and manuscripts relating to Marxism, Socialism and the working class movement.

Also on Clerkenwell Green, at no. 22, is the old **Middlesex Sessions Courthouse** (1779–82), designed by Thomas Rogers with reliefs by Nollekens. It had a reputation for dispensing severe justice: in one year alone 200 people were convicted and transported to America and Australia. Nearby was a prison, the notorious House of Detention, constructed in the 17th century to relieve Newgate. Rebuilt in 1845, it became one of the busiest prisons in the capital.

In Clerkenwell Close is the parish **church of St James's**, with a steeple by James Carr (1788–91). The church is open to visitors when the church office is open (*Mon–Fri 9.30–5.30, ring doorbell for admittance*).

ROSEBERY AVENUE AND EXMOUTH MARKET

Several interesting landmarks cluster around Rosebery Avenue (*map p. 601, F4–F3*), including **Sadler's Wells**, a leading theatre for contemporary dance. The current purpose-built building opened in 1998 and incorporates an earlier 1930s' theatre. The name recalls the area's richness in water: Londoners would come for relaxation and treatments at Clerkenwell's many spas, which were built over natural mineral springs. The first music hall, built in 1683 by Richard Sadler, was built around a medicinal well on this site. On the corner of Rosebery Avenue and Rosoman Street is the neo-Renaissance **Old Finsbury Town Hall**. On Pine Street is the Modernist **Finsbury Health Centre** (by Berthold Lubetkin/Tecton, 1935–8; their first public commission). Also by Tecton is the **Spa Green Estate**, between Rosebery Avenue and St John Street, inventive multi-storey apartment blocks built over a former slum, designed before World War Two but not completed until 1950. The **Laboratory Building** at 177 Rosebery Avenue (1938, built for the Metropolitan Water Board) is now flats.

Exmouth Market, a lively, semi-pedestrian street near the junction of Farringdon Road and Rosebery Avenue, is lined with bars and restaurants.

Mount Pleasant (*map p. 601, F4*) is home to what was once the largest postal sorting office in the United Kingdom, built in 1900 on the site of the Coldbath House of Correction, a prison from 1794–1877. Following privatisation of the Royal Mail, the site is to be redeveloped as luxury flats.

ISLINGTON, HIGHBURY & HOLLOWAY

Map pp. 597 and 601. Underground: Angel, King's Cross St Pancras, Caledonian Road, Highbury & Islington.

Historically a rural area where cattle were rested before being driven to market at Smithfield, Islington in the 18th century was a pleasant countryside suburb near to Sadler's Wells spa. In the 19th century it was developed with elegant terraces and squares and became a place where middle-class City workers lived, due to its proximity to the City. The area became overcrowded and less salubrious later in the 19th century, when the building of the railway at nearby King's Cross displaced large sections of a poor, working-class population, who overflowed into Islington. It was not until the 1960s, when an arty, predominantly left-wing intelligentsia began to rediscover Islington's attractions, that its houses began to be renovated. Today parts of the area are still poor and underprivileged, but on the whole it is a trendy, lively district with plenty of bars, restaurants and shops in its gentrified Georgian streets and squares.

EXPLORING FROM ANGEL UNDERGROUND
Opposite the station is the late 19th-century former Angel Hotel, with a distinctive dome. East of Angel, the **Regent's Canal** passes from City Road Basin (1820; *map p. 597, D2*), a re-developed, former industrial stretch of water and home of the Islington Boat Club, through the longest tunnel on its route, 960 yards, completed in 1818. There is no towpath and the towing horses were led along the area that is now Chapel Market while the bargees propelled their boats by 'legging': lying on their backs and pushing against the wall with their feet. A steam tug was introduced in 1826 and used until the

1930s. The canal emerges from the tunnel at Muriel Street near Caledonian Road (*map p. 601, F2*) and continues to Camden Town, Regent's Park and Paddington.

Running due north from Angel station is **Upper Street** (*map p. 597, D2*), lined with shops and restaurants, leading to Highbury and Holloway Road. **Camden Passage**, a narrow street running parallel with Upper Street on the right-hand side, with a mix of permanent shops, is the site of an antiques market trading on Wed and Sat.

Turn right off Upper Street down Duncan Street to reach **Duncan Terrace and Colebrooke Row**, attractive 18th-century streets which were developed to run either side of the **New River** (its course here indicated by the garden in front of Duncan Terrace; it was culverted in the 1890s). This man-made waterway, 10ft wide and 3ft deep, opened in 1613 to supply London with fresh drinking water from springs in Hertfordshire and Middlesex. It still supplies London with water, now treated before drinking, and flows from Hertford into reservoirs at Stoke Newington. Originally the New River terminated near the Sadler's Wells Theatre (*see p. 375*), where a play was staged in 1613 to mark its opening. It is still possible to walk along large sections of the New River, via the New River Path (*see Canonbury Grove below and Stoke Newington p. 404*). At 64 Duncan Terrace lived the essayist Charles Lamb in 1823; his friend George Dyer, on leaving his house one day, fell into the New River and nearly drowned.

On the green triangle of **Islington Green** is a statue of Sir Hugh Myddleton, chief promoter of the New River, by John Thomas (1862). Essex Road, which forks right, is progressively down-market; along here (nos 161–169) is the Art Deco former **Carlton Cinema** (1930), at the time of writing practically derelict. The building, by George Coles, is in the form of an Egyptian pylon temple, decorated with multi-coloured ceramic tiling.

Opposite Islington Green are the curving roofs of the **Business Design Centre**, an events venue that sometimes stages art fairs. Part of it is housed in the former Royal Agricultural Hall, built for cattle shows in 1861.

Further north on Upper Street, at no. 115 (left), is the **King's Head Pub and Theatre**; performances are held in a back room behind the bar. On the opposite side of the road, on the corner of Gaskin Street, is the red-brick Arts and Crafts former Islington Chapel (c. 1887). Next door is Islington's parish church of St Mary, with an 18th-century tower. The rest was rebuilt in the 1950s after serious war damage. At the rear are public gardens; in Dagmar Passage is the Little Angel Theatre, a puppet theatre for children.

BARNSBURY

The residential area of attractive 19th-century streets between Upper Street and Caledonian Road is known as Barnsbury (*map p. 601, F1–F2*). Much rich architectural detail can be seen in Richmond Avenue, Thornhill Crescent, Thornhill Square and Barnsbury Square, all built in the 1820s–40s. Mountford Crescent, leading off Barnsbury Square, has bow-fronted 1830s' stuccoed villas. Barnsbury Wood is an unexpected tiny plot of inner-city woodland. In the middle of Cloudesley Square stands an early Gothic Revival church (1829) by Charles Barry, architect of the Houses of Parliament; it is based on King's College Chapel, Cambridge. Formerly Holy Trinity,

GIBSON SQUARE
Italianate *tempietto* with pseudo-dome cunningly concealing
a ventilation shaft for the Victoria Line.

it is now the Celestial Church of Christ. Lonsdale Square was built collegiate-style in 1838–45 by R.C. Carpenter; Gibson Square, dating from the 1830s, has, in its central garden, a ventilation shaft for the Victoria Line, disguised as a Neoclassical temple. Of Milner Square (Roumieu and Gough, 1838–44), The architecture historian John Summerson remarked, 'you still could not be absolutely certain that you have seen it anywhere but in an unhappy dream.' The design of long brick pilasters with squeezed-looking narrow windows between them is certainly original; proportionally a little strange. No. 20 is a passageway leading to Almeida Street; the Almeida Theatre was built by Roumieu and Gough as Milner Square's Literary and Scientific Institute.

ON AND AROUND CANONBURY SQUARE

Immediately north of the junction with Upper Street and Canonbury Lane (*map p. 597, D2*) is **Compton Terrace**, an attractive row of early 19th-century houses separated from Upper Street by their gardens. In the middle of the terrace, in Compton Avenue, is the dominatingly incongruous neo-Gothic **Union Chapel** (James Cubitt, 1876–7); it is still a working church but also a music venue and a drop-in centre for the homeless. To the east is **Canonbury Square**, with tall, very handsome townhouses built in 1805–30 around a central garden. Evelyn Waugh and George Orwell were former residents, in the 1920s and 1940s respectively, when the area was down-at-heel; it is far from that now. Along the north side, at no. 39A (Northampton Lodge), is the **Estorick Collection of Modern Italian Art** (*Underground: Highbury & Islington and 10mins walk; open Wed–Sat 11–6, Sun 12–5; admission charge; café and shop; T: 020 7704 9522, estorickcollection.com*), the finest assemblage of early 20th-century Italian art outside Italy. It was formed by the American-born sociologist, writer and art dealer Eric Estorick (d. 1993) and his wife Salome Dessau (d.1989), who began to collect Futurist works on their honeymoon in Switzerland and on their return to England via Milan. Futurism was launched in 1909 when the poet Filippo Tommaso Marinetti published his radical manifesto in *Le Figaro*. Turning its back on Italian heritage and tradition, the movement aimed to be the herald of a new century of technology, industry, energy, speed, action and dynamism. The Estorick has works by Umberto Boccioni, Carlo Carrà, Luigi Russolo, Giacomo Balla and Gino Severini. Chief among the paintings on display are Carrà's *Leaving the Theatre* (1910–11), Boccioni's *Modern Idol* (1911) and Balla's *The Hand of the Violinist* (1912). The collection also contains works by other well-known Italian modern artists, including De Chirico, Modigliani and Giorgio Morandi.

On the east side of the square rises **Canonbury Tower**, with attached buildings in swamp-green stucco. This red-brick 16th-century square tower, 66ft high, is the oldest building in the area, a relic from an ecclesiastical building built for Prior Bolton of St Bartholomew the Great in Smithfield. After the Dissolution of the Monasteries, occupants of the manor house included Thomas Cromwell, Earl of Essex and John Dudley, Earl of Warwick. It was leased to Sir Francis Bacon in 1616–25 and Oliver Goldsmith lodged in rooms in the tower in the 1760s. The interior, with surviving period features, may be seen as part of a pre-booked guided tour with Islington Guides (*T: 020 7359 6888, info@ciga.org.uk, canonburytower.org.uk*).

Round the corner is the attractive, late 18th-century Canonbury House. The 1770s' villas in celadon green stucco at 1–5 **Canonbury Place**, a little cul-de-sac leading left, are built over the southern part of Prior Bolton's building (Weedon Grossmith, co-author of *Diary of a Nobody*, lived at no. 1). Alwyne Place, with big Italianate villas, overlooks a stretch of the New River. From Canonbury Grove on the other side, you can join the **New River Walk pathway**, which passes alongside this original section of the channel; it has been de-silted and the wooden sides restored.

HIGHBURY AND HOLLOWAY

Highbury (*map p. 597, D2*), once woodland belonging to the Knights Hospitallers, was developed as an entity distinct from both Islington and Canonbury from the 18th century; it has some very attractive streets.

Straight over Highbury Corner (the roundabout), with Highbury & Islington station and Holloway Road on your left, is **Highbury Fields**, an ancient open space saved from development in the 1880s by the Metropolitan Board of Works; it is surrounded by handsome late 18th-century terraces. Further north, near Arsenal Underground station, is **Highbury Square**, the historic former home ground of Arsenal Football

Club, one of the richest and most successful premier league clubs in the UK. After the club moved to their new stadium, the Emirates, in Ashburton Grove (*see below*), their original ground was turned into luxury flats incorporating the two listed Art Deco stands; the pitch has been landscaped into a garden.

HOLLOWAY

The name Holloway may derive simply from 'hollow way', a road worn deep and tunnel-like by passing herds of cattle as they were driven south to Smithfield. Holloway Road leads northwest to Archway; it is known for the **women's prison** in Parkhurst Road (top of Camden Road; *map p. 597, D2*), originally built in 1852 as a house of correction for both sexes. Oscar Wilde was imprisoned here. In **Caledonian Road**, known locally as the Cally Road, is Pentonville Prison (just north of Wheelwright St; *map p. 601, E1–F1*), built in 1840. The district was developed and built up very quickly from the 19th century: Holloway is Mr Pooterland, where the fictional Victorian clerk lived and wrangled with uppity tradesmen and domestic servants (*Diary of a Nobody*, by George and Weedon Grossmith). Today it is multi-ethnic and densely populated, with a high percentage of social housing, and although some swear by its unique sense of traditional community spirit, to the unfamiliar visitor it can seem dingy, with pockets of grim deprivation. An Ethiopian community has settled here; historically the cheap rents attracted students. All this is set to change and Holloway and Caledonian Road are said to be next in line for redevelopment; the opening of Arsenal Football Club's **Emirates Stadium** in 2006 may, in part, have acted as a stimulus. The state-of-the-art 60,000-seater stadium, financed by a multi-million pound sponsorship deal with Emirates Airlines, is in Ashburton Grove, built over a former industrial waste estate. It is the third largest football stadium in England and home to Arsenal Football Club, founded in 1886 by workers from the Royal Arsenal armaments factory (*see p. 441*), and known familiarly as the Gunners. When the team moved here, they asked the Royal Artillery Museum for two guns manufactured at the Royal Arsenal to stand guard outside the entrance to the new stadium. The area has exceptionally quick transport links to the centre of town via the Piccadilly Line.

Northwest of Holloway are the Victorian suburbs of Tufnell Park and Kentish Town, on the way to Camden Town.

CAMDEN

Map pp. 600, C2–601, D2. Underground: Camden Town, Mornington Crescent, Chalk Farm. Overground: Camden Road.

Camden Town, usually known simply as Camden, lies northeast of Regent's Park and just above Euston, St Pancras and King's Cross. It is a boisterous area, full of contradictions. On one hand venerated by counter-culture mavens for the live music that buzzes in the noisy bars, pubs and clubs; on the other, its sprawling network of markets along Camden Lock and Chalk Farm Road (*map p. 600, C2–C1*) is a Mecca for thousands of visitors who arrive each weekend, in chaotic search of inspiration amongst the 'vintage' clothes, bric-à-brac, jewellery and junk, at the same time sampling what the food market has cooked up. Camden's grubby urban exterior may have smartened up in the past few years, and there may be more middle-class chain-shops in the High Street, but there is still a distinctly grungy throb at its heart. A step away from the melting pot of tourists, students, media-types and would-be Indie-kids, an altogether more dignified, bohemian feel is found in the side streets and at the peripheries. Here, alongside belts of post-war social housing, are some very attractive streets and mews, home to respected figures in the arts.

HISTORY OF CAMDEN

Camden takes its name from the landowner Charles Pratt, 1st Earl Camden (d. 1794), and was speculatively developed for housing from the late 18th century. By the 19th century its identity was shaped by industry: the Regent's Canal at its northern border opened in 1818–20 and in the 1830s the London and Birmingham Railway was built. Camden became 'the tradesman's entrance to the capital' and an important goods depot. Here working-class and immigrant communities settled, employed by the warehouses and factories lining the banks of the canal and spending their leisure time in the numerous music halls and pubs. Buildings which had initially been built for middle-class families became run-down, shabby and overcrowded. Camden was considered an underprivileged and unfashionable area at least until the mid-20th century.

Outside Mornington Crescent Underground station (*map p. 601, D2*), the main road, Camden High Street, leads north; on your right is the **former Camden Palace** (1900), an old music hall with a green copper dome, now the live music venue KOKO. On your left, the large Egyptian-style Art Deco building, **Great London House**, at the junction with Hampstead Road, is the former Carreras 'Black Cat' Cigarette Factory (c. 1926). The large black cats (restored) are in homage to the ancient Egyptian cult of cat-worship. Behind is Mornington Crescent, built in the 1820s; the artist Walter Sickert, founder of the Post-Impressionist Camden Town Group (*see below*), lived at no. 6.

In Albert Street, with early Victorian terraced housing, is the **Jewish Museum** at nos 129–31 (*map p. 600, C2; open Sun–Wed 10–5, Thur 10–9, Fri 10–2; admission charge; café and shop; T: 020 7284 7384, jewishmuseum.org.uk*), which traces the history of the Jewish community in Britain from 1066 (when William the Conqueror invited the Jews of Rouen to settle in London) and displays an outstanding collection of rare and beautiful Judaica. Nearby Gloucester Crescent, with mid-19th-century Italianate villas, is one of Camden's most desirable addresses. Oval Road leads to the canal where you can join the towpath. You can also walk from here to Primrose Hill (*see p. 275*). The distinctive circular building in Oval Road is Collard & Collard's **former piano factory**. Camden was once the centre of the now defunct British piano-making industry. In the early 20th century, several hundred companies associated with the trade were based here, making a range of instruments from mass-produced 'old Joannas' to concert pianofortes of superior quality. The nearby Regent's Canal provided supplies of timber for manufacture and a means of transport for the finished product. The British firm Challen supplied pianos to the BBC in the 1930s; when the Royal Festival Hall opened in 1951, its instruments were made by Danemann, a company based in nearby Islington.

THE CAMDEN TOWN GROUP

The Camden Town Group of Post-Impressionist artists staged three exhibitions between 1911 and 1913. Three of the painters most closely associated with the group are Spencer Gore, Harold Gilman and Walter Sickert. Their aim was to depict the real lives of the working class: Gilman's *Mrs Mounter at the Breakfast Table* (1917), showing a tight-faced elderly woman, wrapped in a shawl and with her hair bound in an orange headscarf, looking steadily out from behind a large brown teapot, is one such example. Another is *The Fried Fish Shop* (1907) by Stanislawa de Karlowska (not officially a Camden Town artist—women were barred from membership—but married to a member, Robert Bevan). Sickert's famous *Camden Town Murder* series, showing a naked woman stretched on a cheap bed with a fully-clothed man standing or sitting beside it, caused much comment and even led to rumours linking Sickert with the Jack the Ripper killings. Spencer Gore had a more vivid palette than some of the other artists, and many of his works were painted not in the studio but as *plein-air* studies, filled with warmth and sunlight. Paintings by the Camden Town Group may be seen in Tate Britain as well as in Fenton House in Hampstead. In 1913 the group joined forces with other artists, including a number of Vorticists, to challenge the precepts of the Royal Academy. The resulting London Group celebrated its centenary in 2013.

CAMDEN LOCK AND CAMDEN MARKET

Three main roads leading north have their starting point at Camden Town Underground. Camden High Street (Chalk Farm Road) leads to Hampstead. Kentish Town Road (always choked with traffic) leads to the neighbouring suburbs of Kentish Town, Tufnell Park and Archway. Camden Road leads to Holloway and Holloway Road. The house at **39 Hilldrop Crescent**, west off the Camden Road (*just beyond map p. 601, D1*), is where the homeopath Dr Crippen is said to have disposed of the remains of his murdered wife.

Camden Lock itself (*map p. 600, C2*) is a twin lock, constructed c. 1820. It is the only twin lock on the Regent's Canal. Boat services go to London Zoo and Little Venice (*for details, see p. 541*); you can also walk along the towpath. Here, in converted former warehouses and buildings, is **Camden Lock Market**. The rest of Camden Market, really a collection of several markets with masses of stalls (*open daily 10–6; camdenmarket.org*), extends all around and up Chalk Farm Road.

In Chalk Farm Road (near Chalk Farm Tube; *map p. 600, B1*) is the **Roundhouse**, built as a railway engine house and repair shed in the 1840s; it was also used as a bonded warehouse for storing gin. It is now a premier performance venue. Other points of interest are Camden Square and Rochester Square (*map p. 601, D1*), dating from the 1840s; Lyme Terrace, which overlooks the canal; and Camden Mews and Murray Mews, with architects' houses from the 1960s.

EATING AND DRINKING IN CAMDEN, CLERKENWELL AND ISLINGTON

CAMDEN

£ Asakusa. Near Mornington Crescent Tube. Great Japanese restaurant in a shabby building. Good value and popular: best to book. *265 Eversholt St. T: 020 7388 8533. Map p. 601, D2.*

£ The Enterprise. Classic Camden pub attracting a mixed crowd. Can be very busy if there's a band on at Roundhouse, but good atmosphere. *2 Haverstock Hill. T: 0207 485 2659, camdenenterprise.com. Map p. 600, B1.*

£ The Good Mixer. Not as fashionable as it was in the heyday of Britpop, but a good example of an old-school pub with snooker tables (and lots of wannabe musicians). *30 Inverness St. Map p. 600, C2.*

£ Hawley Arms. Lively pub with roof terrace and a music crowd. A good place for fish and chips or a pie and peas. *2 Castlehaven Rd. T: 020 7428 5979, thehawleyarms.co.uk. Map p. 600, C1.*

£ Lock Tavern. Good pub that does food in the garden on sunny days. Live music at weekends. *35 Chalk Farm Rd. T: 020 7482 7163, lock-tavern.com. Map p. 600, C1.*

CLERKENWELL

££ Bistrot Bruno Loubet. Chef Bruno Loubet creates delectable dishes at the Zetter Townhouse. Open daily. *86–88 Clerkenwell Rd. T: 020 7324 4455, bistrotbrunoloubet.com. Map p. 606, B1.* Also at the Zetter Townhouse is the Cocktail Lounge, snug and cosy in winter with an open fire, where you can accompany your drink with Loubet's sharing plates and 'supper bowls'. Same address, different phone (*T: 020 7324 4545*).

£–££ Bleeding Heart. A cluster of places to eat in a courtyard off Hatton Garden. Highly acclaimed, Modern French cooking in the restaurant (Mon–Fri) and Bistro (Mon–Sat) and plainer fare in the Tavern (Mon–Fri). *Bleeding Heart Yard, off Greville St. T: 020 7242 2056, bleedingheart.co.uk. Map p. 606, A2–B2.*

£–££ Comptoir Gascon. Bistro and deli specialising in food and wine from southwest France. Lively and popular. Closed Sun. *63 Charterhouse St. T: 020 7608 0851, comptoirgascon. com. Map p. 606, B2.*

£ The Eagle. Not historic, but the first of London's gastro pubs and still one of the best. *159 Farrindon Rd. T: 20 7837 1353. Map p. 606, A1.*

£–££ Fox and Anchor. Its proximity to Smithfield Market means this pub opens early (7am) on weekdays for hearty breakfasts. The lunch and dinner menu features classic London food: oysters, smoked eel, steak and kidney pie. Also has accommodation. Open daily. *115 Charterhouse St. T: 020 7250 1300, foxandanchor.com. Map p. 606, B2–B1.*

£££ Hix Oyster & Chop House. Mouth-watering dishes from land and sea. Part of chef and restaurateur Mark Hix's portfolio. Good set menus. Open daily. *36–37 Greenhill's Rents (Cowcross St). T: 020 7017 1930, hixoysterandchophouse.co.uk. Map p. 606, B1.*

££ The Modern Pantry. Pleasant, informal lunch place serving good food and good wine. The water comes in lovely big tin ewers. Has a shop attached. Mon–Fri until 3pm. *47–48 St John's Square. T: 020 7553 9210, themodernpantry.co.uk. Map p. 606, B1.*

££ Moro. ■ Justly popular restaurant serving Iberian/Moorish cuisine. Tapas at the bar or a full meal in the restaurant. Highly recommended. No dinner Sun. *34–36 Exmouth Market. T: 020 7833 8336, moro.co.uk. Map p. 601, F3.*

£–££ The Peasant. Bar downstairs serving classic bar meals. Restaurant above with an interesting British-Hispanic fusion menu (the chef is from Chile). Closed Sun. *240 St John St. T: 020 7336 7726, thepeasant.co.uk. Map p. 606, B1.*

££ St John. In a former bacon smokehouse, specialising in offal and unusual cuts of meat, and known for its revival of old English recipes. Real nose-to-tail eating. It has a Michelin star but the atmosphere is unpretentious and un-Michelin-starry. No lunch Sat, no dinner Sun. *26 St John St. T: 020 7251 0848, stjohngroup. uk.com. Map p. 606, B1.*

££ Vinoteca. Great wine and food from this small chain, a joint venture by a chef and a sommelier. There are branches in Chiswick, Marylebone and Soho. Closed Sun. *7 St John St. T: 020 7253 8786, vinoteca.co.uk. Map p. 606, B1.*

ISLINGTON

££ Almeida. Attached to the theatre of the same name, a restaurant offering excellent modern French cuisine. *30 Almeida St. T: 020 7354 4777, almeida-restaurant.co.uk. Map p. 597, D2.*

£ Delhi Grill. A pretty good approximation of an Indian dhaba. Delicious, flavourful street food, to eat in or take away. Open daily. *21 Chapel Market. T: 020 7278 8100, delhigrill.com. Map p. 601, F2.*

££ Drapers Arms. A lovely gastro pub in a pretty tree-lined street. Delicious roasts and good seafood. Pleasant beer garden. Open daily but closes 8.30pm Sun. *44 Barnsbury St. T: 020 7619 0348, thedrapersarms. com. Map p. 601, F2.*

££ Duke of Cambridge. Organic pub. Everything here is eco-friendly, low-mileage, low-carbon-footprint and low key. The food is good too. *30 St Peter's St. T: 020 7359 3066, sloeberry. co.uk. Map p. 597, D2.*

£–££ Elk In The Woods. Excellent breakfasts (poached egg muffins, bacon sandwiches) and a good choice for lunch or dinner, including venison from the Denham Estate in Suffolk. Lots of wood in the décor. You could imagine yourself in a snowbound cabin. Open daily. *37–39 Camden Passage (parallel with/east of Upper St. T: 020 7336 3535, the-elk-in-the-woods.co.uk. Map p. 597, D2.*

£ The Fish and Chip Shop. Whitebait with garlic mayonnaise; shrimp burgers with spicy tartare. This is no ordinary greasy chippy (though they do do takeaways). Supremely prepared fish and trimmings to go with it. *189 Upper St. T: 020 3227 0979, thefishandchipshop. uk.com. Map p. 597, D2.*

££–£££ Frederick's. Modern eclectic cooking and a good wine list. Closed Sun. *Camden Passage (parallel with/east of Upper St. T: 020 7359 2888, fredericks.co.uk. Map p. 597, D2.*

£ The Gate. Inventive, tasty vegetarian. Open daily. *370 St John St. T: 020 7278 5483, thegaterestaurants.com. Map p. 597, D2.*

£ Isarn. Contemporary Thai. Open daily. *119 Upper St. T: 020 7424 5153, isarn.co.uk. Map p. 597, D2.*

£ Ottolenghi. ■ This is the largest of Israeli-born chef and food writer Yotam Ottolenghi's fleet of restaurants (there are other branches in Soho, Belgravia and Notting Hill). Unpretentious, simple food—salads, quiches, vegetable fritters—and absolutely delicious. Open daily but closes 7pm Sun. *287 Upper St. T: 020 7288 1454, ottolenghi.co.uk. Map p. 597, D2.*

££ Smokehouse. Treat yourself to crab on toast and peppered beef. Open daily. *63–69 Canonbury Rd. T: 020 7354 1144, smokehouseislington.co.uk. Map p. 597, D2.*

£ The Standard Tandoori. In a very unglamorous location on the Holloway Road but the Indian food makes it worth it. They do superb butter chicken. *87 Holloway Rd. T: 207 607 1637. Map p. 597, D1–D2.*

£–££ Tenshi. Highly regarded Japanese restaurant. Open daily. *61 Upper St. T: 020 7226 4665, tenshilondon.com. Map p. 597, D2.*

HIGHGATE
Pensive statue in the famous cemetery.

Highgate, Hampstead & the North

Highgate and Hampstead are the cream of the northern suburbs. Further north, Golders Green and Finchley offer comfortable suburban living. To the northeast are Hackney and Stoke Newington, site of the New River. Enfield, on the Essex border, has a fine Queen Anne mansion.

H ighgate and Hampstead were, until the 19th century, very much separate from London. Today, largely due to their active conservation societies—who keep vigilant watch on new developments and on changes to the historic fabric—they still retain a distinct, villagey feel. These districts are lofty both literally and metaphorically: both are known for their free-thinking, intellectual residents, and both command outstanding views of the capital. Shops, pubs and restaurants abound and a day spent traversing the undulating, attractive streets is also excellent exercise. Both areas are spread along the edges of the rural, 800-acre Hampstead Heath, where an exhilarating walk should be on every visitor's to-do list.

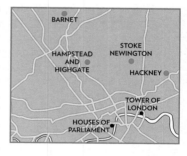

HIGHGATE

Map p. 599. Underground: Archway, Highgate.

Leafy Highgate spreads across the hilltops north of Archway; it adjoins Hampstead Heath on its western side. The district takes its name from a 14th-century tollgate sited along the Old North Road, on land that adjoined the Bishop of London's hunting estate; the Gatehouse Inn, which catered for travellers from the 1670s, commemorates this. Many famous people passed through the growing village along the road to the north, including, supposedly, Richard Whittington, four times Lord Mayor of London (*see below*).

ARCHWAY TO HIGHGATE HILL

Highgate Hill (*map p. 599, F2*) rises steeply from Archway, leading to Highgate High Street. Europe's first cable tramway was installed here in 1884 using the same technology that had been developed in San Francisco in the 1870s. Today, much of the traffic has been diverted along the Archway Road to the northeast, where the viaduct over the cutting (1897; the original was by Nash) affords terrific views.

At the bottom of Highgate Hill, near Archway Underground station, is the drab-looking **Whittington Stone** (middle of the pavement, left hand side of the road), apparently marking the spot where Dick Whittington stopped and listened to the City's bells summoning him back to London. The replica milestone dates from 1821; his cat was added in 1964; the whole is encased in a metal cage. The Whittington Hospital and the Whittington pub have adopted his name.

St Joseph's Church, with its impressive green copper domes, lies just before the junction with Dartmouth Park Hill and Cromwell Avenue. Then, still on the left-hand side, you come to the start of the 29-acre **Waterlow Park**, 'the garden for the gardenless', bequeathed to London County Council in 1889 by Lord Mayor and philanthropic resident Sir Sydney Brownlow. The park stretches all the way down to Swains Lane, where there is an exit opposite the main entrance to Highgate Cemetery (*see below*). In its grounds is the white stucco **Lauderdale House** (1582; much altered), where Nell Gwyn, Charles II's mistress, lived for a short time with her illegitimate son, the Duke of St Albans. John Wesley preached here in 1782. The house is now a community arts and education centre, with exhibition space and a café. Opposite its main entrance on Highgate Hill, note some handsome 18th-century houses (nos 106–110) and the 17th-century Cromwell House.

HIGHGATE HIGH STREET AND NORTH HILL

Highgate High Street (*map p. 599, E2*) is full of quaint shops and buildings—at least, it was until very recently; a few of the ubiquitous chain restaurants have now crept in. Highgate School, in North Road, was founded in the reign of Elizabeth I, in 1565. Sir John Betjeman was a pupil here. At the **Wrestler's Tavern** in North Road, the tradition of the 'Swearing of the Horns' is kept alive in a biannual ceremony. The tradition, mainly enacted for the amusement of customers, was upheld in several of Highgate's pubs and inns from the 17th century. Visitors were granted the Freedom of Highgate after taking an oath of merriment and debauchery, which involved swearing by, kissing or saluting a set of animal horns held out to them by the landlord.

In North Hill is London's premier example of 1930s' Modernist housing: **Highpoint One and Two** (*map p. 599, E1*), built by Berthold Lubetkin for his design practice, Tecton. The apartment blocks were commissioned by Sigmund Gestetner, son of the Hungarian-born inventor of the cyclograph, a duplicating machine. Highpoint One was built in 1935, initially as working-class housing for Gestetner's employees, although they never moved in. The building was greatly admired by Le Corbusier, who visited it and was unequivocal in his praise; it expressed perfectly his vision of tower blocks in park settings. Highpoint Two was completed in 1938 and features caryatids. Both blocks pioneered the use of freely moulded, reinforced concrete, which the *Penguin Dictionary of Architecture* describes as 'prophetic of the 1950s'.

HIGHGATE VILLAGE CENTRE

The Grove and South Grove, with Highgate West Hill between them (*map p. 599, E2*), are at the centre of Highgate Village, preserving handsome 17th- and 18th-century houses. Coleridge lived at no. 3 **The Grove**. The poet had moved to Highgate, firstly to South Grove, in 1816, to live as a house patient with the family of his friend and physician, James Gillman, who helped him try to overcome his opium addiction. Here he continued to write and publish until his death in 1834. He is buried in **St Michael's Church**, a neo-Gothic edifice by Lewis Vulliamy (1832). Also in The Grove lived violinist Yehudi Menuhin (at no. 2). The art critic Roger Fry was born at no. 6.

The **Flask pub** (at 77 Highgate West Hill; not to be confused with the Flask in Hampstead) is one of the highway taverns at which travellers could purchase a refreshing flask of water filled from the area's mineral springs. The building dates from the 1720s and includes part of a 1660s' stable. Dick Turpin, the highwayman, is said to have hidden in the cellar here. Byron, Shelley and Keats drank here when they came to visit Coleridge.

Pond Square, in the middle, is a pleasant bosky quadrangle; the ponds were filled in in the 19th century. Here, in 1626, Sir Francis Bacon is said to have conducted his famous experiment in refrigeration by stuffing a dead chicken with snow (the great empiricist consequently developed pneumonia, and died a few days later). The vicinity is said to be haunted by the ghost of a squawking, half-plucked hen, which appears in extremely cold weather.

At no. 11 is the **Highgate Literary and Scientific Institution**, founded 1839. Its archive of local history holds important documents and pictures from the 17th century to the present day; the library has collections relating to Coleridge and Betjeman.

Off Highgate West Hill is London's second-largest private residence (Buckingham Palace is the first): **Witanhurst**, overlooking Hampstead Heath. This 65-room supermansion, was built in the early 20th century for Sir Arthur Crosfield, whose money came from soap and candles. At the time of writing it was being renovated, and a vast, £50-million double-storey basement was being excavated by its secretive new owner.

HIGHGATE CEMETERY

From South Grove, Swains Lane descends very steeply (it is strongly recommended not to approach Highgate uphill from Swains Lane) to Highgate Cemetery (*map p. 599, E2*). Behind the high brick wall on your right lies the Western Cemetery, the secret, oldest part, which you may only visit as part of a guided tour. On your left is the perimeter of Waterlow Park. The main entrances to both the east and west sections of the cemetery are just beyond, on opposite sides of the road.(*West Cemetery open for tours daily 11–3; at weekends you must book ahead, on weekdays there is no booking; you are asked to turn up and join the next available tour. Tours last approx. 1hr. East cemetery open Mon–Fri 10–3.30, Sat–Sun 11–3.30. West Cemetery tickets include free entrance to the East Cemetery. For the East Cemetery alone, there is an admission charge. To book, see highgatecemetery.org, T: 020 8340 1834).*

The **West Cemetery**, through the neo-Gothic gatehouse, is the oldest section, no longer in use for burials. The rural hillside location, then part of the Forest of Middlesex, was a popular choice for the new cemetery in 1839, designed by the architect Stephen Geary. Initially it was the most expensive and exclusive in London. Here the fanciful high-Victorian funerary landscape is maintained in a romantic, overgrown state. Among the trees and bushes appear huge and ornate tombs and monuments; famous sights include the Egyptian Avenue, flanked by obelisks; the Colonnade; the Circle of Lebanon (around an ancient cedar tree); the Terrace Catacombs and the Mausoleum of Julian Beer, based on the Tomb of Mausolus at Halicarnassus.

The **East Cemetery** still functions as a working burial ground and you may wander here freely (though there is an admission charge). It was opened in 1860. Here is the famous grave of Karl Marx (d. 1883)—a place of pilgrimage for visitors from all over the world. The inscription on the stone reads 'Workers of the World Unite' and the large bust by Laurence Bradshaw, which dominates the cemetery, was added in 1956. Marx's wife Jenny, his domestic servant Helene Demuth, and the ashes of his daughter Eleanor, a Socialist activist who committed suicide in 1898, are also buried here. Buried nearby is George Eliot (as Mary Ann Cross; d. 1880). Many other literary figures have been laid to rest in this cemetery.

HOLLY LODGE ESTATE

Continue descending Swains Lane. The Eastern Cemetery continues for some way on the left, where amongst trees that are filled with the sound of birdsong, are row upon row of lichen-covered headstones interspersed with angels and crosses, overgrown with ivy. Soon on your right, a quiet, private estate composed of avenues of mock-Tudor mansion blocks or 'Tudor cliffs' (disconcerting, like a scene from a zombie film) comes into view. This is the Holly Lodge Estate (*map p. 599, E2*), which runs between Swains Lane and Highgate West Hill. It was built in the grounds of an 18th-century villa, Holly Lodge, which was owned by the wealthy banking heiress and philanthropist Angela Burdett-Coutts. She gave more than £3 million to charitable causes and was known as the 'queen of the poor'. At her death in 1906, her body lay in state for two days and 30,000 people paid their respects. She is buried in Westminster Abbey. The estate was built in the 1920s as housing for female office workers; secretaries and clerks lived here in miserable-sounding bedsits that were considered very modern at the time. John Betjeman, who was brought up nearby, when the housing estate was still a garden, immortalised it in his poem 'NW5 & N6', writing of squirrels in the Burdett-Coutts estate and of bugging his nurse with questions about God. The copyright costs of reproducing a few lines from the poem in print make it impossible to do so here, but all five verses may be searched for and freely enjoyed online.

Further on is Holly Village (junction of Chester Road), a small, neo-Gothic group of houses, behind an elaborate gatehouse, built by Burdett-Coutts in the 1860s for senior workers on her estate.

The area of quiet residential streets stretching to Tufnell Park and Kentish Town is known as Dartmouth Park. Archway, Tufnell Park and Kentish Town Tube stations are all within walking distance.

HAMPSTEAD

Map p. 598. There are several ways to reach Hampstead. The Northern Line (Underground) stops at Hampstead and you emerge at the top of the High Street. Overground rail links deposit you at Gospel Oak and Hampstead Heath stations. You can also walk or take buses from Camden, Chalk Farm, Kentish Town and Belsize Park. The side streets running east along Finchley Road (Swiss Cottage or Finchley Road Underground) all lead up to Hampstead. You can also approach it from Golders Green (it is quicker to get to Kenwood and Hampstead Garden Suburb from there).

Scenic Hampstead, skirting the edges of Hampstead Heath, is one of the highest points in the capital. Its topography preserved it as a village until the arrival of the railway in the 1860s. From the 17th century, this countryside spot, with its clean, fresh air, medicinal spa waters and expansive heath, attracted convalescents and wealthy residents, especially in the summer months, and also inspired artists, musicians, writers and liberal-thinkers and intellectuals of all kinds to settle here. They are nearly all remembered: Hampstead's buildings are simply pocked with blue plaques commemorating former illustrious inhabitants; a cartoon published by the local newspaper *Ham & High* in 1998 depicted a bemused tourist surveying a building plaque with the legend, 'The only house in Hampstead that nobody famous has lived in'.

Today, Hampstead is in effect a large, very wealthy suburban town. In the streets extending down towards the Finchley Road, bounded by Platts Lane, and in the area known as Belsize Park, there are substantial villas and mansions. Old Hampstead, or Hampstead proper, with its narrow, twisting, hilly streets, still retains its village feel and is exceptionally pretty. Strong local interests have ensured that the many attractive houses and cottages have been preserved and that new development has been restricted. The two prominent aberrations are the towering 1970s' block in Pont Street, the Royal Free (an important teaching hospital, but nonetheless an architectural eyesore) and the McDonald's on the High Street, which opened in the early 1990s. A ten-year battle waged before the fast-food giant won the right to open here; initially, its frontage had to be specially designed so that its presence appeared less conspicuous. More of 21st-century Hampstead prospers along the High Street and down Rosslyn Hill towards Belsize Park, where independent businesses have been engulfed by up-market chains of coffee emporia, restaurants, cafés and boutiques that cater for a new strain of resident: bankers, business executives and wealthy expatriates. Property prices in Hampstead are now extremely high and there are more millionaires per capita here than in the rest of London put together. The academic, artistic and literary community that built the area's reputation is being priced out of the market. In spite of this, old Hampstead may still be encountered if you explore the winding back streets, lanes, snickets and corners; this is where you will be rewarded. There are many interesting things to see in Hampstead and a full day here is recommended.

HOLLY HILL AND HAMPSTEAD GROVE

Hampstead Underground station opened in 1907; at 181ft, its lift-shaft is the deepest in London. Heath Street leads south to **Church Row** (*map p. 598, B4*), a very handsome street of early 18th-century brick houses. Lord Alfred Douglas, Oscar Wilde's former lover, lived at no. 26. At the end is the parish church of **St John-at-Hampstead**, by John Sanderson, consecrated in 1747 (Henry Flitcroft was the architect originally approached). The gates and railings are from Canons, the Edgware stately home of the 'princely' Duke of Chandos (*see Cavendish Square, pp. 262–3*). In the peaceful churchyard and its extension in Holly Walk are buried many famous men and women, including John Constable (signposted) and the architect Norman Shaw.

In Holly Place, up narrow Holly Walk, is the Catholic church of **St Mary** (1816; *map p. 598, B3*); it was one of the first new Catholic churches to be built after the Reformation and was the centre of a community of *émigrés* who had fled the Terror of the French Revolution. Further on in Holly Walk is the former **Hampstead Watch House**, where Hampstead's first police force was based in the 1830s. At no. 7 Mount Vernon (Abernethy House, the corner of an elevated row of 1820s cottages), Robert Louis Stevenson stayed when he came to Hampstead to recuperate from illness in the 1870s. **Mount Vernon Hospital** opposite (now luxury flats) was built in the late 19th century to treat consumptives; its large scale, out of keeping with the rest of Hampstead's architecture, was largely deprecated.

No. 6 Holly Hill, a white weather-boarded house, formerly stables, now much altered, was owned and converted into a home and studio by painter George Romney in 1796; later the house became lecture rooms. Constable, Faraday and Elizabeth Fry all spoke here. In Holly Mount is the small and atmospheric **Holly Bush pub** (nooks, etched glass etc.), dating from the late 18th century and also converted from stables. Holly Bush Steps lead to Golden Yard and The Mount, a street of handsome 18th-century houses; Ford Madox Brown incorporated no. 6 into his painting *Work*, begun in 1852.

In Hampstead Grove is Fenton House, Hampstead's oldest surviving mansion.

FENTON HOUSE

Map p. 598, B3. Open March–Oct Wed–Sun 11–5; some weekends in winter. For details, see nationaltrust.org/fenton-house. T: 020 7435 3471. Admission charge.

This handsome red-brick William-and-Mary house, one of the best late 17th-century houses to survive in London, stands at the very top of Hampstead in one of the most attractive parts of the 'village'. From 1936 until her death in 1952, it was the home of Lady Binning, who bequeathed it to the National Trust along with her fine collection of porcelain. Also on display here is the important Benton Fletcher collection of early musical instruments, given to the Trust in 1937. Music students often play the instruments, and it is a memorable experience to visit this airy house and beautiful garden, and to hear from a distant room the evocative sound of a harpsichord or spinet.

Little is known for certain about the early history of the house. It stands on manorial land which between 1682 and 1690 passed through the hands of four different lords, the last of them only six years of age. It was probably built by William Eades, the son of a master bricklayer, apparently without the help of an architect. In the early 18th century it was bought by Joshua Gee, a Quaker linen merchant who went into partnership with George Washington's father, importing pig-iron from Maryland. His initials and those of his wife, Anna Osgood, are worked into the handsome wrought-iron gates at the south entrance from Holly Hill. By 1786 the place was called Clock House. Six years later it was bought by Philip Fenton, son of a coal merchant from Yorkshire, whose family owned it until 1834. During their time here, the Regency loggia between the wings on the east side, which now forms the main entrance, was added. Otherwise the house appears externally much as first built.

Apart from the porcelain and musical instruments, the house also contains paintings by the Camden Town Group of Post-Impressionists (*see p. 382*). The garden is extremely fine and there are 30 varieties of apple tree in the orchard.

FROM FENTON HOUSE TO WHITESTONE POND

Admiral's House in Admiral's Walk (1700; *map p. 598, B3*) was the home of Lieutenant Fountain North, who constructed the deck of a ship on the roof, from where he fired cannon in celebration of naval victories. Presumably Hampstead resident P.L. Travers was drawing on local knowledge when she created the character of Admiral Boon in *Mary Poppins*. Later, Sir George Gilbert Scott lived here. Next door, in Grove House, John Galsworthy completed the *Forsyte Saga*; he died here in 1933.

The views from **Judge's Walk** were painted by Constable, who lived for a time in Lower Terrace; Constable also painted Admiral's House in the 1820s. In Windmill Hill, the little 18th-century cottage called 'Capo di Monte' is where the actress Sarah Siddons stayed when she came to Hampstead for her health; in the 1940s it was the home of Sir Kenneth Clark and later of Marghanita Laski.

The **Hampstead Observatory** in Lower Terrace is open to the public on clear nights at certain times of year (*see hampsteadscience.ac.uk to check; visits are free*). It was opened by the Hampstead Scientific Society in 1910; the telescope dates from the 19th century.

Whitestone Pond, at the edge of Hampstead Heath, was named after a white milestone. At 440ft above sea level, this is the highest point in Hampstead and in London (or so they say; but there are other points that claim this distinction, and it depends on how one defines 'London'). A flagpole marks the spot where the Armada Beacon was lit in 1588, one of several torches that were illuminated on high points across the country, warning of the approach of Philip II's invading Spanish fleet.

THE VALE OF HEALTH

The secluded hamlet known as the Vale of Health (*map p. 598, B3–C3*) was once swampy land known as Hatchett's Bottom. It was drained by 1801 and its new name, Vale of Health, may have been an attempt by its developers to obliterate its unhealthy reputation. In this enclave of houses have lived many artists and writers including, briefly in 1915, D.H. Lawrence and his wife Frieda (1 Byron Villas). Stanley Spencer painted his *The Resurrection, Cookham* in the Vale in the 1920s (it is now in Tate Britain). At 3 Villas on the Heath lived the Bengali polymath and first non-European Nobel Prize-winner Rabindranath Tagore, in 1912.

NORTH END WAY

Jack Straw's Castle (*map p. 598, B3*) is a former pub where many Hampstead artists once drank. In 1673, the highwayman Francis Jackson was hanged near here and his remains were left to dangle for 18 years. Opposite, at the junction with Spaniards Road, is an 18th-century mansion known as Heath House, once the home of the philanthropic merchant family of Hoare, who entertained William Wilberforce and Elizabeth Fry to dinner here.

Off North End Way is Inverforth House (formerly The Hill; *map p. 598, B2*) a huge, early 20th-century mansion built around a smaller property by the soap magnate Lord Leverhulme; it is now luxury apartments. Inverforth Close (left) leads to the **Hill Garden and Pergola**, also built by Leverhulme and now open to the public. This is one of Hampstead's secret gems; a raised terrace and colonnade, 15ft above the Heath, tumbling with fragrant climbing plants. Towards the end of North End Way is the **Old Bull and Bush pub**, dating from the 17th century; a young William Hogarth is supposed to have helped plant the pub garden and Gainsborough, Reynolds and Garrick drank here. This is the hamlet known as **North End**. To the right off North End Road, in Cedar Lodge on North End Avenue, lived the adventuress, philanthropist and benefactor of British aviation Lady Houston, whose fortune was estimated at £300 million in today's money. She lined the coffers of the British aviation team when they competed for the Schneider Trophy; this in turn stimulated the advancement of engine technology and the development of the Spitfire fighter plane used by the Allies during World War Two (it was the backbone of the fighter command during the Battle of Britain). Lady Houston died in 1936, just months after the Spitfire's maiden flight. Also in North End Avenue, Pitt House stands on the site of the house where Prime Minister William Pitt, Earl of Chatham, lay ill for 18 months in 1766–7, refusing to see anyone, including King George III. The great art historian and forensic cataloguer of England's architectural heritage, Sir Nikolaus Pevsner, lived at 2 Wildwood Terrace from 1936 until his death in 1983. In Ivy House (94–96 North End Rd) lived the prima ballerina Anna Pavlova; it is now the London Jewish Cultural Centre. North End Road leads to Golders Green.

Spaniards Road (*map p. 598, B2–C2*) leads from Whitestone Pond all the way to Kenwood House and grounds; the road narrows at the point where an old tollgate stood. Here is the quaint, oak-panelled **Spaniards Inn** (built 1585; *see p. 406*), once the haunt of highwaymen. The Gordon Rioters stopped here on their way to burn Kenwood House in 1780, and were plied with drink by the landlord—a successful diversion. Others who have enjoyed drinking here include Keats, Shelley, Byron and—inevitably—Dickens.

KENWOOD HOUSE

Hampstead Lane. Underground: Golders Green or Archway, then bus 210. Map p. 598, C2. Open daily 10–5. Free. Café and shop. T: 020 8348 1286, english-heritage.org.uk.

Kenwood, an elegant mansion set on a ridge of land with a magnificent prospect over Hampstead Heath towards London, is one of the principal properties of English Heritage. The former house of c. 1700 was remodelled and redecorated in 1764–79 by the Adam brothers, Robert and James, for William Murray, 1st Earl of Mansfield and Lord Chief Justice, who lived here from 1754. The resulting elegant and imposing villa is a major piece of 18th-century Neoclassical architecture and interior decoration, which the Adam brothers regarded as one of their major commissions. The most magnificent of the new ground-floor reception rooms created for Mansfield is without doubt the **Library, or 'Great Room'**, regarded by many as Robert Adam's finest achievement.

The 1st Earl began the landscaping of the **park**, which was continued by the 2nd Earl, aided by the great landscape gardener Humphrey Repton, who was probably responsible for the ornamental flowerbeds of the west garden and the looped foliage passage near the front of the house. The grounds today are a beautiful combination of lawns, a lake, winding rhododendron walks among woodland (recorded here by 1806), an avenue of limes (a favourite resort of the poet Pope), the whole surrounded by Hampstead Heath.

A sale of the house contents was held in 1922 and Kenwood today has none of its original furnishings, save for a few Adam pieces which have fortuitously returned. It is, however, home to the Iveagh Bequest, a major collection of paintings left to the nation in 1927, along with the house, by Edward Cecil Guinness, 1st Earl of Iveagh, who had purchased Kenwood from the Mansfield family in 1925 together with 80 acres of grounds, which were about to be sold as building plots. The house has been open to the public free of charge since 1928.

The Iveagh Bequest

Lord Iveagh, Chairman of Guinness Breweries—and on his death in 1927 reputedly the second richest man in the country—amassed an extraordinary collection of pictures between 1887 and 1891. The collection is particularly rich in 18th-century British portraiture and 17th-century Dutch and Flemish works. The pictures are now displayed throughout Kenwood's historic interiors and include some world-famous masterpieces, such as Rembrandt's *Self Portrait* of c. 1663 and Vermeer's *Guitar Player*, probably a very late work and known to have been in the collection of his widow in 1676. Seventeenth-century works painted in Britain include De Jongh's early topographical view of Old London Bridge (1630s) and Van Dyck's *Henrietta of Lorraine* (1634), a noble full-length which belonged to Charles I. The succession of late 18th-century British works, by Gainsborough, Reynolds, Romney, Hoppner and others, is extraordinary. Gainsborough's *Mary, Countess Howe* (c. 1763–4), one of Kenwood's treasures, dates from the artist's Bath period and is one of his loveliest portraits. The lyrical conversation piece *Going to Market* is a charming mid-period landscape. There are many portraits by Reynolds, including of the celebrated beauty Mrs Musters as Hebe, and Kitty Fisher as Cleopatra; Kitty Fisher was a notorious courtesan who died young, apparently of lead poisoning from cosmetics. There are two Romneys of Lady Hamilton, wife of Sir William Hamilton and mistress of Nelson, and Romney's favourite muse. *Lady Hamilton at the Spinning Wheel* shows her demure, in the guise of a simple country girl. The celebrated actress Mrs Jordan appears as Viola in *Twelfth Night*, painted by Hoppner. Turner's *Iveagh Sea-Piece* (1802) is one of the earliest of his important marine paintings.

EAST HAMPSTEAD AND THE WELLS

From the 17th century, Hampstead was known for its iron-rich mineral springs, but it was not until the early 18th century that the waters were commercially exploited. In 1698 Susanna Noel, mother of the landowning Earl of Gainsborough (then an infant), bequeathed six acres of marshy land around Wells Walk on the understanding that it be used to benefit the poor of Hampstead; the Wells Trust (a charity that still exists today) was born. The charity leased the land, on which a chalybeate mineral spring was located, to a developer to build a heath resort. The resulting spa town, called Hampstead Wells, had an assembly room for socialising and a pump room where the waters were imbibed; in Flask Walk the iron-rich water was bottled for sale in the City. The spa's success soon changed Hampstead from a quiet village into a small town: inns, lodging houses and shops were built to cater for the influx of revellers and invalids. Visitors to this first spa tended to be a rowdy, insalubrious lot, and were so unpopular with residents that in the 1720s the spa's lease was not extended. A second spa was run on much stricter lines, until its popularity finally flagged at end of the 18th century. Those who came to take the cure at this more genteel watering place included Alexander Pope, Dr Johnson and Fanny Burney (Hampstead features in Burney's novel *Evelina*, published in 1778). Today none of the spa buildings remain.

Flask Walk (*map p. 598, B3–C3*), a little pedestrianised street of shops near Hampstead Tube station, leads north from the High Street. Here is the popular Flask pub (the current building dates from the 19th century). In the original pub, the Lower Flask, Hampstead's spa water was bottled for sale. In **Well Walk** is the equally popular Wells Tavern, on the site of a dance hall connected with the spa. The chalybeate spring, located on this street, is commemorated by a Victorian drinking fountain of 1882 (steps leading to Wells Passage); the spa's buildings were located opposite and also in Gainsborough Gardens, which has smart red-brick 1880s' houses. Notable residents of Well Walk include John Keats, John Masefield, J.B. Priestley, John Constable, Margaret Llewelyn Davies (a campaigner who championed the right for women to divorce on the same terms as men and for better maternity care and maternity benefit) and Marie Stopes, pioneer of birth control. **Burgh House**, in New End Square (*map p. 598, C3*), built in 1703, was where the spa physician William Gibbons lived in the 1720s; the garden was designed by Gertrude Jekyll. It is now a community arts centre hosting exhibitions and events. On the first floor is the Hampstead Museum of local history (*open Wed–Fri and Sun 12–5; free; café; T: 020 7431 0144, burghhouse.org.uk*).

The area around **New End** was historically a working-class district. During Hampstead's periods of expansion—connected to the growth of the spa and the arrival of the railway—streets of mean, cramped houses were quickly erected to cope with the population surge; a cholera epidemic occurred in 1849. The buildings were then mostly swept away during a period of rebuilding and town planning the 1880s. The surviving old workhouse, Kendall's Hall, is today a luxury flat conversion.

In Well Road is a fantastical neo-Gothic mansion, **'The Logs'** (nos 17–20). Pevsner called it 'a formidable atrocity'.

Further east at nos 1–3 Willow Rd is a terrace of three Modernist houses, important works by Ernő Goldfinger. No. 2 is where Goldfinger himself, his wife, their children and the nanny, lived. Today it is owned by the National Trust and is open to the public.

2 WILLOW ROAD

Map p. 598, C3. Underground: Hampstead and 10mins' walk. Open March–Oct Wed–Sun, tours at 11, 12, 1 and 2; places assigned on a first-come first served basis. Independent visits from 3pm onwards; last entry 4.30. Admission charge. T: 020 7435 6166, national-trust.org.uk/2-willow-road.

This was the family home of the Hungarian-born Marxist architect Ernő Goldfinger (1902–87), who was a leading exponent of the Modern movement in post-war Britain. Goldfinger designed the house in 1939 and lived there with his wife, the Crosse and Blackwell heiress Ursula Blackwell, until his death in 1987. It is said that the name of the titular villain in Ian Fleming's *Goldfinger* (1959) was a deliberate slight on the character and work of the architect for having demolished a row of cottages to make way for this Modernist ideal home. Controversial though Goldfinger's style was (and remains; Alexander Fleming House at Elephant and Castle, Trellick Tower in Ladbroke Grove and Balfron Tower in Poplar have all been excoriated in their time), there is no better example than 2 Willow Road of the purity and sensitivity that Goldfinger could sometimes employ in his constructions. Far from being a piece of shocking Brutalism, the house shares many characteristics with the elegant Georgian antecedents of which Goldfinger was so enamoured: the brick-faced façade, the deftly-proportioned articulation of the exterior and the play of light inside. As Pevsner pointed out, the architecture is also complemented by a collection of modern art; there are works by contemporaries of Goldfinger such as Henry Moore, Max Ernst and Bridget Riley. The interior remains much as it was during the Goldfinger's lifetime: the plywood chairs, wood-and-leather safari chairs and writing desk are all the work of this architect-cum-designer.

HAMPSTEAD HIGH STREET TO BELSIZE PARK

Hampstead High Street (*map p. 598, C4*) descends to the area known as Belsize Park. It is along this street that 21st-century homogenisation has taken the strongest hold, in the form of coffee-shop, café, restaurant and boutique chains. The little takeaway crêpe stall outside the King William IV pub is now a Hampstead institution.

On the corner of Keats Grove and Downshire Hill is the church of St John (*map p. 598, C3*), dating from the 1820s. **Downshire Hill** itself is lined with lovely 19th-century villas and gardens; at the end is the Freemason's Arms, which has a beer garden. Note no. 49A, by Michael Hopkins, an unobtrusive steel and glass box, partially sunken below the road; it won an RIBA award in the 1970s. Dante Gabriel Rossetti and Lizzie Siddall stayed in a house on the site of Hampstead Hill Mansions shortly after their marriage in 1860. Siddall had convalesced in Hampstead in the 1850s, after contracting pneumonia as a consequence of posing in a bath of freezing water for Millais's *Ophelia* (now at Tate Britain).

In Belsize Park are several large 19th-century mansions, mostly converted into flats. In Lawn Road (*map p. 599, D4*) is the 1930s' white concrete apartment block known as the **Isokon Building**, which was built as communal living for professional workers. Agatha Christie and Walter Gropius were former residents.

KEATS HOUSE
10 Keats Grove. Map p. 598, C4. Underground: Hampstead, Belsize Park (10mins' walk). Open Nov–Feb Fri–Sun 1–5 (Tues and Thur pre-booked groups only), March–Oct Tues–Sun 1–5. Admission charge. T: 020 7332 3868.

This is the house where John Keats, the 'loveliest and the last' (Shelley, 'Adonaïs') Romantic poet, lived from Dec 1818 to Sept 1820. Brief though his residence was, it was here that he wrote some of his richest lyric poetry, including 'Ode to a Nightingale', 'Ode on a Grecian Urn' and 'Ode on Melancholy'. Here he fell in love with and became engaged to his 'Minx', Fanny Brawne and here he became ill with the tuberculosis which would end his life the following year in Rome. He was not yet 26. Originally known as Wentworth Place, the building was constructed as two semi-detached houses in 1815. Keats lived in the smaller of the two, next door to his friend Charles Armitage Brown. Fanny, her siblings and disapproving mother subsequently moved in in Brown's place. The house was restored in 2009 and the garden now has three themed borders: 'Melancholy', 'Autumn' and 'Nightingale'. On display in the museum are Keats' death mask, the engagement ring he gave to Fanny, and letters between the young couple which reveal the poet's passion, insecurity and jealousy. The house also hosts poetry readings.

HAMPSTEAD HEATH

Hampstead Heath (*map pp. 598–9*), rambling over 800 acres, commands superb views of London. It is beloved by Hampstead residents and Londoners alike and over the centuries its wild aspect has captured the imagination of numerous writers and artists. At one time, a community of laundresses would spread their washing to dry on Hampstead Heath, making is look snow-capped from afar. Today it is a popular spot for walking, cycling, kite-flying, jogging, swimming and picnicking. From Parliament Hill, one of the highest points, one can spot numerous landmarks, including the Palace of Westminster and the dome of St Paul's Cathedral, as well as the dominating new skyscrapers in the City and Canary Wharf.

The land around Hampstead was anciently owned by the monks of Westminster, who had a farm here. In 1349, Abbott Simon de Barcheston inadvertently brought the Black Death to Hampstead, when he fled here to escape the epidemic in the City. The Heath is the source of three of London's 'lost' rivers, the Tyburn, the Westbourne and the Fleet (the latter still feeds its ponds), and its sand and clay composition also made it a rich source of mineral spring water. Improved transport links and the arrival of the railway in the 19th century led to Hampstead's popularity with day-trippers, who would come here to escape from London's heat, grime and squalor. During this period, Sir Thomas Maryon Wilson, lord of the manor, wished to turn Hampstead's popularity to his profit by building a network of villas across his land. The rural nature of the Heath would have been altered forever had his project not been vehemently opposed by the local population. Sir Thomas fought tooth and nail for his plans to be approved and the project was only finally given up on his death in 1869. His heir sold the land to the Metropolitan Board of Works, who vowed that it would 'forever keep the Heath open, unenclosed and unbuilt on...and at all times preserve, as far as may be, the natural aspect and state of the Heath, and to that end shall protect the turf, gorse, heather, timber and other trees, shrubs and brushwood thereon.' Today the precious Heath is protected and managed by the City of London Corporation. The Heath & Hampstead Society is also active in the area's preservation.

FROGNAL TO THE FREUD MUSEUM

Frognal (*map p. 598, B3*), a discreet residential enclave, has some interesting architecture. In Frognal Way is a group of 1930s' houses. The most important architecturally is no. 9, Sun House, by Maxwell Fry (1935). Pevsner termed no. 4 'Hollywood Spanish-Colonial'; no. 5 was built by Sir George Gilbert Scott's grandson, Adrian Gilbert Scott, in 1930; no. 20, in Mediterranean style, was commissioned by the singer Gracie Fields in 1934. No. 66 Frognal (Connell Ward and Lucas, 1937) caused a furore when built, its Modernist style offending Sir Reginald Blomfield, who had designed the houses at nos 49 and 51. Further down is the neo-Wren University College School (1905–7). Opposite, at no. 39, is the former home of the children's book illustrator Kate Greenaway; it was built by Norman Shaw in 1884. Shaw's own house, which he designed for himself in 1874–6, is at no. 6 Ellerdale Rd.

In Arkwright Road is the **Camden Arts Centre** (*map p. 598, B4*), which runs education workshops and shows of contemporary art (*open Tues–Sun 10–6, until 9pm on Wed; free; bookshop selling Camden Publications; T: 020 7472 5500, camdenartscentre.org*). If you follow Arkwright Road in the other direction, you come to Fitzjohns Avenue (*map p. 598, C4*), where a small plaque commemorates the **Shepherd's Well**, the purest natural water source in Hampstead.

THE FREUD MUSEUM

20 Maresfield Gardens. Map p. 598, C4. Underground: Finchley Road and 5mins' walk. Open Wed–Sun 12–5. Admission charge. Shop. T: 020 7435 2002, freud.org.uk.

This is the house where Sigmund Freud lived for the final year of his life (1938–9), after fleeing Nazi oppression in his native Austria. His daughter Anna followed him into psychoanalytic practice, living and working here for 44 years, producing ground-breaking work in the field of child psychoanalysis and preserving her father's home as it had been left on his death.

The heart of the house is Freud's **Study and Library**, on the ground floor. Here is the famous Biedermeier-style psychoanalytic couch, given to him by one of his Viennese patients in 1890. The rest of the room is decorated with rich warm rugs, over floor and tables, and with an array of antiquities, including a late 5th–early 4th-century BC Greek terracotta sphinx, a 1st or 2nd-century Roman bronze Venus and a Chinese Buddhist lion paperweight made of jade (Qing Dynasty, 18th–19th centuries). The study also contains the largest remaining part of Freud's personal library, which, along with his couch, was brought from Vienna. Goethe, Shakespeare and the novels of Balzac, Gogol and Anatole France were particular favourites. On the first floor is the **Anna Freud Room**, with Anna's own analytic couch. On the **Landing** hang two portraits of Freud, one by fellow Austrian Ferdinand Schmutzer (1926) and the other by Dalí, a death-foreshadowing image that he sketched on a visit to Freud in 1938, the meeting an historic one for both. Dalí had read *The Interpretation of Dreams* as a student in Madrid, and his art ever since had been driven by the Freudian concept of the unconscious. Freud, hitherto sceptical of being regarded as the father of Surrealism, recorded that 'The young Spaniard, with his candid, fanatical eyes and his undeniable technical mastery, has changed my estimate. It would indeed be interesting to investigate analytically how he came to create his paintings.'

HAMPSTEAD GARDEN SUBURB, GOLDERS GREEN & FINCHLEY

Golders Green (*map p. 598, A1; Underground: Golders Green*) is a comfortable suburb developed in the 19th and 20th centuries, now home to a large middle-class Jewish community (some Orthodox), who settled here from the early 20th century onwards. It claims to offer some of the best kosher shopping in the whole of Europe. In Golders Green is a large bus station, with services to Kenwood and Hampstead Garden Suburb. London's first crematorium was opened in Golders Green in 1902. Sigmund Freud and Bram Stoker (who featured both Hampstead Heath and Jack Straw's Castle in his *Dracula*) were cremated here.

Hampstead Garden Suburb (*map p. 596, C1; Underground: Golders Green, then bus H2 or 20mins' walk*) is a planned development, the brainchild of Dame Henrietta Barnett, a Whitechapel vicar's wife so horrified by housing conditions in the East End that she aimed to create a classless utopia. Building began in 1907, to designs by Raymond Unwin, who had laid out Letchworth Garden City in Hertfordshire. Around Central Square there are buildings by Lutyens, including the Free Church with its dome (interdenominational, in keeping with the founding spirit of the suburb) and the Anglican church of St Jude-on-the-Hill, with its conspicuous spire (1911).

FINCHLEY

Finchley (*map p. 596, C1*) lies strung out along the Great North Road (also known as High Road). Just to the north of Hampstead Garden Suburb, below the North Circular, is East Finchley (*Underground: East Finchley*), where at no. 52 High Road is London's oldest working cinema, the **Phoenix**, in operation since 1910 (*phoenixcinema.co.uk, T: 020 8444 6789*). On the other side of the North Circular, at 80 East End Road further southwest, is the **Sternberg Centre**, proud to announce itself as the largest Jewish community centre in Europe. Here too is the New North London Synagogue, serving a congregation of Masorti Jews (*nnls-masorti.org.uk*).

Further northwest, at no. 17 East End Road, is **Avenue House**, popular for weddings and events (*Underground: Finchley Central*). The fine landscaped grounds and arboretum, laid out by Robert Marnock, are open to the public. The house was built on land originally owned by the Knights Templar. In 1874 Henry Charles 'Inky' Stephens, son of the inventor of the 'blue-black writing fluid' that developed into modern ink, bought the house in 1874 and established a laboratory on the first floor. When he died, he left the house and grounds to the people of Finchley. Today it is home to the Stephens Collection museum (*open Tues–Thur 2–4.30; free; T: 020 8346 7812, avenuehouse.org. uk*).

THE NORTH: ALEXANDRA PALACE, WALTHAMSTOW, BARNET & ENFIELD

Alexandra Palace (*map p. 596, C1; Underground: Wood Green; trains from King's Cross or Moorgate*), familiarly known as 'Ally Pally', is an entertainment venue set in an expansive park. Named after Alexandra, consort of the future Edward VII, it began life in 1873 as an exhibition centre inspired by the Crystal Palace (*see p. 461*). It burned down after only two weeks, was rebuilt and reopened two years later, but was never a commercial success. During the First World War it was used as a prisoner of war camp. In 1936 the world's first high-definition television broadcast was made from here (the transmission antenna survives). Today it hosts a wide variety of exhibitions and events (*alexandrapalace.com*). The views of London from its elevated position are exceptionally good.

WALTHAMSTOW: THE WILLIAM MORRIS GALLERY

Lloyd Park, Forest Road. Map p. 597, E1. Underground: Walthamstow Central and 15mins' walk. Open Wed–Sun 10–5 (guided tours available for pre-booked groups). Admission charge. Tea room and shop. T: 020 8496 4390, wmgallery.org.uk.

The Water House at Lloyd Park is a testament to the writer, social reformer, Socialist and designer William Morris (1832–96), famous for the phrase 'have nothing in your house that you do not know to be useful, or believe to be beautiful'. The designs of the objects of utility and beauty to which he refers, inspired by the forms of nature, traditional craft and workmanship and the aesthetic of the medieval Gothic according to

John Ruskin, and which his company Morris, Marshall, Faulkner and Co. produced from 1861 onwards, include tiles, tableware, stained glass, furniture and wallpaper and are still produced to this day by Morris & Co.

Morris was born in Walthamstow, the son of a wealthy financier. He was a recalcitrant student at the newly-established Marlborough College (Morris preferred to learn his own way, from the independent reading of antiquarian history books and the exploration of local prehistoric landscapes). When his father died in 1847, the family's ensuing straitened circumstances induced his mother to move with Morris and his eight siblings to the Water House, named after its ornamental moat in the grounds, where the Morris family would fish, boat and skate. Morris lived here from 1848–56 but today the open fields and countryside which he would have known have been swallowed up by dense terraced housing, a process of suburban development which began in the 1870s with the extension of the railway. In Morris's words, Walthamstow became 'terribly cocknified and choked up by the jerry-builders'. The house was purchased by the publisher Edward Lloyd, the disseminator of sensationalist serials (known as 'penny dreadfuls') such as *Varney the Vampire or The Feast of Blood* (1845), the precursor to Bram Stoker's *Dracula* and reputedly one of the worst books written in a hundred years. After Lloyd's death the house and grounds passed into public hands.

Much of the contents of the museum comprise the collections of the artist Sir Frank Brangwyn (1867–1956), who was apprenticed to Morris, and A.H. Mackmurdo, an architect, designer and founder of the Century Guild, who had introduced Brangwyn to Morris (one of only five Fretwork chairs made by him is on display here).

The nine galleries are thematically laid out, beginning with the early life and influences of William Morris, moving on to the establishment of his professional career as a designer, to later life as a poet, publisher and radical political activist, and concluding with his lasting legacy. Displays cover the Morris & Co. shop at 449 Oxford St and the famous Kelmscott Press, run from his house in Hammersmith (*see p. 473*), which published the *Works of Geoffrey Chaucer* (1896), with the typeface and page layout by Morris and illustrations by Burne-Jones. The story of the radicalisation of Morris in middle age is also told, showing how his work as a craftsman informed his political beliefs and covering his establishment of the Socialist League in 1884, as well as his arrest for disorderly conduct at a mass meeting of Socialists in 1885.

BARNET

Barnet's location on the main road north from London (*map p. 595, D1*) stimulated local trade and many coaching inns sprang up here; one, the Old Red Lion at the foot of Barnet Hill, was established in the 16th century. The Battle of Barnet, fought on Hadley Common in 1471, was a pivotal conflict of the Wars of the Roses. Warwick the Kingmaker was slain on the field and Edward IV's throne was secured. At 31 Wood St is the **Barnet Museum** (*Underground: High Barnet, then bus or walk; open Tues–Thur and Sun 2.30–4.30, Sat 10.30–4.30; free; T: 020 8440 8066. barnetmuseum.co.uk*) with a display on the Battle of Barnet and other curiosities, including the glove of a Zeppelin pilot who crashed over Potters Bar during World War One.

North of the Barnet Museum, the High Street and then the Great North Road lead to Hadley Green and the **Hadley High Stone** (1½ miles from Barnet), an obelisk commemorating the Battle of Barnet.

Barnet Fair (*first Mon in Sept*) is the descendant of the old Horse Fair, from which the Cockney rhyming slang 'Barnet', meaning 'hair' is derived.

ENFIELD

Enfield still retains something of its old village feel. It is home to the manor of **Forty Hall** (*map p. 595, E1; open April–Oct Tues–Fri 11–5, Sat–Sun and bank holidays 12–5, closes 1hr earlier in Nov–March; closed 1st week of Jan; free; café; T: 020 8363 8196, fortyhallestate.co.uk. Trains from Liverpool Street to Enfield Town, then bus 191 to Forty Hill, from where the house is signposted*), a red-brick mansion, 'but a horse ride from the City', built in 1629–32 for Sir Nicholas Rainton, Lord Mayor of London, President of St Bartholomew's Hospital and a wealthy haberdasher (his name features on the plaque in the entrance to Haberdashers' Hall on West Smithfield). The exterior of Forty Hall is very handsome and the hipped roof is of particular interest, being advanced for its time and an important early example of the style. The interior has been much altered and restored, but some interesting features remain. The Entrance Hall has Rococo plasterwork of c. 1787, with medallions representing the Seasons. The fine carved panelling on the early 17th-century Hall Screen is an outstanding survival from the original house. Other rooms retain plaster ceilings with bold strapwork decoration.

In the grounds is one of the most ancient cedars of Lebanon in the country and scant remains have also been found here of Elsyng Palace, a Tudor royal manor and hunting lodge, where in 1547, in the presence of Princess Elizabeth, Edward VI received the news of the death of his father Henry VIII and of his consequent accession.

Rainton died at Forty Hall in 1646. In **St Andrew's church** in Enfield Town, set back from the market square, you can admire his fine painted family tomb, with stiffly reclining effigies. On market days (Thur, Fri and Sat) you can buy cockles, whelks and other shellfish from one of the stalls—a perfect London snack.

At **Enfield Town railway station** you are treading on ground where Keats trod. The poet attended school in a building on this site from 1803–11. The headmaster's son, Charles Cowden Clarke, became Keats's great friend, to whom the poet acknowledged a debt of sincere gratitude: 'Ah! had I never seen or known your kindness, what might I have been?'

THE NORTHEAST:
STOKE NEWINGTON, STAMFORD HILL & HACKNEY

Once rural woodland, the ancient village of Stoke Newington (*map p. 597, D1; trains from Liverpool Street in c. 15mins*) grew up around Stoke Newington Church Street. Edgar Allan Poe, who went to school here, described it as 'a dreamlike and spirit-soothing place', a place of 'deeply-shadowed avenues', where he would 'inhale the fragrance of its thousand shrubberies, and thrill anew with undefinable delight, at the deep hollow note of the church-bell, breaking, each hour.' Today, with its plethora of small independent shops, pubs, bars and good restaurants serving a wide variety of world cuisine, Stoke Newington's gentrified villagey atmosphere is extremely well maintained—though the streets are shabbier further away from Stoke Newington Church Street. The area is multi-ethnic, with communities of Afro Caribbeans, Cypriots and Asians clustering around Stoke Newington High Street, part of the A10, which is built over Ermine Street, the old Roman road to Lincoln and York. There is a large Turkish population here too, and Turkish restaurants and kebab shops abound.

For centuries Stoke Newington has been a place where outsiders, foreigners and Nonconformists have settled. Jewish refugees arrived at the end of the 19th century, escaping the pogroms of Eastern Europe; in the 20th century ultra-orthodox Jews colonised Stamford Hill (*see below*). Its most famous Nonconformist resident was Daniel Defoe (a road and a pub are named after him), who wrote *Robinson Crusoe* while living in a house on the site of no. 95 **Stoke Newington Church Street**. At no. 184 (the local library) his tombstone from Bunhill Fields is preserved and on display. From the 18th century many wealthy Quakers lived in the area, including Anna Sewell, author of *Black Beauty*, who lived here as a child.

The atmospheric **Abney Park**, to the east along Stoke Newington Church Street, was established as a Nonconformist garden cemetery with arboretum around 1840; the wooded landscape had been laid out in the 18th century. John Loudon, gardener and writer (*see Porchester Terrace, p. 277*), very much admired it. It is now a public park and nature reserve. William Booth and his wife Catherine, founders of the Salvation Army, are buried here. The boarded-up neo-Gothic chapel with 120ft octagonal steeple (William Hosking, c. 1840) claims to be the oldest surviving non-denominational chapel in Europe; it has never been consecrated and was used for funerary purposes, not as a place of worship.

St Mary's Old Church in Stoke Newington Church Street dates from 1560. The 'new' church opposite was designed by Sir George Gilbert Scott in 1858. **Clissold Park**, to the west of the churches, formed the grounds of the local mansion, formerly Paradise House, built for the Quaker, merchant and anti-slavery campaigner Jonathan Hoare, brother of Samuel Hoare (*see Hampstead, p. 394*). The 18th-century villa is now a café and the park has a small menagerie and lake. Part of the New River, a man-made waterway opened in 1613 to supply London with fresh drinking water from springs in Middlesex and Hertfordshire, emerges in the park; further north, it feeds the east and west reservoirs. The **former Stoke Newington Pumping Station** in Green Lanes (skirting the west side of Clissold Park), a castle-like structure, is a valuable example of Victorian industrial architecture. Designed in 1854–6 by Chadwell Mylne, who took inspiration from Stirling Castle in Scotland, it once helped pump the waters of the New River. It has been converted into an indoor climbing centre and is called The Castle.

STAMFORD HILL

Stamford Hill (*map p. 597, D1; trains from Liverpool Street in c. 15mins*), north of Stoke Newington, was once just a sandy ford. In the 18th and 19th centuries wealthy merchants came to live here; today, the most conspicuous aspect of the area is the number of ultra-orthodox Jews you will see going about their business: the square mile comes to bustling life on the Jewish Sabbath (Saturday). Ninety percent of the population here are Haredi Jews: this is the largest ultra-orthodox Jewish community outside Israel and Brooklyn. Behind the façades of the large Victorian and Edwardian houses are synagogues, single-sex schools, community centres and places of religious study, as well as homes. The Haredi live an insular, pious life; they were nearly wiped out during the Holocaust and thriving Eastern European communities were extinguished. The survivors settled in the Israel, the USA and the UK, clinging to their centuries-old traditions and mistrustful of assimilation. Their primary language is Yiddish, religious study is pursued above all else and the trappings of modern secular life are eschewed. They set themselves apart most obviously by their dress. The men, with beards and long, curling side-locks, wear black frock coats and various forms of hat, which some of the married men exchange on Shabbat for the *shtreimel*: the large, circular, real-fur hat that is worn come rain or shine on this holy day (during wet weather it is covered with a transparent plastic bonnet). The women dress modestly in long skirts, jackets, blouses and thick stockings and tend to marry young (at 18 or 20), after which they cover their hair with wigs. They bear an average of six children: fruitful family life is central to this closed community, which already numbers over 20,000 and is expanding. Ex-Chief Rabbi Lord Sachs recently expressed concern for 'the orthodoxy that segregates itself from the world and from its fellow Jews'.

On Dunsmure Road (intersected by the felicitously-named West Bank) there are kosher bakeries, butchers and shops. A multi-million pound six-storey development is due to rise on Stamford Hill itself, with the largest kosher supermarket in the UK, as well as conference facilities and flats with staggered balconies so that the sky will be visible during Sukkot.

HACKNEY

Hackney (*map p. 597, E2; Overground: Hoxton, Haggerston, Hackney Central, Homerton High Street*) developed rapidly in the late 19th and early 20th centuries. After that it went into decline, becoming run-down and with a lingering atmosphere of threat. Furtive-looking men with pit bull terriers would stalk Victoria Park. Today **Victoria Park** is transformed and Hackney Marshes are proud to have the largest concentration of football pitches in Europe. South Hackney has become popular with young professionals and is well stocked with cafés and restaurants. It is also the site of one of London's burgeoning cluster of city farms, **Hackney City Farm** (*1A Goldsmiths Row, hackneycityfarm.co.uk*).

For an outside visitor, the chief reason to come here may be **Sutton House**, which survives largely intact from the early 16th century. The house (*2 & 4 Homerton High St; generally open Wed–Fri 10.30–5, Sat–Sun 12–5; admission charge; café and shop; T: 020 8986 2264, nationaltrust.org.uk*) was built in 1534–5 by Ralph Sadleir, a wealthy soldier and diplomat, secretary to Thomas Cromwell and later King Henry VIII's principal Secretary of State. It was first known as 'the bryk place', being one of the very few brick-built residences in the area (the ragstone tower of St Augustine's church nearby is the only other building to remain from the period). Constructed on the familiar Tudor 'H' plan, the building has been altered several times since—notably around 1620, in 1741–3 and in the early 19th century—but the original form remains remarkably intact. As such it represents an important London example of the development of the medieval hall house, with cross-wings and servants' quarters. The property later passed to Thomas Sutton, who according to John Aubrey was the type for Ben Jonson's Volpone. Of particular interest in the interior is the Linenfold Parlour, which is lined with very fine mid-16th-century carved oak panelling. Originally the wood was painted pale yellow with green in the folds, a colour scheme that can still be seen behind hinged panels in one wall. Quite possibly it was in this room that Sir Ralph Sadleir held negotiations during the Dissolution of the Monasteries, which carved up the wealth of the Church. Also on show are examples of artwork produced in the later 20th-century when the house was occupied by squatters. They named it the Blue House and it became a music venue for punk bands rejoicing in names like 'Sons of Bad Breath' and 'Flowers in the Dustbin'.

Dalston (*map p. 597, D2*) is known for its nightlife and for its 'clown service' on the first Sun in Feb, when jesters, fools and harlequins of all kinds congregate at Holy Trinity church on Beechwood Road (*Overground: Dalston Kingsland*) for a service commemorating Joseph Grimaldi, the pantomime actor who developed the character of the modern clown. He died in Islington in 1837.

EATING AND DRINKING IN HAMPSTEAD, HIGHGATE AND THE NORTH

HAMPSTEAD

Hampstead is home to many pubs, though some of them are tiny and they tend to get crowded. They are nevertheless famous and historic.

£–££ The Old Bull and Bush. This pub, on the border of Hampstead and Golders Green, gave its name to an old music hall song. Modern British cooking. Open daily. *North End Way. T: 020 8905 5456, thebullandbush.co.uk. Map p. 598, B2.*

£ The Flask. Named after the glass bottles in which the Hampstead spa water was once dispensed. The light, airy conservatory is very pleasant. Open daily. *14 Flask Walk. T: 020 7435 4580, theflaskhampstead.co.uk. Map p. 598, B3–C3.*

££ The Holly Bush. Traditional old pub that prides itself on retaining its classic décor. A slice of old England, like the beef. Open daily. *22 Hollymount, T: 020 7435 2892, hollybushhampstead.co.uk. Map p. 598, C3.*

££ Spaniards Inn. This place frequently tops lists as one of the best pubs in the UK to enjoy a roast lunch. Good solid food and wine. Keats is supposed to have drunk here. Open daily. *Spaniards Rd. T: 020 8731 8406, www.thespaniardshamptstead.co.uk. Map p. 598, C2.*

£–££ The Wells Tavern. Award-winning cooking in this revamped pub. Fine roast lunches. Signature Bloody Marys. Open daily. *30 Well Walk. T: 020 7794 3785, thewellshampstead.co.uk. Map p. 598, C3.*

HIGHGATE, ARCHWAY

££ 500 (Cinquecento). At the Archway end of Holloway Road. A real hidden gem: a local Italian whose head chef is a former Jamie Oliver protégé. The food is classy and the place feels authentically Italian. Dinner only Mon–Thur, lunch and dinner Fri–Sun. *782 Holloway Rd. T: 020 7272 3406, 500restaurant.co.uk. Map p. 599, F2.*

£ Côte. Reliable French-style brasserie, one of a chain, with a loyal following. Open daily. *2 Highgate High St. T: 020 8348 9107, cote-restaurants.co.uk. Map p. 599, E2.*

£ The Flask. Historic pub dating back to the 17th century. Coleridge once drank here. Good pub food. Nice garden. *77 Highgate West Hill. T: 020 8348 7346, theflaskhighgate.com. Map p. 599, E2.*

£ Pavilion Café. In the middle of Highgate Wood. Mediterranean food and ice cream. Closes 4pm in winter, 9pm in summer. *Muswell Hill Rd. T: 020 8444 4777. Beyond map p. 599, E1 and map p. 596, C1.*

£–££ St John's Tavern. There are not many good places to eat in Archway, but this is one of them. Pub/restaurant with a daily changing menu. Delicious food with an emphasis on meat and seafood. Good bar menu too. People swear by the scotch eggs. Open daily. *91 Junction Rd. T: 020 7272 1587, stjohnstavern.com. Map p. 599, F2.*

STOKE NEWINGTON

£ 19 Numara Bos Cirrik. Excellent and reasonably priced Turkish restaurant that stays open late. *34 Stoke Newington Rd (continuation of Kingsland Rd; map p. 597, D2). T: 020 7249 0400.*

£ The Londesborough. Consistently good gastro pub. *36 Barbauld Rd. T: 020 7254 5865, thelondesborough.com.*

BANKSIDE
Tate Modern's chimney stack rears skyward
behind the Millennium Bridge.

The South Bank

*This chapter covers Vauxhall, once home to the famous Pleasure Gardens;
Lambeth, with its archbishop's palace; as well as Southwark Cathedral,
Borough Market and the modern art collections of Tate Modern.
Shakespeare's Globe Theatre is also on the riverbank here.*

The south bank of the River Thames from Vauxhall Bridge to Tower Bridge falls into the boroughs of Lambeth and Southwark, both of them historically important districts. In centuries past this area was a place of ecclesiastical power but also of bawdy entertainment, outside the City limits. Theatres and bear-baiting arenas abounded from the Middle Ages and Vauxhall was the home of the famous Pleasure Gardens, one of the most popular places of public entertainment.

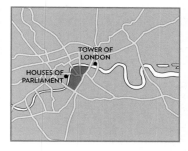

VAUXHALL

Map pp. 597, D3 and 603, F4. Underground/Rail: Vauxhall.

Opposite Vauxhall station is the busy traffic junction and bus shelter known as Vauxhall Cross. Straight ahead is **Vauxhall Bridge** (1906, Binnie and Fitzmaurice), replacing a 19th-century river crossing. It is decorated with allegorical bronze statues representing Pottery, Engineering, Architecture, Agriculture, Science, the Fine Arts and the civic provisions of Education and Local Government. On the right-hand side is Terry Farrell's Post-modern **SIS Building**, in cream stone and tinted green glass, opened in 1994. It is the home of Britain's intelligence service, SIS, generally known by its former title of MI6. The building's stepped geometric form supposedly echoes nearby Battersea Power Station, though it seems to owe more to ancient Babylon; the distinctive façade has featured in several James Bond films. Reflecting it, on the left-hand side of the bridge, is the **St George Wharf** housing development; seven acres of clear and tinted glass, with flock-of-seagulls rooftops. At its centre rises the UK's tallest residential tower block; cylindrical, like a canister of hairspray. Its construction crane was hit by a helicopter in 2013, resulting in the death of the pilot and of a pedestrian in the street below. This part of South Lambeth, historically an industrial, working-class community, is today multi-ethnic and well-endowed with council and social housing estates, though it is being gentrified in part by these riverside developments. They are popular with politicians because of their proximity to Westminster. The **former Elephant and Castle pub** (left out of the station; note the sculptures of elephants with castles on their backs) was, at the time of writing, a branch of Starbucks.

Industries that once flourished in Vauxhall were glass-making (commemorated by Glasshouse Walk, off Albert Embankment), porcelain (the Royal Doulton factory was also off the Embankment) and car manufacture. The Vauxhall Ironworks Co. (later Vauxhall Motors) built its first car in 1903; the factory was on Wandsworth Road, where the Sainsbury's supermarket now stands.

OLD VAUXHALL GARDENS

Behind the station, off Kennington Lane, is a modest green expanse (*map p. 597, D3*). This small rectangle of grassy hillocks with a tarmacked multi-use recreation ground, surrounded by housing estates and with the railway arches running along its western flank, is all that remains of **Vauxhall Pleasure Gardens**.

VAUXHALL PLEASURE GARDENS

'Well, but, Ma'am,' said Mr Smith, 'how do you like Vauxhall and Marybone?
'I never saw either, Sir.

'No—God bless me!-you really surprise me,—why Vauxhall is the first pleasure in life!—I know nothing like it.—Well, Ma'am, you must have been with strange people, indeed, not to have taken you to Vauxhall.'

So wrote Fanny Burney in *Evelina* (1778). Opened in 1661, the Pleasure Gardens' heyday was from 1729–67, when they were owned and run by the shrewd Bermondsey entrepreneur and arts patron Jonathan Tyers (a portrait of him and his family is in the National Portrait Gallery), who turned them into a successful commercial enterprise. They featured the latest in Rococo design and decoration, and for a reasonable entry fee, Londoners from all walks of life could mingle freely in the landscaped grounds, dine in 'supper-boxes', dance, drink, listen to music, admire artworks, watch illuminations and firework displays and even go on balloon ascents. The Museum of London holds several original entrance tickets, from regular ivory passes to upmarket season tickets made of silver and decorated with Neoclassical scenes, the name of the guest engraved on the reverse. In 1738, Tyers commissioned Roubiliac to produce a life-size marble statue of Handel (now in the V&A) to greet guests in The Grove after they arrived by water. Handel's music was often performed here by the gardens' resident orchestra; the dress rehearsal for *Music for the Royal Fireworks* took place at Vauxhall in 1749. Over the years, Vauxhall was visited by Pepys, Goldsmith, Boswell, Walpole, Fanny Burney, Frederick, Prince of Wales, Wordsworth and Charles Dickens. Dickens, in 1836, made the mistake of visiting the gardens by daylight, when all that had seemed so magical by night appeared tawdry and everyday: 'Our favourite views were mere patches of paint...'

Along the eastern edge of the gardens, on Tyers Street, is the **Vauxhall City Farm** (*open Wed–Sun 10:30–4; free, donations welcome*). Following World War Two, the area was little more than a wasteland; this small farm was founded in 1976 as a place where members of the community could come and tend to animals and grow their own produce, a way of bringing nature to the inner city. Today the farm keeps numerous animals, including horses, alpacas, pigs, goats, rabbits, ducks and geese, and offers therapeutic classes in riding and horticulture as well as educational and youth outreach programmes. A group of spinners spins wool from the sheep and alpacas, using vegetable dyes from plants grown on the farm.

Next door and behind the farm is the entrance to **St Peter's Church** (façade best seen from Kennington Lane). Its High Victorian, neo-Gothic design is by J.L. Pearson (1864) and it was built over the slum area that had developed from the former Vauxhall Pleasure Gardens; the altar is on the site of its Neptune Fountain. The church is not always open, but the restored, vaulted interior displays wall-paintings, mosaic and carved stonework. The Vauxhall St Peter's Heritage Centre has exhibitions relating to the history of Vauxhall and Lambeth. The church is known for its music—an appropriate tradition, standing as it does on the site where Handel, Johann Christian Bach and Thomas Arne performed.

LAMBETH

Map p. 604. Underground/Rail: Waterloo, Lambeth North.

Lambeth is a historic area, home to the official residence of the Archbishop of Canterbury, the chief prelate of the Church of England. The name Lambeth may be derived from 'Lamb-hithe', meaning a place where lambs were docked, or from 'Loamhithe', a muddy harbour. It was badly bombed in the Second World War and today is bisected by the railway lines that bring trains to and from the busy Waterloo Station. On the east side of the tracks is **Lambeth Walk** (*map p. 604, B4*), once a lively working-class street, made famous by the song in the 1937 musical *Me and My Girl* (its choreography inspired a strutting dance craze which reached America in 1938). Today the busy street market, with its costermongers, eel and pie shops and tripe dressers, is long gone and the street is quietly occupied by modern social housing, though punctuated by relics from its past: a small parade of 1960s' shops, where in one, local children tinkle away during piano lessons; a tiny terrace of 19th-century cottages; small side streets with names such as Walnut Tree Walk, the ghosts of 17th-century country lanes; and the elaborate, red-brick and stone-clad former Pelham Mission Hall (1910, now the Henry Moore Sculpture Studios; on its façade is an outdoor pulpit from where preachers once addressed shoppers and traders thronging the market below). At the end of Lambeth Walk, the yellow brick Chandler Hall, opposite the China Walk Estate, has a plaque commemorating Charlie Chaplin, who was born and brought up in Kennington (*see p. 462*), which is in Lambeth borough.

Lambeth Walk opens onto **Lambeth Road**, a busy thoroughfare running east–west: if you look east (right), in the distance you will see the Shard. Beyond the junction with Kennington Road is the Imperial War Museum. At no. 100 Lambeth Rd, part of a small Georgian terrace opposite the museum, lived Captain William Bligh, Commander of the *Bounty* (blue plaque); he is buried in the churchyard of St Mary-at-Lambeth (*see Garden Museum, below*).

THE IMPERIAL WAR MUSEUM

Map p. 604, B4. Underground: Lambeth North. Open daily 10–6. Free. Café and shop. T: 020 7416 5000, iwm.org.uk.

The Imperial War Museum operates three sites in London: HMS *Belfast* (*see p. 431*), the Churchill War Rooms (*see p. 149*), and this, its main home. The displays illustrate and record the experience of armed conflict—with particular attention paid to the role played by Britain and the Commonwealth—since the start of the First World War in August 1914. The varied collections tell the story of military and civilian, Allied and enemy, tactical, strategic, social and political aspects of warfare by land, sea and air, employing an extraordinary array of memorabilia, fine art, film, sound archives, background information, interactive audio-visual displays, models and reconstructions. New First World War galleries were opened in 2014 to mark the centenary of the beginning of the 'Great War'.

ST GEORGE'S CATHEDRAL AND HERCULES ROAD

On the corner of St George's Road and Lambeth Road, on the very spot where the 'No Popery' rioters assembled in 1780, stands **St George's Cathedral** (*map p. 604, B4*), of the Roman Catholic archdiocese of Southwark, built by Augustus Pugin in 1840–8, wrecked by bombs in 1941 and freely rebuilt by Romilly Craze using the original design. A spacious edifice, brick outside and stone within, it mixes a profusion of Gothic styles. On St George's Road opposite the cathedral is a Georgian terrace, where at no. 131 lived the master builder George Myers, who worked with Pugin on many of his projects, including Southwark Cathedral.

Christ Church, at the corner of Kennington Road and Westminster Bridge Road, has been rebuilt into an office block. At the junction of Westminster Bridge Road and Kennington Road, opposite Lambeth North Underground, stands the ragstone **Lincoln Tower**, decorated with the Stars and Stripes emblem in red and white stone. It was erected by subscription from Americans as a memorial to President Lincoln, and opened in 1876.

In **Hercules Road**, a plaque on a modern red-brick block notes that William Blake lived on the site in 1793. Opposite, alongside a charming fragment of Georgian terrace, in front of which is a mature fir tree, Centaur Street leads through the clanging railway arch. Straight ahead, Royal Street leads to Lambeth Palace Road and St Thomas's Hospital Accident and Emergency department; left is an entrance to Archbishop's Park. The park (from where there is a good view of Edward Blore's 1830s' Bath stone residential wing of Lambeth Palace) was formerly part of the palace grounds. It was opened to the public in 1901.

GARDEN MUSEUM
Mythical beast and *memento mori*: detail of the
17th-century Tradescant tomb chest.

LAMBETH PALACE

Close to the river, overlooking the Palace of Westminster, stands Lambeth Palace (*map p. 604, A4*), which has been the official London residence of the Archbishop of Canterbury for nearly 800 years; before the bridge crossings were built, the archbishops would travel to Westminster by ferry. Parts of the palace may be visited by pre-booked guided tour (*for available dates, see archbishopofcenterbury.org; tours last approx. 90mins*). The building was begun by Archbishop Langton (1207–29). Altered many times by his successors, it suffered damage during the Civil War and again in the Second World War. Thomas Cranmer wrote his *Book of Common Prayer* here (1549).

Entrance is through the early Tudor gatehouse (c. 1490). The **Great Hall**, rebuilt in medieval style by Archbishop Juxon in 1663, has a roof resembling that of Westminster Hall. The **Library** is thought to be the oldest free public library in the country and contains some extraordinary treasures, including the 12th-century illuminated Lambeth Bible, Elizabeth I's prayer book and the letters that were on Archbishop Laud's desk at the time of his arrest. Also among the palace treasures is a fine series of **portraits of archbishops** by Holbein, Van Dyck, Hogarth, Reynolds, Romney, Lawrence and others. The small Chapel (c. 1230) preserves stalls and other fittings provided by Archbishop Laud (1634). The chapel was the scene of the second trial of Wycliffe in 1378 (the picturesque Lollards' Tower derives its name from the belief that the Lollards, Wycliffe's followers, were imprisoned in it). The beautiful **Crypt** is the oldest part of the building, perhaps as early as 1200.

LAMBETH BRIDGE AND THE GARDEN MUSEUM

Lambeth Bridge (Blomfield et al, 1932) has red-painted arches and balustrades, supposedly to honour the red-upholstered benches in the House of Lords (Westminster Bridge, which is closer to the House of Commons, has a green colour scheme to match the Commons upholstery). On the south side of the bridge, in the deconsecrated church of St Mary-at-Lambeth, is the **Garden Museum**, founded in 1977 by the late John and Rosemary Nicholson, thus rescuing the church from demolition (*map p. 604, A4; open Sun–Fri 10.30–5, Sat 10.30–4, closed 1st Mon of every month; admission charge; café and shop; T: 020 7401 8865, gardenmuseum.org.uk*). The small permanent collection includes material on Joseph Banks (1743–1820), the first professional plant-hunter. Banks accompanied Captain Cook aboard HMS *Endeavour* and named Botany Bay. Artefacts (largely historical garden implements) include a collection of early garden gnomes, a canister of 'Slug Death' (an early pesticide), and two leather 'pony boots' worn by horses that pulled early lawn mowers, to stop their hooves from disfiguring the turf. The north transept is given over to a vegetarian café. Beyond is the entrance to the old graveyard, planted with a replica 17th-century knot garden. Here too is the elaborately-carved tomb chest of the Tradescant family. John Tradescant the Elder (1570–1638) was gardener to Robert Cecil, the first Lord Salisbury, at Hatfield House, and later to Charles I and his consort Henrietta Maria. His son, John Tradescant the Younger (1608–62), was enrolled as a freeman of the Worshipful Company of Gardeners in 1634 and three years later made the first of three voyages to Virginia, bringing back the tulip tree, Michaelmas daisy and Virginia creeper, among other plants and shrubs. The epitaph on the lid reads: 'A world of wonders in one closet shut, these famous Antiquarians that had been, both Gardiners to the Rose and Lily Queen, transplanted now themselves, sleep here.' The elegant Coade Stone (*see below*) tomb of Admiral William Bligh (d. 1817), best known as the captain of the mutinous HMS *Bounty*, stands adjacent to that of the Tradescants. Bligh was engaged on a mission to transplant the first breadfruit trees to the West Indies from Tahiti, as an alternative food source for sugar plantation slaves after American independence threatened the usual supplies. After the mutiny, he and his men were obliged to navigate 3,600 miles by sextant in an open boat for 41 days, living off raw fish, turtles and seabirds.

Opposite the Garden Museum, at no. 1 Lambeth High St, is the **Royal Pharmaceutical Society**. Its small museum on the history of British pharmacy includes examples of 'Lambeth Delftware' pharmacy jars from the 17th and 18th centuries (*map p. 604, A4; free ground-floor exhibit open Mon–Fri 9–5, other displays viewable Tues and Thur by pre-booked tour only; T: 020 7572 7629*).

THE RIVERSIDE WALK TO WESTMINSTER BRIDGE

Across Lambeth Palace Road, the **riverside walk** leads north (right) to Westminster Bridge, affording excellent views of the Houses of Parliament on the opposite bank. In front of Lambeth Pier, from where boat services run up and down river, is the **SOE Monument**, commemorating all those who undertook perilous missions during World War Two. The SOE (Special Operations Executive) recruited male and female volunteers of all nationalities to conduct acts of sabotage in enemy-occupied countries. The bust is of British and French Resistance agent Violette Szabo, who was captured, tortured and then executed, aged 23, in Ravensbruck concentration camp in 1945. Szabo was posthumously decorated by both Britain and France.

The elaborate red-brick buildings behind the wall on the right are the surviving 19th-century ward pavilions of **St Thomas's Hospital** (*see below*). A plaque in the wall opposite Lambeth Palace commemorates Lt-Col John By, founder of Ottawa, who was born in Lambeth in 1779. Another plaque, just before Westminster Bridge, opposite 'Big Ben', commemorates the victims of CJD, the human form of Mad Cow Disease.

Steps lead up to **Westminster Bridge** (Thomas Page, 1854–62, replacing an 18th-century stone bridge), which on its northern side is guarded by the **South Bank Lion**, a large sculpture in Coade Stone (*see below*). It was made in 1837 and formerly adorned the Lion Brewery, which was demolished in 1950. It then stood outside Waterloo Station before being moved to its present site in 1966.

COADE STONE

This artificial, frost-resistant material was first manufactured by Mrs Eleanor Coade in 1769 in a factory on this site. Coade Stone was extolled in its day as the equal of marble for its sharpness of definition. The mixture, to which fine-ground quartz was added, was fired at very high temperatures so that it practically vitrified. In the 18th century its trade name was Lithodipyra, from the Greek meaning stone (*litho*) twice (*di*) fired (*pyra*). The stone, in fact, was semi-ceramic, the secret of its durability. The Coade family was originally from southwest England and it is surmised that they knew of and used china clay, which was—and still is—mined around St Austell in Cornwall. The success of Mrs Coade's enterprise came largely thanks to the enthusiasm for her product of influential architects and sculptors. Robert Adam, on his return from the Grand Tour, found it the ideal medium for producing the ornamental Grecian urns which he made fashionable. Sir John Soane was another user. On the façade of his house in Lincoln's Inn Fields are two Coade Stone figures, and there are others at Pitzhanger Manor, his villa in Ealing. The sculptor John Flaxman also appreciated the material's qualities. His figures of *Tragedy* and *Comedy* on the Royal Opera House in Covent Garden are of Coade Stone.

Coade Stone ceased manufacture in 1840, but its presence still endures. Captain William Bligh's tomb at the Garden Museum is made of it, as is the South Bank Lion.

ST THOMAS'S HOSPITAL AND THE FLORENCE NIGHTINGALE MUSEUM

In Lambeth Palace Road, opposite the Houses of Parliament, is St Thomas's Hospital (*map p. 604, A4*). It is of ancient origin, possibly founded as early as 1106. It moved here from Southwark and the foundation stone was laid by Queen Victoria in 1868. It was built on a 'pavilion' layout devised by Florence Nightingale: to aid ventilation and reduce the spread of disease, wards were organised in long blocks, linked by a corridor, with windows on both sides. Most of the pavilions were demolished when the hospital was rebuilt after the Second World War; the surviving chapel and three original pavilions have been restored.

In the hospital grounds is the **Florence Nightingale Museum** (*2 Lambeth Palace Rd; open Mon–Sun 10–5 (last admission 4.30), free tour by the curator on Mon at 3.30; free illustrated talk by the director on Wed at 3.30; admission charge; shop; café in the hospital; T: 020 7620 0374, florence-nightingale.co.uk*), exploring the achievements of the great nursing pioneer. For her indefatigable campaigns to improve sanitation and hospital management, she became the first woman to receive the Order of Merit (in

1907). The exhibition space (stethoscope audio guides available) is arranged in three 'pavilions' documenting her early life, her work in the Crimea and her legacy: 'Florence Nightingale—that Englishwoman whose name shall never die, but sound like music on the lips of British men until the hour of doom.' The tribute is from the pen of Mary Seacole, herself a Crimea veteran, whose work is also commemorated in the museum.

THE SOUTH BANK

Map p 604, A3–B3. Underground: Waterloo, or Embankment and then cross Hungerford footbridge.

The term 'South Bank' denotes the area running along the Thames opposite Victoria Embankment. Here is a group of arts and performing arts venues covering ground from County Hall to Waterloo Bridge and down towards the Oxo Tower. The former **County Hall** building extends along the river from Westminster Bridge to Jubilee Gardens. The grand, neo-Baroque edifice, faced in Portland stone, by Ralph Knott, was begun in 1912, opened in 1922, but was not fully not completed until the 1930s. The huge, concave river-façade is 750ft long. It was built to house the London County Council, later the Greater London Council, powerful—and now defunct—administrative bodies. Today the complex is a mixture of hotels, flats and tourist attractions, including the Sea Life London Aquarium, the London Dungeon, the London Film Museum and an amusement arcade. Eating and drinking establishments (mainly fast-food, with outdoor seating areas) line the heaving riverside terrace. Further along is the London Eye. Be prepared for long queues at all the attractions.

THE SEA LIFE AQUARIUM AND LONDON EYE

The **Aquarium**, occupying 170,000 square feet, is one of Europe's largest (*open daily 10–7; 10–8 during school holidays; last admission 1hr before closing; tickets may be purchased online, visitsealife.com*). A cascade of waters reveals the huge crescent-shaped twin tanks devoted to the Atlantic and Pacific Oceans, supported by 40 additional exhibits on different regions of the world and different habitats—30,000 specimens in all representing over 350 species. Visitors descend a spiralling walkway through three levels to view the fish and marine life. A touch pool and beach pier allow visitors to handle fish and marine species. Experiences include sound effects, ocean-fresh aromas and a humid Rain Forest. The highlight of the visit is a face-to-face encounter with a shark.

The **London Eye** (*ticket office in County Hall; open 10–8.30, later in summer; tickets may be purchased online, londoneye.com*) is a gigantic observation wheel that overhangs the Thames offering 30-min rides. The 443ft-high wheel, designed by architects David Marks and Julia Barfield, opened in 2000 to celebrate the Millennium. The views of London and beyond, from the glass observation capsules, are outstanding, and on a clear day Windsor Castle can be seen (the Tower of London is more difficult

from its post-war doldrums. Bankside is now a cultural 'destination', home of Tate Modern and the reconstructed Shakespeare's Globe Theatre.

HOPTON STREET AND THE MILLENNIUM BRIDGE

East of Blackfriars Bridge, in Hopton Street (*map p. 604, C3*), are the **Hopton Street Almshouses** of 1752, still in use by pensioners and as sheltered housing. There is a 100-year-old cattle trough on the corner. The **Bankside Gallery** is the home of the Royal Watercolour Society and the Royal Society of Painter-Printmakers (*48 Hopton St; banksidegallery.com*). As well as open exhibitions, it hosts selling exhibitions, mostly of contemporary watercolours and prints. On the riverbank behind the gallery, the **Founder's Arms pub** (*52 Hopton St*) is part of a modern office/housing development, built on the site of a bell foundry where the bells of St Paul's were cast. From the terrace, bar and restaurant there are good views of St Paul's and other City landmarks.

The **Millennium Bridge**, by Foster & Partners with Arup & Partners and the sculptor Sir Anthony Caro, provides a pedestrian link between St Paul's Cathedral and Tate Modern. A flattened suspension bridge, it had a tendency to wobble when it opened in 2000 and after just one weekend had to be closed for adjustments. It reopened in 2001. The bridge was the first Thames crossing to be constructed in over a century and is London's first pedestrian-only bridge. It is designed as a thin metal blade, high above the water, to give maximum views and thrills for those using it. It has a span of 320ft: the Thames is wider at this point than the Seine in Paris.

SHAKESPEARE'S GLOBE

In **Cardinal's Wharf** (nos 49–52 Bankside) are terraced houses dating from 1712. No. 49 stands on the site of the Cardinal's Cap Inn, an Elizabethan tavern and brothel; a plaque falsely indicates that from here Wren watched the building of St Paul's.

Close by is the re-created **Shakespeare's Globe Theatre** (*map p. 604, C3*). The original Globe stood in what is now Park Street, 200 yards away on the other side of Southwark Bridge: a small but lofty circular building, it was built by the Burbages and opened in 1599. Shakespeare was a shareholder and acted at the Globe for many years; several of his plays were produced there. In 1613 it burned down, when a spark caused its thatched roof to catch fire. It was immediately rebuilt, this second time with a tiled roof. The Puritans closed the theatre in 1642 and later demolished it. In 1970 the Shakespeare Globe Trust, headed by the American actor and film producer Sam Wanamaker (d. 1993), was set up to raise funds for the new Globe, which was completed in 1995. It is the first thatched building in central London since the Great Fire and traditional materials and building methods were used throughout—though with modern health and safety precautions. The reconstructed oak and plaster, 20-sided polygonal building is modelled closely on the original Globe and holds 1,500: 500 standing and the rest seated on wooden benches. The central part is open to the skies and performances take place through the summer months. The indoor theatre, the beautifully atmospheric, candlelit **Sam Wanamaker Playhouse**, operates year-round. (*21 New Globe Walk. Guided tours approx. every 30mins, no need to book except for large groups; T: 020 7902 1500. Box office, T: 020 7401 9919. shakespearesglobe.com.*)

Bear Gardens (*map p. 606, C4*) is the site of another early theatre, the Hope (1614), where Ben Jonson's *Bartholomew Fair* was first performed. Bear-baiting began here before 1550 and continued in the theatre itself. Pepys was a visitor in 1666: 'After dinner, with my wife and Mercer to the bear-garden where...I saw some good sport of the bull's tossing of the dogs: one into the very boxes. But it is a rude and nasty pleasure.'

A plaque in **Rose Alley**, parallel with Bear Gardens to the east, recalls the Rose Theatre, put up by Philip Henslowe in 1587, the earliest theatre in the area. The plays of Shakespeare, Marlowe and Kyd were performed here, and Edward Alleyn (*see p. 457*) was a leading actor. It closed in 1606. The remains of the theatre were discovered in 1989 during archaeological excavations for a new office block. A performance and exhibition centre, where visitors will be able to view the remains, is planned.

TATE MODERN

Map p. 604, C3. Underground: Southwark or Blackfriars and walk across the Millennium Bridge. For the Tate Boat, see p. 301. Open Sun–Thur 10–6, Fri–Sat 10–10. Free except for special exhibitions. Cafés, restaurant and shop. T: 020 7887 8888, tate.org.uk.

Tate Modern is one of the most popular museums of modern art in the world. It opened in 2000 in the converted hulk of Sir Giles Gilbert Scott's Bankside Power Station, built after the Second World War to provide the City with electricity. An international architectural competition for the conversion of the site was won by the Swiss firm Herzog & de Meuron, who retained the stark industrial character of the building. Externally it has been little altered. A powerful horizontal mass of red brick, alleviated by immense vertical windows, is bisected by a tall central chimney. A two-storey light box has been added to the roofline, a gleaming white beam at night, housing a restaurant with spectacular views over the river to the City and St Paul's Cathedral.

The entrance is either from the riverfront or through the great west entrance, down a vast concrete ramp straight into the Turbine Hall. Five hundred feet long and 150ft high, this is the heart of the building, the mighty nave of an industrial cathedral. Stripped of its turbine engines, the cavernous space is now a dramatic arena for the display of sculpture and installations of enormous scale, and pieces have been commissioned especially for it.

THE COLLECTION

Tate Modern is devoted to the Tate's collection of post-1900 international art (*for the history of Tate as an institution, see p. 301*). There are many major works, spanning painting, drawing, sculpture, installation and conceptual art, photography, film and video. The collection of Surrealist works is particularly strong, as is the modern and contemporary collection of British art—Henry Moore, Francis Bacon, David Hockney—which Tate represents comprehensively and in depth (although Tate Britain is officially the home of British art, 20th-century British works are shown at

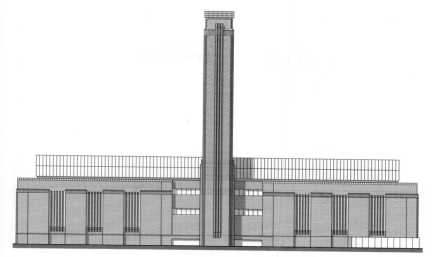

TATE MODERN (BANKSIDE POWER STATION)

both sites). The permanent collection displays are thematic rather than chronological. What follows is a selection of collection highlights.

Early to mid-20th century

All the major -isms are represented, from Impressionism onwards. Monet's *Water-Lilies* (after 1916) and Degas' *Little Dancer Aged Fourteen* (1880–1, cast c. 1922), of bronze, with a muslin skirt and satin hair ribbon, are two of the most famous works in the gallery. Rodin's *The Kiss* (1901–4) shows the lovers Paolo and Francesca from Dante's 'Inferno', naked and locked in their first embrace, their polished bodies contrasting with the hewn rock they sit on.

There are works by the Italian Futurists, examples of Expressionism (Kokoschka), Metaphysical works by De Chirico (*The Uncertainty of the Poet*, 1913; a marble torso in Classical *contrapposto* confronting a sprawling hand of bananas) and Malevich's important *Dynamic Suprematism* (1915/16). Brightly-coloured Fauvist works include paintings by André Derain and Raoul Dufy. Matisse's *The Snail* (1952–3), composed of vividly coloured rectangles of paper arranged roughly in the spiral of a snail, was one of the gallery's major acquisitions. It is one of the artist's cut-outs, produced towards the end of his career, when his hands were no longer steady enough for painting.

The Cubist collection includes works by Braque, Gleizes, Juan Gris, Fernand Léger and Duchamp, as well as a large collection of works by Picasso. *Weeping Woman* (1937), an allegory of republican Spain, is one of several works made following the bombardment of Guernica.

Sculpture includes works by Brancusi, Jean Arp, Lipchitz and Modigliani (his elongated *Head*, c. 1911–12). Marcel Duchamp's celebrated *Fountain*, a urinal, was offered for exhibition in 1917. The most famous of his 'ready-mades', ordinary objects designated works of art by the artist, it is an important precursor to Surrealist works, as well as to conceptual art.

Surrealism and Abstraction

The Surrealist movement was launched in Paris in 1924 by the poet André Breton. Salvador Dalí's dream-like works, windows onto the mind, include his important *Metamorphosis of Narcissus* (1937), while *Lobster Telephone* (1936) confronts the rational with its impossible combination of objects. *Eine Kleine Nachtmusik* (1943) is one of Dorothea Tanning's best known works, showing two girls in a hotel corridor apparently dismembering a giant sunflower. Other artists represented include Miró, Magritte, Picabia and Max Ernst. The sculptor Alberto Giacometti, best known for his skeletal figures, was a former Surrealist, and Tate has a number of his works.

Works by one of the pioneers of abstraction, Kandinsky, include the highly geometric *Swinging* (1925). Other important abstract pieces include works by the De Stijl artist Piet Mondrian. Tate has an important collection of works by the Russian constructivist Naum Gabo, a pioneer of abstract sculpture. Later abstract works include Josef Albers' series of studies for *Homage to the Square*, painted in the 1960s.

American Abstract Expressionist pieces include De Kooning's *The Visit* (1966–7), works by Robert Motherwell and Barnett Newman, and several by Jackson Pollock. His major early drip painting is *Summertime: Number 9A* (1948), the paint splashed in a rhythmic pattern. Vast-scale colour-field pieces include Mark Rothko's famous 'Seagram Murals', commissioned in 1958 for the Four Seasons restaurant in Mies van der Rohe's Seagram building on Park Avenue, New York. The artist is said to have told a friend that he wanted to create 'something that will ruin the appetite of every son-of-a-bitch who ever eats in that room.' When Rothko sampled the restaurant for himself, he changed his mind about the murals' destination. Some of them came to the Tate instead; others are in Washington, still others in Japan. The large, magnificent, luminous works, combinations of maroon and black, are among the gallery's major holdings. In 2012 Vladimir Umanets defaced one of the murals, citing Duchamp's *Fountain* as his inspiration for an act which he claimed was not vandalism, but rather taking a work that someone else had made and 'putting a message on it'. The courts did not take the same view and Mr Umanets was sentenced to two years in prison.

Later 20th century

American Pop Art, inspired by consumerism, Hollywood, advertising and commercial mass production, includes Roy Lichtenstein's well-known *Whaam!* (1963) and Andy Warhol's *Marilyn Diptych* (1962). The Continental European equivalent to Pop was Nouveau Réalisme. Tate has works by, among others, Tinguely, Yves Klein and Arman, one of its leading exponents. British Pop Art includes Richard Hamilton's *$he* (1958).

The large collection of conceptual art includes works by the hugely influential pioneer of performance art, Joseph Beuys, whose installations use organic materials such as fat, wax and rock. Arte Povera, which emerged in Italy in the late '60s and deliberately uses materials of little value, is represented by two of its greatest exponents,

Jannnis Kounellis and Mario Merz. Works incorporating real objects as the stuff of art include Rebecca Horn's *Concert for Anarchy* (1990), a grand piano suspended upside down with its keys spilling out. American minimalist pieces include Carl Andre's infamous 'Bricks' (*Equivalent VIII*; 1966), plain bricks arranged in a neat rectangle, which caused a storm of indignation and hilarity when acquired in 1972, and have ever since been used as evidence by those who wish to argue that modern art is humbug. Other works include Robert Morris's *Untitled* (1965/71), four large reflective cubes of mirror-plate glass on board. The 2009 revival of his *Bodyspacemotionthings*, which invited the active involvement of exhibition visitors, caused controversy following injuries to members of the public as well as to the exhibit itself.

SOUTHWARK & BERMONDSEY

Map pp. 604–5. Underground: Southwark, London Bridge, Borough.

Southwark, on the south side of London Bridge, anciently in the county of Surrey, has as long a history as the City of London itself. The Roman London Bridge, built c. AD 43, connected what was then a series of marshy islands with Londinium (the City). Archaeological excavations have revealed that Southwark was a large Roman settlement, probably an extension of Londinium itself, where abattoirs, cemeteries and taverns were situated. Its name probably derives from 'Sudwerca', meaning a southern defensive fort in Old English. Southwark was the main entry point from the south and coaching inns and hostelries flourished in Borough, its commercial centre. Wharves and warehouses were built along the Thames and in the 18th and 19th centuries Southwark was an industrial centre with breweries and food factories. After serious damage in World War Two and with the decline in trade on the river, Southwark became very run-down until recent regeneration of the area.

SOUTHWARK BRIDGE, CLINK STREET AND ST MARY OVERIE DOCK

Southwark Bridge (*map pp. 604, C3 and 607, D4*) was completed in (1921; Sir Ernest George and Basil Mott), replacing a graceful cast-iron bridge by John Rennie. East of it, in Park Street, a plaque marks the approximate **site of the original Globe Theatre** (*see above*). At 34 Park St, overlooking the river, is the **Anchor Inn**, of 15th-century origin (the present building dates to the 18th century). Park Street was once the location for a number of breweries. Today, under the arches of the Cannon Street railway bridge, is **Vinopolis**, a visitor attraction and venue, spanning 2.5 acres, where you can learn all about wine via wine tasting tours and master classes; or you can simply sample wine in its numerous bars and restaurants.

On the other side of the railway is Clink Street. Today it is a street of 19th-century former warehouses but once it was home to Winchester Palace, the town residence of the Bishops of Winchester from the 12th–17th centuries; it was probably as grand as Lambeth Palace. It was first built in 1144 by Bishop Henry de Blois, brother of King

Stephen. In 1424 James I of Scotland and Joan Beaufort celebrated their wedding feast at the palace; Henry VIII is said to have met his fifth wife, Catherine Howard there. During the Civil War it was used as a Royalist gaol. The building burned down in 1814 but the **remains of the palace's great hall**, including a beautiful 14th-century rose window (restored), survive near the Clink Prison Museum. The surrounding manor of 70 acres, attached to Winchester Palace, was known as the 'Liberty of the Clink' and a pleasure quarter sprang up outside the jurisdiction of the City. Here were the 'stews', largely inhabited by Dutch or Flemish prostitutes, and numerous bear gardens, used also for prize-fights, from which the Bishops of Winchester, as landlords, claimed rents (the prostitutes were known as 'Winchester Geese'). Here too was the **Clink Prison**, partly located below the palace. It was used by the bishops as a place of detention for heretics from the 16th century, and later for thieves and ruffians. The name Clink may have come from 'clinch' or 'clench', rivets hammered in a clinching iron, which held prisoners to the wall or floor. It has since become a term for prisons in general, hence the expression 'in the clink'. The prison was destroyed the Gordon Riots of 1780 and never rebuilt. The **Clink Prison Museum**, in a former warehouse, tells the story of the old prison and the surrounding area (*open July–Sept 10–9; Oct–June 10–6, until 7.30 at weekends; admission charge; T: 020 7403 0900, clink.org.uk*).

In **St Mary Overie Dock**, said to date from the time of Winchester Palace, is a full-scale reconstruction of Sir Francis Drake's ship, the *Golden Hinde*, in which he circumnavigated the globe in 1577–80. Actors in Tudor costume give guided tours around the replica galleon, known as *Golden Hinde II*.

SOUTHWARK CATHEDRAL

Map p. 607, D4. Open daily 8 or 8.30–6. T: 020 7367 6734, cathedral.southwark.anglican.org.

Southwark Cathedral is officially the Cathedral and Collegiate Church of St Saviour and St Mary Overie, Southwark. It has been the seat of a bishop since 1905, when the Diocese of Southwark was established, covering South London and East Surrey. The churchyard is usually full of people sitting and eating delicious snacks purchased at Borough Market next door. Although much rebuilt and repaired, it is the oldest Gothic church in London: an excavated area behind the Harvard Chapel displays remains of a Roman road and parts of the Norman and medieval building fabric. The first foundation here was a 7th-century nunnery, established, according to legend, by a ferryman's daughter; this is where the former name, St Mary Overy, comes from, explained as 'St Mary of the Ferry' or possibly 'St Mary across the Marsh'. In 852–62 St Swithin, Bishop of Winchester, turned the convent into a house for Augustinian canons. In 1106 a priory was built, of which few traces survive. The present choir and retro-choir were built by Peter des Roches, Bishop of Winchester, in 1207; the transepts were remodelled in the 15th century and over the crossing rises a tall 15th-century tower. The nave was entirely rebuilt by Sir Arthur Blomfield in 1890–6. The stained glass is mostly modern, replacing windows destroyed in 1941.

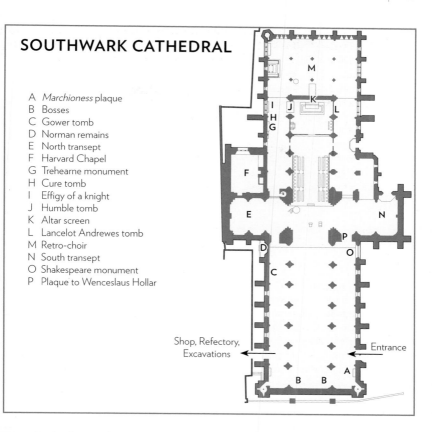

SOUTHWARK CATHEDRAL

A *Marchioness* plaque
B Bosses
C Gower tomb
D Norman remains
E North transept
F Harvard Chapel
G Trehearne monument
H Cure tomb
I Effigy of a knight
J Humble tomb
K Altar screen
L Lancelot Andrewes tomb
M Retro-choir
N South transept
O Shakespeare monument
P Plaque to Wenceslaus Hollar

Shop, Refectory,
Excavations ←

Entrance ←

Nave: In the floor to the left of the entrance is large octagonal **plaque (A)** commemorating those who drowned in the *Marchioness* pleasure-boat disaster of 1989. To the left of it, beside the door to the tower, is a portion of 13th-century arcading. Ranged along the west wall are splendid carved wooden **bosses (B)** from the 15th-century roof.

North side: In the north aisle is the much-restored tomb of the poet **John Gower** (1330–1408) **(C)**, a friend of Chaucer, with a recumbent effigy. Behind the door into the vestry may be

seen the jambs of a Norman door and an ancient holy-water stoup **(D)**.

In the **north transept (E)** stands an oak dresser given to the church in 1588. The monuments here include one to John Lockyer (d. 1672), pill-maker, reclining wearily, with an amusing hyperbolical epitaph.

The **Harvard Chapel (F)** was restored and decorated in 1907 in memory of John Harvard, founder of Harvard University, Massachusetts, who was born in the parish and baptised in this church (1607). During the restoration a Norman column shaft (left of the altar)

SOUTHWARK CATHEDRAL
Face of the devil gobbling Judas Iscariot. 15th-century ceiling boss.

was discovered. The commemorative stained-glass window was presented in 1905. On the right, beside the entrance, a tablet commemorates the playwright and lyricist Oscar Hammerstein.

Choir and retro-choir: The fine **tombs** in the north choir are of John Trehearne (d. 1618) **(G)**, gentleman-porter to James I; Thomas Cure (d. 1588), his emaciated effigy a reminder that death must come to all **(H)**; the wooden effigy of a knight in chainmail (1280, restored) **(I)** and Richard Humble (d. 1616), alderman **(J)**.

The **altar-screen (K)**, erected by Bishop Fox in 1520, is a magnificent piece of work, though much damaged and restored. The statues in the niches date from 1905.

In the south choir aisle is the fine **tomb of Lancelot Andrewes (L)**, Bishop of Winchester (1555–1626), who oversaw part of the translation of the King James Bible, published in 1611.

The beautiful vaulted **retro-choir (M)** has four chapels, dedicated to St Andrew, St Christopher, the Blessed Virgin, and SS Elizabeth of Hungary and Francis of Assisi.

South transept and aisle: The south transept **(N)** was rebuilt in the 15th century by Cardinal Beaufort, whose niece, Joan Beaufort, was married to James I of Scotland in this church in 1424. In the south aisle of the nave, beneath a memorial window to **William Shakespeare** (C. Webb, 1954), is a recumbent alabaster figure of the playwright (Henry McCarthy, 1911) **(O)**, usually holding a fresh rosemary 'quill'; Shakespeare's brother Edmond, a 'player', was buried in the church in 1607. On the pier diagonally opposite is a modern tribute to Wenceslaus Hollar **(P)**, the 17th-century engraver, one of whose famous views of London was taken from the top of Southwark Cathedral tower.

BOROUGH

Many breweries were based in Southwark from the 17th century. In Southwark Street (*map pp. 606, C4–607, D4*), developed by Bazalgette as a modern boulevard in the 1860s, part of the original **Hop Exchange** (R.H. Moore, 1866) survives; behind the impressive iron and stucco exterior, with sculpture of hop-picking in the tympanum, is the large, naturally lit, exchange hall. The building is now used as offices.

Borough Market (*map p. 607, D4*) is probably London's oldest market. A street market selling fruit and vegetables has existed in this part of London since the 13th century. The network of buildings mostly dates from the 19th century. At weekends, the specialist food stalls, cafés, restaurants and bars are thronged with tourists and foodies; delicious cooking smells permeate the whole area and the market is easily found by following your nose (*boroughmarket.co.uk; best days Wed–Sat; closed Sun*).

To the south is Borough High Street, which from Roman times was the great highway to the southeast of England and the Continent. It was the scene of countless processions and pageants in the Middle Ages and was trodden by the feet of many pilgrims on their way to the shrine of St Thomas à Becket in Canterbury. The street once abounded in hostelries and coaching inns, although few remain; many were destroyed in the 'Little Fire of London' that laid waste the area in 1676, the rest were made redundant after the coming of the railway in the 19th century. In a courtyard is the **George Inn** (1676), the last galleried coaching inn left; still a pub but now owned by the National Trust. On the site of Talbot Yard stood the most celebrated hostelry of all, the Tabard Inn, the 'Gentil hostelrye that highte the Tabard, faste by the Belle', the starting-point of Chaucer's Canterbury pilgrims. It survived (as the Talbot Inn) until 1876.

At **103 Borough High St** was the Queen's Head Tavern, owned by the family of John Harvard (1607–38), who was born here. The sale of this property before his emigration to America in 1637 augmented his fortune; at his death, he left money and books to a small Massachusetts college that would become Harvard University.

THE MARHSALSEA AREA

The area around Newcomen Street and Mermaid Court (*map p. 605, D3*) was the site of several notorious debtors' prisons in the 18th and 19th centuries. Here was the Old Marshalsea prison, first mentioned in the 14th century, where Ben Jonson was imprisoned for sedition in 1597. Adjoining it to the south stood the Old King's Bench, the prison to which Judge Gascoigne is said to have committed Prince Henry (afterwards Henry V). Tobias Smollett was imprisoned here in 1739 for libel. In 1758 it was superseded by the New King's Bench, at the corner of Newington Causeway, where John Wilkes was held for libel in 1768–70. The prison was partially burned in the Gordon Riots (1780), fell into disuse in 1860, when imprisonment for debt was abolished, and was finally pulled down. In Union Street to the west stood Horsemonger Lane Gaol, in which Leigh Hunt was confined for two years in 1813 for libelling the Prince Regent as a 'corpulent man of 50, a violator of his word, a libertine over head and ears in debt, a despiser of domestic ties, the companion of gamblers and demireps, a man who has just closed half a century without one single claim on the gratitude of his country' and where in 1849 Dickens witnessed the double hanging of a husband and wife, both convicted of murder. The jeers and hilarity of the crowd shocked him deeply.

In a public garden, before the church of **St George the Martyr** (*map p. 604, C3*), a small part of the walls survive of the White Lion or Borough Gaol, a 16th-century prison to which the New Marshalsea prison was transferred. Dickens's father was confined here in 1824 and it served as the inspiration for the prison scenes in many of the author's novels. While his father was incarcerated, the young Dickens lived in **Lant Street**. He later chose St George the Martyr Church (first mentioned in 1122, rebuilt in 1734–6 by John Price, and since restored) as the scene of the christening and marriage of Little Dorrit. The church is based upon Wren's design for St James's Piccadilly.

Not far from here is the **London Fire Brigade Museum** (*94A Southwark Bridge Rd; pre-booked guided tour only; london-fire.gov.uk*), a comprehensive collection of fire-fighting equipment and memorabilia. Another unusual museum just around the corner is the **Kirkaldy Testing Museum** (*99 Southwark St, entrance on Prices St; supervised visits only; at the time of writing the museum was threatened with closure; see testingmuseum.org.uk for updates*), which houses David Kirkaldy's 350-ton materials testing machine, patented in 1863. The machine tests materials to determine their strength. Parts of bridges, aeroplanes and other civil engineering projects have been tested here.

LONDON BRIDGE QUARTER TO SHAD THAMES

London Bridge Station (*map p. 605, D3*) is the terminus of one of the oldest railways in the world, opened in 1836 between Bermondsey (London Bridge) and Deptford. The station was completely rebuilt after extensive Second World War damage and at the time of writing the sprawling, confusing warren of draughty platforms, which serves 55 million passengers, was being completely overhauled.

St Thomas Street skirts the station to the south. In the roof space of the church of St Thomas (1702–03), up narrow, steep stairs, is the extraordinary **Old Operating Theatre Museum and Herb Garret** (*map p. 607, D4; open daily 10.30–5 except for 3 weeks around Christmas; admission charge; shop; T: 020 7188 2679, thegarret.org. uk*). Before St Thomas's Hospital relocated from Southwark, its buildings and wards directly bordered the church tower, and an operating theatre and herbal pharmacy were created in the church's attic in 1821; female patients were operated upon here, without anaesthetic, in front of medical students. What is remarkable is that this space was forgotten about until 1956, when it was rediscovered and restored. It is the only known example of a Victorian operating theatre in existence; the operating table and spectators' benches are still *in situ*.

A little further on in St Thomas Street stands **Guy's Hospital** (huge modern tower; *map p. 605, D3*), founded in 1726 by Thomas Guy (a City bookseller who made a fortune by his speculations in South Sea stock) to treat 'incurables' from nearby St Thomas's Hospital. John Keats studied here in 1815–16. In the courtyard, surrounded by original 18th-century buildings, is a brass statue of Thomas Guy, by Scheemakers (1733). The Guy's Chapel, also 18th-century, has a marble monument to Guy by John Bacon (1779);

THE SHARD
Teams of abseilers frequently clean its glassy surface.

the chapel was described by Pevsner as 'one of the noblest and most sensitive of its date in England.'

THE SHARD AND HAYS GALLERIA

The area between London Bridge and Tower Bridge is known as the London Bridge Quarter. It incorporates the riverside walk, refurbished warehouses and modern commercial developments. At its centre, towering over London, is Europe's tallest skyscraper, Renzo Piano's **The Shard** (2013; *map p. 605, D3*). This immense glass icicle, which often has its windows cleaned by teams of abseilers, is conceived as a 'vertical city' housing restaurants, bars, offices, a hotel, apartments and shops. A viewing gallery ranges over floors 68–72. Funded by Qatari money, it cost £1.2 billion to build and. At the time of writing, much of it was standing empty.

In Tooley Street, opposite London Bridge Station, is the entrance to **Hays Galleria**, a conversion of shops, offices and restaurants, spanned by an iron and glass arched roof, leading out onto the riverside walk. These buildings were formally warehouses serving Hay's Wharf, built by William Cubitt in the 1850s. Tea clippers from India and China would enter an enclosed dock here to unload their cargoes. Inside, a kinetic bronze ship sculpture (1987) stands on the in-filled former dock, a reference to Hays Galleria's shipping past. The **Horniman at Hays pub** stands on the site of the tea warehouse of Frederick John Horniman (*see p. 459*). It contains friezes commemorating the life and travels of the great merchant and collector.

HMS *BELFAST*

East along the River Walk is the entrance to HMS *Belfast,* part of the Imperial War Museum (*map p. 605, D3; open March–Oct daily 10–6, Nov–Feb daily 10–5, last admis-*

sion 1hr before closing; admission charge; café and shop; T: 020 7940 6300, iwm.org.uk).
The last surviving big gun World War Two armoured warship in Europe, HMS *Belfast*
provides a compelling insight into the nature of war at sea. An 'Edinburgh' class large
light cruiser, she was designed during the mid-1930s in response to the threat posed by
Japanese 'Mogami' class cruisers. Built by Harland and Wolff of Belfast, the vessel was
launched on St Patrick's Day, 17th March, 1938.

On the outbreak of war in September of the following year, HMS *Belfast* formed
part of the maritime blockade of Germany, operating out of the Home Fleet's main
base at Scapa Flow in the Orkney Islands. Badly damaged by a magnetic mine, she was
completely refitted, eventually rejoining active service in 1943 on Arctic convoy duty.
As the flagship of the Tenth Cruiser Squadron, she successfully provided close-range
heavy cover for several convoys of the kind that supplied the Soviet Union with some
four million tons of supplies during the course of the war, including 5,000 tanks and
7,000 aircraft. In the Battle of North Cape in December 1943, she engaged and contributed to the sinking of the German battle cruiser *Scharnhorst*. Only 36 men survived from that ship's complement of almost 2,000. On 6th June 1944, HMS *Belfast*
was one of the first ships to open fire on German positions in Normandy in support of
the D-Day landings. After 1945, she was occupied in peace-keeping duties in the Far
East, helping to evacuate survivors of Japanese prisoner-of-war camps and Chinese
civilian internment centres. A visit gives a vivid impression of life above and below
deck in both war and peace.

MORE LONDON

Continuing east towards Tower Bridge, the thriving area with modern glass offices,
The Scoop amphitheatre and a landscaped park, is known as More London, a 13-acre
development conceived by Norman Foster in the late 1990s. The Kuwaiti property firm
who originally developed the area bought the site back in 2013 for an undisclosed sum
(believed to be in the region of £1.6 billion). The armadillo-shaped structure irrever-
ently dubbed 'the glass gonad' is **City Hall** (*map p. 605, E3*), the headquarters of the
Mayor of London and the administrative body the GLA or Greater London Assembly.
The Mayor of London should not be confused with the Lord Mayor of London, who
is the head of the City of London Corporation (*see p. 20*). The Mayor of London holds
responsibility for a much wider area, though within the City itself, the Lord Mayor
takes precedence. Designed by Foster + Partners, City Hall opened in 2002; its unusual shape minimises the surface area exposed to sunlight and therefore the amount
of energy it consumes.

Further along the waterfront, a new development of luxury apartments and penthouses will rejoice in the prestigious address 'One Tower Bridge'.

BUTLER'S WHARF AND SHAD THAMES

On the east side of Tower Bridge is **Butler's Wharf** (*map p. 605, E3*), a site of 1870s'
warehouses and wharves which has been redeveloped into offices, restaurants, bars
and designer loft-style apartments. The restaurants lining the river have outdoor terraces and good views of Tower Bridge, the City and Canary Wharf. Behind Butler's

Wharf is **Shad Thames**, an atmospheric street lined with old warehouses connected by original iron gantries and overhead bridges, which lends its name to the network of converted warehouses and docks in the vicinity. During the heyday of London's docks, the produce stored and traded here—tea, spices, coffee, dried fruits, etc.—was so plentiful and wide-ranging that the entire area was known as 'the larder of London'. The narrow canyon-like streets and inlets are interesting to explore, especially around St Saviour's Dock. At the time of writing the **Design Museum** was scheduled to move to Kensington High Street.

BERMONDSEY

Bermondsey (*map p. 605; Underground: Bermondsey*) was once the site of a great Benedictine Abbey, dedicated to the Holy Saviour. Elizabeth, widow of Edward IV and the last Plantagenet queen, lived out her last days there. Today, east of St Saviour's Dock, on Bermondsey Wall East, is **The Angel**, an inn first built by the monks. Samuel Pepys was wont to pause here, on his journeys to and from Deptford to visit his friend John Evelyn (*see p. 438*). Here also are scant remains of a **manor house of Edward III** (*map pp. 605, F3*). The site of Bermondsey Abbey today is the scene of the **Bermondsey Square Antiques Market** (*Fridays from 6am; corner of Long Lane*). Until the laws of *marché ouvert* (which gave good title to purchasers of stolen goods) were abolished in the 1990s, Bermondsey Market had a reputation for skulduggery.

Bermondsey was once a centre of the leather industry and many streets bear witness to this: Tanner Street, Morocco Street, and Leathermarket Street (where the old **Leather Hide and Wool Exchange building** still stands; *map p. 605, D3–D4*). The old Leather Market is on Weston Street and there is an old tannery on Long Lane. It was at Bermondsey too that the engineer Bryan Donkin set up his canning factory on Southwark Park Road (*map p. 605, F4*) in 1813, the first ever meat cannery. The British Admiralty placed a large order.

On Thurland Road is **St James's church** (James Savage, 1829; *map p. 605, F4*), with a fine bell-tower and tall Ionic porch, built following the petitions of a committee composed of a wool-stapler, two tanners and sundry others, which formed with the aim of securing a new church for the district. This was one of seven 'Waterloo' churches in south London—and indeed its ten bells are cast from cannon abandoned by the defeated French on the very battlefield. The interior is serene and beautiful with fine pews (*godlovesbermondsey.co.uk*).

Heading north along Bermondsey Street towards London Bridge Station, you come to the Bermondsey branch of the **White Cube** (1970s and Casper Mueller Kneer, 2011; *144–152 Bermondsey St; map p. 605, D4; open Tues–Sun; for more on the White Cube, see p. 219*). Further up still is the Fashion and Textile Museum.

FASHION AND TEXTILE MUSEUM

83 Bermondsey St. Map p. 605, D3. Underground: London Bridge and 15mins' walk. Open Tues–Sat 11–6 (last admission 5.15). Café and shop. T: 020 7403 0222, ftmlondon.org.
The British designer Zandra Rhodes (b. 1940), who put the 'glamour into punk' in the

1970s with her jewelled safety pins and the artful rips in her jeans, established the museum in 2003 to showcase contemporary fashion, textiles and jewellery and to celebrate the work of textile designers, whom she regards as the 'Cinderellas of the business'. The museum holds two permanent collections, the Fashion and Textile Museum Collection and the Zandra Rhodes Collection (*both may be viewed by appointment*). Otherwise, there is a continual run of temporary shows. Exploding out against the tired greys of the surrounding building, this vividly-coloured museum was converted from a 1950s' warehouse by the Mexican architect Ricardo Legorreta, his only commission in Europe. Rhodes still works from a studio above the museum.

EATING AND DRINKING ON THE SOUTH BANK

BANKSIDE

£ **Founders Arms**. Modern pub on the site of the old bell foundry which cast the bells of St Paul's. Wide windows on the water offer good Thames views. Heated outdoor terrace. Pub food: useful for dinner before a play at The Globe. Open daily. *52 Hopton St. T: 020 7928 1899, foundersarms.co.uk. Map p. 604, C3.*

££ **Swan**. Restaurant and bar attached to the Globe Theatre. Modern British cooking using ingredients from local producers and markets: ham hock, cottage pie and English cheeses. No dinner Sun. *12 New Globe Walk. T: 020 7928 9444, loveswan.co.uk. Map p. 604, C3.*

££ **Tate Modern**. Seasonal dishes, plenty of fish and vegetables, in the 6th-floor restaurant with river views. Lunch served daily, afternoon tea and dinner Fri–Sun. Bar open all day for drinks and cocktails. *Bankside. T: 020 7887 8888, tate.org.uk. Map p. 604, C3.*

LAMBETH, SOUTH BANK

£–£££ **Anchor and Hope**. No fuss, no frills, no reservations. Just turn up to enjoy good food in one of London's gastro pubs. Closed Sun. *36 The Cut (Waterloo). www.anchorandhopepub. co.uk. Map p. 604, B3.*

£ **Archduke**. This was the first wine bar in the area when it opened here in 1979 and an architectural pioneer. It now incorporates a restaurant in its brick interior, serving steaks, burgers, chargrills and salads. Open daily. *Concert Hall Approach (corner of Belvedere Rd). T: 020 7928 9370, blackandbluerestaurants.com. Map p. 604, A3.*

££ **Oxo Tower**. Operated by Harvey Nichols, on the 8th floor of an iconic old building (*see p. 420*), the Oxo Tower offers the choice of a restaurant or more informal brasserie, with live jazz in the evenings. Both serve modern British food. Open daily. *Oxo Tower Wharf. T: 020 7803 3888, oxotower.co.uk. Map p. 604, B3.*

££–£££ **Royal Festival Hall**. Skylon restaurant (formal) and grill (relaxed) both offering lunch and dinner, either pre- or post-theatre. *T: 020 7654 7800, skylon-restaurant.co.uk. Map p. 604, A3.*

££ RSJ. Fusion cuisine (okra provençale) and a Loire wine list in an old stable building near Waterloo. Has a loyal following. Closed Sat lunch and all day Sun. *33 Coin St. T: 020 7928 4554, rsj.uk.com. Map p. 604, B3.*

SOUTHWARK, BERMONDSEY

£ The Anchor. Old 18th-century pub building on the site of an even older tavern, proud to record Pepys, Dr Johnson and Sir Joshua Reynolds among its past clientèle. Pub food served daily. *34 Park St. T: 020 7407 1577. Map p. 604, C3.*

£ The Angel. Another pub where Pepys once drank, built originally to slake the thirst of monks from Bermondsey Priory. No food Sun eve. *101 Bermondsey Wall East. T: 020 7394 3214. Map p. 605, F3.*

Borough Market. Oysters, roast meats, tapas, coffee, cakes and more: it is not possible to single out a particular trader or establishment here. There is something for everyone, every day (though individual places have different opening hours). For details, there is an excellent website: *boroughmarket.org.uk. Map p. 605, D3.*

£ George Inn. Historic building: London's only surviving galleried coaching inn, dating from the late 17th century. Open daily. Drink your pint in the shadow of the Shard. *75–77 Borough High St. T: 020 7407 2056. Map p. 605, D3.*

Shad Thames. There are many good places to eat here (*map p. 605, E3*), many of them belonging to a single family of restaurants. Choices include the **££ Butler's Wharf Chop House** (*36E Shad Thames, T: 020 7403 3404, chophouse-restaurant.co.uk*), **£££ Le Pont de la Tour** (French cuisine; *36D Shad Thames, T: 020 7403 8403, lepontdelatour.co.uk*) and **££ Cantina del Ponte** (Italian cooking; *36 Shad Thames, T: 020 7403 5403, cantinadelponte.co.uk*). Here too is the **££ Blueprint Café**. ■ On the first floor of an old banana warehouse, with huge windows giving onto river views (and binoculars to view them through). Modern European cooking expertly executed. Lively and popular. No dinner Sun. *T: 020 7378 7031, blueprintcafe.co.uk.*

£ Shortwave. Café-bar in a popular cinema, good for drinks and snacks. Lunches served Mon–Fri. *10 Bermondsey Square. shortwavecafe.com. Map p. 605, D4.*

£ Southwark Cathedral Refectory. A tranquil place for a simple lunch (soup, salad) or tea and cake. Open daily until 6pm. *Map p. 605, D3.*

£ The Woolpack. Independent pub, not part of a chain, close to the former Leather and Wool Exchange. Mackerel pâté, pies and mushy peas. Open daily. *98 Bermondsey St. T: 020 7537 9269, woolpackbar.com. Map p. 605, D3.*

GREENWICH
The Queen's House and Old Royal Naval College, with Canary Wharf on the further bank.

The Southeast & South

*Covered in this chapter are the historic districts of Deptford and Woolwich;
Greenwich with its naval and royal associations; and Dulwich with its famous
art gallery. Also south of the river are many mainly residential
districts, including Brixton, Clapham and Battersea.*

The most historic part of this large and amorphous district of London is the area immediately along the river, where former naval dockyards and royal palaces illustrate its ancient commercial and administrative importance. Greenwich fully merits a day trip and is rewarding at all seasons. Leafy, genteel Dulwich is home to the oldest public art gallery in London. There are good places to eat in nearby Crystal Palace.

DEPTFORD & ROTHERHITHE

Deptford (*map p. 593, A4–A3; trains from London Bridge in 6mins*) takes its name from the 'deep ford', a crossing place over the Ravensbourne, a tributary of the Thames. Its maritime past is commemorated by a large anchor planted in its High Street: Deptford's Royal Naval Docks were established by Henry VIII in 1513 and they have witnessed at least two scenes now immortalised by historians: the knighting of Sir Francis Drake by Queen Elizabeth I, and Sir Walter Raleigh's flinging his cloak across a puddle to prevent the muddying of the royal feet (though the latter stunt is also claimed by Greenwich). Deptford was the birthplace of the great shipwright Phineas Pett and his son Peter (*see Woolwich, p. 440*). Deptford today has a reputation as a rough area (a reputation sanctified by history: the playwright Christopher Marlowe was fatally stabbed here in 1593, possibly in a tavern brawl), but it is a lively district, proud of its High Street Market (produce, clothing, bric à brac and general stalls; *Wed, Fri, Sat from 7am*). The High Street itself is a wonderful, ramshackle slice of old London: not a chain store in sight, and with an enticing scattering of Afro-Caribbean grocers and Thai restaurants.

Deptford docks were at the height of their prosperity in the 18th century, when they were used for fitting out and provisioning battleships during the Napoleonic Wars (the

Victualling Yard had been set up in the 1740s). In the 19th century the area fell into decline, as newer and larger ships needed docks of greater draught. The docks closed in 1869. The Victualling Yard closed in 1961.

WHAT TO SEE IN DEPTFORD

The Anglo-Catholic **St Paul's Church**, just east of Deptford High Street (*map p. 593, A4*), is a striking building by Thomas Archer (1730), with a tall spire and a semicircular porch of tall Tuscan columns. The interior is very fine. In the churchyard is a plaque commemorating Mydiddee, a native of Tahiti who died in Deptford in 1793, having arrived here with Captain Bligh (of *Bounty* fame; *see p. 414*) aboard the *Providence*. There are also some characteristic tombs in the shape of sarcophagi with headstone and footstone. In Albury Street, also east off the High Street, is a row of 18th-century sea-captains' houses.

St Nicholas's Church on Deptford Green (*map p. 593, B3*) is the old parish church, dating from the late 17th century, with an earlier tower. Christopher Marlowe was buried here in an unmarked grave. The churchyard has more sarcophagus tombs.

From the top of Deptford Green, the Thames path leads off in two directions. To the right it passes the AHOY Centre on Borthwick Street, a charity that offers shipbuilding apprenticeships and sailing and rowing courses for disadvantaged children. Beyond this is a wide foreshore of new housing development, known in estate-agent speak as 'West Greenwich' (the domes of Greenwich and the masts of the *Cutty Sark* are well seen from here). The promenade leads to a curious sculpture group of Peter the Great (Mikhail Shemyakin, 2001) at the corner where **Deptford Creek** enters the Thames. The first London railway was built between Deptford and Bermondsey in 1836. The extension to Greenwich, added in 1838, ran over a bridge across Deptford Creek, with a drawbridge which took several men to operate.

If you follow the Thames Path in the other direction, you cannot walk by the water, but instead pass the site of the old docks (at the time of writing a wasteland known as Convoys Wharf, with plans for re-development) and come to **Sayes Court Park** (just off Evelyn Street; *map p. 593, A3*). It occupies the site of a house once owned by John Evelyn, where Pepys was entertained to dinner. Evelyn's daughter Elizabeth eloped with a young man from the dockyard, much to her father's chagrin. Grinling Gibbons also lived at Deptford, in a house rented from Evelyn. Marvelling at the wood carver's talent, Evelyn presented him to Sir Christopher Wren. Peter the Great stayed at Sayes Court in 1698 when he came to the Royal Dock incognito, to study the craft of shipbuilding. When he and his royal entourage left, it is reported that there was scarcely a window pane left intact, not a chair unsplintered nor a curtain unrent. The Thames Path leads towards Deptford Strand through the Pepys Estate, on the site of the old Victualling Yard, a housing development where the streets and tower blocks have been given nautical names such as 'Windlass Place' and 'Lanyard House'. It was acclaimed as 'an impeccable scheme' in 1967. Today it is plastered with official signs warning of anti-vandal paint. A survival from more prosperous times is **The Colonnade**, leading off Grove Street (opposite Windlass Place; *map p. 593, A3*), a terrace of 18th-century houses for officers of the Victualling Yard.

SURREY QUAYS AND ROTHERHITHE STREET

Map p. 597, E3. Overground to Surrey Quays. Underground: Canada Water.

Between Deptford and Rotherhithe are the sprawling **Surrey Quays**, a residential development and 'leisure park' on the site of once bustling docks: many are now filled in, though Canada Water, South Dock and Greenland Dock survive, with a marina and water sports centre. The first dock on the site was the Great Howland Dock, built in 1696. It was the largest commercial dock in the world when it was built, with berths for 120 ships. It became Greenland Dock in 1725, when the South Sea Company leased it for their whalers: the stench from the vats of boiling blubber being rendered down for soap, drifted for miles. Today nothing more noxious wafts across the water than the smell of cooking oil from the Moby Dick tavern. Later the docks complex was enlarged to receive timber from Canada, the Baltic and Scandinavia: Quebec Pond, Russia Dock and Norway Dock were added. The dockyard finally closed in 1970.

The Rotherhithe Peninsula juts into the Thames opposite Wapping, to which it is connected by tunnel (*see below*). Rotherhithe Street leads north across it (*its route can be followed on Bus C10 from Canada Water, which stops at the places described below*). **Surrey Docks Farm** is a working animal farm in the heart of London (*open daily 10–5 in summer, 10–4 in winter; free but donation requested; café; T: 020 7231 1010, surrey-docksfarm.co.uk*). Further on at Cuckold's Point (so named because King John is said to have donated the land to a local miller to compensate him for the seduction of his wife) is the Hilton Docklands Hotel, occupying the old **Nelson Dock** (*map p. 593, A2*), once a shipyard (it retains its dry dock and narrow draw dock). The Georgian Nelson House (1740s) in the hotel forecourt was probably once the home of a wealthy shipwright. On the peninsula tip are many restored riverside houses. **Lavender Pond Nature Park**, just inland from the tip, was once a shallow pool belonging to the old timber docks, used to prevent merchandise from drying out. It is now a wetland reserve with walkways over the reed beds. The pond was formerly connected to the Thames by a channel, navigable by small boats and lighters. In 1928 the Port of London Authority built the Pump House to regulate water levels in the docks (previously subject to tidal fluctuations) and the channel was closed. The **Pump House** still stands, open as a museum of Rotherhithe history (*Mon–Fri 10–4, T: 020 7231 2976, thepumphouse.org.uk*), fascinating for anyone who remembers Peek Frean biscuits (their factory was nearby). The pump itself is now outside the Brunel Museum in Rotherhithe (*see below*).

ROTHERHITHE CENTRE

Map p. 597, E3. Overground: Rotherhithe.

Historically, Rotherhithe was known as Redriff. Its centre, around the Overground station, is an attractive enclave of cobbled streets and converted mills and warehouses. In Tunnel Road, behind the station, is the **Brunel Museum** (*open daily 10–5; admission charge; brunel-museum.org.uk*). It occupies the former engine house (with slender tin smokestack) of Marc Brunel's Thames Tunnel (1825–43), the first underwater tunnel in the world, for the construction of which he invented the tunnelling shield. The museum offers a film and small exhibition on the construction of the tunnel, which almost cost Brunel his life when the Thames waters burst through the roof in 1828.

The force of the water pushed him up the tunnel shaft and ejected him from the top. Brunel's Thames Tunnel was at first a foot tunnel and was later adapted for the railway. Today part of it can be seen at Wapping station and guided tours are sometimes organised (*see museum website for details*).

Near the Brunel Museum is the Anglo-Catholic **St Mary's Church** (*stmaryrotherhithe.org*), where the captain of the *Mayflower*, Christopher Jones, worshipped and was buried (plaque at the end of the north aisle, beneath a fine sea captain's memorial). The church dates from 1715 (tower and spire later). Prince Lee Boo, a native of the Pacific islands who died in Rotherhithe in 1784, is buried in the churchyard. The church interior is very fine, with a wooden-framed barrel roof held up by four massive pillars—tree trunks encased in a plaster shell and given gilded Ionic capitals. A clock ticks gently on the organ loft. Opposite the church is the **old Free School**, founded in 1613. The building is of the early 18th century and features statues of a girl and boy pupil in their uniforms at the first-floor level. The Watch House Café adjoins it.

On the other side of the church is the 18th-century **Mayflower pub**, which overlooks the river (*see p. 470*). It was re-named to commemorate the famous ship which sailed from the Thames to Portsmouth and from there with the Pilgrim Fathers to America in 1620. The **Hope (Sufferance) Wharf** warehouse, in yellow stock brick, has been restored as flats. A sufferance wharf is one where dutiable goods may be unloaded to relieve congestion at licensed docks.

Rotherhithe has traditionally catered to the spiritual needs of Scandinavian seafarers. The Danish Seamans' Mission survives on Rope Street and on Albion Street are the Finnish Seamans' Mission and the Norwegian church of St Olav (by the entrance to the Rotherhithe Tunnel, a road tunnel built in 1904–8).

WOOLWICH

Map pp. 597 and 595. DLR: Woolwich Arsenal. Rail: trains from London Bridge, Charing Cross, Cannon Street and Waterloo East to Woolwich Dock and Woolwich Arsenal.

Woolwich has a distinguished naval and military past and is also known for its football team, Arsenal (established by workers from the Royal Arsenal factory in 1886, which moved to north London in 1913; *see p. 380*). The Woolwich Building Society, founded in 1847, kept the name of the district on people's lips with its famous advertising catchphrase of the 1980s: 'I'm with the Woolwich.'

Henry VIII established a **dockyard** at Woolwich in 1512. The *Henri Grace à Dieu* or *Great Harry*, the fleet's flagship, was built here and later the *Sovereign of the Seas*, designed in 1637 by Phineas Pett and his son Peter (both buried at Deptford). The dockyard closed in 1869. Munitions manufacture began at Woolwich in 1696, at what became known as the **Woolwich Arsenal** (*map p. 595, F3*). In 1716 Vanbrugh was appointed to design new foundry buildings after a severe explosion at Moorfields (where guns were then made) made it imperative to transfer all works out of central London. During the First World War some 80,000 workers were employed at the Arsenal; fear of air-raids during the Second World War caused manufacture to be spread more evenly throughout the country. The Arsenal closed in 1967 and is now a museum (*see below*). **Woolwich Market** received its first Royal Charter in 1618; today it thrives in Beresford Square, in the shadow of the Arsenal gates (*daily except Sun*). It has stalls selling produce, flowers and general goods.

ROYAL ARTILLERY MUSEUM

Map p. 595, F3. Trains from Charing Cross or London Bridge to Woolwich Arsenal and 5mins' walk. Open Tues–Sat 10–5 (last admission 4). Admission charge. Café and shop. T: 020 8855 7755, firepower.org.uk.

The Royal Regiment of Artillery or the Royal Artillery, often known colloquially as the 'Gunners', is the artillery arm of the British Army with a distinguished history stretching back to the creation of two field companies in Woolwich in 1716. The museum in its honour was founded as a teaching collection in 1776 by Lieutenant General Sir William Congreve. His son, Colonel Sir William Congreve, developer of the Congreve rockets used during the Napoleonic wars, succeeded his father as Superintendent of the Military Machines and had the collection installed in the Rotunda (*viewable by appointment*), a strikingly original building by John Nash (1820). It remained the museum's home until early 2001, when the collection moved into the buildings of the Royal Ordnance Factory at the Royal Arsenal.

The displays are introduced by a 15-min presentation called 'Field of Fire', an audio-visual display in a large, darkened auditorium that gives visitors a loud and vivid impression of gunners and gunnery in action, complete with smoke plumes, piercing searchlights and bomb-shake effects. The History Gallery, on the balcony level overlooking the main hall, describes the development of artillery pieces from the trebuchet through cannons and mortars to the Maxim machine gun. In 1250 the English Franciscan friar and philosopher Roger Bacon is supposed to have 'discovered' the recipe for gunpowder, concealing it in a secret code. Whatever the truth, an explosive combination of saltpetre, nitrate, sulphur and charcoal was in use by the end of the same century.

On the ground floor, the Gunnery Hall is home to a formidable collection of retired artillery pieces of the 20th century.

Not far from the museum, on John Wilson Street near the river, is the **old Odeon Cinema** (now a religious centre) by George Coles (1937). The **Woolwich Ferry** crosses the Thames here, a free service for vehicles and passengers operating every 5–10mins. A ferry crossing was first established here in the 14th century. You can also cross under the river via the Woolwich foot tunnel. On the north bank, the Royal Docks complex is not far away (*see p. 125*).

THE THAMES BARRIER

One mile further upstream is the massive Thames Barrier (*map p. 597, F3*), which stretches across the River Thames and is raised when necessary to protect London from surge tides. The Barrier came into operation in 1982, originally designed to be raised once every few years. The winter of 2014 broke all records for the number of consecutive occasions on which it was closed. It is one of the largest moving flood barriers in the world, spanning 568 yards across the Thames, with ten massive steel gates. The **Thames Barrier Information Centre** (*1 Unity Way; open Thur–Sun 10.30–5; last admission 4.30*) offers an audio-visual presentation and working models illustrating the history of the river and the threat of flooding. The café overlooks the Barrier.

GREENWICH

Map p. 593. DLR from Bank or Tower Hill to Island Gardens (then walk through the foot tunnel) or direct to Cutty Sark or Greenwich. You can also come by river: Thames Clipper services from Embankment, London Eye, Blackfriars, Bankside, London Bridge, Tower and Canary Wharf (journey time c. 40mins from Embankment).

Greenwich was once a fishing village, lying along the line of the Roman Watling Street. Its pleasant location beside the Thames brought it to royal attention in the 15th century. Humphrey, Duke of Gloucester, son of Henry IV, built himself a mansion and enclosed the park as a hunting ground. It was from Greenwich that Willoughby and Chancellor set sail in search of the Northeast Passage in 1553; it was possibly here that Sir Walter Raleigh gallantly put down his cloak for Elizabeth I to walk over—and certainly here that he was arrested by James I on his return from Guyana, having failed to find the gold of El Dorado. George I landed here from Holland on his way to claim the crown of the United Kingdom.

Today the magnificent buildings of the National Maritime Museum, the Old Royal Observatory, Queen's House and Old Royal Naval College have earned UNESCO World Heritage status under the soubriquet of 'Maritime Greenwich'. The views from either side of the river are exceptional: from the north bank at Island Gardens of the beautiful symmetry of Greenwich, or in the other direction, from Greenwich Hill, of the soaring geometry of Canary Wharf. Greenwich is a deservedly popular destination, often very full indeed on summer weekends. As well as the museums and historic buildings, there are some good pubs and restaurants, a market and of course the spacious park.

GREENWICH WATERFRONT

The elegant masts and rigging of the ***Cutty Sark*** are a Greenwich landmark. This was the fastest of the great tea clippers, which raced each other annually to bring back the lucrative new-season China tea crop from the Far East. She is now the only clipper to survive and is open to visitors (*map p. 593, B3; DLR to Cutty Sark; open daily 10–5, last admission 1hr before closing; café and shop; tickets can be booked in advance via rmg.co.uk/cuttysark or on T: 020 8312 6608*). *Cutty Sark* was built by the firm Scott & Linton at their shipyard on the Clyde, and launched in 1869. Her name comes from the short shirt of Paisley linen worn by the witch Nannie in Robert Burns' poem 'Tam

O'Shanter'. Nannie serves as the ship's figurehead, grasping the tail of Tam's grey mare in her hand. Elegant and sleek, with a great expanse of sail, the *Cutty Sark* had a maximum crew of 28. At her fastest she covered 368 miles in a day. She worked in the China tea trade between 1870 and 1877, then carried coal from Shanghai to Sydney, wool between Melbourne and New York and, from 1885–95, wool between Australia and London. She has been in dry dock at Greenwich since 1954, her hull now encased in the glass-walled lobby and shop, making her appear berthed on a crystal lilo. Her lower hold is home to a small theatre.

The glass-domed brick rotunda in front of the *Cutty Sark* is the entrance to the **foot tunnel** under the Thames, completed in 1902 (there is a matching rotunda on the opposite bank). Access is via lift or stairs. The **Thames Path** leads east past a couple of rib shacks and burger bars, passing an entrance to the Old Royal Naval College with a good view of the Queen's House. The walk continues all the way downstream to the Thames Barrier (*see above*). The Greenwich Peninsula, stretching northwards as the river bends around it, affords views of the **O2 Arena**, a concert venue. The four tall chimneys in the foreground belong to **Greenwich Power Station**, still in operation providing backup electricity for London Underground.

The **Trafalgar Tavern** (built 1837), with iron balconies, overlooks the river. It became famous for its whitebait dinners, popular with ministers in Queen Victoria's reign. Other famous customers include Thackeray and the ubiquitous Dickens. The Thames Path leads behind it, past the cosy Yacht pub and a couple of rowing clubs, to emerge by the striking **Trinity Almshouses**, founded by Henry Howard, Earl of Northampton in 1616. The Cutty Sark pub is a few hundred yards further along (*signed*).

OLD ROYAL NAVAL COLLEGE

King William Walk. Map p. 593, C3. Grounds open daily 8–6; Painted Hall, Chapel and Queen's House daily 10–5, Sun 11am service in the Chapel. NB: sometimes closed for functions; check website. Free. Café and restaurant. Guided tours can be booked. T: 020 8269 4799; ornc.org.uk.

Greenwich has had royal associations since the 15th century, when Humphrey, Duke of Gloucester built the palace of Bellacourt. Here he came with his second wife Eleanor and enjoyed a life of ease and pleasure until Eleanor was arrested on charges of sorcery. Her alleged accomplice the 'Witch of Eye' was burned at Smithfield and Eleanor dragged out the rest of her days a prisoner. Henry VII renamed the palace Placentia. It was the birthplace of Henry VIII and Elizabeth I, and a favourite location for jousting, tilting and hunting for Tudor and early Stuart monarchs. In 1614 James I presented Greenwich to his consort, Anne of Denmark, it is said in apology for having cursed her in public for accidentally shooting his favourite hound on a hunting jaunt. It was Anne who commissioned the Queen's House from Inigo Jones. The palace became the official reception point for important visitors, such as foreign ambassadors, who arrived downriver at Gravesend. After the Restoration, Charles II demolished the Tudor buildings and began work on a vast new palace, designed by John Webb. Greenwich Park, which stretches up the hill beyond the Queen's House, was given axial tree-lined avenues, grass terraces, or Giant Steps (the remnants of which can be made out to the east of the Observatory), and an elaborate parterre with fountains designed by the French court garden designer André le Nôtre.

Greenwich is also the home of Greenwich Mean Time. The foundation of the Royal Observatory within the park in 1675, and the presence of the Navy on the palace site since 1694, placed Greenwich at the heart of astronomical discovery and maritime endeavour. Today the buildings of the Old Royal Naval College, together with the Queen's House, constitute a unique ensemble of works by leading architects: Inigo Jones, Wren, Hawksmoor. The magnificent river view of them inspired Canaletto (the view that he painted is on show in the Queen's House).

HISTORY OF THE ROYAL NAVAL COLLEGE

The hospital was established by Queen Mary II in 1694 as the Royal Hospital for Seamen, a charitable institution for injured Royal Navy sailors, their widows and children. She gave over land at Greenwich for the purpose, John Webb's vast palace for Charles II having been abandoned in 1669 with the completion of only one block. Mary died in 1694 but her husband, William III, respected her wishes. Sir Christopher Wren was appointed Hospital Surveyor, with Nicholas Hawksmoor as Clerk of the Works. The Queen's House, however, remained in royal ownership and its vista to the river was to be preserved. Wren incorporated it in his plans as a distant visual centrepiece, with in front of it four symmetrical blocks, the two furthest from the river (the King William and Queen Mary courts) with matching domes and colonnades. On the river, the King Charles Court (Webb's earlier building) was mirrored by Queen Anne Court. Building was a piecemeal exercise which spanned 55 years and which witnessed successive surveyorships (Vanbrugh 1716, Colen Campbell 1726), but the resulting ensemble is one of the grandest Baroque sites in England. Greenwich Hospital's magnificence reflected the charitable munificence of the Crown and the importance of the Navy. The King Charles block, altered and enlarged, was the first to be completed; in 1705 the pensioners moved in.

In 1869 Greenwich Hospital closed and in 1873 the site became home to the Royal Naval College, which occupied the buildings until the mid-1990s. In 1997 the buildings were transferred to the Greenwich Foundation, established to administer the site and to oversee its conversion for the University of Greenwich (which now occupies the King William, Mary and Anne blocks) and Trinity Laban Music Conservatoire (King Charles block). Visitors can see the grounds as well as the Painted Hall and Chapel.

The main entrance to the Old Royal Naval College is via the west gates on King William Walk, which date from 1751 and were moved to their present position in 1850. Their gigantic celestial and terrestrial stone spheres, 6ft in diameter, have their latitudinal and longitudinal lines marked in copper bands. Just inside on the left is the Visitor

OLD ROYAL NAVAL COLLEGE
William III, in Roman guise, arrives in England.
Painted by James Thornhill (1718–24).

Centre. Beyond it, just ahead, is the main complex of the old Greenwich Hospital, with a statue of George II by Rysbrack (1735) in the centre of the Grand Square (wrapped in polythene in winter). This is a good place to pause to get your bearings. There are four blocks or courts: the Painted Hall is on the right and the Chapel is opposite it. On the left is the Trinity Laban Conservatoire of Music and Dance (the pleasant tinkling of pianos can often be heard).

The Painted Hall

The Painted Hall occupies the length of one wing of King William Court. Painted by Sir James Thornhill in stages (for £3 per yard) between 1708 and 1726, it is one of the most magnificent and impressive Baroque painted interiors in the country, and Thornhill's masterpiece. Its hugely complicated iconography necessitated the publication of Thornhill's 'Explanation' of it in 1726/7.

The larger, **Lower Hall**, where the pensioners ate, was painted first, between 1708 and 1714, the ceiling glorifying the Protestant constitutional monarchy of William and Mary (*Peace and Liberty Triumph over Tyranny*), and the Naval and maritime foundation of Britain's power and mercantile prosperity. Below the seated figures of the monarchs, a cowering Louis XIV clutches a broken sword and Architecture points to a large elevation of the King William block. The appearance of Tycho Brahe, Copernicus and John Flamsteed on the ceiling (on the end nearest the entrance vestibule) alludes to the importance of astronomy to maritime navigation. Flamsteed holds a document inscribed 'Apr: 22 1715', the date of his predicted eclipse of the sun (which proved accurate).

The **Upper Hall**, where the officers ate, was completed in 1718–25. Queen Anne and her husband, Prince George of Denmark, Lord High Admiral, appear on the ceiling; the Prince of Orange, later William III, is welcomed by Britannia on the south wall (left), in grisaille, and on the north wall (right) George I lands at Greenwich. The great west wall, mainly the work of Thornhill's assistant Dietrich Ernst André, celebrates the Protestant Hanoverian succession, with George I and his family surrounded by Peace and Justice and other Virtues, with the great dome of St Paul's Cathedral, symbol of Anglicanism (and Thornhill's other great painting commission; *see p. 36*), rising in the background. Thornhill himself appears to the right of the steps.

The **entrance vestibule**, painted with cartouches inscribed with benefactors' names, with seated charity boys, was completed by 1726.

From 4th–7th January 1806, Nelson's body lay in state in the Painted Hall before being taken by funeral barge to St Paul's Cathedral. The 1810–12 **Nelson Pediment** above the colonnade of the King William Court (you have to be inside the courtyard to see it) was designed by West. Forty feet wide and ten feet high and stylistically heavily influenced by the Elgin Marbles, recently arrived in London, it shows Neptune delivering Nelson's mortal remains to Britannia. It is made of Coade Stone (*see p. 415*).

THE BAROQUE IN ENGLAND

The art and architecture of the Baroque, with all its theatricality and direct appeal to the senses and emotions, took hold in Britain following the triumphant restoration to the throne of Charles II in 1660, when 'all arts seemed to return from their exile'. An international court language which bolstered the absolutist regimes of much of Europe, the Baroque flourished in Britain until the early 18th century. The period witnessed the architecture of Sir Christopher Wren, Nicholas Hawksmoor and Sir John Vanbrugh, the vast illusionistic mural paintings of Antonio Verrio, Louis Laguerre and Sir James Thornhill, and the virtuoso limewood carving of Grinling Gibbons. In 1660 Charles II and his courtiers set about equipping the Stuart monarchy with a magnificent setting suitable for the restored regime, inspired by the visual splendour witnessed at the courts of Europe. Baroque culture, with its emphasis on vastness of size, immense cost and grandeur, as well as the theatrical etiquette and ceremony which accompanied it, was used by the Stuart court to underline the power of the monarch and reinforce it in the minds of the people. Outside London, Verrio decorated the ceilings of the remodelled Windsor Castle with vast allegorical scenes celebrating the might of the Crown. In London, following the Great Fire of 1666, Sir Christopher Wren's new St Paul's Cathedral rose glorious from the ashes, a magnificent symbol of the Anglican nation, its great dome decorated by Thornhill. William and Mary created a splendid Baroque palace at Hampton Court, in conscious competition with Louis XIV's Versailles, with painted ceilings and sculpture symbolic of William as the Protestant victor of Europe. Greenwich

Hospital, with Thornhill's supreme masterpiece, the Painted Hall, reflected the magnificence, munificence and charity of the Crown.

In an age which, following the 1688 Glorious Revolution, saw the curbing of the absolute authority of the Crown and the championing of civil liberty, Whig adherents increasingly viewed the reigns of the earlier Stuart monarchs as periods of aggressive Roman Catholicism, tyrannical government and extravagant ostentation. The Baroque fell from favour and in its stead came Palladianism, rooted in the ideals of ancient Rome and hailed as a purer and more restrained form of art. Symptomatic of this change was the renewed interest in the unsullied Classicism of the architecture of Inigo Jones, particularly championed by Lord Burlington and his circle, who saw in its 'still unravished' lines a style and culture which better reflected the decorum and gravitas of the new Augustan age.

The Chapel

The Chapel is directly opposite the Painted Hall, in the Queen Mary block, the least magnificent of the four courts and externally a simpler (cheaper) version of the King William. Originally completed in 1750, the Chapel was gutted by fire in 1779 and remodelled by James 'Athenian' Stuart (author, with Nicholas Revett, of the influential *Antiquities of Athens*). The distinctive bracketed gallery repeats the earlier one, but the plasterwork ceiling is Stuart's design, its delicate neo-Grecian modelling in startling contrast to Thornhill's overwhelming Baroque. The 25ft altarpiece, *St Paul Shipwrecked at Malta*, was commissioned from Benjamin West in 1781, and the statues of *Faith, Hope, Charity* and *Humility* in the vestibule were also designed by him.

THE NATIONAL MARITIME MUSEUM

Romney Road. Map p. 593, C3–C4. Open daily 10–5 (last admission 30mins before closing; ground-floor galleries and Sammy Ofer wing open until 8pm on Thur). Free. Café, restaurant and shop. rmg.co.uk.

The National Maritime Museum, which opened in 1937, tells the story of the Royal Navy, of Britain as a seafaring power and of the history of maritime exploration, navigation, astronomy and the measurement of time. As well as the main museum, it includes the historic Queen's House, where its important collection of maritime art is displayed, and the Royal Observatory. The museum's 2.5 million objects include cartography, ship models and plans, an exceptional collection of scientific and navigational instruments, important collections relating to national heroes such as Nelson and Captain Cook, paintings and an important library housing books and manuscripts dating from the 15th century onwards.

The main entrance takes you into Neptune Court (Rick Mather, with the Building Design Partnership), a vast space spanned by a steel-framed glass roof. Exhibition spaces and micro-galleries are arranged in and around this, and off it opens the Sammy Ofer wing, named after the Romanian-born Israeli businessman who donated many millions of pounds to the Maritime Museum and helped fund restoration of the *Cutty*

Sark following fire damage in 2007. Money from the family foundation also secured two paintings by Stubbs of a dingo and a kangaroo, documenting discoveries by Captain Cook and representing the first depictions of the animals in Western art. At the time of writing, the works were expected to be put on display in the Queen's House.

Ground floor

As soon as you arrive, your ears are assailed by the sound of crashing waves, an audio innovation of the 1990s. In the Neptune Court, large-scale highlights from the collection are displayed, including the working paddle engine from the steam paddle-tug *Reliant* (built in 1907 for service on the Manchester ship canal) and Prince Frederick's barge, a 'floating coach' designed by William Kent in 1732 with carved and gilded work by James Richards, the King's Master Carver. Used for state occasions on the Thames, it would have been accompanied by another barge with a 'set of Musick'.

Many of the displays in the museum are particularly appealing to school parties. To the sound of creaking decks, 'Explorers' gives a brief overview of the history of exploration, from Vasco da Gama and Christopher Columbus to Sir John Franklin's ill-fated 1845 attempt to find the Northwest Passage. In cases set into ice-lined walls, with the sound of howling wind, are items such as the snow boot of one of Franklin's party who died in Starvation Cove. Important early navigational instruments are on show in 'Voyagers', as well as the magnificent late 16th-century Drake Jewel and Cup: the former sun-shaped, decorated with rubies and opals, the reverse containing a miniature of Elizabeth I; the latter a coconut shell set elaborately in silver, the cover surmounted by an exquisite model of the *Golden Hind*. Presented to Sir Francis Drake by Elizabeth I to mark his historic circumnavigation, it is rather lost in a muddled showcase captioned 'Anticipation', with a fly whisk collected by Captain Cook in Tonga displayed alongside. 'Maritime London' contains an evocative painting of Deptford docks in 1794. A small and interesting display of photographs tells the story of the wartime Arctic Convoys.

First floor

Arranged at either end of the 'Great Map' are two themed galleries. 'Traders' explores the story of the East India Company, apologetically interpreting Britain's commercial history as a tale of rapine and diplomatic ineptitude. A highlight is the 1819 figurehead of HMS *Seringapatam*, a carved representation of Tipu Sultan holding a parasol and riding a roc, a mythical bird; and a fine bust of Queen Victoria by Boehm (1874), displayed alongside a quote from Nehru: 'It is significant that one of the Hindustani words which has become part of the English language today is loot.' The other gallery, 'Slavery, Trade, Empire', deals with Britain's voyages across the Atlantic, presenting explorers' fascination with and respect for the new cultures that they encountered as well as the greed for their goods and exploitation of their people that resulted.

Second floor

'Nelson, Navy, Nation' traces the rise of the Navy and the status of the sailor. Displays include much memorabilia connected to Britain's great naval hero, Horatio Nelson.

QUEEN'S HOUSE
Detail of the 'Tulip Staircase'.

Rather frantic sound effects attempt to recreate the atmosphere of a warship in the thick of an engagement. The most compelling exhibits are the clothes Nelson wore at the Battle of Trafalgar, the fatal musket ball hole visible just below the left epaulette of his coat. Touchingly personal items include a letter from his abandoned wife, Frances Nisbet, and Nelson's last letter to his daughter by Emma Hamilton, Horatia.

THE QUEEN'S HOUSE

Map p. 593, C3. Open daily 10–5 (last admission 30mins before closing). Free.

The Queen's House, a perfectly proportioned architectural masterpiece, is usually taken as the first—and one of the finest—truly classical Renaissance buildings in England. Designed by the great architect Inigo Jones on his return from his influential last trip to Italy (*see p. 365*), it symbolises the refined aesthetic of the early Stuart court. The Queen's House was in fact built in three main stages for successive queen consorts: Anne of Denmark, wife of James I; Henrietta Maria, wife of Charles I; and Catherine of Braganza, wife of Charles II. Anne of Denmark was granted Greenwich as her private residence in 1613 and commissioned the building in 1616. It stands almost exactly on the site of the gatehouse of the old Tudor palace, which marked the demarcation between the private palace gardens and Greenwich Park, to which the queen desired easy access. The Queen's House is in fact two buildings, one on the palace side, the other on the park side, linked by first-floor bridges which span what was then a public highway. On Anne's death in 1619 only the bottom storeys of the two blocks were complete. In 1629 Greenwich was granted to Henrietta Maria, and work resumed. Between 1629 and 1638 the upper storeys were added, including the central bridge room and the elegant loggia overlooking the park, and a programme of elaborate interior decoration was undertaken.

The interior

The double-height, single-cube galleried Hall, the centrepiece of the Queen's House, had its black and white marble floor laid in 1636–7, its pattern mirroring the white and gold compartmented ceiling above. The latter originally contained a cycle of nine canvases, *The Allegory of Peace and Arts under the English Crown*, by Orazio Gentileschi, a friend and follower of Caravaggio. Removed in 1708, when the Queen's House became the official residence of the Governor of Greenwich Hospital, they were re-installed at Marlborough House, where they still are today. Other important Gentileschis were commissioned for the house, including the large *Finding of Moses*, which was sold at the 1649 Commonwealth sale following Charles I's execution (it is now in the National Gallery). The Hall was used for the display of Classical and modern sculpture. You enter it from the so-called 'Tulip Stairs' (though the motif in the fine wrought-iron balustrade is in fact probably intended as a fleur-de-lys, Henrietta Maria's family emblem). Off the gallery are the principal rooms. The **Queen's Bedchamber** has a coved ceiling painted with important Italianate grotesque work, possibly by John de Critz, Serjeant-painter to the king. The most sumptuous room is the **King's Presence Chamber**. The beams of its compartmented ceiling bear festoons of fruit and flowers and the frieze and cornice cartouches have the monograms of Charles I and Henrietta Maria.

The collection

The Queen's House displays the National Maritime Museum's excellent collection of paintings, including marine scenes, portraits of naval heroes and portraits and landscapes relevant to Greenwich's royal history. William Dobson's portrait of the elderly Inigo Jones (c. 1644) is among the exhibits. Works by Lely include his early portrait of Peter Pett, shipbuilder of Woolwich, with the *Sovereign of the Seas* in the background. James II himself appears in a swaggering, almost comic, full-length by Henri Gascars. *The Somerset House Conference* (1604) shows delegates at the peace negotiations held between England and Spain after the death of Elizabeth I. Not to be missed is Canaletto's charming view of Greenwich Hospital (1750–2). Reynolds' portrait of Rear-Admiral the Hon. Augustus Keppel (1752–3) shows him full-length before a stormy sea and is said to be the picture which established Reynolds as a leading artist. Also among the portraits is Hudson's likeness of the unfortunate Admiral Byng, who failed to prevent the French capture of Minorca, was court-martialled and shot in 1757; and Nathaniel Dance's famous portrait of Captain Cook (1775–6). A display devoted to the Van de Veldes, the first great marine artists to work in Britain, who settled in London in 1673/4, occupies the room they were given by Charles II to use as a painting studio (on the lower floor). Also downstairs is a seapiece by Dominic Serres, the only marine artist to be admitted as a founder member of the Royal Academy.

GREENWICH VILLAGE

In the centre of Greenwich, **St Alfege** in Church Street (*map p. 593, B4; open 11–4, st-alfege.org*) marks the spot where Alphege, Archbishop of Canterbury, was murdered by invading Danish Vikings in 1012. Henry VIII was baptised in the medieval church; Thomas Tallis, the great composer of English sacred music, is buried in the vault and preserved at the west end is a keyboard that may have been played by him and by Princess Elizabeth. The current church, designed by Hawksmoor and completed in 1714, was restored after heavy war damage. Also buried in the vault is James Wolfe, who lived in a house on Croom's Hill and who died claiming Quebec for the English. Just inside the entrance to the church is a plaque commemorating John Julius Angerstein, benefactor of the British Museum (*see p. 168*), another local resident, who was buried here in 1823.

Diagonally opposite the church, on Church Street, is an archway leading to **Greenwich Market**, in a covered Victorian market building. Once a produce market, its stalls now sell books, clothing, bric à brac and handicrafts, and more shops and food stalls line the periphery. An admonitory motto, 'A false balance is abomination to the Lord but a just weight is his delight' is inscribed over the exit to College Approach.

Croom's Hill has some attractive Georgian houses and, opposite the theatre, the **Fan Museum**, dedicated to the history of fans and fan-making (*12 Croom's Hill; open Tues–Sat 11–5, Sun 12–5; T: 020 8305 1441, thefanmuseum.org.uk*). The Orangery is open for afternoon tea (*Tues, Sat, Sun, booking advised*). At the top of Croom's Hill is **Macartney House** (*map p. 593, C4*), where General Wolfe once lived. There are entrances along Croom's Hill to Greenwich Park (*see below*)

THE ROYAL OBSERVATORY

Map p. 593, C4. Open daily 9–5 (last admission 30mins before closing). Admission charge for Flamsteed House and Greenwich Meridian; Planetarium free. Shop.

Standing high on Observatory Hill, with a spectacular view over the Hospital, the river and London stretching into the distance, is Flamsteed House, the earliest building of the Greenwich complex which comprises the Royal Observatory. Built in 1675–6 by Sir Christopher Wren, with the assistance of Robert Hooke, it was the first purpose-built scientific research facility in the country. The Observatory at Greenwich is no longer used to make positional observations (due to atmospheric pollution, the Royal Observatory began the move to Herstmonceaux, Sussex, in 1948), but its historic build-ings remain a site of extraordinary significance for the history of astronomy, time-keeping and the calculation of longitude. At the International Meridian Conference in Washington in 1884, Greenwich was recognised as marking the Prime Meridian, Longitude 0°, and Greenwich Mean Time was internationally adopted.

HISTORY OF THE OBSERVATORY

The Royal Observatory was the product of the 17th-century scientific revolution, a great era of investigation and discovery. One of the crucial problems demanding a solution was the calculation of longitude, vital for accurate navigation at sea which, for a maritime nation, was of obvious importance. The Royal Observatory was founded by Charles II, with John Flamsteed appointed the first 'Astronomical Observator' in 1675, with this specific task in mind. Flamsteed's aim was to facilitate the calculation of longitude through lunar observation, specifically the annual passage of the moon against the stars, by compiling accurate star catalogues and lunar tables. He moved into Flamsteed House, his official residence, in July 1676 and began his observations from the top floor observatory in September.

Outside the gates of the courtyard is the **Shepherd 24-hour clock**, erected in 1852, the year the Greenwich Time Service started sending signals. Greenwich is the official starting point of each new day. The large red Time Ball on the east turret of Flamsteed House is the world's first visual time signal. Since 1833 it has been hoisted half-way up the mast at 12.55, to the top at 12.58, and dropped at precisely 1pm.

The entrance route funnels you through the ticket office and round into the cobbled courtyard, which you enter with Flamsteed House on your left and the Meridian Building on the right. A brass line in the ground marks the **Prime Meridian**. It runs straight through the Meridian Building, linking the North and South Poles and marking the division between the Eastern and Western Hemispheres. Visitors can thus stand astride the line, in two hemispheres at once (there are usually large numbers of people photographing each other doing so). The Meridian is seen most dramatically at dusk, when the green laser beam projected from the Observatory stretches into the evening sky, across Greenwich Hospital and the river towards the distant lights of the tall modern buildings of Canary Wharf.

Flamsteed House

On entering the house there is a display of portraits of Astronomers Royal. The **downstairs apartments** have been fitted up to look much as they might have done in Flamsteed's day and also under the tenure of Nevil Maskelyne, fifth Astronomer Royal. Upstairs is the spectacular **Octagon Room** (known by Flamsteed as his Octagonal Great or Star Room): Wren's fine, airy interior with tall windows was suitable for observing the heavens through long telescopes. The plasterwork ceiling has a frieze of roses, oak leaves and the royal arms, and there are full-length portraits of Charles II and James II after Lely (the latter a copy of 1984). The three clocks, with 13ft pendulums behind the walnut-grained wainscot, were used by Flamsteed for checking the regularity of the Earth's rotation. The original movements and dials were made by the great Thomas Tompion but in 1719, after Flamsteed's death, were sold by his widow (Flamsteed had paid for his own instruments). One was purchased by the British Museum in the 1920s and another was returned to the Observatory in 1994 and is displayed in a case with its movement and pendulum visible. Flamsteed's immense contribution to astronomical observation was published soon after his death (*Historia*

Coelestis Britannica, 1725; *Atlas Coelestis*, 1729) and he is celebrated on the ceiling of Thornhill's Painted Hall (*see p. 446 above*).

From the Octagon Room stairs lead down to displays of historically important time-pieces, particularly those which illustrate the quest to calculate longitude, given impetus after the drowning of Sir Cloudesley Shovell and his crew off the Scilly Isles in 1707. In separate cases are John Harrison's four ground-breaking marine chronometers (on loan from the Hydrographer of the Navy), which changed maritime navigation forever. Instead of using the moon as an astronomical clock, Harrison, a Yorkshire carpenter and self-taught clockmaker, worked towards the perfection of a clock that would keep accurate time while on a temperature-variable rolling ship at sea. His first prototype, H1 (1730–5), was based on his early wooden clocks but was fitted with a temperature compensation device. It was followed by H2 in 1737–40, and H3 between 1740 and 1759. The latter can be seen in the background of Harrison's portrait by Thomas King, as well as the precision pocket watch made for him, according to his specifications, by John Jefferys. H4 was Harrison's triumphal marine timekeeper. In the form of a compact watch, inspired by the Jefferys watch, it has pivot-holes of rubies and pallets of diamonds. It was H4 that was awarded the £20,000 prize for solving the Longitude problem, which the Board of Longitude had been seeking to give away since 1714.

The Meridian Building

Flamsteed had made further astronomical observations from the courtyard. Early views of the Observatory show his 60ft refracting telescope appearing above the courtyard wall. He also erected the northeast Summer House, his solar observatory; a Sextant House, for his seven-foot Equatorial Sextant; and a Quadrant House. The latter was added to by succeeding Astronomers Royal: Edmund Halley (d. 1742), of comet fame, and James Bradley. These buildings now make up the Meridian Building, where Bradley's Mural Quadrant and 12½-ft Zenith Sector Telescope (1727) can be seen; and successive Transit Instruments, culminating with Airy's Transit Circle. Observations made on the latter had the effect of moving the Greenwich Meridian 19ft east, the equivalent of .02 seconds, and its optical axis still defines the Greenwich Meridian. Inside the distinctive onion-shaped Dome of the Great Equatorial Building (*access up stairs from the Meridian Building shop*) is Sir Howard Grubb's great 28-inch refracting telescope of 1893, which was used at Herstmonceaux until 1971 and then returned to Greenwich.

In 1894–9 two ornamental structures of red brick and terracotta were added to the complex: the Altazimuth Pavilion and the South Building. Between them is the **Planetarium** (*free admission*).

GREENWICH PARK

Outside the Royal Observatory enclosure is a **statue of General Wolfe** by Tait McKenzie, presented by the Canadian nation in 1930 and unveiled—a nice touch—by the descendant of Montcalm, the commander of Quebec who met his death in the tussle with Wolfe. From here a broad, tree-lined avenue leads through Greenwich Park to Blackheath Gate. Greenwich is a royal park, first enclosed by Humphrey, Duke of Gloucester as a hunting ground in 1433. With its steep topography, it offers superb views of the Thames. It was laid out by Sir William Boreman to a plan by André le Nôtre, commissioned by Charles II in the 1660s. Signs indicate the park's salient features: the Flower Garden, Deer Enclosure, Roman remains (virtually nothing to see) and **Queen Elizabeth's Oak**, a tree under which Henry VIII is said to have danced with Anne Boleyn, and where Queen Elizabeth picnicked as a child. It collapsed in 1991 and now lies where it fell, enclosed by railings, a short walk southwest of Maze Hill Gate. At the time of writing it was home to a family of wrens. Just outside Maze Hill Gate is **Vanbrugh Castle** (*map p. 593, C3–C4*), recognisable by its green turret, built in 1726 by Sir John Vanbrugh when he was Surveyor of the Royal Hospital.

On the west side of the park is Ranger's House (*see below*). Close by are the remains of a sunken bath house built for Caroline of Brunswick, consort of George IV, and a bronze sculpture by Henry Moore: *Large Standing Figure: Knife Edge.*

RANGER'S HOUSE

Chesterfield Walk. Map p. 593, C4. Trains from Charing Cross or London Bridge to Greenwich or Blackheath. Open April–Sept Mon–Wed and Sun 11–3.30. Admission charge. T: 020 8294 2548, english-heritage.org.uk.

Standing between Blackheath and Greenwich Park, over which it has fine views to the Royal Observatory, Ranger's House is a handsome mansion built in 1700–20 for Captain, later Admiral, Francis Hosier. Due to its proximity to the royal palace, and later to the Naval College and surrounding shipyards, it was a spot favoured by courtiers and seafaring men. The core of the house is Hosier's, who made a fortune through the sale of ships' cargoes. The fine red-brick exterior has a Portland stone centrepiece, a modest Baroque flourish, with a carved mask of Neptune above the entrance door. In 1748 the house was owned by Philip, 4th Earl of Chesterfield, politician and wit and author of the celebrated letters to his son, who built the south wing of yellow brick. Chesterfield spent every summer here for the last 23 years of his life. The north wing was added in the 1780s. In 1807 the house was leased by Augusta, Dowager Countess of Brunswick, sister of George III, and in 1815 it became the official residence of the Ranger of Greenwich Park, by now purely an honorary office. The first Ranger to take up residence was Princess Sophia Matilda of Gloucester. Other occupants of the house include the young Prince Arthur of Connaught, Queen Victoria's third son, and Field Marshal Viscount Wolseley, who relieved General Gordon at Khartoum.

The Entrance Hall, with its chequered black-and-white stone floor, dates from Hosier's day. To the right of the Hall is Hosier's Crimson Camblet Parlour, used by Chesterfield for cards, which leads to the New Gallery, a spacious room with triple bow windows in the centre and at each end. Here Chesterfield displayed his Old Master paintings, with sculpture busts and porcelain in the niches. The 1710 Oak Staircase leads up to the Long Gallery or Passage, which retains its original early 18th-century panelling. Off it Hosier had a 'Cockloft', a gazebo from which he could train his telescope on ships on the Thames.

The Wernher Collection

The Wernher Collection of pictures, jewellery and *objets d'art* is on permanent loan here from the Wernher Foundation. Sir Julius Wernher (1850–1912) was a German diamond merchant who made his fortune (£11 million at his death) in South Africa in the 1870s when his operation merged with De Beers. He settled in England and in 1903 purchased the great Bedfordshire mansion Luton Hoo, which was redecorated in lavish style. Luton Hoo was sold in the 1990s and several of the most important items from the collection were auctioned. What remains is nonetheless impressive. There are pictures by Joos van Cleve, Hans Memling and Gabriel Metsu; English works by Reynolds, Romney and Hoppner; 18th-century French tapestries; Renaissance bronzes, ivories and enamels; and an important collection of enamelled and gem-studded Renaissance jewellery.

BLACKHEATH & ELTHAM

Blackheath (*map p. 593, C4; trains from London Bridge or Charing Cross to Blackheath in 15–20mins*) is an attractive residential suburb nestling on the edge of the heath itself, an almost treeless grassy plateau of some 280 acres. The Roman Watling Street crossed Blackheath and both Roman and Saxon remains have been found here. During the Peasants' Revolt in 1381, Wat Tyler assembled his supporters on the heath before advancing on London. It was the scene of royal celebrations such as the welcome for Charles II in 1660. The heath also had a bad reputation for highway robberies. The Royal Blackheath Golf Club was the first in the country when it opened here in 1607 (it is now in Eltham). Blackheath Rugby Club prides itself on being the oldest in the world. Today the heath is known for its spectacular fireworks displays on 5th November, Bonfire Night (*see p. 554*). It is also a favourite place for kite-flying. The start lines for the London Marathon are ranged around Blackheath.

Around the east and south side of the heath are some handsome 17th- and early 18th-century villas. Morden College on St German's Place was built in 1695 by Wren with a colonnaded courtyard to house 'decayed Turkey Merchants who had fallen on hard times'. Sir John Morden, its benefactor, was himself a 'Turkey merchant'. It continues in the same spirit today, being a residential home for the elderly. The Princess of Wales pub on the south side of the heath (*1A Montpelier Row*) is a good place to stop for a drink or a bite to eat.

ELTHAM

Eltham (*map p. 597, F4; trains from Charing Cross to Eltham in c. 25mins*) is a busy suburb—and probably has always been thus. Ideally located on the way from London to the coast, it was used by kings and their troops for 200 years, on their way to overseas battles. Court Yard, just off the High Street, leads to the remains of Eltham Palace (*see below*), once a royal manor and now one of London's finest Art Deco houses. Well Hall

Road leads north from Eltham High Street for half a mile to **Well Hall Pleasaunce** (*wellhall.org.uk*), a small local park with a medieval moated garden, formerly the grounds of Well Hall mansion, the home of William Roper, who married Sir Thomas More's daughter Margaret in 1521. The surviving 16th-century barn is now a restaurant (*T: 0845 459 2351, tudorbarneltham.com*) and it preserves a small stained-glass window featuring Margaret Roper. Well Hall was also the home of E. Nesbit, author of *The Railway Children*. It was demolished in 1931.

ELTHAM PALACE

Court Yard, off Court Road. Trains to Eltham from Charing Cross, then bus 126, 161. Open April–Oct Mon–Thur and Sun 10–6, Oct 10–5, Nov–March closed but with some limited opening during that period; check website. Admission charge. Café serving light lunches and teas. T: 020 8294 2548, elthampalace.org.uk.

The manor of Eltham was one of the oldest estates belonging to the Crown and by the 14th century was one of the largest and most frequented of the English royal palaces. Originally a moated manor house, it was a favourite Christmas residence of English sovereigns from Henry III to Henry VIII. Chaucer was clerk of the works to Richard II here, and here Henry IV entertained the Byzantine emperor Manuel II Palaeologus. After Agincourt Henry V stayed at Eltham before his triumphal entry into London. The Great Hall, the most evident feature of the medieval palace which remains today, was constructed by Edward IV in 1475–80. Henry VIII was the last monarch to spend much time at Eltham, and after the Civil War both the palace and its grounds were given over to agricultural use. The Great Hall was used as a barn and romantic views of it as such were made by several artists, including Turner.

In 1933 the site was purchased by the wealthy Stephen Courtauld (brother of Samuel Courtauld, founder of the art institute) and his wife Virginia. They conceived a spectacular and luxurious house, designed by Seely & Paget. The aim was to construct a glamorous and modern home while retaining as much as possible of the medieval palace. The result is an extraordinarily eclectic mix. The interiors were created by a team of artistic advisers, personal friends of the Courtaulds, including Winifred Knights and her husband Thomas Monnington, the Swedish interior designer Rolf Engströmer (head of the Swedish company Jefta) and the Italian decorator Peter Malacrida. Malacrida, then working for the company White Allom, had been a neighbour of the Courtaulds in Grosvenor Square. The house became the stage for extravagant weekend parties, the quality of its materials and craftsmanship matched by the luxury of the innovative 1930s' technological features: an internal telephone system, concealed ceiling lights, underfloor heating, speakers which broadcast music throughout the ground floor, and a centralised vacuum cleaner with sockets in each room. The Courtaulds left Eltham in 1944.

The tour takes in the reception rooms, bedrooms, Virginia Courtauld's luxurious onyx bathroom, and Mah-Jongg's quarters, designed for the Courtaulds' pet ring-tailed lemur, bought at Harrods in 1923. 'Jongy' enjoyed central heating, a bamboo forest mural and a bamboo ladder leading down to the Flower Room. He accompanied his owners everywhere and had his own small deckchair for foreign cruises.

DULWICH, FOREST HILL & CRYSTAL PALACE

Map p. 597. Trains from Victoria to West Dulwich or from London Bridge to North Dulwich and 10mins' walk.

Dulwich is an attractive residential suburb, well kept and villagey, with white-painted signposts whose arms are fashioned to look like pointing fingers. There are some handsome houses and a general air of leafy prosperity. Dickens frequented the predecessor of the Victorian Crown and Greyhound pub, and he chooses Dulwich as the place of Samuel Pickwick's retirement, in 'one of the most pleasant spots near London'.

In 967 King Edgar granted the manor of Dulwich to one of his followers; later it belonged to Bermondsey Abbey before the land was purchased by Edward Alleyn, the actor and theatre manager, in 1605. Alleyn founded Dulwich College, partly as a school for the poor and partly as almshouses. The old College buildings stand in the intersection of College and Gallery roads. The new Dulwich College in College Road, designed by Charles Barry (son of the architect of the Houses of Parliament) in an ornate Italian style (1842 with extensions in 1870), includes the chapel in which Alleyn is buried. Famous former pupils include Raymond Chandler and P.G. Wodehouse. The trust still collects a toll from cars using the privately-owned section of College Road. This is the last surviving toll-road in London.

DULWICH PICTURE GALLERY
Map p. 597, D4. Open Tues–Fri 10–5; Sat, Sun and bank holidays 11–5. Admission charge. Café/restaurant and shop. T: 020 8693 5254, dulwichpicturegallery.org.uk.
According to the American architect Philip Johnson (1906–2005), 'the Dulwich Picture Gallery set forever the way to show pictures'. Designed by the great architect Sir John Soane in 1811–13, this is the oldest public art gallery in the country. Purpose-built for the display of pictures, Dulwich opened its doors to the public in 1817 (seven years before the National Gallery), and in June of that year its first annual dinner took place. Over 30 guests, including many Royal Academicians, feasted on turtle soup and venison. Today, Soane's great building sits in spacious grounds in a gracious area of old Dulwich. The modern café wing (Rick Mather 2000) wraps itself round the east and north edges of the grounds, against the building of old Dulwich College. To celebrate the bicentenary year in 2011, the Gallery commissioned the Lumsden Design team to create a new entrance hall and shop.

History of the collection
Now an independent charitable trust, until 1994 Dulwich was part of Alleyn's College of God's Gift (which included the school, Dulwich College), a 17th-century educational and charitable foundation established in 1619 by Edward Alleyn. Alleyn (d. 1626) was an actor of renown and also wealth, manager of the Rose, Fortune and Hope playhouses (rivals to the Globe) and, alongside his father-in-law Philip Henslowe, joint master of the 'Royal Game of Bears, Bulls and Mastiff Dogs' (which incorporated lion-baiting).

He bequeathed to his college his collection of pictures, which included a set of English monarchs. In 1686 the Alleyn pictures were joined by works from the collection of the actor William Cartwright, including a portrait of the actor Richard Burbage.

Sir Francis Bourgeois' bequest in 1811 of over 350 Old Master pictures transformed the College collection. Bourgeois, an artist of moderate ability (several examples of his work are in the collection), was the protégé of the ambitious art dealer Noel Desenfans, with whom he collaborated. Between 1790 and 1795 Desenfans was collecting on behalf of Stanislaw II Augustus, King of Poland, who wished to establish a National Gallery of Poland; but with the partition of that country and the forced abdication of the king in 1795, Desenfans was left with the pictures. He passed them to Bourgeois, who in turn bequeathed them to Dulwich College to 'go down to Posterity for the benefit of the Public' (the educational impulse behind the gift remains present in the gallery's innovative educational programmes).

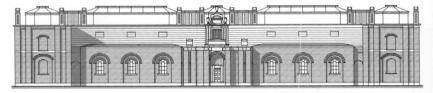

DULWICH PICTURE GALLERY: EAST FRONT

The building
Soane's task was to design a new gallery for the pictures which was also to incorporate a mausoleum for the tombs of Bourgeois and Desenfans and later Desenfans' wife (d. 1813), all of whom had been Soane's friends. This dual purpose, and the association between death and art, excited Soane, and Dulwich became his 'favourite subject'. Due to lack of funds, the actual building (which cost less than £10,000) is stark and austere with little embellishment: though celebrated today, it was not truly Soane's wish. The main galleries, a succession of plain interlinked spaces, had top-lighting in the form of large lanterns, influential for later gallery design in Britain; and the mausoleum was centrally placed on the west side, flanked by almshouses (a key function of Alleyn's college), now converted to galleries. The contrast between the 'dull, religious light' of the mausoleum, filtered through amber glass, and the daylight clarity of the gallery, was deliberate. Internally the gallery has been restored as far as possible to its original early 19th-century appearance, including the smoky dark red of some of the walls.

Collection highlights
The pictures at Dulwich include about 56 of those intended for Poland (others were sold at auction in 1802) and those Bourgeois continued to collect. Highlights of the French works include works by Claude and his circle; Charles Le Brun's *Massacre of the Innocents* and Poussin's *Nurture of Jupiter* and *Triumph of David*, showing David parading the head of Goliath through Jerusalem. The collection has a particularly strong collection of Dutch and Flemish pictures: several works by Cuyp and Ruisdael

and atmospheric winter scenes by Teniers the Younger. Aert de Gelder's *Jacob's Dream* is memorable, with its huge sky and angel appearing in a dazzling, bright light. By Rembrandt is the well-known *A Girl at a Window*, signed and dated 1645. There are several works by Rubens, including *Venus, Mars and Cupid* and *Hagar in the Desert*. Italian pictures include Guercino's *Christ and the Woman Taken in Adultery* (c. 1621), Sebastiano Ricci's *Resurrection* (an oil sketch for the painted apse in the chapel of the Royal Hospital, Chelsea), Veronese's *Saint Jerome and a Donor* and a very striking portrait of a young man against a bright blue ground, attributed to Piero di Cosimo. Another popular work, and much copied, is Murillo's *Flower Girl*, possibly modelled by the artist's daughter Francisca, who later became a nun.

The British pictures include Van Dyck's extraordinary *Venetia Stanley, Lady Digby, on her Death-bed*, painted in 1633, two days after she died in her sleep. Gainsborough's excellent full-length *The Linley Sisters*, portraits of the musical daughters of a friend of the artist, was bequeathed by William Linley in 1831. Sir Joshua Reynolds' great *Mrs Siddons as the Tragic Muse* is a replica of the one now at the Huntington Art Gallery in California, which Desenfans ordered from Reynolds in 1789.

FOREST HILL

The suburb of Forest Hill (*map p. 597, E4; trains from London Bridge to Forest Hill in c. 15mins*) became home to German merchants and artisans in the 19th century. Their Lutheran church, the Dietrich-Bonhoeffer-Kirche, occupies a building of 1959 in Dacres Road. Forest Hill is also home to the idiosyncratic Horniman Museum.

HORNIMAN MUSEUM & GARDENS

100 London Rd. Map p. 597, E4. Train to Forest Hill from London Bridge and 10mins' walk. Bus: 176, 185, 312, P4. Open daily 10.30–5.30; gardens open Mon–Sat 7.15–sunset, Sun 8–sunset, Nature Trail open 9–4. Museum and gardens free; admission charge for aquarium. Shop and café. T: 020 8699 1872, horniman.ac.uk.

As the plaque on the façade of the main building indicates, the Horniman Museum & Gardens was left to the people of London in 1901 'for ever as a museum for their recreation, instruction and enjoyment'. A museum of anthropology, natural history and musical instruments, it was established in 1888 by Frederick John Horniman (1835–1906), a Somerset-born tea merchant (his company was the largest in the world in its time) and avid collector. Horniman amassed around 30,000 objects in his lifetime, including birds and butterflies, musical instruments, glass and porcelain and Egyptian and Classical antiquities. The museum building (1901), a truly modern construction in its time, is an example of English free style architecture. Its architect, Charles Harrison Townsend, was dubbed one of 'the prophets of the new style' by the German architect Hermann Muthesius. The main feature of the façade is the large Byzantinesque mosaic by Robert Anning Bell, *Humanity in the House of Circumstance*, which symbolises the course of human life. 'Humanity' is flanked by the Gates of Life and Death and tended by figures personifying the Fine Arts, Poetry, Music, Endurance, Love, Hope, Charity, Wisdom, Meditation and Resignation.

CRYSTAL PALACE
Detail of one of the surviving sphinxes on the terrace below the palace site.

Horniman opened the gardens to the public to mark the Diamond Jubilee of Queen Victoria in 1897. There are six 'Display Gardens', including the Medicinal Garden, the Materials Garden, with a wide range of plants used for textiles and building materials, and the Sound Garden, with large-scale musical instruments to play. Other features of note include the glasshouse conservatory (1894); the octagonal Bandstand (1912) designed by Charles Harrison Townsend; and the Dutch Barn (c. 1895), which Horniman transported back from Holland. The South Downs picnic area provides glorious views of Kent.

The collections

The **Natural History Gallery**, on the ground and first floors, is suffused with a Victorian taxidermy aesthetic and is testimony to the vanguard work of the British naturalists of the 19th century and dominated by the overstuffed wrinkleless walrus from Hudson Bay, which has been on display since the museum's opening in 1901. The first-floor display has examples from the whole animal kingdom, classified according to the Linnaean system: protozoa to mammals by way of molluscs. Here too is the famed mid-19th-century German **Apostle Clock**, complete with mechanical figures of the Apostles which, apart from Judas, at 4pm each day, bow to the figure of Christ.

The basement **Aquarium** features seven aquatic habitats from around the world. Here are beautifully coloured dart-poison frogs from Central and South America, the grotesque giant frogfish, found in tropical coral reef areas such as the Red Sea, and the gorgeous moon jellyfish, an inhabitant of UK coastal waters. The **African Worlds Gallery**, situated on the lower ground and ground floors, presents a selection from the estimated 22,000 African and African-influenced objects that make up almost a third of the museum's ethnographic collections. The **Centenary Gallery** on the lower ground floor has Horniman's original collection of over 16,000 butterflies, beetles and insects, as well as rare birds in bell jars. The most unusual object here is the so-called Torture Chair, with a dubious provenance once ascribed to Cell 23 of the dungeons of the Spanish Inquisition. It is now believed to be a 19th-century fake, but incorporating a genuine garotte.

The **Music Gallery**, arranged thematically, displays around 1,300 objects from the museum's collection of some 8,000 musical artefacts from all periods and cultures, the largest collection of its kind in the UK.

SYDENHAM AND CRYSTAL PALACE

Sydenham (*map p. 597, E4; trains from Victoria or London Bridge to Sydenham*) was once a spa—the health-giving water now forms pools in Sydenham Wells Park. After the Great Exhibition of 1851, the Crystal Palace was moved to the area. Thousands of Londoners travelled here to visit it and many settled in big houses in Sydenham and Norwood.

CRYSTAL PALACE

The spacious Crystal Palace Park, with its large sports stadium, lies directly outside Crystal Palace railway station (*map p. 597, D4–E4; trains from Victoria or London Bridge to Crystal Palace; Overground to Crystal Palace; park open daily until dusk; boats for hire April–Sept*). The park was designed by Sir Joseph Paxton in 1852 to complement the Crystal Palace, the huge glass and iron building, also designed by Paxton, which had been the centrepiece of the Great Exhibition of 1851 in Hyde Park and which was moved here in 1854. It perished in 1936 in a fire, which could be seen from as far away as Brighton. On the **site of the palace** today, only the grand approach stairways and parts of the parapets remain, the stone plinths mostly empty save for the statue of a turbanned man and the headless form of an elegantly-draped woman. Above these are two sphinxes and further up again is an overgrown grassy platform with a single white-painted replica corner of metal framework, indicating where the structure of the Crystal Palace once stood. The **Crystal Palace TV transmitter** towers above one end of the terrace. John Logie Baird, the inventor of television, had studios here which were lost in the fire (the studios moved to Alexandra Palace; *see p. 401*). The **Crystal Palace Museum** on Anerley Hill is open at weekends. A huge bust of Sir Joseph Paxton by W.F. Woodington (1869) stands at the foot of the terrace steps below the car and coach park. At the time of writing, plans by the Chinese developers Zhong Rong to 'rebuild' the Crystal Palace were being debated and contested.

In the other direction, past the stadium (*signed*), is the **Dinosaur Park**, a pond with an island in its centre, inhabited by concrete models of huge prehistoric creatures designed by Benjamin Waterhouse Hawkins in 1854. They are quite an extraordinary sight. Information boards provide a link to an audio trail.

SOUTH LONDON

Kennington, Walworth, Brixton, Peckham and Camberwell are all south London suburbs, all with distinct characters, none of them destinations in their own right, but all with features of interest.

KENNINGTON

Kennington (*map p. 597, D3; Underground: Oval*) is a scruffy, somewhat down-at-heel part of London. As you emerge from the Underground station, you will see **Kennington Park** in front of you. This was formerly an execution ground and was also a popular public assembly point. The great radical preacher George Whitefield (*see p. 344*) addressed crowds numbering tens of thousands here in 1739. Chartists gathered here in 1848. Opposite rises **St Mark's church**, with its Doric portico and Ionic bell-tower. It is a 'Waterloo' church (*see p. 419*) built by D.R. Roper in 1824. Charlie Chaplin was born in Kennington in 1889, the son of an alcoholic music hall performer who died of dropsy aged 37. The last time his son saw him alive was in the Stag's Head on Kennington Road. The Surrey Cricket Club was established at the **Oval Cricket Ground** in 1845.

In Vassall Road off the Camberwell New Road is the church of **St John the Divine** (G.E. Street 1870–4), admired by Pevsner as one of the best Victorian churches in south London. Today its gates are kept padlocked and unless a service is in progress, it is difficult to get in. The restored spire features gargoyles of prominent public figures, including HM The Queen (clutching a corgi) and the Prince of Wales.

ELEPHANT & CASTLE AND WALWORTH

Elephant and Castle (*map p. 604, C4; Underground: Elephant and Castle*) is the area of south London that spreads around the large and busy traffic roundabout of the same name. The skyline is punctuated by the looming silhouette of **Strata** (*8 Walworth Rd*), a residential skyscraper built in 2010 whose roofline features three large wind turbines. Lauded by some, dismissed as a gimmick by others, the building is not generally greatly liked. Another controversial modern block stands hunkered down on the east side of the roundabout: with its blue balconies, this is Ernő Goldfinger's Alexander Fleming House, which was received with ecstasy in architectural circles in the 1960s, though loathed by those who had to inhabit it. It now goes by the name of **Metro Central Heights**, has been repurposed as a condominium, and its apartments sell for substantial sums.

The **Old Kent Road** (*map p. 605, D4*), formerly the Roman road to Dover, led from the Elephant and Castle to Canterbury. This was the route taken by Chaucer's pilgrims, who halted at 'St Thomas a Watering', now the Thomas à Becket bar and club, open until the small hours, with a salvage-architecture interior (*320 Old Kent Rd, corner of Albany Rd*). Famous boxers once trained in the gym above the pub. Ben Jonson once lived in lodgings on the Old Kent Road.

Walworth is known for its **East Street Market** (*Tues–Fri 8–5, Sat 8–6.30, Sun 8–2; Underground: Elephant & Castle, then walk or bus down Walworth Rd*). Officially the market has been running since 1880, though its origins are much older, from the days of the medieval drovers who would pasture their cattle on Walworth Common. The market sells mainly clothes and market produce.

On Liverpool Grove (*east off Walworth Rd, between East St and Albany Rd; map p. 597, D3*) is **St Peter's church**, built by Sir John Soane in yellow stock brick with an Ionic screen porch (1825). Further south along the Walworth Road is the **Cuming Museum** (*155–157 Walworth Rd; T: 020 7252 2332; closed at the time of writing*), destroyed by fire in 2013, though due to re-open after renovation, thankfully with its collection intact. This small local museum is based on the collection of Richard Cuming (d. 1870) and his son Henry (d. 1902), who between them amassed an eclectic range of nearly 25,000 objects and curios encompassing natural history, ethnography, archaeology, decorative and popular art and British social history. Henry Cuming left the collection to the local borough, together with a sum of money for the employment of a curator, and the museum was opened in 1906 by Lord Rothschild. The 'Billy and Charleys' fakes are medieval pilgrim badges, small shrines and other oddments, forged by William Smith and Charles Eaton, two illiterate mudlarks from Shadwell, who duped the entire country in the 19th century. The museum continues to collect material relevant to the past and recent history of Southwark and its local communities.

BRIXTON

The visit of Nelson Mandela to Brixton (*map p. 597, D3–D4; Underground: Brixton*) in 1996 was a symbolic recognition of the district's role in the struggle for black rights in Britain. The life and culture of Brixton is inextricably associated with the immigrants from the West Indies who came to these shores in the 1940s and '50s, the so-called 'Windrush Generation' (the *Empire Windrush* was a ship which docked in Tilbury, Essex in 1948, with 500 Jamaican passengers aboard). Today around a quarter of Brixton's population is of African and Caribbean descent; there is also a sizeable Portuguese community. The shops, street markets, pubs and restaurants all reflect this ethnic mix. **Brixton Village** (formerly Granville Arcade) contains a wide range of value-for-money coffee shops and boutique eateries, serving a wide range of fresh produce, such as goat curry, jerk chicken with rice and grilled fish.

In its origins, Brixton, in common with other south London suburbs, was a fashionable residential area in the 18th and 19th centuries. Large villas along Brixton Hill and in Angell Town were built for City merchants but the arrival of the railway brought cheaper housing in densely-built terraces. Famous residents include Van Gogh, who lived at 87 Hackford Rd in 1873 (he was 20). Here he fell in love with Eugenie Loyer, the daughter of his landlady, a love unrequited.

Brixton's most famous street is **Electric Avenue**, immortalised in a song of the early 1980s by Guyanese-born Eddie Grant. It took its name from the fact that it was one of the first London streets with electric lighting when it opened in 1888. Though the elegant Victorian canopies and the upmarket department stores, Bon Marché and Quin & Axtens, are long since gone and the street's notoriety as the 'Oxford Street of the south' is a distant memory, there are still remnants of its handsome past, such as the Ritzy Cinema, built in 1910.

Brixton Station Road Market sells food, household goods and more, always lively, with a farmers' market on Sun (*brixtonmarket.net*). **Brixton Windmill** (*Blenheim Gardens, west off Brixton Hill*) was built as a flour mill in 1816 and was in use until 1934. Now restored to working order, it can be visited on open days (*see brixtonwindmill. org*). **Brixton Prison** (1820), in Jebb Avenue off Brixton Hill, once housed a treadmill.

The **Black Heritage Centre** (*at the time of writing due to open on Windrush Square*) has an important collection documenting the history, culture and art of the African and Caribbean diaspora in Britain, particularly rich in oral histories. One of the collection founders was the Jamaica-born historian and educationist Len Garrison (1943–2003), who was determined to reveal the 'hidden history' of Black heritage in Britain. The library of the Runnymede Collection, also scheduled to move here, is the most important archive on multiculturalism and race relations in the country.

Nearby **Brockwell Park and Hall** (20mins' walk; *map p. 597, D4*) provide a leafy retreat. Known as 'Brixton's Beach' from its swimming lido, the Park Estate is graced by a late Georgian mansion in a free Grecian style. It was built by D.R. Roper for John Blades, a glass manufacturer of Ludgate. The grounds are now a public park.

In Stockwell (*map p. 597, D3; Underground: Stockwell*) is the **Type Museum**, exploring man's relationship with the printed word and graphic symbols (*100 Hackford Rd, T: 020 7735 0055, typemuseum.org; closed for refurbishment at the time of writing*).

CAMBERWELL

Camberwell (*map p. 597, D3; trains to Denmark Hill from Victoria or Blackfriars in c. 10mins*), between Brixton and Peckham, is an inner city residential area, once empty and rural and appropriated as a hunting ground by King John. In the 18th century Camberwell was known for its market gardens. Terraced housing development began in the 1780s and in the 19th century the area became a fashionable, middle-class place to live. More recently it has been run-down and deprived, the place where Danny in the cult film *Withnail and I* invents the Camberwell carrot. Today, however, Camberwell has experienced something of a resurgence and many of the Georgian and Victorian properties have been renovated. The area is enriched by the presence of Camberwell College of Arts and two important hospitals: the student buzz extends to a few lively bars and restaurants on Camberwell Church Street. Camberwell also gives its name to the Camberwell Beauty (*Nymphalis antiopa*), a butterfly that only occasionally migrates to British shores.

Camberwell Green, now a traffic island, was the site of fairs from 1279; they rivalled the popular events at Greenwich but were stopped in 1855. In **Denmark Hill** (south from Camberwell Green) are King's College Hospital (founded 1840) and the psychiatric Maudsley Hospital (founded 1923); in Champion Park is the William Booth

Memorial Training College, designed by Sir Giles Gilbert Scott in 1932 with statues of the Salvation Army's founders, General and Mrs Booth, outside. John Ruskin lived at no. 28 Herne Hill, the continuation of Denmark Hill, and also at no. 163 Denmark Hill; both houses have gone but he is commemorated by Ruskin Park.

Some impressions of Camberwell's fashionable past may be glimpsed in **Camberwell Grove**, where the politician Joseph Chamberlain was born in 1836 (at no. 188). The parish church of **St Giles** in Church Street was built in 1844 by Sir George Gilbert Scott on the site of an older church destroyed by fire; it has stained glass designed by John Ruskin (*see above*). On Peckham Road is the **South London Gallery**, known for its programme of contemporary and live art shows (*66–67 Peckham Rd; open Tues–Sun 11–6; café; T: 020 7703 6120, southlondongallery.org*). Robert Browning was born in nearby Southampton Way in 1812.

PECKHAM

Peckham (*map p. 597, E3; trains to Peckham Rye from Victoria in 13mins*) is named after the ancient River Peck. Along with Camberwell it was once a hunting ground of King John and later became an area of market gardens, where melons and figs were grown. Some fine houses were built here in the early 19th century. Thomas Tilling's first omnibus service ran from Peckham to the City in 1851 and the railway arrived in 1862. By the late 20th century, Peckham had become a multi-ethnic neighbourhood, infamous for its complicated traffic system and large estates of council housing providing theatres for gang and gun crime. Today, the London press forecasts gentrification in the form of 'Peckhamania' and waxes enthusiastic about a hip, arty scene with independent bars, restaurants and shops springing up around **Bellenden Road** (a pleasant, quiet area of handsome 19th-century houses just behind Peckham Rye station, bordering East Dulwich). It was around here that Elizabeth Cadbury, Quaker and wife of the chocolate manufacturer, was born. Frank's Campari Bar, on **Rye Lane**, opens during the summer months as a pop-up cocktail bar under a red tarpaulin on the 10th floor of a multi-storey carpark. The branch of the budget clothing store Primark on Rye Lane is by George Coles, designer of Art Deco former cinemas in Kilburn and Islington.

In **Meeting House Lane**, running north from Peckham High Street, stood the Meeting House used by the Quaker William Penn (founder of Pennsylvania) before his fiery tracts led to imprisonment in the Tower in 1668.

Peckham Rye Common, where a young William Blake had a vision of angels, was saved from encroaching developments in 1868. The area has found its way into fiction with Muriel Spark's *The Ballad of Peckham Rye* (1960).

Nunhead Cemetery, between Linden Grove and Limesford Road, was founded in 1840 and is one of the largest of London's Victorian burial grounds. Part of the area is a nature reserve and it has been described as the 'Highgate of the south'. The entrance gates, lodges and Kentish ragstone chapel are by James Bunning. Among the lime trees is buried Thomas Tilling (d. 1893), who pioneered the horse-drawn bus. The Scottish Martyrs' Memorial, an obelisk erected in 1851, commemorates five political reformers (two of them Scots) who were transported to Australia for sedition in 1793.

BATTERSEA, CLAPHAM & WANDSWORTH

Battersea, a former island in the Thames marshes, riverside Wandsworth and lastly Clapham, strung out along a Roman military road with its Georgian houses and famous common, are all residential districts grown up around former villages, estates and farms. Time was when it was a social embarrassment to live south of the river; today the areas are mainly prosperous and sought-after. 'The man on the Clapham omnibus', a term first coined in a legal context in the late 19th century, is taken to stand for the average unexceptional, but reasonable and decent, human being.

BATTERSEA

Map p. 596, C3. Trains to Battersea Park or Queenstown Road from Waterloo in 5–10mins.

Battersea (opposite Chelsea) is an ancient settlement, as indicated by the recovery in 1857 of the Iron Age Battersea Shield (now in the British Museum). Famous landmarks include Battersea Power Station and Battersea Park. Before becoming an industrial area based on the Nine Elms railway yard, Battersea served as a market garden for London; here were fields of watercress and lavender.

The first **Battersea Bridge** was built in the 18th century by Henry Holland; the present iron bridge was built by Bazalgette in the 1880s and replaced the wooden structure depicted in many paintings. Along the Thames here many modern apartment complexes have been built. At the time of writing a pedestrian bridge was planned.

In Old Battersea near the river, on the site of an Anglo Saxon church, stands **St Mary's Church** (Battersea Church Road), built by Joseph Dixon in 1775–6, in yellow brick with classical details. The east window has 17th-century heraldic glass and there are monuments from the earlier church. J.M.W. Turner was inspired to paint his Thames sunset by the view from the church window, and the poet William Blake married the daughter of a local market gardener here in 1792. The manor house which stood next to the church is now demolished. The Vicarage and Devonshire House are attractive 18th-century houses. In Vicarage Crescent is the 17th-century Old Battersea House. Battersea Square has upmarket shops and restaurants.

BATTERSEA PARK

Battersea Park (*open 8am–dusk; boats for hire in summer; fountain displays spring–autumn*) occupies the long riverside stretch between Albert Bridge and Chelsea Bridge. The 200-acre park has attractive gardens, a children's zoo and a boating lake, and hosts regular antiques fairs and art exhibitions. Before it was landscaped in the mid-19th century, it was notorious as Battersea Fields, according to one commentator 'a place that surpassed Sodom and Gomorrah in ungodliness and abomination', filled with illicit drinking dens frequented by such inveterate imbibers as Charles Dickens. Also here, in 1829, the Duke of Wellington fought a duel with the Earl of Winchilsea

BATTERSEA POWER STATION

over the subject of Catholic emancipation. The area became the centre for the new craze for bicycling in the 1890s and in 1951 was laid out as pleasure gardens for the Festival of Britain. The Victorian Pump House (1861) is now a contemporary art space. The Peace Pagoda, with wind-bells, overlooking the Thames, was erected by Japanese Buddhists in 1985. The park now includes a Herb Garden, Old English Garden and Winter Garden. Barbara Hepworth's *Single Form* (beside the lake) was made in commemoration of Dag Hammarskjöld, the UN Secretary General who was killed in an air crash in 1961. On the north side of the lake is Henry Moore's *Three Standing Figures*. There is a café on the east shore, La Gondola al Parco. The *Brown Dog* statue (Geraldine James, 1985), north of the English Garden, is a replacement for an earlier monument to a brown terrier who died in the vivisection laboratories of University College. The statue was destroyed by vivisectionists in 1907.

BATTERSEA POWER STATION

The four white chimneys of **Battersea Power Station**, east of Chelsea Bridge, dominate the river skyline from many aspects. Although now the structure has achieved iconic status, it caused widespread public dismay when it opened in 1933, because of fears of pollution as well as its gigantic size. This 'Temple of Power' was designed by Sir Giles Gilbert Scott. Its four fluted chimneys are 335ft high. At the time of writing the derelict building was finally being redeveloped, to open as a residential complex.

At the former railway yard at Nine Elms is the **new Covent Garden Market**. The famous produce market moved here from central London in 1974. It now houses wholesale traders.

Battersea Dogs' Home, on Battersea Park Road, takes in over 20,000 stray dogs and cats a year and finds new homes for them.

CLAPHAM

Map p. 596, C3–C4. Underground: Clapham Common, Clapham South, Clapham North. Trains to Clapham Junction from Victoria and Waterloo in 10mins.

In the last 20 years Clapham has become a desirable residential area and there are 'villagey' pockets of thriving independent bars, restaurants, shops and boutiques: look in Northcote Road, Battersea Rise, St John's Hill, Clapham High Street and Clapham Old Town. In Clapham South, **Abbeville Road** has become a little enclave in its own right, filled with restaurants and referred to as 'Abbeville Village'.

    Clapham Common is recorded in the Domesday Book. It covers 220 acres and has never been cultivated. Once it was notorious as a cruising ground (in the 18th century the phrase 'been to Hadham and come home by Clapham' was slang for contracting gonorrhea). Today it is used for sports, fairs and circuses; the bandstand has been restored. Around its perimeter are some attractive private houses dating back to the late 18th and early 19th centuries, when Clapham was 'a pretty suburb' (according to Thackeray). Samuel Pepys retired to Clapham and lived in a house in North Side, overlooking the Common, until his death in 1703; the mansion was demolished in 1754. On the site of no. 29, formerly 'The Elms', the architect Charles Barry lived, and died in 1860. In the plain brick church of the **Holy Trinity** (Kenton Couse, 1774), the Clapham Sect, a group of evangelical Christians who counted anti-slavery campaigner William Wilberforce among their number, met in the 19th century. **Clapham Junction** is the busiest railway junction in the UK.

WANDSWORTH

Map p. 596, C4. Underground: East Putney; trains to Wandsworth Town from Waterloo in c. 15mins.

Wandsworth takes its name from the River Wandle, whose delta was first settled in the Bronze Age. The river was much exploited for industry: in the 18th century the arrival of Huguenot refugees led to a great growth in textile manufacture here; the Wandle came to support some 65 water mills between Wandsworth and Merton to the south. Bleaching, dyeing and brewing were carried on here and there were also iron and copper foundries. The last brewery, Young & Co's Ram Brewery, closed in 2006, after 425 years. Today the riverside around **Wandsworth Bridge** (Thomas Peirson Frank, 1940) has been developed with modern apartment complexes and the riverside walk to Battersea has been opened up. The Ship Inn is an 18th-century pub with a river terrace. The Victorian streets behind Wandsworth Town station are attractive and gentrified and there are expensive pockets around East Hill, Spencer Park and St John's Hill, all with independent shops, bars and restaurants. The **Royal Victoria Patriotic Building**, a huge, mid-19th-century neo-Gothic former asylum by Rohde Hawkins, dominates the northern edge of Wandsworth Common; Rudolf Hess was interned here for a time during World War Two. The history of the area can be further explored at the **Wandsworth Museum** (*38 West Hill; open Tues–Fri 11–4, Sat 11–5; admission charge; café and shop; T: 020 8870 6060, wandsworthmuseum.co.uk*), in a late Georgian mansion. The **De Morgan Foundation Collection** of paintings and ceramics by the Arts and Crafts artists William and Evelyn de Morgan is housed in the same building.

EATING AND DRINKING IN SOUTHEAST AND SOUTH LONDON

BATTERSEA, CLAPHAM, WANDSWORTH

There are some good restaurants on Northcote Rd and Battersea Rise, between Wandsworth and Clapham commons (*map p. 596, C4*). £ **Lola Rojo** serves superb tapas (*78 Northcote Rd, T: 020 7350 2262, lolarojo.net*). £ **The Breakfast Club** serves breakfasts from 8pm and continues dishing up until the evening (*5–9 Battersea Rise, T: 020 7078 9630, thebreakfastclubcafes.com*). Cheap pizzas are the stock in trade of the lively £ **Buona Sera** (*22 Northcote Rd*). ££ **Soif** serves good Mediterranean-inspired cuisine (*27 Battersea Rise, T: 020 7223 1112, soif.co; closed Mon midday and Sun eve*). On the south side of Wandsworth Common is the Michelin-starred French-influenced ££–£££ **Chez Bruce** (*2 Bellevue Rd, T: 020 8672 0114, chezbruce.co.uk; map p. 596, C4*). £ **The Ship** is a pleasant riverside pub by Wandsworth Bridge (*41 Jews Row, theship.co.uk*). £ **Bradys** on Smugglers Way serves good fish and chips (*bradysfish.co.uk; map p. 596, C4*). East of Clapham Common is the £–£££ **Abeville Kitchen**, with a modern European menu (*47 Abbeville Rd, T: 020 8772 1110, abbevillekitchen.com; map p. 596, C4*).

CAMBERWELL, HERNE HILL

£ **The Florence**. A good place for a Sunday roast, if you are in the area (Herne Hill, right opposite the north side of Brockwell Park). Open daily. *131–133 Dulwich Rd. T: 020 7326 4987, florenceherne hill.com. Map p. 597, D4.*

££ **Camberwell Arms**. Camberwell's best gastro pub. Operates the same no-reservations policy as its sister establishment the Anchor and Hope at Waterloo. Good food and wine. Open daily (kitchen closes 4pm Sun). *65 Camberwell Church St (between Camberwell New Rd and Peckham Rd; map p. 597, D3). thecamberwellarms. co.uk.*

CRYSTAL PALACE

Between Crystal Palace and Gipsy Hill is the so-called 'Crystal Palace Triangle', formed of Church Road, Westow Street and Westow Hill. The best restaurants are located here (*map p. 597, D4*). The £–££ **Crystal Palace Market** (*3–7 Church Rd, T: 020 3475 7080, the crystalpalacemarket.com*) offers good fresh fish, burgers and more (choose what you want and they will cook it for you), and the pop-up stall **Margosa Dining** serves authentic Sri Lankan curries made to a secret spice blend.

£–££ The Alma. Refurbished pub with good food. Open daily. *95 Church Rd. T: 020 8768 1885, thealmapub.com.*

£ The Sparrowhawk. Another fine pub, known for its duck confit and its sharing platters. Open daily. *2 Westow Hill. T: 020 8761 4831, thesparrowhawkpub.co.uk.*

£–££ Joanna's. An old Crystal Palace favourite, in business for many years. Good for steaks and celebrations. Open daily. *56 Westow Hill. T: 020 8670 4052, www.joannasuk.com.*

£ Tamnag Thai. Very good Thai restaurant with wonderful interior decorations: Buddha statues, temple lamps and upside-down parasols on the ceiling. Open daily. *50–54 Westow Hill. T: 020 8761 5959, tamnangthai.com.*

In the railway station is **£ Brown & Green**, a good brunch café where you can eat in or buy food to take away.

DULWICH

££ Belair House. Fine, glamorous dining (midday and evening) in an equally fine 18th-century villa by Richard Shaw. Closed Mon. *Gallery Rd. T: 020 8299 9788, belairhouse.co.uk. Map p. 597, D4.*

£ Crown and Greyhound. If you're ticking off all the places where Dickens lifted a glass, this is one of them. The drinks menu might have been more traditional in his day. Now they offer potato vodka and hot buttered lemonade. Food too. Open daily. *73 Dulwich Village. T: 020 8299 4979, thecrownandgreyhound.co.uk. Map p. 597, D4.*

Gail's Artisan Bakery is one of a chain, even though its homey name suggests otherwise—but it is a pleasant place for tea (in a pot) and cake. Open daily (*91 Dulwich Village, gailsbread. co.uk*).

£ Rocca offers pasta, pizza and other Italian favourites. *75–79 Dulwich Village. T: 020 8299 6333, roccarestaurants.com. Map p. 597, D4.*

GREENWICH

££ Inside. *The* place to eat in Greenwich, according to the food guides and Greenwich locals. Delicious Modern European dishes and friendly service. Closed Mon. No dinner Sun. *19 Greenwich South St. T: 020 8265 5060, insiderestaurant.co.uk. Map p. 593, B4.*

£–££ Trafalgar Tavern. The upstairs dining room is airy and pleasant, with good river views. Whitebait is still on the menu, as it has been since the 19th century. Open daily (kitchen closes 4pm Sun). *Park Row. T: 020 8858 2909, trafalgartavern.co.uk. Map p. 593, C3.*

£ Heap's Sausage and Café. Martin Heap is passionate about sausages— and he makes extremely fine ones. Here you can see how it's done, buy fresh ones to take away, or eat in at the café. *8 Nevada St. T: 020 8293 9199, heapssausages.com. Map p. 593, B4.*

ROTHERHITHE

£ The Mayflower. Lovely, friendly old pub: a real sailors' snug inside, with an airy upstairs dining room overlooking the river and a beer garden terrace. Dates back to the 17th century. Close to the Brunel Museum (*map p. 597, E3*). Open daily (closes 8pm Sun). *117 Rotherhithe St. T: 020 7237 4088, themayflowerrotherhithe.com.*

The Southwest & West

The southwest of London comprises largely attractive and affluent suburbs, both north and south of the river, stretching from Hammersmith to Twickenham. All have points of great historic interest.

Hectic Hammersmith, and Chiswick with its lovely vestiges, are both situated on the north bank of the Thames. To the south are riverside Barnes, Putney and Mortlake, Wimbledon with its famous tennis courts and Richmond with its equally celebrated deer park. The Heathrow flight path is very apparent in this part of London: jets fly low in rapid succession over Isleworth, Kew and Richmond.

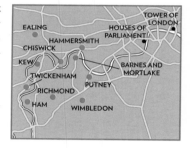

HAMMERSMITH

Map p. 596, B3. Underground: Hammersmith.

Hammersmith is a busy commercial and residential suburb on the A4, the Great West Road out of London. The concrete 1960s' Hammersmith Flyover dominates the centre, causing optimists to liken Hammersmith to downtown Manhattan. Several international blue chip companies have their headquarters here and Hammersmith supports two Underground stations (Hammersmith & City and Circle lines and Piccadilly and District lines), a major bus terminus and a shopping mall (Broadway Centre), two theatres (the Lyric and Riverside Studios), a music and comedy venue (HMV Apollo), several historic buildings and an attractive stretch of riverside townhouses, boating clubs and pubs. The influential River Café, an Italian restaurant co-founded by Rose Rogers (wife of architect Richard Rogers, whose firm's practice is nearby) and the late Ruth Grey, is south of Hammersmith Broadway on Thames Wharf (*see p. 511*).

King Street, the main local shopping parade, leads west and eventually becomes the Chiswick High Road. Further north, at 27 Stamford Brook Rd, is the house where Lucien Pissarro, son of Camille, lived. It became a meeting place for artists of the day, including Sickert, William Rotherstein, Charles Ricketts and Charles Shannon.

ST PAUL'S CHURCH

On one side of the flyover stands **The Ark** (*201 Talgarth Rd*), a striking office building in the shape of a plate-glass boat, designed by Ralph Erskine and built by Swedish developers Åke Larsson (1991). In the other direction, in Queen Caroline Street, is **St Paul's Church** (*sph.org*). Dating to 1883, it has recently been heavily restored and a modern extension added with café, bookshop and meeting rooms to accommodate the needs of the swelling evangelical congregation. The entrance to the church is through the café and the combination of carpeted interior, electric musical instruments and amplifiers in front of the altar and walls lined with solemn Neoclassical monuments, is unexpected. On the north wall is a memorial to the civil engineer William Tierney Clark, who built the first Hammersmith Bridge and contributed much to Hammersmith's 19th-century infrastructure. The carved pulpit is from Wren's All Hallows, Thames Street. In the northwest corner, by glass doors leading to the porch, is a bust of Charles I, erected by the pioneering Royalist merchant trader Nicholas Crisp (d. 1666), who built the first chapel on the site. Upon his instructions, his embalmed heart was buried in the urn below the bust to be taken out each year and refreshed with wine. His heart has since been reunited with his remains elsewhere. The marble egg-cup font in the porch is from Crisp's chapel.

Bradmore House (facing St Paul's Church) has a 17th-century façade which was restored in the 1990s. Original panelling from the house is in the Geffrye Museum in Shoreditch. It now houses a Chinese restaurant offering an all-you-can-eat buffet.

HAMMERSMITH BRIDGE AND THE RIVERSIDE WALK

Green-painted **Hammersmith Bridge**, London's first suspension bridge, was originally designed in 1824–7 by William Tierney Clark (who went on to design Budapest's Chain Bridge across the Danube). It soon became a popular vantage point from which to view the annual Oxford and Cambridge boat race. When it became too small for the volume of traffic, it was dismantled and the present structure was built by Sir Joseph Bazalgette in 1887. It incorporates piers and abutments of Tierney Clark's bridge.

Westwards from the bridge, the Thames Path forms a pleasant two-mile walk towards Chiswick. The **Blue Anchor pub** was founded in 1722 and was where Gustav Holst composed part of his *Hammersmith Suite*. Further on, **Furnival Gardens** provide breathing space between the river and the constant traffic of the Great West Road. Named after the social reformer and scholar Dr F.J. Furnivall (d. 1910), whose eponymous sculling club was based nearby, the gardens and small pier were built in 1951 to commemorate the Festival of Britain and to cover what was once 'Little Wapping', Hammersmith's old wharf. There was once a busy creek here, where Stamford Brook joined the Thames, allowing barges to sail as far as King Street at high tide. Opposite, across the main road, stands the Art Deco **Hammersmith Town Hall** (E. Berry Webber, 1939). Note the double staircase flanked by sculptures of Old Father Thames. A pedestrian underpass allows closer access.

The small paved alley with an entrance to the 18th-century **Dove Inn** is all that remains of old Hammersmith. The pub, once a coffee house, boasts being the smallest in London and is reputedly where Charles II had assignations with Nell Gwyn. It is

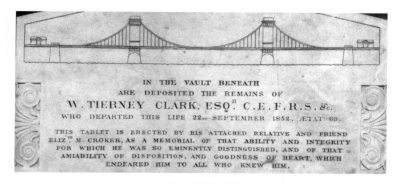

IN THE VAULT BENEATH
ARE DEPOSITED THE REMAINS OF
W. TIERNEY CLARK, ESQ^R C.E. F.R.S. &c.
WHO DEPARTED THIS LIFE 22ND SEPTEMBER 1852, ÆTAT 69.

THIS TABLET IS ERECTED BY HIS ATTACHED RELATIVE AND FRIEND
ELIZTH M. CROKER, AS A MEMORIAL OF THAT ABILITY AND INTEGRITY
FOR WHICH HE WAS SO EMINENTLY DISTINGUISHED, AND OF THAT
AMIABILITY OF DISPOSITION, AND GOODNESS OF HEART, WHICH
ENDEARED HIM TO ALL WHO KNEW HIM.

HAMMERSMITH
Plaque in St Paul's church to William Tierney Clark, who
built the first Hammersmith Bridge.

also where Thomas Arne composed 'Rule Britannia'. If you can get a place (*T: 020 8748 9474*), the balcony affords a good aspect of the river. The other half of the building was where the **Doves Press** was located and a blue plaque commemorates this. Founded in 1900 by Thomas Cobden-Sanderson and Emery Walker (*see 7 Hammersmith Terrace below*), friends of William Morris, the Doves Press was renowned for its unique font, the Doves Type, which was used in its Arts and Crafts publications, including the Doves Bible. When the press closed in 1916, Cobden-Sanderson destroyed the type by throwing the blocks into the Thames from Hammersmith Bridge.

The alley leads into Upper Mall. William Morris lived at no. 26, **Kelmscott House**, from 1878–96 and died there; he named the house after his country home in Oxfordshire. The basement is home to the William Morris Society and lectures and events take place here. Earlier it was home to Sir Francis Ronald, inventor of the telegraph (part of his original telegraph is in the Science Museum). Catherine of Braganza, wife of Charles II, lived in a house (now demolished) on Rivercourt Road after the death of her husband. Latymer Preparatory School (*36 Upper Mall*) stands on part of the site.

Some way further on, **Linden House** (c. 1730) is home to the London Corinthian Sailing Club and the Sons of the Thames Rowing Club.

Continuing close to the Thames, you come to the **Old Ship Inn** (17th century and rebuilt 1850) and the **Black Lion pub** (c. 1793), standing on either side of what was the West Middlesex Waterworks (1906), also designed by Tierney Clark. Water was once pumped under the Thames from reservoirs across the river in Barnes. Both pubs have extensive outdoor seating overlooking the Thames and are popular all year round, but especially in good weather.

The path now doglegs into **Hammersmith Terrace**, a row of mid-18th-century townhouses. The English Arts and Crafts typographer and friend of William Morris,

Emery Walker, lived at no. 7 and the interior has been preserved as it was in his lifetime (*for further information and to book a tour, see emerywalker.org.uk*). Another typographer lived at no. 3: Edward Johnston (1872–1944) who, in 1916, created the typeface still used (in a variant form) by London Underground.

CHISWICK

Map p. 596, A3–B3. Trains to Chiswick from Waterloo in c. 25mins. Underground: Turnham Green then 20mins' walk, or to Hammersmith and then along the Riverside Walk. Bus 190 from Hammersmith Broadway.

Old Chiswick, by the river, is hemmed in by the busy A4. Historically a rural community of fishermen, watermen and farmers (Chiswick means 'Cheese Farm' in Old English), its idyllic setting made it popular as a country retreat for wealthy Londoners from the 16th century.

CHISWICK MALL

The riverside walk from Hammersmith continues into Chiswick Mall. Despite close proximity to the relentless main road, the setting is tranquil with views of Barnes's wooded towpath on the opposite bank. Elegant 17th–19th-century villas line the cobbled street, many covered in climbing plants such as honeysuckle and wisteria. Their lush private gardens are along the water's edge on the opposite side of the road (residents usually open their gardens to the public once a year in the spring). Parts of the Mall are unembanked and can flood during high tide (it is not uncommon to see swans swimming along it)—which is worth bearing in mind if driving or parking a car.

Walpole House, one of the finest villas on the Mall, was the home of Barbara Villiers, Duchess of Cleveland, Charles II's mistress, who died here in 1709, and is a fine example of the Restoration period. It was named after a later resident, the Hon. Thomas Walpole (d. 1803), nephew of Sir Robert Walpole, 1st Earl of Orford, the first Prime Minister of Great Britain. Walpole House later became a school and one of its pupils was the novelist William Makepeace Thackeray. Thackeray is said to have based Miss Pinkerton's Seminary for Young Ladies in his novel *Vanity Fair* upon Walpole House.

On **Chiswick Eyot** (pronounced 'eight'), a small island in the Thames, osier willows were cultivated for basket-making until the 1930s.

Award-winning beer and real ale, such as Chiswick Bitter and London Pride, are brewed at **Fuller's Griffin Brewery** (Chiswick Lane). Beer has been brewed on this site for over 350 years. Tours start in the brewery's pub, the Mawson Arms, where Alexander Pope once stayed (*tours Mon–Fri, approx. 2hrs with tasting afterwards, advance booking essential; fullers.co.uk, T: 020 8996 2175*).

The famous Thornycroft boatyard was on **Church Wharf** (now 1980s' townhouses) and the first torpedo gunboat with a water tube boiler (HMS *Speedy*) was built here in 1893 (she fell victim to a mine in the North Sea in 1914).

At the end of the Mall stands the parish church, dedicated to **St Nicholas**, patron saint of sailors and fisherman. It was rebuilt in the 1880s but the tower is from the 15th century. The churchyard contains William Hogarth's tomb (d. 1764; clearly visible on the left-hand side up the flight of steps), which is marked by a pedestal and urn with a palette and brushes on the side. The weathered epitaph, by Garrick, reads:

Farewell great Painter of Mankind
Who reach'd the noblest point of Art
Whose pictur'd Morals charm the Mind
And through the Eye correct the Heart.

Nearby is the bronze tomb chest of the artist Whistler (d. 1903). Two of Oliver Cromwell's daughters are buried here without monuments—as are, according to some, the headless remains of Oliver Cromwell himself (*for the fate of his head, see p. 142*). Also in the graveyard lies Henry Joy (d. 1893) the trumpeter who sounded the Charge of the Light Brigade.

CHURCH STREET AND THE HOGARTH ROUNDABOUT

The notorious 18th-century highwayman Dick Turpin is reputed to have frequented **The Old Burlington** on Church Street, an Elizabethan building, once the Burlington Arms tavern. Church Street leads to the congested Hogarth Roundabout. The construction of the Great Western Road (A4) was proposed in the 1930s but abandoned after strong local opposition. After the area sustained extensive bomb damage in World War Two, the planning finally went ahead in the 1950s, ripping through this part of historic Chiswick. Left off the roundabout is the tiny **Chiswick Square** (1680s), with Boston House (1740s) at its centre. A plaque on one wall states that 'into this garden Thackeray in "Vanity Fair" describes Becky Sharp as throwing the dictionary'. The claim to fame as the original Miss Pinkerton's Academy is disputed with Walpole House (*see above*). On Hogarth Lane is **Hogarth's House** (*map p. 596, B3; open Tues–Sun and bank holidays 12–5; free; T: 020 8994 6757*), a modest, Queen Anne building, fragile and small amid the traffic. This is the 'little country box by the Thames' that Hogarth used as a summer retreat from 1749–64. A high wall surrounds the house and garden, where a mulberry tree from Hogarth's day survives. A fire in 2009 mercifully destroyed little, and the house contains Hogarth's palette, paintbox and punchbowl as well as prints and engravings. *The Man of Taste* mocks Lord Burlington and his favourite decorative painter, William Kent (who, through Burlington's promotion of him, won commissions from Hogarth's father-in-law, Sir James Thornhill). Burlington's support of Italianate art was a favourite subject of Hogarth's needling wit. His Palladian mansion (Chiswick House) is in the park just to the southwest.

CHISWICK HOUSE

Map p 596, B3. Burlington Lane. Trains to Chiswick from Clapham Junction or 15mins' walk from Turnham Green, Chiswick Park or Gunnersbury Tube. House open April–Oct

Sun–Wed 10–5, at other times by appointment. Admission charge. Gardens open daily 7–dusk, free. Café. T: 020 8995 0508), chgt.org.uk.

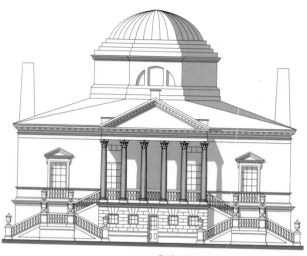

CHISWICK HOUSE: ENTRANCE FAÇADE

Chiswick House is the greatest architectural statement of Richard Boyle, 3rd Earl of Burlington (1694–1753), the early 18th-century 'Apollo of the Arts'. Heavily influenced by the architecture of ancient Rome and that of Palladio, which he had seen on his tours of Italy (returning from the second trip in 1719), as well as the architecture of the great Inigo Jones, Burlington conceived Chiswick as an embodiment of his architectural ideals. The villa, with ornate interiors and Jonesian ceilings painted by Burlington's protégé William Kent, was originally attached to the estate's Jacobean mansion (since demolished) and was used as a temple of the Arts, an intellectual retreat where Burlington displayed his fine pictures and sculptures and entertained friends, including the poet Alexander Pope. On Burlington's death the estate passed via his daughter to Lord Hartington, later 4th Duke of Devonshire. Throughout the 18th and 19th centuries the house was a centre of English social life. In 1809 Charles James Fox died here and Edward VII, as Prince of Wales, spent time here, as did the Tsars of Russia. The Chiswick estate remained with the Dukes of Devonshire until 1929. Burlington's pictures and much of the furniture designed for the house by Kent have either been dispersed or are in the Devonshire collection at Chatsworth. Several loans from the latter, however, and the odd chance purchase of important pieces original to the house, give a sense of the villa as it was in its 1730s' heyday.

Palladio's Villa Rotonda outside Vicenza is usually cited as the main inspirational source, but in fact the villa is Burlington's own unique interpretation of several models. The central octagonal dome is flanked by four chimney stacks in the shape of obelisks, while an elaborate double staircase rises to the first-floor entrance, under a crisply carved Corinthian portico. At the foot of the staircase, to either side, are statues by J.M. Rysbrack (c. 1730) of Burlington's architectural heroes, Palladio and Inigo Jones.

INTERIOR OF THE VILLA

A sequence of nine rooms of a studied, intellectual magnificence is arranged around the octagonal domed **Upper Tribune**, with light flooding in from its Diocletian windows, its walls punctuated by four pedimented doorways, based on Jones designs. Classical busts sit on gilded brackets and above them hang large pictures from Burlington's collection. They include *Charles I and his Family*, after Van Dyck; *Liberality and Modesty*, after Veronese; *Louis XIII and Anne of Austria* by Poussin's master Ferdinand Elle; and Kneller's *The Moroccan Ambassador* (1684), an equestrian portrait of Mohammed Ohadu, famous for his displays of horsemanship in Hyde Park.

The **Gallery** runs the full length of the garden front and is one of the most important rooms in the house. A tripartite space with a rectangular, apsed centre, with flanking circular and octagonal cabinets, it is a rigorously controlled architectural enfilade. The actual dimensions are small but an effect of grandeur is achieved through the skilfully judged proportions and the richly carved and ornamented surfaces, decorated in white and gold. The ceiling painting is a copy of Veronese's *Defence of Smyrna*, attributed to Sebastiano Ricci, who also decorated Burlington's townhouse (now the Royal Academy; *see p. 213*). The surrounding ceiling panels, within compartments with ornamentation derived from Jones, are by Kent. The magnificent carved and gilded marble-topped tables, designed by Kent, were made for the house in 1730.

The **Green Velvet Room**, with marble chimneypieces based on Jones designs, contains eight charming paintings of the gardens commissioned by Burlington from Pieter Andreas Rysbrack, brother of the sculptor. The **Blue Velvet Room** has an elaborate ceiling design with console brackets with Kent's *Architecture* in the centre. The carved and gilded pedimented doorways are surmounted by portraits, held by putti, including Inigo Jones by William Dobson and Pope by Kent.

THE GARDENS

The gardens at Chiswick mark a departure from the intricate, formal designs of the Baroque age in the direction of a more 'natural' landscape, with semi-contrived wildernesses, lakes and groves and expansive vistas, dotted with statuary. They have been hailed as the founders of the Landscape Movement, the inspiration for New York's Central Park and much besides. In the early 1730s, Kent was hired to complete for Burlington a suburban retreat. Many of the features can still be seen, including the broad avenue lined with urns and sphinxes, culminating in a semicircular exedra, originally of myrtle but now of yew, framing casts of Roman busts (originals inside the villa) of Caesar, Pompey and Cicero. The bridge over the canal was built by James Wyatt in 1774. At the canal's south end is the Cascade, two triple-arched storeys of rough masonry down which water flows. North of the house is the Inigo Jones Gateway, brought to Chiswick from Beaufort House, Chelsea in 1736, a gift of Sir Hans Sloane and the subject of a verse by Pope. The conservatory, added in the early 18th century, is famous for its camellias.

KEW

Map p. 596, A3. Underground: Kew Gardens. River boats from Westminster Pier in c. 90mins (no service in winter; for details, see p. 541).

Kew owes both its botanic garden and the attractive village setting at Kew Green to the existence of nearby Richmond Palace. The handsome 18th-century houses surrounding the quintessentially English village green, where cricket is sometimes played, were built for members of the King's Court when the Hanoverian royal family made Kew their home. The main gate to Kew Gardens is here.

The parish church of **St Anne's** dates to 1714; Queen Anne granted the plot of land on which it is built. Buried here are the painters Thomas Gainsborough (d. 1788) and John Zoffany (d. 1810), as well as Jeremiah Meyer, miniature painter to Queen Charlotte, and Francis Bauer, George III's botanical artist.

In Ruskin Avenue are the **National Archives** (formerly the Public Record Office), holding documents pertaining to a thousand years of British history, including the Domesday Book. The public may visit free of charge (*Tues–Sat; nationalarchives.gov. uk*) to consult original documents; only five percent of the records are online.

ROYAL BOTANIC GARDENS

Entrances are on three sides: the Main Gate is on Kew Green; Victoria Gate is entered from Kew Road (a short walk from the Tube station). The Lion Gate is south of Victoria Gate and the Brentford Gate is on the Thames side, access from Ferry Lane. Gardens open daily from 9.30; closing time varies according to season, approx. 4pm in winter, 6pm in summer. Tickets on the gate or online: kew.org. Cafés and restaurants.

Kew's splendid 300-acre gardens, with glorious seasonal displays, both wild and exotic, occupy a bend in the Thames between Kew and Richmond. They contain the largest and most diverse botanical collections in the world and grow over 30,000 species of plant and 9,000 species of tree; some of the rarest are under cover in the magnificent Victorian glasshouses. The herbarium preserves seven million plant specimens for study. Kew is internationally recognised as a centre of botanical research and scientific excellence and is a world leader in plant conservation. Its 'unique cultural landscape', with several listed historic buildings, including Kew Palace, has been recognised as a UNESCO World Heritage site.

> ### HISTORY OF KEW GARDENS
> The history of the gardens is really an amalgamation of several royal initiatives added to and enriched by successive generations, but it is generally accepted that the foundations of the botanic gardens were laid in the 1750s when Augusta, Dowager Princess of Wales and mother of George III, was living on the estate and developed a nine-acre garden around the White House, a Palladian villa by William Kent,

that stood opposite what is now known as Kew Palace. Sir William Aiton was her head gardener and Sir William Chambers the architect. Over six years he built 25 ornamental buildings. Some of these mid-18th-century follies survive, including the Pagoda, the Orangery, the Ruined Arch, the Temple of Bellona and the Temple of Arethusa. The site was considerably enlarged by George III, who combined it with the Richmond Lodge estate and employed 'Capability' Brown to remodel the Old Deer Park. He and Queen Charlotte frequently stayed at Kew Palace (formerly the Dutch House). Sir Joseph Banks, who accompanied Captain Cook on his round-the-world voyage, was gardener from 1772–1819, when plants were collected and cultivated from South Africa, Australia and the Pacific. In 1841 the now extensive Kew Gardens were handed to the nation and expanded to 300 acres. In the same year, Sir William Hooker became Director of the new National Botanic Institute and the Royal Botanic Gardens.

Among Kew's historic achievements were the introduction of the bread fruit tree to the West Indies in 1791 (the purpose of the *Bounty* voyage), quinine to India in 1860 and rubber trees to Malaysia and Sri Lanka in the 1870s; in the late 19th century Kew played an important part in restoring the European wine-growing industry with imported American rootstock, after vines were destroyed by phylloxera.

KEW PALACE

The red-brick building (*admission free with a Kew Gardens admission ticket; closed Nov–April*) is a fine example of the 'artisan mannerist' style popular in the early 17th century and worthy of comparison with Forty Hall (*see p. 403*). A royal residence from the early 18th century, it is all that remains of George II and George III's palace at Kew. Formerly known as the Dutch House, it was built in 1631 for Samuel Fortrey, a City of London merchant of Flemish descent. The date is carved in the brickwork above the door, as are Fortrey's initials, entwined with those of his wife in a lover's knot. By the mid-18th century this fine three-storey villa, with its rubbed brickwork and Dutch gables, was being used as an annexe to the royal residence known as the White House or Kew House, built in the 1730s by Frederick, Prince of Wales. It was the childhood home of George III and later the nursery for his own children and his retreat during the onset of his nervous disorder, porphyria. Fanny Burney, Assistant Mistress of the Robes to King George's beloved wife, Queen Charlotte, wrote in 1786 that 'the Royal family are here always in so very retired a way, that they live as the simplest gentlefolks.' Queen Charlotte spent the last six months of her life here in 1818, a year in which the palace also saw the marriages of two of her sons, the middle-aged Dukes of Clarence and Kent. The latter married Princess Victoria of Saxe-Coburg and their daughter later became Queen Victoria, who opened the palace to the public in 1899. The palace has recently undergone an extensive programme of restoration and re-presentation. The façade has been re-covered with its distinctive red ochre wash over the Flemish-bond brickwork. Inside, the focus is on the turn of the 19th century, when the house was most frequently in use by George III, Queen Charlotte and their children. Welcoming guides greet the visitor wearing period costume, mob caps etc., and in the majority of rooms jarring audio aids play on a continuous loop,

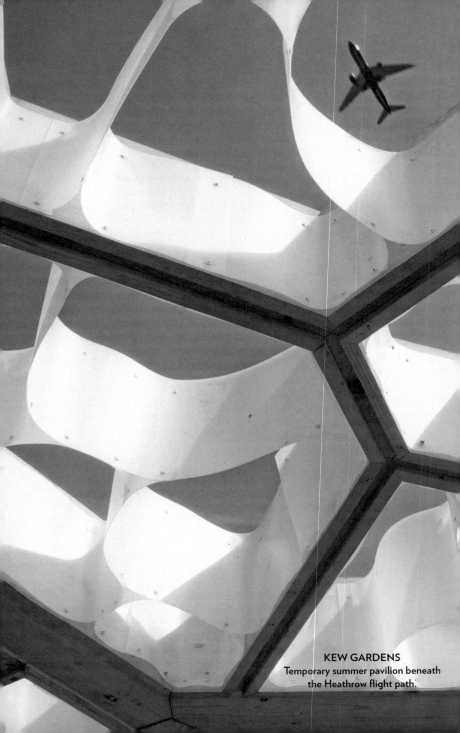

KEW GARDENS
Temporary summer pavilion beneath
the Heathrow flight path.

narrating the history of George III and his family at Kew; the voices assume German accents when playing royalty, northern English accents when playing their servants. Notwithstanding all this there are attractions, and these include a waxwork of George III taken from Madame Tussaud's life cast; the shirt he wore during his illness; and a 1780s' dolls' house with tiny embroidered furnishings made by George III's daughters. The wallpaper, carpets and curtains have been recreated from surviving fragments and contemporary descriptions, and the 18th-century brass door locks, engraved with the crest of Frederick, Prince of Wales, have been preserved. The second floor, where the princesses stayed, has been reopened for the first time in 200 years; the suites of wood-panelled rooms, left bare, afford good views of the Thames.

Behind the palace is the **Queen's Garden**, created in 17th-century style. Nearby are the recently restored **Royal Kitchens**, built in the 1730s to cater to Frederick, Prince of Wales and the royal family when they stayed here. The rusty hip bath in the silver scullery is alleged to have been used by George III. The **Orangery** (now a restaurant) was built by Chambers in 1761.

QUEEN CHARLOTTE'S COTTAGE AND THE PAGODA

Queen Charlotte's Cottage, on the other side of the gardens about a mile from Kew Palace, is a quaint cottage with a thatched roof. It was contrived and built by Queen Charlotte in 1771 as a rustic retreat. Here the royal family would come for breakfasts, picnics and to take tea. In the upstairs Picnic Room the walls, ceiling and door frames are naïvely rendered as an arbour of nasturtiums and convolvulus. The artist is believed to have been Princess Elizabeth, a daughter of George III and Queen Charlotte, who painted similar decoration at Frogmore House, Windsor in 1805. The Cottage once overlooked a menagerie which had kangaroos in the 1790s; today the wooded grounds are a misty sea of flowering bluebells in May.

The ten-storey **Pagoda**, 164ft high, in the corner near the Lion Gate, was built by Sir William Chambers in 1761 as a surprise for Princess Augusta. It is built to one of the designs Chambers brought back to England after his journey to China. Near to the Pagoda once stood a wooden painted folly, the Gothic Cathedral, designed by Johann Heinrich Müntz, who was also employed for a time by Walpole at Strawberry Hill.

THE GLASSHOUSES

Kew's collection of spectacular glasshouses is deservedly world-famous; between them they house four acres of the gardens and some of the rarest plants.

Near the Pagoda, the enormous **Temperate House** was designed by Decimus Burton. Building started in 1860 but was not completed until 1898. It is planted according to geographical zone: Australasia, the Americas, South Africa, New Zealand and Asia. In the centre, the huge Chilean wine-palm (*Jubaea chilensis*) was raised from seed in 1846. *Encephalartos woodii*, a type of cycad, is the rarest plant at Kew; it is extinct in the wild. The challenge is to get it to cone because in the wild cycads bear male and female pollen on different plants and this plant is a lone male. The Toromiro, a small flowering tree from Easter Island, is also extinct in the wild. The more modern

Evolution House, behind the Temperate House, tells the story of plants from the first life forms 3.5 billion years ago.

North of the Evolution House, in the centre of the gardens, is the **Xstrata Tree-Top Walkway**, created by Marks Barfield Architects, the designers of the London Eye. It allows one to view the garden from canopy level.

Near Victoria Gate, the **Palm House**, its distinctive curving roofs reflected in the nearby Palm House Pond, was completed in 1848 to a design by Decimus Burton and built by the engineer Richard Turner, who came up with the idea of wrought-iron ribs as used in shipbuilding to cover the maximum space without internal supports. Pevsner thought it was 'much bolder and hence aesthetically more satisfying than the Crystal Palace ever was.' It creates steamy, humid conditions similar to a tropical rainforest: tall canopies of palms reach up to the roof and underneath grow rubber trees, bananas, mangoes, jackfruits, breadfruits, durians and spices. Many of the plants grown here are threatened in the wild and some are extinct. Here too is an antique and massive pot plant, a South African cycad, brought to Kew in 1775. The Marine Display, in the basement of the Palm House, has seahorses and jellyfish as well as living algae, seaweed and coral.

Next to the Palm House is the humid **Waterlily House**, with waterlilies and lotus. It was built in 1852 with ironwork by Richard Turner. The **Princess of Wales Memorial Garden** (1987), a complex, state-of-the-art construction with a boiler underground, houses ten environments from desert heat to tropical rainforest under one glass roof. The cacti, succulents and lithops are one of the best collections of semi-arid plants in the world. It has an aquatic display of fish and poison-dart frogs from South America.

The **Davies Alpine House** (2006) won a RIBA award for its innovative design, which regulates the temperature in order to grow tender Alpine species. Also in this corner of the gardens, in an austere Neoclassical building, is the so-called **Museum No. 1**, originally the Museum of Economic Botany, founded in 1841 by Sir William Hooker, who assembled a collection of specimen textiles, gums, dyes and timber intended to complement the living plants in the gardens. Hooker had a particular interest in the commercial usefulness of plants. The museum was the first of its kind in the world, and the collections grew rapidly, with contributions encouraged from all corners of the Empire. Many, such as an intricate Hindu temple carved out of vegetable ivory, were also received from the Great Exhibition of 1851. Today an exhibition entitled 'Plants and People', in themed showcases, displays changing selections from the collections.

ART GALLERIES AT KEW

The **Shirley Sherwood Gallery** opened in 2008 as the first gallery in the world dedicated exclusively to botanical art. Designed by Walters and Cohen, the blinds and glass automatically react to light in order to preserve the fragile paintings and drawings within. Here are exquisite works from Kew's premier—and hitherto little-known—collections of historic, scientifically-accurate botanical illustrations; many have never been published. Francis Bauer (d. 1840), 'Botanick Painter to his Majesty' and tutor to Queen Charlotte and William Hooker, had such an accurate eye that his drawing of a pollen grain was later proved by a scanning electron microscope to be entirely accurate. Works by Georg D. Ehret, Pierre-Joseph Redouté and Walter Hood Fitch are also shown and the Roxburgh drawings, presented to Kew by the East India Company in 1859, are sometimes on display. Fine contemporary botanical works from Dr Sherwood's extensive private collection are in the Link Gallery, which connects to the Marianne North Gallery next door.

The **Marianne North Gallery** is situated, at the artist's request, in a quiet corner away from the main gate. Red brick with a veranda, typical of European dwellings of that period in India, the building was expressly designed to display Marianne North's oil paintings, 832 studies of nature from life in countries all over the world, executed between 1871 and 1885. Many were painted in circumstances of considerable discomfort and hardship, so Marianne North also wanted the gallery to remind visitors of the hospitality offered to the weary traveller in far-flung places. Neatly labelled and arranged in geographical order, her direct, colourful, uncomplicated oil paintings, none much larger than twelve inches by six, fill the walls completely above the dado, itself made of some 250 vertical strips of different types of timber.

At the far end of Kew Gardens, the **Old Deer Park**, along the river, links Kew with Richmond. These are the former gardens of Richmond Lodge, parkland conceived by 'Capability' Brown of which nothing remains except for the King's Observatory (Chambers, 1769), marooned in a golf course. Plans are afoot to restore it within a more worthy setting.

KEW BRIDGE AND BRENTFORD

Strand-on-the-Green (*map p. 596, A3*), a dulcet stretch of fine riverside houses and a smattering of pubs, is best approached from Kew Bridge. Among the famous residents of its 18th-century houses was the artist John Zoffany, at no. 65 (1790–1810). **Kew Railway Bridge**, spanning the river, in green wrought-iron lattice, opened in 1869. On Kew Bridge Road, the tall chimney of the old Kew Pumping Station is prominent. The building has been restored to house the **Kew Bridge Steam Museum** (*T: 020 8568 4757, kbsm.com*), with restored beam engines of the Grand Junction Water Works, which began supplying water to west London in 1837. The great Cornish pumping engines are run one weekend a month, the rotative engines usually every weekend (*for schedules, see website*). Further down Kew Bridge Road, which becomes Brentford High Street, is the **Musical Museum** (*either walk or take bus 267 to the Musical Museum stop*), with a collection of working Wurlitzers and pianolas (*open Fri–Sun 11–5; shop; T: 020 8560 8108, musicalmuseum.co.uk*). Further down Brentford High Street is the entrance to Syon Park.

SYON PARK AND HOUSE

Map p. 596, A3. Trains from Waterloo to Brentford or Syon Lane then 20mins' walk or bus 267 from Hammersmith to Brent Lea. Underground to Gunnersbury and then bus 237 or 267. Usually open mid-March–Oct on certain days of the week, but these are subject to change and the house is often used for filming. Check website or phone ahead.

Admission charge. Garden Centre Refectory serves drinks, snacks and light lunches. T: 020 8560 0882, syonpark.co.uk.

The London seat of the Dukes of Northumberland, set in 200 acres of parkland, Syon is chiefly famous for its magnificent Adam interiors and furnishings, its collection of British historical portraits, and grounds laid out by Lancelot 'Capability' Brown. This is the only surviving ducal residence in Greater London. The house occupies the site of a medieval abbey (named after Mount Zion in the Holy Land), founded by Henry V in 1415. After the Dissolution of the Monasteries the estate became Crown property, and it was at Syon that the unfortunate Catherine Howard, fifth wife of Henry VIII, was held between her trial and execution. Richard Reynolds, a monk at the abbey, is honoured as one of the five 'proto-martyrs', the first Catholics to be executed at Tyburn in 1535. In 1547 the estate was granted to Lord Protector Somerset (*see p. 188*), and after his execution in 1552 it was presented to John Dudley, Duke of Northumberland (no relation to the present family). His daughter-in-law, Lady Jane Grey, was offered the crown at Syon. The estate was acquired by the powerful Percys, Earls of Northumberland, in 1594. The 1st Duke of Northumberland commissioned Robert Adam to refashion the interiors in 1761. The somewhat gaunt exterior, comprising a castellated block with square corner turrets, dates from the mid-16th century and does nothing to prepare visitors for the splendours of Adam's state rooms. The Northumberland lion (made of lead) which tops the east front of the house is from Northumberland House on the Strand, the family's townhouse, demolished in 1874.

The Adam rooms

Within the shell of the Jacobean house, Adam created a thoroughly Neoclassical interior. The **Great Hall**, in the form of a Roman basilica, is austerely decorated in tones of white and black, with Roman statuary and fine plasterwork. A striking contrast to this cool restraint is the lavish **Anteroom**. Twelve columns of *verde antico* marble (some ancient, dredged from the Tiber and brought to Syon in 1765), cleverly arranged to transform the rectangular space into a square, support jutting entablatures and heavily gilded free-standing classical figures. The richly coloured floor is a magnificent example of scagliola work. The **Dining Room**, Adam's first interior at Syon, is decorated in white and gold with copies of antique statues, ordered by Adam, in niches. The **Red Drawing Room**, next in the sequence, has a coved ceiling with intricately-painted medallions by Cipriani, a fireplace with ormolu decoration by the famous Matthew Boulton, doorcases with large panels of ivory with applied gilded lead ornament, in Italian Renaissance style, and an exceptional Adam-designed carpet made by Thomas Moore of Moorfields, signed and dated 1769. This room also contains Sir Peter Lely's double portrait, *Charles I and James Duke of York*, painted probably in 1646 when the King was under house arrest at Hampton Court. Occasionally he was allowed to ride to Syon to see his children in the care of Algernon Percy, 10th Earl of Northumberland.

The **Long Gallery**, with its intricate enrichment of almost every surface (in the words of Adam, decorated 'in a style to afford great variety and amusement'), is one of the highlights of the house. In the original Jacobean long gallery, Adam punctuated

garden front. It has been returned as far as possible to Adam's original pea-green colour scheme with pier glasses for easier viewing of the paintings that hang here.

The **Drawing Room**, counterbalancing the Eating Room and designed around the same time, is much richer in concept, with a ceiling modelled on the Temple of the Sun at Palmyra. The carpet was designed by Adam in response to the ceiling and was manufactured by Thomas Moore of Moorfields. Horace Walpole considered the room 'worthy of Eve before the Fall'. The tall pier glasses are also by Adam, along with the inlaid, purely ornamental commodes. The grate in the chimneypiece, itself not entirely of a piece with the room, is made of paktong, an alloy of copper, zinc and nickel, the only one of such pieces by Adam to remain *in situ*. A number of Child family portraits are hung here, original to the house and on loan to Osterley from Lord Jersey. Among them is Allan Ramsay's *Francis Child III* (1758).

From here you enter the sumptuous **State Apartment**, already practically out of fashion when commissioned by Robert Child in 1772 but providing three superb examples of Robert Adam's style at its most confident and mature. The **Tapestry Room** has a delicate ceiling and the carpet was again designed by Adam to mirror it. On the walls are Gobelins tapestries designed by the painter François Boucher and representing the Four Elements in the shape of the loves of the gods: *Venus and Vulcan* (Fire), *Aurora and Cephalus* (Air), and *Vertumnus and Pomona* (Earth). The mirror on the window wall stands in for Water. The eight armchairs are backed with oval frames holding Boucher's *Jeux d'Enfants*, designed for Madame de Pompadour in the early 1750s: the cartoons were not released for use by other clients until 1770. The **State Bedchamber** is dominated by the domed State Bed of 1776, one of Adam's most ambitious pieces of furniture. The last room, the **Etruscan Dressing Room**, has striking wall decoration inspired by ancient Greek vases, Roman *grottesche* and the engravings of Piranesi. It is the only surviving example of this type of design by Adam.

Designed by Charles Holden and Stanley Heaps, architects for the London Underground, **Osterley station** (*map p. 594, C3*) is one of number of Underground buildings erected in the 1920s and '30s according to a rational Modernist plan. Constructed of brick and concrete, it features a square-plan tower with an illuminated obelisk which at night transforms it into a sort of land-locked lighthouse.

GUNNERSBURY & EALING

Gunnersbury, Chiswick Park, Turnham Green and Ealing are attractive west London residential suburbs. In **Gunnersbury Park** (*map p. 596, A3; Underground: Gunnersbury Park*) the Gunnersbury Park Museum (*open April–Oct 11–5, Nov–March 11–4*) has a small a local history collection housed in a venerable old 19th-century mansion. Originally a Palladian villa stood here, built as a summer residence for Princess Amelia, daughter of George II. She made improvements to the grounds, originally laid out by William Kent: the Doric temple on the edge of the round pond is a survivor of her scheme. The villa was demolished in 1801 and the present two Regency houses were built. In 1835 Nathan Meyer Rothschild bought the larger of the two and Sydney Smirke added the orangery. Later the Rothschilds also acquired the smaller mansion and continued to live here until 1917.

North of Turnham Green Underground station, nestled in the crook of Fielding Road and Abinger Road, is **Bedford Park** (*map p. 596, B3*), famed as being the first planned garden suburb in the world, with red-brick houses by a number of architects, including Norman Shaw.

EALING

Ealing (*Underground: Ealing Broadway*) is renowned as the 'Queen of the Suburbs', a reputation gained in the 19th century with the coming of the Great Western Railway (1838), turning what had been a sedate market-garden parish with Anglo Saxon origins into a bustling municipal borough—the first in the County of Middlesex—for the new Victorian middle classes.

Ealing for many means the **Ealing Studios** on Ealing Green (*map p. 596, A3; limited opening in Feb during the Ealing Music and Film Festival; ealingmusicandfilmfestival. org*). Film-making at Ealing dates back to the silent era, though its golden age came in the late 1940s–mid-1950s with *Passport to Pimlico* (1949), *Kind Hearts and Coronets* (1949), *The Lavender Hill Mob* (1951) and *The Ladykillers* (1955). The studios are now home to the Met Film School.

North of the studios is **Pitzhanger Manor**, built by the architect and collector Sir John Soane (*see below*). The continuation of Ealing Green to the south is St Mary's Road, where **St Mary's Church** is an extraordinary 'Byzantine shrine' (S.S. Teulon, 1866) on the site of a medieval church destroyed in the Civil War. The church of **All Saints** on Elm Grove Road, on the south side of Ealing Common (*map p. 596, A3*), stands on the site of the former home of Spencer Perceval, the only British Prime Minister to be assassinated, who lived there until his untimely end in 1812. The church was the bequest of his youngest daughter, Frederica, who lived at Pitzhanger. Among its possessions are Perceval's death mask and his official red leather attaché case.

PITZHANGER MANOR
Map p. 596, A3. Walpole Park, Mattock Lane. Underground: Ealing Broadway and 10mins' walk. Closed for refurbishment at the time of writing. T: 020 8567 1227, www. ealing.gov.uk/pmgalleryandhouse.
In 1800 Sir John Soane bought Pitzhanger Manor House. It was a homecoming for him, for, at the age of 15, he had been apprenticed to George Dance the Younger, who had built Pitzhanger's modest south wing extension. Soane later described Dance's interior as displaying a 'profusion of ornaments, exquisite in taste and admirable in execution'. However, he demolished the rest of the pre-1768 'incongruous mass of buildings' and over the next four years set about erecting an Italianate villa which would advertise his fascination with ruins and the effects of space and light. For almost

a decade he used it as a weekend family refuge, a house to entertain friends and a show-case for his ever-growing collection of art and antiquities. When the house was sold in 1810, its collection removed to Lincoln's Inn Fields (*see p. 197*).

Pitzhanger was purchased in 1843 by Spencer Horatio Walpole for his four unmar-ried sisters-in-law, all daughters of Spencer Perceval (*see above*). The sisters lived at Pitzhanger on a peppercorn rent. During their tenure, Soane's courtyard, with its col-onnade of mock-ancient columns, was demolished and replaced with a building which now houses the contemporary art gallery. Frederica, the youngest of the sisters, died in 1900. The house is now managed by Ealing District Council as a museum and cul-tural venue, known as **PM Gallery and House**. It is home to the largest collection of **Martinware pottery** in the UK. The Martin brothers, Wallace, Walter, Edwin and Charles, artist-potters based at Fulham and later Southall, specialised in producing salt-glazed stoneware vases, dishes, grotesque face jugs and their so-called bird-jars, all done in browns, greens, greys and blues. The restoration and remodelling of the manor, led by the architects Jestico + Whiles, intends to return the house and gardens to their Regency splendour, faithful to Soane's original vision. Soane's façade is still extant, of three bays in yellow London stock brick, across which stretches an Ionic screen with a massive, mannered entablature and sculptured figures of Coade Stone (*see p. 415*) modelled on the Erechtheion caryatids.

WALPOLE PARK

Walpole Park, named after Pitzhanger Manor's sometime owner, Spencer Horace Walpole (*usually open 7.30–dusk*), lies to the rear of PM House and was once part of its grounds. In the mid-18th century it consisted of formal gardens, cedar trees and a rec-tangular kitchen garden (which can still be seen today). On his purchase of the manor house, Soane worked closely with the landscape architect John Haverfield and made notable changes, including a small serpentine lake (now a stream) with a rustic bridge arching over it, surfaced in flint, rubble and dressed stone to give an antique effect. His mock Roman ruins and fragments, to give the impression that an ancient temple had been discovered in the grounds, are no longer extant and his planned melon grove did not materialise. Today there is a children's play area and café.

BARNES & MORTLAKE

Barnes and Mortlake are pleasant, quietly affluent residential suburbs. Mortlake will be a familiar name to all those who follow the annual Oxford and Cambridge Boat Race (*see p. 496*). Barnes is known for its wonderful Wetland Centre.

BARNES

Map p. 596, B3. Trains from Waterloo to Barnes and Barnes Bridge in c. 25mins. Bus 290 or 283 from Hammersmith Broadway bus station.

Until the opening of Hammersmith Bridge in 1827 and the coming of the railway in the mid-19th century, Barnes was an isolated rural area known for its market gardens. It is still one of London's most tranquil riverside suburbs, a picturesque, affluent 'village' on the south side of the Thames, where one may enjoy scenic riverside walks in a countryside setting. Its chief attraction is the London Wetland Centre, a wildlife paradise in the midst of the capital, with terrific opportunities to spot interesting and sometimes rare wild birds.

The 19th-century chimneyed Barnes Station appears marooned in the middle of **Barnes Common**. The common, 100 acres of unenclosed land, is Barnes's southerly nature reserve and is about a 10–15mins' stroll from the village centre along Station Road or Rocks Lane, or a few minutes by bus (*bus stop outside station*). Barnes Bridge, the next railway station, is on the river, adjacent to Barnes Terrace.

If you arrive across Hammersmith Bridge, look out for the **Harrods Depository** on the left, clad in distinctive orange terracotta tiles with twin cupolas and tinted blue windows. Built in 1894 to store large items of furniture for the eponymous department store in Knightsbridge, it was converted into luxury flats and penthouses as part of the Harrods Village estate in the 1990s. Hammersmith Bridge leads straight into the bosky main avenue, Castelnau (generally pronounced 'Castle-Now', although 'Castle-Know' or 'Castle-Gnaw' are probably more correct), which takes its name from a family of aristocratic French Huguenots who settled here in the 17th century. At the very end of Castlenau, on Queen Elizabeth's Walk (junction with Red Lion pub and Church Road), is the London Wetland Centre.

LONDON WETLAND CENTRE

Map p. 596, B3. 10mins' walk from Barnes Station or bus 283 from Hammersmith Broadway bus terminus. Open daily except 25 Dec; check for summer and winter opening hours. Children under 16 must be accompanied by an adult. Café and shop. T: 020 8409 4400, wwt.org.uk. It is recommended that you bring your own binoculars, but these can be hired from the In Focus shop, above the main gift shop. The main walkways are flat and paved with tarmac. The 'wilder' parts have hard stony paths and the hides are not suitable for small children or large parties.

The peaceful Wetland Centre is a first-class example of urban regeneration, successfully bringing the countryside to London—which is quite a feat, lying as it does beneath the Heathrow flight path.

The 100-acre site, managed by the Wildfowl and Wetlands Trust (WWT), founded by the late conservationist and ornithologist Sir Peter Scott, is built over four disused Victorian reservoirs. The landscaped reed beds, marshes, pools, lakes and gardens support a diverse ecosystem and are a haven for birds, reptiles, amphibians, dragonflies, butterflies and water voles. Highland cattle graze the wildflower and water-meadows. Since the Centre opened in 2000, over 200 species of wild bird have been spotted, many not seen anywhere else in London, and many thrive here in nationally significant numbers. Wild ducks, geese and swans arrive from Europe to over-winter and during this period the centre teems with waterfowl including widgeon, teal, pintail and shoveller. One of the Centre's rarer winter visitors—and the Holy Grail of birding—is the Great Bittern. This shy bird had been hunted to extinction in the UK but over the last century about 44 breeding pairs have returned. Six birds have been recorded wintering in the reed beds. In spring and summer the Centre is home to summer migrants from Africa, including sand martins, swifts, warblers and swallows, and the marshes resonate with the peculiar croaking of marsh frogs. 'Wetlands of the World', the left arm past the Welcome Centre, is divided into paddocks containing some of the most internationally endangered species of wildfowl. These birds are not native to the UK and are part of the WWT's global conservation programme. The right arm of the Centre (past the excellent Water's Edge Café) has three interactive areas for children to explore. Past these are reed beds, the lagoon walk and the unmissable Peacock Tower, a multi-storey hide offering panoramic views.

BARN ELMS

Barn Elms playing fields, the expansive open space opposite the entrance to the Wetland Centre, bordered by Queen Elizabeth's Walk and Rocks Lane, was the site of the old medieval manor of Barnes, destroyed by fire and demolished in 1954. The estate was leased to Sir Francis Walsingham, Elizabeth I's Secretary of State and spymaster, in 1579 until his death in 1590. The Queen herself was a visitor. Later inhabitants and visitors included John Evelyn, Samuel Pepys, George II, Handel and the Hoare banking family. Another house on the estate, long since demolished, was Jacob House, home of Jacob Tonson, publisher, bookseller and founder of the Kit-cat Club. The Club met here for ten years and members had their portraits painted by Sir Godfrey Kneller (some of them are now in Room 9 of the National Portrait Gallery). The Home Farm (also demolished) was leased by the writer, pamphleteer and radical rural rider William Cobbett, in 1827–31, for experimental husbandry and the growing of maize.

CHURCH ROAD AND BARNES HIGH STREET

Church Road, opposite Queen Elizabeth's Walk, is a winding Edwardian parade of shops and cafés. **St Mary's Church** stands in an attractive churchyard with a large yew tree. The church was seriously damaged during a fire in 1978 and the interior, with Edwardian pews and other wooden fittings, was completely destroyed. The modern, reconstructed space incorporates some original soot-blackened stonework and monuments. During the rebuilding, some of the medieval fabric was exposed and may be seen on the interior walls (paintwork on south wall). At the end of Church Road on the left are the village green and duck pond. **Milbourne House**, facing the pond and opposite the Sun Inn, is the oldest private house in Barnes. The present building (17th century with later additions/restorations) was the home Henry Fielding. A resident of the earlier 16th-century building was Robert Beale, Francis Walsingham's secretary (*see Barn Elms, above*), who witnessed the execution of Mary, Queen of Scots.

Barnes High Street leads to **The Terrace**, a charming row of 18th-century townhouses, some bow-fronted. Gustav Holst lived at no. 10 and Dame Ninette de Valois, founder of the Royal Ballet, at no. 14 (both with blue plaques). Barnes Bridge, the railway and pedestrian bridge connecting Barnes with Chiswick, was first built by Joseph Lock in 1849 and replaced in 1895 by the London and South Western Railway. There are plenty of pubs and restaurants in this area to choose from. White Hart Lane, a street of pastel-coloured Victorian cottages known as Little Chelsea, and also the official boundary between Barnes and Mortlake, boasts a couple of interesting antique shops.

MORTLAKE

Map p. 596, A3–B3. Trains from Waterloo via Clapham Junction. Bus 209 from Hammersmith Broadway via Barnes. It terminates in Avondale Rd, off Mortlake High St.

Mortlake, a residential area bordering Barnes, has a few interesting buildings and a couple of churches, all of which may be seen from the short High Street, which runs parallel to the river. At no. 123 Mortlake High Street (the Barnes end) stands 'The Limes' (1720 and later), a riverside house, now offices. In 1827 Turner painted two views of the Thames here. The paintings are now in the collections of the National Gallery of Washington and the Frick Collection, New York.

The ancient manor of Mortlake, which included Putney and Wimbledon, was the property of the Archbishops of Canterbury until 1536, when Cranmer transferred it to Henry VIII. The riverside location of the **Stag/Budweiser brewery**, with its distinctive chimney and redundant mid-Victorian buildings (off Mortlake High Street, near the roundabout and junction with Lower Richmond Road), stands on the grounds of what would have been their residence. At the back of the brewery, down Ship Lane, is **The Ship**, a popular 18th-century riverside pub near the finishing line of the Oxford and Cambridge boat race (*see p. 496*) and with views of Chiswick Bridge.

In 1543, Henry VIII decreed that the parish church, **St Mary the Virgin**, which also originally stood on the site of the brewery, be transferred to its current location in the middle of Mortlake High Street. The church has been much altered, notably by Sir Arthur Blomfield in 1905–6, but the tower, with its attractive cupola and belfry, is believed to have been constructed using brick from the original church. On the north wall are monuments to Henry Addington, 1st Viscount Sidmouth, who during his term as Prime Minister (1801–04) negotiated the Treaty of Amiens, an accord which secured a brief interlude of peace during the Napoleonic Wars. A rectangular brass, midway up the north wall, commemorates Edward Myles (d. 1618), servant to Henry, Prince of Wales and his younger brother Prince Charles, later Charles I. Dr John Dee (d. 1608), the great Elizabethan scholar, mathematician and alchemist, interested in magic and angelic communication (the character of Prospero in Shakespeare's *Tempest* is said to have been based on Dee), was a local resident and is believed to be buried in the chancel. Dee's library of over 4,000 books was one of the finest in Europe and Elizabeth I came to Mortlake to consult him on matters of astrology. The obsidian mirror which Dee used for divination is on display at the British Museum. When at Cambridge, Dee devised 'miraculous' stage effects for a performance of a play by Aristophanes. People began whispering that he was a sorcerer, a reputation he never shook off. Aubrey describes him as 'tall and slender, a very handsome man,' with 'a long beard as white as milk'. In the churchyard are several weathered tombs and a weath-

MORTLAKE
Detail of the tent-tomb of Sir Richard Burton.

ered map of their locations. Alderman John Barber (d. 1740), Lord Mayor of London and friend of Jonathan Swift, is buried here. Barber's patronage of the arts was patronisingly mocked by Pope in the *Dunciad*: 'so by each Bard an Alderman shall sit, A heavy Lord shall hang at ev'ry Wit'.

In 1619, under James I, a **tapestry works** was established at Mortlake staffed by skilled Netherlandish weavers. The Prince of Wales, later Charles I, was a patron. The tapestry buildings stood along the river opposite the church: the lone survivor is no. 119. Despite the excellence of the tapestries produced, the works went into decline after the Civil War and by 1703, Queen Anne authorised their closure. Examples of Mortlake tapestry can be seen at Ham House, Kensington Palace and Hampton Court.

An extraordinary late 19th-century mausoleum designed as an Arab tent may be seen at the Catholic church of **St Mary Magdalen**, on North Worple Way (*map p. 596, B3; from the bus terminus, walk parallel to the railway line and turn right*). The butterscotch-coloured stone monument, with ruched exterior detail giving the impression of draped fabric, dominates the peaceful Victorian graveyard and is almost as high as the row of terraced cottages in the street behind. It is decorated with various Eastern and Christian motifs including a Star of Bethlehem, a Crucifix and gilded Muslim crescents. Inside are the coffins of the explorer, traveller and translator of *The Arabian Nights* Sir Richard Burton (1821–90) and his wife Isabel, and various objects including an altar, Middle Eastern lamps, coloured glass vessels and camel bells, which were fixed to a battery in order that they would tinkle when the tomb door was opened. The interior may be viewed through a plate-glass window (originally stained glass) at the back, via a fixed iron step ladder. The tomb was erected by Lady Burton after her husband's death and she visited frequently, sometimes sitting inside amongst the tinkling bells. She was buried alongside him in 1896 (her coffin is the more ornate of the two).

PUTNEY & WIMBLEDON

Putney (*map p. 596, B3; Underground: Putney Bridge*) is known for its heath (adjoining Wimbledon Common to the north) and for its bridge across the Thames. The original wooden bridge of 1729 was the first river crossing since London Bridge (though further out, at Kingston, there had been a bridge since the early Middle Ages). The current **Putney Bridge**, five spans in grey stone and Cornish granite, links Putney with Fulham (*NB: Putney Bridge station is on the Fulham side of the river*). It was built by Bazalgette in 1882–6.

Putney was the birthplace of Thomas Cromwell in c. 1485; his early life here is documented in Hilary Mantel's historical novel *Wolf Hall*. The **church of St Mary**, by the bridge, has a 15th-century tower; the rest was rebuilt in the 19th century and again after a fire in 1980. During the Civil War, Oliver Cromwell's New Model Army had their headquarters in Putney and the Putney Debates—a series of constitutional discussions—were held in the church in 1647. Edward Gibbon was born in Putney in 1737.

The Embankment, a picturesque spot on the water west of Putney Bridge, lined with small boathouses, a couple of pubs and gardens, overlooks the green expanse of Bishop's Park on the opposite bank. At high tide the river often washes along here, in places ankle-deep. A path leads to Hammersmith Bridge (and a cut-off along the way, about a 30-min stroll, takes you to the London Wetland Centre; *see p. 492*).

All Saints' Church on Putney Common (south of Lower Richmond Road; consecrated 1874) is richly decorated in the Victorian Arts and Crafts tradition. The architect was G.E. Street in collaboration with Edward Burne-Jones and William Morris; many of the stained-glass windows are by Morris & Co.

The poet Swinburne lived at 'The Pines' on Putney Hill from 1879 until his death in 1909, tended by his friend Theodore Watts, whose aim was to save him from his alcoholism. In **Putney Vale Cemetery** (*map p. 596, B4; open Mon–Sat 8–dusk, Sun 10–dusk; bus 85 or 265 from Putney; wandsworth.gov.uk*), the sculptor Joseph Epstein (d. 1959) is buried (Block AS, south of Alexander Way, southern boundary of the cemetery), as is Howard Carter (d. 1939), discoverer of the tomb of Tutankhamun (Block 12, south of Central Drive).

THE OXFORD & CAMBRIDGE UNIVERSITY BOAT RACE

Each year in the raw weather of early spring, crowds throng the Tideway between Putney and Mortlake to see the Oxford and Cambridge eights battling with each other over the four-mile course. The race was first held in 1829 at Henley; today's course, from Putney to Mortlake, was established in 1845 (a victory for Cambridge). Since 1856 (also a victory for Cambridge) the Boat Race has been annual, interrupted only during the two World Wars. Oxford wear dark blue shirts and Cambridge light blue, the same colour as their blades. The crew must be composed of members of the respective universities, graduate or undergraduate. The first woman took part in 1981, coxing Oxford to victory. A separate all-female race is to be held from 2015. The University Stone, just upstream of Putney Bridge, marks the race's starting point.

WIMBLEDON

Map p. 596, B4. Underground: Wimbledon, Southfields, Wimbledon Park. Trains to Wimbledon from Waterloo in c. 16mins.

Wimbledon is one of the most attractive suburbs of London, part urban settlement, part country village, home of lawn tennis, site of the 'turfy plateau' of Wimbledon Common, and the inspiration for Elizabeth Beresford's burrow-dwelling Wombles, popularised in a succession of children's books and a TV series in the late 1960s and early '70s. The Common includes wooded areas, scrub and heathland, ponds, mown lawns and recreation facilities. The majority of the land is a conservation area due to its rich plant and animal life, including eight varieties of bat. In the past (due to its remoteness from London), Wimbledon Common was popular with duellists. The first recorded was in 1652, when George Brydges, 6th Baron Chandos, killed Colonel Henry Compton over Mary Carey, Lady Leppington. In 1798, William Pitt the Younger fought the Whig MP George Tierney over his lack of patriotism, and in 1809 an argument over the deployment of British troops during the Napoleonic Wars led Lord Castlereagh (a crack shot) and George Canning (first time with a pistol) to exchange gunfire here. The latter was wounded in the thigh.

On the northeast edge of the Common is **Wimbledon Windmill** (*Windmill Rd; Underground/railway station: Wimbledon then bus 93 (about 30mins); open March/ April–Oct Sat 2–5, Sun and bank holidays 11–5; admission charge; shop; T: 020 8947 2825, wimbledonwindmillmuseum.org.uk*), the old village mill, built in 1817 and the only hollow-post flour mill remaining in this country. It houses a museum of wind-mills, milling and local history (including displays of Girl Guide and Scouting memo-rabilia; Baden-Powell wrote part of *Scouting for Boys* here in 1908) and you can try your hand at milling flour with some grain, a saddle stone, mortar and hand quern.

An unexcavated iron-age hill fort known as **Caesar's Camp** (no connection to the Romans) is situated on the Royal Wimbledon Golf Club (south part of the Common).

SOUTHSIDE HOUSE

3–4 Woodhayes Rd. Map p. 596, B4. Underground/railway station: Wimbledon, then bus 93 in 15mins. Open Easter–end Sept Wed, Sat, Sun and bank holidays for 60-min guided tours at 2pm, 3pm and 4pm. No need to pre-book, but phone to check house open, as it is often hired for private events. Admission charge. T: 020 8946 7643, southsidehouse.com.
At the south edge of Wimbledon Common stands the two-storey Southside House, faced in plum-coloured brick. The property is said to have been bought in 1665 by Robert Pennington, a Chancery official and loyal supporter of Charles II during his exile in Holland, who employed Dutch architects to create a William and Mary façade (the year 1687 is carved on one of the chimneypieces inside). The house has remained in the hands of the Pennington family ever since. In 1910 Hilda Pennington Mellor married the Swedish physician Dr Axel Munthe, author of the bestselling autobiog-raphy *The Story of San Michele* (1929). The house as it appears today owes most to the son of Hilda and Axel, the war hero Major Malcolm Munthe, who fought behind enemy

lines in Sweden and Norway for the Special Operations Executive and was awarded the Military Cross. After the War he set himself the objective of creating a 'cultural ark' in his four family homes of Hildasholm in Sweden, Castello Lunghezza near Rome, the manor house of Hellens in Herefordshire, and here at Southside, which is now run by the Pennington-Mellor-Munthe Charity Trust, presided over by Major Munthe's son Adam.

The house boasts a fine small collection of British painting. In the Dining Room there are some elegant full-length portraits by Van Dyck and his studio. In the same room is Burne-Jones's *St George and the Dragon* (1868). The house also contains a number of objects with colourful and elaborate provenances: Anne Boleyn's vanity case, which she had with her in the Tower before her execution; the pearl necklace which Marie-Antoinette wore at the guillotine and which was presented to John Pennington by Josephine Bonaparte; the emerald and gold ring of Alexander I, the last King of Serbia (assassinated in 1903), whose proposal of marriage Hilda Pennington Mellor declined; and a portrait and letter of Charles-Geneviève-Louis-Auguste-André-Timothée d'Éon de Beaumont, usually known as the Chevalier d'Éon (1728–1810), the French diplomat and spy who spent one half of his life dressed as a man and the other half attired as a woman. The sumptuous Prince of Wales Bedroom preserves the memory of the visits of Frederick, Prince of Wales, heir to George II. Lord Nelson, Sir William Hamilton and his wife Emma were guests at Southside when they were living at nearby Merton Place (demolished) in the years before Trafalgar. The platform upon which Lady Hamilton performed her classical 'attitudes' is in the Music Room, as is her portrait by Romney, for whom she sat over a hundred times.

WIMBLEDON VILLAGE

Some attractive old buildings survive in Wimbledon Village. On the High Street is the 17th-century **Rose and Crown pub**, where Swinburne drank before alcoholic dysentery took him (*see p. 496*). On the same side of the High Street is the Dutch-gabled **Eagle House**, formerly the Rev. Thomas Lancaster's School for Young Noblemen and Gentlemen, where the young Arthur Schopenhauer received a clumsy and inadequate education in 1803: no science of any kind was taught, canings were frequent, and the experience left him with a loathing of the Anglican Church. 'When English people display on the Continent their...stupid bigotry,' he later wrote, 'they should be treated with undisguised derision until they are shamed into common sense, for such things are a scandal to Europe.' North of the High Street, at 14 Calonne Rd, is the beautiful **Wat Buddhapadipa**, the first Buddhist temple to be built in the UK. It is open for visits daily (*buddhapadipatemple.org*).

Wimbledon's main fame, of course, comes from the annual championships at the **All England Lawn Tennis Club** on Church Road, held in June–July since 1877. There is a museum. (*Underground: Southfields and 15mins' walk; Wimbledon (also railway station) and 20mins' walk. Open daily 10.30–5, last entry 4.30; open until 8pm during championships, or until close of play if earlier. During championships open to ticket-holders only. Admission charge. Café and shop. T: 020 8946 6131, wimbledon.com.*) The museum explores the history and development of tennis from the gentlemanly pastime of 'real tennis' in 16th-century France to the multi-million dollar international business of today. There are autographed mementoes from Wimbledon champions such as Björn Borg and John McEnroe, the *enfant terrible* of SW19. Of especial interest are the reconstructions of a wooden racquet-maker's workshop and a gentleman's changing room from c. 1900, and the costume gallery recording the changes to ladies' tennis dress over the past 120 years. The museum can be seen as part of a tour which takes you to Court I, the Winter Gardens, the Press Interview Room and the International Box of the world-famous Centre Court.

RICHMOND UPON THAMES

Map p. 596, A4. Underground: Richmond or trains from Waterloo or Victoria in c. 25mins (trains from Victoria change at Clapham Junction). Between April and Oct, Richmond can also be reached by boat from Westminster Pier.

Richmond upon Thames is an attractive riverside suburb with a royal past that can still be traced at Richmond Green and Richmond Park. It has good shops, plenty of pubs and restaurants, a theatre, the Thames for riverside walks and boating, and Richmond Park for walking and cycling.

The area around **Richmond Green** is rich in history and architecture, making it an unspoilt and attractive green 'square'. There was jousting here in Tudor times, and two centuries later cricket: the Cricketer's Inn is on one side of the Green. Shops fill the alleyways which lead through to George Street and the Quadrant, the main shopping area. On the Little Green is the terracotta façade of Richmond Theatre, built by Frank Matcham, architect of the London Coliseum, in 1899.

On two sides of the Green and in adjoining alleyways are attractive 17th- and 18th-century houses, including Old Palace Terrace (1692), Old Palace Place (1700) and Old Friars (1687), on land which once belonged to the order of Friars Observant. The well-proportioned houses in Maids of Honour Row, fronting the Green, were built in 1724 for the ladies-in-waiting of Caroline of Ansbach, when she was Princess of Wales.

RICHMOND PALACE

The remains of Richmond Palace are essentially rebuilt Tudor fragments, though the origins of a palace here go back further. Edward III built what was then known as Sheen (or Shene) Palace in the 14th century, but as early as 1125 Henry I had stayed in Richmond. After Sheen Palace was destroyed by fire in 1497, Henry VII had it rebuilt and renamed it Richmond Palace after his Yorkshire earldom. It became one of the favourite palaces of the Tudor monarchs. Elizabeth I kept a wardrobe of several thousand dresses here, and died here in 1603. After the execution of Charles I, the main buildings were demolished. The monarchy returned to Richmond in 1720 when George, Prince of Wales, the future George II, took over Richmond Lodge in the Old Deer Park. George III also used the lodge, but preferred Kew Palace.

Old Palace House and Palace Gatehouse were built into the surviving wall of Henry VII's palace. Next to them, turn left through a surviving arch of the **Outer Gateway** (above which is Henry VII's coat of arms) into **Old Palace Yard**. Here, the left-hand block is called The Wardrobe, renovated in the 1680s but retaining Tudor brickwork. At the bottom of the yard stands Trumpeter's House (1702–4), built on the former Middle Gate. Next door (right) is Trumpeter's Inn; it is in 18th-century style but was built in the 1950s. Past the bollards, Old Palace Lane, with attractive 19th-century cottages and the White Swan pub, leads left down to the Thames.

OTHER THINGS TO SEE IN RICHMOND

The attractive **riverside**, with grassy slopes, restaurants and pubs, is mainly a result of re-development in 1988 by Quinlan Terry and comprises some 20 buildings in different styles, pleasing in scale and arranged around four courtyards. It is a popular spot and is crowded in fine weather. **Asgill House** is built on the site of the water-gate of Richmond Palace. This fine mansion was designed by Sir Robert Taylor in 1757–8 for Sir Charles Asgill, Lord Mayor of London. Just before **Richmond Bridge**, a graceful curve with five arches (James Paine, 1777), are boathouses where one may hire rowing boats and bicycles. Boat trips are available here to Teddington and Westminster.

In Paradise Road is **Hogarth House** (1748), the home of Leonard and Virginia Woolf from 1915–24. It was here that they founded the Hogarth Press. In the Vineyard are three groups of pretty almshouses of various dates, and in Ormond Road, just off Hill Rise, attractive 18th-century houses. The local parish church, St Mary Magdalen on Church Walk in the centre of the town, has a 15th-century flint and stone tower. The church of St Matthias is by Sir George Gilbert Scott (1861–2). In the Old Town Hall on Whittaker Avenue is a **museum** (*open Tues–Sat 11–5*), where the local history of Ham, Petersham, Richmond and Kew is explored.

RICHMOND HILL

The view from Richmond Hill is famous: a fine prospect of the winding Thames with watermeadows, Petersham Common (the neo-Gothic Petersham Hotel of 1864 is by John James, who designed the Langham Hotel) and Ham on one side; Marble Hill house and park on the other. At the top of Richmond Hill are two fine houses, both of the 1770s: The Wick, by Robert Mylne; and Wick House, built by William Chambers for Sir Joshua Reynolds. The huge neo-Renaissance Star and Garter Home (Sir Edwin Cooper, 1921–4) is a dominant landmark from both the road and down on the riverbank. It still houses invalid servicemen. Opposite is an attractive group of 18th-century terraces, now mostly hotels, and on the roundabout an elaborate RSPCA fountain, with gilded griffins (T.E. Colcutt, 1892), erected to quench the thirst of horses having toiled up the hill.

RICHMOND PARK

Richmond Park comprises 2,500 acres of rolling natural parkland with historic trees (*15mins' walk to Richmond Gate from Richmond Underground station; further gates at East Sheen, Roehampton, Kingston Hill, Kingston and Ham*). It was once a royal hunting ground, enclosed in 1637 by Charles I. Some oak trees are said to date back to the Middle Ages and several hundred red and fallow deer roam freely. There are also large flocks of screeching green parakeet; wilds birds, not native to the UK, but which number several thousand in West London. In popular myth, they are said to be descendants of captive birds kept at Ealing or Isleworth studios, where *The African Queen* was filmed in 1951. In the centre of the park are the man-made Pen Ponds, where fishing is allowed by permit. The Isabella Plantation and Woodland Gardens are impressive from March–May, when hundreds of azaleas and rhododendrons bloom.

Several buildings stand within the park, including the White Lodge, built in 1727–9 as a hunting lodge for George II, influenced by Chiswick House across the river. Queen Mary, George V's consort, grew up here and her eldest son, later Edward VIII, was born at the house. It is now the Royal Ballet's Lower School.

Pembroke Lodge was the home of Lord John Russell and the childhood home of his grandson, the philosopher Bertrand Russell. It now houses a café and offers a splendid view over the Thames Valley; on a fine day one can make out Windsor Castle. Just north of it, a prehistoric barrow known as **King Henry's Mound** provides high ground from where it is said that Henry VIII watched the rocket announcing Anne Boleyn's execution. A telescope on the summit offers a protected view of St Paul's Cathedral, ten miles away in the City (really worth a look). The frame shows the famous cathedral standing alone, without the surrounding high-rises.

PETERSHAM AND HAM

Southwest of Richmond lie two attractive riverside villages. Petersham (1 mile) and Ham (2 miles). **Petersham Nurseries**, reached by walking across the long grasses of the watermeadows, is a charming rural-feeling garden centre with an award-winning restaurant (*see p. 511*). From Ham there is a ferry to Twickenham (*see p. 541*).

HAM HOUSE
Map p. 596, A4. Bus 371 from Richmond to the Ham Street stop. House generally open mid-March–end Oct 12–4 daily except Fri; garden, café and shop open all year 10–5. Opening times vary and tours are sometimes available. Check website for details. Admission charge. T: 020 8940 1950, nationaltrust.org.uk.

Ham House is a remarkable 17th-century survival, having remained almost untouched since the 1670s. It preserves much of its original interior decoration and furniture (early inventories indicate how it was arranged) as well as its garden layout. The original 1610 Jacobean house, built by Sir Thomas Vavasour, Knight Marshal to James I, was remodelled first by William Murray, 1st Earl of Dysart in 1637–9, and more substantially by Elizabeth, his daughter, and her second husband, John Maitland, Duke of Lauderdale, from 1672. Both periods of rebuilding and redecoration were according to the latest fashions, with no expense spared. The remarkable survivals from both these schemes make Ham a key house for the study and appreciation of grand 17th-century interior decoration. The Green Closet contains miniatures and cabinet pictures. There is also a reclining chair made for Catherine of Braganza.

NETHERLANDERS IN BRITAIN

A distinct feature of the artistic community in England in the 16th and 17th centuries was the presence of foreign artists and craftsmen, of which the majority were Netherlandish. England had enjoyed commercial and artistic links with Flanders since the Middle Ages and the city of Antwerp was a base for English bankers and merchants, particularly those in the cloth trade. Netherlandish artists and craftsmen, who provided a level of skill which to some extent native artists lacked, were encouraged to settle in England and to work for the court and for private patrons. Guillim Scrots, formerly court painter to the Habsburg court at Brussels, worked for Henry VIII and Edward VI, while Hans Eworth, from Antwerp, was painter to Mary I. Religious and political events in the Low Countries provided added reasons for Netherlanders to emigrate. Large numbers of Protestant refugees arrived from those parts of the Low Countries under Habsburg rule. The etcher and painter Marcus Gheeraerts the Elder fled to London from Bruges in 1568 and his son, Marcus Gheeraerts the Younger, was to become the leading artist under Elizabeth I. John de Critz, whose sister married Gheeraerts the Elder, arrived from Antwerp and headed an artistic dynasty active in England for several generations. Legislation designed to protect native workers restricted the activities of 'alien' artists and craftsmen, who could only set up workshops if they assumed English citizenship. Many therefore lived in parishes beyond the jurisdiction of the City guilds.

The focus of London's Netherlandish community was the Dutch Church, Austin Friars (*see p. 65*). Not all Netherlandish artists and craftsmen were religious refugees, however. London offered career opportunities for artists such as Daniel Mytens and Van Dyck, as well as for specialists in genres other than portraiture. The renewed cultural programme of the court following the Restoration of Charles II in 1660 attracted skilled artists and craftsmen, and Dutch and Flemish artists were at the forefront of the development of British marine and landscape painting.

TWICKENHAM

Map pp. 596, A4 and 594, C3. Trains from Waterloo in c. 30mins to Twickenham or St Margaret's. Bus H37 from Richmond. You can also walk along the Thames Path from Richmond (about a 30-min stroll), or take the ferry boat from Ham (see p. 541.

Twickenham, the home of English rugby since 1909, is a prosperous riverside town beyond Richmond. When Richmond and Hampton Court were royal palaces, courtiers came to live in Twickenham and some fine villas were built in the 17th–18th centuries. Famous past residents include Sir Francis Bacon and 'the three Yahoos of Twickenham' (so called by Lord Bolingbroke), John Gay, Jonathan Swift and Alexander Pope. Today, Twickenham has three fine houses to visit: Marble Hill House, Orleans House and Strawberry Hill House, and offers some pleasant riverside walking.

EXPLORING THE TOWN: WEST TO POPE'S GROTTO

On leaving Twickenham station, turn right, and about a 10-min walk along Whitton Road is **Twickenham Stadium**, known as 'Twickers'. The 82,000-seater stadium is the headquarters of the Rugby Football Union and the largest rugby union venue in the world. The World Rugby Museum (*open Tues–Sat 10–5, Sun 11–5; admission charge*) has a collection of rugby memorabilia and the Twickenham Experience offers tours of the stadium. Beyond, in Kneller Road, is **Kneller Hall**, owned by Sir Godfrey Kneller, the royal portrait painter, in 1709–11 and significantly remodelled by George Mair in 1847–50. Since 1857 it has been the home of the Royal Military School of Music.

If you turn left out of Twickenham station, London Road leads to the river. In York Street, opposite the petrol station, is the entrance to **York House**, behind a wrought-iron gateway. It was built in the 17th century and owned by Lord Clarendon until 1689. Other residents include the sculptor Anne Damer (from 1817), the Comte de Paris (from 1864) and the Indian merchant Sir Ratan Tata, who designed the gardens (1906–13) in Italian style (*see below*). It is now council offices and has been much altered, with suburban red-brick extensions and white-painted shutters. Riverside leads east to Orleans House (*see below*).

In Church Street, surrounded by mature yew trees, is the church of **St Mary the Virgin**. The Kentish ragstone tower is medieval; the 18th-century red-brick Neoclassical main body, with pedimented projecting sides facing the village and river, was built by John James, architect of St George's Hanover Square, after the old church collapsed in 1713. Entry to the galleried interior, where Alexander Pope is buried, is limited and the church is not open during the week. Also commemorated here are Mary Beach, Pope's nurse for 38 years, as well as the actress Kitty Clive and Thomas Twining of the tea family.

Church Street, with small shops and a couple of pubs, curves westwards, giving a sense of the old village. Continue down Church Lane to the river and at no. 25 The Embankment, is the **Twickenham Museum** (*open Tues–Sat 11–3, Sun 2–4; free; twickenham-museum.org.uk*), with local history archives relating to Twickenham, Whitton, Teddington and the Hamptons. Across the water is **Eel Pie Island**, once only accessible by boat. From the 17th century it became a place of revelry and had its own public house. In the 19th century it catered for large boat parties who arrived by steamer to enjoy the famous eel pies; in the 1960s the Eel Pie Island Hotel attracted 'swinging' London, who came to party and to listen to The Who and the Rolling Stones perform. Today the island is accessed by a footbridge and there is no pub or hotel, just boatyards, private residences and artists' studios.

Continue west and the **site of Alexander Pope's villa and grotto** is about 15–20mins' walk. Pope lived in Twickenham from 1719–44, leasing land beside the road now called Cross Deep. Here he built himself a Palladian villa (demolished 1808) and linked it with a riverside garden via a subterranean grotto. Much of the grotto still exists beneath buildings owned by Radnor House School but it may only be visited by special prior arrangement or during Twickenham's Festival Week in June each year (*requests for visits: Radnor House School, Pope's Villa, Cross Deep, Twickenham, Middlesex, TW1 4QG; info@radnorhouse.org, T: 020 8891 6264*).

RIVERSIDE AND YORK HOUSE GARDENS

Heading east, the Embankment leads past the Barmy Arms pub to the road called Riverside from where there is access to the Italianate **gardens of York House**, laid out in 1910 by Sir Ratan Tata. Here, unexpectedly, is a fantastic statuary composition featuring enormous nude female nymphs clambering up a rockery-cum-cascade with scallop shells and leaping winged horses in white Carrara marble; mallard ducks float peacefully in the pool beneath all the fevered activity. A 'Chinese' stone bridge arches from the gardens across Riverside to York House itself.

Continue east along **Riverside**, under the bridge now, and past attractive houses and villas. Sion Row is a pretty terrace dating from the 1720s; the White Swan pub (with riverside seating) also dates from the 18th century (*NB: this area is prone to flooding at high tide*). Soon you come to the pleasant woodland gardens of Orleans House (*see below*).

ORLEANS HOUSE GALLERY

Map p. 596, A4. Trains to St Margaret's from Waterloo in c. 30mins and then 20mins' walk, or walk along the Thames Path from Richmond Bridge. Open Oct–March Tues–Sat 1–4.30, Sun 2–4.30; April–Sept Tues–Sat 1–5.30, Sun 2–4.30. Free. Café and shop. T: 020 8831 6000.

Alas, the Octagon Room, designed by James Gibbs c. 1716–21, is all that remains of Orleans House, built by John James for James Johnston, Secretary of State for Scotland to King William III. The original two-storey red-brick house (demolished in 1926 by a firm of gravel merchants) was noted for its simplicity and for its Thames view. Gibbs' Baroque addition, the Octagon, owes much to his training under the Roman architect Carlo Fontana, a pupil of Bernini. Gibbs's task was to provide a fitting forum for a sumptuous dinner party for the then Princess Caroline of Brandenburg-Ansbach, consort of the future George II. The resultant domed room has an ornate plasterwork interior by the Swiss-born Giuseppe Artari and Giovanni Bagutti, whom Gibbs described as 'the best fret-workers that ever came to England'. Other notable features include portrait medallions of the future George II and his wife, probably by Rysbrack. A further portrait bust, above the east door, may represent Louis-Philippe, Duc d'Orléans, King of France from 1830–48, who lived here in 1800–14 and 1815–17 and after whom the house is now named.

On witnessing the demolition of Orleans House, the Hon. Mrs Nellie Ionides, a collector of Chinese porcelain who lived at Riverside House next door, came forward to save the Octagon Room, making regular use of it in the 1950s to host Edwardian-style dinner parties. On her death she bequeathed it to the borough of Richmond upon Thames on condition that it was used as a public art gallery. The gallery now displays selections from its important collection of paintings, drawings and prints, mostly early 18th-century to present-day local topographical views, including works by Leonard Knyff, Samuel Scott, Peter de Wint and Corot. Peter Tillemans' 18th-century *The Thames at Twickenham* is the earliest-known view of the area: it aims to capture what Colen Campbell, in his *Vitruvius Britannicus* (1715), called 'the most charming part of the Thames, where the eye is entertained by a thousand beauties'.

Past the Octagon, and past Orleans Gardens (with a café overlooking the river), is a view of Ham House (*see p. 502*). A **ferry** takes passengers across the river for a very small fee (*see p. 541*). Then, on your left, is Marble Hill House, a glistening white Palladian mansion set in 66 acres of public park.

MARBLE HILL HOUSE

Richmond Road. Map p. 596, A4. Trains to St Margaret's from Waterloo in c. 30mins and then 10mins' walk, or walk along the Thames Path from Richmond Bridge. Ferry from Ham (see p. 541). Open April–Oct Sat 10–2, Sun 10–5, by guided tour only. Admission charge. Café and shop. T: 020 8892 5115, english-heritage.org.uk.

Marble Hill (built 1724–9) is a fine example of an English Palladian villa, the fruit of the singular will of Henrietta Howard, Countess of Suffolk, mistress of George II. The design of the house has been attributed to both Henry Herbert, Earl of Pembroke, the 'architect earl', and the Palladian architect Colen Campbell (who remodelled Lord Burlington's town residence on Piccadilly, now the Royal Academy). The tripartite façade is divided both horizontally and vertically; it is faced with stucco and dressed in stone. The north front sports a giant Ionic order of four pilasters, complemented on the south front by a rusticated arched door. All sits compactly under a pyramidal roof.

The house and its mistress

Henrietta Howard (1688–1767), wife of Charles Howard, fifth son of the Earl of Suffolk, had become, at the accession of George I, a Woman of the Bedchamber to the Princess of Wales. By 1720 the Prince of Wales, the future George II, was said to be spending 'every evening of his life, three or four hours in Mrs Howard's lodging'. Doubtless Mrs Howard was seeking solace from her marriage to an uncongenial and spendthrift husband (she was once reduced to selling her own hair to keep creditors at bay). Her liaison with the prince offered financial stability. The £11,500 worth of South Sea stock that he gave her was more than sufficient to purchase the 25 acres next to the Thames to build her Palladian-style summer villa.

An early Hanoverian blue-stocking, Mrs Howard was said to keep a 'philosophical' expression and, in her own words, enforced 'every argument with that gesticulation of the hand for which I am so famous'. A patron and correspondent of men of letters, she gathered about her at Twickenham a circle of like-minded companions, including Alexander Pope, the Earl of Chesterfield, John Gay and Jonathan Swift. Pope's 'On a Certain Lady at Court' refers to Mrs Howard and his 'Bounce to Fop' is an epistle addressed to her lap-dog Fop from Pope's own Great Dane, Bounce. Her relationship with the king had ended in 1734, George reputedly bemoaning that she had become an 'old, dull, deaf, peevish beast'. Her second marriage, to George Berkeley, was happy and she retired to Twickenham for the remainder of her life. Horace Walpole, her near neighbour at Strawberry Hill, was a regular visitor; between 1759 and 1766 he filled his notebooks with her conversation and anecdotes.

Tour of the house

The **Hall**, with its four columns, is decorated with marble profile reliefs of Jupiter, Juno, Ceres and Bacchus (French c. 1720), installed in the room in 1750–1. To the left is the **Breakfast Parlour**, symmetrically laid out and decorated with an acanthus leaf frieze and decorated capitals on the columns. On the opposite side is the **Dining Parlour**, created for the Countess in 1750–1 by Matthew Brettingham.

The grand mahogany staircase leads to the first-floor **Great Room**, a perfect cube of 24ft with a coved ceiling, reputed to have been modelled on the double-cube room designed by Inigo Jones at Wilton House, Salisbury. The principal pictures here, including the *capriccio* views of Roman ruins by G.P. Panini (1738) set over the doors and chimneypiece, were returned to the house in stages, as they appeared on the art market. Copies after Van Dyck and Rubens by Charles Jervas were on display here in the Countess's day (the works after Van Dyck seen here now are not original to the house). The highlight of the room is the carved and gilded decoration by James Richards, Grinling Gibbons' successor as Master Carver to the Crown: friezes and panels of flowers and foliage above the pictures and pier glasses, eagles above the doors and antique masks in the cornice. Owls appear on the inside of the shutters and two large putti lean on the overmantel pediment. The marble-topped console table, with heavy Kentian gilded carving incorporating a peacock, the attribute of Juno, one of an original set of four, was returned to the house after its discovery in Australia.

Lady Suffolk's Bedchamber retains its screen of Ionic columns at the north end marking the bed space. There are two jib-doors, one of which leads to the service wing, the other to **Miss Hotham's Bedchamber**, where Henrietta's great-niece and companion once slept. From the mahogany staircase the Stone Staircase leads to the **Picture Gallery**, where visitors could originally view full-length portraits of George II, Queen Caroline and Henrietta herself—as well as a splendid panorama of the Thames and beyond through the windows.

In the **gardens**, laid out by Charles Bridgeman with the involvement of Alexander Pope, was a grotto, accidentally rediscovered in 1941 following the felling of a tree, and re-excavated in 1984. Now restored to an approximation of its original c. 1739 appearance, it has walls lined with shells and a floor with circles of pebbles. The original cavern-mouth entrance was decorated with coral, flints and blue glass. Another garden feature, since disappeared, was the Priory of St Hubert, a 'gothic' barn dedicated to the patron saint of hunting, a sport which Henrietta is said to have pursued with a violent passion.

STRAWBERRY HILL HOUSE

Waldegrave Rd. Map p. 594, C3. Trains from Waterloo to Strawberry Hill in c. 30mins and then 10mins' walk (signposted). Open March–Nov Mon–Wed 2–6, Sat–Sun noon–6, garden open all week 10–6. Café open Sat–Wed 10–5.30. Shop. Tickets are timed-entry and self-guided, purchase from gift shop or online. Guided tours Wed 10am and Sat 10:30am. Also 'Twilight Tours' available with a free glass of Prosecco on arrival (check website). House may be closed at short notice for private functions (check website). T: 020 8744 1241, strawberryhillhouse.org.uk.

In 1747 Horace Walpole, collector, antiquarian, man of letters, Whig politician (son of the Prime Minister Sir Robert Walpole) and coiner of the word 'serendipity', leased a modest house in Twickenham for use as his summer retreat. Twickenham, lying as it did between the royal palaces of Richmond and Hampton Court, was a fashionable resort during the 18th century and fine mansions and villas lined the banks of the Thames here; Walpole considered it an English Brenta, the canal that connects Venice with its hinterland and which is lined with Palladian summer villas. In contrast to the prevailing fashion for Palladianism, however, Walpole set about transforming his cottage, known locally as Chopp'd Straw Hall, into a diminutive Gothic castle. Over the next 40 years he clad and expanded the exterior with turrets, tracery and battlements and the interior was fancifully remodelled and Gothicised according to an amateur Committee of Style formed of himself, the architect John Chute, the illustrator Richard Bentley and Mr Robinson of the Board of Works, who took care of structural and building matters. The artist and architectural designer J.H. Müntz was a member for a time, when Walpole was still delighted with him. Later Walpole decided that he was idle. Details from famous Gothic buildings including Old St Paul's, Canterbury Cathedral, Rouen Cathedral, York Minster and Westminster Abbey were copied and rendered in wood, *trompe l'oeil* and *papier-mâché*, but never so authentically as to be uncomfortable to live with. The prevailing themes were of mystery and surprise, light and shade, and of 'sharawaggi' or 'want of symmetry'; sheep and cows were grazed in the surrounding gardens and meadows to give a 'becoming' view.

At Strawberry Hill Walpole housed and exhibited his eclectic and vast collection of fine ceramics and porcelain, miniatures by Hilliard and Isaac and Peter Oliver, paintings by Reynolds, Lely, Poussin, Van Dyck, Hogarth and Gheeraerts. He also owned a number of curiosities such as the obisdian mirror of Dr Dee (*see p. 494*), now in the V&A, the red hat of Cardinal Wolsey and the spurs that William III used on his horse Sorrel during the Battle of the Boyne. He entertained foreigners, royalty and members of the aristocracy and at one party greeted guests wearing leather gloves that had belonged to James I and a limewood cravat carved by Grinling Gibbons to resemble Venetian lace (also in the V&A). Walpole is documented as having been outbid at auction for Oliver Cromwell's nightcap. He wrote *The Castle of Otranto* while living here (1754–6) and printed it on his private printing press, the Strawberry Hill Press.

The house became famous in Walpole's lifetime not only as an avant-garde and influential work of Gothic Revivalism but also as a tourist attraction and a folly. Visitors were shown around in groups of four by the housekeeper. Walpole catalogued the house and its contents and printed his *Description of the Villa* on his printing press. Today the *Description* provides a fascinating insight into Walpole's long-dispersed art collection and how it was displayed. It has been reprinted in its entirety and is available for purchase in the gift shop (an abridged version is part of the ticketed, self-guided tour of the house).

After Walpole's death, the house passed to his ward, the sculptor Anne Seymour Damer. It later passed to George, 7th Earl Waldegrave, who in 1842 sold off Walpole's collection in its entirety at a historic, 24-day auction. After Waldegrave's death in 1846, his widow renovated and enlarged the house with Victorian additions.

Today, the Strawberry Hill Trust has undertaken a restoration programme to return the house to its appearance of the 1790s, the decade of Walpole's death. At the time of writing, the house gleams with white lime-wash. The garden is also being restored and has been replanted with an avenue of limes that existed in Walpole's day. Due to 20th-century development, however, there is no longer a river view. Nor are there cows.

Highlights of the interior

Past the Little Cloister, with the Abbot's Garden on your right, the visitor enters the 'gloomth' of the **Hall**, where the reproduction *trompe l'oeil* wallpaper is hand-painted with Gothic arches (during restoration some original fragments were uncovered). The windows on either side of the door were once fitted with 16th-century Flemish stained-glass saints; in the 1750s the shockwaves from a gunpowder explosion on Hounslow Heath (modern Heathrow Airport) were felt at Strawberry Hill and much of Walpole's antique glass was blown out, including the saints, which Walpole described as having been 'martyred'. In the **Great Parlour**, leading off the Hall and used as the dining room, note the window tracery design of the backs of the black chairs, which would have cast dramatic shadows on the walls by candlelight. Back in the Hall, the elaborate **staircase**, with models of antelopes along the balustrade, was designed by Bentley and leads up to the splendid library with Gothic-arched fitted bookcases and a painted ceiling depicting Walpole's crusading ancestors. The **Holbein Chamber** was once hung with tracings of original drawings by Hans Holbein. Through a dusky corridor one arrives, in a burst of unexpected colour, into the **Gallery**, Walpole's state room, with its restored gilded fan-vaulted *papier-mâché* ceiling and crimson walls. The **Tribune Room** housed Walpole's treasured coins, medals, enamels and miniatures in a fine rosewood cabinet. On the ground floor, the new **Museum Room**, once the servants' hall, narrates the history of the house and its various owners via interactive displays. There is also access to Yale University's public database of Walpole's collections, which plans to list every artefact that was once at Strawberry Hill with its current location, if known.

EATING IN SOUTHWEST AND WEST LONDON

BARNES, MORTLAKE

£–££ Annie's. Bright but cosy brasserie in Mortlake, serving 'Briterranean' food. *36–38 White Hart Lane (south from Mortlake High St). T: 020 8878 2020, anniesrestaurant. co.uk. Map p. 596, B3.*

£–££ The Depot. Bar and restaurant offering good food and wine, a convivial atmosphere and river views. Open daily. *Tideway Yard (bottom of Mortlake High St; map p. 596, B3). T: 020 8878 9462, depotbrasserie.co.uk.*

£–££ Olympic Studios. The top floor of this famous former recording studio, in the heart of Barnes, is now a cinema. The ground floor is a restaurant serving very good (and very good value) food. Ella Fitzgerald, Stevie Wonder, Roxy Music and Pink Floyd all recorded here. Open daily. *117–123 Church Rd. T: 020 8912 5161, olympiccinema.co.uk. Map p. 596, B3.*

£ The Ship. Old 18th-century pub on the finishing line of the University Boat Race at Mortlake. Good pub food. Open daily. *10 Thames Bank, just east of Chiswick Bridge. T: 020 8876 1439. Map p. 596, A3.*

££ Ye White Hart. Elegant old pub offering sophisticated food and river views. Open daily. *The Terrace (Barnes riverside, eastern continuation of Mortlake High St). T: 020 8876 5177, whitehartbarnes.co.uk. Map p. 596, B3.*

CHISWICK

Good pubs include the **Mawson Arms** on Chiswick Lane or **The George and Devonshire** on Burlington Lane.

£ Chiswick House Café, a piece of bright white geometry in the grounds of Chiswick House (*map p. 596, B3*), serves snacks, sandwiches and modern British cooking (breakfast and lunch). *Burlington Lane. T: 020 8995 6536, chiswickhousecafe.com.*

£–££ High Road Brasserie. Potted rabbit, *croque monsieur* and cassoulet. Good French-influenced cooking in relaxed surroundings. Open daily. *162–170 Chiswick High Rd. T: 020 8742 7474, brasserie.highroadhouse. co.uk. Map p. 596, A3–B3.*

££ La Trompette. Michelin-starred restaurant proud to offer 'some of the best food in London'. But not at West End prices. Open daily. *3–7 Devonshire Rd. T: 020 8747 1836, latrompette. co.uk. Map p. 596, B3.*

££ Vinoteca. Part of a small chain, but a good one (other branches in Soho and Farringdon). Modern British cooking and excellent wines. Open daily. *18 Devonshire Rd. T: 020 3701 8822, vinoteca.co.uk. Map p. 596, B3.*

HAMMERSMITH

£ Black Lion. Fine old pub on the river between Hammersmith and Chiswick. Beer garden and skittle alley. Open daily. *2 South Black Lion Lane (south of the Great West Rd). T: 020 8748 2639, theblacklion-hammersmith.co.uk. Map p. 596, B3.*

£ Blue Anchor. Historic old pub just beside Hammersmith Bridge, right on the waterfront. Open daily. *13 Lower Mall. T: 020 8748 5774, blueanchorlondon.com. Map p. 596, B3.*

£–££ **Dove Inn**. Classic pub food—burgers and Sunday roasts—with nouvelle offerings as well. Fine riverside setting. Open daily (closes 8pm Sun). *19 Upper Mall, south of the Great West Rd. T: 020 8748 9474, dovehammersmith.co.uk. Map p. 596, B3.*

£ **The Gate**. The original of two vegetarian restaurants (its sister is in Islington). Cleverly constructed dishes in a light, loft-style space in a quieter part of Hammersmith, south of the flyover. Open daily. *51 Queen Caroline St. T: 020 8748 6932, thegaterestaurants.com. Map p. 596, B3.*

£ **Old Ship**. One of Hammersmith's many riverside pubs. Come here for a cheese and pickle sandwich and a pint, and watch the river flow by. Open daily. *25 Upper Mall, just west of Hammersmith Bridge. T: 020 8748 2593, oldshipw6.co.uk. Map p. 596, B3.*

£££ **River Café**. A Michelin-starred institution, which brought Italian cuisine to the UK. The *River Café Cookbook* quickly became a classic cook's resource. Advance booking essential. No dinner Sun. *Thames Wharf, Rainville Rd, between Fulham Palace Rd and the Thames Path. T: 020 7386 4200, www.rivercafe.co.uk. Map p. 596, B3.*

KEW

££ **Glasshouse**. In the same family as La Trompette (*see Chiswick, above*), Michelin-starred and offering an excellent and good-value set lunch. Open daily, evenings also. *14 Station Parade, just north of Kew Gardens station. T: 020 8940 6777, glasshouserestaurant.co.uk. Map p. 596, A3.*

PUTNEY, WIMBLEDON

£ **Côte**. One of a chain of competent French brasseries. Open daily. *8 High St (Wimbledon). T: 020 8947 7100, cote-restaurants.co.uk. Map p. 596, B4.*

£–££ **Duke's Head**. Handsome old Putney riverside pub, at the starting point of the University Boat Race. Good pub food (they are proud of their steaks). Open daily. *8 Lower Richmond Rd. T: 020 8788 2552, dukesheadputney.com. Map p. 596, B3.*

£ **Star and Garter**. Another Putney pub at a good vantage point for the Boat Race start. Artisan cheese boards, cold meat platters and good pub grub. Open daily but kitchen closes 8pm Sun. *4 Lower Richmond Rd. T: 020 8788 0345, thestarandgarter.com. Map p. 596, B3.*

RICHMOND, PETERSHAM

£ **Petersham Nurseries Café**. Seasonal dishes and a good sprinkling of edible flowers. A member of the Slow Food scheme. Lunch only (but occasional supper clubs). Closed Mon. *Petersham Rd. T: 020 8940 5230, petershamnurseries.com. Map. 596, A4.*

£ **White Cross**. Comfortable riverside pub just north of Richmond Bridge. Open daily. *Water Lane. T: 020 8940 6844, thewhitecrossrichmond.com. Map p. 596, A4.*

TWICKENHAM

The £ **Eel Pie pub** serves Dorset beer from a family brewery and good, honest pub food. Open daily (until 8pm Sun). *9–11 Church St (south of York St). T: 020 8891 1717, theeelpie.co.uk. Map p. 596, A4.*

HAMPTON COURT
View of Sir Christopher Wren's south front.

Hampton Court

Hampton Court Palace, sprawling and magnificent on the Thames bank, is from a distance a fantasy of Tudor turrets and twisted chimney stacks. A boat trip here on a fine day is an experience not to be missed.

Formerly the extravagant home of Cardinal Wolsey, Hampton Court was requisitioned by Henry VIII in 1528, following Wolsey's failure to obtain an annulment of Henry's marriage to Katherine of Aragon. It was here that Henry VIII was betrothed to his third wife, Jane Seymour and here, a year later, that Jane died giving birth to Edward VI. Shakespeare may have acted in his own *Measure for Measure* in the Great Hall. Hampton Court was a favoured royal residence of the later

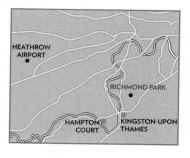

Tudors and early Stuarts, a pleasure palace with tennis courts, bowling alleys, a tilt yard and parks stocked with game. From 1645 Charles I was imprisoned at the palace and, following his execution, it became Oliver Cromwell's country residence. From 1689 Hampton Court was transformed for William III and Mary II by Sir Christopher Wren into a modern Baroque palace, its size and splendour in conscious competition with Louis XIV's Versailles. Suites of King's and Queen's state apartments were created, outstanding ornamental gardens with topiary and fountains, and a maze which is still one of the palace's best-known features. The court last visited Hampton in 1737. The state apartments were opened to the public in the 19th century, shortly after the accession of Queen Victoria, while other parts of the palace were awarded as 'grace and favour' apartments to pensioners of the Crown and others. It was in one of these that, in 1986, a fire broke out, which caused catastrophic damage to some of the King's Apartments. Following meticulous restoration, the rooms now offer a true sense of the exuberant and rich interiors of the time of William III.

Getting there and tickets

Map p. 594, C4. Trains from Waterloo to Hampton Court in c. 35mins. Underground: Richmond and then bus R68. Boats from Westminster Pier (map p. 604, A3). Open April–Oct Mon–Sun 10–6, Nov–March Mon–Sun 10–4.30; last admission 1hr before closing. Tickets can be pre-booked on T: 0844 482 7799 from UK or +44 20 3166 6000 from overseas. Admission charge. Cafés and shop. T: 0870 752 7777, hrp.org.uk.

HISTORY OF THE TUDOR PALACE

The first buildings at Hampton belonged to the Knights Hospitaller of St John of Jerusalem, who acquired the manor in 1236 and used it as a grange. By the 15th century the great barn had been replaced by residential buildings, used by the abbots as a rural retreat. In 1494 Sir Giles Daubenay, Henry VII's Lord Chancellor, purchased an 80-year lease on the property and transformed it into a major courtier house. It was in 1514–15 that Hampton Court's association with royalty and political life began, with the acquisition of a 90-year lease by Thomas Wolsey, Henry VIII's Lord Chancellor. Appointed Cardinal by Pope Leo X in 1515, Wolsey transformed Hampton Court into a complex of buildings of international importance. As well as a private residence, he envisaged the palace as a show house for entertaining kings and prelates and for receiving foreign dignitaries. Built by architects and master craftsmen associated with the country's most important buildings, Hampton Court had innovative features and Renaissance embellishments not seen in England before. Its succession of courtyards and elaborate, turreted gateways provided accommodation for the court and lavish apartments for the king (which remained the apartments of the monarch until the reign of William and Mary). The long gallery, erected in 1515–16, was glazed on either side. Gardens were laid out and a moat and ponds for fish constructed, the latter providing freshwater shrimps and carp. These major alterations were undertaken in two principal phases: in 1515–22, the last date being that of the visit to Hampton Court of the Holy Roman Emperor Charles V (nephew of Katherine of Aragon); and a second phase, until 1527, when Wolsey received the huge entourage of the French court. The palace was furnished with costly magnificence. Tapestries were purchased abroad for staggering sums, while Wolsey's own apartments were hung with cloth of gold.

In September 1528 King Henry ordered Wolsey to vacate the palace for the duration of the visit of the papal delegation, in London to discuss the royal divorce. From that time on Henry assumed ownership of Hampton Court. Alterations and additions were made and practical improvements were undertaken, such as the construction of the Great House of Ease (communal lavatories).

EXTERIOR OF HAMPTON COURT

The main entrance is through **Trophy Gate (1)**, built for William III. At its far end is the west front of the palace, built by Wolsey and completed and altered by Henry VIII. The central **Great Gatehouse (2)**, of mellow brick with limestone dressings, was originally two storeys higher but nevertheless preserves an excellent sense of the imposing silhouette it would have presented to visitors. The fine moated bridge, built by Henry VIII, is guarded by the King's Beasts. On the turrets to either side are terracotta roundels by the Florentine sculptor Giovanni da Maiano, two of eight imported and set in place in 1521 (others appear in the succeeding courtyards). Henry VIII's arms were inserted in 1530. Visitors pass through to **Base Court (3)**, originally cobbled but which remains much as Wolsey built it. Straight ahead is the **Anne Boleyn Gate**, built by Wolsey but so called because the fan-vaulted ceiling was added after Anne became queen in 1533. It bears her badge of a falcon and the intertwined initials H and A. Its small 18th-century bell-tower contains an original bell of the Knights Hospitallers.

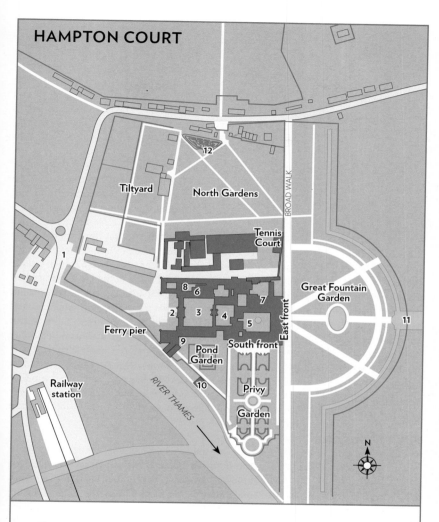

HAMPTON COURT

1 Trophy Gate
2 Great Gatehouse
3 Base Court (Anne Boleyn Gate)
4 Clock Court (entrance to Tudor apartments)
5 Fountain Court
6 Great Hall
7 Chapel Royal
8 Master Carpenters' Court
9 Lower Orangery (*Triumphs of Caesar*) and Great Vine
10 Banqueting House
11 Long Water
12 Maze

Though now much altered, **Clock Court (4)** was the principal court of Wolsey's palace. The west range has Wolsey's arms above the gate, supported by cherubs and surmounted by his cardinal's hat. Henry VIII's Astronomical Clock, made in 1540, its dial altered, shows the hour, month and day, the number of days passed since the beginning of the year, the houses of the zodiac and the phases of the moon. The east side was remodelled in Tudor style by William Kent in 1732. It replaces the magnificent apartments constructed by Wolsey for Henry VIII, their former great feature being tall glazed windows which in their day would have amazed and astonished. On the north is the buttressed mass of Henry VIII's Great Hall. The colonnaded south side was constructed by Wren for William III.

Eager to avoid the smog of London and the damp of Whitehall Palace (William III suffered from chronic asthma), William and Mary ordered Wren to 'beautify' Hampton Court in March 1689. Wren transformed it into a modern Baroque palace, architecturally influenced by Continental precedents. Continuing through to **Fountain Court (5)**, visitors find all trace of the Tudor palace removed, supplanted by the arched cloisters and Baroque façades of Wren's new courtyard. The tall first-floor windows are those of the State Apartments, above which were the lodgings of important courtiers and officeholders. On the south side, carved wreaths surround twelve (much faded) *Labours of Hercules* by the French Baroque decorative artist Louis Laguerre, part of the heroic iconography glorifying William III that appears throughout the late Stuart palace. An exit on the east side leads to the gardens and Wren's imposing east and south fronts, among the most important examples of Baroque architecture in the country. The **east front** is architecturally the more elaborate, with a great central pediment filled with a sculptural relief, *Hercules Triumphing over Envy*, by Caius Gabriel Cibber, supported by giant Corinthian columns. The **south front**, which contains the King's Apartments, with views over the elaborate Privy Garden, has over the central window a carved trophy of arms with a Latin inscription, *'Gulielmus et Maria Rex et Regina Fecerunt'*, glorifying William and Mary's building project.

THE TUDOR INTERIORS

The surviving apartments of Henry VIII are approached via Clock Court, up the staircase in Anne Boleyn's Gate. They lead to the **Great Hall (6)**, the largest room in the palace, begun in 1532. The remarkable hammerbeam roof, one of the finest in existence—but which serves no practical function—was designed by the King's Master Carpenter, James Nedeham, and is richly decorated with carved pendants, the royal arms and heraldic badges. The exceptional Flemish 'Story of Abraham' tapestries, woven in Brussels in the 1540s with silver and gold thread, were among the most expensive tapestries commissioned by Henry VIII.

Beyond Horn Court (where old Tudor antlers were stored at the time of William III) is the **Great Watching Chamber**, the only one of Henry VIII's state apartments to survive. It was a room at the heart of court life, where senior courtiers would have dined and where the Yeomen of the Guard were stationed, controlling access to the king in the Presence Chamber beyond. The decorated ceiling is original, as are the 16th-century tapestries, but the deep heraldic frieze has been whitewashed.

The Pages' Chamber was where courtiers waited before being presented to the king. The **Haunted Gallery** is named after the shrieking ghost of Catherine Howard said to inhabit it. Catherine, Henry VIII's fifth wife, was held at Hampton Court, in her lodgings, before her execution on charges of adultery. Sixteenth-century Flemish tapestries, probably owned by Elizabeth I, show scenes from Virgil's *Aeneid*. Important Tudor pictures from the Royal Collection hang here, including (though the selection can change) the *Family of Henry VIII*, showing the king enthroned, flanked by Jane Seymour and his only son, the future Edward VI, with, to the sides, his daughters Mary and Elizabeth; and the famous *Field of the Cloth of Gold* and *The Embarkation of Henry VIII*, showing the English fleet preparing to leave for Calais.

The **Chapel Royal (7)** was built by Wolsey and is still in use (*services at 8.30, 11 and 3.30 on Sun*). Its most magnificent adornment is the astonishing fan-vaulted ceiling, carved and decorated with gilded pendants, installed by Henry VIII in 1535–6. The high altar, with its oak reredos by Grinling Gibbons and painted angels by Sir James Thornhill, was installed by Queen Anne, who also altered the upper Royal Pew, where the monarch would attend services. Its painted ceiling is also by Thornhill.

The Wolsey Rooms

The Wolsey Rooms occupy the site of Wolsey's private apartments, built in the 1520s. Refitted in the 18th and 19th centuries, they nevertheless retain some original Tudor features: linenfold panelling, plain early 16th-century fireplaces and a ribbed ceiling with early Renaissance decorative motifs. Important pictures displayed here (though again, the choice is liable to change) include Leonard Knyff's large bird's-eye panorama of Hampton Court, c. 1703.

The Tudor kitchens

The kitchens (entered from the Master Carpenters' Court; **8**) fed Henry VIII's court of 1,200 people, who dined in the Great Hall and the Great Watching Chamber. The Boiling House was the Tudor butchery, where great cauldrons of stock and stew were also prepared. Fish Court houses various kitchen departments, such as the spicery, the pastry house and the fish larder. The Great Kitchens, a vast, cavernous space with huge hearths and spits, is divided into three spaces, the third being the oldest, part of Wolsey's kitchens built c. 1514. Dishes were elaborately dressed and garnished in the Dressers, then passed out to the Serving Place to be taken to diners via the North Cloister. The vaulted Great Wine Cellar contains great oak barrels hooped with willow.

INTERIORS OF THE LATE STUART PALACE

The transformation of Hampton Court from an old-fashioned shrine to the Tudor monarchy into a great Baroque palace which challenged the supremacy of Louis XIV was undertaken for William and Mary from 1689 by a team of great architects and designers: Sir Christopher Wren, Nicholas Hawksmoor, the virtuoso carver Grinling Gibbons, William Talman and the leading Baroque decorative artist Antonio Verrio. Queen Mary had keenly overseen progress at the palace until her premature death, of smallpox, in 1694, when work virtually ceased until late 1697 when William, his

European wars over, took a renewed, personal interest. In January 1698, after fire had virtually destroyed the chief royal residence, Whitehall Palace, Wren submitted an estimate for the completion of the interiors. Tapestries from the Royal Collection were used throughout the rooms, as well as pictures. The Master of the Great Wardrobe, Ralph, Baron (later Earl, then 1st Duke of) Montagu, took charge of the furnishings. Former Ambassador in Paris, he promoted French Huguenot artists and craftsmen. Throughout the State Apartments is elaborate upholstery, expensive carved giltwood furniture supplied by Jean Pelletier and exceptional mirrors by Gerrit Jensen (*for more on Huguenot and Netherlandish artists and artisans in London, see pp. 111 and 503*). The court removed to Hampton for the first time in April 1700 and thereafter it was William's habit to spend spring and early summer and autumn here, until his death following a riding accident in the park in 1702.

The King and Queen had their own suites of rooms, reached by separate staircases. Access to the apartments was governed by strict court protocol. Most visitors could mount the Great Stairs and linger in the Guard Room, but further progression was governed by rank. The closer one got to the private apartments of the monarch, the more exclusive the room and the richer its furnishing and ornamentation. The King's Private Apartments, where only the most favoured were admitted, were the most lavish of all. All the state apartments at Hampton Court illustrate these conventions to rich and grand effect.

The King's Apartments

The spectacular **King's Staircase** was decorated by Verrio in 1700–2. An overwhelmingly Baroque space, designed to awe visitors, its walls and ceiling illustrate Alexander's triumph over the Caesars paralleled with William's over the Roman Catholic James II, and celebrates the king as Protestant champion of Europe. The *Banquet of the Gods* is on the ceiling. The fine wrought-iron balustrade is by Jean Tijou. The **King's Guard Chamber** was where the Yeomen of the Guard were stationed, letting past into the state rooms only peers, officeholders, privy councillors or gentlemen of good quality and fashion. The oak panelling is decorated with more than 3,000 pieces of arms, arranged in patterns by John Harris, Master Gunner of Windsor Castle.

The **King's Presence Chamber** was used for formal ceremonial occasions. Facing the entrance is the king's throne, made in 1700. Courtiers would bow three times in its direction, even when it was unoccupied. Opposite it is Sir Godfrey Kneller's enormous *William III on Horseback*, a prominent, heroic image of the monarch. The tapestries, the *Labours of Hercules* and *Triumph of Bacchus*, originally belonged to Henry VIII. The **King's Eating Room** was where the king dined in public, a ceremony not undertaken by William frequently. Above the chimneypiece is a portrait of Christian IV of Denmark, brother of James I's queen, Anne of Denmark, set within a majestic overmantel of carved limewood by Grinling Gibbons: brilliantly realised drops of leaves and flowers, with a cresting of arching wheat and palm fronds. The 'Acts of the Apostles' tapestries are of 17th-century Brussels manufacture (*see below*).

The **King's Privy Chamber** was the most important ceremonial room in the palace. It was here that the king received foreign ambassadors at their first, official, entrance and where other court functions, such as the performance of Birthday Odes, took place. The tapestries are part of Henry VIII's *Story of Abraham* series intended for the Great Hall. The Privy Garden is visible from the window. The richly carved overmantel is by Gibbons.

> ## THE MORTLAKE TAPESTRIES AND 'ACTS OF THE APOSTLES' CARTOONS
> Shortly after Giovanni de' Medici, son of Lorenzo the Magnificent, became Pope Leo X, he commissioned, in 1516, ten cartoons from Raphael, depicting the Acts of the Apostles, for tapestries for the Sistine Chapel. The tapestries were woven in Flanders in the workshops of Pieter van Aelst. Charles I purchased the cartoons in 1623, and had tapestries made up from them at Mortlake: lavish and costly items that made copious use of metallic thread. The Mortlake manufactory had been set up by Royal Charter four years previously. It had 18 looms, an artist's studio, and employed over 50 Netherlandish weavers. Among them was Louis Dermoulen, who specialised in heads, and Pieter de Craigt, who specialised in flesh parts. Mortlake's golden era began in the 1620s, under the directorship of Francis Cleyn, who was chief designer there until his death in 1657. He was appointed on the strength of the new working cartoons which he produced from the Raphael series. Raphael's own cartoons were restored later in the century by order of William III and brought to Hampton Court. Monumental examples of High Renaissance art in England, they were held up as exemplars of artistic excellence. Sir James Thornhill studied them when working on the dome of St Paul's, and in 1729 he was granted a Royal Warrant to make copies. He hoped to make them more accessible to art students, and as such a focus for academic instruction. These great works of art—the gestures of the figures and their composition—made an impact on English art for generations.

Only court officeholders, privy councillors and Secretaries of State were admitted to the **King's Withdrawing Room**, where social gatherings would take place and cards would be played. The tapestries are from the 'Acts of the Apostles' series. The carved overmantel is a masterpiece by Gibbons, with leaves and fruit hanging in dense ropes and crisply carved complex gatherings of fruit and flowers. The **King's Great Bedchamber** next door, one step further into the sanctum, admitted privileged courtiers only, by way of the King's Back Stairs. This magnificent space was a ceremonial room where the king was dressed in front of courtiers, who were kept at a distance behind a rail. The gilded furniture and mirrors, by Gerrit Jensen, are the finest in the apartments, including one 13ft high, incorporating, in strips of blue glass, the king's monogram and crest. The great state bed, with plumed finials, soars towards the richly painted ceiling by Verrio, *Endymion in the arms of Morpheus*, Greek god of dreams and sleep. Below is a remarkable carved frieze by Gibbons, of scrolling acanthus, songbirds, blossoms, fruit and ears of wheat. The **King's Little Bedchamber** was where the monarch actually slept. Displayed on the chimneypiece are rare pieces of oriental porcelain from Mary II's collection. The Verrio ceiling, an excellent piece of painting unusually well preserved, shows Mars and Venus, with cupids, billing doves and orange trees in the cove.

The **King's Closet** was his private study, where he would receive ministers and secretaries of state. The Back Stairs lead to the **King's Private Apartments** on the ground floor. Most of the paintings are from William's collection, as are those in the Middle Closet. The long and airy Orangery has a series of sculpture busts of philosophers by Hubert Le Sueur ('Praxiteles Le Sueur', as he liked to sign himself) and the original Privy Garden statuary (in the garden itself are copies). The King's Private Drawing Room and Private Dining Room were where William entertained unofficially, the latter hung with Sir Godfrey Kneller's important *Hampton Court Beauties*, a series of full-length portraits of the principal court ladies, commissioned by Queen Mary.

The Queen's Apartments

Intended for Mary II, who died in 1694 before the completion of the palace, some of the Queen's Apartments were used by William III but the rest remained empty. In 1715–18 they were set up for the use of the Prince and Princess of Wales, later George II and Queen Caroline, and on George II's accession to the throne they were redecorated and refurbished for Caroline. The **Queen's Staircase**, originally panelled and whitewashed, was painted by William Kent in 1734 to create a more lavish entrance. The vast allegorical oil painting, *Mercury Presenting the Liberal Arts to Apollo and Diana*, by Gerrit van Honthorst (1628), shows Charles I and Henrietta Maria as Jupiter and Juno with the Duke of Buckingham as Apollo. The **Queen's Guard Chamber** is where the Yeomen of the Guard were stationed to control access to the queen. They appear on the extraordinary chimneypiece, possibly made by Gibbons, the design sometimes attributed to Sir John Vanbrugh, who was also responsible for the room's architecture. The sober **Queen's Presence Chamber** was also designed by Vanbrugh, who was employed at the palace early in the reign of George I.

The **Public Dining Room** was used by George II and Queen Caroline when they dined in the presence of the court. The **Queen's Audience Chamber** was used for the reception of important visitors. It retains Queen Caroline's crimson throne canopy. The **Queen's Drawing Room** is the central room on Wren's east façade. Aligned with the Long Water, dug for Charles II, the view from the window shows the avenue of yews and other trees stretching into the distance. The queen's 'drawing rooms' took place here, where ladies of the court gossiped and played cards. The painted ceiling and walls, the latter in imitation of tapestries, were executed by Verrio and a team of assistants from 1703. Commissioned by Queen Anne, who succeeded William III, the theme is royal naval power. Anne's husband, Prince George of Denmark, features prominently as Lord High Admiral. Prince George was fond of Hampton Court and these apartments were set up for his use. This was Verrio's last commission—he was by this time an ageing man with poor eyesight—and the work has, with justification, been much criticised (although it is much restored, George II having covered it up with wallpaper).

The **Queen's State Bedchamber** has its original bed, made in 1715, and a painted ceiling by Sir James Thornhill, *Leucothoë Restraining Apollo from entering his Chariot*, with oval portraits of members of the Royal family in the cove. The **Queen's Gallery** was used by William III, who displayed here Mantegna's *Triumphs of Caesar* (*see p.*

522). The 18th-century Brussels tapestries, episodes from the story of Alexander the Great, were hung here by George I. The **Queen's Closet** is hung with needlework panels made for Mary II, in the style of the French Huguenot Baroque designer Daniel Marot, who worked for the queen when he was briefly in England.

THE GEORGIAN ROOMS

These rooms comprise the apartments occupied by George II and Queen Caroline—who last visited the palace with the court in 1737—and the new apartments created in 1732 by William Kent for their second son, William Augustus, Duke of Cumberland. The **Duke's Bedchamber** has an elaborate Palladian bed niche. The **Wolsey Closet** is a 19th-century assembly of salvaged Tudor fragments which evokes a 1530s' royal closet.

The **Communication Gallery** was built for William III in the 1690s. It displays Sir Peter Lely's exceptional *Windsor Beauties*, a set of pictures of court ladies commissioned by Anne Hyde, first wife of James II, in the early 1660s. Notable figures such as Frances Stuart, Duchess of Richmond and Charles II's mistress Barbara Villiers are included. The **Cartoon Gallery** was built by Wren as William III's private picture gallery. It was soon altered specifically to take Raphael's 'Acts of the Apostles' cartoons (*see p. 519*).

The **Queen's Private Apartments** were built by Wren for Mary II. They are presented today as occupied by Queen Caroline in the 1730s. The Queen's Private Drawing Room is hung with rare 18th-century crimson flock wallpaper and has a large 17th-century Isfahan carpet. Her Private Bedchamber is hung with Mortlake tapestries of c. 1685. Above the chimneypiece, set within a dense roundel of carved flowers by Gibbons, is a portrait of Queen Caroline by Joseph Highmore. The Queen's Dressing Room and Bathroom preserve a silver-gilt toilet service made c. 1695 by Daniel Garnier and engraved in 1740. Beyond the Private Dining Room and Sideboard Room is the Queen's Private Oratory, with a lofty carved and moulded dome, where Caroline would hear sermons and services from her chaplain.

THE PALACE GARDENS

Henry VIII laid out elaborate ornamental gardens which comprised a privy garden, a public garden, pleasure gardens and a tiltyard for jousting and tournaments. Beyond lay parkland. The gardens today reflect their Baroque transformation under William and Mary, who laid out the great avenues of trees to the east—such a defining feature of the present Hampton Court—as well as the Privy Garden's elaborate parterre to the south and the Wilderness to the north.

South Gardens

The **Privy Garden**, the King's private garden, was completed for William III in 1702, its magnificent symmetry of design seen to best effect from the windows of the King's Apartments. Recent restoration has re-established the great ornamental parterre, with its box and gravel arabesques, carefully placed clipped evergreens, its fountain basin at the centre, and elegant statuary. The great screens at the bottom of the garden, by the Thames, of wrought iron with elaborate gilded panels, are by Jean Tijou, originally made for the east front Fountain Garden. The **Pond Garden** was where Henry VIII's freshwater ponds were, which provided fish for the kitchens.

The **Lower Orangery** (**9**; *entered from Base Court*) houses Andrea Mantegna's magnificent *Triumphs of Caesar* (c. 1486–94), exceptional Italian Renaissance works made for the Gonzaga court at Mantua, purchased by Charles I in 1629 with other works from the Gonzaga collection. Their triumphal allegory reflected the king's military prowess. The **Great Vine**, in its purpose-built glasshouse, is from a cutting of the Black Hamburg vine at Valentine's Park, Essex. Planted by 'Capability' Brown in 1768, it is the oldest vine in the world and is tended by a resident keeper. On the east facing wall of the vine-keeper's house is the Great Wisteria, only a couple of decades younger.

The elegant **Banqueting House (10)** is a pleasure pavilion on the edge of the Thames. Its three rooms are richly decorated, with Gibbons carving and Verrio decorative work.

Great Fountain Garden

The semicircular area immediately east of the palace was laid out as the Great Fountain Garden for William III, an expansive parterre with twelve marble fountains. The scheme was simplified by Queen Anne, who dug the encircling canal. The central **Long Water (11)** was created for Charles II in the 1660s. At the north end of the Broad Walk is the Royal Tennis Court, built in the 1620s and still in use today.

North Gardens

The northern gardens occupy the site of the Wilderness, in place by 1686 but to which William III made alterations, a plantation of hollies and bay trees with winding paths and openings in elaborate, symmetrical patterns, a great yew tree at its centre. The feature which remains today is the world-famous **Maze (12)**, the oldest planted maze in the country, although its hedges have been renewed over the centuries. Originally of hornbeam, it was entirely replaced with yew in the 1960s, although hornbeam was partly reintroduced in 2005 and is being monitored to see how well it responds to the constant stream of visitors. Also introduced in 2005 was an audio installation by the sound artists Greyworld: lost visitors will hear fragmented music, distant laughter and the rustle of silks.

KINGSTON UPON THAMES

Map p. 594, C4. Trains to Kingston from Waterloo in c. 25mins.

The Royal Borough of Kingston upon Thames is one of the oldest royal boroughs in London. Its local museum was opened in 1904 and houses three permanent exhibitions and a collection of topographical paintings of the local area, as well as playing host to an art gallery for temporary displays of contemporary community art.

KINGSTON MUSEUM
Sallie Gardner, a horse owned by Leland Stanford, running at Palo Alto in 1878.
Images by Eadweard Muybridge.

KINGSTON MUSEUM

Wheatfield Rd (5mins' walk from the station). Open Tues, Fri and Sat 10–5, Thur 10–7; closed bank holidays. Admission charge. Shop. T: 020 8547 5006.

The exhibition 'Ancient Origins' examines the life of Kingston from Palaeolithic times to the Saxon period. Items on show include Mesolithic flint axe-heads, Bronze Age spears, three Saxon swords and some Roman coins. The **Eadweard Muybridge exhibition** celebrates one of Kingston's most famous past residents. Born Edward James Muggeridge in 1830, Muybridge moved to New York and later San Francisco to work in the book trade, becoming interested in landscape photography, from which profession he made his fortune. Challenged to establish whether a running horse ever has all four feet off the ground at any one time, Muybridge set up a camera shed at the stud farm of the tycoon and founder of Stanford University, Leland Stanford, and proved to the world that a horse can indeed fly. He later produced *Animal Locomotion* (1887), 751 plates of animal and human locomotion, based on studies carried out at the University of Pennsylvania. Muybridge bequeathed to the museum his lantern slides, his zoöpraxiscope (a device which could display photographic motion pictures) and a number of plates from *Animal Locomotion*.

The 'Town of Kings' exhibition narrates the story of the town of Kingston from its early origins (a period in which seven Anglo Saxon kings were reputed to have been crowned in its precincts) to modern times. One can view a life-size model of one of the seven crowned monarchs, King Aethelstan (895–939), the reconstruction of a medieval kiln and a penny farthing and boneshaker bicycle.

WINDSOR
Mute swans on the Thames.

Windsor & Eton

Facing each other across the Thames are Windsor, with its famous royal castle, and Eton, with its equally famous boys' school.

Windsor, 21 miles west of central London, although not within the Greater London area, is an easy day trip. Anglo Saxon kings settled at Old Windsor, three miles from the current town, but after 1066, when William I built a fortress at New Windsor, the royal household moved here. As well as Windsor Castle, rising majestically over the town, Windsor's attractions include shops, restaurants, hotels, a theatre (Theatre Royal), riverside walks and boat trips and a racecourse. It is connected by footbridge to Eton.

Getting to Windsor, eating and drinking

Map p. 594, A3. Trains from Waterloo to Windsor & Eton Riverside in c. 45mins, then a 5-min walk to the centre; the road snakes uphill along Thames Street, past the George V memorial fountain, with the walls of the castle rising on your left, until you reach the High Street. There are also trains from Paddington (change at Slough) to Windsor & Eton Central, directly opposite the castle on the High Street.

Most of the station buildings have been converted into Windsor Royal Shopping, an arcade of shops, restaurants and cafés. Also here is the Royal Windsor Information Centre: Old Booking Hall, 52A Windsor Royal Shopping, Thames St. T: 01753 743900. There are also places to eat in Windsor old town.

WINDSOR CASTLE

Open March–Oct 9.45–5.15, last admission 4pm; Nov–Feb 9.45–4.15, last admission 3pm. Admission charge. The castle is often wholly or partially closed; check website. Tickets may be booked online. T: 020 7766 7304, royalcollection.org.uk. Changing of the Guard takes place Mon–Sat at 11am in April–July and on alternate days at other times of year. Check the website for schedules. The ceremony lasts approx. 45mins.

The history of Windsor Castle spans a thousand years: it is the oldest and largest occupied castle in the world. Thirty-nine British monarchs have lived here; HM The Queen is in official residence at Easter and for the Garter Service (*see below*) in June. She also uses the castle to entertain visiting heads of state and foreign dignitaries and members of the Royal Family host charitable receptions in the Royal Apartments, which are furnished with artworks from the Royal Collections. It is also the Queen's favourite palace for private weekend use and when she is in residence the royal standard flutters from the Round Tower.

THE ORDER OF THE GARTER

The Order of the Garter was founded by Edward III in 1348 and is the oldest and the highest British Order of Chivalry. Its motto is *Honi soit qui mal y pense* ('Shame on him who thinks ill of it'). The words were first spoken, according to the popular story, by Edward III when dancing with his daughter-in-law, whose garter slipped to the floor. Kind Edward picked it up and tied it around his own leg. Membership today consists of the Sovereign, the Prince of Wales and 24 'companions', either men or women, chosen by the Sovereign from among those who have held public office, who have contributed to national life or who have personally served the Sovereign. The patron saint of the Order is St George and its spiritual home is St George's Chapel, Windsor. In June, the Knights of the Garter gather at Windsor Castle, where new Knights take the oath and are invested with the insignia. A lunch is given in the Waterloo Chamber, after which the Knights process to a service in St George's Chapel, wearing their blue velvet robes (with the badge of the Order—St George's Cross within the Garter surrounded by radiating silver beams—on the left shoulder) and black velvet hats with white plumes.

Windsor Castle occupies a naturally defensive position, a chalk cliff rising 30m above the Thames. It was built by William I from 1070–86 to defend the western approach to London and formed part of a larger network of Norman fortifications. The original wooden fortress was built according to standard Norman motte-and-bailey design although the keep that surmounts the artificial earth mound (motte) was unusually defended by two baileys (today the Upper and Lower Wards). Henry II rebuilt the castle in stone and in 1170 the wooden Norman keep was replaced with the Round Tower. Henry III improved and extended it (the D-shaped towers in the walls tend to be from Henry III's reign and the square towers from Henry II's) but preserved the original plan of two baileys and a motte hill. Under the 14th-century warrior king Edward III, William of Wykeham, Bishop of Winchester, transformed Windsor from a defensive fort into a Christian Gothic palace and built the royal apartments in the Upper Ward. During the Civil War, Windsor Castle was used as a Royalist prison; Charles I spent his last Christmas here as a prisoner (1648) before his execution the following January. After the Restoration in 1660, Charles II, influenced by what his cousin Louis XIV was doing at Versailles, turned the castle into a grand Baroque palace to glorify and accentuate the permanence of the restored monarchy. Gentleman-architect Hugh May oversaw the transformation. George IV created sumptuous royal apartments here and during his reign the exterior of the castle was re-Gothicised and towers and battlements were added to create a romantic castle ideal. The present aspect of the building dates from the extensive restorations undertaken by Jeffry Wyatt, who changed his name to Wyatville. During Queen Victoria's reign the castle fulfilled a twofold role of private royal retreat and magnificent palace for the ceremonial entertaining of visiting dignitaries. In the 1840s the state apartments were opened to the public.

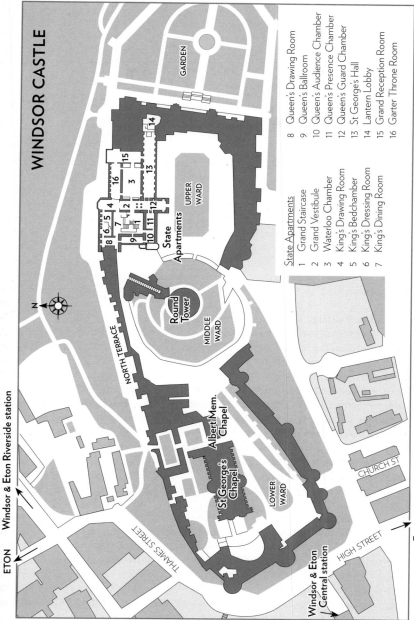

WINDSOR CASTLE

State Apartments

1 Grand Staircase
2 Grand Vestibule
3 Waterloo Chamber
4 King's Drawing Room
5 King's Bedchamber
6 King's Dressing Room
7 King's Dining Room

8 Queen's Drawing Room
9 Queen's Ballroom
10 Queen's Audience Chamber
11 Queen's Presence Chamber
12 Queen's Guard Chamber
13 St George's Hall
14 Lantern Lobby
15 Grand Reception Room
16 Garter Throne Room

ETON   Windsor & Eton Riverside station

Windsor & Eton Central station

Frogmore

CHURCH ST

HIGH STREET

THAMES STREET

NORTH TERRACE

N

GARDEN

UPPER WARD

State Apartments

Round Tower

MIDDLE WARD

Albert Mem. Chapel

St George's Chapel

LOWER WARD

In November 1992 a fire started in Queen Victoria's private chapel and spread to St George's Hall, the Grand Reception Room, the State Dining Room, the Crimson Drawing Room as well as rooms on neighbouring floors, causing millions of pounds' worth of damage. By fortunate coincidence, the rooms that were gutted and most badly damaged had been due for electrical rewiring so had been emptied of their contents, and thus many treasures survived. The castle has since been repaired and restored by teams of craftsmen, either in a neo-Gothic style using medieval building techniques, or as recreations of the way the rooms looked during the reign of George IV. Today the fabric of the castle is in better shape than it has been for two centuries.

VISITING THE CASTLE

Once past the ticket office, through the airport-style security checks and past the audio guide hut, the visitor climbs Castle Hill and circles the Middle Ward. Here there is a good view of the Round Tower, built in 1170 by Henry II and extended upwards by George IV for pictorial effect. Today it houses the Royal Archives. The moat has always been dry and is planted as a lush ornamental garden with a small a trickling waterfall on one side. The grassy mound blooms with seeded daffodil, narcissus and primrose in the spring. Go through an archway in the curtain wall to enter the North Terrace, developed from the reign of Henry VIII, commanding splendid views towards Eton and beyond. On your right is the entrance to Queen Mary's Dolls' House and the State Apartments.

Queen Mary's Dolls' House

Queen Mary's Doll's House, never intended as a toy, was given to Queen Mary in 1924 and exhibited at the British Empire Exhibition the same year. It was designed by Sir Edwin Lutyens on a scale of 1:12 (it measures 8ft by 5ft) as an accurate replica of a contemporary aristocratic London house. It is fully plumbed with hot and cold running water, has electric lights, two lifts and is filled with miniature furnishings and objects made by leading artists, craftsmen and designers of the day. The wine in the cellar is genuine, the books in the walnut-panelled library were specially handwritten by prominent authors (including J.M. Barrie, Hilaire Belloc, Sir Arthur Conan Doyle and Rudyard Kipling), the tiny clocks are by Cartier, the silverware by Garrard and the provisions in the kitchen are all British brands in accurately reproduced packaging. In the maid's closet is the latest in cleaning devices: a working electric vacuum cleaner. The miniature garden was designed by Gertrude Jekyll and has birds nesting in the trees.

Drawings Gallery

The Drawings Gallery, in a vaulted undercroft designed by James Wyatt for George III, holds temporary exhibitions of works from the Royal Collections. In the China Museum is the Rockingham Service, commissioned by William IV in 1830 from the Yorkshire pottery. This ambitious porcelain dinner service, decorated with symbols representative of Britain's far-reaching empire, from Indian scenes to exotic fruits, sugar cane and pineapples, bankrupted the family who ran the pottery, but it was finally completed and delivered to Queen Victoria in 1837.

The Grand Staircase and Waterloo Chamber

Ascend the **Grand Staircase**, with a huge statue of George IV (1832) by Chantrey on the half-landing, past suits of armour made for Henry VIII and Henry, Prince of Wales, to reach the **Grand Vestibule**. Here, beneath James Wyatt's plaster fan-vaulted ceiling, a late work for George III, are displayed all manner of arms, armour and trophies, some intricately gem-set. In the showcase on your left is a relic from the magnificent palace of Tipu Sultan: a large gold tiger's head with rock crystal fangs which once adorned the great Tiger of Mysore's throne. In the showcase opposite is a mounted bullet: the very **musket ball that killed Lord Nelson**. It was extracted from Nelson's left shoulder on the deck of HMS *Victory* at his death in 1805; it is difficult to make out but it is said that a tiny fragment of Nelson's uniform is still attached to it.

The splendid **Waterloo Chamber**, designed by Wyatville, displays superb portraits by Sir Thomas Lawrence of the monarchs, statesmen and commanders who contributed to the defeat of Napoleon Bonaparte. On the east wall is a portrait of the Duke of Wellington, leader of the allied forces at the Battle of Waterloo in 1815. The limewood carvings, by Grinling Gibbons and his assistants (1680s), are relics from the Royal Chapel demolished in the 1820s. The roof was designed and decorated by the firm of Crace, who worked for George IV at the Royal Pavilion, Brighton. This room was spared in the 1992 fire due to the thickness of its medieval walls.

The State Apartments

The State Apartments, grand Baroque sequences of rooms, now much altered, were built for Charles II and Catherine of Braganza between 1675 and 1678. They were richly decorated by the Neapolitan mural painter Antonio Verrio, with additional limewood carvings by Grinling Gibbons and his assistants and hung with sumptuous tapestries and textiles and recovered works of art that had once belonged to Charles I. Today the rooms display numerous masterpieces—paintings, furniture, objects— from the Royal Collections. In the **King's Drawing Room**, where Charles II received important visitors, is Van Dyck's famous study for a bust of Charles I in three positions. The organ clock (c. 1740), with a rock crystal casket, is believed to be by Charles Clay and plays ten tunes, five of which are arrangements by Handel. In the casket is the Bible used by General Gordon at Khartoum. The **King's Bedchamber** was hung in crimson silk for George III; the bed was installed for a state visit by Emperor Napoleon III and Empress Eugénie; the green and mauve silk hangings are the colours of the Third Empire. The **King's Dressing Room**, hung with Northern Renaissance paintings, including Brueghel's *Massacre of the Innocents* (1565–7), is probably where Charles II slept. In the **King's Closet**, Charles II's most private room, are fine Italian Renaissance paintings; Bronzino's *Portrait of a Lady in Green* (c. 1530) was originally in the collection of Charles I. In the wood-panelled **King's Dining Room** is one of the three surviving ceilings by Antonio Verrio. Painted in the 1670s, it depicts a banquet of the gods. On the walls, the festoon carvings by Grinling Gibbons and his assistants incorporate life-like renderings of crustaceans and fish.

In the **Queen's Drawing Room** are fine Tudor and Stuart royal portraits. The **Queen's Ballroom** has a superb collection of portraits by Van Dyck, including *The*

Five Eldest Children of Charles I (1637). Also worthy of mention is the solid silver furniture—tables and mirrors—the ultimate symbols of wealth and power and rare survivors from the late 17th century. The fashion for silver furniture was started by Louis XIV at Versailles; many sets were subsequently melted down for currency. The **Queen's Audience Chamber** and the **Queen's Presence Chamber** both retain their painted ceilings by Verrio: Queen Catherine is depicted in glorified compositions at the centre of both. Both rooms also retain carving by Gibbons and his assistants; the tapestries are later acquisitions by George IV. The **Queen's Guard Chamber**, which in the 17th century would have served as entrance to the queen's apartments, was altered to its current neo-Gothic appearance by Wyatville. Here is a large bust by Chantrey of Nelson (1835) and decorative wall displays of arms; the examples in the display cases came from George IV's collection at Carlton House. Above the busts of Wellington and Marlborough hang the annual rent banners for Stratfield Saye and Woodstock. The bust of Churchill is by Oscar Nemon (1953).

The 185ft **St George's Hall**, created by Wyatville for George IV from two separate rooms, is used for state banquets, when it is filled by an enormous dining table that seats 160, groaning with fine porcelain, plate and crystal from the Royal Collections. The hall was gutted in the 1992 fire and has been restored; the neo-Gothic hammer-beam roof, by Giles Downes of the Sidell Gibson Partnership, was constructed in green oak using medieval techniques. It is decorated with hundreds of heraldic shields of Knights of the Garter since 1348; the plain white shields represent those of 'degraded' knights who have been struck from the Order over the centuries.

The **Lantern Lobby**, formerly the Victoria Chapel, is where the 1992 fire started. Also by Downes, it is said to be inspired by the octagon in Ely Cathedral and the Abbey of Batalha in Portugal, and provides a processional route between the State and the Semi-State Apartments. It also functions as a treasury and displays fine examples of silver-gilt plate from the Royal Collections.

The Semi-State Apartments

The Semi-State Apartments, created by Wyatville as George IV's private rooms, are used by HM The Queen for entertaining and are open to the public only during the winter months. They were severely damaged by the 1992 fire but their contents—which had been moved out—survived largely intact and this was the chief impetus behind the decision to restore them to their late-Georgian gilded glory. What the visitor sees today is largely how the rooms would have appeared during the reign of George IV; some of the furnishings were originally at Carlton House.

The next room on the main tour is the Rococo-revival **Grand Reception Room**, exemplifying George IV's own preferences for all things French, with 18th-century panelling imported from Paris. It has been perfectly restored since the fire and the parquet floor is original; the singed blocks were simply turned over. It is used by HM The Queen to greet guests before a state banquet.

Finally, the **Garter Throne Room** is where new Knights and Ladies of the Garter are invested. It was Queen Victoria's throne room, and it is here that she received visitors on the Indian ivory throne.

St George's Chapel

St George's Chapel, in the Lower Ward, is a superb Perpendicular building, begun in 1475 by Henry Janyns for Edward IV and continued in the early 16th century by William Vertue. It is one of the most perfect extant specimens of 15th–16th-century Gothic architecture in England. Ten British monarchs are buried here.

The **west window** preserves pre-Reformation glass of 1503–9 depicting not only kings and their people, but also popes and saints. The nave has a fine ribbed vault with liernes and carved bosses bearing emblems of Henry VII. Between the nave and the north aisle is the **tomb of George V** (d. 1936) by Lutyens and Reid Dick, and of his consort Queen Mary (d. 1953), for whom the Dolls' House was made. In the **Urswick Chapel** (first north) is Matthew Wyatt's tomb of Princess Charlotte, George IV's only child, who died in childbirth in 1817, aged 21, occasioning a huge outpouring of public grief. She lies under an all-covering shroud from which only four fingers protrude, but also rises to heaven, accompanied by angels, one of whom carries the stillborn baby.

The choir is separated from the nave by a neo-Gothic screen (c. 1785–90). Off the north choir aisle is the **Memorial Chapel of George VI**, where Queen Elizabeth, the Queen Mother and the ashes of Princess Margaret are also interred. In the north choir aisle itself is the **Chantry Chapel of William, Lord Hastings**, with contemporary paintings of his execution in 1483. He was put to death by Richard III on charges of having conspired against the king's life. A superb pair of gates (1482) fronts the **tomb of Edward IV** (north of the high altar). Above the royal pew is a wooden oriel provided by Henry VIII for Katherine of Aragon to watch the Garter ceremonies.

In the centre of the floor of the **choir** is a vault containing the remains of Henry VIII and Jane Seymour (the wife who bore him a son) together with Charles I and a still-born child of Queen Anne. In the Royal Vault are the remains of George III and Queen Charlotte, George IV and William IV. The three tiers of carved wooden stalls (1478–85 with 18th-century adjustments) are surmounted by the helmets, crests and banners of the Knights of the Garter, whose installations have taken place at Windsor since 1348. At a member's death their 'achievements' are removed but the brass stall plate, with the member's name, arms and date of installation, is retained as a memorial; there are about 600 heraldic stall plates here. The reverse stalls are those of the royal family, the sovereign's stall marked by the Royal Standard.

In the south choir aisle is the **Chantry of John Oxenbridge**, with paintings of 1522. It also contains the great sword of Edward III and a simple slab marking the **tomb of Henry VI**, founder of Eton College. On the south side of the high altar is the **tomb of Edward VII** and Queen Alexandra.

In the **ambulatory**, the east wall once formed the west front of Henry III's Chapel (1240–8) and retains its original doors. The **Albert Memorial Chapel**, conceived by Henry VII as a burial place for Henry VI, was later completed by Cardinal Wolsey. Wolsey's tomb, which had never been used, was broken up during the Civil War: its black marble sarcophagus now forms part of Nelson's tomb in the crypt of St Paul's. Queen Victoria had the chapel converted into a memorial to Prince Albert (d. 1861), who is buried at Frogmore (*see below*). The chapel also contains the tombs of the Duke of Clarence, eldest son of Edward VII, who died of influenza in 1892 aged 28 (tomb by

Alfred Gilbert, sculptor of 'Eros' in Piccadilly), and of Leopold, Duke of Albany, Queen Victoria's haemophiliac son, who died in 1884 aged 30.

FROGMORE HOUSE

To the north and east of the Castle is the Home Park. In the south part is **Frogmore House** (*access along Windsor High St and then Park St; guided tours in summer; see royalcollection.org.uk for details*), used as a retreat by Queen Charlotte, consort of George III, and her unmarried daughters. Queen Charlotte was a great botanist and created splendid gardens here. Queen Victoria loved Frogmore: the 'Indian Kiosk' in the garden is her addition. Also in the garden is the **Mausoleum** (*not open to the public at the time of writing*), a centrally-planned tomb chamber where the Prince Consort and Queen Victoria lie side by side in their sarcophagi. Also buried here are the Duke of Windsor (the former King Edward VIII; d. 1972) and his wife, the former Mrs Wallis Simpson (d. 1994).

WINDSOR TOWN

At the foot of Castle Hill, a **statue of Queen Victoria** by Sir Joseph Boehm (1887) stands on what was the centre of the medieval marketplace. The **Guildhall**, on the High Street, opposite the Castle Hotel, was designed by Sir Thomas Fitch in 1686 and finished by Sir Christopher Wren in 1707. It is adorned with statues of Queen Anne and Prince George of Denmark and has royal portraits and collections of Windsor's silver plate in its museum.

Windsor Old Town consists of a network of cobbled streets and attractive and tightly-packed old houses. In Church Street is the **Old King's Head**, with a copy of Charles I's death warrant, signed by Oliver Cromwell, on the wall opposite Church Street Gardens (a small public square). Next door is Burford House (1640), where Nell Gwyn, mistress of Charles II, once lived. The parish church of **St John the Baptist** in the High Street contains a *Last Supper* attributed to the painter and tapestry designer Francis Cleyn. The mosaics in the chancel and apse are by Antonio Salviati.

The **Household Cavalry Museum** in Combermere Barracks, St Leonard's Road, can be visited by appointment (*T: 01753 755112*).

South of Windsor is **Windsor Great Park**, crossed by The Long Walk, planted with elms by Charles II and replanted after 1945 with horse chestnut and plane trees. It stretches for almost three miles. At the end of it is a great statue of George III (known as 'The Copper Horse') by Westmacott. It shows the monarch in the Roman attitude of *acclamatio*, arm outstretched.

Between Windsor and Staines is **Runnymede** (*map p. 594, A3*), where King John fixed his seal to the Magna Carta, the great charter of English liberties, on 15th June 1215.

North of Windsor Castle, **Windsor Town Bridge** (1824; *pedestrians and cycles only*) crosses the Thames to Eton.

SWAN UPPING

Swan Upping is the name given to the ceremony of the swan census which takes place every year on certain reaches of the Thames. It traces its origins back to the 12th century, when the sovereign claimed ownership of all Mute swans (a culinary delicacy). Swans are no longer eaten, but the census still takes place annually in the third week of July. Royal ownership of the swans is symbolically retained, and is held together with the Worshipful Companies of Vintners and Dyers, two of the City of London's ancient livery companies (*for more on these, see p. 21*). 'Swan Uppers' representing HM The Queen and the two livery companies, all clad in splendid scarlet uniforms, embark in six skiffs, propelled by oars, to find and mark all new cygnets on the Thames. When the skiffs row past Windsor Castle, the Swan Uppers utter the traditional salute: 'Her Majesty The Queen, Seigneur of the Swans!' The ceremony takes five days. All cygnets are marked with a small nick in the beak, are examined for disease or injury (the Queen's Swan Warden is a qualified professor of ornithology), and are returned to the water.

The aura of bygone ritual, the prop-box costumes and the man-powered boats may make the ceremony appear little more than pantomime. But it fulfils an important function. Swans are not endangered but their habitats are threatened by increased river use by humans and their lives are put at risk by stray lengths of fishing line. The Swan Upping ceremony carefully and scientifically monitors how well they are faring and does much to ensure the survival of this wild species. Watching the ceremony, in any case, is a thrilling spectacle.

ETON

Eton College, probably the most famous school in England, was founded by Henry VI in 1440 to provide an education to poor scholars. It remains single-sex (boys only) and all its pupils are boarders. It is the best known of all the English public schools, famous for its uniform of morning coats and pinstripe trousers. The term 'public school' was originally used to indicate that entry was not subject to religious or professional restrictions. Today it means that a school is independent and fee-paying.

Over the centuries Eton has educated a great many statesmen, soldiers, poets, ne'er-do-wells and public servants. Famous old Etonians include the Duke of Wellington, Beau Brummell, George Gordon (instigator of the eponymous riots) and the poet Thomas Gray, who wrote his 'Ode on a Distant Prospect of Eton College' on seeing a group of schoolboys out on the playing field, laughing and shouting, full of the innocence and irresponsibility of youth. 'Alas, regardless of their doom, the little victims play!' he wrote, glumly: 'No sense have they of ills to come, nor care beyond today.'

Getting to Eton, eating and drinking
Map. p. 594, A3. Trains from Victoria to Windsor & Eton Riverside in c. 50mins. Or cross the pedestrian Windsor Town Bridge from Windsor, which leads directly into Eton High Street, lined with shops and tearooms. Guided tours of Eton College can be booked. Admission charge. For details, see etoncollege.com.

THE ETON EXPERIENCE

by Charles Freeman, Old Etonian and freelance historian.

The battle of Waterloo was, they say, won on the playing fields of Eton. My own first encounter, as a 13-year-old, with the soggy pitches where a melée of adolescents swarmed to and fro in Eton's own version of football, the Field Game, suggested that Napoleon would have made short work of us. The essence of Eton is that it tolerates diversity and a bit of disorganisation—not attributes of much use on a battlefield.

Eton is tribal. One is very conscious of joining an institution that for over five and a half centuries has attracted an extraordinary variety of Englishmen, and, increasingly, others from further afield. This long history gives it the confidence to accept diversity and reject uniformity. Many of the most important activities are run by the boys themselves. I never had the sense that any Head Master, even the redoubtable Robert Birley, Head Master when I first arrived, who had served with distinction as an educationalist in post-war Germany and later went out to fight for human rights in South Africa, was really in charge. Where Eton life matters is in the 'house', usually made up of some 50 boys, its character wholly dependent on the quality of the House Master. Some clearly did not care what went on: when my second House Master, an energetic Welsh historian and cricket enthusiast, Ray Parry, took over his house, he told how one of his first tasks had been to clear out the empty gin bottles. It is in the house that the tone is set that will determine whether a boy settles happily at Eton or not. I was lucky with Ray Parry and I stayed in touch with him until the end of his life.

Within the house—many of which were in dreadful condition in the '60s—each boy has his own room. This is one of the great secrets of Eton's success. The rooms were hardly grand. A 'Boy's Maid' woke one with a jug of hot water for the basin, which was heated by a coal fire which one lit and made up oneself. The bed folded up into the wall to give more room. Yet one had private space. And with so many chores done for one, there was ample time to fit in reading. One 'half' (as Etonians have persisted in calling 'terms' ever since they were increased from two a year to three in the 18th century) I developed a passion for the novels of Nevil Shute and got through 14 of them largely without interruption. In the afternoons we would 'mess' together for tea, that is, cook up something in the small kitchen (there was one on each floor) with one's chosen companions.

Yet much of this freedom came from a lack of rigour in the schoolrooms (some of them the originals)—very different from what is expected at the school today. In the '60s, education was much more haphazard. The ability to teach never appeared to be high on the criteria for employment as a teacher and some teachers were simply recycled old boys. Classics still dominated the curriculum. Much time was wasted in attempting to translate English prose into Latin verse and some of the Classics teachers, expert at the most obscure linguistic aberrations of Greek and Latin grammar, seemed to have no knowledge of the great civilisations themselves. It was always a tense moment at the beginning of each 'half', when one looked to see who would be teaching one and whether a term would be wasted or full of interest. Every now and again one struck lucky. I became completely absorbed by the Minoans and Mycenaeans in my first year because a teacher inspired me, and an excellent course on the literature of the '20s and '30s began just before I left. My biggest regret, as an avid reader, is never having been introduced to English literature earlier—it was simply not on the curriculum when I arrived. Yet a course on archaeology was offered and we were allocated a neglected room behind the School Hall, which (in the way things tended to happen at Eton) actually held one of the finest collections of Egyptian antiquities in the country, the Myers Bequest. Now it has at last been recognised for its quality and pieces have been lent out to international exhibitions.

I had a similar experience at the College Library, whose outstanding collection of books goes back to the 16th century. I had entered a national essay prize for which some original academic work was required and heard that the Library had one of the best collections of political pamphlets on the English Civil War in existence. I chose them as my subject. Thus it was that two evenings a week for a 'half', I waited outside the Library door until the College Librarian, a Dr Prescott, unlocked it and handed me my volumes. He never asked me how I was getting on and I never saw a single other visitor to the Library while I was there—but I do now know perhaps more than most people about Civil War pamphlets. Today the Library has been taken in hand, new collections added and its riches displayed.

To get to the Library I had to walk through School Yard, with its statue of Henry VI, who founded a school for 70 poor scholars in 1440. The imposing 16th-century Lupton's Tower stands at the far end, the rooms of the Collegers (boys who have won scholarships) to the left and the magnificent 15th-century College Chapel on the right. It was a special experience when the evening sun was setting. The Chapel is only half the size Henry intended it to be but one of its treasures is a magnificent array of faded wall paintings by Flemish masters dating from the late 15th century. Covered over at the Reformation, it was only in the last century that they were fully restored. The chapel also has fine 20th-century windows, some designed by the renowned John Piper, to replace those shattered by a bomb in the Second World War.

Eton tends to get stuck in old traditions. A bitter campaign was waged by diehards when the school abandoned holding the first lesson of the day before breakfast. Fagging, where the older boys were allowed to ask newcomers to run their errands for them, has disappeared—and presumably boys are not allowed to cane other boys as they used to. However one tradition that is returning is that of providing the college with a leaving portrait. In its heyday in the 18th and 19th centuries, this custom endowed the school with masterpieces from some of the finest artists of the day: it is an outstanding collection. Some sitters were more disgruntled with the commitment than others. It cost ten guineas more to have one's hands included in the portrait and it is fun to see how some of the subjects have resolutely tucked theirs away. Now once again, portrait painters are being given their chance with these 18-year-old subjects. Some may one day be Prime Minister, some actors, others academics or explorers and some will undoubtedly end up in prison. There is no guessing where an Eton education may lead.

PRACTICAL
INFORMATION

Getting Around

GETTING TO AND FROM THE AIRPORTS

Heathrow

Heathrow Airport (*map p. 594, B3*) is well connected to central London. All its terminals are on the Piccadilly Line of the Underground (which is why Piccadilly Line trains are so often clogged with suitcases). The journey is not swift, however. It is much quicker (though more expensive) to take the Heathrow Express train, a frequent service between the airport and Paddington Station (*map p. 602, B1; journey time c. 15mins*). Tickets can be bought in the airport arrivals hall and on the Paddington station concourse; or book online. (*For details, see heathrowexpress.com.*)

Gatwick

Gatwick Airport is 28miles south of London but with good connections. Frequent Gatwick Express trains (*gatwickexpress.com*) run from the airport to Victoria Station (*map p. 603, E3; journey time c. 30mins*). Tickets can be bought from the airport arrivals hall or from the Gatwick Express booths at Victoria railway station; or you can book online. A slower but cheaper connecting service is operated by easyBus, which runs coaches to Earls Court (*map p. 602, A4*) every 15–20mins (*journey time c. 65mins; easybus.co.uk*).

Luton

The airport is slightly over 30miles north of London. Trains link Luton Airport Parkway station with St Pancras International (*map p. 601, E3*) in c. 40mins (there are also trains to London Bridge and to Blackfriars, but they tend to be slower services). There is no exclusive Luton Airport train service: the route is served by national rail and this is a major commuter route to and from London—so if your journey from the airport is early in the morning or if you are travelling to the airport during the afternoon rush hour, you may find that the train is very crowded.

Tickets can be purchased in the airport arrivals hall or at Luton Airport Parkway station, which is situated a mile or two from the airport itself. A shuttle bus makes the connection (bus stops just outside the airport terminal/railway station building). The shuttle service is not free: when buying your train ticket, specify that you want to travel all the way to/from Luton Airport (not Parkway), and the shuttle bus fare will be included in the ticket. If your ticket is only to/from Luton Airport Parkway (the terminus of the train), you will need to scrabble for change to pay the bus driver. There are also coach services from Luton Airport to central London, operated by easyBus to/from Baker Street (*map p. 603, D1; journey time c. 50mins; easybus.co.uk*) and National Express (to/from Victoria Coach Station and other stops on the way; *nationalexpress. com*).

Stansted
Stansted Express trains run frequently between London Liverpool Street (*map p. 605, D1*) and the airport (*journey time c. 50mins; stanstedexpress.com*), which is some 40miles north of London. Coaches operated by easyBus link the airport with Baker Street (*map p. 603, D1; journey time c. 75mins; easybus.co.uk*). There are also National Express coaches to/from the airport and Victoria Coach Station, with several other stops in between (*nationalexpress.com*).

London City
Docklands Light Railway (DLR) trains link London City Airport (*map p. 597, F2*) with the centre of town.

USING PUBLIC TRANSPORT

All travel within London comes under a single umbrella, operated by Transport for London (*tfl.gov.uk*). A single type of ticket is valid on all forms of transport. Ticket desks are located at Underground stations and you can also buy tickets directly from bus drivers. Buying tickets can be time-consuming and fiddly: there are often long queues at the ticket desks, the machines are not as user-friendly as they might be and the more cantankerous-natured bus drivers insist on the exact change. If you are going to be travelling quite a bit, or if you are in London for any length of time, it is a good idea to invest in a Travel Card or an Oyster Card.

Travel Cards
These are available for a single day or for 7 days. If you travel after 9.30am on week-days, or at a weekend, you can get an off-peak card, which is cheaper. Travel Cards are priced according to zone, and thus it is useful to work out which transport zones you will be visiting. London is divided into 9 zones, with Buckingham Palace and St Paul's Cathedral in Zone 1 (the most central) and Hampton Court in Zone 6, the outermost zone covered in tis guide. Maps showing the zones are posted in all stations and at bus stops. Travel Cards covering the inner zones are cheaper than cards which cover all of them.

Oyster Cards
These pay-as-you go cards can be purchased at London Transport ticket offices or online (*tfl.gov.uk*). You put a certain amount of money on the card when you buy it and top it up as needed, either at machines in the Underground stations or again online.

They are convenient and time-saving, covering all zones and automatically calculating the cheapest fare. Place your Oyster Card on the sensor to open the turnstile.

THE LONDON UNDERGROUND

This is the oldest metropolitan underground system in the world. Its network of tunnels is vast, the number of passengers that it handles every day is vaster, and yet somehow it manages to operate (mostly efficiently) 365 days a year, despite a number of antiquated features, miles of tunnels to walk, long escalators, and frustrating numbers of stairs (frustrating if you are travelling with suitcases or pushchairs). Some stations (e.g. Covent Garden) have no escalators, only lifts (or stairs). It is also worth knowing that two of the lines (the Northern Line and the District Line) have split routes, and at times you need to change trains on the same line to get to the destination you want. Maps of the Underground (based on a famous schematic design of 1931 by Harry Beck) are posted in all stations and free paper copies are readily available for you to slip into your pocket and carry with you. There is also a London Tube Map app.

TRAVELLING ON OVERGROUND TRAINS

The 'London Overground' is the name used to designate a network of suburban trains serving more outlying destinations (e.g. Hampstead Heath, Crystal Palace). On Tube maps it is indicated by parallel orange lines. Ordinary London Transport tickets are valid on these services. London Transport tickets may also be used on National Rail services within London (travelling from Clapham Junction to Barnes, for example) but are not valid on the Heathrow Express, Stansted Express or Gatwick Express, or on National Rail airport services to Luton.

LONDON BUSES

The London double decker bus is famous and most visitors want to ride on one at least once. The original Routemaster bus of the 1950s, with its open boarding and exit platform at the back, has almost completely disappeared, though it survives on one lone route: no 15 between Trafalgar Square and Tower Hill. In 2010 the New Routemaster came into operation. It also has a boarding platform, which you can use to board the bus if you have an oyster card (if not, you must show your ticket to the driver) and via which you can jump off. At the time of writing new Routemasters were in use (not always exclusively) on the following routes: 24 between Pimlico and Hampstead Heath; Route 11 between Liverpool Street station and Fulham Broadway; Route 9 between Trafalgar Square and Kensington High Street; Route 390 between Notting Hill Gate and Archway; Route 38 between Victoria and Hackney.

TRAVELLING BY TAXI

London's **black cabs** are unique and famous. All the major railway stations have taxi ranks. Cruising cabs patrol the streets: look to see whether the orange light on the roof is illuminated. If it is, flag the cab down and the driver will stop where he conveniently may. It is customary to tell the driver where you want to go (speak to him through the front window) before you get in. In most cabs, there is a control panel which allows you to talk to the driver or seal yourself in hermetic silence. There is a meter, always placed so as to be readily visible from the back, which allows you to monitor the price of your journey. When you arrive at your destination, get out and pay the driver, again through the front window. It is customary (but not obligatory) to give a small tip. This need be no more than rounding up the fare to the nearest pound. If you have a large suitcase, the driver can stow it in the space beside him in the front. London taxis may also be booked in advance. For a list of numbers, visit the website: *www.tfl.gov.uk/modes/taxis-and-minicabs/book-a-taxi*.

Independent **minicab** firms abound offering competitive fares that are often cheaper than black cabs. Addison Lee (*addisonlee.com*) is probably London's premier minicab company and gives consistently good service. An important note: it is very important to ensure that your minicab is licensed and the driver and vehicle are insured, so always make your booking in person at the minicab office or by telephone or through an app such as Cabwise or Addison Lee's app. It is illegal for minicab drivers to approach you on the street or outside restaurants, bars and venues: these are unlicensed drivers and for your own safety, you must not use them.

DRIVING IN LONDON

Traffic proceeds at a snail's pace through the capital's streets. Parking is difficult and most of the central areas of town are covered by the 'congestion charge', a fee levied on motor vehicles using central London roads on weekdays between 7am and 6pm. The Congestion Charge Zone is signed by a large white C inside a red circle. If you are going to be driving in London, you can pay the charge online: *see tfl.gov.uk*.

CYCLING IN LONDON

Cycling is becoming ever more popular in London. As commuter routes become steadily more crowded, many people (at any rate, the youthful and the able-bodied) are opting to cycle to and from work. Pedestrians and motorists alike should take care. Cycle lanes crop up all over the place and cyclists all too frequently take risks, cutting across traffic, weaving in and out of lanes and swerving onto pavements.

At many points all over town you will see ranks of bicycles sporting the blue Barclays logo. The ranks are known as 'docking stations' and the bicycles are dubbed 'Boris bikes', from the Mayor of London Boris Johnson who pioneered the scheme of bicycle lending. Bicycles may be hired for short journeys (you will need a credit card) and returned to any available docking station (maps of the network are provided). The scheme works well and is popular. For details, visit the website: *www.tfl.gov.uk/barclayscyclehire*.

GETTING AROUND BY WATER

Not so long ago, London was all but divorced from its river. Now the Thames Path has been opened up for walkers and cyclists along large stretches of river, both right in the heart of the city and in the more outlying districts. Walking along the Thames in parts of the City of London or on the other side of the river, in Southwark, one gets a full appreciation of the tidal nature of the waterway. Wide expanses of the bank are exposed. In fine weather, the silty foreshore is colonised by sunbathers.

BOATS ON THE THAMES

Many boats ply the Thames, both pleasure craft and working commuter services.

Thames Clippers run commuter services between Putney and Blackfriars, Greenwich and the London Eye, and St George Wharf (Vauxhall) and Bankside (Tate Modern). For details and timetables, see their website (*thamesclippers.com*) or consult the timetables at the river piers at any of the stops mentioned above, and also at Tower Pier, Millbank (Tate Britain), Embankment (Houses of Parliament), London Bridge, Canary Wharf and Chelsea Harbour. Thames Clippers also operate sightseeing cruises and the Tate Boat (*see p. 301*).

Thames River Boats operate services to Kew, Richmond and Hampton Court. Services run from Westminster Pier (*map p. 603, F2*) between April and October (*for details, T: 020 7930 2062, wpsa.co.uk*).

City Cruises (*citycruises.com*) offer sightseeing tours on the river from Westminster, London Eye, Tower and Greenwich piers; and **Bateaux London** (*www.bateauxlondon.com*) offer a variety of scheduled dining cruises (choose between the Lunch Cruise, the Sunday Lunch Jazz Cruise, the Afternoon Tea Cruise or the Dinner Cruise). They are not cheap but extremely good fun and the dinner cruises afford excellent views of the Thames by night.

Ferries operate in east London between Woolwich and North Woolwich (*map p. 597, F3*): daily services, free, last boat at 7 or 8pm, *www.royalgreenwich.gov.uk*. In west London, Hammerton's Ferry takes passengers between Ham and Twickenham (*map p. 596, A4*) for a very small fee, every weekend until 5pm, on weekdays April–Sept until 6pm, *T: 020 8892 9620, www.hammertonsferry.com*.

BOATS ON THE CANALS

Waterbuses from Camden Lock (*map p. 600, C2*) or Little Venice (*map p. 596, C2*), all converted narrowboats, run approx. hourly April–Sept, less frequently in the colder months. They call at London Zoo (*for details, see londonwaterbus.com; T: 020 7482 2660 for information; T: 020 7482 2550 to make a group booking*). For details of the **Jason's Trip** canal tour, see p. 282.

Accommodation

There are hundreds of places to stay in London. This guide cannot possibly list them all. What is given below is a selection of some of the finest, chosen for their character, their location, their charm, their value for money or simply for the visitor experience they provide. The listing is divided geographically, based on the chapter scheme of the guide.

Price categories (double room per night) are a guideline only:

££££	£600 and over
£££	£300–600
££	£150–300
£	£150 or under

HOTELS IN THE CITY AND EAST LONDON

££ Fox and Anchor. Six comfortable, individually designed rooms above this popular pub in lively Clerkenwell. Breakfasts from 7am. *115 Charterhouse St. T: 020 7250 1300, www.foxandanchor.com. Map p. 606, B2–B1.*

£–££ Malmaison. Boutique hotel in a former nurses' home on the edge of trendy Clerkenwell and close to the City. Comfortable beds, moody lighting, fast wifi, 24-hr room service. Cocktails and steak are served in the hotel's Stripbar; bar and brasserie dining in the more relaxed Mal Lounge. *18–21 Charterhouse Square. T: 084469 30656, www.malmaison.com. Map p. 606, C1.*

££–££££ The Rookery. Located in Clerkenwell and close to the Barbican and the City. Friendly, quiet, tastefully furnished with antiques—more like an impeccable private club than a hotel. A best-kept secret to those in the know. Concierge, 24-hr room service, use of the conservatory, rooms and suites. *Peter's Lane, Cowcross St. T: 20 7336 0931. www.rookeryhotel.com. Map p. 606, B1.*

£££–££££ Threadneedles. Five-star boutique hotel in the heart of the Square Mile, part of the Marriott chain. In a marble-clad former bank, period features include a mid-19th-century stained-glass dome above the lobby. Rooms vary from standard doubles to penthouses and have every amenity.

Bonds Bar and Restaurant serves breakfast, lunch and dinner. *5 Threadneedle St. T: 0207 657 8080, www.hotelthreadneedles.co.uk. Map p. 607, D3–E3.*

££–£££ The Zetter Hotel. Affordably plush hotel in a fashionable location. 59 designer rooms ranging from modest to rooftop luxury, some with private patios, all with state-of-the-art technology. Extravagant range of guest services including 24-hr room service, free Broadband internet access (wired and wireless), iPod docking station and speakers, oversized duck-down pillows, personally selected Penguin paperbacks, complimentary spring water from The Zetter Borehole, walk-in 'Raindance' showers, mist-free bathroom mirrors. Breakfast is complimentary if you book online. On site is the Bistro Bruno Loubet Restaurant and the Atrium Bar. *St John's Square/86–88 Clerkenwell Rd. T: 020 7324 4444, www.thezetter.com. Map p. 606, B1.*

£–£££ The Zetter Townhouse. Award-winning boutique hotel across the square from the Zetter. 14 rooms in a Georgian house ranging from luxurious crash pads to deluxe suites. Fabulous cocktail lounge. *49–50 St John's Square. T: 020 7324 4567, www.thezettertownhouse.com. Map p. 606, B1.*

HOTELS IN MAYFAIR AND ON PICCADILLY

£££–££££ Claridge's. First opened by William Claridge in 1856, this famous hotel has been a favourite with crowned heads, deposed crowned heads, flappers and film stars ever since. Spencer Tracy famously said he would prefer to go to Claridge's than to heaven. With interiors by Diane von Furstenburg and David Linley. Restaurant, bar, fumoir and health club. *Brook St. T: 020 7629 8860, www.claridges.co.uk. Map p. 603, D1.*

£££–££££ The Connaught. Famous luxury hotel, in business since 1815. General de Gaulle set up residence here in 1940. Michelin-starred restaurant (Hélène Darroze at the Connaught), spa and champagne bar. *Carlos Pl. T: 020 7499 7070, www.the-connaught.co.uk. Map p. 603, D1.*

£££–££££ The Ritz. Perhaps the most famous hotel in London, overlooking Green Park and Piccadilly. To read about it, turn to p. 214. *150 Piccadilly. T: 020 7493 8181, www.theritzlondon.com. Map p. 603, E2.*

HOTELS IN SOHO AND COVENT GARDEN

£££ Covent Garden Hotel. One of the hotels in the Firmdale group: a number of stylish townhouse hotels in prime central locations, conceived and designed by Tim and Kit Kemp. This one has the trademark Firmdale stone fireplaces and public honesty bar. Comfortable, stylishly-appointed rooms. Restaurant. First-floor guest drawing room and library. *10 Monmouth*

St. T: 020 7806 1000, www.firmdalehotels.com. Map p. 603, F1.

£££ Dean Street Townhouse. The former Gargoyle Club is now a stylish restaurant and hotel. Rooms are not super-sized (a fact they fully acknowledge, with their classifications of 'Tiny', 'Small', 'Medium' and 'Bigger') but they are cleverly furnished—and should you want your bathtub in the middle of the room, your wish is granted in the 'Bigger' category. Otherwise there are rainforest showers. *69–71 Dean St. T: 020 7434 1775, www.deanstreettownhouse.com. Map p. 603, E1–F1.*

£££ Haymarket Hotel. A member of the Firmdale group (*see Covent Garden Hotel, above*). Stylish interior décor in the 'modern English' idiom (boldly clashing colours and patterns) in an elegant building by John Nash. Restaurant, bar and swimming pool.

Right in the middle of Theatreland, just off Haymarket. *1 Suffolk St. T: 020 7470 4000, www.firmdalehotels.com. Map p. 603, F1–F2.*

££–£££ Hazlitt's Hotel. Very civilised small hotel with devoted following in an excellent central location: the hotel occupies a group of Georgian townhouses in the heart of Soho. Inside is an old-fashioned oasis with friendly service. Concierge, 24-hr room service, library, honesty bar, rooms and suites. *6 Frith Street. T: 020 7434 1771. www.hazlittshotel.com. Map p. 603, F1.*

£££ The Soho Hotel. One of the Firmdale group (*see Covent Garden Hotel, above*). Large windows give an airy feel and let in plenty of light on dull London days. Bar and restaurant. *4 Richmond Mews (between Dean St and Wardour St). T: 020 7559 3000, www.firmdalehotels.com. Map p. 603, E1.*

HOTELS AROUND OXFORD STREET, IN MARYLEBONE AND NOTTING HILL

££ The Arch. Luxury here means flat-screen TVs you can watch from the tub in your black marble bathroom. Restaurant and gym. Comfortable beds with angleable reading lights. Close to Marble Arch (hence the name). *50 Gt Cumberland Pl. T: 020 7724 4700, www.thearchlondon.com. Map p. 602, C1.*

££ Chandos House. Comfortable, beautifully-appointed rooms in a building just north of Oxford Street belonging to the Royal Society of Medicine and used by them for functions and conferences. Accommodation is available to

non-members. The house was designed by Robert Adam and the reception rooms and finer bedrooms have marble fireplaces and painted ceilings. Every comfort, excellent location. Breakfast is served at a long communal table. *2 Queen Anne St. T: 020 7290 3820, www.chandoshouse.co.uk. Map p. 600, C4.*

£££ Dorset Square Hotel. One of the seven London boutique hotels belonging to the Firmdale portfolio (*see Covent Garden Hotel, p. 543*). Comfortable and centrally-located, in two Regency townhouses. The rooms are furnished in contemporary English style. The items of cricket memorabilia in the main areas are a reference to the square's past as Thomas Lord's original cricket ground (see p. 270). Most of the rooms overlook the square; some of the cheaper rooms are quite small. The Potting Shed bar and restaurant is open all day and serves delicious British food and afternoon tea. *39–40 Dorset Sq. T: 020 7723 7874, www.firmdalehotels.com. Map p. 600, B4.*

££ The Mandeville. Luxury hotel with a bar and restaurant that has been well received. But despite the marble bathrooms and power showers, the rooms are not overdone and the overall effect is warm and cosy. In Marylebone. *Mandeville Pl. T: 020 7009 2200, www.mandeville.co.uk. Map p. 603, D1.*

£ New Linden. In the same group as the Mayflower and Twenty Nevern Square. Clean, colourful, contemporary design in a classic Notting Hill townhouse. Lounge and outdoor terrace. *59 Leinster Sq. T: 020 7221 4321, www.newlinden.com. Map p. 602, A1.*

££ The Portobello. Boutique hotel in Notting Hill, decorated with English taste (and tolerance of things being slightly rough round the edges). Rooms are categorised Good, Better, Great and Exceptional. Singles also available. Continental breakfast is included in the room price; full English for an extra charge. *22 Stanley Gdns (between Ladbroke Grove and Kensington Park Rd). T: 020 7727 2777, www.portobello-hotel.com. Map p. 596, B2.*

HOTELS IN KNIGHTSBRIDGE, KENSINGTON AND CHELSEA

£ B+B Belgravia. Comfortable B&B accommodation in three Georgian townhouses. No lifts. Guest lounge and garden. Slightly further down the same street, studio-type accommodation is also offered at The Studios@82. *64–66 Ebury St. T: 020 7259 8570, www.bb-belgravia.com. Map p. 603, D3.*

£££ Blakes. Luxuriously-appointed hotel north of the Fulham Road. The décor in the rooms ranges from elegant to over-the-top (the so-called 'Parisian' rooms are the best). Bar and restaurant. *33 Roland Gdns. T: 020 7370 6701, www.blakeshotels.com. Map p. 602, B4.*

££–£££ The Capital. Small boutique hotel, still owned and run by its origi-nal founder, in Knightsbridge. Ideally located for museum visiting and for shopping (they offer a personal shopper for Harrods and Harvey Nichols. Restaurant (Outlaw's; Michelin-starred) and bar. *22–24 Basil St. T: 020 7589 5171, www.capitalhotel.co.uk. Map p. 602, C3.*

££–£££ The Gore. Opulent décor, lots of rich-coloured fabrics and throws across the beds. There is even a 'Tudor Room' complete with minstrel's gallery and oak four-poster. Bistro and bar (the latter the scene of a Rolling Stones album launch in 1968). Well located for the South Kensington museums and the nearby famous shops. *190 Queen's Gate. T: 020 7584 6601, www.gorehotel.com. Map p. 602, B3.*

£££ **The Goring**. Family-run small luxury hotel in Belgravia, in business since 1910. This was the first hotel in the world to provide a private bathroom for every bedroom: the heir to the throne of Norway acknowledged that it was more luxurious than Buckingham Palace. Restaurant (traditional British) and gardens. *Beeston Pl. T: 020 7396 9000, www.thegoring.com. Map p. 602, E3.*

££ **Knightsbridge Hotel**. A member of the Firmdale group (*see Covent Garden Hotel, p. 543*), offering the customary comfort and eclectic décor. A stone's throw from Harrods. Handy for the South Kensington museums. Afternoon teas are served (beef and horseradish sandwiches). *10 Beaufort Gdns. T: 020 7584 6300, www.firmdalehotels.com. Map p. 602, C3.*

£££–££££ **The Milestone**. Small luxury hotel overlooking Kensington Gardens, repeatedly voted one of the best in London, best in Britain, best in the world. Individually designed rooms and suites. Restaurant, bar and spa. *1 Kensington Court. T: 020 7917 1000, www.milestonehotel.com. Map p. 602, A2.*

£–££ **The Nadler Kensington**. Easy, unfussy, uncomplicated hotel in a very central West London location. Modern décor in an old Kensington townhouse. Single rooms available at excellent rates. *25 Courtfield Gardens. T: 020 7244 2255, www.thenadler.com. Map p. 602, A3.*

£££ **Number Sixteen**. A member of the Firmdale group (*see Covent Garden Hotel, p. 543*). Stylish, welcoming décor. Garden and conservatory. Afternoon teas. A graceful home from home just off the Old Brompton Road. *16 Sumner Pl. T: 020 7589 5232, www.firmdalehotels. com. Map p. 602, B3.*

££ **The Pelham**. Luxury boutique hotel in South Kensington, very close to the museums. Eclectic design, a fusion of classic and contemporary. Bar 15 serves brunch and evening snacks. Library, guest drawing room and honesty bar. *15 Cromwell Pl. T: 020 7589 8288, www.pel-hamhotel.co.uk. Map p. 602, B3.*

HOTELS IN BLOOMSBURY AND FITZROVIA

£–££ **Arosfa Hotel**. Georgian town-house, the former home of the painter John Everett Millais. Offers simple B&B accommodation in its 15 rooms. Rooms and bathrooms are small, but the location is excellent—and it is refreshing to read a hotel website which doesn't promise 'pampering' and 'decadence'. Full English breakfasts. Garden. *83 Gower St. T: 020 7636 2115, www.aros-falondon.com. Map p. 601, D4.*

£–££ **Arran House**. Excellent value in the heart of Bloomsbury. Small hotel in two typical London townhouses, one the former home of an East India merchant, the other of a naval officer who lost his life at Trafalgar. Steep stairs, soggy arm-chairs, simple rooms and full English breakfasts. And a summer rose garden. *77–79 Gower St. T: 020 7636 2186, www. arranhotel-london.com. Map p. 601, D4.*

£££ Charlotte Street Hotel. Very 'Bloomsbury', the public rooms hung with original artworks by Vanessa Bell, Roger Fry and Duncan Grant. Nicely-appointed bedrooms. Restaurant, bar, gym. A member of the Firmdale group (*see Covent Garden Hotel, p. 543*). *15–17 Charlotte St. T: 020 7806 2000, www.firmdalehotels.com. Map p. 601, D4.*

£ Jesmond Hotel. Another good-value Bloomsbury offering on Gower Street. Family-run B&B offering very simple rooms (some with shared bathrooms) and a friendly welcome. Garden. *63 Gower St. T: 020 7636 3199, www.jesmondhotel.org.uk. Map p. 601, D4.*

£ The Penn Club. Quaker-affiliated club in the heart of Bloomsbury. Non-members are welcome to stay in one of the very simple rooms (some with shared bathrooms). Stairs only (no lift). A simple breakfast is served (porridge and kippers on the menu). Free wifi. Latest check-in 10.30pm. *21–23 Bedford Pl. T: 020 7636 4718, www.pennclub. co.uk. Map p. 601, E4.*

MORE OUTLYING HOTELS, NORTH OF THE RIVER

£–££ High Road House. Hotel and Members' club on Chiswick High Road, 20mins from Heathrow and from Central London. The 14 bedrooms are cosy and comfortable. Non-members are welcome and may use the members' private bar and restaurant and meeting space provided they abide by the house rules: no photos, no mobile phones, no suits. Downstairs is the popular High Road Brasserie, open to the public, offering good all-day dining and a bar. *162–170 Chiswick High Rd. T: 020 8742 1717, www.highroadhouse.co.uk. Map p. 596, A3–B3.*

£ Hotel 55. Small hotel in Ealing. Contemporary, eclectic design. Kingsize beds and free wifi. Garden, restaurant (Momo; Japanese) and bar. *55 Hanger Lane. T: 020 8991 4450, www.hotel55-london.com. Map p. 596, A2.*

£ The Mayflower. Small, comfortable hotel in Earl's Court. No fuss or frills and very fair prices. In the same group as the New Linden and Twenty Nevern Square. *26–28 Trebovir Rd. T: 020 7370 0991, www.themayflowerhotel.co.uk. Map p. 602, A4.*

£ The Rockwell. Restfully decorated hotel near Earl's Court Tube. Neither minimalist nor maximalist: just plain and uncluttered. Bar, restaurant and garden. *181–183 Cromwell Rd. T: 020 7244 2000, www.therockwell.com. Map p. 602, A3.*

£ Twenty Nevern Square. In the same group as the Mayflower and the New Linden, and sharing their Anglo-Indian aesthetic. Simple décor, richly-coloured cushion fabrics and bedspreads. Located very close to Earl's Court Tube. Bar and courtyard garden. *20 Nevern Sq (north of Trebovir Rd). T: 020 7565 9555, www.20nevernsquare.com. Map p. 602, A4.*

HOSTEL ACCOMMODATION

There are a number of hostels all over town offering short-and longer-term accommodation both for students and general tourists of all ages. The websites below contain descriptions of each hostel, to help inform your choice:

www.hostelbookers.com/hostels/england/london
www.hostelworld.com/hostels/london.

BED AND BREAKFAST ACCOMMODATION

If you don't mind staying a little way out of the centre of town, a traditional English B&B can be a good option. It provides an opportunity to get to know a local family and to experience the lives of Londoners. The city and its suburbs are amply stocked with B&Bs, of varying degrees of simplicity and splendour, with prices per night that vary accordingly. To find what you are looking for, try the London Bed and Breakfast Agency (*www.londonbb.com*).

London Food & Drink

D ining in London is extraordinarily good. The capital has not only overtaken Manhattan in the gastronomic stakes but, with over 60 Michelin-starred restaurants, it is now ranked alongside Paris in terms of fine dining. A survey in 2014 of the world's 100 best restaurants included eight London establishments: The Ledbury in Notting Hill; Dinner by Heston Blumenthal in the Mandarin Oriental Hotel on Hyde Park; Restaurant Gordon Ramsay in Chelsea; Alain Ducasse at the Dorchester in Mayfair; Le Gavroche and Nobu, also in Mayfair; Amaya in Belgravia and Zuma in Kensington. However, this is only half the epicurean story because the gourmand on a budget may have an equally appetising time here: in London you can find any type of cuisine at any price level: French, Italian, Japanese, Moroccan, Lebanese, Chinese, Belgian, Taiwanese, Vietnamese, Modern British, Pan European, North American, Spanish, Peruvian, Fusion, etc. The outward-looking nature of this famously 'insular' island race means that everything is given an airing, from eclectic and experimental to homely and unadorned—and all of it downright delicious. It is quite simply getting difficult to eat badly in London. For inspiration, reviews and offers, see *www.squaremeal. co.uk* and *www.toptable.co.uk*.

As noted above, London eating can be frighteningly expensive; but it can also be astonishingly good value. Partly this depends on the area of town (Mayfair and Kensington are pricey; outlying districts much less so). But wherever you go, there are always plenty of simple cafés, sandwich bars and street markets offering simple meals, as well as traditional pubs or high street chains (e.g. Pizza Express, ASK, Strada, Prezzo), where menus tend to be comfortably affordable. In restaurants with more pretension, you can expect to pay around £100 for a two-course dinner with wine for two people. A number of places offer set menus, which tend to be good value. Note that in many establishments a service charge, typically of 12.5 percent, is automatically added to your bill. This will be indicated either on the menu or on the bill itself.

A selection of restaurants is given at the end of each chapter. In a city such as this, where the offering is so varied and so immense, no listing can ever hope to cover all the possibilities: instead we have chosen places that are known to the authors and editors of this guide, where we have been well served and which we would happily visit again.

Restaurants listed in this guide are categorised as follows:
£: *à la carte* main courses for under £12–£14;
££: mains for between around £14 and £25;
£££: mains for over £25.

FARMERS' MARKETS

Street food is extremely popular in London and the city plays host to a large number of local farmers' markets. Here you will find stalls selling fresh, seasonal produce to householders as well as freshly-prepared food for the casual and curious visitor to eat on the spot: pies, soups, scotch eggs, sandwiches, cakes and drinks. Farmers' markets are typically held from around 9am to 1 or 2pm. The calendar of farmers' markets given below was current at the time of writing. For details and updates, exact locations and maps, see *lfm.org.uk*.

On Tues: London Bridge (south side), South Kensington;
On Thur: Bloomsbury;
On Sat: Ealing, Hampstead, Highgate, Notting Hill, Pimlico, South Kensington, Twickenham, Wimbledon;
On Sun: Blackheath, Brixton, Chiswick, Islington, Marylebone, Queen's Park.

Other famous London food markets (Borough, Brixton) are covered in the text and are listed on pp. 556–7.

AFTERNOON TEA

This 'quintessential' English ritual came into being in the mid-19th century, as dinner times moved later and later into the evening and something was needed to fill the gap between luncheon and the evening meal, to avoid what the 7th Duchess of Bedford referred to as 'that sinking feeling'. Nearly every luxury or boutique hotel in town now offers their version of the congenial ceremony of the teapot and the cakestand; the pleasurable consumption of finger sandwiches, scones with cream and jam, cakes and pastries and, of course, perfectly brewed loose-leaf tea. For more information, and tips on tea-related etiquette, see *afternoontea.co.uk*.

BLUE GUIDES RECOMMENDED

Restaurants and pubs that are particularly good choices in their category—in terms of location, charm, value for money or the quality of the experience they provide—carry the Blue Guides Recommended sign: ■. These have been selected by our authors, editors or contributors as places they have particularly enjoyed and would be happy to recommend to others. We only recommend establishments that we have visited. To keep our entries up to date, reader feedback is essential: please do not hesitate to contact us (*www.blueguides.com*) with any views, corrections or suggestions.

General Information

CHOOSING A SEASON

London is always crowded, particularly in the summer, when visitor numbers swell, and during school holidays and half terms, when long queues can form outside the more popular museums. The weather is famously changeable. Winter can be relentlessly raw and damp, summers disappointingly cool and wet. Crisp, sunny days in spring and autumn are the finest, when Constable-like formations of clouds scud across a bright blue sky and the green of the many parks and trees is truly glorious.

EMERGENCIES

For all emergencies, whether you require an ambulance, a fire engine or a police officer, T: 999: the switchboard will coordinate the help you need.

FESTIVALS AND EVENTS

There are events, festivals and pageants taking place in London all the time. Some of them are held annually, others occur on a pop-up basis. To find out what is going on, take a look at any one of the following websites: *www.timeout.com*, *www.visitlondon. com*, *www.londontown.com* or *www.allinlondon.co.uk*. For a list of public holidays, see p. 556. Below is a short list of some of the best, most famous and most traditional of the annual celebrations, events and fairs hosted by the city.

University Boat Race: The popular annual rowing contest between Oxford and Cambridge University dates from 1829 and takes place at a weekend just before Easter; usually the last Sat in March or the first Sat in April. The 4-mile course, following the bend in the Thames from Putney Bridge to Chiswick Bridge, is thronged with spectators and the riverside pubs overflow with revellers. The race is beamed live around the world by the BBC and large TV screens are erected in Bishop's Park (Fulham) and in Furnival Gardens (Hammersmith); a festival atmosphere reigns in both these open-air venues, with pop-up stalls selling refreshments. Both crews of eight are referred to as 'blues'; Oxford's colour is dark blue and Cambridge's is light blue. The coin toss before the race determines the side of the river on which the crews start. The Fulham/Chiswick side is known as Middlesex and the Putney/Barnes side is known as Surrey, and during the race each crew must stick to their side unless they obtain a 'clear water' lead, by which they may switch station. The race is timed to start on the incoming flood tide and the crews compete for the fastest current in the middle of the river; if the boats become dangerously close and their blades look as though they might clash, the teams incur the wrath of the umpire who warningly booms 'Oxford' or 'Cambridge' through his megaphone. The main race is preceded by the two competing reserve crews, Isis (Oxford) and Goldie (Cambridge). March or April; *www.theboatrace.org*.

State Opening of Parliament: The State Opening of Parliament is a historic ceremonial pageant in which the three constituent parts of Parliament, the Sovereign, the House of Lords and House of Commons, meet to formally begin the parliamentary year. The ceremony occurs on the first day of a new parliamentary session or soon after a general election. The Queen, escorted by the Household Cavalry, processes from Buckingham Palace to the Houses of Parliament. She rides in Queen Victoria's Irish State Coach behind a coach transporting the royal regalia: the Imperial State Crown, the Cap of Maintenance and the Sword of State. The procession proceeds along the Mall, through Horse Guards Parade, along Whitehall and down Parliament Street and members of Britain's armed forces 'present arms' as she passes. When she enters the Palace of Westminster through the Sovereign's Entrance, a 41-gun artillery salute is fired in Hyde Park and at the Tower of London and the Royal Standard is raised to fly over Westminster for the duration of her visit. The Queen proceeds to the Robing Room where she assumes the Imperial State Crown and the Robe of State before leading the Royal Procession through the Royal Gallery to the chamber of the House of Lords. Black Rod, the Queen's parliamentary representative, then goes to summon MPs from the House of Commons. The doors to the Commons chamber are ritually slammed in his face to symbolise the Commons' right to exclude royal messengers; the last time the Sovereign entered the House of Commons was in 1642, when Charles I attempted to arrest five MPs. After rapping three times, the doors are opened and Black Rod leads the members of the Commons to the Lords chamber where both houses listen to the Queen's speech. The speech, which she delivers from the Throne, is in actual fact written by the government and sets out its proposed parliamentary agenda for the new parliamentary session. Afterwards, trumpeters sound the Queen's departure, the royal standard is replaced by the Union Jack and a new parliamentary session begins. Dates vary; *www.parliament.uk*.

Chelsea Flower Show: Britain's most prestigious annual flower show has been held in the grounds of the Royal Hospital, Chelsea since 1913. It is organised by the Royal Horticultural Society and held over 4 or 5 days in May; members of the Royal Family attend the opening. British and international gardeners and horticulturalists compete for a range of prize medals. One of the most famous categories is the prize from the most original show garden. May; *www. rhs.org.uk*.

Trooping the Colour: Trooping the Colour is a pageant held every June on Horse Guards Parade as a public and official celebration of the Queen's birthday (her actual birthday is on 21st

April). The phrase 'trooping the colour' has its origins in ancient military tradition when the colours—flags—of regiments were used as rallying points on the battlefield. Thus it was vital for every soldier to recognise his colour, and to ensure he did so, ceremonies were held in which the colours of the regiment were processed—trooped—slowly down the ranks for all to see. Today's ceremony starts at approx. 11am, when the Queen and other members of the Royal Family process in carriages and on horseback from Buckingham Palace down Whitehall to Horse Guards Parade. The Queen is greeted by a royal salute after which Foot Guards and the Household Cavalry perform a musical troop on the parade ground. The Queen rides back to Buckingham Palace at the head of the Household Division and joins her family on the balcony of the palace to watch an RAF fly-past. June; *www.trooping-the-colour.co.uk.*

Masterpiece: This is London's most prestigious art and antiques fair, held over several days at the end of June/ beginning of July in purpose-built marquees erected in the South Grounds of the Royal Hospital, Chelsea. Dealers and exhibitors from all over the world congregate to display the very best in painting, sculpture, design, antiquities and jewellery. Upmarket dining establishments such as The Ivy, Scott's, Harry's Bar and Le Caprice host pop-up restaurants and bars to revive flagging enthusiasts. Entry fee, advance booking essential. June or July; *www.master-piecefair.com.*

Wimbledon Lawn Tennis Championships: The prestigious inter-national two-week tennis championships, held each summer, is the oldest tennis tournament in the world and the only remaining tennis championship to be held on grass. A quintessentially British affair, it has been held at the All England Club since 1877. Players abide by a strict all-white dress code—and if the Queen or the Prince of Wales is watching from the Royal Box, players are expected to bow or curtsey before play. Spectators gorge on strawberries and cream and nationalistically get behind the British underdog (though Scotland's Andy Murray has reversed the pattern of late). Office workers find excuses to be off work in order to watch the BBC's live, back-to-back coverage. Play is often suspended due to the notoriously changeable British weather: since 2009 Centre Court has had a retractable roof which is closed when raining. June–July; *www.wimbledon. com.*

The Proms: The 'Promenade Concerts', always known as the Proms, are a festival of summer Classical music held at the Royal Albert Hall and in Hyde Park. They have been running since 1895, when they were founded by the impresario Robert Newman, who hired Henry Wood as conductor. Mid-July–mid-Sept; *bbc.co.uk/proms.*

Notting Hill Carnival: From small beginnings in 1965, this has risen to become Europe's biggest street party (*for details, see p. 279 and www.thenot-tinghillcarnival.com*). Aug.

Pearly Kings and Queens Harvest Festival: The London Pearly Kings and Queens Society Costermongers Harvest

Festival Parade is the flagship event of London's Pearly royalty, usually held on the last Sunday in Sept. 'Pearlys' (*see p. 50*) from all London's boroughs dress up in their best mother-of-pearl finery and congregate in Guildhall Yard, where from 1pm traditional Cockney entertainment takes place. They then process, accompanied by marching bands, City dignitaries and donkeys and dogcarts laden with autumn produce, from the Guildhall to St Mary-le-Bow Church for a Harvest Festival service at 3pm. The event is free to the public but all donations go to charity. Sept; *www.pearlysociety.co.uk*.

London Open House: An annual event whereby members of the public may visit buildings, institutions and gardens that are otherwise closed. It is a fantastic way to get to see inside many of London's shuttered or secret architectural gems, free of charge. Buildings that have been opened in previous years include the Gherkin, the Foreign Office and 10 Downing Street, as well as many private houses. Usually held in Sept; *www.londonopenhouse.org*.

Turner Prize: An exhibition of works by the four artists shortlisted for this prestigious contemporary art prize is hosted at Tate Britain, usually from Oct until shortly after the announcement of the winner in Dec. The prize was set up in 1984, to be awarded to any British artist under 50 whose output over the past year has been judged outstanding. The show often raises eyebrows and is always worth seeing. Oct–early Jan. **The Frieze** contemporary art fair takes place in mid-Oct in Regent's Park (*friezelondon.com*).

Bonfire Night: *'Remember, remember the fifth of November, Gunpowder, treason, and plot. I see no reason why gunpowder treason should ever be forgot.'* So runs the old rhyme. This annual event, held on 5th Nov, historically celebrates a failed attempt on the life of James I when a group of English Catholics planned to blow up the House of Lords during the State Opening of Parliament on 5th Nov 1605. After the so-called 'Gunpowder Plot' was discovered and foiled, Guy Fawkes, who was in charge of the explosives, and several of his co-conspirators, were hung, drawn and quartered. Thereafter, 5th Nov became a day of public commemoration and in communities across Britain schoolchildren would make an effigy of Fawkes, known as 'the Guy', to be ritually burned on a public bonfire. Today, very few bonfires are lit due to health and safety regulations but the event is marked by a series of impressive public firework displays held on the Sat nearest to Nov 5. The displays in Battersea Park and on Blackheath are recommended. Nov.

Remembrance Sunday: Remembrance Sunday, the second Sunday in November, is when the nation remembers all those who have given their lives in defence of their country. A National Service of Remembrance is held at the Cenotaph in Whitehall, where a wreath is laid by The Queen. Members of the Cabinet, Opposition Party leaders, former Prime Ministers and certain other ministers and the Mayor of London are invited to attend, as are representatives of the Armed Forces, Merchant Navy, Air and Fishing Fleets, and members of faith communities. High Commissioners from

Commonwealth countries also attend the ceremony and lay tributes. Sunday nearest to 11th Nov.

Lord Mayor's Show: Steeped in 800 years of history, this is one of London's premier pageants, usually held on a Saturday in early Nov. The newly elected Lord Mayor (*see p. 20*), accompanied by a procession over three miles long, processes from the City to Westminster where he or she swears allegiance to the Crown. The procession starts out at approximately 11am from Mansion House and makes its way, via St Paul's Cathedral, to the Royal Courts of Justice. It returns via the Embankment between 1–2.30pm. Afterwards fireworks are held on the river. Check website for details of the Lord Mayor's flotilla, an ancient part of the ceremony, which has recently been reintroduced. Nov; *www.lordmayorshow.org.*

New Year's Eve: Hordes of revellers line the banks of the Thames around Westminster, the South Bank and beyond, in anticipation of Britain's biggest and most spectacular fireworks display, which heralds the New Year after Big Ben tolls midnight. Afterwards the crowd comes together for a rendition of *Auld Lang Syne.* Space is very limited; it is recommended to plan well in advance and check for road, bridge, station, and Tube closures. The restaurants and bars along the South Bank usually have private viewing platforms and pedestrian access is restricted to diners; again, book well in advance. 31st Dec; *www.london. gov.uk.*

MUSEUMS AND GALLERIES

Many of London's finest and most famous museums can be visited free of charge: the British Museum, National Gallery, National Portrait Gallery, V&A, Natural History Museum and Science Museum are all examples. The same is true of most churches (though not all; the ticket prices for Westminster Abbey and St Paul's Cathedral are particularly hefty). Opening times for museums and galleries and other institutions have been included with the descriptions in the text, but of course these are always subject to change and it is always worth phoning ahead or consulting the website before your visit. This is particularly true of locations in high demand for official or corporate events (the Royal Palaces are a good example).

The **London Pass**, valid for 1, 2, 3 or 6 days, allows free entrance to a number of top sights, including Westminster Abbey, Shakespeare's Globe, the Tower of London, London Zoo and Windsor Castle. It is available either with or without a free travel pass on top. There are different prices for adults' and children's cards. Passes can also be bought online and shipped to you ahead of your trip. For details, see *londonpass.com.*

OPENING HOURS

London is a city that seldom truly sleeps and many shops and restaurants are open all day, every day. If a museum, gallery, restaurant or other commercial establishment has a regular closing day, this is indicated in the text. Parks are generally open from around 8am until dusk.

PUBLIC HOLIDAYS

England has relatively few public holidays and there is no National Day. Even on the days which are designated holidays, you will find that most shops, restaurants and major museums remain open. The curiously unhistoric-sounding tradition of the 'Bank Holiday' began in 1871. There are four of these, always occurring on a Monday so as to create a long weekend. On Bank Holidays, banks are indeed closed. Public holidays in England are as follows:

1st January	New Year's Day
Good Friday	(the Friday before Easter)
Easter Monday	Easter Bank Holiday
1st Monday in May	May Day Bank Holiday
Last Monday in May	Spring Bank Holiday
Last Monday in August	August Bank Holiday
25th December	Christmas Day
26th December	Boxing Day

SHOPPING

Napoleon might have sneered when he spoke of the British as a 'nation of shopkeepers', but London understands retail like nowhere else on the planet. The customer's convenience is paramount and endlessly attended to. Shops are open every day and sometimes well into the night; convenience stores abound; all manner of items are stocked under a single roof making one-stop shopping easy and normal; shop assistants leave you to browse on your own (but are available to help when required); no one minds if you leave without purchasing anything; and the quality of what is on offer is phenomenal: portable goods from every corner of the globe. London is tirelessly and expertly commercial in its instincts.

The best-known **shopping districts** are Oxford Street, with its famous department stores (*see p. 256*), St James's, with its traditional gentlemen's outfitters (*see p. 216*), and Knightsbridge, which is home to Harrods, Harvey Nichols and Peter Jones (*see p. 293*). But every district of London has its shops. Many of them belong to national chains, which can lead to a depressing monotony. But quirky one-offs are still to be found, for example the splendid James Smith & Sons umbrella seller near the British Museum (*see p. 345*).

London is also home to a burgeoning number of **street markets**. These are mentioned in the text of the guide. The genuine bargains, cutting-edge fashions and plethora of individual traders have departed from Portobello Road, Carnaby Street and Covent Garden, whose names have become too famous now to sustain any kind of haphazard originality. But below, for handy reference, is a short list of some of the best and most famous of the markets:

Brixton	see p. 464
Borough	see p. 429
Brick Lane	see p. 109

TELEPHONES

The dialling prefix for London is 020.
Dialling London from within the UK: (020) + number.
Dialling London from outside the UK but within Europe: (00) + (44) + (20) + number.
Dialling London from the US: (001) + (44) + (20) + number.

THEATRES AND THEATRE TICKETS

The demand for tickets to West End shows is always high and competitive. One can buy direct from the theatre box office or via various websites such as Time Out (*www.timeout.com/london*), Lastminute (*www.lastminute.com/site/entertainment/theatre/*), Ticket Master (*www.ticketmaster.co.uk*) or from the TKTS booth in Leicester Square (*map p. 603, F1*), which also offers tickets for selected shows at half-price or discounted rates (*see www.tkts.co.uk*). If you haven't booked anything in advance and feel like seeing a show, it is worth going along to see what is available. It is a good way to be spontaneous in a city where high demand makes spontaneity difficult.

To find out what's on, *Time Out* is probably the best source of listings information. It is available in printed magazine form, or online (*see website above*). Another good website, particularly for those less familiar with the city, is *www.visitlondon.com*.

TIPPING

Tipping is less bountiful in Britain than in North America. In restaurants the bill now increasingly includes service: always check whether this is the case before leaving a tip. If not, it is customary to leave the equivalent of ten percent of the total on the table to convey appreciation. Taxi-drivers are very happy to be tipped but it is not automatically expected and it is fine just to round up the fare. In hotels, porters who show you to your room and help with your luggage will appreciate a small token of thanks.

Glossary

Annunciate, of the Virgin, shown receiving the news that she is to bear the Son of God

Anodised, treated with an electrolysing process to increase durability and resist corrosion

Anthemion (pl. anthemia), type of decoration originating in ancient Greece, resembling leaf or honeysuckle fronds fanning out from a central stem

Apulian, from Puglia, southern Italy

Architecture terrible, style recommended by the 18th-century French architect J.F. Blondel as suitable for prisons or houses of correction, for its dour and forbidding aspect

Architrave, the horizontal beam placed above supporting columns, the lowest part of an entablature (*qv*); the horizontal lintel above a door or window

Archivolt, moulded architrave carried round an arch

Art Deco Stylised, often geometric art and architecture of the 1920s and '30s

Art Moderne 'Machine Age' art, a 'poor man's Art Deco', stylised and geometric, of the late 1920s and '30s

Art Nouveau design style originating in the late 19th century, curving and feminine, asymmetrical, making use of floral motifs, leaves and vine tendrils

Arts and Crafts, design movement originating in the late 19th century emphasising handicrafts and artisanal workmanship, a reaction to the growth in mass production

Atlantes, sculpted figures of the god Atlas, used as supporting columns

Baldachin, canopy supported by columns or other uprights

Basilica, originally a Roman building used for public administration; in Christian architecture, an aisled church with a clerestory and apse

Bas-relief, sculpture in low relief

Bauhaus, design school founded by Walter Gropius which came to be associated with clear, clean, austere Rationalism

Boss, carved or otherwise decorated block at the join of two vault ribs

Caduceus, the staff of Hermes/Mercury, a winged rod with snakes twining around it

Canopic jar, ancient Egyptian urn used to preserve the entrails of the mummified deceased

Canted, inclined, oblique, slanted

Capital, the top or head of a column

Capitolium, in the Roman world, a temple dedicated to the 'Capitoline triad': Jupiter, Juno and Minerva

Capriccio, an artistic fantasy or caprice, typically a townscape incorporating buildings from different cities

Caryatid, supporting column in the form of a sculpted female figure

Cenotaph, literally 'empty tomb', a monument to someone whose body is lost or buried elsewhere

Champlevé, metalwork technique whereby elements of a design are scraped hollow, then filled with enamel before firing

Chancel, part of a church to the liturgical east of the crossing (*qv*), where the clergy officiate

Chiaroscuro, distribution of light and shade in a painting

Cloisonné, type of enamel decoration, where areas of colour are partitioned by narrow strips of metal

Clerestory, upper part of the nave wall of a church, above the side aisles, with windows

Coade Stone, artificial stone formerly manufactured at Lambeth (*see p. 415*)

Composite, order of architecture combining elements of the Corinthian and Ionic

Corinthian, ancient Greek and Roman order of architecture, a characteristic of which is the column capital decorated with sculpted acanthus leaves

Cosmati, Cosmatesque, inlaid marble work using mosaic, coloured glass and stone to decorate pavements and other surfaces

Couchant, heraldic term to describe a beast as lying down

Cove, in a ceiling, concave ornamental moulding applied at the point where the ceiling and the wall meet

Crenellated, of a wall or parapet, indented with alternate crenels (the indented sections) and merlons (the sticking-up sections), so as to form a battlement

Crossing, the part of a church where the nave (central aisle) and transepts (side arms) meet

Curtain wall, a non-load-bearing wall, essentially an infill or screen between supporting piers or partitions

Decorated, late 13th–14th-century style of Gothic architecture characterised by rich, flowing tracery (*qv*)

De Stijl, the art and aesthetic of an avant-garde group of early 20th-century Dutch artists, among them Mondrian and Theo van Doesburg

Diaper, decorative style, particularly of brickwork, consisting in repeated geometric patterns of lozenges

Doric, ancient Greek order of architecture characterised by fluted columns with no base, and a plain capital

Entablature, the continuous horizontal element above the capital (consisting of architrave, frieze and cornice) of a Classical or Neoclassical building

Early English, Gothic architectural style of the 12th–13th centuries characterised by lancet (narrow, single-aperture, pointed) windows without tracery or plain Y-shaped tracery

Easter sepulchre, tomb recess in a church reserved for the ritual 'burial' of Christ in medieval Good Friday services

Evangelists, the writers of the gospels, Matthew, Mark, Luke and John, often represented in art by their symbols: a man's head, a lion, a bull and an eagle

Exedra, recessed area projecting from a room, a large alcove

Faïence, glazed decorative earthenware or terracotta, named after the town of Faenza, Italy, where it originated

Flemish bond, style of brickwork where the bricks in each row (course) are placed alternately long-short-long

Greek cross, cross with vertical and transverse arms of equal length

Grisaille, painting in tones of grey

Grotesque, grotesques (*grottesche*), painted or stucco decoration in the style of that found during the

Renaissance in Nero's Golden House in Rome, then underground, hence the name, from 'grotto'. The delicate ornamental decoration usually includes patterns of flowers, sphinxes, birds, human figures etc, against a light ground

Hammerbeam, type of roofing where the rafters are supported on short projecting struts

Hexastyle, having six columns

Inflected, of an arch, curving inwards before its point, a style much seen in Gothic and Moorish architecture

Ionic, an order of Classical architecture identified by its capitals decorated with volutes (scrolls)

Intarsia, inlay of wood, marble or metal

Krater, large ancient Greek vessel for mixing wine and water

Latin cross, cross where the vertical arm is longer than the transverse arm

Lierne, kind of ribbing in a vault producing an intense veined pattern, with ribs running out from each other

Listed, of a building, indicating that it has been placed on the roster of national monuments

Lost wax, method of metal casting whereby a mould is made around a wax model, which is then melted away so that molten metal to be poured in

Lunette, semicircular space in a vault or ceiling, often decorated with a painting or relief

Mascaron, decorative element in the form of a carved head or face

Mews, street of buildings comprising former coach houses and stables

Misericord, decorated wooden block attached to the underside of the seat in a choir stall, against which choristers can lean for support during long periods of standing. From the Latin

word for mercy

Norman, the name given to the Romanesque (*qv*) architecture of Normandy and Britain

Oculus, round window or other aperture

Ogee, of an arch, shaped in a double curve, convex above and concave below

Oriel, a window projecting from an upper storey

Palladian, of architecture, pertaining to the ideas of Andrea Palladio (1508–80), whose airy, geometric, symmetrical forms sought to revive the architecture of ancient Rome

Pediment, gable above the portico of a classical building; also above a window, either triangular in form or curved (segmental)

Pendentive, concave spandrel (*qv*) beneath one of the four 'corners' of a dome

Perpendicular, 14th–15th-century style of Gothic architecture characterised by long horizontal and vertical elements dividing traceried panes

Pier, a square or compound pillar used as a support in architecture

Pilaster, shallow pier or rectangular column projecting only slightly from the wall

Pietre dure, hard or semi-precious stones, cut and inlaid to decorate cabinets, table-tops, etc.

Porphyry, an extremely hard, dark blue or purplish igneous rock

Putto (pl. putti), sculpted or painted figure, usually nude, of a baby boy

Quatrefoil, four-lobed design

Quire, part of a cathedral reserved for the singers, usually with stalls. Also written 'choir'

Quoins, from the French *coin* (corner), stones placed in courses at the outer corners of buildings

Ragstone, irregularly shaped blocks of hard grey limestone used as a facing

Rebus, a badge or device which indicates the surname of its user by means of a pun

Reredos, panel or screen behind an altar, which may stand alone or be part of a larger retable (*qv*)

Retable, screen behind an altar, often a frame or setting for the reredos

Rococo, frothy, highly ornamented design style of the 18th-century

Romanesque, architecture of the Western (not Byzantine) Empire of the 7th–12th centuries, preceding the Gothic. In England it is often known as Norman

Rood-screen, a screen below the Rood or Crucifix, dividing the nave from the chancel in a church

Royal peculiar, a place of worship under the jurisdiction of the sovereign instead of that of a bishop

Rustication, the grooves or channels cut at the joints between huge blocks of facing masonry (ashlar)

Scagliola, a material made from selenite, used to imitate marble or *pietre dure* (*qv*)

Sedilia, recessed bank of seats with stone canopies, for officiating clergy

Serlian window, tripartite window with a taller, arched central section flanked by two flat-topped apertures of lesser height

Sgraffito, decorative plasterwork whereby two-tone designs are etched onto a wall surface

Soffit, the underside of an arch

Spandrel, surface between two arches in an arcade or the triangular space on either side of an arch

Squint, angled aperture cut in the chancel wall to allow a sightline to the altar

Starling, bulwark around the piers of a bridge

Stoup, vessel for Holy Water, usually near the entrance of a church

Tessera (pl. tesserae), small cube of marble, glass, etc. used in mosaic work

Tondo (pl. tondi), a painting or sculpture in the form of a roundel

Tracery, system of carved and moulded ribs within a window aperture dividing it into patterned sections

Transenna, open grille or screen, usually of marble, in an early Christian church

Transept, the side arm of a church leading to right (liturgical south) or left (liturgical north) of the nave

Trefoil, decorated or moulded with three leaf or lobe shapes

Triforium, upper-level arcaded aisle, below the clerestory

Triton, a sea god

Trompe l'oeil, literally, a deception of the eye: illusionist decoration, painted architectural perspectives, etc.

Tuscan, plain order of architecture with an unfluted column rising from a base to an simple, unornamented capital

Tympanum, the area between the top of a doorway and the arch above it or the triangular space enclosed by the pediment

Ushabti, figurine from an ancient Egyptian tomb intended to perform manual tasks for the deceased in the afterlife

Verde antico, a green marble from Thessaly in Greece

Vermiculated, carved with a wormlike design

Vitrolite, opaque glass used as a structural component, typical of Art Deco

Volute, tightly curled spiral scroll

Kings & Queens of England

HOUSE OF WESSEX

Edward the Confessor	1042–66
Harold II	1066 (killed in battle)

HOUSES OF NORMANDY–BLOIS

William I (the Conqueror)	1066–87
William II (Rufus)	1087–1100
Henry I (Beauclerk)	1100–35
Stephen	1135–54

HOUSE OF PLANTAGENET

Henry II	1154–89
Richard I (Coeur de Lion)	1189–99
John	1199–1216
Henry III	1216–72
Edward I	1272–1307
Edward II	1307–27
Edward III	1327–77
Richard II	1377–99 (deposed)
Henry IV	1399–1413
Henry V	1413–22
Henry VI	1422–61
Edward IV	1461–83
Edward V	1483 (?murdered)
Richard III	1483–5 (killed in battle)

HOUSE OF TUDOR

Henry VII	1485–1509
Henry VIII	1509–47
Edward VI	1547–53
Lady Jane Grey	July 1553
	(reigned 9 days, executed 1554)
Mary I	1553–8
Elizabeth I	1558–1603

HOUSE OF STUART

James I (James VI of Scotland)	1603–25
Charles I	1625–49 (beheaded)

INTERREGNUM: PROTECTORATE OF CROMWELL

HOUSE OF STUART (RESTORED)

Charles II	1660–85
James II	1685–9 (deposed)
William III and Mary II	1689–1702 and 1689–94
Anne	1702–14

HOUSE OF HANOVER

George I	1714–27
George II	1727–60
George III	1760–1820
George IV	1820–30 (Regent from 1811)
William IV	1830–7

HOUSE OF SAXE-COBURG GOTHA

Victoria	1837–1901
Edward VII	1901–10

HOUSE OF WINDSOR

George V	1910–36
Edward VIII	1936 (abdicated)
George VI	1936–52
Elizabeth II	1952–

Index

Numbers in bold are major references. Numbers in italics refer to illustrations.

DOCKLANDS & GREENWICH

LONDON OVERVIEW

A | B | C

Sarratt · Radlett

594 · Amersham · Little Chalfont · Grand Union Canal · Watford · M1 · Colne · Elstree Aerodrome · Borehamw

Watford Junction · Cassiobury Park · A41 · Elstree

Chorleywood · Bushey · Elstree

1

Chalfont St. Giles · Rickmansworth · Moor Park · South Oxhey · EDC

A413 · Maple Cross · NORTHWOOD · HATCH END · HARROW WEALD · pp.596–597

Chalfont St. Peter · HAREFIELD · Ruislip Lido · Ruislip Woods · PINNER · HARROW

M40 · Denham Aerodrome · Grand Union Canal · ICKENHAM · RUISLIP · WEMBLEY

Gerrards Cross · Denham Park · RAF Northolt · NORTHOLT

arnham ommon · Denham · A40

2 · Stoke Poges · Iver Heath · Black Park · UXBRIDGE · HILLINGDON · YEADING · GREENFORD

arnham Royal · Langley Park · M25 · COWLEY · HAYES · A312 · Grand Union Canal · EALING · EAL

Slough · Iver · YIEWSLEY · SOUTHALL · Gunne Pa

Langley · Richings Park · WEST DRAYTON · M4 · HARLINGTON · HESTON · Osterley Park · BRENTFORD

Eton College · M4 · Datchet · A4 · Colnbrook · Osterley · Isleworth · Syon Park · Kew Garde

Eton · W. & E. Riverside · The Queen Mother Res. · T5 · T1-2-3 · Heathrow Airport · A30 · HOUNSLOW · ISLEWORTH · RIC

W. & E. Central · Windsor Castle · Windsor

3 · Old Windsor · Wraysbury · Wraysbury Res. · M25 · T4 · Bedfont Lakes · FELTHAM · Hounslow Heath · Twickenham Stadium, Mus. of Rugby · TWICKENHAM · Ri

The Long Walk · Thames Path · Runnymede Park · Egham · Thames · Staines · A308 · Ashford · A316 · Strawberry Hill · KIN

Windsor Great Park · Kempton Park · HAMPTON · Bushy Park · Kingston · King

Virginia Water · Queen Mary Res. · M3 · Sunbury · Hampton Court · Hampton Court Park · Thames Path · SU

Virginia Water · Shepperton · Thames Path · Queen Elizabeth II Res. · Molesey · Hampton Court · Thames Ditton · Thame

4 · M3 · Chertsey · Walton-on-Thames · Ember · Sandown Park · A309

Sunningdale · Chobham · Common · Addlestone · Weybridge · Esher · Claygate · CHESS

Ottershaw · M25 · A3 · A243

Chobham · Woodham

© Crown copyright 2014 Ordnance Survey 100043799.

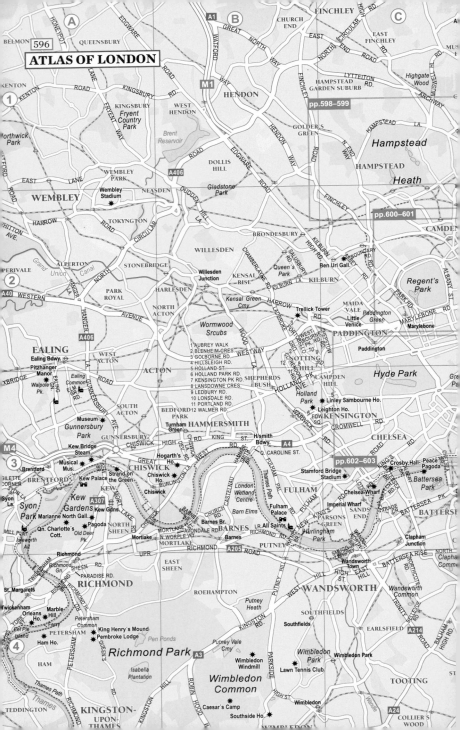

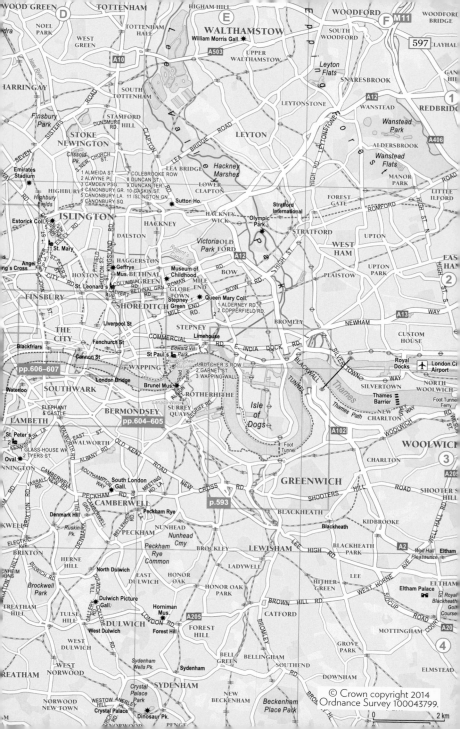

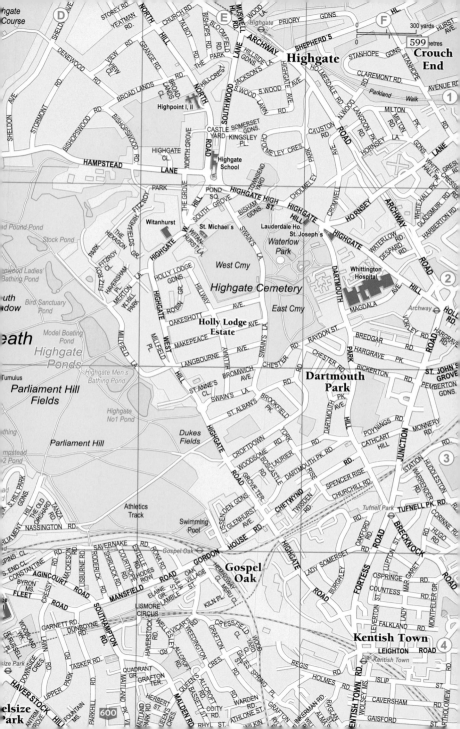

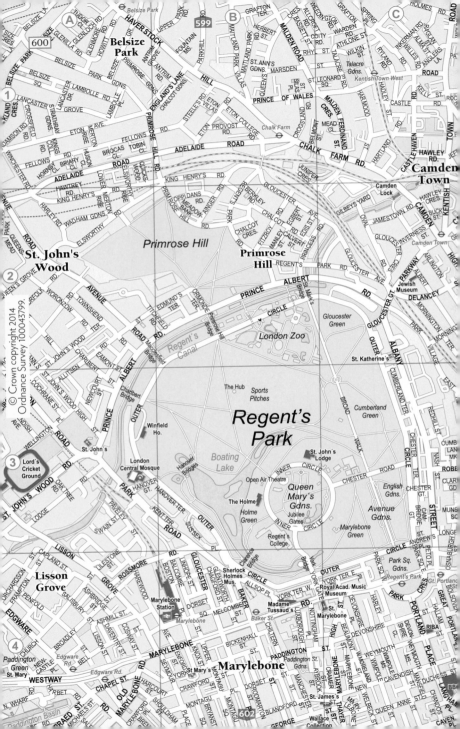

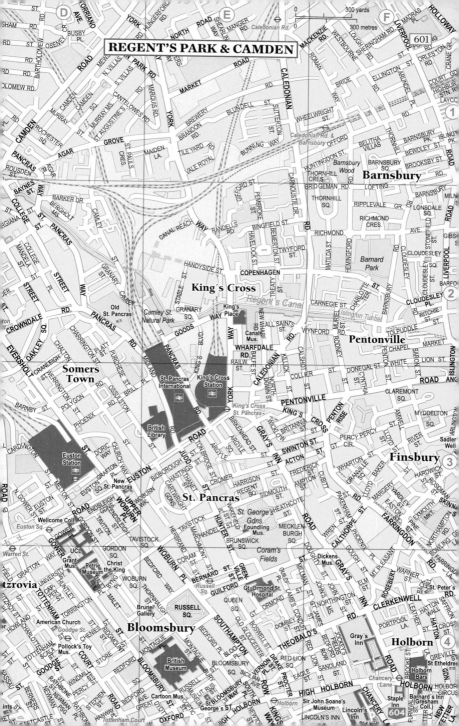

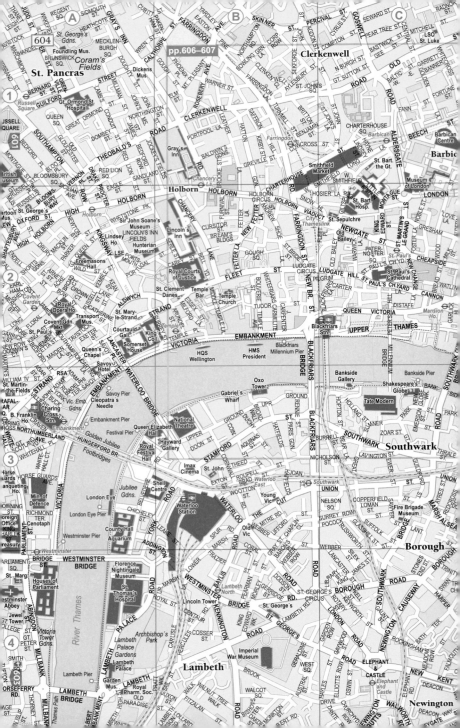

CENTRAL LONDON

Crown copyright
4 Ordnance Survey.
100043799.

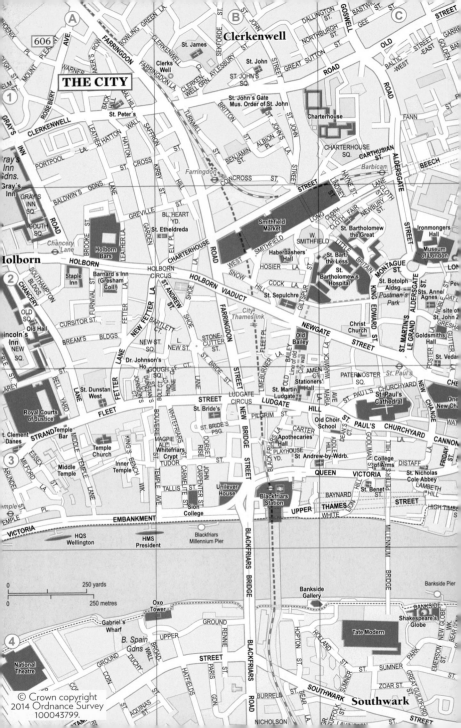

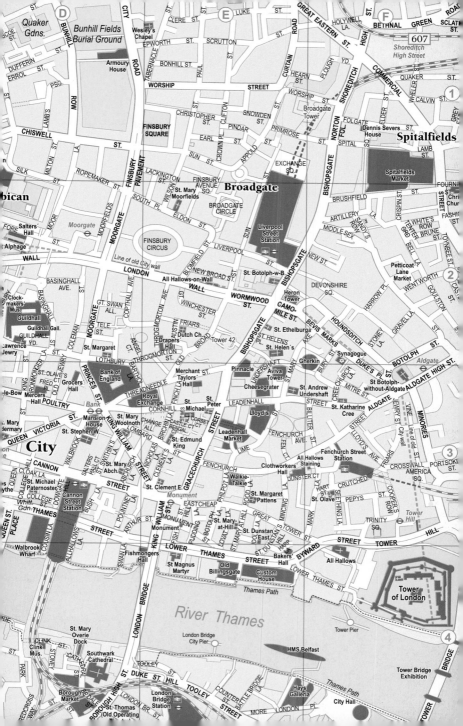

SELECT BIBLIOGRAPHY

Bold, John et al: *Discovering London's Buildings in 12 Walks*, Frances Lincoln, 2009

Bradley, Simon and Pevsner, Nikolaus: *London 1: The City of London*, (Pevsner Architectural Guides: Buildings of England), Yale 1997

Bradley, Simon and Pevsner, Nikolaus: *London: The City Churches*, Yale, 1998

Bradley, Simon, Pevsner, Nikolaus, Schofield, John: *London 6: Westminster*, (Pevsner Architectural Guides: Buildings of England), Yale, 2003

Brown, Maisie: *Barnes and Mortlake Past: With East Sheen*, Historical Publications, 1997

Coke, David and Borg, Alan: *Vauxhall Pleasure Gardens A History*, Yale, 2011

Glinert, Ed.: *The London Compendium*, Penguin, 2003

Halliday, Stephen and Hart-Davis, Adam: *The Great Stink of London: Sir Joseph Bazalgette and the Cleansing of the Victorian Metropolis*, The History Press, 2013

Impey, Edward and Parnell, Geoffrey: *The Tower of London: The Official Illustrated History*, Merrell Publishers Ltd, 2000

Keay, Anna: *The Crown Jewels*, Thames and Hudson, 2012

Kenyon, Sir Nicholas, ed.: *The City of London*, Thames and Hudson, 2011

London: British History Online: *www.british-history.ac.uk*

Longstaffe-Gowan, Todd: *The London Square*, Yale, 2012

Millar, Stephen: *London's Hidden Walks*, vol. 1, Metro Publications, 2011

Oxford Dictionary of National Biography

Powell, Kenneth: *21st Century London, The New Architecture*, Merrell Publishers Ltd, 2011

Rule, Fiona: *London's Docklands A History of the Lost Quarter*, Ian Allan Publishing, 2013

Wade, Christopher: *The Streets of Hampstead*, Camden History Society, 2000

Willey, Russ: *The London Gazeteer*, Chambers, 2007